William Howard Taft and the
First Motoring Presidency, 1909–1913

For Gabriela & Christopher
and
With love and gratitude to
Judith & James Bromley and John Bromley

William Howard Taft and the First Motoring Presidency, 1909–1913

by Michael L. Bromley

McFarland & Company, Inc., Publishers
Jefferson, North Carolina, and London

The present work is a reprint of the illustrated case bound edition of William Howard Taft and the First Motoring Presidency, 1909–1913, *first published in 2003 by McFarland.*

LIBRARY OF CONGRESS CATALOGUING-IN-PUBLICATION DATA

Bromley, Michael L.
William Howard Taft and the first motoring presidency, 1909–1913 / by Michael L. Bromley.
p. cm.
Includes bibliographical references and index.

ISBN-13: 978-0-7864-2952-3
ISBN-10: 0-7864-2952-6
(softcover : 50# alkaline paper)

1. Taft, William H. (William Howard), 1857–1930 — Views on automobiles.
2. Presidents— United States— Biography.
3. United States— Politics and government —1909–1913.
4. Automobiles— Political aspects— United States— History — 20th century.
5. Automobile industry and trade — Political aspects— United States— History — 20th century.
6. Automobiles— Social aspects— United States— History — 20th century.
I. Title.
E762.B85 2007 973.91'2'092 — dc21 2003008595
British Library cataloguing data are available

Cover photograph: William Howard Taft and aide Archie Butt (lower left) in Denver (Denver Public Library, Western History Collection R-501071); foreground and background ©2007 PhotoSpin

Manufactured in the United States of America

McFarland & Company, Inc., Publishers
Box 611, Jefferson, North Carolina 28640
www.mcfarlandpub.com

Acknowledgments

The author thanks Thomas Jefferson, the Department of Defense, and Roget for, respectively, the Library of Congress, the Internet, and always another good word, sometimes even the perfect one. The Montgomery County Public Library at Rockville, Maryland, is most appreciated for its extensive newspaper microfilm archives. The author hopes all those dimes he fed the machines may one day help the library buy new machines that won't break down quite so often.

Automotive historians Keith Marvin and Beverly Rae Kimes were the author's motoring conscience and ever-ready mental encyclopedias. Keith, you motoring fiend, this book should be dedicated to you! Many thanks to the esteemed beating hearts of the Society of Automotive Historians, Kit Foster, Sinclair Powell, and Leroy Cole. Proving there is no money in this business, their references and thoughts were invaluable. The author is nevertheless indebted to them. Henry Merkel generously provided photographs, history, and precious insight to the White Company and its marvelous cars. Charles Lemaitre gave the author an unforgettable ride in his 1911 36 H.P. Pierce-Arrow and a wonderful afternoon amidst his incredible collection of automobiles and automotive art and photographs. Richard Wells also gave the author an amazing ride in his 1911 White "OO" steamer. He kindly let the author sit in back, doing his best imitation of William Howard Taft, while the great and smooth steamer took the winding Massachusetts roads. And yes, it's a great ride! Mr. Wells patiently demonstrated, from beginning to end, how the car works. White enthusiasts Nick Howell, Pat Ferrell, and Ron Thurber are also gratefully thanked for assistance and information. Robert Rogers and Judith Selleck of the Heritage Plantation, Sandwich, Massachusetts, are thanked for information and views of the original Taft steam car, which is on display at that great automotive collection. Stephanie Chontos of the Henry Ford Museum and Greenfield Village kindly shared information on one of that museum's prize pieces, the 1912 Baker Electric, and on the history of the Model N and the Model T. Golf writer and historian James Finegan kindly and patiently taught the author about the history of that favorite game of Taft's. Karen Kimball helped with research and otherwise shared enthusiasm for this project.

Special thanks go to Miss Constance Carter, head of the Science Reference Section at the Library of Congress, for enthusiasm and the biggest smile on the fifth floor of the Adams Building. Miss Carter is Old School Library, and she brings to life two characters dear to the author, Helen "Hyphen" Anne Hilker, who made the Library laugh and otherwise kept its public posture correct, and Verner W. Clapp, the author's grandfather, the Library personified, and the father of modern librarianship. Fred Bauman, Ernie Emrich, Jeff Flannery, Ahmed Johnson, Patrick Kerwin, and Bruce Kirby are fine and beyond helpful stewards of the Library of Congress Manuscript Reading Room, where the microfilm machines whirl and produce Taft's life.

Unlike some in the business, historian H.W. Brands kindly bothered to answer this pesky author's questions. He is a credit to his profession. Carl Sferrazza Anthony has to be the most gracious, kindliest, and most sympathetic historian out there. He answers his mail, too. More importantly, his encouragement, enthusiasm, and directions were vital. Towering over the study of the era is Dr. David Burton and his numerous histories of Roosevelt, Taft, and Wilson. Dr. Burton kindly took time out from his work on the Taft letters and directed the author, sight unseen, to exactly the right place. Thank you, Professor.

Cathy, D.J., Debs, George, Hoopes, Seany, Erin, Kerry, and Cristina are thanked one and all for words and bundles of confidence and faith. Cathy, thank you. The author asks the reader to look up Cristina under "Gutiérrez Richaud." She is a poet among the great ones, and writes to die for. "Late Night" Neci Crowder of the great WHFS has been a friend to this work and, with her music and her laugh, a guiding angel through the late night sessions that were the writings of this book. Professor Rosenfeld, thank you. Prayers to our men and women out there yet fighting and risking their lives to preserve the American Founding and Nation. As Taft said in 1912, it's worth saving.

Dear old Uncle John, your nephew thanks you. You salvaged this work, even if you didn't mean to. Look carefully, and you will find one or two things—but no more—critical of Taft (these two parentheses are for you!). Mirta and the kids are thanked for their endless patience, although with the children it is generally impatience, just as it should be—they *are* perfect, you know. Whenever the author opens his copy of Pringle's second volume on Taft, he finds pasted on the first page a note from Gabriela: "*I love you! Hurry up!*" (I'm trying, dearest, I'm trying.) Christopher and Gabriela know more about Captain Butt than any other children in the whole world. And they love to say his name, particularly when discussing his promotion to Major. To Ben and Shevi, Susan and David, and all the kids, and to the Ladds one and all, especially Michael for his enthusiasm and encouragement, thank you. Indebtedness and love forever to Mom and Dad.

Bethesda, Maryland, 2003

Table of Contents

Part Three: The Third American Revolution (that almost was)

Preface

Our dear readers are welcomed to one of the 21st Century's first encounters with a hundred years ago. It was an odd time, the early twentieth century, but it seems so only because own times are so odd. To see it better I invite you to join this book's underworld of notes and back-page references. Ignore them if you must; if you choose to join the fine print, I think your experience will be richer for it. Please see the glossaries and appendices for a guide and reminder that will explain the maze of names, things, and events that make up the Taft presidency. I hope it helps.

Sources chosen for this work are principally those used by other Taft biographers. Much of the material and many of the quotations are the same. One cannot tell the story without them. The difference here is context and attitude. The emphasis has been to follow the news, for which the *New York Times* is the chosen record. The paper's general aspect was pro-business, vehemently anti-tariff, and otherwise purposelessly non-partisan. I hope to have developed for the reader a feeling for the flow of events during the Taft period and the evolution of its attitudes. Looking backwards, historical events are flat. The aim here is a more saturated view of those times. History should, like wood, take its paint deeply. My highest aspiration in this work is to add color to the history of our 27th President.

This is a positive account of Taft. I ask only for an open mind. If it is your first encounter with him, welcome. If you and he are already acquainted, you will find herein sunshine in his four years and not the despair he is supposed to have suffered throughout. The principal difference between this work and others is that this book was not written with the assumption that the Taft presidency was a failure. Even Henry Pringle, whose 1939 biography of Taft is the authority, and to whom this work is indebted, started backwards. If Taft was a loser, so be it, but let him, not the biographer, prove it to you. When he left office, Taft was not just a happy man, he was contented and proud. It couldn't have been all that bad, now, could it?

Taft was an eminently principled and equally practical man. He abhorred politics and played it vigorously. He was a party loyalist and turned to the opposition to secure his agenda. He was dedicated to the democratic spirit and fawned over his monied patrons. He was progressive in what the Constitution allowed, beyond which he "stood pat." The past was vital to Taft as example and rule, but he never

A Motoring Administration

With the induction into office today of William H. Taft as president of the United States, the United States will have an administration which has endorsed the motor car by putting it into service at the White House instead of the horse, an innovation which is all the more startling because of the attitude of the Roosevelt regime toward the car. President Taft is an ardent motorist and in the last campaign he used the car in many instances, as did the opposition candidate, William J. Bryan—in fact, it may be said it was a motoring campaign. Elected to the presidency, Taft insisted upon having a motor stable and, despite the opposition on the part of some of the senators, congress appropriated $12,000 for motor cars for the president. These machines already have been bought—one of them a White steamer and the other a Pierce-Arrow six-cylinder. Vice-President Sherman has bought a Peerless.

Announcement of the new "Motoring Administration." (From *Motor Age*, March, 1909) cowed to convention for its own sake. He believed in women's causes and equality for blacks, although both were to exercise their rights in another room. He loved to motor, could walk six miles at pace, and was an uncommonly competent horseback rider. Taft adored Theodore Roosevelt and expelled the man from his party.

You will find that this work is often critical of Roosevelt. I have no intention to chisel his face from Mt. Rushmore. As President he was an inspiration and a leader to his generation. He was a dreadful ex-President. Taft, in defeating Roosevelt for the Republican nomination in 1912, and reclaiming that party, defined American politics for the rest of the century. The man whom history has derided as a reluctant, ineffective President yet acclaimed for being the only President to become Chief Justice was not nominated by his party for both positions by chance. Taft was made Chief Justice in 1921, his very dream, by the party he salvaged in 1912. There is no accident here, no casual passing of time and men.

William Howard Taft — 27th President, 1909–1913. (Courtesy Library of Congress)

The words Taft and leadership are not often spoken together. Let them be spoken. Taft led his nation to progress in welfare, law, and justice. When the hour called for generalship, he answered with authority, especially during the 1912 election, when Taft salvaged the Republican party from an agitation that nearly killed it. More importantly, during that fight Taft reminded his country of the meaning and nature of its political form. He defined constitutional, popular government and defended it against one of the greatest assaults it has suffered in its short history.

Irony is the flavor of the Taft presidency. He disliked strife and politics. He got and gave both in abundance. He didn't like the income tax, and he didn't want the federal government to pay for interstate roads. He launched them both. He was a progressive, and he buried the progressives with his conservatism, all the while advancing their cause in the law. But irony is not the final product of the Taft presidency. Taft kept his nation from the extremes of his age. His presidency was critical to what we call America today. If I must identify his single most important achievement, it is this: he distilled the era of its extra-constitutional meanderings and prevented that dipsomaniac slide toward state control and the weakening of the courts and the Constitution that were among the lesser impulses of the progressive movement.

Next best thing? He set the country rolling to motorized glory.

Michael Bromley
Summer 2003

I shall be content to await the writing of the Administration's history.

—William Howard Taft,
November 7, 1912

Introduction

First Motoring

Somewhere along the way, the American leader was going to get a motor car. It might have been William McKinley, but he was shot soon after his first motorized rides. Next in line, Theodore Roosevelt refused the honor. Were it not for his predecessor, Woodrow Wilson might have spent his eight years in office following a horse. If so, Warren Harding would have been the man. Harding loved motor cars, and not just because the golf course was nearer by motor. As it was, Harding's political mentor, William Howard Taft, made the first presidential move to motors in 1909.

Taft attributed his automobiling to an "accident of office and the generosity of a Republican Congress" that granted him the funds he spent on some of the best motor cars in the world. Yet Congress only gave the man what he asked. Without his word there would have been no White House garage in 1909. Without those cars, the politics of the automobile would have continued to be defined by populist politicians who scorned motors—and who took gleefully to them after Taft mounted the Great Seal upon his machines. Only after Taft could motoring be spoken among the right thinking and in the halls of Congress.

Taft declared, "I am sure the automobile coming in as a toy of the wealthier class is going to prove the most useful of them all to all classes, rich and poor." To the political classes, however, the motor car was repugnant. The great social advance that Taft saw clearly and Henry Ford made real was delayed by Roosevelt-era politics that equated automobiles with privilege. The automobile changed America. It cannot be ignored. History treats it as an inevitability, an accident of technology and culture.

In March of 1909, that outcome was not clear. Automobiling was encroaching, capturing many, but culture didn't want it. It was still a choice. As David McCullough said, "The hardest thing to convey in writing history or teaching history is that nothing ever had to happen the way it happened." Taft chose it.

Contrary to his claim that he would never have joined the "carriage class" were he not made President, ten months before taking the oath Taft was hanging out at Brooks Brothers, sorting through the auto scarves bin. His motoring modesty was an obligatory apology for what was seen as an elitist diversion. He knew the automobile meant much more, including "an industry that contributes greatly to the wealth of this country, and adds much to its manufacturing product." Such a statement was not obvious in those days, or at least not in good political company. To Taft the automobile was a "wonderful development."

This is the story of the man during his four years in the White House, much of that time spent in the back seats of automobiles. Please join in this overdue thanks to William Howard Taft, and not just from the motoring world.

Part One
The Eye of the Storm

1

Motoring Unspoken

...but I know from experience that only us millionaires can be automobilists...
—Simeon Ford to the Automobile
Club of America, 1904[1]

The Autumn New York Horse Show was preeminent among the society-based trade exhibitions. Viewing booths went for upwards of $10,000 for the week-long event, and the fashions displayed were absolute. Come the automobile shows, starting in 1900, where novelty, excitement, and money were on the podium and in the newspaper headlines, the staid displays of the equestrian age had been eclipsed; the carriage trade reacted in kind. In 1903 it was reported that a stylish déclassé had descended upon the haughty gathering, and, like Rousseau's literal-minded pupil Marie Antoinette for whom peasantry was play, a second-hand carriage marked the exquisite in four-legged transportation. Nothing new was to come in carriages and Society knew it.[2]

A few years later a spin down 8th Avenue at sixteen miles per hour—double the speed limit, that is—was no longer the subject of editorial debate, church sermons, and vindictive legislative oratory, except, as we shall see, on Capitol Hill. The issue had gone from one of extermination to adaptation: how to get along with the damned things. Although still thought the realm of "those who can afford it," fascination with automobiles by the "many who cannot" was noted.[3] It wasn't just the rich who went to automobile shows; a general curiosity was aroused. Questions of retirement were for the horse.

Despite a rough economy and industry predictions of a slow down, the January 1908 New York auto shows were the most successful ever. Automobiles were taking over public fascination and the streets. Throwing rocks at passing cars was reduced from political statement to simple hooliganism. A horse-drawn cab strike later that year proved to New Yorkers that they could get along just fine by automobile. Above all, the middle class was ready to motor. In 1908 the high of quality and

1. *Automobile*, 1/30/04, p. 155. The comment was said in a sarcasm based on an accepted truth of the day.
2. "Fashions in Carriages," *New York Times* (*NYT*), 10/25/03 (1904). For our purposes this source will be referred to in the text as the *Times*.
3. "Automobile Talk," *Washington Evening Star*, 1/8/09, quoting the *Springfield Republican* (hereafter the Washington paper will be called the *Evening Star*).

moderate of price Buick sold as much as any.

The idea of the "poor man's automobile" had been around since the early days. An entire category of under-$500 motorized buggies, called the "buggyabout," "buggymobile," or "power carriage," fully emerged in 1906. Characterized by high-wheels, small motors, and the inoffensive look of a horse buggy, these motors were designed to meet the budget, needs, and sensitivities of the common man. One maker called its 14-horsepower buggyabout the "The Farmers' Auto."[4] A 1908 observer counted a million carriages made in 1905 and said it "shows that there is still a tremendous field which the automobile builder may invade and reasonably hope to capture by quicker, cheaper and more economical methods of mechanical transportation."[5] Underpowered and mostly with two-seats, the buggyabout failed as the bridge from horse to motor. It kept too much of the horse.

Responding to his own instincts and increasingly loud calls for the Everyman's car, Henry Ford launched the Model N in 1906. Rather than build a carriage up, Ford built an automobile down. "A four-cylinder runabout for $500!— it seemed too good to believe," wrote Ford's biographer. Indeed, the next year Ford's sales quadrupled.[6] When Ford announced a hundred dollar increase, there was concern it couldn't be done, or it would have to be done by someone else.[7] The Model T, introduced in 1908, answered the question — sort of. It was the best car for its $825 price, the best car for under $2,000 the company bragged.[8] In June, 1908 the *Automobile* declared,

> Whether there will ever be such a thing as the "poor man's automobile," has been discussed pro and con ... and nothing that has happened in the interim can be considered as sufficient cause for altering opinions there set forth. But that the time has come when it will be possible for the man in ordinary circumstances to maintain an automobile that is neither a cheap, low-powered car or one that is merely a low-priced imitation of better things, has actually arrived, now appears to be fact."[9]

As late as 1910 it still had to be said; it was still a matter of faith: "There is no doubt, though, that the man who can successfully solve this knotty question and produce a car that will be entirely sufficient mechanically, and whose price will be within the reach of the millions who cannot yet afford automobiles, will not only grow rich but be considered a public benefactor as well."[10] The car for the masses was an answer to a question nobody asked.[11] Anybody who really wanted an automobile could get one. If the $250 buggyabout didn't do it, and if the $850 Ford was too

4. "Characteristics of the American Runabout," *Automobile*, 10/17/07, pp. 523–524.
5. "Horse-Drawn Statistics That Indicate Auto's Growth," *Automobile*, 2/6/08, p. 189.
6. *Ford: The Times, the Man, the Company,* by Allan Nevins, pp. 324, 645. The motor buggy didn't last, and here's why: a 1907 study demonstrated that of the most inexpensive runabouts only the Ford Model N had a four cylinder engine. Its big-name competition came from the single and two-cylinder offerings from Cadillac, Brush, Reo, and Buick. Another look found that among the under $1,000 category, only four "are really four-seated touring cars." Of four cylinder cars only the Ford cost under $1,000 ("Medium-Priced Cars are Increasing," *Automobile*, 10/31/07, p. 661). The secret to the Ford was that it produced the most horsepower per both price and weight. The Ford was not yet considered the farmer's car (see "To Secure Good Roads: Make Farmer an Autoist," *Automobile*, 10/31/07, p. 666).
7. "Ford Runabout Price Raised A Hundred," *Automobile*, 1/31/07.
8. Nevins, p. 388.
9. 6/18/08, p. 858.
10. Nevins, p. 449, quoting *Harper's Weekly*, 1/1/10.
11. Henry Ford did not create the Everyman's car. He perfected it. Ford called his a "universal" car both for its standardization of manufacture and for its usefulness to buyers. Ford's early 1909 explanation was that

much, the classifieds were full of affordable used cars. The problem was not price.

Buggyabouts aside, there were essentially two types of automobiles in 1908, runabouts, a common name for the Ford "N" and "T" cars, and tourers. Touring cars, whether open or closed, were invariably described in news accounts as "big"—as in expensive. Limousines, a subcategory of tourers, were just then replacing the horse-drawn coach as formal carriage and cost four, seven, or even eight thousand dollars. That kind of money wouldn't turn the head of a respectable heiress, but it was serious cash to everyone else. A basic multi-passenger touring car started at $1,500.[12] Add a few extra cylinders, a roof, armchairs upholstered by Gobelins, a liquor cabinet by Baccarat and Hiram Walker, a foot warmer, an umbrella holder, a Cuban-stocked humidor, gold-plated vanity case, silver mirrors, cigar lighters, and a nice little cut glass vase, and you might as well have been riding J.P. Morgan's yacht down Fifth Avenue.

A motorist was usually someone who rode in the back seat with a chauffeur at the wheel. The rolls of automobile clubs were filled with "automobilists" who had no idea how to drive a car. For those who did, the chauffeur, also called a mechanic or "motor man," rode alongside to take over if the ride went bad or tiresome.[13] The mechanical side of motoring was beyond a gentleman's meaner desires. Riding a mile a minute was a thrill, but there was no romance in grease. For city use, parking, traffic, and cops were as problematic as today with the added joy of horses, trolleys, and pedestrians unused to darting cars; so the chauffeur.

Ladies and gentlemen were to be driven. The limousine's form was all about carriages, whose styles and conventions had to be incorporated before motor cars could fulfill that luxurious mission. The deciding change in automotive design that conquered the carriage was the side-entrance limousine. Early limousines mimicked carriages with exterior-perched chauffeurs and ornate interiors, but proper dress and manner could not be maintained while climbing rear steps or over a folding front seat. The side entrance ensured a lady's dignity, allowing her a graceful step from curb to carriage above and away from the horse-dirtied streets.

Courts of Europe—often, the more minor the fiefdom the greater the display—were dedicated to motor cars, using them for all but the most formal occasions. Edward VII of England bestowed Royal patronage upon the Daimler Company and the British Automobile Club. This was a matter of absurdly great significance to the automobile, as if the wave of the Royal hand had created the thing. With the King's approval everyone got on board, including the capricious and brilliant Prime Minister Arthur Balfour, who paid homage to the King's indulgences and upped the ante: even Edward was shocked when the PM pulled up to the palace in

11. (*cont.*) "nothing is skimped, except extravagance, and that is entirely eliminated" ("System the Secret of Ford's Success," by Henry Ford, *NYT*, 1/3/09). In 1902, Ransom Olds built a decent, inexpensive car, but he was too early for mass consumption. The 1909 Brush sold for less than a Model T, and its makers dreamed of mass production. Ford and these others aside, used cars constituted the first cheap cars. A study in France in 1908 demonstrated that the average life of a motor car was almost five years. Of great concern to sellers of new cars was that good, sturdy cars were passed on to second-hand owners (see "Motoring," *Evening Star*, 12/20/08). It was another decade before the "T" approached the price of a buggy.

12. The average price of automobiles sold in 1907 was $2,138, having risen from $1,351 in 1904. By 1910 it dropped to $1,483. See appendix for chart.

13. This practice led to some confusion as to what to do with the chauffeur when the owner was driving. The usual solution was to put him in the front passenger seat (the rear being out of question). In 1906, a Frenchman solved the issue by creating a "chauffeur's seat" which was mounted on the running board to the side of the driver (see "What to do with the Chauffeur," *Automobile*, 7/19/06, p. 87).

a motor car.[14] He was only following a logical extension of the King's motoring enthusiasms. Automobile promoter and inventor of the Rolls-Royce "Flying Lady" mascot, Lord Montagu, wrote that automobilism "owes much of its wonderful success" to the King's patronage.[15] Emanuel of Italy owned automobiles, while in Spain Alfonso XIII set his reputation as the leading Continental scorcher, chief enthusiast, and preeminent automotive fiend.

In France, the world leader in the new technology and its fabrication, the government was favorable to the motor car in matters of law and society. President Loubet of France repressed his known preference for horse and carriage and opened the annual *Salon de l'Automobile* with alacrity and enthusiastic pronouncements of French superiority in the field. Although he arrived at the 1903 show in a horse-drawn landau, his presence, and that of three of ministers, gave an immeasurable boost to the country's acceptance of automobiling and its industry. In 1905 his entrance came by way of a landaulet motor car.[16]

On the eve of the 1908 New York to Paris race, France's automotive pride was spoken by its Ambassador, Jules Jusserand, to the Automobile Club of America (ACA). The audience included the conservative and very rich Senator Chauncey Depew and retired General Nelson Miles, the first and most vigorous American government promoter of automobiles. The Ambassador raised his glass to "France, the Mother of the Automobile."[17] That France was the motherland of the automobile there was no argument from American motorists. In the New World, the American President rode a horse.

In 1902, an automotive press lamented,

> The French are justly proud of the intelligence displayed by their highest government officers in lending the dignity of a State function to the festivals which mark the victories of automobilism. The contrast between this attitude and the cold indifference shown by the State and Federal authorities in the United States, is striking, and what this means to an industry which necessarily must struggle against prejudices and caution of capital before it can attain the vast national importance to which it is destined, is evidenced in the jubilation of the standard bearers in France over the recognition accorded it."[18]

And again in 1903 with,

> What consolation is it to Americans that nearly all the crowned heads of Europe have proved their modernity, when the head of our own Republic clings to the horse, or takes long walks afoot, under the delusion evidently that a motor vehicle affords too little scope for the cultivation of strenuosity?[19]

Theodore Roosevelt demonstrated an all-consuming energy that satisfied

14. *Eminent Edwardians*, by Piers Brendon, 1980, p. 99.
15. *Stretching It: The Story of the Limousine*, by Michael L. Bromley and Tom Mazza, 2002, p. 173.
16. "The Salon de l'Automobile at the Grand Palais," *Automobile*, 12/27/02, "Le Sixième Salon de l'Automobile," *Figaro*, 12/10/03 and "President Loubet, of France, Arriving by Automobile Landaulet to Officially Open the Paris Automobile Show," *Automobile*, photo caption, 12/21/05, p. 685.
17. "Greatest Auto Race, Jusserand Calls It," *NYT*, 1/26/08 and "A.C.A. Banquet a Gathering of the Old Guard," *Automobile*, 1/30/08. Depew replied to the Ambassador's toast with, "America, the User of the Automobile." Five years before, General Miles was ridiculed for suggesting that the automobile might replace the Army mule (see "Horses vs. Machines," *NYT* editorial, 8/30/03). Miles first proposed U.S. Army use of the "motor wagon" in 1895 ("The Use of the Motor Vehicle in the United States Army, 1899–1939," by Norman Miller Cary, Jr., p. 10). He estimated in 1901 that the country wasted $500,000,000 annually on the inefficiency that was mud ("Miles on Good Roads," *NYT*, 4/19/01). That insight was not generally recognized for another decade since nobody considered that automobiles would provide efficient ground freight and, besides, the railroads were the great evil of the day, and high shipping costs were blamed on them.
18. "The Salon de l'Automobile at the Grand Palais," p. 2.
19. *Automobile*, 8/29/03, p. 218.

outdoorsmen, reformers, and journalists. He was at best useless to his nation's motorists. When his predecessor, William McKinley, took a ride with F.O. Stanley in a Locomobile steam car in 1899, it was thought that the chief representative of the great republican experiment had blessed the horseless carriage. Then along came Roosevelt — on horseback.

* * *

A facile way to prove one's "modernity" was to buy an automobile. Show up at Tuxedo Park in it and you were the rage. Suffragettes took gleefully to the motor, making it an instrument of liberation and shock. England's leading lady agitator, Mrs. Emmeline Goulden Pankhurst, "rode like an empress" in her motor car with a chauffeuse at the wheel.[20] The social

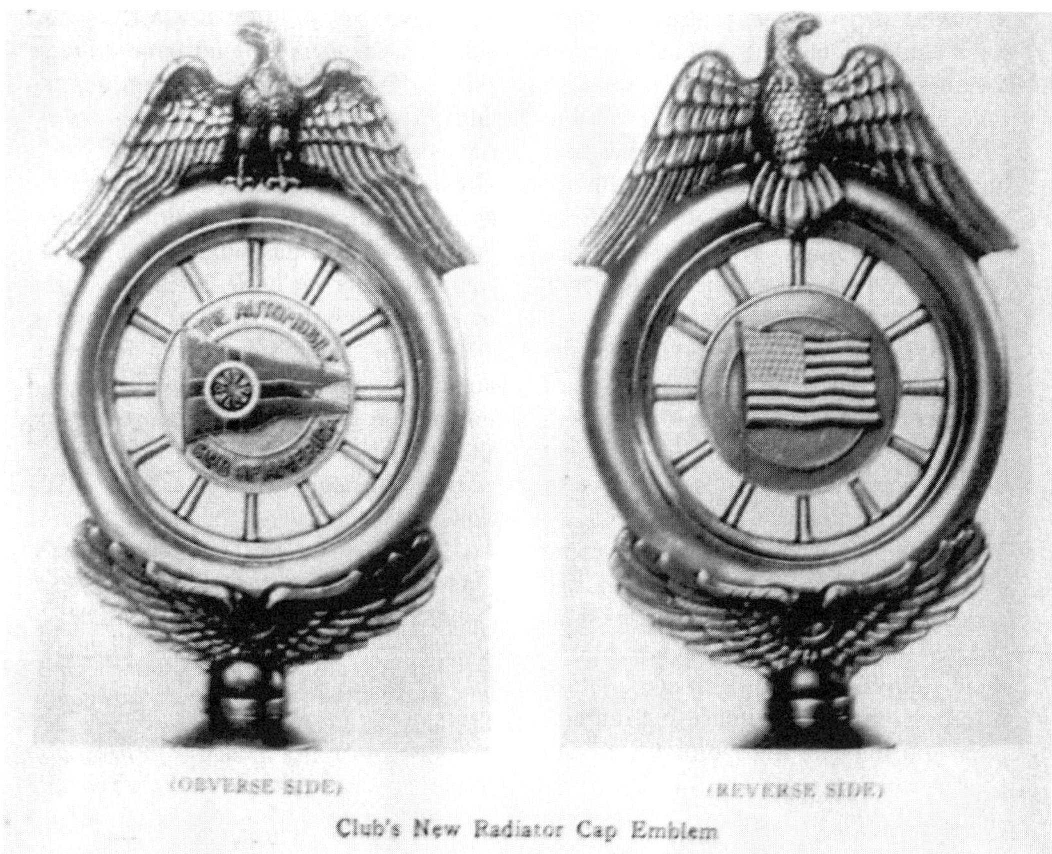

What made automobiles so distasteful and subject to class-consciousness was their exclusivity combined with high visibility. Expensive limousines, huge touring cars, and "freak" racers were in-your-face, fume-spitting, noise-making and very conspicuous consumables. Nobody cared if J.P. Morgan used a $5,000 carriage, but put him in an automobile of equal value and it was, well, like having J.P. Morgan blow his horn down your street. Pictured here is the mascot used by members of one of the most exclusive clubs in the world, the Automobile Club of America. This emblem didn't grace just any automobile. Members of the Club did as much to launch the Motor Age as any others. (From *Club Journal*, 1911)

20. Mrs. Pankhurst's landaulet was a present from an American disciple. The chauffeuse's parents suffered trebly from their daughter's base and manly profession and the passenger she served, that "dreadful woman" (Brendon, p. 172). For the contrarian view of women drivers, see "Bars Women Chauffeurs: Cincinnati Mayor Says They Should Run Sewing Machines," *NYT*, 3/10/08.

import of the automobile was unbalanced. It was both a new wealth toy and malcontent's rattle.

Roosevelt was no anti-modernist. Change was his instinct and political ally. His greatest accomplishment was the Panama Canal, a world wonder. His most ridiculous act was an attempt to reform the English language. He was devoted to assembling an American Armada, the Great White fleet, with the most technologically advanced ships. He was "greatly interested" in a display of inventor Hiram Maxim's latest "noiseless rifle." He watched a Kinetoscope picture show at the White House. His Army tested automobiles, and his generals otherwise delighted in them. So why no presidential automobile? In 1908, Roosevelt's new aide-de-camp, Captain Archie Butt, complained, "Governor Magoon in Cuba has far more in the way of automobiles and carriages than has the President of the United States. In fact, the President has no automobiles at all and while he has never said so much yet it is evident that he thinks it a piece of cowardice on the part of Congress...."[21] The Captain didn't realize what was going on.

Roosevelt was an indefatigable poser, "one of the greatest experts in publicity there ever was," according to his daughter Alice.[22] He crafted his image as frontiersman, Rough-Rider, and sportsman. He did nothing in public without purpose. His greatest stunt was to carry on a speech after being shot in the chest in 1912. He bellowed, "I do not care a rap about being shot, not a rap.... What I do care for is my country."[23] The crowd went crazy. There being no question that Roosevelt truly believed in the "strenuous life," let us just say that he didn't mind that his every hike, climb, and horseback ride was recorded in the newspapers. Exaggerated loyalty to horses was part of this manly act. The flip side to the daring of the automobile racers such as William K. Vanderbilt and Barney Oldfield was a reputation of automobiling as effete dandyism.[24] Roosevelt dared not issue any feminine auras, especially around voters. Horse and saddle were it.

Roosevelt's masculinity was all very well, but what really moved him was the insidious symbolism of the automobile as a toy of the rich. His public revulsion to it lay in the political trenches he dug on the populist side of class warfare. A man of the people wasn't to be seen enjoying Edwardian indulgences. As de Tocqueville noted,

> In the United States, the more opulent citizens take great care not to stand aloof from the people; on the contrary, they constantly keep on easy terms with the lower classes ... in democratic times, you attach a poor man to you more by your manner than by benefits conferred ...

21. *The Intimate Letters of Archie Butt*, 12/4/08, p. 214, 2/28/09, p. 361 and "Wolf Hunt at White House," *NYT*, 12/9/08, and unpublished passage, Butt letter of 6/8/08. Archie Butt was military aide and confidant to Roosevelt and Taft. He wrote extensive letters to his mother and, when she died in late 1908, to his sister-in-law, Clara. His letters were published in two sets. The first, *The Letters of Archie Butt*, was from the final year of Roosevelt's presidency and will be cited as *Letters*. The second was from the Taft period and is entitled *Taft and Roosevelt: The Intimate Letters of Archie Butt, Military Aide*. Unpublished letters and passages are from the Butt Papers, Georgia Department of Archives and History, Atlanta, Georgia. The Kinetoscope, a trademark, flashed still photos sequentially to show motion. This exhibit was of a man fighting a wolf with his bare hands.
22. *Mrs. L: Conversations with Alice Roosevelt Longworth*, by Michael Teague, p. 72.
23. *Maniac in Milwaukee Shoots Col. Roosevelt*, *NYT*, 10/15/12.
24. Boy Scouts founder Lord Baden-Powell feared that young motorists would "grow brains instead of brawn" (Brendon, p. 208). In 1903, the *New York World* accused motorist William K. Vanderbilt of putting on ten pounds and labeled it "autofat." As for Roosevelt's view of unmanliness, he labeled critics of his actions in Panama "shrill eunuchs" (from *T.R.: The Last Romantic*, by H.W. Brands, 1997, p. 487).

In 1899 motorists celebrated that President William McKinley (1897–1901) took a ride in a Locomobile steamer. "Now that the horseless carriage has won the approval of the Chief Magistrate, its popularity will gain a decided impetus," crowed the ***Horseless Age*** magazine. McKinley's successor, Theodore Roosevelt (1901–1909), rode in an automobile on August 22, 1902, at Hartford, Connecticut. He was photographed there in a Columbia electric, made by the biggest name in automobiles, the Electric Vehicle Co. Delighted that the national leader seemed again to approve the machines, the ***Automobile and Motor Review*** reported, "These photographic views, it is said, give for the first time in history, the pictures of a President driven in an automobile instead of a vehicle drawn by horses." Unfortunately for the industry, Roosevelt wasn't photographed in a motor car again until 1906 — in "Porto Rico," as pictured here. This time it was in a White steam car, likely belonging to the American territorial governor or the U.S. Army. But why was the President otherwise rarely seen in automobiles in the United States after 1902? Roosevelt's "strenuous life"— and, more importantly, the politics thereof — precluded automobiles. To the politically sensitive, automobiles were a symbol not of progress but of predatory wealth. (Courtesy Library of Congress)

> that population does not ask them for the sacrifice of their money, but of their pride.[25]

Roosevelt was no commoner. His family was of the original Manhattan Dutch aristocracy. His Harvard degree and, better yet, Porcellian Club membership were as elite as they come. Roosevelt carefully maintained proper social form, fretting over decorum and the social blunders of others. He kept the posture and air of a president, as was his duty. When calling on ambassadors he rode in the official White House formal brougham carriage with a coachman and liveried footman.[26] He loved the exclusive game of tennis, and he kept it out of the news. Roosevelt

25. *Democracy in America*, by Alexis de Tocqueville, 1835 (from the New American Library version, edited by Richard D. Heffner, 1956).
26. See Butt, *Letters*, 12/12/08, p. 242.

Some of Roosevelt's Cabinet weren't so cautious of the undemocratic associations of automobiles. Secretary of State Elihu Root was a confirmed motorist, one of the earliest important politicians to use one regularly in Washington, starting in 1906. Taft was especially keen about the machines. In addition to using the Army steamers, he took rides in the Columbia touring car of his Washington friend William J. Boardman, and, in 1908, in Boardman's new Packard limousine. Pictured here in 1912, Elihu Root walks to a waiting limousine. (Courtesy Library of Congress)

was a social patrician and a political populist.

Not so his delightfully unruly First Daughter, popularly known as Princess Alice. Alice deliciously satisfied both convention and outrage. She was an effective political ambassador for her father, and the prize of New York's new money, whom he despised.[27] She arrived at Newport parties by automobile — sublime for the blatant reverse condescension to the newly rich and better yet for the car thing — ever more shocking for Daddy's disapproval. Alice's love for driving cars was equal parts rebellion, insult, and the sheer joy of the thing. The motor car was perfect for her.

When Roosevelt forbade smoking in the White House, Alice smoked on top of it. Where her pet snakes and betting at the races tried her father's patience, her motoring exploits sent him over the edge. She rode against her father's automotive disdain in gleeful rebellion. Not that anyone confused Alice's pranks for aristocratic vanity, but motoring — especially in Newport — was not the page one news her father was looking for. Little that Alice did went unnoticed. Reporters followed her everywhere, and she fed their libelous minds with antics close enough to their fabrications, such as that she danced alone for the men on the roof of Grace

27. See Butt, *Letters*, 1/28/09, pp. 312–313.

Vanderbilt's mansion. Alice was a master flirt and drove the boys— and girls—crazy. Her jealous cousin, the family prude Eleanor, once lamented that Alice was "crazier than ever ... I saw her ... in Bobbie Goelet's auto quite alone with three other men!" In 1903 the news was that Alice trekked from Boston to Newport in a friend's imported Panhard automobile in record time.

Buying or pretending to buy automobiles was a particularly joyous occasion for Alice. She cajoled a salesmen into giving her one on consignment, a red "United States Long Distance touring car." The $2,500 purchase made the papers— as did the retraction when the President stepped in to reverse the deal. Alice sent the bill to her grandfather, who financed many of her caprices. Her grandmother, who had no interest in Alice's games, returned the invoice. Alice was enraged. It didn't matter, for there was always the motor of fellow mischieveuse Maggie Cassini in which to cruise Washington streets, with suitors and cops in chase.[28]

So here was the President's daughter cavorting through Society and the scandal sheets, riding, driving, and buying automobiles. On top of it all, she invariably mixed with her father's politics. Her hanging out with E.H. Harriman's daughter, he of the railroad trust the President was in the process of "busting," made her father

Despite his horse-bound ways, the automobile crept up around President Roosevelt. At his 1905 inauguration, a White Model "E" steamer led a military procession, the only automobile in a parade full of whooping "rough riders" on horseback. At the wheel was Walter White, one of three brothers who ran the famous sewing machine company's automobile division. Walter White was an indefatigable promoter. He ran the mails in London, a Vanderbilt Cup race, and long distance trials to prove the quality of White cars. One of White's most prestigious customers was the U.S. Army. (Courtesy Henry Merkel)

28. This section from *Princess Alice*, by James Brough, 1975, pp. 148–149, 157, 168; "Alice," by Howard Teichmann, 1979, p. 38; *Alice Roosevelt Longworth* by Carol Felsenthal, 1988, pp. 63–64; "Miss Roosevelt's New Fad," *NYT*, 5/31/03; "Alice Roosevelt Becomes a Motorist," *Automobile*, 6/6/03, p. 610; and "President and the Press Agent," *Automobile*, 7/4/03, p. 20. The latter article noted that the President's anger over Alice's automobile purchase was at not just at her but at the company official who publicized it. "We imagine that should the President run across this gentleman he will be likely to get a brief insight into the strenuous life," wrote the *Automobile*.

seriously worry about his daughter's effect upon the 1904 election. That election was more important to him than anything, for it was to free him of McKinley and the title "His Accidency." The election he won, and by a landslide, all the more for his daughter's fame.

* * *

Meanwhile, automobiles ran across the nation and through the headlines, with or without Alice, and almost wholly without her father. The virtues and evils of automobiling kept newspaper editors and letter writers busy, and spiked advertising dollars and newsstand sales. While the gasoline motor revolutionized old tools such as trucks, omnibuses, ambulances, and farm equipment, the image of the automobile was decidedly and in the worst way patrician.

Automobiling had barely made it from the sports to the news sections, when the evil "scorcher" took over, "the worst enemy of the sport...."[29] In 1902, the *Times* railed,

> The worthless sons of an earlier generation of rich men in this country used to manifest their high spirits and low breeding by getting drunk and becoming disorderly in public places, to the annoyance and disgust of decent people. That sort of thing was tolerated for a time, and then the police and the police courts put an end to it.... There are fifty or a hundred times as many rich men's sons now ... those among them who are cads and rowdies are justly regarded as about the least useful class of society. A good many of this class have taken to automobiles....[30]

Next to offend were their chauffeurs, low-bred servants to the rich who governed car and master alike, and who maimed innocents in the streets. "Chauffeurs Lord It Over Their Employers," declared the *Times* in 1906.[31] Extending their hegemony from machines to their mechanically-ignorant masters, chauffeurs refused to wash cars, spat upon the livery they were asked to wear, and demanded ever greater pay. "My chauffeur acts as though he were conferring an honor upon me in consenting to drive my car," grumbled an ACA member. "The more we give chauffeurs the more they want," a garage manager complained. If that wasn't bad enough, along with the attitude was its ultimate expression in "joy riding," unauthorized use of a car. Owners noted that even when they weren't out motoring the gasoline bills remained high. During idle times, some chauffeurs offered the car for hire. Others used it to impress the ladies, such as an imported French chauffeur who found himself in doubly deep trouble when he was caught speeding and joy riding with a couple of girls along.[32]

Stealing away in the boss's car became a subject of considerable attention in the press, the courts, and state capitals. In New York joy riding was labeled an official menace. Rhode Island banned operation of motor vehicles without the owner's consent. While courts in Pennsylvania and Maryland contemplated whether or not joy riding was theft, New Jersey codified it as an offense punishable by up to three years in prison. A company was formed in Manhattan "to spot machines and inform owners of their chauffeurs' actions."[33] Garages promised to monitor chauffeurs and report unauthorized use.

Newspapers publicized every automobile death. Monday morning readers

29. "Automobile Topics of Interest," *NYT*, 7/13/02.
30. *NYT*, editorial, 6/1/02.
31. *NYT*, 8/12/06.
32. "French Chauffeur Arrested," *NYT*, 10/9/02.
33. See "Motoring," *Evening Star*, 3/21/09, 4/18/09.

were treated to lurid accounts of the weekend's carnage.[34] The joyful horror included blown tires, overturned cars, and dead motorists, such as one Mr. Harmon whose demise came of a popped tire outside of Boston. As the car "skidded badly," Harmon and a passenger bailed out, "fearing it was going to turn turtle," and abandoning Mrs. Harmon who remained in the car, unhurt.[35] That automobilists mostly killed themselves soothed but would hardly contain the outrage. Intimations of a link between alcohol and auto accidents provoked further indignance. "One automobilist recently made the sage remark that there would be fewer accidents if the principle were recognized that cocktails and gasoline did not mix," wrote the *Times*. "How many fatalities may have been due to more or less generous mixing of fiery fluids probably will never be known."[36]

In every place and way the automobile seemed an illegitimate wild child in need of the civilizing effects of legislatures and police. Motor clubs fretted over speed-crazed scorchers and delinquent chauffeurs. Self-policing was the topic for these groups, who feared that if there were no restraint the state would do it for them. Overly spirited drivers were expelled, such as one irrepressible scorcher who was tossed from a New Jersey club for having hit a spectacular 90 M.P.H. on Ocean Avenue at Long Branch.[37]

Automotive law was haphazard and irregular, varying from town to town and state to state. Until reciprocity deals were struck amongst the states, some of which held out until the 1920s, it was necessary to register a car wherever it was driven. To run a car throughout the Washington area, three tags and licenses were needed, one each for Maryland, Virginia, and the District of Columbia. One car seen there sported eight plates.[38] Speed laws were locally designated, there being towns that banned automobiles altogether. This brought about cries for federal standards and rules, a natural for the nationalist-minded progressives.

Instead, automobiles were problems for the rich who'd have to fend for themselves. Automobiling was political taboo—except for ridicule. Politicians scorned motors as a threat to horse and farm, and used anti-automobile rhetoric as voter bait. "I am tired of having half a dozen high collared fellows riding around in automobiles," Rep. Stanley of Kentucky complained during a House debate over an agricultural appropriation, "eating canvasback duck and drinking champagne, and then going up in the country and telling the farmer how to milk his cow."[39] Get caught in a car and you were to be hung by Harriman's high collar or drowned in Vanderbilt's champagne.

At the White House, Roosevelt might have chosen otherwise with automobiles. He might have followed that adventurous instinct that tempted him into an electric automobile in a parade in Hartford, Connecticut, in 1902. He might have been taken with his daughter's motoring enthusiasms as he was, briefly, in 1905, when

34. See "Scorching Through 1902: 'The Automobile Terror'" by Michael L. Bromley, *Automotive History Review*, 2003.
35. "Automobile Accidents for Ninety Days," *NYT*, 9/1/07.
36. Continuing, "Many of the accidents, however, which have filled the Monday morning papers with such harrowing details were undoubtedly due to the incapacity of the drivers to see straight ahead, for it is equally true that the man at the wheel must have his lights as bright and steady as the brilliant acetylene light in front of the car to light up the road ahead" ("Automobile Accidents for Ninety Days").
37. "Auto Club Expels Thomas," *NYT*, 12/8/09.
38. "More Laws for Autos," *Evening Star*, 3/23/09.
39. "Laughs at the 'Uplift,'" *Evening Star*, 3/2/09.

At first automobiles were considered harmless extensions of the bicycle craze. Eccentrics and the ever odd American inventor such as the Stanley brothers and Henry Ford raised curiosity, not ire. Into 1902 automobiling was reported in newspaper sports sections. Soon, the machines intruded the headlines and the streets. They were not welcomed. This c. 1904 view of Broadway at Prince Street in New York City gives us a good idea of how automobiles might fit in: with difficulty. Autos not only competed with horses for street space, they did so in a different time zone: motorists complained of horse-era speed limits that were impossibly slow. Trolley cars, meanwhile, sped along, maiming and killing with greater efficiency than automobiles. Automobiles caught the bad press. Trolleys, you see, were not instruments of privilege. When President Roosevelt's carriage was hit by a trolley, killing a Secret Serviceman, the President blamed the driver, not the technology. When automobiles killed, the entire species was condemned. (Courtesy Library of Congress)

he took a ride in a 40 H.P. Columbia up the conduit road along the Potomac River. Or he might have tried out the wheel of a White steamer somewhere else than in Puerto Rico, as he did in 1906. In no case was there any follow-through. As with his first rides in Washington, back to the horse it was.[40]

These episodes were few and generally unpublicized. Roosevelt preferred it that way. Upon heading out on his first ride in Washington, a White House policeman put a hand over the lens of a photographer who tried to record the event. "One would expect that the Chief Executive of the United States, because of his established strenuous disposition, would have taken to the automobile with unhesitating alacrity," wrote the *Automobile*. "But President Roosevelt has surrendered gradually, and even now his use of the motor-driven vehicle is more or less spasmodic."[41] The city of Washington's low automobile population placed it "behind other cities of much less importance," observed the *Automobile* in 1905.[42] The District's first automobile club was started in 1906. Its rolls remained distinctly free of public figures. Politicians

40. "The President's Ride," *Automobile and Motor Review*, 9/20/02, p. 14, and "President Takes to Auto," *Automobile*, 5/28/05, pp. 681–682. A month later his car was stopped by a policeman for doing twenty-five along the Conduit road. He told the chauffeur to slow down, and went his way. Upon reaching Great Falls, Maryland, he climbed out and walked a few miles before being picked up again by the automobile ("President Held Up," *Automobile*, 6/29/05, p. 791). There is some confusion over Roosevelt's ride in Puerto Rico, as the event is often cited as having taken place in Cuba. He stopped at Puerto Rico on his return from Panama. In neither place did he step from U.S. territory. The Puerto Rican visit was heralded as "An American President's First Visit to an American Colony" (*Harper's Weekly*, 12/22/06, p. 1856).
41. "The Strenuous President and the Automobile," *Automobile*, 5/3/06, p. 746.
42. 9/14/05, p. 297. The *Automobile* estimated there were about 2,000 automobiles in Washington. The number of registered cars was actually half that, which only strengthens the complaint (see appendix).

with the motor bug only did so vicariously through the garages of the local rich. Roosevelt's "intense loyalty to the horse," a journal later complained, "...put a damper on all forms of motoring enthusiasm ... [he] went so far as to almost never ride in an automobile."[43]

The day he left office, Roosevelt was said to have declined an offer for a motor ride to the train station. "I came to the inauguration in this horse-drawn vehicle and I will leave in it," he said that stormy day of March 4, 1909.[44]

43. "Prominent People Who Use the Automobile," *American Motorist*, Feb. 1910, p. 66. The article continued, "The only exceptions were in a few instances when committees that received him on his speech-making tours had provided no vehicles except motor cars and thus left the strenuous one no alternative."
44. The source was a White House chauffeur, George Robinson, who fudged on some stories he told as an old man in the 1960s. The sentiment was entirely accurate (*Presidents on Wheels*, by Herbert Ridgeway Collins, 1971, p. 134).

2

From Whence a President

I do not believe there can be found in the whole country a man so well fitted to be President.

—Theodore Roosevelt on William Howard Taft, June, 1908[1]

The United States at the turn of the 20th Century was a world power, even if no one realized or dared to acknowledge it.[2] At home, George Washington's warning against "foreign entanglements" was still taken seriously. The Old World that was about to implode into the worst span of violence and murder in history—a self-destruction that unleashed the American Century—was on an edge of collapse as yet unforeseen. While England tripped over Africa and India, Spain lost just about everything, and Russia was embarrassed by the Japanese, the other late-coming colonial powers such as Belgium, Holland, and Germany were yanked around by the likes of Venezuela, China, Morocco and other unruly overseas possessions and national novelties. America, still an historical curiosity, was, as ever, concerned only with herself.

Following McKinley's reluctant war against Spain that brought the first American colonies, Roosevelt wielded the country's latent might to arbitrate several international conflicts, netting a Nobel prize along the way. He sent the American fleet around the world, an unprecedented act, provocative and bold. But the real game was in dollars. It was reported in 1908 that one third of the world's cash circulated in the United States.[3] The American genius for money making was far more menacing than the Monroe Doctrine or the U.S. Navy.

Where the computer age brings efficiency to old things, the turn of the 20th Century was all new things. Americans turned scientific rationalism into real advance, with electricity, margarine, telephones, photostat copiers, and modern medicine the product. Like sorcerers, industrialists conjured machines, rails, skyscrapers, consumer products, and money, unheard of money, seemingly out of the air. Solutions were everywhere. Cities

1. *The Life and Times of William Howard Taft*, by Henry F. Pringle, p. 356.
2. McKinley knew it. On the taking of the Philippines he said, "And so it has come to pass that in a few short months we have become a world power..." (*In the Days of McKinley*, by Margaret Leech, 1959, p. 464).
3. "Currency of Nation," *Evening Star*, 12/10/08.

could be sculpted, cancer could be cured. Even pitcher Christy Mathewson's vicious spitball could be explained by physics.[4]

The show was impressive, but to wary eyes that peeked behind the curtains it could not possibly go on. The historically minded Henry Adams gazed upon a display of monstrous electric motors at the 1900 World's Fair and saw in them progress and destruction.[5] A disturbing social disorder emerged from beneath the smoke. Business and science that could solve all problems were the cause of all problems. Dread fear overcame many. A new, unsure word hit the lexicon, "pragmatic."[6] For those not inclined towards reality, another word seemed pure, "socialism." What science wrought politics would heal.

The period was fallow. While a middle class discovered itself and the newly rich gave meaning to consumption, sucked into the industrial machine were farm boys who traded Jeffersonian liberty for hourly wages and immigrants and Southern blacks who flooded Northern cities and competed for the same. The far West, smacked against the ocean wall, struggled for a new order somewhere between corporate mines, rails, and cattle and the idealized and cruel equalities of the old frontier. Anarchists, unionists, suffragists, prohibitionists, and socialists got busy mucking about, kicking up noise and class envy. The grievances were real, but the choir was doped on change and propelled by enthusiasms that exceeded the means.

The old order reacted with its own sometimes serious, sometimes flippant, and often ludicrous enthusiasm for novelty — so long as there was no compromise as measured by its political and social authority. Its subscription to new thinking might be summed up by Mrs. Campbell's "My dear, I don't care what they do, so long as they don't do it in the street and frighten the horses."[7] Social awareness consisted of "slumming," stealth excursions across the tracks akin to a visit to the zoo, and vain philanthropies such as to bring about social betterment through song or loaning automobiles to striking workers. These were the days when John D. Rockefeller tossed about nickels with the advice to put them in the bank.[8]

On the one hand were the "octopuses" — the monopolies, and the attack upon which propelled Roosevelt to enormous popularity. These "trusts," which arose upon the capital of the incredible American business expansion, sought greater returns, efficiencies, and reduced competition through large organizations, in the modern tongue a conglomerate or holding company. The "robber baron" label mistakes wealth for corruption; the two went hand-in-hand as ever, but specifically, not universally. The excesses of the Gilded Age came not in money corruption so much as the amazing number of zeroes that followed the dollar signs and the political dominance that trailed behind it. For the corrupt, gobs of lubricant greased the way with bought judges, politicians, customs agents, and regulators. Nothing new there. For the rest, the law protected their ways. Yes, business was well represented in Congress and well protected by property rights–defending courts, a certain Judge Taft included when

4. Matty's spitball was rewarded with an automobile bought by admirers ("Secret of 'Matty's' Curves Scientifically Solved," 8/18/12 and "Baseball an Aid to Auto Industry," 10/20/12, *NYT*).
5. See "The Dynamo and the Virgin," Chapter XXV, *The Education of Henry Adams*, by Henry Adams, rep. 1974.
6. For a contemporaneous, popular view of the word, see "What's Pragmatism, Anyway?" *NYT*, 11/10/07.
7. Attributed (see *Bartlett's*, 16th edition, p. 590:7).
8. Piers Brendon wrote of an English suffragette who sought "to restore to the brutalized urban masses their lost sense of the pulsating joy of Merrie England by means of folk songs and Morris dances" (see Brendon, p. 161 and "Rockefeller Tips 5 Cents," *NYT*, 12/10/08).

William Howard Taft. U.S. Solicitor General, Federal Judge, Governor of the Philippines, Secretary of War ... and now, President of the United States of America. Ambitious? You bet. But the big guy didn't stop there. In 1921 he became Chief Justice of the Supreme Court. Most associations with Taft include a 350 pound-capacity scale, a White House cow, and a very large bathtub. Try this: Great American. "Corpulent," "affable," "lazy" and other such descriptions should be dispelled — Taft was a dynamic, ambitious leader and a visionary in law, society — and automobiles. He was also nearly arrested for picking flowers. When he stole buds from a Department of Agriculture garden to bring to his wife, the watchmen hollered and threatened arrest. "I am put here for a purpose, and I have to obey my orders whether it is the President or not," he said. Taft laughed, "Right you are. Do you want me to go to the station house with you?" (Courtesy Library of Congress)

he rode the Federal Circuit Court in the 1890s.

Latter-half 19th Century politics were driven by the long fight against the railroads, headed principally by Western agrarian interests exercising new found power, that of shipper over carrier and that translated politically into "the people" over "the interests." In the 1880s the fight spilled into Washington. The railroads were the first of the period's businesses to patently present a challenge to federalism, being undisputably engaged in interstate commerce. And they brought their clients with them across those state lines, be it Chicago meatpackers or Kansas farmers. The impact and symbolism of the railroad, good and bad, cannot be underestimated. The tentacles of the octopuses were spread by rail. Rockefeller grew Standard Oil to dominance in large part through manipulation of railroad rates. Pittsburgh steel went for and by rail. The names Depew, Vanderbilt, Harriman, and Hill were of the railroads. The first national strike started at a rail car maker and was spread across the country along rail lines that carried its Pullman cars. Roosevelt's first anti-trust client was the railroad conglomerate, Northern Securities.[9] The Panama Canal was seen as the way to break the back of the railroads. With the money, the railroads had the political power. With the political power, the railroads became the political target.

Roosevelt seized the moment under the standard of regulation. His conservation policies were as much to preserve nature as to protect it from the monopolies. Exploitation of Alaskan coal was fine so long as it was not by anyone named Guggenheim. The trust busting itself was not the clear-cut forest it would seem. Where Roosevelt gave new life to the 1890 Sherman Anti-Trust Act, he sought to manage the trusts as much as to destroy them. His Bureau of Corporations would,

9. Morgan's gigantic steel and rail industry mergers were the catalyst for the trust-busting, although Roosevelt only went after the railroad conglomerate. Following Roosevelt's anti-trust case against the company, Senator Mark Hanna wrote, "I warned Hill that McKinley might have to act against his company... Mr.

through scientific investigation, bring order to the dichotomy between the abuse and license of big business.

Roosevelt's success was to braid these tensions into a political rope of great resilience. Had McKinley's detached manner taken on the 20th Century the balance may have shifted more to the radical; more likely, his quiet resolve would have steadied the intoxication of change. As it was, his assassination served as a mandate for action. Between the murders of Lincoln and McKinley, anarchists claimed a Russian Czar, a King of Italy, a President of France, a Prime Minister of Spain, and an Empress of Austria. Their new word "terrorism" would mar the next centuries.[10] When it came to assassins, labor agitators, and William Jennings Bryan, even Republican conservatives welcomed Roosevelt's, to them, embarrassing moralizing. In a marvelous display of commotion, Roosevelt lashed out in all directions.

The Roosevelt chief executive, like Andrew Jackson, defied the country's republican traditions. This anti-elitist President managed to wield the power of a king — more than any monarch around, in fact. A remark by the French Ambassador to President Taft that the American leader held more power than any other, including the English King, the German Kaiser, and the recently neutered Russian Czar, would have been absurd two Presidents earlier; after Roosevelt it was fact. Roosevelt imagined a strong presidency guided by the public good as much as by Congress and the Constitution. There was more than a little irony to Senator Augustus Bacon's reply to Roosevelt's kidding about the Senator's "turning pale" when Roosevelt took the oath of office. "On the contrary, Mr. President," Bacon laughed, "I never felt so relieved in my life."[11]

William Howard Taft appeared just the man to follow Roosevelt. Although he tempered his rhetoric with "the guarantees of the Constitution," Taft was a true believer in Rooseveltian policy and person, even if the two were frequently indistinguishable. It was understood that Taft would not imitate Roosevelt, a relief to many, especially in Congress, but there was no doubt that he would follow Roosevelt's policies — indeed, he would put the rhetoric into law. To those worried that Taft might not live up to his example, Roosevelt replied, "The system may be different, but the results will be the same."[12]

Nevertheless, the colossal 1912 battle between the two men was previewed in President-elect Taft's January 1909 ad

9. (*cont.*) Roosevelt's done it" (from *Hanna* by Thomas Beer, p. 246, as per *Theodore Roosevelt: A Biography*, by Henry F. Pringle, p. 254; note that citations henceforth for "Pringle" refer to the Taft biography, *The Life and Times of William Howard Taft*; if the source is from Pringle's Roosevelt biography, it will be noted *Roosevelt*).

10. "The Assassination of Kings and Presidents," *Century Magazine*, Vol. LXIII, 1902, p. 18. A prayer that terrorism ends with the centennial of the McKinley assassination. Terrorism being war by other means, it represents either a failed political solution or a failed political movement. In the United States, anarchy's revolution never rose because of the political system's incredible ability to absorb dissent and refashion it in mainstream politics. There is no deeper grave for radicalism than American politics (or the American university).

11. Butt, *Letters*, 1/11/09, p. 282. On the whole, Roosevelt played it according to Hoyle. It is difficult to point to specific instances of his extra–Constitutional acts. He did, he didn't, and sort of, sometimes. The change he brought was in attitude. For example, a dreaded thought that the Government would take over coal mines spurred the conclusion to a 1902 strike in which owners were otherwise unwilling to compromise (when McKinley and Hanna thwarted a similar strike in 1900 the difference from Roosevelt was in volume not effect; as ever, Morgan played the reaper). Or, Roosevelt reserved massive areas of public lands from development just before signing a law that prohibited it, and he organized executive commissions without sanction from Congress.

12. Butt, *Letters*, 1/11/09, p. 283.

monishment to the impatient: "I know that sometimes the Constitution seems to be in the way of direct operation ... [and] seems to work against the rapid carrying out of some of the reforms," he warned, but the Constitution that "has in the past been capable ... to meet the emergencies" would do so again.[13] To the governor of Kansas, who demanded change, change, change, the President-elect wrote,

> We must work along with our Constitution as it is. It is a most wonderful instrument, most elastic for accomplishing purposes that were only dimly in the minds of its framers, and I think after you contemplate the history of the country one of the wisest features of the instrument is the difficulty with which it can be amended.[14]

Taft was elected on Roosevelt's coattails, openly calling it his job to put into law the moral awakening Roosevelt had stirred in the people. Roosevelt's Secretary of Commerce and Labor, Oscar Straus, said of Taft, "He will write in to the statutes the great moral principles his predecessor has written in the hearts of the people." Just how were those "moral principles" to be translated into law? The problem was that the morally aroused weren't disposed to talk process and law. They wanted the world, and they wanted it now. President-elect Taft was aware of their passions and their impatience for orderly reform. Before taking office he reminded the nation that its Constitution was "a most wonderful instrument, most elastic for accomplishing purposes that were only dimly in the minds of its framers...." Taft is quoted in this cartoon saying, "We have gotten along pretty well with that Constitution." Theodore Roosevelt read that newspaper. Did he approve? (From *Evening Star*, 11/28/08)

* * *

States' rights fifty years before fought the wrong battle and lost to abolition and nationalism, which in turn gave to a peculiar mix of Reconstruction, Jim Crow, industrialism, and the 14th Amendment. While Southern Democrats remained fiercely loyal to the states' rights banner and Northern Republicans defended high tariffs and capital, otherwise known as "property rights," the West, with its own concerns and no longer isolated, especially from Eastern markets and banks, was becoming a third political axis. The "Western" power base consisted of mid-country and populist opposition to Eastern power

13. The reforms Taft referred to were "the conservation of our natural resources and perhaps the regulation of railroads and the meeting of those evils, those abuses, which have crept in with our marvelous progress in the combination of capital" ("Taft Stands by Constitution," *Evening Star*, 1/15/09).
14. The Governor wanted to limit federal judicial terms (Taft to WR Stubbs, 1/4/09). Remember this line

structures, and the far–West, with its new Senate seats that gave the region a force in Washington proportionally in excess of its economic output and population. By 1909, the Republican party was splintering along these grains. The "regulars" or "Old Guard" represented the status quo, with its long incumbency and hold on the majority in Congress. Bucking that grip were the Republican "insurgents," so-called for voting against the party leadership. This group consisted mostly of newcomers to Congress and was predominantly of the middle–West.

Atop the Republican establishment were Senator Nelson W. Aldrich and Speaker of the House Joseph G. "Uncle Joe" Cannon. (None dared give Aldrich a nickname.) The two men dominated Congress. At a White House dinner Aldrich flatly declared to President Taft that there would be no amendments to a bill. Observing this, Senator Elihu Root grabbed Cannon by the hand and led him to Aldrich. "Mr. Czar, let me introduce you to your fellow Czar."[15] These were the "standpatters," and they were as committed to their ideals as any others. Chauncey Depew defined the breed as "one who, like a Puritan, would die for dogma and go into obscurity for a principle."[16]

Nelson Wilmarth Aldrich. "Standpatter" supreme, "the High Chauffeur of the Golden Juggernaut," and the Republican leader of the Senate. Aldrich was in 1909 the Senate King of kings, Czar of czars. He was never caught in a cartoon with a smile. (Arthur Dove cartoon, c. 1909, Courtesy Library of Congress)

Although sold to the public by their detractors as representing all that was wrong with the country, the standpatters did not hold for corruption or abuse. Their finger in the dike was a principled attempt to preserve prosperity, property rights, and the Constitution, all of which they saw threatened by immoderate reformers. Cannon summed it up with, "I'm goddamned tired of listening to all this babble for reform. America is a hell of a success."[17]

This old school Republicanism was expressed in the party's 1908 platform:

> This great historic organization, that destroyed slavery, preserved the Union, restored credit, expanded the national domain, established a sound financial system, developed the industries and resources of the country, and gave to the nation her seat of honor in the councils of the world....

But the sentence was completed by the new Republicanism of Roosevelt:

> ...now meets the new problems of government with the same courage and capacity with which it solved the old.[18]

14. (*cont.*) when you get to the part of this book about the Progressive Party's call for easier amendment of the Constitution.
15. Butt, 6/25/09, p. 131.
16. "Tribute to Sherman at Republican Club," *NYT*, 11/25/12. "Standing pat" was generally a reference to tariff questions, but by the time Depew said this the operative word was "conservative."
17. *William Howard Taft: An Intimate History*, by Judith Icke Anderson, 1981, p. 139.
18. *National Party Platforms*, compiled by Donald Bruce Johnson and Kirk H. Porter, 1973, p. 157.

Joseph Gurney Cannon. "Uncle Joe" was the Speaker of the House. "I'm goddamned tired of listening to all this babble for reform. America is a hell of a success." (Clifford Berryman cartoon, c.1909, Courtesy Library of Congress)

Between these bookends, somehow, old Republican principles, under whose "guidance ... the American people have become the richest nation in the world" would meet "new problems" with new ideas. Without incongruity, Taft accepted the nomination on both premises.

Across the legislative isle was the Democratic party. At its essence the party was still Jefferson's heir, defenders of states' rights, the farmer, and the philosophy of "don't tread on me." Democrats spent the previous fifty years besieged by Republican and federal political dominance. Occasionally a Democrat made it close to the top post, generally on behalf of opposition to Republican hegemony or the populist movements of low tariffs, silver currency, labor, and the farm. The successful exception was Grover Cleveland, an Eastern, conservative reformer. The chief practitioner of Democratic populism was William Jennings Bryan of Nebraska, one of the new West.

The Republican insurgents met between Bryan and Roosevelt, leaders who skated above their party's core on the veneers of popular appeal. Their constituency was change. The insurgents ran to inevitably similar destinations as the Mugwumps, earlier Republican defectors who were left abandoned in their protest, and the Populists of the 1880s and 1890s agrarian, anti-railroad revolts who were absorbed into Bryan's Democracy. The Democrats found themselves frequently in bed with insurgents whose political foundation lay in a similar appeal to the common man, only through the national rather than the state capitals.[19] "An insurgent has not the manhood to be a Democrat," chided Henry de Lamar Clayton. "He is too much of a coward, but he realizes that people are sick of Republican misrule. The insurgent is willing to tear down the chosen leader of his party and refuses to aid in carrying out the policies of his party."[20]

Taft came into the mix on behalf of Roosevelt's policies. He was above all an ardent Republican. He was sympathetic to the insurgents but realized the need to work with the regulars who held power. He was friendly to the Democrats, especially Southerners who he felt were unjustly exiled by Republican politics, but he wouldn't budge on the Constitution and its Jim Crow–defying 15th Amendment

19. A 1905 Gridiron joked that a debate between Roosevelt and Bryan was futile. "What's the use? They're both on the same side" (from *The President Speaks Off-the-Record*, by Harold Brayman, p. 58).
20. "Calls Cannon Meanest Man," *NYT*, 7/19/10.

William Jennings Bryan. Nobody, nobody, could rile up the masses like W.J. Bryan. Only he was never able to rile up enough of them to get him into the White House. He lost, for the third time, on the Democratic ticket in 1908. His most promising issue in 1908 was tariff reform. Taft stole it from him by promising the same. Here he is during the campaign. (Courtesy Library of Congress).

and the guarantee of black suffrage. He was of the old West of Ohio and unfamiliar with the new West of Minnesota and California. Taft saw it his job to make in law the moral awakening which he said was Roosevelt's greatest achievement, the unspoken and deadly inescapable logic to which being that Roosevelt failed to put that movement into law.

To that end Taft purposefully sought legal talent for his Cabinet. He wanted a team of lawyers whose expertise could transform rhetoric to statutes. He wrote the Governor of Missouri, Herbert Hadley, a lawyer whom he wanted in the Cabinet,

> My idea is to get five as good lawyers as I could get in the country, who have had large experience in corporate matters, who subscribe to my views on the subjects as indicated in my Inaugural Address which you will read, and who know enough about law to draft the needed amendments to the statutes; whose standing before the business community is such as to commend the result of their judgement, and to enable me, therefore, to get the suggested amendments through both Houses of Congress. *It is the business of my Administration to do something, and to embody what we do in statutory form.* There is no need to advise you, for you are a lawyer, that the difference between proclamation and result in the form either of a statute or a judgement is very wide. The President has preached a crusade and has nerved the people up to demand reform. Now it falls on me to clinch the matter by securing the necessary statutes, and that is

> a very different thing from carrying on a popular propaganda[21] [italics added].

Taft defined "the matter" by his 1908 platform. A political instrument, it was a compromise between conservatives and liberals. Both sides saw it as a betrayal. Taft defined his presidency by it.

Shortly after the convention, insurgent Senator Robert La Follette wrote Taft to implore him to support a cause of his the platform had ignored:

> You could do no single thing which would go so far to disarm the opposition and *repair our barren legislative record*, and the bad work of the convention. There is widespread distrust of the reactionary spirit that controlled the Chicago convention[22] [italics added].

On the other side, it was generally assumed that Speaker Cannon would scuttle the platform just as easily as La Follette wanted to amend it in the opposite way. Taft aimed to steer between these extremes in order to fulfill his pledges, which Roosevelt himself fully endorsed. Honest and unusually resolute, Taft ultimately prevailed. By the end of his term his promises were substantially enacted into law. And he may well have carried his program into a second term but for the one man who started the whole thing. During Taft's four years this man was like a grenade on the table, quiet if unmolested, but ever a deadly potential. In 1912, Theodore Roosevelt pulled the pin.

* * *

In 1906 Congress appropriated nearly $2,000,000 for Army field maneuvers. The tests included automobiles, among which were two White steamers purchased by the War Department that June.[23] It was largely found that the automobiles were only useful for staff movements, not general transport. The only other official automobile news from Washington that year was a restrictive automobile law for the District of Columbia. Sponsored by Rep. Thetus Sims, the law promised to protect D.C. residents from the automobile menace. "If there is anything the matter with this bill, it is that it is too lenient, he huffed"[24]

The Roosevelt Government came as

21. Taft to HS Hadley, 2/23/09, Taft Papers, Library of Congress (LC). See also Taft to WR Nelson, 2/23/09, for Taft on the lawyer Cabinet. In the letter, Taft criticized Roosevelt's Justice Department, which, Taft felt, needed to be "reorganize[d] on a basis for accomplishing things. It has needed it for a number of years." Roosevelt biographers have criticized Taft for his lawyer-cabinet as a betrayal of Roosevelt (see Brands, p. 666).
22. La Follette to Taft, 7/17/08. See *The Big Stick and the Congressional Gavel* by Carl E. Hatch which reviews the "Do-Nothing" 60th Congress about which La Follette here complains. "It has been generally conceded that Roosevelt and Congress by May, 1908, were mutually disgusted with one another," wrote Hatch (p. 48). Hatch's book filled an historical gap left open by other historians, as most treatments of Roosevelt tend to gloss over this aspect of his final two years in office. Hatch avoided judgement, although he concluded that Roosevelt won the popularity contest with Congress, a victory that boomeranged on him in 1912.
23. "Opportunities for Motor Trucks in Army Manouevres," 6/20/06, pp. 930–931 and "Automobiles in the Army Manoeuvres," 10/24/06, pp. 503–504, *Horseless Age*. "Commanding generals have been requested to make reports to the War Department on the merits and demerits of cars used by them" ("War Department Buys Autos," *Automobile*, 6/28/06, p. 1007). Afterwards, an Army Captain told *Horseless Age*, " in my opinion the main reliance of the army between terminal stations and the front will always be upon beasts of burden." The Government also purchased a Royal Tourist and a Franklin light truck for the war games. Through the Roosevelt years, the Army policy on automobiles was that they were for personal transport, and their use had to be justifiably cheaper than other means of transport, such as for ambulances. Historian Norman Cary wrote, "The only exception... was if the automobile functioned as the most feasible method for an officer or enlisted man to perform his duties" (Cary, p. 24).
24. "Simms Bill Passes Without Dissent," *Automobile*, 3/15/06, p. 512. The bill passed the House as Sims wanted it, although the Senate cut its more drastic elements.

close as it ever would to automobiles in 1905 when it was learned that petroleum-less Germany was keen about running motors, lamps, and heaters on denatured alcohol. The idea hit the United States with an uncommon force in 1906. Congress debated relieving alcohol intended for "industrial purposes" of vice taxes. The President gave the movement his "hearty sympathy," and he set the Department of Agriculture to look into it. Prohibitionists were appalled. Farmers were thrilled. Motorists were delighted at the news from the Secretary of Agriculture that corncobs could be turned into motor fuel at three cents a gallon. Coincidently, 1906 was the year the Government sued the Standard Oil Company for violation of the Sherman anti-trust law. It was a nice fit, this finding an alternative to kerosene and gasoline. And it went away in 1907 as Department of Agriculture tests turned up little of substance. Standard Oil was relieved of the corncob threat. The *Times* joked, "Many persons have often imagined from the reckless way in which some automobiles are piloted through the city streets that they were being run, to some extent, at least, upon whisky...."[25] If farmers could benefit from fueling automobiles, that was one thing, but Roosevelt never got any closer to finding virtue in them than to hope for cheap fuel culled of Kansas fields.

By the latter half of his second term, Roosevelt abandoned any realistic legislative program. His triumphs and his losses, both substantial, were secure. He became less vigilant about his public posturing, more vigorous with his public moralizing, and more careless in seeking out enemies. Even if he didn't endorse the automobile, he allowed it around him. Secretary of State Elihu Root motored to and from the Executive offices.[26] Secretary of War Taft took rides in Army motors. During the summer vacation at his Long Island home in 1907, Roosevelt allowed the two Army White steamers to be used as utility cars for visitors.

> One of the fixtures of the "summer capital" at Oyster Bay, ever since President Roosevelt's return to his home on June 12 last, has been two 30-horsepower White steamers, fitted with seven-passenger Pullman bodies. They are "on the job" every day in the week from 7 A.M. to 1 o'clock the next morning, and the reception they meet with at the hands of the various government officials who are conveyed in them is often amusing. "A regular government star route conveyance," is the way Secretary of War Taft characterized them to Postmaster-General Meyer, as they entered one of the cars at the Oyster Bay station last week. There is a sign at the gate to the presidential estate which reads, "No Automobiles Allowed," but it does not apply to the two government White steamers' arrival at the Roosevelt home.

The steamers were Taft's babies, and he was mad about them. "I wish Sagamore Hill was further away from the station," he said upon arrival.[27] In a few weeks, Roosevelt himself made news for trying out the steamers. He was henceforth seen arriving and departing

25. From "Denatured Alcohol in Germany," *Automobile*, 10/26/05, "Report on Farm Motors Favors Free Alcohol," 5/31/06, *Automobile*, 3/15/06, p. 504, "Free Alcohol Bill Passes," *Automobile*, 5/31/06, "Alcohol When Used as a Motor Fuel," *Automobile*, 9/20/06, p. 380, "U.S. Government Tests Alcohol as Fuel," *Automobile*, 9/26/07, p. 416 and "Whisky as Auto Fuel," *NYT*, 2/17/07.

26. Root rented an electric brougham in 1906 for $350 a month, placing him at the fore of motoring politicians. In 1907 he purchased a Packard "30" touring car, which he either replaced or supplemented with a Packard "18" limousine in 1909 for $4,400. Root loved to motor. Later, he enjoyed to drive between Washington, New York, and his home at Clinton, New York. "One of the great things about motoring," he wrote, "is that in hot weather you can make your own breeze by moving swiftly without having to feel sorry for the horse" (from *Elihu Root*, by Philip C. Jessup, 1938, pp. 461, 502 and *The Papers of Elihu Root*, LC).

27. "The White machines are considered absolutely indispensable to the expeditious handling of government work at Oyster Bay, and one or both of them meet every arriving train all day long, besides performing numerous other forms of service" ("Secretary of War Taft Likes the White," *Automobile*, 8/22/07, p. 284).

from the Oyster Bay train station in them, so much so that the *Times* announced in 1908 that he was "taking" to autos.

Once again, the automobiles were left behind, as Roosevelt's attentions wandered elsewhere, such as to bear hunting in Georgia. And, again, the automotive press was disappointed. "While President Roosevelt has occasionally used automobiles, particularly during the summer seasons spent at Oyster Bay, he has consistently refrained from purchasing one for the White house stables," complained the *Automobile* in November, 1908. By contrast, the winner of the 1908 election, a man who was known to be "fond" of automobiles, would purchase two for the White House. It "will give a big boost to the automobile industry," the magazine predicted.[28]

* * *

Having announced in 1904 that he would not seek a third term, Roosevelt's chief concern in 1908 was to secure an heir, a process known today as "legacy building." He publicly announced that his retirement would come in the form of an African safari and set about privately nailing down that legacy. Root, an attorney, was thought overly tangled with New York "interests" to be his successor, and didn't want it, anyway. Senator Philander Knox, who as Attorney General directed Roosevelt's first anti-trust case, was likewise perceived as too close to his old corporate accounts. Another choice, New York Governor Charles Evans Hughes, was off the short list as he was more a rival than an heir. Roosevelt required greater loyalty. William Howard Taft was his man.

Taft was a superb administrator and diplomat. He proved himself through deft handling of the Philippines "situation" as its first territorial governor, and then as an effective and loyal sergeant to Roosevelt in the Cabinet. Taft and Roosevelt had become friends while sharing political quarters in the Harrison Administration, Taft as Solicitor General and Roosevelt as Civil Service Commissioner. Both were young, ambitious, and politically wired. Taft admired Roosevelt's intellect, energy, and sense of honor. Roosevelt loved Taft's loyalty, steady friendship, humor, and absolute correctitude.

Nomination to the candidacy of Vice President was often a political burial ritual. For Roosevelt in 1900 such was his privilege. He feared that the New York political conductors had interred him there. After that election, the Taft name was spoken for President in 1904. And Roosevelt knew it. While his friend was making headlines sorting out the Philippine mess, Roosevelt was stuck presiding over the Senate, rarely able to cast either a vote or a news story. Looking across the band of rivals, Roosevelt's calculating mind included Taft among competitors. For his part, Taft made light of the possibility but always with an open eye. Though outwardly modest and self-deprecating, skyward were Taft's ambitions.

With McKinley's death, Taft and Roosevelt switched fates. Now it was Roosevelt in '04. His every move was designed towards that election. Taft was yet thought of as a potential rival.[29] To Roosevelt and

28. "Man Unnamed Will Select Cars for President-Elect," 11/19/08, p. 723. Roosevelt seems to have committed automotive abandon in DC, perhaps for the first time in over two years, when on November 14 he and his wife took one of the steamers to Alexandria, VA. Ten days later, Mrs. Roosevelt and her son, Quentin, motored to a luncheon in Baltimore (Butt, unpublished passage, 11/24/08). And in December, again finding himself in need to quickly run to Alexandria, Roosevelt jumped into a Signal Corps motor that sped him across the Potomac ("Motoring," *Evening Star*, 12/20/08).

29. As late as January, 1904, there was speculation of Taft as a replacement candidate for Hanna and Roosevelt (see "Mr. Hanna's Candidate," *NYT* editorial, 1/20/04).

Taft's wife, Helen, where Taft was headed meant everything. So in 1902, when Roosevelt offered a spot on the Supreme bench, Mrs. Taft and the rest of the Taft clan saw exile. Everyone was working around Taft's move to the Court for political reasons— except Taft. He had a job to finish and a loyalty to repay to the Philippine people.[30] He denied himself his dream job on the Court. Soon thereafter, Roosevelt again offered a place in the Court, and Taft again deferred his ambition —for the court, not the presidency — to his immediate responsibilities.

In 1906, the War Department purchased two White Model "G" steam cars for Army exercises. The following Summer, the steamers were sent to Oyster Bay to shuttle visitors to and from Roosevelt's home and the railroad depot. Their most enthusiastic user was Secretary of War Taft, who loved them so much he bypassed the local station for a longer automobile ride. Soon, Roosevelt, too, was seen in the cars riding to the station, as pictured here. Nevertheless, the "No Automobiles Allowed" sign that graced the entrance to Roosevelt's home didn't come down. He used them more frequently the following Summer, which prompted the *Times* to write, "The President has said that he did not care to use an automobile so long as there were good horses to be had but it seems that he is beginning to take a fancy to riding in one or the other of the two touring cars stationed here for the use of the secret service men. On several occasions recently he has made use of them." With the exception of at least two motor rides during the early summer of 1905, until the very end of his term of office, Roosevelt steadfastly avoided using automobiles in Washington. (Courtesy Henry Merkel)

Next came a situation that left no options. Elihu Root who with Secretary of State John Hay, both from the McKinley administration, had done so much to give legitimacy to the Roosevelt regime, retired. The vacancy at the War Department begged the talents of Taft, who again objected to his removal from the Philippines. Root and Roosevelt insisted that Taft could better serve the Filipino people from Washington. The logic and necessity of the situation won out. Mrs. Taft was thrilled. A Cabinet position was the correct trajectory.

Roosevelt by 1905 was self-sure and had carved out of the White House the pulpit from which he launched a thousand ships. Taft was no longer anything but an asset. The War Secretary was dedicated to the boss and a believer in the cause. He traveled the country as the Administration hound dog, explaining and promoting Roosevelt's policies. He enjoyed this work and found the travels expedient. He was in politics now. And in 1906 he again denied himself a seat on the Supreme Court. When Roosevelt made the offer, with the additional promise of the Chief Justiceship if the opportunity came, Taft confronted a Faustian choice. That the Court was his for the asking is incredible enough; that the alternative to it was the presidency is amazing. With the understanding that should he lose the election he would lose all opportunity for the Court, Taft

30. To Taft the Philippines was a test of the American ideal. Taft first declined the job because he did not believe in the occupation. McKinley told him that he, too, had not wanted to take the islands, and for that very reason he needed Taft there. To McKinley and Taft; the success of the Philippines occupation was a measure of the viability of self-government.

tempted ambition, fate, and the American electorate.[31]

Come 1908, Taft's ascension was all but a formality. With Roosevelt's man Henry Cabot Lodge in the Chair at the Republican Convention, Taft secured the nomination with ease. That autumn, and largely financed by his brother, Charles, Taft ran an effective campaign against William Jennings Bryan. As ever, Taft fretted about his chances.[32] When all was said and done, he took about the same slice of the vote as Roosevelt had in 1904.[33] Taft was Teddy-light, just perfect, then, for a nation enamored of its energized Chief Executive but ever wary he might go over the edge, and the country with him. Notably, Taft ran ahead of his party. The Republican majority in Congress was shaved slightly, and Democrats won key gubernatorial contests, including in Taft's home state, Ohio.

The Golf Cabinet. From left to right, Gen. Clarence Edwards, Capt. Butt, Senator Jonathan Bourne, and President Taft. Meetings were convened at the Chevy Chase Country Club. (Courtesy Library of Congress)

31. Mrs. Taft intervened personally in this one. She met with Roosevelt, after which Roosevelt wrote a lengthy letter to Taft discussing his potential for good in the presidency and the bench (see Roosevelt to Taft, 3/15/06 and Pringle, pp. 314–317). In her memoirs Mrs. Taft wrote, and apparently without sarcasm, but who knows, "The subject of my husband's appointment to the Supreme Bench cropped up with what seemed to me to be rather annoying frequency" (*Recollections*, Mrs. William Howard Taft, 1914, p. 304). For one such instance, see "Taft to Succeed Fuller: Rumor Busy In Washington Making Him Chief Justice" (*NYT*, 6/17/05). The next day's headline produced, "Taft Not For Bench; Story Angers Friends: Supreme Court Tale a Trick of Foraker's Friends, They Say" (*NYT*, 06/18/05). Indeed, Roosevelt's enemies wanted Taft shipped off to the Court. As for Taft, he wanted the Chief's place, not just any spot on the bench. The precedent was that Associate Justices were not to be promoted. Roosevelt assured Taft he would give it to him, anyway, as soon as the Chief Justiceship came available (it did not until Taft's presidency, and he elevated an Associate Justice). Charles Taft advised Taft not to look upon an Associate position as an obstacle to being Chief, and not to look upon either position as being an obstacle to running for President (Charles Taft to Taft, 3/12/06). Take your pick. Taft had the additional reasoning not to accept the Court appointment that there was significant legislation before Congress regarding the Philippines that needed his attentions as Secretary of War. The author suggests that historians would better understand Taft were they not to let his close-calls with and ambitions for the Court get in the way of their judgement of his presidency. He was no less a President for it. As his friend, Jack Hammond put it, "the popular estimate of Taft as president is more or less confused with a conviction that he would have accomplished greater things as a jurist" (*The Autobiography of John Hays Hammond*, p. 549).
32. For his campaign jitters, see Taft to Mabel Boardman, 7/14/08 and Taft to Charles Taft, 8/28/08. Taft's attitude towards the future was generally fearful optimism.
33. In 1904 Roosevelt beat Alton B. Parker by 7.6 to 5.1 million popular votes and 336 to 140 electoral votes. Taft beat Bryan 7.7 to 6.4 million popular votes and 321 to 162 in the Electoral College. The extra million votes for Bryan represented the populist side of Democracy that had abandoned, in a Bryan-led protest, the more conservative Parker in 1904.

* * *

Taft worked hard in the campaign, traveling plenty and giving speeches, but not much more than he had while War Secretary, when he was called, "The Chief of the Department of Travel."[34] His greatest pleasure came from playing golf. Roosevelt fretted over Taft's politically obtuse delight in the game, which he felt weakened the candidate in the West. Typically, Roosevelt had swayed his own penchant for a sport into political currency. Although he declared, "I never let a photograph of me in tennis costume appear," he allowed insiders and a knowing press to speculate jealously over the "tennis cabinet," consisting of his playground buddies. "Besides," he advised Taft, "you never saw a photograph of me playing tennis. Photographs on horseback, yes, tennis, no, and golf is fatal."[35] Instead, Taft publicly declared it "democratic."

"There is nothing more democratic than golf; there is nothing which furnishes a greater test of character and self-restraint."—W. H. Taft.

As for golf, President Taft was a fanatic. He loved it as much as motoring. Roosevelt warned Taft not to play golf while running for President, as its patrician associations would offend western voters. Taft not only didn't care, he disagreed. Instead, he called it "democratic." To a fellow golfer he wrote, "there is nothing more democratic than golf; that there is nothing which furnishes a greater test of character and self-restraint, nothing which puts one more on an equality with one's fellows, or, I may say, puts one lower than one's fellows, than the game of golf." Taft fully intended to share his love for the "ancient and honorable game" with his fellow citizens. He wrote a newsman in December, 1908, "I intend to make a popular game in this country — golf." (From *Evening Star,* 12/11/08).

Golf was a new game outside of Scotland, scattered about by migrants from the homeland. As with other leisure sports, golf was patrician. The amateur was a gentleman and the professional the hired help. It was not until the 1920s that professionals were allowed inside the clubhouse. Before then, the closest the sport came to mass appeal was in 1913 when former caddy Francis Ouimet amazingly won the U.S. Open.

The game yielded no public benefit to Taft, and he sought none from it. He just liked to play — and curse — golf. "I don't know of any game that is so provocative of profanity as golf," he liked to say. "I don't know any game that makes one so ashamed of his profanity."[36] But is, or was, golf "democratic"? Forget about country clubs and knickers. Taft didn't care about privilege, and he was not defending it in golf. To him, what the game represented was a fundamental challenge of the individual against himself. Every golfer starts from the same tee and faces the same

34. *Harper's Weekly*, 5/11/07, p. 685.
35. "Golf as Test of Character," *Evening Star*, 12/11/08, Brands, p. 630, Roosevelt to Taft, 9/5/08, and Hammond, p. 540. Hammond wondered that by Roosevelt's advice, Taft ought have taken to "tennis or running, or pole vaulting."
36. "Taft at Gateway of Yosemite," *NYT*, 10/7/09.

When Taft broke 100 at the world-class Myopia Club in Massachusetts, over $1,000 changed hands in the club house. Taft's choice of Augusta for his winter home is self-evident to the modern golfer. Of the difference between Roosevelt's tennis and Taft's golf, Capt. Butt wrote,"Whereas in the old days I had corns on my right hand from tennis ... there are corns on the left hand, the change of hand showing the change of administrations." If he ever tired of the golfing, Butt got his revenge when he nailed the President with a golf ball. "He hasn't the slightest idea of the etiquette of the game," Butt complained of Taft's habit of walking ahead of other players. "I put a brassie shot right into the fat part of his leg just above the knee. He squealed when I hit him, but said it was his own fault." Pictured here is the President-elect on the links at Hot Springs, Virginia, in December 1908. (Courtesy Library of Congress)

obstacles, the epitome of democracy. Taft wrote a fellow player,

> Preceding the late election campaign, there were many of my sympathizers and supporters who deprecated its becoming known that I was addicted to golf, as an evidence of aristocratic tendencies and a desire to play only a rich man's game. You know, and I know, that there is nothing more democratic than golf; that there is nothing which furnishes a greater test of character and self-restraint, nothing which puts one more on an equality with one's fellows, or, I may say, puts one lower than one's fellows, than the game of golf.[37]

At every opportunity throughout his presidency Taft promoted the game, its benefits, particularly for the man over fifty, and the establishment of public courses to share it with all. As had Roosevelt's appearance at a polo match and, later, a football game, spiked a brief popularity in those sports, following Taft around the links was a sudden interest in the game.

During the campaign and into his presidency, editorial and public sentiment towards his golfing was positive. The press kept tabs on his partners and scores, noting improvement in his swing and exercising no complaints over his company. The Gridiron Club, a group of Washington correspondents that held banquets for off-the-record ribbing of politicians, celebrated Taft's golfing with a skit about his caddie and left the golfing alone. There being no golf industry to support, no jobs to protect, and no tariffs to erect, his golfing went unscathed. Golf became a publicity problem — and a personal refuge — when something else went wrong. The cartoonists' quill turned bitter in response to other issues, not to the golfing itself.

37. "I have had a good many invitations recently, but none more tempting than that of the St. Andrews Golf Club. When I learn that your club — the oldest in this country — is only twenty years old, and realize that I have been playing golf since '96, I am surprised. I would, in respect to any other matter feel very much discouraged having attained in so long a time so little excellence, but golf is different from other games. Pope's lines have a greater application to it than to any other sport I know: 'Hope springs eternal in the human breast; Man never is, but always to be blest'" (Taft to AG Fox, 12/5/08; the letter was reproduced in newspapers).

3

How Dare They?

Then there was Helen Taft. She relished the life of the governess in the Philippines, where she lived in a Spanish palace and her husband was worshiped by the locals. Once in Washington as a Cabinet wife she was damned well going to make First Lady, too. Pretty, smart, refined, and farcically stuck up, she weeded her way through Washington without crafting enemies or friends outright amongst the various political wives with whom she was supposed to make pretty. She wore the political pants in the family. She regularly attended sessions of Congress, and detested men-only affairs which excluded her from her husband's political gatherings. She declined a scheduled motor ride with "the ladies of New Orleans" to follow instead her President-elect husband to a country club for a reception. She had no business there. Nor would she stay away.[1]

It is said that no one wanted the presidency for Taft more than his wife, and that the person who wanted the job the least was Taft himself.[2] If true, to what effect? The most that can be credited to that view is that Taft had a strong woman in his wife. She was ambitious for her man, and she got one to match. That she made him President is nonsense. That she encouraged, assisted, and pushed him onward is but a reflection of a fine partnership.

Taft was devoted to his wife. His love for her was absolute. This adoration has given biographers much grief, one of whom miserably turned to Freud for explanation. Taft was loyal, considerate, and loving. It was that simple, or as simple as a marriage can be. Actually, what has confused historians comes of what confounded his contemporaries. It took Captain Butt a while to catch on, and when he did he learned the secret to William Howard Taft. Taft was easygoing — so long as the going was his.

1. "Taft Quits Dixieland," *Evening Star*, 2/13/09. She detested women-only affairs, such as Edith Roosevelt's weekly Cabinet wives meetings, which First Lady Taft discontinued right off. Needless to say, Helen Taft and Edith Roosevelt could chill a room when together. Alice, by then Mrs. Nicholas Longworth, loved Taft and hated his wife. The feelings were all-round mutual.

2. "It was his wife, his brothers, and TR who were determined that he be President," wrote historian Will Manners. "Big Will Taft merely wished for peace, the calm, the dignity of a judicial career." It gets worse: Manners continued that on March 3, 1909, Taft "found himself ... only hours from the presidency" (William Manners, *TR and Will: A Friendship That Split the Republican Party*, p. 7). If Taft did magically appear in the White House the next day, so what? The notion that Taft only wanted to be a judge and not President — encouraged by Taft himself when he was on the Court in the 1920s — has been a blind on the history of his presidency, a rationalization for events and not relevant to them.

Butt wrote that while riding, "nine times out of ten," the President would follow him. That one time in ten Butt had to backtrack to follow Taft, the Captain learned, was when his way was not the President's way. The other nine were Taft's way as well, only Taft was happy to let Butt find it first. With his wife, Taft was no different, except that he never let disagreement get between them. When he argued with her he did so with tact and humor. Mrs. Taft got a most caring husband, a President, and a Chief Justice. Her ambition for him was a complement to, not the cause of, his own. Together they planned his career. As he did with his brothers, Taft shared with his wife the details of his political life and correspondence that he received from the field.[3] The decision making he reserved for himself. Nobody made William Howard Taft. He didn't mind that others thought it. As Butt wrote, it was the "absence of littleness which makes him wholesomely big."[4]

Helen Herron Taft. In her day, she was called "exquisite." Historians since have called her a lot of other things, from "domineering" to "nervous." It is said she personally arranged her husband's career. It is said she brought automobiles to the White House, trading advertising for discounts. Innocent as charged. Helen Taft was a strong woman, a smart woman, and a woman very involved in her husband's career, proving only a fine example of what lies behind a great man. And she was quite a mother, too. Her children were all prominent citizens. The youngest, Charlie, was mayor of Cincinnati. The middle child, Helen, became one of the nation's first woman deans of a prominent college. The eldest was "Mr. Republican" himself, Senator Robert A. Taft. (Courtesy Library of Congress)

* * *

Helen Taft could be all that Alice meant by her "hippopotamus face" imitation.[5] Cheever Cressy of South Hamilton, Massachusetts, tells of his mother who cared for the children of a neighbor to the Taft "Summer White House" in Beverly, Massachusetts. The President loved to sit on the porch and enjoy the company of children, who would "bounce on his lap — what there was of it, anyway," says Cressy. Mrs. Taft would variously pour out the door, heel across the porch, then storm off just as quickly. To the young mistress it was quite the act.[6]

Beyond her supercilious facade, which Archie Butt finally attributed to shyness, Mrs. Taft had a superb eye for the aesthetic

3. See Taft to Helen Taft, 3/30/08. In a note attached to a long political memo, Taft wrote, "Respectfully referred to my better half." The letter, by CW Raymond to AI Vorys (3/26/08), was full of political suggestions, such as to have more photographs of Taft sent out to the press. "People seem to be hunting for just such 'dope,'" wrote Mr. Raymond. "They want to see pictures of the man 'in action.' They want the human side. It appeals to them. They understand that...." Taft thought his wife ought see it.
4. Butt, 6/1/09, p. 104.
5. Teague, p. 184.
6. With thanks to Mr. Cressy for relating this story. Cressy owns and runs Aachen Books of South Hamilton, MA.

and impeccable taste. She was an excellent musician and a founder and manager of the Cincinnati Orchestra Association. She spoke several languages. To her, form was everything, from signing her autobiography "Mrs. William Howard Taft" to proper display of her position as First Lady. She was brutalized in her day and in contemporaneous memoirs for changing White House conventions. Only a strong, smart woman of that day would have dared. She was all that, Dolley Madison one hundred years later.

Helen Taft attended sessions of Congress. She sat in on her husband's political meetings. She threw a magnificent wedding anniversary party at the White House that was the climax of her teenage fantasies to be First Lady. She conceived of Washington City's cherry trees. Heading into the White House, she intended to make of the position not just a social mistress but an office. Starting with an announcement that she would dedicate herself "to the betterment of the conditions of working women," she meant to be a modern First Lady.[7]

As she plotted her entrance to the White House, the aristocratic earthiness of its occupants had to be on her mind. Beyond Roosevelt's White House antics, such as wrestling matches and the children riding bicycles through the halls, the Roosevelts were sticklers for form. Slights of decorum and diplomacy were serious and never ignored. Roosevelt stampeded a man from a Washington social club on account of a family feud from New York, for he refused to be "exposed to the possibility of meeting him there." Longtime White House usher Ike Hoover, who was otherwise devoted to Roosevelt, wrote in his memoirs, "The formalities were so keenly observed that they were sometimes tiresome to everyone rather than pleasant or brilliant."[8]

Although no less concerned with form, where the Roosevelts came in shades of brown, Mrs. Taft wanted stronger colors. One report caught her tone:

> The circumstances may be somewhat different under the new administration now at hand, for Mrs. Taft is a woman of distinctive personality, and it is predicted that she will restore to the White House that atmosphere of refined and dignified yet democratic simplicity which won such universal popularity for that feminine idol — Mrs. Grover Cleveland.[9]

Ultimately, the Tafts' changes were well received. Of a January 1910 diplomatic reception, Butt wrote that it "was pronounced by everyone, save Alice Longworth, the most beautiful reception ever held in the White House ... there was none of that formality and stiffness which have made the receptions ... in the past a thing of horror...."[10]

* * *

In January of 1909, conversations in Washington society and among the White House staff hummed with speculation and fear of the changes to come. If Taft made of himself a facsimile of Roosevelt, he would have been hanged for a pretender. If he adjusted the Roosevelt portrait an inch he was to be shot as a traitor. From Cabinet selections and diplomatic appointments to the White House china, the Tafts were interlopers.

The usher Hoover took this bitterness to his grave five administrations later. His

7. "Mrs. Taft Volunteers Help," *Evening Star*, 3/16/09.
8. "The Tafts Reconstructing Society in Washington," *NYT*, 1/1/11 and *Forty-Two Years in the White House*, by Irwin Hood (Ike), 1934, p. 33.
9. "The New Belle of the White House," *Evening Star*, 2/28/09.
10. Butt, 1/5/10, p. 251.

reminiscences are the fodder of so much historical evidence of the sins of the Tafts. So twisted was the man's attitude that he abused Taft for sharing a laugh with Speaker Cannon. When one of Taft's secretaries resigned, it was to take a position, not as a bank president, but "with financial interests in New York." Taft was condemned for offending the Quakers when Captain Butt went to church in uniform. And Hoover was deeply offended that President Harrison's widow was seated at the wrong spot at the table. Somehow it all constituted conspiracy and ill-attitude. It is beyond silly. Hoover's attitude was corrupted to the point that in 1910, after ex–President Roosevelt visited the White House, he told Butt, "It is the only happy day we have had" since Roosevelt's departure.[11]

We can balance Hoover's dissatisfaction with the Tafts with the enthusiasm for them of Elizabeth Jaffray, who came new to the Taft White House untainted by the

Mrs. Taft participated closely in her husband's political career. He made her proud, in or out of automobiles. (1910, from Eastport, Maine; Courtesy Library of Congress)

11. Hoover, pp. 40–57 and Butt, 11/24/10, p. 562. Hoover's treatment of the Tafts is so slanted it ought be discounted or taken with reservation. His unhappiness with the Tafts was real, but the conclusions and memories he drew were severely biased by it. For example, of Mrs. Taft's entrance he wrote, "she made plans to revolutionize the place. She seemed to have forgotten entirely that the White House is ... a public institution...." (p. 41). Butt held the opposite view, saying that the success of the Diplomatic dinner was due to its having been "like a reception in a private home" (1/5/10, p. 251). Hoover's account of Roosevelt's 1910 visit to the White House offers a clue as to the origin of this attitude. He told Butt that Roosevelt "recalled every old servant by name, even the scullery maids...." (Butt, 11/24/10, p. 561). Taft was indifferent to such politicking, sincere or not. On a boat to Panama, it was reported to Butt that the crew was upset the President paid them no attention. "It is not natural that he should," wrote Butt. "He is built on different lines from the other...." Roosevelt always inculcated himself to the commoners around him, from Rough Riders to scullery maids. Taft suffered not having done so, as Butt explained, only in comparison to Roosevelt's "methods" (Butt, 11/20/10, p. 559).

Roosevelt cult. Another of Mrs. Taft's changes in the White House was to exchange the steward for a housekeeper. She found one to her liking in Jaffray at "an exclusive employment bureau in New York."[12] Jaffray's published reminiscences are wholly glad of the Taft period. Roosevelt holdovers who refused the neutral view ended dissatisfied. Those of more generous impartiality saw good and bad in both. A moderate observer, Secret Serviceman "Jimmy" Sloan, spoke highly of Taft the man and prejudicially of Taft the politician, especially when compared to the master spinner, Roosevelt. He was critical of Taft, but without malice. He compared Taft and Roosevelt and concluded that Roosevelt would take Taft to the cleaners and steal the 1912 nomination in a heartbeat, if he chose. Sloan remained a Roosevelt partisan, but he was not resentful of Taft. "In many ways...," he said, "I like this man much better than the other. He's finer on some points, but he does not see as the other saw things."[13]

Hoover's mind was fixed against the Tafts before they walked through the front door. Even Captain Butt suffered this preconviction. Although he felt that Mrs. Taft's plans to switch the "frock coated ushers" for liveried doormen — to the horror of those compelled to be horrified at such things—"would certainly look much better," he feared that Mrs. Taft's changes would not be for the better. In early December 1908 he wrote:

> I am to call on Mrs. Taft at 5:00 this afternoon. She wants to talk about the personnel of the White House, and I hope it will not offend her by speaking the truth, but I shall certainly advise against any radical changes, and if Mr. Taft gets a tip from me I feel that things will remain very much as they are.... I wish I were not so fond of the President and his family, for I cannot help feeling a bit jealous toward the Tafts.[14]

Butt already knew the Tafts, having served under the Governor in Manila and the War Secretary in Cuba. He felt indebted to Mrs. Taft for her having visited his beloved mother and for always asking after her. Nevertheless, her reputation was set in him:

> I am sure that it is going to be a difficult thing to get along with them, especially after the delightful service with the Roosevelts. Still it is unjust to prejudge them, but I have heard such funny stories about them in the Philippines. It seems that they think aides were made for the role of domestics, and that would certainly not suit me. I remember seeing Major Noble when he returned from the Philippines and he certainly looked cowed and hucked. I have heard that Mrs. Taft did not hesitate to skin him well if he did anything she did not like.[15]

Given the predisposition, it would be hard to like Helen Taft. She was forthright and demanding. Archie's impression in December was that she "is very blunt in her manner and comes to the point at issue without much diplomacy." Hoover and the rest cowered from her before her arrival. In January, Butt wrote of the White House staff, "They are all stampeded from accounts they get of Mrs. Taft."[16]

This was no unique manner in 1909. Without the prejudgement, Mrs. Taft would have fared equally well as Mrs. Roosevelt, another wonderfully Edwardian stuffed bird. Butt wrote,

12. *Secrets of the White House*, by Elizabeth Jaffray, p. 5. Carl Anthony called her a "terrorizing housekeeper"—Mrs. Taft's own, then! (*First Ladies*, 1990, p. 314). Hereafter referred to as "Anthony" in notes section.
13. Butt, 1/12/10, p. 262.
14. Butt, *Letters*, 11/30/08, p. 205, 12/7/08, pp. 228–229. See also "Taft Shifts Staff," *Evening Star*, 3/3/09.
15. Butt, unpublished passage, 2/15/09.
16. Butt, unpublished passages, 12/8/08 and 1/27/09.

> Somehow I am glad I never knew the Roosevelts until after they were in the White House, or possibly I may have seen some difference in them too. But their old intimates tell me it has made no difference to them whatever in the matter of their personal friendships, yet I occasionally hear regrets that they have become so exclusive. It must be the same to all.[17]

Edith Roosevelt was thought, if unfairly, to be humorless, if not dull. She was a sweet woman, but even the stuffy Henry Adams said she "needed a crown." Roosevelt himself joked that she had a "humor which is more tyrannical than half the tempestuous women of Shakespeare." When Elihu Root laughed at his satisfaction that her husband was sidelined by a fall for the relief it gave from exhausting outdoor treks, she took deep offense.[18] Mrs. Roosevelt had instituted substantial changes in the management of the White House, but where her austerity drew sympathy Helen Taft's direct manner brought enmity.

Butt, though, warmed to Mrs. Taft. "I have always found her thoughtful and kind and I believe she will make a very popular mistress of the White House," he concluded in January.[19] And although he vacillated from that view through the following month, the "Taft smile" completely won him over. "All my theories about Mrs. Taft vanish when I see Mr. Taft," he wrote in February. "And he has a wonderful way of dispelling all forebodings."[20] Butt's initial reaction to Mrs. Taft's front was turned to respect by her resoluteness. By February, he wrote,

> It will be interesting to watch Mrs. Taft in the White House. I do not think she is going to be a popular First Lady, but I predict that she is going to make a fine mistress of the White House, and in short time will not only have the White House but the office as well entirely under her control. If we can only keep her from making speeches and hold her down to the simple duties of First Lady, I shall be content, but I fear she has a leaning toward the betterment of the working girl class through the lecture platform.[21]

Not a great endorsement, and a backtrack from before, but Archie was open to her. We can see how she was not winning hearts. If Butt couldn't make up his mind about her, certainly the longtime Roosevelt crowd remained defiant. That he had been exposed to Roosevelt's charm less than a year meant the infection had not taken to the spine as with others. "And the influence of Mr. Roosevelt over those around him is masterful and his friends become fanatical — e.g., to wit — I," he admitted.[22]

Mrs. Taft's reputation also suffered in contrast to her instantly likeable husband. "You know, Archie, that I think he has the most lovable personality I have ever come in contact with," Roosevelt told the Captain. "I almost envy a man possessing a personality like Taft's. People are always prepossessed by it. One loves him at first sight...."[23] Dissatisfaction with Taft was projected upon his wife, or excused as a result of henpecking. Adams wrote of a friend who was awaiting Taft's decision whether to keep him as Ambassador to France, "Harry has not heard a word about

17. Butt, unpublished passage, 2/15/09.
18. Anthony, p. 312, Butt, 1/29/12, p. 832, and Pringle, pp. 275–276 (from William Howard Taft to Helen Taft, 9/24/05).
19. Butt, unpublished passage, 1/27/09.
20. Butt, "Letters," 2/16/09, p. 344.
21. Butt, unpublished and undated letter from early Feb. 1909.
22. Butt, "Letters," 1/5/09, p. 273.
23. Butt, "Letters," 1/5/09, p. 272.

himself, and is waiting the pleasures of our great masters — or mistresses." Cabot Lodge later wrote that the ambassador was dismissed because of a minor slight rendered to the Tafts years before, the insinuation being that Mrs. Taft commanded her husband's dark side.[24]

One occasion Mrs. Taft vetoed a Cabinet appointment. Archie described the moment, when he encountered Mr. Taft laughing hysterically:

> He grabbed me by the hand and when he could control himself, said, "Nothing to laugh at! I think it is the funniest thing I ever heard...." Then turning to me he said: "I was Cabinet-making early this morning, and I had thought that I had settled one place at least.... She simply wiped him off the face of the earth and I have got to begin all over again. The personal side of politics has always been funny to me, but nothing has been quite as funny as to have a man's career wrecked by a jealous wife."
>
> "Not jealous at all," said Mrs. Taft, "but I could not believe you to be serious when you mentioned that man's name. He is perfectly awful and his family are even worse. I won't even talk about it."[25]

Butt's story, rather than to affirm Lodge's view, offers a constructive look at the Tafts' interaction. Taft deferred to his wife when he wanted to. And in this case he found amusement in it. For Butt it was an enlightening and amusing incident which speaks volumes about all three. No sooner had Butt gone to work for the new President than Taft's bountiful charms set permanently upon him.

Another example of the Tafts' working partnership was the choice of Augusta, Georgia, for their 1908 Winter vacation. Mrs. Taft thought it was too far from Washington. Taft ignored her objections. She ended up loving it there. In a letter that explains so much of the Tafts, their personalities, their relationship, and their humor, Taft wrote his sister-in-law from Augusta,

> We are enjoying the Christmas very much, because we have our three children with us. The only difficulty seems to be that I am the only person that will talk. All others sit quietly around and either munch candy or read novels or do picture puzzles, or, in Nellie's case, criticize my efforts at cabinet making. I am really enjoying our stay here exceedingly. Nellie thinks it is a[s] stupid as going to church. Indeed, she says that church is the only excitement there is. I play golf every day.... Yesterday we went over to Aiken and there we met the remnants of the Four Hundred ... we attempted to learn of the scandals and complications that have arisen in the divorce courts and elsewhere among the coterie that live there ... since Nellie has become the first lady of the land she seems to have a yearning for that sort of society. Whether it is going to lead her into domestic complications, or not, I don't know.[26]

Historians have accused Mrs. Taft of everything from making her husband President against his will to single-handedly negotiating a corrupt purchase of White House automobiles.[27] If she was all this, why then, is she not held as a towering example of feminine advance? The accusations are as petty as they are wrong. Mrs. Taft was involved in the purchase of

24. *Henry Adams and His Friends*, p. 653. Pringle dismissed this story (p. 547). In 1910, Taft wrote, "I had no idea that [Roosevelt's] heart was set on White. If I had known it I would not have relieved White, but I suppose I was doing exactly what he approved when I put Bacon in White's place, because Bacon is one of the men whom he has always praised to the skies" (Taft to Charles Taft, 9/10/10).

25. Butt, *Letters*, 12/10/08, pp. 233–234.

26. Taft to Mrs. Charles Anderson, Jr., 12/27/08.

27. A typical commentary is "Taft might never have become President without the prodding of his wife" (*Presidential Wives*, by Paul F. Boller, Jr., Oxford University Press, New York, 1988, p. 206). First Lady

President-elect Taft loved motoring, and automobiles fit his wife's conception of modernity. The pair worked with Roosevelt's aide-de-camp, Capt. Archie Butt, and Taft's friend, Gen. Clarence Edwards, to find the right cars for a President. Taft's choice was the White Company, as he loved its steamers, the preference over at the Army. The White Company took great care of the President-elect, lending him cars during his pre–Inaugural get-away at Augusta, Georgia, and in New York City. Pictured here is the Taft family in a loaned White touring car at Augusta, Georgia, likely during the winter of 1909. This photograph was widely circulated in the form of a post card — and with the Great Seal surreptitiously added to the door, which has caused a confusion that this was the White House automobile. It was not. Anyway, this and similar photographs taken at Augusta in December 1908 reminded Americans that their incoming President approved of automobiles. (Courtesy Henry Merkel)

the automobiles, for example, and she took the decision on a summer cottage.[28] To a Congressman who lobbied on behalf of an automobile manufacturer, and with typical humor, Taft simultaneously sent it to his wife and blew off the request:

> I have your letter ... in respect to Woods Motor Vehicle Co. I have turned the letter over to Mrs. Taft, who has interested herself in the matter of the selection of vehicles for the White House. I hope you will not think that this is a complete abdication of my powers in the office of President, but when I do have to give up a thing I want to give it up freely, and I wish, therefore, to say that I have turned this matter completely over to Mrs. Taft.[29]

As he would with the cars, Taft stepped in only when he wanted something for himself.

* * *

The aftermath of the November election offered no quiet to Taft. Starting with the writing of countless thank you notes, December turned hectic as he left the golfing at Hot Springs, Virginia, to install himself on the third floor of the William Jarvis Boardman home in Washington. These friends and political supporters and their famous daughter, Mabel, entertained, hosted, and generally provided for the Tafts when in Washington. Boardman was a Cleveland attorney made good, who set up shop in Washington, like other rich families of the age, to establish a bloodline in the nation's central city. Taft enjoyed the

27. (*cont.*) historians can be forgiven this view, as their subject was assertive and did influence her husband's career. The most bitter treatment, however, was by Margaret Truman, who said that Mrs. Taft "extracted" from Congress money for automobiles and resorted to "commercialization of the presidency" in a "deal" with the manufacturers for a "handsome discount" in exchange for advertising rights. "Nellie was acting more like a Queen than a First Lady," Truman wrote (*First Ladies*, by Margaret Truman, Random House, New York, 1995, pp. 108–109).
28. "The question of summer homes I transmit to Nellie for consideration," Taft wrote his brother, recusing himself (Taft to Horace Taft, 1/13/09).
29. Taft to FW Upham, 12/22/08.

old man, calling him "Foxy Grandpa."[30] They played golf and socialized throughout Taft's tenure at the White House. Daughter Mabel was a leader of Washington society and a social crusader. She salvaged the American Red Cross from the ego of Clara Barton and turned the organization into a singularly well organized and effective force in human affairs, worthy of the very best in Barton. Outside his family, Mabel was Taft's closest confidant. If it were possible in those days—and it was certainly a reflection of Taft's views toward women — Mabel was one of his closest friends. Alice Longworth called Mabel the "Pompadour" of the Taft administration.[31]

From the Boardman house, that of brother Henry ("Harry") in New York City, and during his winter getaway at Augusta, Taft carried on the tedious work of becoming President. He was forced to stand for countless portraits and photographs. He fended off favor seekers and disparate expectations. As he was carrying on for Roosevelt, the most difficult and delicate task was choosing a Cabinet. And to sustain that greatest of Roosevelt legacies, one that Taft as War Secretary had managed for four years, he left for Panama in late January. There was much discussion as to whether the Canal work should proceed according to the planned lock system or as a sea-level waterway. With doubts of the engineering program, huge monies spent, and election-year charges of corruption, the country was anxious about the project. Taft intended to reassure the public, Congress, and the House Appropriations Committee, especially, that things were in order.

The transition got messy early. When Taft's brother Charles joined an ugly Senate battle in Ohio, Roosevelt made it worse by denying too strenuously that he had argued with Taft over the matter. The denial confirmed to many minds that there was a rift. Privately, Taft felt that Roosevelt objected to his brother's candidacy over a misunderstanding that came of a meeting between the two. None of it was helpful to Charles' Senate ambitions. After Roosevelt was told that the Ohio Society of New York supposedly refused to toast his health, his animosity for Taft's brother was fixed. Not only was Charles at the banquet, but Henry Taft was the group's president.[32]

The worst of it came over the question of who was responsible for Taft's election, a petty question that plagued everyone but Taft and especially Charles Taft and Roosevelt. "I see a tendency, and I think it but natural, on the part of the friends of Taft to discredit what I did for him in the campaign," Roosevelt told Archie in January. Irritation turned to insult in Roosevelt's mind when Taft wrote a few months later that he was indebted to both men for his ascendancy to the office. Word filtered back that Roosevelt took offense at the idea that his successor had two parents. Charles did some good hating right back. "What troubles Charles," Taft kidded him, "he is afraid Roosevelt will get the credit of making me President and not himself." Taft tired of this discussion, now carried five months into his presidency. "Old fellow," he said, "I will not goad you into any discussion of this subject again, for we have had some heated talks on it before, haven't we? And I will agree not to mini-

30. Butt, 8/10/10, p. 473.
31. Butt, 10/10/10, p. 473 and 1/5/10, unpublished letter. The "Pompadour" remark regarded a weekly political "salon" Mabel held. Taft attended whenever he could. Insurgents and regulars, including the Czar himself, Aldrich, occasionally showed up (Butt, 3/7/10, unpublished passage). For her Red Cross work, Mabel was honored with the personal commendations of the King of Italy, the Emperor of Japan, and the Belgian Queen.
32. Butt, *Letters*, 1/30/09, p. 313 and "Taft's Brother Elected," *NYT*, 12/1/08.

mize the part you played in making me President if you will agree not to minimize the part Roosevelt played."[33]

Taft couldn't win for winning. While he earnestly prepared for a presidency fairly won but that an ambitious family and the outgoing President and his choir projected upon him, everyone else argued over who was responsible for it. Taft imagined they all had a say, but, in the end, it was he. It wouldn't matter. The Roosevelt loyalists were sour winners, and Taft suffered in being a gentleman about it all. Butt felt that Taft was justified in becoming his own man. As for Roosevelt, the Captain didn't see any problem other than what the sycophants might arouse. The building animosity came not from Roosevelt but his entourage, whom Taft friend General Clarence Edwards derided as the "Incense Swingers." Edwards explained to Butt that these were "largely of the New England element, possibly more the Harvard type, who are supposed to stand around the President as acolytes do about a priest and swing incense at him and about him, while the center figure stands with this skirts outspread to receive the adulation ... and who never think the President makes a mistake."[34]

In January, Lodge returned from Augusta disgusted at having spent two days without seeing the President-elect, and when he got the interview it was under the guard of Mrs. Taft and brother Charles. Lodge, who already declined Taft's offer of Secretary of State, claimed that Taft would keep only George Meyer from Roosevelt's Cabinet. Mrs. Roosevelt laughed it off. Her husband said nothing. Butt took offense at Lodge's attitude. "I felt rather disgusted that Senator Lodge should come home and stir up discord between the two families."[35]

Any theory on the origins of the Taft-Roosevelt break must accommodate an innate prejudice of the Roosevelt groupies. The choice of the West, Theodore Roosevelt, was brought up politically by Boston and New York elites, his literary friends who excused his hunting and populism as a gentleman's quirks. Chief among the Incense Swingers was Gifford Pinchot, a snob. Roosevelt's mentor, Henry Cabot Lodge, was a snob. Above them all towered Henry Adams, descendent of Presidents, the most Boston of Bostonians, the snobbiest of them all. For Lodge and Adams, particularly, Roosevelt's departure was a disaster. That he was to be replaced by an Ohioan was a calamity.

Worse, the Ohio President found his Secretary of State in the city of steel. "I am sorely beset," wrote Adams. "I am obliged to look directly in to four years of Ohio Fog. Four years of Bill Taft will kill me — thank God for that! — but four years of Bill Taft with Philander Knox on top of him, make a nightmare such as Sinbad never dreamed...." Ohio was just bearable, as Adams was plenty used to such Presidents. But Pittsburgh, too? And the Vice President was from *Utica*. How the old set shuddered. Smoke stacks and iron mills ought be neither seen nor heard; these are intellectual curiosities, only.[36]

Adams' excuse for dissatisfaction was that Taft "has done, undone, and left undone, a quantity of things that bewilder

33. Butt, *Letters*, 1/30/09, p. 314 and Butt, 6/1/09, p. 103.

34. Butt, *Letters*, 11/25/08, pp. 194–195. For Roosevelt's professed disinterest and the growing animosity of the Incense Swingers towards Taft's cabinet making, see Butt, 1/11/09, p. 283.

35. Butt, *Letters*, 1/5/09, p. 272. Consistency is always a problem in personal squabbles: by Lodge's view of Mrs. Taft, what was Mrs. Roosevelt doing in a political discussion?

36. For Roosevelt's view on the geographic dispersion of evil, see Butt, *Letters*, 1/28/09, pp. 312–313. "While Pittsburgh is vulgar and common," he said, "it is not so sordid as New York." The comment was made in front of a guest from New York, Mrs. Fred Vanderbilt, a queen of the new rich, a set which, Butt said, Roosevelt "despises." The irony is not that Mrs. Vanderbilt was at the table, but that she was at the table at all.

me ... but if the new President is so bent on making a clean sweep of Roosevelt's men, why did we elect him expressly to carry on the Roosevelt regime?"[37] What really bothered Adams was revealed with, "In a few days more, Washington will groan with dullness without him." Adams was out. "These ruptures of social relations depress me horribly. They are nearly always final." Later in the year, he resigned himself to his self-imposed exile. "Cincinnati and Pittsburgh will insist on regarding us as outsiders — Roosevelt men, and what can we do about it?"

Roosevelt deferred all decisions to Taft, including, and contrary to his later assertions, the choice of the Cabinet. In late December, he wrote to Taft, "Ha ha! *you* are making up your Cabinet. *I* in a light-hearted way have spent the morning testing the rifles for my African trip. Life has compensations!"[38]

Supremely confident, the President-elect kept up the Taft smile and forged ahead. Meanwhile, the incoming First Lady carefully planned her White House. She calculated costs, decorum, tradition and her own priorities. She upheld Mrs. Roosevelt's china and banished the caterers. That practice, to which the Roosevelts resorted for large dinners, she considered poor in taste and costly. By expanding the White House kitchen she not only saved on the catering, she dissolved from the White House an unpalatable bourgeois habit.[39]

Next on the shopping list was a new set of wheels.

36. *(cont.)* See *The Age of Reform* by Richard Hofstadter, 1955, p. 92–93 for a review of these attitudes. He wrote, "...both the imperialist elite and the Populists had been bypassed and humiliated by the advance of industrialism...."

37. *Henry Adams and His Friends*, pp. 638–640, 668. Of Roosevelt's Cabinet, Taft kept only the immensely popular Agriculture Secretary James Wilson, a McKinley appointee, and Postmaster General Meyer, whom Taft moved to the Navy Department. The one "Roosevelt man" Taft most wanted in wanted out, Elihu Root. Other cabinet members, such as James Garfield, Taft disliked or, as with Luke Wright, he thought useless. "The reason why I kept Garfield out of the Cabinet was because I knew him," Taft wrote to his brother, Horace (2/1/10). Additionally, two of the most important "Roosevelt men," Kellogg and Lodge, both declined Taft's invitation. Aside from the Cabinet selections and Taft's being from Ohio, Adams complained that Taft surrounded himself with lawyers and that he "went off to Panama to decide an engineering matter for which he was incompetent...." That last was particularly silly, for War Secretary Taft had been personally responsible for the Canal and the matters of its "engineering," not to mention that President-elect Taft went there in part at Roosevelt's insistence. Adams was just being prissy.

38. Roosevelt to Taft, 12/28/08. Although that letter came before Lodge's trip and Taft's final decisions, Roosevelt did not change this attitude into January, when Roosevelt said, "If Mr. Taft were to ask my advice as to his Cabinet I would not know what to say. I would possibly suggest to him to retain the present Cabinet and to make changes as he saw fit, but he cannot ask me and I cannot volunteer advice in the matter. If he should ask my advice he would feel compelled to take it, whereas if he asks Root's advice he can take it or not as he chooses. No, Taft is going about this thing just as I would do, and while I retained McKinley's Cabinet the conditions were quite different. I cannot find any fault in Taft's attitude to me (Butt, *Letters*, 1/25/09, pp. 307–308). Roosevelt did make at least three Cabinet suggestions: that Taft definitively avoid two men, one on account of the "Secret Service affair" and another on account of his opposition to Taft's nomination — both being personal offenses to Roosevelt, not Taft, and that he keep George Meyer (see Roosevelt to Taft, 12/15/08 and "Roosevelt Keeps Foe Out of Cabinet," *NYT*, 2/20/09). Taft complied.

39. Deriding a catered New York party, Butt wrote, "I can detect a caterer's dinner by the way the caviar is placed on the toast" (Butt, *Letters*, 11/21/09, p. 216).

4

The Captain and the Cars

The automobile, the manufacture of which has become one of our leading industries, is destined to assume a very important part in the economic welfare of the world.

— Secretary of War and presidential aspirant
William Howard Taft, March, 1908[1]

Throughout it all in Washington, New York, and Georgia, Taft was seen in or getting in and out of automobiles. In New York, it was in a "fast" automobile preceded by bicycle policemen (how "fast" could that be?). From Augusta came a photograph of the Taft family in an automobile. "President-Elect Taft Believes in Autoing," ran a headline. Postcards of the image circulated the nation. Upon his arrival to Atlanta it was directly from the train to the automobile of a prominent host. Then it was tours of the countryside by motor. In Washington it was in the Boardman's "high-powered automobile," a Packard limousine.[2]

Taft's War Department coachman was an Irishman named Quade. He was a loyal employee and trustworthy driver, although Mrs. Taft complained that "he took great pride in the speed" of his horses and would "swing around corners and dash past street cars and other vehicles."[3] Taft, we find out later, greatly enjoyed this business. It was in Washington as War Secretary that he proved his modernity and discovered automobiles. The U.S. Army was up on the technology and had been toying with motor cars for tests since the McKinley days. Lately, use of these autos was a mark of rank. When Major General Frederick Grant, an early promoter of automobiles, showed up at a Chicago post, he demanded an Army motor. His compatriot, Major General J. Franklin Bell, also motored about, only he made the mistake of flaunting it and his chauffeur, George Robinson, to his boss, the Secretary of War. Coming into the White House, Taft pulled rank and took the chauffeur. Bell was consoled with a new

1. "Taft Sends Letter by Race Leaders," *NYT*, 3/28/08.
2. "President-Elect Taft Believes in Autoing," *Automobile*, 12/31/08, p. 976, "Boardman House Taft's Temporary Headquarters," *Evening Star*, 2/28/09 and "Executive Machines," *Auto News of Washington*, April 1909, p. 3. For Washingtonians, the Boardman's Dupont Circle address was 1801 P Street.
3. *Recollections*, p. 278.

White limousine delivered to him in February of 1909.[4]

Following a luncheon in his honor at the White House on December 12, 1908, Taft took Butt aside to say that he "was going to give up horses and use automobiles at the White House." Butt already knew, as General Bell had earlier floated the idea with the White House on Taft's behalf. And, as was his way, Butt was already on it. Two days before Taft's announcement, he had phoned Mrs. Taft at the Boardmans to inquire her opinion as to "how small a number of automobiles the White House could get along with next year."[5]

Starting in 1899, the U.S. Army experimented with automobiles. Led by motoring enthusiast Gen. Nelson A. Miles, the Army, its generals in particular, tested and enjoyed the new technology. Pictured here is a U.S. Signal Corps 40 H.P. Royal Tourist that was purchased for the 1906 Army maneuvers. The *Automobile* wrote that the motor "proved invaluable to General Funston and his staff, who use it to travel from camp to camp." Despite these tests, the Army did not seriously develop its use of the automobile until Taft took office. Under Woodrow Wilson, however, there was a lapse in the experimentation and purchases that left the Army motor-handicapped going into the 1916 Punitive Expedition in Mexico and World War I. (Courtesy Library of Congress)

Taft advised Butt to discuss the matter with Roosevelt's secretary, William Loeb. The two "thought it best to start modestly with Congress and ask for only twelve thousand, which ought to buy three large cars and several runabouts, for each factory will sell to us very cheaply for the advertisement which is in it." Butt reported that as of the 28th of the month, "there has been no serious objection to the appropriation of $12,000 for the motors." Once he learned how much automobiles cost he revised his opinion as to how many cars could be purchased for $12,000. "Mrs. Taft wants to get four motors out of this amount," he wrote. "There is only one way to do it; that is, to take the cars at a reduced rate and permit the makers to advertise the fact that their cars are being used for the White House."

Why $12,000 is unclear. The first "official" mention of the automobiles, likely coming from the War Department, mentioned two cars.[6] Loeb's formal request to Congress on the 27th of November asked for the continuation of an existing $25,000 presidential travel fund with

4. *The United States Army and the Motor Truck*, by Marc K. Blackburn, 1996, p. 9, "Taft's Daredevil Chauffeur," *NYT*, 8/15/09, "A White for the White House," *Automobile*, 2/23/09, p. 251, and the "Motoring," *Evening Star*, 12/28/08. Two other White Model 'M' steamers were delivered to the Army in January of 1909.

5. Butt, *Letters*, 12/10/08, p. 235, 12/12/08, p. 244, and 12/28/08, p. 257 and Loeb to Taft, 11/27/08.

6. *Automobile* announced, "An officer of the War Department, whose name is kept secret until certain plans can be formulated, and who is said to be an authority on automobiles, has been detailed to select two cars for Mr. Taft..." ("Man Unnamed Will Select Cars for President-Elect," 11/19/08, p. 723). This seems to have been the first notice of Taft's intention to use automobiles, saying it came of an "official announcement." The story was dated November 14. The news got out, as Taft received a letter dated the 16th trying to sell a car (see FW Carpenter to WR Mason, 11/19/08).

permission to purchase "an automobile."[7] Somewhere between Loeb's letter and Butt's conversation with Mrs. Taft of December 11, the need for more cars and, thus, more money arose. "Three large cars and several runabouts" would break $12,000. Perhaps they didn't at first realize what cars cost. Or expectations ran ahead of reality. The Tafts had never owned an automobile, and although Butt once roamed England in one, his personal relationship to motors was vicarious. He had experience with the Quartermasters' motors, but nothing by way of how to squeeze four or five cars into twelve grand. A couple of Buicks and one or another little Oldsmobile might fit, but there was no question as to those makes, and imports were out of bounds. Mrs. Taft didn't take kindly to Butt's suggestion that she'd have to settle on a pair of $2,800 Ford Sixes.[8] The nation's leader should be driven in nothing less than a Peerless, a Locomobile, a Pierce-Arrow, or a Packard. A Pierce started at four thousand, while a Locomobile could go for double that.

Archie Butt would have to find a way. He always found a way. "Whatever Major Butt did was done faultlessly — always," wrote Mrs. Taft.[9]

* * *

"Archibald Willingham Andrew Brackenbreed.... Butt!" Alice chanted, mocking a name that sounded like "a load of coal falling downstairs." Butt was of a good but not wealthy Georgia family. He was born in 1865 and liked to think he had a part of the Confederacy in him. He was tall, upright, and a dedicated bachelor wholly devoted to his mother whom he supported since the age of fourteen. He was a loyal soldier, an even more loyal friend, and "through and through a gentleman." He loved his uniform, "the broader and yellower the stripes the better." He shared Taft's fine sense of humor. He was principled, disciplined, decorous, and of "integrity unassailable."[10]

Butt possessed "unusual social gifts." He worked as smoothly without as within proper society, knowing when and when not to let loose. He was as capable to represent the President to a foreign embassy as to partake in a bachelor's party where his drunken friends literally tossed around the room an equally drunken Japanese minister, and their shot glasses into the fire place. He took offense at the slightest slight, especially to a lady. He was one of the few who could play along with Alice in her social games — and who earned her respect for it. He also managed to outwit her once or twice, including to pour pitchers of water on her as she tried to break into his house on a prank. He was everything a black man on the street whom Butt befriended meant when he said, "Dere goes de man what's de highest wid de mighty an' de lowest wid de lowly of any man in d's city."

He was very Southern, which in 1908 meant that he was proud of the South and patriotic to the bone to the Union. There was in those days great romance in a Southern heritage. Roosevelt's familial pride lay in his mother's Georgian ancestry and her family members who

7. Loeb to Tawney, 11/27/08.

8. See Anthony, p. 314. The story among First Lady historians, which the author was unable to verify, although it makes sense, is that when Archie told Mrs. Taft she'd have to take the Fords she replied, "absolutely not" (from "Helen Herron Taft: Influence and Automobiles," by Walter Ostromecki, Jr., Manuscripts, Summer 1991).

9. *Recollections*, p. 333.

10. This section from Teague, "Mrs. L," pp. 141–142, Butt, *Letters*, introduction, pp. ix, xxi–xxiii, Butt letters of 2/21/09, 1/2/10 and 6/27/11 (published and unpublished), and White House memorandum, 3/3/09.

fought for Dixie. Butt wore his thoroughbred Southernness plainly. And like most people in Southern white society, he was an outright racist.[11]

Butt was a journalist by profession. Before joining the Army he worked in Washington as correspondent for a conglomerate of Southern newspapers. He next served as a secretary to the U.S. Ambassador to Mexico, a southern Civil War general who recognized Butt's gifts. He there wrote a critique of the Mexican economy, "Where Silver Rules," that was indicative of his open, inquiring mind. He went in to the project dedicated to Democracy's "free silver." He concluded that the monetary policy was ruinous.[12]

Captain Archibald Willingham Butt, military aide to Presidents Roosevelt and Taft. Elevated to Major in March 1911. Butt was a journalist by training and early profession, and to him we are indebted for copious letters on the daily life of President Taft. Butt's presence with the President was constant. He was assistant, friend, sounding board, and motoring and golf partner. "I cannot tell you, Archie," Taft said to him, "what you have meant to me...." At a press dinner in 1911, Butt's old newspaper boss Col. Watterson said of him, "He has been greater than President: the guide, philosopher, and friend of a pair of Presidents ... it was his gentle influence which kept Theodore Roosevelt from declaring himself a dictator. It is said that William Howard Taft considers him his mascot, and looks to him to insure his re-election." Butt's journalist friends made fun of him and his uniform in the news. One mocked, "...In the hearts of the women there is enshrined a vision — said vision being known by the imposing cognomen of Archibald Willingham De Graffenried Clavering Butt. They say in Beverly that Apollo was not in Capt. Butt's class — admitting, of course, that Apollo never had a chance to appear in blue and gold with brass buttons — and certain among them pronounce his name as though it were spelled Beaut, a delicate and touching tribute to his Gibbonesque figure." Butt's final act of gallantry came on the *Titanic.* (Courtesy Library of Congress)

Butt signed up for service at the tail end of the Spanish American War and was appointed a Captain of volunteers. He was sent to Manila in charge of a transfer of mules from Oregon to the new island possession. His first official act demonstrated both his skill and impulsiveness. He disobeyed orders to land in Hawaii for recuperation and instead steamed straight to Manila, expertly managing both animals and teamsters to a happy arrival in the Philippines. Applause rather than reprimand followed, and the government adopted his views on bypassing Hawaii. When a typhoon struck Manila, Butt was found the next morning still amidst his all-night custody of the teamsters and their precious charge. He was commissioned to the Quartermaster Corps

11. Of a dinner party at which a black man entertained, Butt wrote, "Seeing a negro man pass in and out among the tables singing and playing smart rather arouses my southern prejudices. I am sure the New Englanders present thought it quite the nicest dinner of the season" (unpublished passage, 1/2/10).
12. Pamphlet stamped Mexico City, 1896.

in 1901.[13] His next assignment was Depot Quartermaster at Washington in 1904. He was the lowest-ranking officer to have held that position. Two years later he jumped, literally — arriving two days in advance of his superior with a landing program already worked out — at the assignment for an intervention in Cuba.

Whatever Archie Butt had going for him, it took him far and quickly. After two years in Cuba he was returned to Washington, now as the personal military aide to the President. Already well known from his previous tour as a journalist and with the title of the President's aide-de-camp added to his poised, uniformed presence, Butt became a social prize in the city. Mr. and Mrs. Roosevelt came to rely on his diplomatic talents and administrative skills, and from the short time he spent working for them he earned the highest Roosevelt praise that, "If ever again it should befall me to command troops I should desire him to serve under me." In 1911, Taft proudly signed his commission as Major.

There was one other side to Butt's personality that commended him to presidents. As one historian put it, he was "a shrewd horse trader who readily adapted his abilities at negotiation to the White House budget...."[14]

* * *

In charge of the White House stables, the task fell upon Butt when Taft announced the horses were to be turned out for automobiles, as well as the delicate business of their purchase. Which automobile the President chose was no small matter. A Daimler advertisement from 1906 highlighted the benefits of a conspicuous clientele: "The Car of Kings; The King of Cars," ran the headline to an ad that listed as Daimler owners, His Majesty the King of England, who owned seven, the Prince of Wales, with four, and over one hundred princesses, dukes, earls, lords, M.P.s and esquires, many of whom owned two or three Daimlers. In all, the advertisement spoke of some one hundred-fifty Daimlers owned by England's finest. "Looking over the list of purchasers," read the copy, "is like reading the pages of Burke's Peerage."[15] There was a lot of cash sitting in those blue-blooded garages. American companies looking for a spot in the White House garage dreamed of similar glory. The President might not have an official warrant to grant, but this was the greatest man in the nation, with or without birthright. His motoring outfit would be noticed.

The automobile industry applied in force. Butt was inundated with solicitations. It all turned into a perfectly Washington circus. Congressmen petitioned for constituents and friends. The rest wrote letters, called the White House, and otherwise drove Butt crazy. One likely candidate was the maker of the more practical of the high-end machines, the George N. Pierce Company, winner of numerous Glidden Tours and whose six-cylinder Pierce-Arrow 48 H.P. Suburban (limousine) sold for $6,100.[16] The company lobbied hard. Buying into Butt's theories of the advertising value in the deal, in De-

13. His commission was on February 2, 1901. The preface to his published papers states that he was commissioned in 1900. Butt's commission was by request of Governor Taft, who on January 7, 1901, wrote Secretary of State Root with the recommendation based upon Butt's excellent record in the Philippines.
14. *The President's House*, by William Seale, p. 727.
15. Advertisement, *NYT*, 1/21/06. The Daimler Co. was originally a British licensee of the German Daimler and was the predominate British luxury make until WWII. Its entry to the U.S. market was marred by a conflict over licensing rights with the German company.
16. Pierce-Arrow 48 H.P. Suburban advertisement, *Country Life in America*, Oct. 1908.

cember Pierce offered a mighty discount on a veritable show piece, the prize of the New York Automobile Show, a $10,000 limousine called the "Louis XVI" or "Boudoir" car. Green and gold with accents of satinwood without, within came brass, gold plate, velvet and painted ceiling and walls in an "historically correct Louis XVI style." Not exactly the egalitarian economobile. For $2,500, it might just work.[17] Meanwhile, Taft had his own ideas. He sent Butt a letter of introduction to the maker of his favorite car:

> This will introduce you to Mr. W.C. Sterling, of the White Steamer Company, who has talked with Mrs. Taft and me in respect to the automobiles for the White House.[18]

Whites had served Taft's War Department admirably. When in New York or Boston, Taft was in the good hands of White representatives and cars. In Georgia, the company had one of its famed steamers placed there for him "on loan." The War Department man who drove one of the White steamers at Oyster Bay the previous summer unpacked, prepared, and chauffeured the car for the incoming President. Maybe it was a coincidence that the White Company was from Taft's home state. Maybe there was nothing to the geographic loyalty, even if he weren't so enamored of the cars. When it came to politics, it's not that Taft didn't care, it's that he didn't care to notice. In February of 1909, Taft was inducted into the Masonic Order — hardly democratic.[19] Likewise he took to the automobile with no concern for its political impact. He did it because it was the right thing to do, and if $12,000 was needed, $12,000 would be asked of Congress. If the White Company was a friend, a White would go in the President's garage. Taft's only concern was that whatever the deal it must be clean. He instructed the Captain,

> ...my understanding is that the form of the appropriation is such as to make it impracticable to adopt a plan that the White Steamer Company suggest, of their furnishing for a certain sum a year new machines, to be renewed each year, without the expense of repair, and we only to put upon the payroll the operators. I have said to Mr. Sterling that we have no objection to his taking up this proposition with you again, to see if it is practicable, but if not will you be good enough to explain to him the plan you have, which you explained to me, in respect to the invitations of bids from the three companies you have in mind, including the White Company?

Even so, Taft not so mildly instructed Butt to work it out with Sterling:

> Both Mrs. Taft and I feel extremely friendly to the White Steamer Company because of the accommodations that they have furnished us and because of the very great satisfaction that their car, which we used in New York, Washington, and Au gusta, has given us.

A few days later, Taft made the order more direct. "A letter from Mr. Taft to-day rather upsets some plans," Butt wrote, "for he wants us to buy only White Steamers for motors. I have been harassed to death by automobile people and I will be glad to have something settled definitely."[20]

17. Butt, unpublished passage, 12/25/08 and "How One Maker Supplies Artistic Luxury," *Automobile*, 1/14/09. The $10,000 is from Butt; the *Automobile* later listed the price at $12,500 ("The Pierce Boudoir Car," 1/21/09, p. 162)
18. Taft to Butt, 1/4/09.
19. "Taft Mason At Sight," *Evening Star*, 2/1/09. This caused some grumbling among the Masons. One complained, "He got all the fun without any of the hard work."
20. Butt, unpublished passage, 1/11/09.

* * *

Whites, like their boiled-water brethren, Stanley, made excellent touring cars. Steam engines were strong, silent, and fast. The White Model M could power a car load of motorists, including Taft, one of the largest enthusiasts in the land, and run for great distances, needing only an occasional refill of water for steam and fuel for the burners. Additionally, with few moving parts, steamers were most reliable, especially compared to the quirky, complex gasoline machines. Steam's defect was that it was not practical for on-off city use, for starting the engine literally required building up steam. If you've ever waited on boiling water in the kitchen you'll understand why city folks shied from steamers. Winter posed the additional problem of freezing. Even with a chauffeur around, the quick-starting gasoline car was the more suitable platform for the city, especially to power limousines whose primary role and social significance was in the city.[21]

Taft's love for the steamer was from touring — driving around to pass an afternoon for relaxation and fresh air. His greatest joy was to sit in the back and let the countryside fly on by, enjoying what he called "atmospheric champagne."[22] He loved speed, and he was uninhibited by foul weather. Open air driving was considered a panacea, recommended by doctors and considered a healthful activity by practitioners. For Taft, the benefits of fresh air came secondary to his love for just being there, loving every second of cruising along country roads.

Taft's choice for the touring car and that it be a White was immutable. But a motoring President — and his wife — must also employ a formal coach, which meant a limousine. And for Mrs. Taft there was also to be a landaulet and an electric, a collection that constituted the fewest number of automobiles she "could get along with." The order that all the motors be Whites was dropped. Taft had what he wanted in the tourer. The other cars were up to Mrs. Taft. To the discriminating lady of 1909, each of these types of automobiles served a social role. The limousine was all that was exquisite in motors. The landaulet was show. The electric was for a lady to be on her own.

In the limousine, the Tafts could reign with the dignity of any rulers in a formal coach. The closed passenger compartment brought distinction to the passengers, and a proper set of coachman and footman fit nicely in the half-enclosed front seats. The landaulet, however, was all Mrs. Taft's. It was the motoring equivalent to the landau carriage whose retractable roof gave either protection or air, whichever was suitable, and most suitable meant the top down, being seen. The landau was for shopping, rides in the park, and "calling," that twisted Victorian ritual of having servants exchange cards as a form of social interaction between their employers. The landaulet's collapsing rear

21. For the advantages of steam, see "The Steam Car Superior to Gasoline Cars from Standpoint of Flexibility and Ease of Control," *NYT*, 10/18/08. The author was none other than Windsor T. White. He discussed steam's "noiselessness... smoothness... simplicity of operation... flexibility" and pointed out that there is no cranking and a single throttle. "It does not take any time to 'build up speed,' as does the gasoline car..." he wrote. And, all importantly, "There has never been an explosion of a generator of the White car, and never can be." White Company historian Henry Merkel disagrees with the author's conclusion that steam was inconvenient for the city. Mr. Merkel points out that anyone who could afford a White kept a chauffeur who suffered its inconvenience for the owner. Additionally, steam cars, as Windsor White noted, had no gear changes, which meant smoother starting and stopping, and were more useful than gas cars for "constant use," such as for taxicabs and buses. Nevertheless, and for whatever the reason, gasoline made the winning case with the consumers of the day.

22. Taft papers, "Official Functions," 9/22/09, p. 164 (reel 599).

roof was crucial, for while the footman delivered her calling card, the top of the lady's hat should be perceived, through a peaked drape, perhaps, perched on a head whose chin tilted upwards at exactly twelve degrees, hands folded astride, she perfectly ensconced in the back seat. The landaulet was for the lady who took to fads, a seasoned accent to her modernity.[23]

The electric was a wholly different vehicle of pretension. Electrics were limited in range and power. Electrics, though, were free of noise, cranks, clutches, and fire — not unimportant when the pilot light of a steamer was in plain view and "explosive" gasoline engines ran literally on internal combustions.[24] Electrics were clean, smooth, and started at a switch. This was a singular machine for a lady. In her electric, she could wander streets free of chauffeur and men altogether. Going her own way, a lady could prove her modernity and independence. An electric was like having the right hat.

All that for $12,000? The White tourer that Taft was certain to buy was the Model 'M,' the best and biggest steamer on the road. It went for $4,000, as advertised during the January auto shows, leaving hardly enough to cover another three cars, chauffeurs and upkeep.[25] Captain Butt was stuck trying to fit a round peg in the square hole. Some other way had to be found.

Taft was decisive in his needs and indifferent to those of others. As was his way with matters beyond personal concern, he left it up to his wife to decide on the other cars. Despite Butt's discussions with Mrs. Taft of the prior week over four cars, a press notice of the pending purchases dated December 20, 1908, spoke of two motors. With her husband fixed on the White, she was limited to that car which was most appropriate for her arrival to the Capitol on March 4, the limousine. Butt's quest was thus temporarily narrowed. The $12,000 might do.

Along with the request to Congress for funds and the precious time spent on the matter by the exiting President's private secretary and military aide, Taft had one other important government official working on the motors, General Edwards, Chief of the Army Insular Division. Edwards was a close Taft friend, chief golfing pal, and, of course, from Ohio. Edwards had his own car from the War Department and had spent hours motoring with Taft, a practice they continued into Taft's term. The big gun was now out on behalf of the President-elect's automobiles.

On the 3rd of February, General Edwards cabled the boss, who was in the Canal Zone with her husband, Mr. Taft. To her attention, he wrote,

> White House carriages — Private will be sold February 22, Public carriages not fit for use. Meantime nothing to ride in — but[t] recommends purchase White tour-

23. The absurdity of the practice was exceeded in 1909 when an outmoded fashion, to some commentary, was resurrected, the infamous "double card." Here's how it worked: "If one woman were calling upon another, or at a house where there was no man for whom cards would be left, she should send in the double, which amounts to one of her husband's and one of her own being left for each woman... But should there be a man in the house, the number of cards instantly becomes uneven, for only one of hers is required, while there must be two more of her husband's, certainly one for the host and hostess. This means that more of the man's are needed, and to preserve unity the visitor should, according to one set, leave her own single card and two of her husband's, as has been done for years past..." ("Mr. and Mrs. is Proper on One Calling Card," *Evening Star*, 2/19/09).

24. Worried that it led to an incorrect public notion that automobiles exploded, the *Automobile* wrote, "The word 'explosion,' in connection with gasoline, is nothing but a figure of speech." Nitro-glycerine explodes by itself, it said, not gasoline, which only explodes with an external source of oxygen (editorial, 6/9/10, p. 1059).

25. White 40 H.P. Model "M" advertisement, *NYT*, 1/17/09.

ing and Pierce-Arrow limousine to be kept in local garage company's expense until after March 4th. Pierce-Arrow best bargain to be had today. Decide on these two cars and other things can be taken up on your return but it should not be delayed. I concur. Tentative orders given.[26]

Perhaps Archie thought it was settled now. Not so fast. Taft himself cabled back two days later:

> Whatever inconveniences, cannot settle limousine matter until return. You can close as to the White touring car.[27]

26. Edwards to Helen Taft, 2/3/09. The "but" was "Butt."
27. Taft to Edwards, 2/5/09.

5

Two Cars for a Tariff

When the Tafts enter the White House there will begin an automobile administration.

—*Washington Evening Star*[1]

The first issue Taft aimed to tackle as President was the tariff. Tariffs were considered by proponents "protective" and immutable shields to the American economy. Roosevelt was neither willing nor in any position to work with Congress on the tariff, leaving it to Taft to grapple. Instead, Roosevelt used the tariff as leverage for other legislation. During the 1905 honeymoon, he floated a tariff trial balloon. It was a standard Roosevelt political operation: let out an unofficial idea and see what gives. The House leadership put a stop to any such idea and Roosevelt backed off. In exchange for his railroad reforms the tariff went untouched. The *Times* lightly reported, "President Roosevelt favors the earliest possible action looking to revision.... While the President is deeply in earnest in his desire for tariff revision, he regards the question as one of expediency *in which no great principle is at stake*.... The freight rate question he does not regard as one of expediency. He holds that it is a subject in which a great moral principle is involved...."[2] [italics added]. Translation: if you want railroad reform, lay off the revenue bills. He made the trade.

Modern associations with tariffs revolve around free trade deals and an occasional spat over steel, automobiles, bananas, computer chips, and cheese. For Americans of the 19th Century, the tariff was *the* political issue, one that twisted and tore the Union as much as any. Over high tariffs coastal New England threatened secession in 1814. South Carolina talked divorce over the "tariff of abominations" of 1828, and another of 1832. The two-party political axis was entrenched on either side of the tariff issue, one to protect industry, growth, and jobs, and the other in defense of consumers, farmers, and exporters who demanded parity with the lower duties of other nations. Almost every social and political division was somehow twisted around the tariff. Taft's goal and that of other Republican reformers was to rid the country of disruptive tariff fights by instituting a rational, scientific tariff.

1. "Motoring," *Evening Star*, 12/20/08.
2. "President Gets Poll of House on Tariff," *NYT*, 1/11/05.

Taft's problems all started with the biggest thing Roosevelt failed to do. Roosevelt here proclaims, "The tariff cannot with wisdom, be dealt with in the year preceding a Presidential election." He had been dodging the issue since 1905. The "standpatters" rejoiced. These were the Republican "Old Guard," the Republican leaders who believed that prosperity depended on a protective tariff. The "tariff revisionists" were stunned. The tariff problem fell upon Taft, who announced it his most important first step as President. He immediately called a special session of Congress to address this most pressing and fundamental question. (c. 1907 Clifford Berryman cartoon, Courtesy Library of Congress)

The "Commoner" or the "Peerless Loser," depending on your point of view, William Jennings Bryan, had thrice won the Democratic nomination and thrice lost the national election based upon various schemes for free trade, free silver, a free Philippines, and a not-so-free government-owned railway system. The Republicans were hardly clean on these populist stands. It was Grover Cleveland who saved the nation from their perverse scheme of 1890 that bought votes for high tariffs with silver to appease the populists in an attempt to re-elect Harrison. That tariff, the McKinley Act, blatantly called for high rates in order to reduce a government surplus, supply-side theory in reverse. Its prohibitively high duties were meant to suppress imports, which would, in turn, suppress government revenues. It worked marvelously. Along with the Sherman Silver Act of 1890, which mandated purchase of silver by the government — and drained the Treasury of its gold — the Panic of 1893 resulted.

When it came to government money, hypocrisy reigned, never more evident than amidst tariff revision. All tariff politics were local. Free traders with everything else, Louisiana Democrats took leave of their party for any tariff bill that included high sugar duties. Eastern Republicans wanted hides duty-free, while their Western brethren howled at the thought of cheap foreign skins. Otherwise, Westerners considered it a moral right that finished leather goods have low duties. And so on went the tariff dance for every product in its every form for every state and district across the country. Congressmen voted for protection against everything made, grown, raised or produced at home and for "free listing," the removal of duties, of anything imported. Figure out those demographics and there you have a deep comprehension of the history of American politics. There was no good answer. The tortured components to the tariff were the sum of the national mood. When Taft came in, the temperature of tariff reform was moderate. Get it done, get it done quickly, and get it done quietly. On this promise Taft was elected by a concurring majority. There would be and there never could be a happy ending to this episode. With tariffs, no one was going to walk away happy. The issue was larger than Taft's election year good will. It soaked it all up early.

While Taft stood with all his weight upon the Republican platform, the tariff plank nearly came unglued early. Empowered by Bryan's fatal announcement that the tariff was not the issue of 1908, Republican standpatters were able to control the issue and force into the platform a vague call for ""revision."[3] After the election they asserted that the "revision" plank did not necessarily mean down.[4] Taft flatly announced that the changes would be "honest" and "downward." The tariff would go accordingly or there would be "no revision at all," he announced in December. This was not a negotiation. Congress and his party must abide. Taft wanted a construction whereby tariffs be calculated by "the difference between the cost of production of the article in this country and such cost abroad." Included in that definition was to be, by some measure or other, "a reasonable manufacturer's profit."[5] When it came time for the real thing, of course, Taft alone cared for his promises.

Everybody applauded the president-elect's reasonableness, for he would "take fixing of rates out of politics." The thing is, Taft really meant it. To the lawyer, judge, and career civil servant, this all seemed most reasonable, and it played well in editorials. Needless to say, the "interests" went to work on the matter, tearing it every which way but Taft's, and always in the direction of the greatest "reasonable" profit, be it political or financial, be that change up or down.

* * *

The Association of Licensed Automobile Manufacturers (ALAM) was a trade and lobby group that to those of 1909, had they cared to look, had all the appearances of a trust.[6] Wrapped around the 1895 Selden automobile patent which covered all gasoline motor cars, the ALAM kept a tight collar on the industry. Only a few, including Ford, Maxwell-Briscoe, Reo, Mitchell, and the French maker, Panhard et Levassor, refused to play ball. The price of independence was time in court for violation of the patent. Imported competition was tamed by a 45 percent duty that Congress obediently conferred to domestic producers.[7] In December of 1908, the ALAM announced itself happy with the existing levy on imports but demanded "that motorcars and their parts be placed in a separate classification," a tremendous request, the equivalent to official endorsement of the industry.[8]

3. Taft stole the issue with his call for revision. Bryan dumped it and instead declared himself for public ownership of the railroads. Instead of forcing the Republicans to define "revision," Bryan unwittingly empowered tariff standpattism (see Pringle, pp. 346–347).
4. The wording of the tariff plank bedeviled Taft. The platform called for a revision but without any suggestion as to whether it be up or down. Until Taft laid into the idea, standpatters, including Cannon and Aldrich, claimed that there never was a promise for a downward revision. There was a need for lateral changes, for tariff revision meant not just rates. Republicans pointed to changed business conditions that required a reformulation of the schedules, that is the categories of products. Some were obsolete, while others went missing altogether. Legitimate revision meant to update schedules as well as rates.
5. "Taft Tariff Talk Stirs Ohio Society," 12/17/08 and "Taft Gives His Ideas of Tariff Revision," 12/18/08, *NYT*.
6. At a tariff hearing in Congress, auto importers labeled the ALAM a "trust" ("Auto Makers Interested in Tariff Revision," *Automobile*, 12/10/08, p. 826), as did Henry Ford in public statements ("From Both Sides of the Selden Patent Fence," *Automobile*, 5/2/07, p. 734).
7. In 1908, 1,706 automobiles were imported into the United States for a value of $3,965,468. These figures, interestingly and in reflection of lower prices forced on foreign makes by domestic competition, were up in number but down in unit value from 1907's 1,473 imports at a value of $4,829,437, and 1906's 1,561 cars worth $5,488,690 (from "Importation of Automobiles," *Evening Star*, 1/20/09).
8. "Tariff Engaging Motorcar Makers," *NYT*, 12/11/08.

Before a hearing in Congress, head of the ALAM's tariff committee, Packard President Henry B. Joy, demanded a 60 percent tariff. Unfortunately for him, a prominent member of his manufacturing community — one who was just inventing the world's greatest industrial conglomerate, General Motors— testified to the Ways and Means Committee that only a 20 percent duty was needed. Representing the Buick Motor Company was W.C. Durant, an audacious man who looked beyond to a future of his company's dominance. He infuriated his competitors with the testimony and insult, "The present rates are not protecting the American workman and they are not protecting the American consumer. They are in protection of enormous profits and ridiculously bad management."[9]

Committee Chairman Sereno Payne, whose name would be forever linked to Taft's tariff revision, found himself agreeing with Durant, except that he believed additional revenue was necessary from imported cars "to counteract the annual deficiencies." To this, Durant made the sublime retort, "I don't think it is right to make us come here and testify our sources of income out of our pockets." The remark didn't go over very well, for Payne's motoring constituents needed no alms for sustenance and gasoline. This was not an oppressed group, and their cause drew no sympathy in Congress. To protect labor was noble and good; it was quite another thing to count pennies for motorists. The surgeon needed no chloroform when extracting that money.

By February the ALAM was getting edgy. Joy wrote Taft to complain. His petition was considered important enough to be relayed to Taft during his voyage to Panama. Taft's reply commenced with a gratuitous display of Joy's importance. "I received your telegram from Detroit, Mich., sent to me at Charleston, and forwarded to me by wireless on board the U.S.S. North Carolina." Then the blow off:

> I quite realize the necessary halt that consideration and discussion of any new tariff bill brings about in business. All I can say is that I hope the prompt passage of a satisfactory bill will make the halt in the present instance as short and as little injurious as possible.[10]

The pandering businessman out-pandered by the politician. Beautiful Taft, and the hallmark of the subsequent four years. Care, measure, tact — and an ill-fated hope that things would work out just fine. Let one aspect of this exchange make clear that President-elect Taft brought something new to the automotive industry: a willing ear and a fair reply.

* * *

All the schemes and negotiations for the new automobiles had been going on under the assumption that the $12,000 would somehow materialize by the good graces of Congress and by Four March, the date of the Inaugural. Loeb worked with Butt and the House Committee on Appropriations Chairman James Tawney of Winona, Minnesota, to quietly push it through the committee and into a bill. Smiling upon Taft's request, the House granted $12,000, "for the purchase, care and maintenance of automobiles for use of the President."[11] Newspapers across the country noted this remarkable change at the White House. "Taft Asks for Autos," ran a headline the next day:

9. "Asks Low Duties on Automobiles," *NYT*, 12/20/08.
10. Taft to HB Joy, 2/6/09.
11. From original language of the H.R. 26399.

> A sum approximating $12,000 will be spent on automobiles for the use of William Howard Taft when he becomes President. This amount is carried in this year's Urgent Deficiency bill, in order that the vehicles may be ready for the bulky Executive as soon as he takes the oath of office.[12]

The request was initially placed before both houses as part of the Legislative, Executive, and Judicial bill, but Taft's agents convinced Tawney of the necessity to coincide the funding with his entry to office, not July 1, as would have been the case with the general funding bill. Tawney slipped the matter into the Urgent Deficiencies bill, a stopgap measure to carry over certain funding through to July, the end of the fiscal year. In pursuit of his automobiles, Taft was defended magnificently by Tawney, who, in turn, had good reason to help the incoming President.

Tawney was not just looking forward to the change at the White House, he was desperate for it. The triumvirate of the House hierarchy was the Speaker, the Whip, and the Chairman of Appropriations. With the key to the national treasury, Tawney was the iron in Cannon's fist. These men held to the 19th Century view of the People's House as the nation's true center of power, and to which the President was *a priori* a constitutional annoyance. So long as the President signed legislation he was tolerated. Should he ignore the will of Congress, or ask anything of it, he was a tyrant. Roosevelt was nothing less than a usurper.

Those antagonisms exploded during Roosevelt's final months in office. He left the White House with practically the same violence he entered it with. He went ballistic at Congress over the body's censorship of the use of the Secret Service for investigations outside its mandate. He hurled a libel suit at newspaper accusations of impropriety in the original Panama Canal deal.[13] He dared the Senate to impeach him over the disposition of documents held by the Bureau of Corporations.[14] He accused the Army of sloth. He toyed with the insurgents to allow them to think that he supported an overthrow of Speaker Cannon.

Roosevelt and Tawney ever kept restless company. In 1905, Tawney grabbed hold of Roosevelt's finger-in-the wind tariff polling and nearly forced him into a special session on it, thus adding to the newly reelected President's woes with that Congress. The agitation led to Roosevelt's devil's bargain with Cannon not to touch the rates. Tawney led another insurrection against a Roosevelt-Cannon deal on a Philippines measure and a statehood bill that would have admitted New Mexico and Arizona as a single state.[15] Tawney

12. "Taft Asks for Autos," *NYT*, 1/17/09.
13. In October, 1908, the *New York World* published an account of a blackmail plot that intimated that Roosevelt's brother-in-law, Douglas Robinson, and Taft's brother, Charles, had something to hide over the original 1902, forty-million dollar contract for the rights to the old French canal company, a deal brokered by J.P. Morgan. The issue culminated with an election-eve editorial by the *Indianapolis News* that questioned the final destination of the government payment. Roosevelt sent the Justice Department — against its better judgment — into a libel suit against Pulitzer and his *World* and the editors and owners of the *News*. It was one of Roosevelt's ugliest ventures. The suit was based upon an old 1825 statute and the nebulous and very dangerous theory that claimed jurisdiction because the newspapers had circulated on government property. A Justice Department attorney in Indiana resigned rather than proceed with the case. It ended in 1911 in the Supreme Court resoundingly in Pulitzer's favor (see Pringle, *Roosevelt*, pp. 334–338).
14. See Butt, 1/23/09, pp. 305–306.
15. "President Gets Poll of House on Tariff," 1/11/05, "Speaker Will Block House Insurgents," 1/8/06, "Roosevelt and Cannon Vainly Wave Big Stick," 1/14/06, and "President Charges Bribery in Congress," 1/15/06, *NYT*. The insurgency bit both Cannon and Roosevelt. Roosevelt's threats to withhold patronage backfired, and, although the Philippines bill eventually went through, due in part to Taft's insistent lobbying, only Oklahoma, along with the Indian Territory, was given statehood. For Roosevelt's problems with the end of the 58th Congress, see Pringle, *Roosevelt*, p. 366.

otherwise went the party way, which frequently put him into opposition with Roosevelt over spending matters, especially Roosevelt's budget-busting battleship requests. Tawney complained, "I am tired of these annual wars with Japan, which always occur simultaneously with the consideration of the naval appropriation bill by Congress. All the rest of the time our relations with Japan are friendly, but as soon as we begin to consider the naval appropriation bill then we learn from the press and other sources that war is imminent."[16]

It got downright nasty when Tawney was singled out for abuse in Roosevelt's January 1909 "Secret Service" message, which led to a vindictive reply by Tawney described as "a speech that has the distinction of being the only congressional effort of the kind in history that contained absolutely no adjectives."[17] Congress was used to Roosevelt's methods and had by 1908 tired of them entirely. Threats to withhold patronage and charges of corruption lost their sting as Roosevelt's incumbency turned lame. When Roosevelt hauled out the old corruption standard, Congress bit back.

The affair came of a dispute whether Secret Service activities in Justice Department investigations exceeded the Service's mandate. In April of 1908, Tawney put a restriction into an appropriations bill that limited funding to already proscribed Service jurisdiction. Roosevelt objected privately to Cannon, but otherwise followed the rules. Agents on assignment for other agencies were transferred to those departments.[18] Throughout the year, intimations simmered over Secret Service activities. The escalating rhetoric culminated in a December message to Congress in which Roosevelt declared that Congress was protecting corrupt members from scrutiny, a jibe well-understood to be directed at Tawney. A story flew from "high Administration officials," said the *Times* on the front page, that Roosevelt was preparing to expose dirty secrets up on Capitol Hill.[19] Chief Wilkie and his agents were gathering "interesting information concerning Congressmen," especially as regards "the interests" and their relations to Congress. The House demanded proof. There was none, of course, but there was also nothing to the vigorous rumors circulating on the Hill as to politically motivated investigations, including one story from Tawney's hometown. When Roosevelt gave his January reply, the House voted over-

16. "Passed by the House," *Evening Star*, 1/22/09. Hatch dismisses congressional interference with Roosevelt's four-battleship-a-year program. He wrote that Congress' arguments were "lamely argued" and its reasoning was "nonsense" (p. 44). Hatch accepts Roosevelt at face, citing a Message to Congress. Taft understood it differently. He told Speaker Cannon, "About the only promise which Roosevelt extracted from me, and about the only one I gave, was not to divide the fleet between the Atlantic and the Pacific... and to try to add two battleships a year until completion of the canal... Now what I want of you is to pull off your coat and work for those two battleships." Cannon couldn't believe what he'd just heard! "Nothing illustrates better than this the difference between our last two Presidents. Roosevelt never wanted but two at a time and yet he always asked, even demanded, four a year, hoping thereby to get two. You, on the contrary, want two and ask for two... I am inclined to think we can put it through in spite of Tawney." Taft replied, "Yes, I know Tawney is opposed to the idea, and I cannot ask him to change his ideas on the subject, for he has always opposed the building of these ships. I think his opposition to the policy was the real cause for disaffection between Roosevelt and him, but I think I can counteract his influence." He didn't have to, as Tawney went along with two battleships (from Butt, 3/9/10, pp. 303–304).
17. "Heard and Seen Here and There," 1/23/09, *Evening Star*.
18. Roosevelt to Cannon, 4/29/08 and 4/30/08, per Hatch, p. 50 and Treasury Department Memo, J Wilkie to "Special Operatives," 6/27/08, National Archives and Record Administration (NARA), Committee on Appropriations, RG 233, Box 514.
19. "Roosevelt Message Stirs Up Congress," 12/9/08 and "Roosevelt To Tell Congress's Secrets," 12/13/08, *NYT*.

whelmingly to refuse to accept it, a terrific rebuke. Like the libel suit, it was not Roosevelt's shining moment.[20]

Next, Tawney put into a Sundry Civil bill an amendment that prohibited funding of executive commissions not specifically authorized by law. In what was a substantial Congressional victory, Roosevelt gave in and signed the bill. It was an assault upon his farm, conservation, and other commissions that Congress the year before had refused to fund and that Roosevelt organized and paid for outside of official appropriations. Roosevelt had so far gotten away with it. Only he blew it that February by demanding funding for the National Conservation Commission. The commissions held no legal authority, but Roosevelt considered them important to his moral crusades.[21] More importantly, they reflected the drifting final years of his presidency, when he lost control of Congress and his agenda found no reward in law. The commissions were all gesture, as was their banishment. Neither Roosevelt nor the Incense Swingers would forgive the Appropriations Chairman for it.

When Taft demanded official recognition of the Motor Age he needed Tawney's permission. The November 27 request went out from Roosevelt's secretary, Loeb, at a time when the President and the Appropriations Chairman still inhabited the same planet. It conveniently followed an eight page notice from Tawney to Taft that pledged support for tariff revision — in exchange for peace from up the block on Pennsylvania Avenue. "I want to assure you of my personal good faith," Tawney wrote the President-elect. "You would be perfectly safe in making public a statement expressing your confidence in the republicanism and good faith of the representatives of the Republican Party in the House in the matter of carrying out the declaration of the party respecting tariff revision and every other declaration made by the party in its national platform and"— read here —"that under no circumstances would you take any interest or active part in the organization of either branch of the legislative department."[22] Leave us alone, particularly regarding the election of the Speaker, and we will give you your tariff revision.

This was an interesting proposition. Tawney assured the President-elect, "This would not only establish the best of feeling between you and the Congress, but would stop this unnecessary agitation." Not shades, but plain colors of Roosevelt here. "Unless some statement of this kind is

20. See Pringle, *Roosevelt*, pp. 483–485. The rumors of a Secret Service investigation of Tawney started when an out-of-state private detective went looking into theft at a local department store at his hometown. In the January message, Roosevelt attacked him by saying that Tawney misrepresented the facts regarding a Bureau of Engraving scandal and a letter from the Secretary of Treasury admitting to improper investigations. The President's implied charge was fraud, and it was repeated by others as such. It was not, but Tawney took terrific heat from some press. He successfully sued for libel a Minnesota paper that repeated the charges. From Butt's account Roosevelt truly believed Congress had something to hide, only the best he could do was abuse corruption in general, saying "the higher up the criminal... the more necessary it is to strike him down" and point to the Service's role in a 1905 investigation that led to the conviction of two Senators. Roosevelt's conviction that Congress was hiding corruption became an obsession. Following the January message Butt wrote, "He thinks it is the most important issue which has ever presented itself to him" (Butt, *Letters*, 12/11/08, p. 240, 1/11/09, p. 281).

21. Reformers looked to commissions to protect from political influence. "Experts" would study problems as science, not politics. Commissions were politics by another name. Taft believed in commissions, and even Aldrich took to the commission for his currency reform. For an enthusiastic look at commissions, see "The Short Ballot in American Cities," *American Review of Reviews*, Jan. 1912, pp. 82–84. Hofstadter noted, "Frank Hague use his position as commissioner of public safety, i.e., the police and fire departments – as a stepping-stone toward that execrable regime for which he became notorious" (p. 267, fn, 6).

22. Tawney to Taft, 11/25/08.

made by you in the near future this attempt on the part of the half breed republican news papers to create friction between the legislative and executive branches of the government will continue and it may prove disastrous," Tawney concluded. "It is my interest in your success and in the success of the Republican Party and because I believe there is serious danger threatening that success in the future that I have written you as I have."

Then came the Secret Service affair which led to Tawney's adjective-bereft reply to Roosevelt. The controversy was not the cause of the animosity; it turned a mutual distaste to dire hatred. By then Taft's automobile plan was irrevocably launched. Besides, and amazingly, Taft walked into office wholly free of these antagonisms. As Secretary of War and Administration mouthpiece, Taft was in the forefront of some serious Roosevelt controversies. But no one on Capitol Hill confused Taft's lash for Roosevelt's whip. Taft brought none of that baggage with him. And he intended to follow Tawney's advice to lay off the Congress, so long as Congress kept to the platform and to "honest" tariff reform. Peace was to reign. The lions and the lambs would bed together.

6

Peace at Last

Congress spent most of the winter session fighting the President, funding pet projects, arguing, mounting filibusters, and generally shaming each other, itself, and the President; in short, being Congress. The President-elect dodged the strife entirely, but not because he wanted to avoid conflict. He was both unafraid of Congress and aware of the dangers therein, having been abused by it over the Philippines and, particularly, the Brownsville affair, another Roosevelt act of righteousness gone haywire.[1] Taft would keep his campaign promises. Nevertheless, there was some other business left tangled by the outgoing Administration.

In Georgia and on the way to and from Panama, Taft explained his views on race relations and the South in general. He spoke to anxious Southerners who felt their parole had expired. Taft walked the tricky line between his personal sympathy and Southern enmity for blacks. One Taft comment in North Carolina incited an anti-black mutiny in the Annapolis legislature, which interpreted it as endorsement of separatist policies. Taft squarely denounced the Marylanders. On another occasion, Taft spoke to a black technical school in Georgia, over which the *Washington Evening Star* described his "most profound sympathy for the struggle upward of the negro race." Taft said,

> I do not think it inappropriate to refer to some of the expressions that fall from the lips of men prominent in political life that are utterly lacking in any sympathy of that kind and that are cruel and abrupt in their meaning.... I refer to those gentlemen who deem it necessary to affirm that in the interest of this country the negro race should have no education.[2]

Taft refused to dodge "the negro question." He also refused to use race as a political wedge. "I am not going to put into places of such prominence in the South where the race feeling is strong, Negroes whose appointment will only tend to increase that race feeling...."[3] If practicable, and in the North where Republicans didn't often turn to them, he aimed to appoint

1. See glossary and Pringle, *Roosevelt*, pp. 458–464. Secretary Taft was not altogether comfortable with the Administration's position on Brownsville (see "Roosevelt and Taft Said to Have Clashed," *NYT*, 11/21/06).
2. "Charmed by Georgia Girls," *Evening Star*, 1/20/09.
3. Taft to WR Nelson, 2/23/09. Butt described Taft's warm receptions in the South and accounted it to his position on blacks. "He dislikes the Negro, and his highest ambition is to eliminate them in politics," he wrote glowingly. Archie mistook Taft's rejection of old school Reconstruction politics for racism (Butt, 11/14/09, p. 204).

blacks. Where not, he would refuse. A Roosevelt appointment had especially disgruntled Southern whites, that of William Crum, a black, as collector of the port of Charleston. Taft asked Crum, whom Roosevelt had first dispatched to Charleston without Senate confirmation, to step down.[4]

Taft was not promoting segregation, as Wilson would in a few years. He was applying his principles to a reality he faced. And he put his appointments where his ideals were. He appointed a black, William H. Lewis, to the position of Assistant Attorney General, and, to the amazement of some, sent Lewis around the country to speak on behalf of the Administration.[5] He appointed a Southern Democrat, Jacob Dickinson, to head the War Department. Taft's own party's dwindling vote in the South was losing black as well as white votes, which was due entirely to the spoils system that constituted the Republican operation in the South. The Texas party, for example, was a one-man show. While the votes disappeared, the machine man, Rough Rider Cecil Lyon, tightened his hold on federal patronage, and, some said, his cut on those salaries.[6] It was Reconstruction at its worst, and politically, it was a failure. The sole function of black appointments had become by 1909 internal Republican politics.

The *Times* praised Taft's policy. "Up to the present time the Republican Party in the South has been closely identified with office holding and with the negro vote led by negro office holders. If Mr. Taft can alter that he will set on foot an important and fruitful change." It was all part of Taft's scheme for "a tolerance of political opinion" in the South. "The real spirit of Appomattox ... will manifest itself in political independence the country over," he told the Union League, "so that we shall not know each other by sections in political matters but by difference only in principles." At a banquet in Augusta, he told the crowd plainly, "If I can convince the southern people that this administration is as much concerned with the welfare of the people of the south, as it is with the welfare of the people of every other section, I have accomplished all that I can hope to." He closed this line with a slice of Taftian naivete. "The votes and the political matters can take care of themselves."[7]

Yes, the votes took great care of themselves. In 1910 the city of Richmond embraced the President. "Taft is simply a bully fellow," declared a Democrat at a banquet. "He is the kind of a man you love." Another replied, "You bet he is. But by the way, are you going to vote for him next time?" The other looked back, incredulous. "Vote for him? Vote for him? I'd rather see him in hell first."[8] Taft sailed these hot-cold waters during his Southern visits. He was rejoiced in Atlanta with a 'possum feast (which he worked off

4. Pringle, p. 390. The fight between Roosevelt and the Senate over Crum started in 1902, when Roosevelt sent Crum's name to the Senate for Collector of Customs. Then, it was a product of the pre-nomination maneuvering with Mark Hanna over Hanna's hold on Republican appointive politics (see "William D. Crum: A Negro in Politics," by Willard B. Gatewood, *Journal of Negro History,* Oct. 1968). The appointment was also aimed at South Carolina Senator Ben Tillman, whom Roosevelt despised. Senate Republicans tangled with Roosevelt over the intrusion and in defense of their consent powers more than over the appointment itself. Crum was confined finally in 1905.
5. "Negro Official to Speak," *NYT*, 11/16/11. Also, Taft refused to appoint to the high court a judge who upheld Jim Crow laws in an Ohio railroad car case (*American Review of Reviews,* March 1912, p. 271).
6. See "Theodore Roosevelt, William Howard Taft, and the Disputed Delegates in 1912: Texas as a Test Case," by Lewis L. Gould, *Southwestern Historical Quarterly,* Vol. LXXX No. 1, July 1976, p. 36.
7. "Mr. Taft and the South," *NYT* editorial, 4/13/09, "Union, Taft's Text on Grant's Birthday," *NYT*, 4/28/09, "Augusta Claims Taft," *Evening Star*, 1/21/09.
8. "Love for Taft, No Vote," *NYT*, 11/30/10.

dancing past midnight), toasted in New Orleans (and stuffed with bouillabaisse), and hailed in North Carolina, all without upsetting his Northern base — or taking a Southern vote.

Taft's goal was nothing less than a political realization of the ideals imbedded in his proposal for a memorial to span the Potomac, a revival of Andrew Jackson's dream for a bridge "symbolical of the firmly established union of the North and South."[9] Taft considered it his task to finish Lincoln's reconciliation that was lost to Andrew Johnson's rout by Northern radicals. His brother Horace was keen on these efforts. "The policy you set forth shows a better spirit than has been shown in the southern matters since Lincoln was shot," he wrote. "I cannot see how it can fail to produce most remarkable results."[10]

Next, the economic situation Taft inherited in 1909 was confused. Government and business were lions circling each other. Business was more concerned with recovery from the Panic of 1907 than with the 1908 election, so long as Bryan didn't win, and it was learning to accommodate federal intervention by trying to shape it. Principally, the anti-trust situation remained unclear. The largest government case, against Standard Oil, yet brewed in court.

Certainly, Roosevelt was the capitalist's equal in haggling skills, but for him business was foreign. He privately admitted bewilderment at the workings of the economy.[11] Business was politics, just like anything else, with all the messy alignments that entailed. His nationalist inclination was to partner with business, the intent of his Bureau of Corporations. He learned more economics than he ever cared to know during the panic of 1907. Attempts to lay the downturn on him went nowhere, but there was enough blame in currency to fuel hearings in Congress and to stymie new reforms.[12]

Taft knew no more of economics than Roosevelt, although his experience to build self-sufficiency in the Philippines had given him a close look at the relationship between government and business, particularly concerning tariffs. Taft looked upon business as neither inherently mean nor ultimately sovereign. It was a matter of law. He let it out that the Constitution would not be flexed to accommodate unions, monopolies, or unwarranted government interference. It belonged to Rockefeller as much as to any other American. The policy was that the law would be enforced. Coming into the presidency his overriding concern was that tariff revision disturb business as little as possible.

Largest among the President-elect's reconciliation moves was to rebuild a bridge to Congress. New ways had to be found. Taft had no sympathy for the reactionaries in Congress. He also knew that Roosevelt's methods had produced few results since the 1906 mid-term elections. The bickering between Capitol Hill and the White House left Taft with a divided party and the compromise platform on which he was elected. Consequently, Taft's mandate was limited to that of Congress. Roosevelt may have built the biggest bonfire in town, but he left Taft walking on coals.[13]

9. "Washington," by W. H. Taft, *National Geographic Magazine*, March 1915, p. 251.
10. Horace Taft to Taft, approx. Jan. 1909.
11. Pringle, *Roosevelt*, p. 432.
12. See "President Found at Fault," *Evening Star*, 2/20/09. Currency reform was the only measure of twenty recommended by Roosevelt in his messages to the 60th Congress that made it into law intact, and it did so because it was Congress' legislation not his. Roosevelt's recommendation for currency reform was purposefully vague, asking for "immediate attention" without specific form (see Hatch, pp. 43, 46).
13. Hatch suggests that Roosevelt's 1908 attacks on Congress were motivated by a fall in popularity in late 1907, and again following his December, 1908 Message (Chapter III, especially p. 77).

The popular legislative body is a lot of things, but mostly it is organized chaos. Rules in the House are sacrosanct, and whoever wields them — that is, whoever has the votes— dictates the flow of business. Cannon managed the House with a poised ruler. The insurgents aimed to break this "one man" control. Cannon was not disliked personally so much as his taut management. His wit was famous, as was his practice to hold back from floor discussions until ready to end a matter with a vicious one-liner. He was crude but endearing and very funny. Even the *Times*, which viewed all things by the tariff and "Cannonism," admitted an affection for the old guy who proclaimed himself too young to take up golf.[14] Nevertheless, the differences between the Speaker and the insurgents went beyond House rules. Were they content with the directions of his leadership, the insurgents would have had no objection to the rules.

That Speaker Cannon held the votes for reelection in the upcoming session was apparent to all. It would be his fourth term, a historical dominance. Taft was inclined to challenge him for the sole reason that he worried that Cannon would stand in the way of his agenda. Taft wrote to Elihu Root, "My attitude is one of hostility toward Cannon and the whole crowd unless they are coming to do the square thing.... If they play fair I will play fair, but if they won't then I reserve all my rights to do anything I find myself able to do."[15] In addition to his November letter to Taft, Tawney visited Roosevelt to negotiate the *détente*. Roosevelt conveyed the message to Taft with his fullest approval.[16] The old dogs chose to play tame, and just in time. In exchange for the leadership's pledge to sustain the platform, Taft agreed to lay off. Horace Taft wrote his brother of the victory. "Nothing is more gratifying than the promises to be good that are being daily made by Cannon and the other standpatters."[17]

No sooner than Cannon's dominion was renewed, Taft was accused by the insurgents of betrayal. Three years later, Taft reflected on what happened. He wrote to Mabel,

> It was about two years after I came into office that I heard from Congressman Madison that just the day before the inauguration he and Gussie Gardner and some other progressives went to Mr. Roosevelt and asked him to intervene with me to assist them in defeating Cannon for Speaker; that Mr. Roosevelt said that he agreed with them but that he was not quite sure that he could convince me; but that he would see me about it; and that thereafter he sent for them and told them that he had seen me but that it had done no good.

Roosevelt, Taft realized too late, was walking both sides of the street. While deals were cut with the Speaker, sympathies were sent to the insurgents. Taft continued to Mabel,

> They may have misunderstood him, and probably they did, and that he said, assuming from conversations which we had had before, that I had a different plan

14. "Uncle Joseph Cannon," *NYT* editorial, 8/4/09. Cannon would turn 73 that Spring. He lived until 1926, every bit as prickly as he was in his youth as Speaker. He tried golf in 1911 and pronounced it, despite his 26 strokes to the first hole, "a great game, a great game" ("Cannon Plays Golf," *NYT*, 9/6/11).
15. Taft to Root, 11/23/08, per Pringle, pp. 405–406.
16. Roosevelt to Taft, 11/10/08. Roosevelt advised, "It would of course be well if there was some first class man to put in [Cannon's] place as Speaker; but we can not think of putting in some cater-cornered creature like Burton; and, moreover, if it is evident that four-fifths of the Republicans want Cannon I do not believe it would be well to have him in the position of a sullen and hostile floor leader bound to bring your administration to grief, even tho [*sic*] you were able to put someone else in as Speaker."
17. Horace Taft to Taft, 12/1/08.

> and that I would not do anything about it. Naturally I wouldn't, when at his advice I had sought Cannon out and agreed that if he would help the administration measures I would stand by the caucus and not interfere with the regular course in Congress.[18]

That the insurgents misunderstood or not is irrelevant. Roosevelt worked them like penned animals. When he left the zoo, he left the cages unlocked.

* * *

From their firm hold on the minority House Democrats could only watch and hope for a rupture between Republicans. On February 27, 1909, there went a typical exchange between the Speaker and a frustrated Democrat, akin to the statement of earlier Speaker Thomas B. Reed that "the right of the minority is to draw its salaries, and its function is to make a quorum."[19] Amidst the reading of the Deficiency bill, John Wesley Gaines of Tennessee strode onto the floor chewing an unlit cigar and demanded to question Chairman Tawney. Cannon laid into Gaines on this violation of a rule against questions on the first reading of a bill. "I did not know I was out of order," retorted Gaines. Cannon replied that Gaines had been around long enough to know better. "It takes a student like the Speaker," went Gaines sarcastically, "to know what the rules are, and he has to study them every minute, with somebody to prompt him." Cannon's patience was already tried by late-night sessions, the constant bickering, and the attempts to outmaneuver him by Democrats and insurgents. "The gentleman from Tennessee is not only absolutely discourteous, but misstates the facts," he said. Now followed some sublime Congress-speak, the idiom of the third person and the normally controlled insult. "The gentleman from Tennessee," Gaines shrilled, "is no more discourteous to the Speaker than the Speaker is discourteous to him and the gentleman from Tennessee has not misstated the facts."

Gaines was not the most pleasant man to listen to. His voice "filled every reach and corner of the House and spilled out profusely into the corridors."[20] One story of his speaking style went that a visitor to the Capitol heard him through the closed doors of the House chamber. "What kind of show is that 'er, anyway?" This latest harangue threw Cannon into "a real passion." The Speaker retorted, "The chair desires at all times to be as impartial as he can, but the practice has grown up occasionally for a member, on the supposition that the Speaker's tongue is tied, to insult him and the Speaker will not submit to it. He will not permit any one to insult him." Cannon again demanded order. Gaines wouldn't let go. "The tongue of the gentleman from Tennessee is tied and he is insulted by the chair," he shouted. Now he expressed the rage of both Democrats and insurgents. "The speaker has done it for twelve years!"[21]

Cannon called for order one more time, but Gaines screamed back, "The Speaker will be in order, too!" At this, Cannon pulled the trigger. He turned to the Sergeant-at-Arms. "Put him under the mace and see that he remains in order." The mace, or "the bird," as House aides tagged it, is the House symbol of authority, a four-foot pole with a silver eagle mounted atop that rests beside the Speaker's chair when the House is in session. Rarely is the mace employed against a member. This was perhaps the first time

18. Taft to Mabel Boardman, 4/14/12.
19. *The Wit and Wisdom of Congress*, edited by Edward Boykin, p. 165.
20. "Capitol Callers and Their Queer Questions," *Evening Star*, 2/21/09.
21. Twelve years of Republican Speakers Reed, Henderson and Cannon. From "Cannon, Made Angry, Suppresses Gaines," *NYT*, 2/28/09

In a 1909 exchange between Speaker Cannon and a frustrated Democrat, Cannon declared, "The Speaker will not ... permit any one to insult him." The Democrat cried out, "The tongue of the gentleman from Tennessee is tied and he is insulted by the chair. The speaker has done it for twelve years!" Cannon is pictured here taking up the golf stick. The ball is labeled "insurgency." It all fell apart for him in March of 1910, when the Democrats were joined by enough insurgent votes to take away the Speaker's strongest power, appointment to the Rules Committee. With the Republican party imploding over the insurgent revolt, and using the discontent over the Payne tariff as the wedge, Democrats turned the House of Representatives upside down in the November elections. (Clifford Berryman cartoon, Courtesy Library of Congress)

in a generation. With Cannon banging his gavel, and the Sergeant-at-Arms approaching with the mace, Gaines ran to his seat. Although blame was laid upon Gaines for the incident, it was emblematic of the frustration of Cannon's opponents. Likewise in the Senate were complaints lodged that the leadership held key positions, leaving for the rest meaningless committee posts and bureaucratic tasks such as Indian school house investigations and the building of Civil War memorials. The treatment, insurgents and Democrats felt, amounted to house arrest.

Taft asked the same thing of regular and insurgent alike: the platform. To get it he'd face the devil he knew to get the tariff he wanted. As he roped the regulars to fulfill his promises, he lost the insurgents. Had Roosevelt been as blunt with the insurgents as he was with Taft on the need to work with Cannon, none of this may have mattered. Taft was plain to insurgents and their sympathizers; Roosevelt was not. As Taft doused the flames Roosevelt lit at the one end of the bridge, the other was set afire.[22]

* * *

In retrospect, Taft's entrance to the White House seems to have gone wrong from the beginning. While Roosevelt lit up the Capitol and signed last-minute Executive Orders, Mrs. Taft was accused of everything short of treason for wanting to

22. Taft understood the dynamic and made a rational choice. On March 21, 1909, he wrote to Roosevelt, "I have no doubt that when you return you will find me very much under suspicion by our friends in the West... Indeed I think I am already so because I was not disposed to countenance an insurrection of thirty men against 180 outside the caucus. I knew how this would be regarded, but I also knew that unless I sat steady in the boat and did what I could to help Cannon and the great majority of the Republicans stand solid, I should make a capital error in the beginning of my administration in alienating the goodwill of these without whom I can do nothing to carry through the legislation to which the party and I are pledged...." (Taft to Roosevelt, 3/21/09). Taft actively tried to persuade the insurgent press to go along. Writing to W.D. Foulke, an Indiana newsman who soon turned on him, Taft explained, "The question with me is practical, not theoretical, and I ask you how a man of sense, looking at the situation as it is, can expect me to do otherwise than support the regular organization in the House." Taft knew he was dealing with emotion, not reason. "One slight difficulty about reformers (I have felt the lack myself)," he warned Foulke, "is the indisposition to look ahead.... and to magnify the importance of one particular thing which is immediately before them as compared with the whole plan of progress" (Taft to Foulke, 3/13/09).

switch the ushers for footmen. The sitting President was insulted when the incoming President's hostess, Mabel Boardman, committed social blasphemy by proposing the date of a Taft visit with the President rather than waiting to receive an invitation. Taking offense was not obligatory.[23] Worse, Taft made the news when he visited the White House and found that the President was out for a ride. With the Incense Swingers fuming, Taft absorbed rumor and intrigue over his audacity to want a Cabinet of his own choosing and dinner plates, curtains, and servants to suit his wife.

None of this was apparent in early 1909, when Taft was applauded for moving forward on the tariff, sustaining the Panama Canal project, and bringing the South back to the national fold. On top of all this good feeling was the Capital city's largest concern, how best to celebrate the 100th anniversary of Lincoln's birth. Congressmen fell over themselves trying to out-dedicate one another to the great man. Plans for a Lincoln monument were debated, memorial stamps were issued, and preparations were made to engrave on the copper penny Lincoln's homely face. The only serious friction in town involved the Roosevelt side shows, whose star performer was acting out his final days as agitator-in-chief.

Furious members vented foul language and disrespect on the floor of Congress when discussing him. One Democratic outburst labeled Roosevelt a "pygmy scion of a race of Dutch Burghers." It got so bad that a rule was proposed in the Senate to prohibit "referring offensively" to the Executive.[24] The general opinion was that a good congressional slap was due the President, although some members had headier thoughts of censorship and worse. The winning argument against further retaliation was that Congress should hold itself above the President's behavior.

Finally, even Roosevelt got testy. Perhaps he was weary of the constant fight. At the January Gridiron his Country Life Commission was ridiculed. He usually took their jokes in stride, such as that of a list of American Presidents that read, "T. Roosevelt & etc.," and a skit that consisted of the smashing of typewriters, a parody of his adventures in spelling reform. This was messing with his legacy. As he became annoyed with the skits of farmers ridiculing the dandy "uplifters," echoes rang of his angry encounter at a 1907 Gridiron with Senator Foraker that ended with a breach of protocol when the President was denied the evening's final word. The Secret Service affair was reenacted with detectives whose investigations of Congress revealed no counterfeiters, only "a few four flushers." A Teddy Bear sang, "Oh, Tawney, Jim Tawney, Jim Tawney." A generous atmosphere prevented any serious moods as the Club presented Roosevelt with an inscribed gridiron "on which to broil lion steaks and rhinoceros chops."[25]

Then Cannon engineered another offense from which Roosevelt never recovered. In an uncharacteristic act of political bungling, just amidst the Secret Service spat Roosevelt sent to the Speaker a request to keep certain items from the mansion, including a sofa his wife particularly liked. On the House floor Cannon said the President's request seemed fine but it was

23. She told Roosevelt that only one evening was open. Taft and Roosevelt sorted it out in a series of kindly letters that resulted in an invitation to Mr. and Mrs. Taft to spend the night of March 3 at the White House (Butt, *Letters*, 12/5/08).

24. "Assailing President, Willett Choked Off," *Evening Star*, 1/18/09 and "Rules to Muzzle Senators," *Evening Star*, 2/1/09. The House voted to redact Willett's insult from the Congressional Record.

25. Tawney was at the dinner. According to the rules, newspapers reported only on the skits. Roosevelt's anger is from "The President Speaks Off-The-Record," p. 70. See "Grill Roosevelt and Fairbanks," *NYT*, 1/31/09 and "Toasts and Roasts at Gridiron Feast, *Evening Star*, 1/31/09.

a matter for the Appropriations Committee, as in Jim Tawney. Members ripped into laughter, knowing exactly the reactions of both Tawney and Roosevelt. "Without delay the President replied that he withdrew his request and would let the matter drop," recorded the *Times*.[26]

Among the aimless grievances served out at the end of his term was Roosevelt's frustration at the unenthusiastic enforcement of his orders to the Army for physical training. West Point was not exactly an egalitarian model. In those days there was no distinction between an officer and a gentleman. Military rank was a privilege, just as in Washington's day. Butt, who got where he was in no small way from his social rank, criticized one military family whom he considered "ambitious socially." The offense came in the indiscretion, not the act.[27] Dissolution in the services, moral and physical, was not hard to find. Opportunity for complaint surfaced when Roosevelt's orders for horse "tests" went ignored by the military and ridiculed in Congress. There could be no greater joy for him than to punish Congress and the intemperate alike, all the while certifying his own vigor.

He led the Captain and two Naval officers on a grueling, one day, one hundred mile horseback ride through the January Virginia countryside.[28] The idea was for the President to castigate officers who ignored the order for three days of thirty mile rides by running himself ninety miles in a single day. The party wore down several teams of horses, nearly froze in a blizzard, and went sore for days after.[29] Roosevelt made his manly, futile testimony. He loved it.

The press enjoyed "the Ride," answering it with both applause and ridicule. A sampling of editorial reactions included:

> The President rode horseback ninety-eight miles in one day, and was able to sit down comfortably for a late dinner. What's the use of Congress trying to spank a man like that?
>
> What does Roosevelt want of an auto? Any one can do ninety-eight miles in seventeen hours in one of those things.
>
> It is difficult, of course, to surpass the President in the matter of erratic performance, but there is reason to believe that between ninety-eight miles on horseback and a meal of 'possum a good many people would choose the ride.
>
> T.R. rode a hundred miles in a day, but Taft beat him to a frazzle by dancing until 2 o'clock in the morning.[30]

The next month, Roosevelt's War Secretary, Gen. Luke Wright, ordered that military officers based in Washington be forbidden from using automobiles except on official duties.[31]

* * *

Throughout, Taft set about his business. Nothing had ever not worked out for him, so why shouldn't this? Amidst the Messages, the Libel Suit, the Ride, the cursing in Congress, calls for censorship, and toasts of "to the lions" as a send-off for Roosevelt's Africa trip, Taft stood apart from it all. History points to all the problems and Taft's single term of office. As seen by the Butt letters, which turned ever more endearing towards Taft, things were

26. "Cannon Joke on President," *NYT*, 1/17/09. In 1910, Taft ordered a duplicate and sent it to Mrs. Roosevelt as a Christmas gift.
27. Butt, *Letters*, 11/24/08, p. 190.
28. Archie later wrote that it was he who suggested the Virginia route (Butt, 7/22/11, pp. 702–703).
29. Butt, *Letters*, 1/12/09, 1/14/0, pp. 283–296.
30. *Evening Star*, 1/24/09, quoting from various newspapers.
31. "How Foreign Governments Employ the Automobile," *NYT*, 2/28/09.

moving along just fine. Correspondence between Roosevelt and Taft was jovial. The press celebrated the Tafts. Above all, at the Capitol both parties saw blessed relief in the change up Pennsylvania Avenue. With the exception of a hard minority who wanted the exact opposite, a new normalcy was expected by all.

The political city yearned for peace. "Farewells have been said to the 'Big Noise,' who was the nearest approach to perpetual motion ever allowed to enter the Patent Office," wrote a Washington commentator.[32] At the "Amen Corner" banquet in New York, a dinner similar to the Gridiron, a cast of the "short and ugly, the malefactor of great wealth, the scoundrel, the muck-rakers, the soft body and the hard face, the weakling and the mollycoddle, the libeler, the nature-faker, the perverter of truth and the nation traducer" sang to the tune, "Give Us a Drink, Bartender,"

> Give us a rest, dear Teddy, dear Teddy,
> We're tired of noise, you know;
> They're going to turn off the limelight,
> Teddy,
> and give Billy Taft a show.[33]

In Washington, the welcome mat was out for the incoming President. The *Evening Star* noted, "Praise for Judge Taft is now as nearly unanimous as a public man has a right to expect. It is a melancholy fact that in a month or two he will be obliged by the necessities of high office to select a few enemies."[34]

32. "'Possum Wallow,' U.S.A.," by "General Debility," *Auto News of Washington*, April 1909, p. 2.
33. "Foolery Holds Sway," *Evening Star*, 2/28/09.
34. Editorial, 1/13/09.

7

The People's House v. The Motor Age

The tremendous good will of Congress toward the incoming President can be measured by its several acts of generosity. The first was a bill introduced by Senator Bourne to double the President's $50,000 salary. At Conference, the House and the Senate split the difference and Taft got a $25,000 raise, something Congress denied Roosevelt. Only one President had ever before been given a raise, Ulysses Grant. Another piece of kindness sent Taft's way was this little business of automobiles.

Butt's December observation that there was "no serious objection" to the $12,000 didn't gel. Unlike the salary matter over which the Senate was complacent and the House the spoiler, when it came to motor cars, fraternity lay in the House. Anti-automobile sentiment took voice on the 21st of January when the Senate voted down the measure. It refused Taft's autos "on the theory that it recognized the present as a 'horseless age.'"[1]

Senator Tillman offered a way, if not to stop, then to slow automobiles: "With a shotgun." He talked of one of his constituents who "hitched up" his wagon and "put his trusty shotgun ... to his shoulder. Those automobile fellows got mighty polite after that." Instead of cars, voted in was a cool seven grand for local snow removal. Evidently the Senators were tired of having to jump over snow banks in order to climb into their carriages. Amidst these debates, both the House and the Senate studied a request from the Department of Agriculture for half a million dollars to fight the hoof and mouth disease that plagued, yes, horses. The *Times* put it mildly, "The automobile has not made many friends in the Senate."

On February 2, in a debate described as a "spirited" and "fun," the House took up a rebuttal to the Senate changes in the Urgent Deficiencies bill, H.R. 26399.[2] At play on the chamber floor was far more than a simple matter of $12,000 and two

1. "Taft To Have Automobile," *Evening Star*, 2/5/09, "No Autos for Taft," 1/22/09 and "Tillman's Motormania Cure," 2/5/09, *NYT*.
2. This section from "Congressional Record," (*CR*) 2/2/09, pg. 1723–1755, "Autos for Taft Voted In House," 2/3/09 and "Taft Will Have Autos," 2/6/09, *NYT*, and "Heard and Seen Here and There," 2/6/09 and "Vote Autos For Taft," 2/2/09, *Evening Star*. The *Times* called the discussion "short and spirited." The *Evening Star* described it as "fun" and having gone for "some length."

automobiles. As in the Senate, for some representatives the government shall never endorse the vile contraptions. For these holdouts it was horse and mule. Other objections were procedural, partisan, and in general protest of giving anything to the Executive branch. The more serious of these questions centered on the intricacies of the power balance in the House. The minority was forever conjuring technical objections, but it had lately been joined by the insurgents.

Things got going with Tawney's call for unanimous consent to tell off the Senate, which had generally tampered with his Deficiencies bill, and, in particular, Taft's motor cars. This would send the bill to Conference and another round of votes. The motion to repudiate the Senate changes was immediately challenged. Georgia Democrat Bartlett went straight to the problem: "Mr. Speaker, reserving the right to object, I understand this is the urgent deficiency bill which contained a provision for $12,000 for the purchase of two automobiles.... Now, does the gentleman request the House to disagree to that amendment as well as the others?" In a beautiful show of how these things happen, Tawney responded with disagreement to that amendment "and to all other Senate amendments." No uppity Senators were going to mess with Tawney's bill. Bartlett demanded a vote on the automobiles alone. "Mr. Speaker, I do not want the gentleman to give any promise for anybody but himself. Can the gentleman say that we will have an opportunity to vote upon that amendment? Because if that amendment remains in when the conference report is presented, we will have to vote it up or down." In other words, don't force the motor cars down our throats in order for us to get the rest of the bill.

After some parliamentary bantering over the form of the earlier voting, Bartlett objected that the Legislative, Executive, and Judicial bill already "contained $35,000 for carriages and automobiles." Tawney clarified that the "statement was made by myself on the floor — $25,000, not $35,000. But that will not be available until the 1st of next July, and will provide only for maintenance of such vehicles as the President may employ or purchase."[3] Bartlett got nasty. "The statement was made somewhere else that it would be a violation of the rules to mention, by a Member of Congress, that the legislative, executive, and judicial appropriation bill did carry $35,000 for carriages and automobiles for the executive mansion." Tawny replied, "My recollection is that the amount is $25,000. However it is the same amount that has been appropriated in previous years for that service. But that appropriation will not be available for the purchase of these automobiles until July, and the current appropriation for that service is not available because the language in which the current appropriation is made does not authorize the purchase of automobiles."

"I merely want to say," continued Bartlett, moving to semantics and sarcasm, "because this is the only opportunity, that for one I do not want to agree that the purchase of automobiles is so urgent as to put it in the urgent deficiency bill. I do not want to give unanimous consent, although I know that is the usual way, to agree to disagree to the Senate amendment." A well spoken surrender by a practiced member of the minority. Tawney recognized the swipe for what it was, and switched the stick for the carrot. "I do not think the gentleman from Georgia is disposed to inconvenience the Chief

3. Press accounts also confused these figures. The $35,000 figure was from the usual appropriation for maintenance of the White House physical plant and grounds.

Executive in the matter of conveyance. As I said, the incoming President proposes to abandon horses for reasons that the gentleman well knows: he does not wish to violate the law against cruelty to animals."

To the ensuing laughter, Bartlett backed down, repeating without effect that he be allowed to vote against the automobiles. Democratic floor leader Champ Clark of Missouri stepped in for Bartlett and demanded a reply, to which Tawney reiterated that the House would stand up to the Senate in defense of the proposition. Clark, who was known to speak of Taft's "garooge," shifted to another line of questioning, whether there would be "the usual appropriation for horses and this additional appropriation for automobiles?" Tawney answered that the general funding was "so worded as to make it impossible to purchase automobiles out of it," and what was needed was the authority to do so, not more money.

Now Thetus Sims of Linden, Tennessee, champion of restrictive automobile statutes in the District of Columbia, stood to speak for the Luddites. Linden was the home to Tennessee mules that "are famous all over the South, principally for the way they can kick," an apt metaphor for its representative. Linden, a columnist described it, consisted of "mules to the right of us, mules to the left of us; mules to the front of us." Sims was well liked in Congress as earnest and sincere, which usually earned his colleague's forgiveness for his not infrequent lapses into "intellectual coma." Motorists were unforgiving. They loathed him for his anti-automobile speeches and penchant to do everything within his powers to restrict, nay, evict motor cars. In 1906 Sims tried to limit the free flow of motor cars along Pennsylvania Avenue to vehicles of one-half horsepower, with all others required to be preceded by mounted police and sounding a fog horn.

"There are some folks in Washington who are too prone to criticize Mr. Sims for his aversion to motor cars," mocked our columnist. "The apparatus isn't yet made that can go around a curve under its own power as slowly as Mr. Sims would have it do." But Sims might be forgiven this view and not just because he was from Linden, circa 1805. Walking at his "usual rate of a block and a half an hour," the portly Sims was once landed upon by a "sixty-horse-power motor car at sixty miles an hour. There was a fearful crash, and for a moment the air was full of gasoline and people." The car was trashed, the owner hospitalized, and Sims, "standing mid the wreckage, discovered, after a careful inspection, a snag in his Sunday pants. Ever since then Mr. Sims has been dead against the automobile. Sunday pants do not grow on trees in fair Linden, Tenn." All were prepared for the arguments to follow.

In his first response to Tawney, Sims took to the rules. He quizzed Tawny on the definition of a deficiency and forced Tawney to admit that the automobile need was not exactly a deficit. "I so stated at the time," declared Tawney, backing off. Well then, declared Sims, "I think in all fairness, as the gentleman brought in the deficiency bill, we had a right to rely on him that there was nothing in it but deficiencies, and that was why a unanimous vote of the House was had." Lest he accuse the Chairman of subterfuge — which was exactly the accusation — Sims quickly added, "There was nothing wrong about it, of course — but I do think the House ought to have an opportunity to vote to concur in the Senate amendment."

Presently, Sims and Tawney launched a volley of accusations over whether there had been proper discussion of the matter before the previous vote in favor of the automobiles. Tawney stated that "this particular item was discussed at some length, and was about the only item that was discussed." Sims insisted there was a breach of rules in that "it was supposed to be a deficiency item and not subject to a point of order" which would have been made had the bill been properly discussed. "The discussion of this provision took place after the reading of the time," repeated Tawney. "And too late to make a point of order," retorted Sims. "The point of order would have been made had it been known it was not a deficiency item."

Now Mann, an independent-minded Illinois Republican, inserted a new objection, this one going straight at Taft on both counts of motor cars and the salary increase. "Is not the question that is in the legislative bill in relation to salaries, the salary of the President, involved in this proposition; and if the House agrees to the item for automobiles, is not that a step in the direction of not agreeing to the exorbitant increase of salary?" Tawney parried this with, "I do not know that I can answer that one way or the other. I will leave that to the gentleman from Illinois to answer."

Moving on, Tawney went to the offensive. "Mr. Speaker, in view of the fact that gentlemen on the other side, either because of being asleep or for some other cause, did not know or now pretend they did not know, that this provision carried in the urgent deficiency bill was not in the deficiency bill, although it was discussed, I ask unanimous consent that this amendment be considered in the House as in Committee of the Whole and acted upon at this time."

Debate, digression, and rancor were House specialities, especially over a subject that provided so many juicy opportunities for ridicule and specious argument. Tawney tried to move on, but the Democrats wouldn't let go without scoring a few points. The objection was raised to Tawney's move for unanimous consent, and a discussion ensued over which motion had precedence, Clark's to agree with the Senate or Tawney's to reject it. Such things mean much to legislators. While this went on, demands were made several times that the clerk re-read the Senate amendment and the full language of the original House bill, a tedious exercise. The Speaker allowed Clark's motion, but gave the floor to Tawney, who yielded five minutes apiece to Democrats Clark, Fitzgerald, and Sims.

Clark went first. "Mr. Speaker, I have no sort of objection to the President of the United States having an automobile if he wants it; but what I do object to is to make the usual appropriation for horses and then make the extraordinary appropriation for automobiles." Clark foresaw a slippery descent into ever more White House automobiles. "I do not know that the next President of the United States would prefer an automobile to a horse, but I have observed this ... if you make an appropriation for a thing once the tendency is to keep on making that appropriation, so far as I know, until the end of the world."

Continuing, Clark said, "If the President-elect can not use horses, then we ought to cut off the appropriation for horses and give him automobiles. If that is his preference, I am willing to do it. But I do object to this doubling up.... I do not know exactly what the reason for this automobile appropriation is. It was intimated by the chairman of the Committee on Appropriations that if we did not pass it, it would be inflicting cruelty, as I understood him, on animals." Having thus swung at Taft, Clark next went after Roosevelt. "That may mean that the incoming President is of such ample proportions that it is dangerous to any horse he would ride. If that is true, he does not need as big an appropriation for horses as the celebrated equestrian who occupies the White House now. There is no possible danger, as I take it, of President Taft ever riding 98 miles in a day or two days or three or four or five

James Beauchamp "Champ" Clark. On the Democratic side at the House was the Minority Leader from Missouri. Clark expertly led his Democrats through the tariff battle and the Republican insurgency against the rule of Speaker Cannon — right into the Speaker's seat himself in 1911. The tariff put him there. The question was, would he take a seat in the Speaker's automobile? Not for a year. (Courtesy Library of Congress).

days or a week; but the objection and the only objection I have to it is that it doubles up this appropriation, and you ever do it once, you have got to go on doing it forever."

Tawney responded tirelessly: "It does not double the appropriation," to which Clark shot back, "It adds to it." Tawney explained again that the money spent on automobiles would save on horses. Clark baited Tawney to prove that he, as Chairman of Appropriations, could save money on the cars over the horses. Tawney didn't take, denying responsibility for administering the money. This, in turn, led to a discussion of the difference between chauffeurs and hostlers and who actually owned the horses at the White House stables, anyway. Tawney again read from the bill to clarify that the sum was $25,000 and not $35,000 as stated by Bartlett and that it did not include automobiles, thus the need for the $12,000 specifically for new automobiles.

John Fitzgerald, from Brooklyn, known as the "liveliest democratic member of the committee," interjected on Tawney's behalf.[4] Stating that he had not originally opposed the measure "because I did not believe it was adding additional expense to the Government," Fitzgerald explained the reason the funds were necessary immediately was that, "In the legislative bill for the next year the word 'automobiles' is included where it has not hitherto been in the law." That is, Taft had no authority to buy automobiles until July. Without getting into the urgency for Spring motoring, he then went after Roosevelt, of which the newspapers took note for the accusation of misconduct by the President: "From some more or less distinct or obscure source I have received either the information or the intimation that the horses for the White House are not purchased entirely, if at all, out of the appropriation in the legislative bill."

To the reader of these accounts in 1909 the charge was clear. Fitzgerald was saying that Roosevelt used Army funds for personal advantage, at worst, and against Congressional authority in the least. Nobody cared about the horses; the insinuation led straight back to the Secret Service and commissions authorizations.[5] Fitzgerald let loose a sarcastic indictment:

4. Fitzgerald shared a place of honor with Tawney in Roosevelt's Secret Service message.
5. It was true in at least one instance. Captain Butt purchased a personal horse for the President at a show in Philadelphia that was paid for by the Quartermaster. The issue resurfaced during the 1912 election.

> I do not know whether the mounts of the President, purchased out of the Army fund, have amounted to $12,000 in four months, $12,000 in twelve months, or $12,000 in seven years in which he has been in office, but I have no doubt that if it had been necessary it would have amounted to that much. I say this not intending any reflection upon the present Chief Executive. If he needed those horses either for his official duties or to keep himself in that vigorous condition so essential to the proper discharge of the duties of the Chief Executive, I would say that he certainly was justified in purchasing the horses.... Perhaps it may be that such horses are not purchased at all for the White House. It may be that when the President, for instance, desires in one day to ride 98 miles and use three relays of horses, instead of using the horses purchased for the White House, or his own personal mounts ... directs the Quartermaster-General to have suitable mounts for the President stationed at various places and certain times, to enable him, "to ride and spread the alarm, through every Middlesex village and farm...."

These lines from Longfellow's poem aroused great laughter and applause, and must have been like water to the thirsty for that Roosevelt-weary Congress. Members on both sides of the isle were thrilled by Fitzgerald's ridicule. "Mr. Speaker," Fitzgerald continued to more applause,

> The money expended for the White House ... is so obscured in the mysteries of many appropriation bills that I doubt if any man in Congress is able to state the exact sum which is used for the support of the President. Believing this, believing that it would conduce to the comfort, happiness and well-being of the Chief Executive of the United States, and especially if it would make him of a more peaceful and complacent disposition after the 4th of March than he has been prior to the 4th of March, I believe that $12,000 could be well expended, not in four months, but every month....

Thus having leant his support to Taft's funding, Fitzgerald apologized to his own, saying that his explanation was "in justice to those Members on this side of the House who have the right to know my reasons."

Fitzgerald's attack on Roosevelt quenched the Democrats, leaving room now for Republican Joseph Keifer to respond where Tawney had failed to the criticisms of the funding as neither urgent nor a deficiency. "In some sense that is true, but in a broad sense, it is not exactly true," went the old hand, former Speaker, and skilled sophist. With a graceful, reverse logic — or the appearance of logic, lawyer-speak, that is, he explained away the funding as a deficiency because it reflected an "anticipatory appropriation" to the funding of July. His argument — honest, he said it — was that since the Congress authorized to spend the money later, if it were spent now it would be both deficient and urgent. "Now, if this appropriation goes in this urgent deficiency bill, we will have purchased the automobiles we have already authorized to be purchased, and will not need to expend any of that $25,000 in the next fiscal year appropriated to buy automobiles. So in that sense it may be called, 'urgent deficiency.'"

5. (*cont.*) General Wood was called on to affirm that, "Colonel Roosevelt, neither while President of the United States, nor at any other time, asked me to sign [there's the escape clause] a requisition for a riding horse or horses for his personal use, or for any other purpose" (Wood to Stimson, 8/13/12). Actually, Roosevelt did loot the Quartermaster's stables, but so did other presidents (See Butt, unpublished passage, 6/8/08). There has always been a nebulous but largely innocent intermingling of the resources of the White House and its executive branches. At any given moment the President was surrounded by Secret Servicemen from Treasury Department, military aides and physicians from the Army and Navy, and policemen from the District of Columbia. For a 1909 view see "The White House and the President's Salary Cost Country $230,000 Annually," *Evening Star*, 2/21/09.

Keifer next took on opposition to motor cars directly. "Now, it is not worth while, Mr. Speaker, to here discuss the question as to whether the next President of the United States is in favor of automobiles at his stables rather than horses and carriages, for we all know the automobile has come to stay." While agreeing with Clark that "we will keep appropriating for them for the Presidents through all time," Keifer marvelously turned that around as a reason for spending the money without delay. "I do not think that there is any economy in refusing the appropriation now, as we simply give in advance of the next fiscal year, and we will therefore curtail the expense, so much desired by the gentleman from Missouri [Clark], and do it a little in advance." Breathtaking.

Keifer next defended Taft against charges of exclusivity, the sin of automobiles. "Somebody has said that the next President of the United States does not believe in horses and carriages. He is a horseman. He is able to ride a horse, I think, as well as some of the rest of us on this floor; and I do not know whether he would take a hundred-mile test ride or not, but he would be likely to try to do it if anybody bantered him."

Somehow convinced that the motors would mean neither more spending nor greater imperialism at the White House, Clark announced, "Mr. Speaker, in view of the numerous explanations that have been made on the other side and the luminous explanation made by my friend from New York [Fitzgerald], I withdraw the motion to concur in the Senate amendment." Clark's avowal constituted his party's endorsement of Taft's automobiles. But before Tawney could move on that announcement, Sims threw in another wrench. "Mr. Speaker, I would like to renew it."

Whether Tawney or the chamber expressed exasperation at this point is not recorded. "I have no objection to Mr. Taft riding in an automobile," Sims said, "if he is willing to take the risk, while he is a private citizen, but when he becomes the President of the United States the whole country has got an interest in him, and we all know that the automobile is a dangerous method of travel, not only to the people who occupy it, but to everybody along the line of travel. They are a first-class, all-round, genuine nuisance in a thickly settled city, and rather ought to be prohibited by Congress than encouraged. I am opposed to Congress ever going on record as favoring the automobile as a means of travel in a crowded city, and especially the capital of the United States, that we holdup as a model to all the other cities of the United States."

A reporter said this "threw the House into prolonged laughter." The Congressional Record notes laughter and applause, but not snickers, which surely followed the question next posed by Mann: "Does the gentleman think the President ought to be required to use Tennessee mules?" Sims, "growing somewhat hot," replied directly, "I do not ask the President, nor would I require him, to use Tennessee mules, nor do I propose to prohibit him from using them." Mann slipped in, "He might do worse."

Sims was serious. "I propose to prevent a congressional mandate requiring him to use automobiles." He continued,

> I want to protect him from the implied command of the legislative body to adopt a dangerous method of traveling, not only to himself, but to the people among whom he would travel. This automobile nuisance is simply getting more intolerable every day. When a street car stops to take on or let off passengers, an automobile is right there and dashes by without waiting for passengers to get out of the way.... I know of a man not much less in body than the President-elect who while getting off a street car came near

> being run over by an automobile, and I happened to be that gentleman [laughter]. I have, therefore, a personal interest in this matter. I do not want by congressional action to say to all the automobile fanatics in this country that we hereby encourage you to go on with your reckless disregard for comfort and human life. Let us act boldly and vote down this item and not intimate that we are trying to put the responsibility off on Mr. Taft. He is a large man physically as well as mentally; he is equal in his physical powers to his size, and he rides horses gracefully and safely. I have seen him ride them; he is not afraid of them; but he can get into a carriage if he wants to; and if he can not, we will build a platform and take him in on that.

Mann couldn't resist. "We got a big enough platform for him last summer." Sims was quick with his retort, "But you are trying to get him off by putting him on a platform that may destroy him." Mann drew more laughter with, "You tried last summer, but never could get him off." Not only was Sims setting himself up, he was proving the legitimacy of the automobile. Rep. Olmsted piped in with, "I would like to ask the gentleman from Tennessee, a pretty well-developed man, if he does not think that he would be safer riding up Pennsylvania avenue in an automobile of his own than he would be on horseback among automobiles of other people?" Sims started at this, then paused, catching himself amidst the laughter. Sims replied, "I think he would, especially if the other people who use them are of the Washington school." With time expired for Sims, Tawney again tried to settle the matter.

Unfortunately, Gaines was now seized by indignance. Of Tawney he demanded, "I want to know if the gentleman declines or not to give me a piece of information that I am trying to get at?" Tawney could only mutter back, "I beg your pardon. I wanted to close debate. I will give the gentleman any information I have." Gaines, who had not only recently faced Cannon's mace but had lost the 1908 election and was on his way back to Nashville, returned to the question of the horses. Tawney replied that he'd already answered the question. By now, the chamber was tiring and restless, and Gaines complained of "so much confusion in the chamber" that he couldn't hear. "There always is when the gentleman takes the floor," slammed Tawney.

Gaines went on anyway. "I would like to know what is going to be done with those twelve horses." Tawney and Gaines went back and forth over the fact that Tawney had no idea what Taft would do with the horses, and that they were already paid for in the previous year's budget, and that Taft intended to use automobiles. "We give him automobiles in lieu of the horses?" demanded Gaines. "We give him the automobiles in lieu of the horses," repeated Tawney. Said Gaines, "This is lieu of horses. Is that the programme?" "That is the programme."

Gaines demanded, "How many automobiles do you propose to buy?" Tawney explained that was up to the President and then took the floor away from Gaines by yielding one minute to Rep. Kustermann, on whom he could count for a badly needed burlesque. "Mr. Speaker, I consider this appropriation which is asked for automobiles a very reasonable one if it includes the furnishing of gasoline at the present price." This reference to the tariff and Rockefeller brought an extended laughter. "If petroleum and gasoline are placed on the free list, as they should be, we can then reduce the appropriation for the automobiles a few thousand dollars." A reporter wrote, "It took the House about five minutes for the gale of laughter that followed this solemn utterance to spend itself."

When things calmed down, Tawney moved to close the matter. "Now, Mr. Speaker, I demand the previous question."

The Speaker repeated Clark's motion to concur in the Senate amendment. Tawney added, "I hope that will be voted down." Sims wasn't through. He knew he was about to lose the vote but he was going to make it hurt as much as possible. "A division," he demanded. The Speaker had no choice but to follow the request for a roll call. Twenty-seven Democrats joined Sims against 185 votes of no. "the mule of Tennessee, and elsewhere lost out," concluded the *Evening Star*.

Taft's deal with the House leadership was paying off. He was to get his motors and his tariff revisions—at least as far as the House of Representatives was concerned.

8

The Senate of a Great Country!

I have got all the bids in for the motor cars for the Tafts and just as I was ready to decide the matter the Senate struck out the appropriation for the motors and everything has to come to a standstill until the appropriation is reinstated in conference. Senator Hemenway told me that it was merely a matter of policy to kill the appropriation in the Senate but that it will be put back in the bill in the Conference. On this assurance I have ordered a White Touring car and a Pierce Arrow limozine [sic].

—Capt. Archie Butt[1]

The House having twice voted the funding for Taft's motors, the Senate was certain to succumb at the Conference Committee. The *Evening Star*'s joke that "Senator Bailey will not go so far as to try to demonstrate that automobiles are contrary to the Constitution" proved exact. The Senate grudgingly handed Taft the keys. The *Times* declared, "After swearing by all the nine gods of war that President Taft should get around as best he might, but that never, never, never would it consent to give him $12,000 for the immediate purchase of automobiles after March 4, the Senate to-day surrendered."[2] The journal *Motor Age* celebrated:

> The entire motor car world will rejoice over the fact that congress has at last passed the urgent deficiency bill, which contains an appropriation of $12,000 for the purchase and maintenance of motor cars to be used by President-elect Taft.... This is a signal victory for those members of congress who fought vigorously to secure an appropriation that would enable President-elect Taft to displace the White House horses and carriage with motor cars, and marks a distinct step forward for the motor car.[3]

The anti-motoring days of Roosevelt expired, courtesy of Taft's joy at the wind in his hair. Motoring enthusiasts considered the victory double, for the White

1. Unpublished letter, 1/27/09.
2. Editorial, *Evening Star*, 1/26/09 and "Taft Will Have Autos," *NYT*, 2/6/09.
3. "Congress Decides To Buy Cars for Taft," *Motor Age*, 2/6/09.

House cars and that Congress spent time talking about automobiles. *Motor Age* continued,

> The present session of Congress now drawing to a close has been remarkable for the amount of time devoted to a discussion of the motor car question. Hardly a week has gone by without an animated discussion about the motor car, and while many Senators and Representatives have jumped into the limelight with a bitter denunciation of this modern mode of locomotion, it is interesting to note that the motor car has more friends in Congress than it has enemies.

The Senate had not condoned Taft's automobiles. Taft, the House, and the inevitability of it all forced the issue. It was more a capitulation than an endorsement from the upper house. Senators soon enough found occasion to vent on the evil machines. Unrelated to Taft's cars, there came a few days later before the Senate an appropriation bill for the District of Columbia. When Senator Tillman discovered an item for $300 for the District's motoring board, he decided to torment Bailey of Texas. Tillman was in no mood to defend automobiles; he just enjoyed goading his fellow Democrat on them.

Unlike Sims, Bailey's constituents did not all ride mules. Bailey was no Luddite — although close. The reasoning by which Bailey carried the Senate motorphobia was a devotion to Jeffersonian ideals of the American farmer, self-reliant, inviolate of city corruption and free unto himself ... not to mention the Senator's considerable interests in horse stables. Bailey's less philosophical reasons aside, he failed to recognize, as the farmers were themselves to discover while enriching Henry Ford, that the internal combustion engine would broaden American lives immeasurably.[4] That this tremendous change was occurring had not yet been noticed by the Baileys of 1909, for whom the ideals of the farm were happily entrenched in centuries past.

To Bailey, automobiles were just fine in the city so long as they sufficiently maimed the subjects of mammon. He'd be damned if the devil machines were going to be unleashed upon countryside and farm. "I am for the man who tickles Mother Earth with the plow and makes her laugh rich harvests. Down with the automobile! You can't grow 'em on the farm." Tillman, who was seated beside the stirred Bailey, chided him, "Ah, but the Senator is opposing the march of science?" The pair carried on these lines for an hour, jibing, prodding, and joking with each other. At the end, Bailey mockingly demanded that Tillman "retire to the cloakroom," a reference to Tillman's infamous 1902 Senate floor fistfight. Laughing, Tillman declined.[5]

Bailey was set on protecting the horse business, which, like its carriage industry brethren, was about to get run over by automobiles. That the Senator rose in public outrage against motor cars went beyond any realistic hope for annulment of the drastic change. The difference was that it was being talked about. Besides, most of Bailey's horse-raising constituents hadn't

4. Gasoline motors were in common use as stationary and marine engines starting in the 1890s. The first gasoline-powered farm tractors were built in 1902. Steam tractors were long in use, but they were expensive, bulky, and a burden to run. To avoid the difficulty to start the machines, some farmers left their steam engines running all night. The automobile's specific utility to the farm was for transportation, but the ascendancy of the internal combustion engine revolutionized farm machinery. For our purposes the reference to farmers regards passenger cars. For a look at the conversion of farm machinery from steam to gasoline, See "Farming With Automobiles," *American Review of Reviews*, Jan. 1911, p. 62.
5. "Scan Bill Closely," *Evening Star*, 2/5/09. In 1902, Tillman slugged his fellow South Carolina Senator, John McLaurin, right in the face.

raised a shotgun at one in years. As testified by Senator Francis Warren, automobiles were quite the benefit to the farm. Warren's ranch in Wyoming used motors to round up lost cattle.[6]

* * *

Had anyone in Roosevelt's government any interest in making the popular case for automobiles, the best opportunity came during the election year of 1904 at the St. Louis World's Fair, where America and its Patent Office were on show. A centennial celebration of the Louisiana Purchase, the Fair ran for seven months during which the Olympics were played, the Liberty Bell was presented, and the latest technologies, from refrigeration to electricity to automobiles, were demonstrated. A big deal, this. Planning went for seven years, and Congress invested $5,000,000 in it.[7]

In April, 1903, Roosevelt attended the dedication ceremonies for the next year's Fair. While there, he addressed a Good Roads Conference that was aiming to catch some press over the affair. The President spoke stirringly of the benefits of roads, trolleys, telephones and rural free delivery. Roads, he said, were "plainer than anything else" Rome's enduring mark.[8] Not automobiles. Not even General Miles, who also spoke at the Conference, mentioned them. Behind scenes, the National Association of Automobile Manufacturers (NAAM) successfully lobbied for space for an automobile exhibit at the Fair. That Autumn, the U.S. Army turned down an offer to monitor a NAAM-sponsored endurance test.[9]

On April 30, 1904, Roosevelt launched the Fair by telegraph. Taft was dispatched to appear on his behalf. Alice showed up and made a tremendous hit. Her entrance was by carriage with two automobiles in train. William Jennings Bryan was there along with his entire Democratic party, which held its convention at St. Louis. Roosevelt appeared at the close of the Fair in late November, after he was freed from the front porch to which he was bound during the election. Throughout, there was no mention of automobiles by the politicians, not from the President, the Secretary of War, or the Democrats.

Such publicity came from the motorists themselves in the form of an automobile tour to St. Louis organized by the American Automobile Association (AAA), a conglomeration of local motor clubs. From as far away as Boston, Minneapolis, and Birmingham, motorists set out for St. Louis. Of the New York contingent sixty-six of seventy-seven automobiles made it to Missouri over horrific roads. That group included the famed long-distance motorist, Charles Glidden, who made his fortune in a highly favorable association with Alexander Graham Bell and who was amidst a circumnavigation of the globe he started in 1902.[10] The success of the run inspired Glidden to offer a silver trophy for another tour. The subsequent Glidden Tours brought annual headlines for motoring, roads, and manufacturers.

6. "The Senate of a Great Country!" *Automobile*, 1/28/09.
7. From "The St. Louis Games Were All American," *Sports Illustrated*, 7/19/96, and *AAA and the Glidden Connection* by Dave Stucker, web publication, www.vmcca.org, 2000.
8. "President Roosevelt Reaches St. Louis," *NYT*, 4/30/03. He kept to this rhetoric through his term. In 1907 he spoke at an Agricultural College of "All kinds of agencies, from rural free delivery to the bicycle and the telephone..." that would benefit the farmer (from *Theodore Roosevelt Cyclopedia*, Roosevelt Memorial Association, p. 175). The bicycle?
9. "Demonstration Cars at St. Louis Exposition," *Automobile*, 5/2/1903, p. 496 and "The Use of the Motor Vehicle in the United States Army, 1899–1939," p. 17.
10. *Charles Jasper Glidden*, by Tedd Delong, web publication, www.vmcca.org, 2001. By 1908 Glidden and his wife had driven 42,367 miles in thirty-five countries ("Gliddens Again Off on the 'Round-the-World Trail," *Automobile*, 1/9/08, p. 60).

Serious mud. Seriously bad roads. This photo, captioned in *American Motorist* as "The Slough of Despond," featured one of the 1909 Glidden Tour "pathfinders," the cars that blazed a trail that year from Detroit to Denver. The Glidden Tours served to raise public awareness of the viability of automobiles — and the horrible state of the nation's roads. The problem was that politicians didn't want to pay for roads that would supposedly only benefit wealthy motorists. As automobiles churned up mud and dust, states expected motorists to pay for the roads they destroyed. Automobile licensing and other fees were put back into dirt and stone roads that automobiles destroyed again. The "Good Roads" movement desperately sought help from the Federal treasury for decent roads. (From *American Motorist,* July, 1909)

The hardy motorists paraded through St. Louis on August 12 in celebration of the proven viability of their mounts. Some 140 cars were exhibited at the Fair itself amongst displays of the world's fastest railroad steam engine, a working turnstile, Lincoln's private rail car, and other machines and industrial wonders. The public found great interest in the automobiles and their ability. On the downside for the motorists came word that the apparent winner of the Olympic marathon arrived looking unusually fresh, as he had made eleven miles by automobile.

Frustrated by road conditions, tolls, and the interstate maze of speed limits, registrations, and license plates, motorists turned to Congress for liberation. Uniform rules, national speed limits, and federal roads seemed to this group the only relief to their pain. When it came to autos, the generally rich and independent-minded motorists punted federalism like the progressives who saw the states as useless for overcoming the *problèmes du jour.* But Congress wasn't listening. Aside from political distaste for the subject and a few tariff dollars, Congress had yet to figure out how to cash in on automobiles.[11] Canals, harbors, railroads, and any other

11. For some still-born pre–1909 automobile legislation see "Bill Empowering Interstate Commerce Commission to Issue Federal Automobile Licenses," *Automobile*, 12/14/05, p. 675 (the magazine complained of its "radical provisions... The 'Morell Bill' is simply the outcome of the 'regulating' craze that has struck the Fifty-ninth Congress"); "Will Ask Congress To Pass Auto Bill," *NYT*, 1/24/07 (a AAA sponsored "Federal automobile law"); and "Autoists To Argue For Federal Bill," *NYT* 3/9/08 (regarding the Cocks bill, another AAA work). None of these bills escaped the committee room. Numerous "good roads" bills of interest to motorists went before Congress, but automobiles were like the derelict uncle nobody dared mention.

apparition that in the slightest resembled interstate commerce or was connected to the post office were easy pork in a constituent's barrel. On Capitol Hill motor cars didn't pay.

The fight over the automobile took place in the cities and the states, where motoring forces eventually garnered the strength to squeeze out a few accommodating laws. Local governments learned what every good municipality today with an inch of jurisdiction on an interstate swears by: the automobile as rolling cash machine. Like chaste early adolescents sworn off vice, tobacco, and their parents' martinis, governments first treated automobiles like the minister's son. The miscreant was condemned in proper company, unmentionable in class, and envied at the playground. When the hyperbole of the automobile detractors wore thin and the things didn't just go away, governments came to see motors differently. Maybe there was something here ... something like money. After a taste or two, the virtue of abstinence lost its urgency. A few drinks more and addiction set in; the more cars the better the fix. Soon drunk on fees, fines, regulations, and valuation taxes, States held automobiles for ransom.

The next discovery was of the far more lucrative side of motoring — roads. Once road building for motors became politically expedient, every monied connection to road construction was soon at the Governor's doorstep. As with railroads, the politics and corrupt possibilities of road building were stunning. If new property had to be purchased to lay or widen a roadbed, suddenly farm, forest, and swamp looked like a pretty good investment. To the bankers, a bond or two floated over the Statehouse made a nice backdrop to the balance sheet. Investors invested, brokers commissioned, contractors contracted, workers worked, and governments governed. All involved were happy — and richer for it.

In 1909, only the few motor-friendly states had tasted these heady fruits. Well on the way, though not having completely replaced carriages, automobiles for city use in 1909 were making the winning case. Cars stacked easier, fit in smaller spaces, and were more easily serviced than horses, despite their complexity. Expensive property was freed of stables, which spurred development. City streets that were not already paved had a new reason for attention, for which politicians found ready support from builders and commercial users. The business of automobiles was self-perpetuating. From repair, parts, and fuel to storage and used vehicle sales, automobiles were a working Ponzi scheme.

A look at an automotive accessories catalog gives a pretty good idea of what countryside motoring was about. Outside of running gear and mechanics, survival gear dominates these catalogs. Headwear, goggles, gloves, raincoats, and dust shields belie the less enjoyable side of the country drive. A report of a European tour described a car caked in mud and dust at the end of a day's running.[12] In America, it was worse and worser. "Monroe street especially was a mire apparently without bottom," wrote the driver of the 1904 St. Louis "pathfinder" car of an Illinois road. "The wheels spun around and we pushed behind, but with both axles buried in mud the car remained stationary." The mud was knee-high, and it took a rope, two pulleys, a telegraph pole, and three shoulders to extract the car.[13]

Cities experimented with macadam, corduroy, wood planks, brick, concrete, asphalt, bitumens, and any various combi-

12. See "A Family Motor Tour Through Europe," Leo Hendrik Baekeland, *Horseless Age*, New York, 1907.
13. "On the Road to St. Louis— VII," *Automobile*, 7/9/04, p. 37.

nations thereof for lasting, smooth road surfaces capable of supporting automobiles, horses, carriages, bicycles, and delivery wagons. Some solutions fell short for lack of endurance, others for slickness, pliability, or expense. Regardless, dense populations and small urban expanses allowed for experiment and cost. In the country, where automobilists sometimes resorted to fixing the roads themselves, if a road was "improved" it was for short distances only. The best results tended towards patchworks of various surfaces along larger paths of mud or dust. In 1911, T. Coleman du Pont offered to pay for a hundred-mile stretch of road to finally abate the Delaware reputation summed up by the comment of a mud-caked motorist upon arrival to Wilmington: "The road's better than it used to be. I didn't have to use chains."[14]

Into the 19th Century, the turnpikes of the early days that served as interstate corridors were replaced by canals and rail. Jefferson's four day ride from Monticello to Washington was an easy day's jaunt by train. Roads became local connectors between rails and waterways. The 1880s bicycle craze spurred the repair of some country roads, but as there was no real transport need fulfilled by bicycles the movement exercised no political or economic force. As always, the better roads were for profit or tax — the turnpikes.

Federal intervention, dormant since Jefferson's Cumberland Road, the first national road, came by way of the Postal Department which was constitutionally mandated to build roads for mail delivery.[15] The Service's mission was greatly expanded in 1896 under the Rural Free Delivery Act. Southerners who first viewed it as more federal intrusion were quickly swayed by the enormous benefits both in road building and mail service.[16] For Northerners, among the primary benefits of the act was that delivery could be year-round, even during the messy thaws. These improvements were not to the benefit of automobilists who needed more than a clear path through the woods. As demonstrated by Roosevelt's 98-mile horse ride and a 1911 Taft automobile venture over the same country, horses were better than motors at forging streams and mud. A typical 1908 countryside auto run went something like this:

> Last Spring a motoring party, after plowing through the mud of Maryland roads, and enjoying the comparative luxury of a Pennsylvania "pike," encountered a stretch of such awful "going" that the end of all things seemed near at hand. The car was jounced from rut to rut. Great stones gave the chauffeur the task of his life to prevent disaster. He wrestled with the wheel and brake and lever, and managed to make progress, a triumph of mind and machinery over matter. Somebody in the car remarked that it was a long way between toll gates, whereon the chauffeur, a product of the smoothly paved town, emitted an irrepressible sniff. Asked the cause of his derision, he said: "Toll gates! I'm getting wise to this toll stunt! When the roads is good they charges for 'em, and when they's like this they ain't got the nerve to ask for money." Just then the car gave a particularly vicious jolt over a well concealed "thankee-marm," and the

14. "The Only Routes Now Necessitate a Wide Detour," *NYT*, 3/12/11.
15. "For Good Roads," by George C. Diehl of the AAA in *Harper's Weekly*, 4/6/12, p. 12. Madison, Clay, and Calhoun all declared themselves in favor of a national road (see *Automobile*, 10/26/05, p. 472).
16. "The first rural delivery service established in the United States was October 1, 1896," stated Assistant Postmaster General DeGraw in February of 1909. "The first rural delivery service established in the south was October 19, 1896, at Clarksville, Johnson County, Arkansas, when three routes were put into operation, and during that fiscal year several experimental rural routes were established in nearly all of the other southern states." With these successful examples, into 1902 "the department was literally overwhelmed with petitions for the service" (from "Expanding Rural Routes for Free Delivery," *Evening Star*, 2/21/09).

> chauffeur's speech was choked. When he had regained even keel he added, sententiously: "If they'd have spent on the roads some of the graft money they put into that Capitol building it would have been better for this State."

The writer then turned to political and economic concerns of far greater import than an uncomfortable afternoon drive:

> The toll road is an anachronism, and, although it is the best type of highway in most sections, it is usually an abomination. A cross-state journey by motor should become part of the duty of every commonwealth legislator. When they have been shaken to jelly or mired for hours or slewed into deadly peril in consequence of the neglect of the roads by past generations of lawmakers and taxpayers perhaps these men will recognize the fact that the American roads are a disgrace to our civilization. The farmers are appreciating the need of better highways, and the motorists are demonstrating effectively in the same interest.... What is needed is a more intelligent popular understanding of the economic truth that was enunciated by the chauffeur-commentator just quoted.[17]

If only Congress and the states would listen. Roads for farmers and postal delivery were one thing, but sympathetic ears would not be turned towards "autocrats," "speed demons," and "scorchers." Suspend judgement here, and imagine the issue like today's treatment of tax cuts: roads for automobiles were for the rich. It was a tough sell no matter how great the benefit to all citizens.

* * *

Some years before that ugly Pennsylvania ride the nation's top scorcher had had enough. In addition to holding various world speed records this man was a principal subscriber to speeding tickets from towns across the Northeast. Weary of constables and the politics of automobiles, William K. Vanderbilt dropped out. He first demonstrated his disgust with the legalities and general prejudices against motoring in 1902 by announcing his resignation from the sport. The speed disease was strong, and he never left. Within two years he was back at it with the biggest road race in the country, the Vanderbilt Cup. He felt that America lagged in the automotive game. His Long Island races were intended to popularize automobiles and prod

William K. Vanderbilt was the preeminent automobilist of the early 1900s. When he felt his motoring nation lagged behind Europe, he launched the Vanderbilt Cup race to promote the domestic industry. At first, European makes won the Cup, but the Americans soon caught on. Vanderbilt is at the wheel here, c. 1906. (Courtesy Library of Congress)

17. "The Great Road Question," *Evening Star*, 12/20/08. The writers noted, "The Federal government is working to hasten the day of emancipation from toll gates and mud holes," a reference to the Office of Public Roads, nominally started in 1893, and dedicated to the development of road technology — but not road building.

domestic producers to compete with the Europeans. The races were a sensation. Tens of thousands showed up to witness the madness. By the third running things got out of control; 200,000 spectators crowded the lanes, and one man was killed.[18]

Amidst similar tragedies in Europe and the anti-motoring sentiments in the press and government, Vanderbilt was convinced to build his own road upon which to race and otherwise run his automobiles as he saw fit. Shortly after the 1906 race, and joined by fellow enthusiast Henry Ford as a director, Vanderbilt formed a corporation to create the world's first motor car–dedicated roadway. With two and a half million dollars the company set about acquiring rights and land and began to lay the best roadbed in the world. Some land owners, mostly farmers, joined the effort and donated or sold rights through their property, buying in to the theory that it would increase the overall value of their land. Others refused. Lacking eminent domain to force owners to cough up land for the public good, the private road was forced into a convoluted path of willing participants.

Vanderbilt's road was an exercise in motoring liberty. On his road there would be no hay wagons, no horses, no intersections, no policemen, and no speed limits, just miles of smooth-like-glass, dust-free automobile intoxication, "where dirt and noise can be left behind, and where the fingers can coax the throttle without the eye being in mortal terror of alighting on a blue uniform...."[19] The Long Island Motor Parkway featured bridges and overpasses, novel concepts whose sole purpose was the uninhibited flow of automobiles. Why bother with an overpass if limited to eight miles an hour? And what need for such limits with no obstacles? It was a brilliant solution to the both motorist and anti-motorist nightmares. For good measure, the first-ever highway rest stop was added, an upscale restaurant and club that lay at the end of this bodacious highway named "Petit Trianon."[20] With the singular motives of speed and profit Vanderbilt aimed to cut across Long Island a luscious, sixteen-foot automobile swath. Empowered by fortune, he broke no law, took no tax (while paying plenty), and abused no power. In fact, the Parkway had everything going against it in public perception and government antagonism, or the indifference of both. It was an astonishing project.

By October 1908, only nine miles were built, and, due to difficulties in acquiring rights of way, plans were shortened to forty-five snaking miles to connect the odd tracts. By the time Taft took office, the company was shipping out the attorneys to assure investors and the motoring public that, despite the need for another million dollars, the Parkway would be completed.[21]

18. For a great read on Vanderbilt's racing and races, see "Willie K.: The Saga of a Racing Vanderbilt," by Beverly Rae Kimes, *Automotive Quarterly*, Vol. 15, No. 3.

19. "Over the Long Island Parkway Course," by H.A. Grant, *Automobile*, 6/27/07, p. 1043. With no need to accommodate horses, the first surfaces were oiled and tarred, a far more economical method than macadam (see "Parkway to be Coal-Tarred," *Automobile*, 11/29/06, p. 737 and "Mr. Vanderbilt on the Long Island Parkway," *Automobile*, 12/13/06, p. 845). The first use of cement came on bridges and in a five-mile roadbed built for the 1908 Vanderbilt Cup called the "cement stretch." It was a breakthrough use of the material ("Long Island Motor Parkway Has Its Racing Initiation," *Automobile*, 10/15/08, p. 522 and "Some Striking Features of the New Motor Parkway on Long Island," *NYT*, 9/20/08).

20. Now, *that* name will get some class envy going... ("Motor Parkway Opened," *NYT*, 6/1/12).

21. From "Motoring," *Evening Star*, 2/28/09. The brief notice reads, "Assurance is given by the attorneys for the Long Island motor parkway that despite the announcement that $1,000,000 is needed to complete the roadway, the directors have no intention of abandoning the project and are confident of being able to finish it."

The business and political climate was still uncertain for the project.

* * *

Congress rewarded itself plenty with travel reimbursements and pay raises. Criticisms of these treasury raids pierced the thick hides of few, if any, members. Congressmen went mute during the votes and deaf when the news hit the presses. Not so over automobiles. Until Taft's motors came before it, Congress would walk a mile to avoid automobiles. So when Uncle Joe hoped to ride the wake of the Taft automobile appropriation by slipping into a legislative funding bill a little self-gratuity, "for the purchase of a horse and carriage, or other vehicle" for the Speaker's office, Senator Bailey blew an artery. He tearfully spoke of the "abomination" that were the machines whose use "should be curtailed, if not abolished."[22] Not even Taft drove his car through the Senate on the first try. Cannon was out of his league.

Between ridiculously low speed limits, awful roads, and horses, cows, and dogs, early motorists ever faced an unwelcome path. Vanderbilt had a solution: he'd build his own road. The Long Island Motor Parkway with its automobile-only, cop-free motoring splendor was the result. Pictured here are two views of the glorious project, which spanned about forty-five miles across Long Island. Among its distinctive innovations were motor-only traffic, replacement of grade-crossings and intersections with bridges and on-off ramps, and the world's first rest-stop, a luxurious club house at the end of the road, called "Petit Trianon." It was a magnificent project. (From *Club Journal,* June 10, 1911)

Anti-motorists Bailey and Sims should have been laughed off the floor years before. Entering the second decade of the Motor Age, that constituents rewarded intransigence, newspapers repeated slanders, and filibusters were performed in protest cannot be entirely explained by a natural development of the nation's attitudes. The great man of progress, Theodore Roosevelt, cannot be absolved of this. Had his enthusiasm and moral leadership embraced the motor car, America would have had a better jump on the technology. Had he walked the isles of an automobile show, honored the industry with an official motor, or spoken up against the demagogues, his citizens may have more quickly and better benefited from the automobile and better roads built for it. Whatever the case, Roosevelt scorned motors. This prime national example, whose daily health, social schedule, and every word were studied in newspapers across the country, for seven precious years ignored the new century's most important social and technological advance.

22. "The Senate of a Great Country!" *Automobile*, 1/28/09

With an expected 1909 production of 80,000 cars at a value of over $100,000,000, the U.S. led Germany at 25,000 and France with 40,000 vehicles, although with higher unit values, these production numbers approached the U.S. total dollar value.[23] By comparison to their overall economies and populations, France and Germany were way ahead of the game, especially in technology. The American numbers are all the more impressive when considering the political environment in which the industry operated. On the roads, chickens had the right of way. In the courts and newspaper editorials, motorists were guilty as charged. On the docks, the Treasury Department treated automobile imports with contempt, arbitrarily naming values and refusing to discount mileage logged on the Continent. In Congress, the incoming President had to fight for a lousy twelve thousand bucks for a decent ride.[24] With its 40,000 registered cars and even more oppressive, anti-automobile laws, London proved that a king's motoring example could defy stupid law.[25] The United States had no such leadership.

Sure, motor cars served the richer. Yes, death and pollution followed them on the nation's highways. The motor-intoxicated devils who flew down country roads testing new carburetors and a farmer's intolerance turned their whacked ideas into liberation of the rural poor and the otherwise small-town stuck. The "autocrats" who provocatively tooled along Pelham Avenue in backseat splendor did more for the great American worker than any anarchist. We can begin with the simple benefit that those imperialist road machines cleared city streets of hay-consuming, methane-producing, solid waste-spewing horses, and thus saved from disease and filth the teeming, trashing, city poor.

Call it a historical irony that among those who benefited the most from automobiles were its ideological opponents and their protectorates. In 1904, Governor Robert La Follette conducted an "auto stumping" tour of Wisconsin farming districts during his reelection campaign. The motor car didn't hear a peep from him since. Or at least not until 1910, when his fellow progressive Hiram Johnson vented populist rage across California in an automobile campaign.[26] What changed?

There was nothing distinct in 1909 in automotive technology or business methods. Advance was incremental, not revolutionary. The other great 20th Century

23. "Motoring," *Evening Star*, 1/31/09. Production estimates were more generally said to be 75,000 cars for 1909.

24. Politics do matter. France early embraced the automobile. It led the world in exportation of automobiles through to WWI. During that war, the country was saved from the German invasion in part by mobilization of automobiles on its automobile-friendly roads and by its military's early embrace of the technology. When Germany put its nationalist mind to the automobile the great 1930s Mercedes-Benz and the Autobahn were the result, not to mention the German Army's quick mobilization over it. When after WWII, Great Britain and France turned to the luxury motor car for a tax base and political punching bag, their automotive industries collapsed; the great Renault was turned into a midget, and limousine companies in Paris drove clients in Cadillacs. Not until the 1950s and President Eisenhower, with his memories of a horrific 1919 motor trek across America and the smooth roads he saw in conquered Germany, and the fear of his own country's inability to defend itself from border to border, did the United States fully commit at the national level to freeing the country of dirt and two lane roads. In the 1970s the United States repeated the mistakes of post–WWII England and France and set itself to the destruction of the large passenger car under the political guise of fuel efficiency (CAFE standards). Detroit faltered, Japan jumped in, and the American consumer turned to SUVs and stretch limousines. Populism and automobiles ever mix like oil and water.

25. "Motoring," *Evening Star*, 2/14/09.

26. "Campaigning By Automobile," *Automobile*, 8/27/04, p. 243, *La Follette's Autobiography*, pp. 336–337, and *The New Nationalism*, by Theodore Roosevelt, edited by William E. Leuchtenburg, 1971, pp. 6–7. La Follette's car was loaned "by friends" ("Minor Mention," *Horseless Age*, 7/20/04, p. 71).

innovation, the airplane, had been around since 1903. There should be no surprise that the Wright Brothers' fame came first in France, and that the first official presidential recognition of their achievements came after March 4, 1909.[27] You see, "air sailing" was also a game for the rich, and its promoters were the exclusive, rich man's automobile clubs.

Along with road building, an important transportation technology that was stifled by the class-envy stigma against automobiles was that great 20th century innovation, the airplane. Before 1909, the Wright brothers went largely unnoticed by their fellow Americans. Not so in France, that motor-friendly land that embraced the pair and their amazing machines. Back in America "air sailing" found hospitality only among elite automobile clubs. This lovely portrait of automobilists shows the association. Put a motor boat on the lake and you have the three great transportation revolutions launched by the internal combustion engine. Elites embraced and nurtured motoring. Taft set it free for everyone. (Courtesy Library of Congress)

Roosevelt was ecstatic about another new transportation technology. For this business he heartily applauded massive public expenditures. He celebrated its appearance and cheered it in public. "Marvelous" he said of it in Los Angeles. In New York, he rode it in public.[28] He gladly allowed White House funds be expended for its use by his staff. Even after being nearly killed when his carriage was run over by one, he unloosed no condemnation of the machines. Of course, a trolley car was no upper-class privilege. Nobody would be denied a vote for riding one. The driver took his ire, not the machine.

It was Thomas Edison's mastery of electricity that allowed for the placement of small, easily operated trains in the cities. This was a tremendous development, one that changed city planning and the habits of the people before the automobile came along. The trolley was to be the liberator of the masses, a noble technology that would benefit all and deny none. Tracks were laid, electric wires hung, and horses shoved aside to accommodate the trams. Tunnels were built in New York, platforms were raised in Chicago, and tracks were run up and down Pennsylvania Avenue in Washington. Los Angeles and Cincinnati built world-class trolley systems that created the first metropolises by making local the outlying towns.

There was outcry and legislative argument over this new technology, but it was generally adopted amidst declarations of great public benefit, including in the nation's model city, Washington, D.C., where nothing happens without the approval of Congress and its strange mix of leadership from across the continent. When the call was made for patching the entire country

27. As with the automobile, the U.S. Army was the first government organization to endorse the new technology. And, as with the automobile, the President of the United States through 1908 paid it no mind.
28. *Asphalt Nation*, by Jane Holtz Kay, p. 152.

You may recognize that double "R" on the grill. It was before the famed "Flying Lady" was mounted up front, but there in the back seat were three famous men who marked the convergence of earth and atmospheric motoring: Charles S. Rolls and Orville and Wilbur Wright. In 1910, Rolls sadly made the ultimate sacrifice to aeroplaning. Another important automobilist to back the Wrights was Henry Joy, President of Packard. (Courtesy Library of Congress)

with trolley lines, the American politic took joy, not horror, at the vision. Trolley cars, meanwhile, maimed and murdered, and their owners monopolized the systems through graft and abuse of the public trust. Until 1910 more New Yorkers were killed every year by trolley cars than by automobiles. Newspapers sensationalized these incidents, but nowhere to the degree as for automobiles, and without moral condemnation. Lacking for good copy was political advantage and the curse of class distinction.[29]

If in Senator Bailey's testament against Taft's motors we flip horse and automobile, we see how seven years of a contrary example stifled the Motor Age, or how Taft's embrace launched it:

> When the president turns his horses out to die, then everybody who wants to imitate the President does the same thing, and the example extends itself down, not only to everybody who can afford to buy a motor car, but to a good many people who cannot afford to buy one. Thus you are depriving the farmers of a valuable customer for one of the necessary products of the farm.[30]

Then again, it could have been worse.

* * *

Law, attitude, and public sentiment in 1909 favored the horse and trolley over the automobile. Motorists pointed out that speeding on a horse was subject to a maximum $10 fine in New York City, while the same infraction by an automobilist could cost up to one hundred dollars. In Washington, a set of motorists complained of being held up from taking a road while a carriage slipped by. "Why the discrimination?" they asked.[31] The warning by a state highway official to the Amateur Motor League convention in New York in 1904 had played out fully by 1909:

> You are desirous of aiding this industry, but you must remember how valuable is the co-operation, the good-will, and assistance of those who own property on the public highways, and use the same for other purposes than pleasure and with other means of conveyance. When bicycle riders started scorching, the result was disaster, but the general use of bicycles brought discretion and consideration. The result must be the same with you, or it will bring forth the most drastic legislative enactments which can be enforced.[32]

29. To their credit, reformers attacked the trolley monopolies ("Automobile Death Harvest Doubled in Three Years," *NYT*, 2/2/03).
30. "Congress Decides to Buy Cars for Taft," *Motor Age*, 2/11/09
31. *The Horseless Age*, 2/24/09, p. 287 and "Washington Autoists and Their Cars," *Evening Star*, 8/1/09.
32. "Anxious For Good Roads," *NYT*, 1/30/04.

In 1906, Woodrow Wilson, future President of the United States, declared, "Nothing has spread socialistic feeling in this country more than the automobile. To the countryman they are a picture of the arrogance of wealth, with all its independence and carelessness." He would learn better, but not before Taft taught the nation to drive. During Taft's presidency, automobiles became normal, as seen in this 1913 photo of New York's Fifth Avenue. Note the sight-seeing bus to the left and the horse-drawn cart to the right. (Courtesy Library of Congress)

Although law was closer to prohibition than unrestrained scorching, condemnation of automobiles and laws against them grew with every accident. For motorists it was guilt by association. One scorching accident and the entire class was on detention. While the ACA swore to "good roads, good laws, and good behavior," it was said that the "autocrats" were doing nothing more than fomenting socialism. Well, that is, according to the President of Princeton University in 1906. They'd better tone down the act, you see, or the exclusivity of automobiles will create a jealous backlash by the proletariat:

> Nothing has spread socialistic feeling in this country more than the use of automobiles. To the countryman they are a picture of arrogance of wealth, with all its independence and carelessness.[33]

This man, one Woodrow Wilson, soon to be known as "Would Run" Wilson, was politically ambitious and knew exactly what he was saying.[34] His kind lost the 1908 election, but not to motorists. That the winner was a motorist was providential. It might have been different. It might have been that an antimotorist demagogue took office. "I am a Southerner and know how to shoot," said Wilson of reckless automobilists. Would such a President have halted the automobile's progress, or merely slowed it by riding like a hay wagon in its path?

Had things really progressed from 1905, when the Washington, D.C. superintendent of police ordered officers to arrest as many motorists as possible when the local Auto Club announced plans for a "run"? Chicago-area police regularly shot at automobiles that year. "Autophobia Rampant in Illinois," lamented the *Automobile*. Or maybe the Motor Age would have been held up by a continuance of the malevolent regard for it from the Government. In 1906 acting Postmaster Hitchcock praised the success of an automobile mail delivery test outside of Baltimore. Then he

33. "Wilson Blames Speeders," 2/28/06 and "Motorists Don't Make Socialists, They Say," 3/4/06, *NYT*. The comment came at a talk Wilson gave, entitled, "The Young Man's Burden," presented at the most conspicuously and arrogantly wealthy of places, the Waldorf-Astoria.

34. Wilson's hyperbole lives on as an expression of the evil that are automobiles a century into their historic service to mankind in the current anti-automobile rhetoric of the "green" movement. The author of the automobile-condemning book, *Asphalt Nation*, was compelled to give up her own car only after someone asked her about it. (Wilson nicknames from Taft to Helen Taft, 8/16/11. He was also called, "Dr. Syntax" and "The Open Mouth." Taft was fearful of Wilson. "He is evidently quite popular... He speaks too well.")

announced, "Carriers who desire to use automobiles must provide them at their own expense." Great. Or the politics of automobiles might have stayed the way of New Jersey State Senator Frelinghuysen, who like Woodrow Wilson, coveted the governorship. The Senator met with the New Jersey Automobile & Motor Club and used less than encouraging words such as "discussing ... learn the views ... receptive mood ... under consideration." The *Automobile* advised its readers that "all politicians are more or less alike in their methods" and not much help to motorists.[35] Come 1909, the briefs were in, but the jury was still out.

Still, there was no stopping them. Despite his motorphobia, Frelinghuysen owned a motor car. His problem was with politics, not automobiles. Not even Wilson and his self-righteous bullets were going to stop the scorch-crazed roadsters and chauffeured riders. It was too fun, too convenient, and they could afford it no matter the tax. This group that would go so far as to build its own roads might also learn to fire back. But maybe the contagion could have been slowed from its spread to everyone else. When Taft came to bat, it was two-on, one-out, and all that was needed was an outfield looper to win the game. He might have hit into a double play.

Then, the rising tide of automobilism, the enthusiasm for better cars and its bounty of lower prices and more practical machines might have been quelled. Were the President to pronounce it un-democratic and ungodly, all those Buick and Ford buyers might have been shamed into riding trolleys and horses, for a time, anyway, and at a crucial time for the automobile industry. A President Bailey might have declared the menace official and launched a congressional posse in pursuit of Sims's wildest anti-motoring arraignments. That kind of President might not have been the 1908 Democratic candidate, Bryan, but he or another might well have used the full force of office to condemn the machines. Certainly, automobiles would not have followed Bryan into the White House. Sims' speed limits might have retarded the development of better brakes and safety glass, among innovations, and without any savings in life. Henry Joy's 60 percent duty might have been notched up to 100 percent, just the remedy to kill innovation. American automobiles might have been taxed as a vice. Detroit might today be Toronto or Toulouse.

Senator Bacon's reaction to Taft's automobile appropriation illustrates how in 1909 automobiles were just able to stare down the evil eye. Bacon spotted the political convenience to agree with everything Bailey had to say about motors and even to add a few kicks for show. But in the end, Bacon explained with affected agony, Congress can't stand in the way of progress. "If found efficient, the government should adopt them wherever practical," he admitted.[36]

35. From "Washington D.C., 1,000-mile Non-Stop Run," 12/28/05, p. 731, "Autophobia Rampant in Illinois," 8/10/05, p. 173, "Mail Carriers Must Buy Their Autos," 9/13/06, p. 345, and "The Way of a Politician," 3/12/08, p. 366, *Automobile.*
36. "The Senate of a Great Country!" *Automobile,* 1/28/09.

9

Steam, Gasoline and New Stable Boys

Dear Mr. Taft! I see him now, a great big pink porpoise of a man sitting in the back of an open touring car with his hands on his rotund belly.
—Alice Roosevelt Longworth, reminiscing[1]

America of March 3, 1909, was on the verge of automobilism, although no one knew or would admit it. With Army generals pulling rank on each other for a motor, with members of the President's Cabinet sniffing gasoline on the side, and the President's wife sneaking rides to Baltimore and back, motoring was an underground rage. It might have seemed that the only people in Washington who had never touched an automobile were Bailey, Sims, and Roosevelt.

It took the golf-playing, motor riding, political monochromatic William Howard Taft to liberate the motoring nation from Roosevelt's prejudice and Wilson's blasphemy. Without Taft's request, the motorists in Congress would have remained shut in the closet. Taft's cars, rammed through Congress thanks to Tawney's peace smoke with the President-elect, smothered the political argument against automobiles. The congressional parking lot was already, although quietly, stocked with a few automobiles. After Taft opened the doors, it filled with them.

It turns out that Senator Bacon had a car. Roosevelt's friend and last Secretary of State, Robert Bacon, had one. Secretary Meyer bought a Pope "model 67" that March. Speaker Cannon had a car and wanted a new one on the House. James S. Sherman joined Taft as Vice President in a fantastic new Peerless limousine bought off an auto show floor that Winter. Senators Depew, Root and Knox were long time motorists. Rep. Carter Glass bought a White steamer in July.

Although no longer her father's problem, Alice Longworth owned an electric in which she tooled around Washington on one escapade or another. Indeed, a living icon of the republic and leading intellect, Henry Adams, was a convinced motorist. Stuffier than Alice's worst hippopotamus face and smarter than anybody, Adams had

1. Teague, p. 139.

the speed disease. "My idea of Paradise," he wrote, "is a perfect automobile going 30 miles an hour on a smooth road to a 12th-century cathedral."[2] Another leading Washington player, Larz Anderson, bought a new car practically every year, starting in 1899, after he fell in love with the machines he saw in Paris.[3]

But would William Jennings Bryan? He purchased one in March. Yes he did. It was an electric coupe from the great maker of battery-run cars, Detroit Electric. Prior to this, it was said that "he has been partial to horses."[4] Not anymore.

Why do we know all this? Because following the announcement of Taft's intention to use automobiles at the White House, newspapers and motoring journals were suddenly full of names and notices of prominent men and women becoming automobile owners for the first time — or admitting to it.

* * *

When Congress went public with Taft's automobiles, everyone with an interest in motoring took note. Manufacturers not already in the insiders game sent petitions, which Taft's secretary forwarded to the much harassed Captain Butt. Chauffeurs saw gold therein as well. The Taft papers contain dozens of letters from chauffeurs, so it can be imagined that many more of these ambitious mechanics, a most precocious bunch, pestered their congressmen for an inside track to the nation's top driving job. They wrote the incoming President:

> Honored Sir: — The final motion of Congress granting you a private motor car fund was of special interest to me. I do not wish to appear at all presumptive in addressing the highest executive of our nation, but would venture to say that I have a great desire to be your chauffeur the coming season.... The slightest consideration by Your Excellency would be greatly appreciated and it would be a pleasurable honor to send any particulars desired. Most Respectfully, Laurence E. Sloan

> Honorable Sir — Having learned that you would use an Automobile, the coming summer, and thinking that you will need a competent chauffeur, and as I have had quite a bit of experience in that line, I thought I woud [*sic*] write you concerning the situation.... I drove [my employer's] car on his Honey moon trip ... but owing to the breaking of a small spring on the intake valve, which took six days to be replaced from New York. — aside from the small spring above mentioned — the car ran beautifully and there was not an hours delay delay [*sic*] owing the cars lack of condition.... Trusting to hear from you soon, I am, respectfully yours, Charles M. Miller

> Dear Sir — I ask your pardon for writing you, and beg of you not to make this public. I cannot help writing you sir, because I admire you as much, and I believe what isn't worth trying for, is not worth getting.... I am a chauffeur here in the city and hear they are going to have automobiles for your use, when president, and would like very much to obtain a position driving for you, or your family. I am not quite twenty two years of age yet, but I am a good and careful driver, and of good apperence [*sic*]. I don't smoke and do not use intoxicating drinks of any kind.... I have much higer [*sic*] ideals than that of a

2. *Henry Adams in Love*, by Arline Boucher Tehan, Universe Books, New York, 1983, p. 201. Adams seems to have first bought one, a Mercedes 18 H.P., in Paris in 1904 (see *Letters of Henry Adams*, edited by Worthington Chauncey Ford, Houghton Mifflin Company, Boston, 1938, p. 437).
3. See *The Andersons*, web publication by the Museum of Transportation, Brookline, MA, www.mot.org, 2001.
4. See "Motoring," 3/21/09 and 3/28/09 and "Washington Autoists and Their Cars," 8/1/09, *Evening Star*, "Two Motor Cars for Taft," *Motor Age*, 2/25/09, and "Prominent People Who Use the Automobile," *American Motorist*, February, 1910, pp. 65–67.

chauffeur, but I wish to start at the bottom, and work my way up.... Hoping to hear from you, I remain, Very respt. Your's [*sic*] Dan'l N. Farrell.[5]

Most of these letters were addressed to "Hon. W. H. Taft" or "Mr. W. H. Taft, President-elect," forwarded to, simply, "Washington, D.C." One chauffeur sent his letter to "Sixteenth and 'K' Street North West, Washington D.C.," Taft's private residence, which was openly listed in the phone book under "War Secretary."[6] Return addresses were generally at a garage, which in those days was the chauffeur's work station, be his private or commercial employment. One chauffeur tried the Ohio connection. Using inside information, this man addressed his petition to the power-maker, Taft's private secretary, Fred Carpenter. Typed on his employer's letterhead, W.J. Fiedler wrote,

Dear Sir: — Will you kindly consider this application for a position as Mechanic and Chaffeur [*sic*] in the White House garage. Should further references as to character, experience and ability be desired, I can furnish others of same character as the one enclosed. Thank you in advance, Yours respectfully, W.J. Fiedler

Handwritten below his signature, Fiedler made his play:

Mr. Butlter [*sic*] who has kindly given me this letter is the only brother of Mr. Taft's friend J.G. Butler Jr. of Youngstown, Ohio.

The reference letter came from Fielder's boss, J.W. Butler of the Butler-Clark Company, "First Class Sight-Seeing Auto Service," of Cleveland, Ohio:

Dear Sir: — Regarding the enclosed application of Mr. W.J. Fiedler for a position as mechanic and chauffeur in the White House garage, we take pleasure in testifying as to his exceptionable ability both as mechanic and driver. His character is of the best and he is obliging, careful and industrious. During his service with us we have felt that our cars were looked after as carefully as though we were personally in charge of them. It will be a pleasure to hear of his success with the matter in hand. Yours Very Truly, J.W. Butler, Pres. & Gen. Mgr.

Fiedler's "exceptionable" ability notwithstanding, Carpenter didn't give this applicant special notice.[7] Everybody within a stone's throw of Taft was asking something for someone, and the claimed friendship of Butler's brother to Taft was just another drop of oil in the machine. As to the other petitioners, Carpenter replied to Fiedler,

I beg to acknowledge receipt of your favor of the 29th of January and to say in reply that at the proper time full consideration will be given to your application for a position as chauffeur at the White House.[8]

In those days there was much trouble to find a good chauffeur. Although the position was not privileged, it was a great job for a working man. They were notoriously scrappy, smoked cheap cigarettes, and spoke some other kind of English. If trained in mechanics the chauffeur knew nothing of service. If a domestic the automobile was originally as foreign to him as it was to the lady of the house. The choice was often between polished boots or a functioning automobile. The one made for an elegantly mannered driver who raised

5. Letters, Sloan to Taft, 2/27/09, Miller to Taft, 2/24/09, and Farrell to Taft, 2/3/09.
6. *Boyd's Directory*, 1908. Taft's address was 1603 K St., N.W.
7. Exceptionable means "open to exception, objectionable," the opposite of "exceptional" ... so much for sounding sophisticated.
8. Fiedler to Carpenter, 1/29/09, Butler to Carpenter, 1/29/09 and Carpenter to Fiedler, 2/1/09.

his elbows to get the car moving and apologized after running down pedestrians. The other was an uncouth coal miner's son who spat and cursed in front of the children but could rebuild a broken spring out of a coat hanger and thread a needle on a dirt road between a donkey cart and a milkmaid at forty miles an hour.

While from Panama Taft ordered confirmation of the White purchase and Mrs. Taft contemplated her limousine, solicitations and catalogs from auto makers rolled in, including one from the hometown Cincinnati Peerless dealership.[9] Another letter came from E.R. Jackson, representing the Sharp Arrow Automobile Company, and was addressed directly to Carpenter:

> Upon the advice of my friend Congressman Ira W. Wood I am addressing you concerning the recent appropriation of $12,000 to purchase automobiles for Judge Taft. I represent the Sharp Arrow Automobile Co. of this city, manufacturer of the "Sharp Arrow," which holds the American road record for stock cars, 188 miles in 199 minutes, made on October 10th, 1908. I am very anxious that at least one of the cars purchased for Mr. Taft shall be a "Sharp Arrow," and shall take great pleasure in showing my appreciation of any assistance you may give me toward completing the sale. Kindly advise me as to what line of action you deem best for me to follow.[10]

Aside from the scantily clothed bribe, the writer was counting on a little political help, and not just from his friend, Representative Wood. He wrote the letter on the stationery of "The Republican Club" of Trenton, New Jersey. Carpenter deferred the matter to Butt, replying as to the choice of vehicles, "I do not know how far he has progressed."[11]

* * *

The price settled with the White company was good, but not nearly so much as to make it a crime. Taft got a "Model 'M' 40 H.P. seven passenger steam touring car" at a thousand dollar discount from the advertised price of $4,000 — plus a removable top, acetylene headlights, two brass oil lights, a brass taillight, a Prest-O-light tank, speedometer, clock, and a lit electric gauge, all of which could easily add another thousand bucks retail. It was a pretty good deal, although still at a profit for the White company, which like most in the industry sold cars at double the cost.[12]

The "M" was a fine machine, capable of a mile-a-minute, smooth as only steam could be smooth, quiet as the wind, and strong enough to haul the 300-plus pound Taft and five guests across Potomac lowlands, through the winding Rock Creek Park, or up Connecticut Avenue to the golf links at Chevy Chase. In this machine Taft would know the breeze, his best relief from the Washington vapors that would pollute his term of office. In this machine Taft would lead his nation into the Motor Age.

The White steamer was the product of two generations of engineering genius and mechanical expertise. White was a leading manufacturer of sewing machines whose founder was boosted to success by an unlikely ally, Susan B. Anthony. Ms. Anthony saw liberation for the sisterhood in Thomas White's sewing machines. Mr. White saw money in that freedom. With Anthony's petition on one side and White's sales pitch on the other, flyers promoted the cause of both. By the end of the century the "White Mafia" had become a Cleveland social fixture. But the White genius wasn't going to be spent on golf with fellow Cleve-

9. Carpenter to Butt, 12/28/08.
10. ER Jackson to Carpenter, 2/10/09.
11. Carpenter to Jackson, 2/11/09.
12. White House expense voucher, 4/7/09, NARA, "White House Dispersing Officers Accounts" (RG130).

landers, the Rockefellers (John D. bought two White steamers in 1908), or bridge with the Akronite Firestones, for Thomas' sons were as enterprising as the father.[13]

Son Rollin had the automobile disease — and engineering genius to apply to it. He also had access to manufacturing space, engineers, machinery, machinists, tools, dies, an international sales and distribution network, and serious capital to throw at it. Rollin worked out an efficient design for a steamer, and with his father's blessing, set about perfecting it. Thomas White had built a fortune on making a better machine. Sewing machine patents that protected huge profit margins expired in the 1870s and prices dropped from some sixty-five to twenty-five dollars a machine. Only the very best could compete as had White at those prices. When it came to motor cars, no inferiority would be allowed, not in the product and most definitely not in anything associated with the White name. The important business was in sewing machines, not automobiles. No risk was to be taken by an association with a breaking-down, misfiring motor car that couldn't make it up a hill.

The exigence led Rollin to steam. It was a more mechanically reliable and mature technology than gasoline. Not before an unreal fifty — no Cadcam — test cars were built and refined were the cars put on the general market. Son Windsor took up management and son Walter set out to promote. Whites were proven in races, hill climbs, and reliability trials. One went into William K. Vanderbilt's garage — the highest possible praise.[14] The 1905 Model G, rated at 30 horsepower, held the world record for the closed oval track mile. At over seventy miles an hour, the steamer outdistanced 90-horsepower gasoline competition from Fiat and Mercedes. On hill climbs, Whites regularly topped the rest with huge leads. Along with the Stanley, whose steamers set Daytona Beach speed records well into three digits, the rest of the motoring world tired of being pushed around by steam. Races were divided into separate categories, and steamers were sometimes banned altogether. A reading of 1900s automotive journals makes evident the unusual command of Whites in all forms of automobiling, from tours, climbs, and Army trials, to society and races. The venture was so successful the White Company was incorporated as a separate entity in 1906.[15]

Following a severe wreck which neutered the company driver, Thomas White withdrew the company from speed competition. He feared for the intrepid Walter, who, in place of that pained chauffeur, had run a difficult Vanderbilt Cup race. Well beyond the days of having Walter run the mails for a month in London to prove the machines useful, the company turned to the more practical affairs of trials and tours, often with Walter at the helm. A White ran up Pennsylvania Avenue with a military delegation at the 1905 Roosevelt inaugural parade with Walter himself at the wheel. The War Department was convinced and became a regular client after its purchase of the two Model "G" steamers in 1906. So was one Earl Russel, who put the number one 1908 London tag, "A 1," on his White.[16]

13. "White Mafia" as described by Beth King. This section with thanks to her and fellow White family descendent, Henry Merkel, for great White stories and information. Mr. Merkel is a leading steam car aficionado, and the author is indebted to him for instruction, information, and photographs. Thanks also to Richard Wells for the demonstration of how a White steamer works, and for a great ride in his fabulous 1910 "OO" steamer. (Rockefeller's steamers from "Brief Items," *Automobile*, 7/23/08, pg 143; although propelled by steam, the cars were fueled by kerosene, so John D. was not avoiding his own product.)

14. "Willie K.: The Saga of a Racing Vanderbilt."

15. "Now Known as the White Company," *Automobile*, 11/29/06.

16. "White Steamer First Car in Britain," *Automobile*, 1/28/09.

The advantage to steam was ease of operation and power. Practicality and range were its issues. White resolved to overcome these limitations. Rollin applied himself to making the cars accessible to everyday use. His solutions were ingenious. The most critical issue Rollin addressed was the boiler. The standard steam boiler was essentially a pot of water on a stove. The Stanley followed this pattern, but with a series of vertically mounted tubes through which heat was run to boil the surrounding water. Rollin's solution was to switch the equation: the water was run inside the tubes. These "coils," a series of circular steel tubes, held no more than a gallon of water. With less water and greater surface contact to the heat, steam was raised quickly. The coils were compact and unlikely to rupture or explode.[17] The next problem to be resolved was water consumption. It wasn't always the worst problem what with troughs for horses along highways, but steamers needed frequent refills. The White solution was to recycle. A condenser captured escaping steam from the motor and returned it to the boiler. The condenser looks and acts just like a standard radiator, thus the car's outward resemblance to a gasoline motor.

Another engineering advance of the White was employment of a two-step application of steam to the cylinders. Rather than sending steam simultaneously to each of the two cylinders, the White system injected steam sequentially. The steam escaping the first, smaller cylinder carried unused energy, enough so that the second cylinder, with its larger size, achieved equal power to the first.[18] Called a "compound engine," this type of motor was common to marine steam engines and was unique to land vehicles in the White. The two cylinders were of cast iron and mounted within an aluminum crankcase, one of the earliest applications in the industry of this metal that was once considered as precious as platinum.[19] The White managed even greater power from the pistons by pushing each with steam injected from both top and bottom. Remarkably clever all around.

The White design was holistic. With the exception of fuel burned to an amazing one million BTU's (a good sized modern home heater might be in the range of 150,000 BTU's), what was put into the system was returned to it. The engineering was circular from the burner to the cylinders and back again through the condenser. The heart of Taft's Model M was the "flow motor," Rollin's ingenuous system for controlling the burner, coils, and steam power. The flow motor measured the movement of water to the coils, which in turn controlled the burner and its production of steam, all according to the driver's demands on the engine. The mechanism removed from the chauffeur the need to directly manage the balance of steam production and its application. When steam was needed, more water was automatically sent to the coils and the burner activated.

17. The danger of boiler explosion comes not from steam but water. Steam is vaporized water, that is, it has already expanded. With less water in the White's coils there was less potential explosive force from water turning to steam. Although Stanleys rarely, if ever, exploded, the general design was more dangerous than the White. The Stanley avoided explosions from the strength of the boiler tank. The White avoided it in the coil design.

18. Henry Merkel explains that displacement (bore and stroke), used to measure power in gasoline engines, is irrelevant with steam engines. Although the steam moving into the second cylinder carried less energy, with its larger area the second cylinder achieved the same amount of power. "Less force over larger area equals the same amount of power," Mr. Merkel explains. The 1909 "M" had a 3½ inch bore "high-pressure" first cylinder and a six-inch bore "low pressure" second cylinder. Stroke for both was 4½ inches ("The 1909 White Steam Cars," *Automobile*, 8/27/08, p. 302).

19. Rollin White was on the Board of Directors of the Aluminum Company of America. Other early pioneers in the use of aluminum in engines were Pierce-Arrow and the Wright brothers.

The fuel tanks were pressurized. To the chauffeur's delight there was an air pump for inflating tires. A series of pumps managed the flow of air, water, oil, and fuel through the system in order to maintain an equilibrium of 600 psi of steam at any moment. Additionally, there was a cooling fan, pilot light, burner controls, oil injection and retrieval systems, fuel vaporizer, and other mechanisms to turn water to steam and steam to water again, not to mention the application of that force to the rear wheels. All this complex engineering was aimed at ease of operation. Although starting and shutting down the White was more time consuming than a gasoline engine, driving it was a simple affair.

The White's two gears were for low speed operation and regular running, which for the passenger as well as the chauffeur was a great distinction over gasoline cars. The ability of a chauffeur to smoothly shift gears in a gasoline car was of the highest order. In a steamer there was no need. Throttling steam into the pistons gave a continuous application of power for unparalleled, clutch-free smoothness, one of the holy grails of the pre–1950s automotive industry. Before commercial development of automatic transmissions the luxury car makers minimized gear shifting with huge, eight, twelve, and sixteen cylinder, torque-laden, not high horsepower engines, which spared passengers the bounce of gear changes.

Whites were known for going easy on tires, for the weight distribution was evenly spread across the front-mounted engine and condenser, the center vaporizer, and the rear transaxle transmission. A side-benefit to this layout was that, with its compact engine, the steamer's hood was barely longer than the diameter of the front wheel. The automobile bonnet was first developed to house bulky gasoline engines and that new technology in cooling systems, the radiator. Previously, engines were fitted under the carriage, thus the "horse wanted" look of early autos. With the White's short front the rest of the 122-inch wheelbase could be dedicated to people space. Taft, of course, appreciated the extra room. The rear seat which Taft would so come to love was wide, rounded, and a perfect fit for the big man. The car's heavy-duty springs were to be much in demand under President Taft. He was going to be in fine company in his Model "M."

* * *

Renamed in 1909 as the "Pierce-Arrow Motor Car Company," in reflection of the prestige of its car, Pierce-Arrow was among the top manufacturers, and, given evidence of its Glidden Tour wins, arguably maker of the best built car in the country. The greatness that was the Pierce-Arrow came of an insistence upon excellence like that of a rare few in automotive history. The authority behind this exigence was Col. Charles Clifton, in 1909 the Pierce-Arrow Treasurer and the company's guiding force into its command of the luxury car market this lasted into the 1930s. Spread across 100 acres outside of Buffalo, Pierce-Arrow owned one of 1909's largest, newest, and most advanced automobile manufacturing plants. Like White, Pierce came to automobiles through manufacturing and engineering. For Pierce it was appliances and bicycles that led to motor cars. After reviewing the competition and experimenting in steam, the company decided upon gasoline.

As did the rest, Col. Clifton recognized the opportunity to outfit the President's garage. But Clifton would be neither outbid nor out-maneuvered. He was a scrupulous correspondent, and he demanded the best of his subordinates and agents. If a pint of oil was needed it was sent to the White House garage without delay. If Clifton was traveling when a telegram arrived from Pennsylvania Avenue, he responded at the first opportunity with profuse apologies for any lost time, if only a day late. When the White House needed a Pierce-Arrow limousine for the going price of a Ford, Clifton delivered.

As Mrs. Taft wandered through New York automobile showrooms in January, she viewed cars in a seller's market. The excitement of the annual auto shows kept prices high in anticipation of the coming Spring motoring season. In October of 1908, Pierce advertised its 48 H.P. "Suburban" limousine for $6,100. A 36 H.P. 6-cylinder landaulet was advertised for $4,600. As late as February 16, the choice of a limousine was yet undecided upon. Writing that day of the inaugural program, Archie noted that he and Mrs. Taft "will go alone in the motor car, one which she will pick out while she is in New York...." Time was running short, for the limousine was needed in Washington by March 4.

Pierce-Arrow made the decision self-evident. Clifton nailed it with an incredible offer, a deal that was as sweet as they come. The Tafts would have a 48 H.P. limousine for $2,500, the same price as offered for the Louis XVI car, and in time for the inauguration. Only, two cars were needed, for Mrs. Taft's displays required the formality of a limousine as well as the show of a landaulet. Clifton would meet that extravagance with a 36 H.P. landaulet to be delivered later for a slight $2,000. A summer, seven-passenger touring body that

After his White, Taft left it to his wife, Butt, and Edwards to figure out what other cars to get. A proper garage needed a tourer, a limousine, a landaulet, and, for a modern First Lady, an electric car. Electrics were for a lady. Mrs. Taft drove her Baker electric victoria around Washington and Beverly, Massachusetts, during summers. This marvelous act of independence was called "democratic" in the press. Wrote the *Times,* "No greater contrast can be found between the pomp and state of a European court and the democracy of America than to see the wife of the President driving her own automobile in the streets of Washington." The electric was purchased locally in 1909. Its 1912 replacement today resides at the Henry Ford Museum at Greenfield Village, Michigan. Pictured here is the full White House set, probably taken in the Spring of 1909 — a most complete garage. (Courtesy William Howard Taft National Historic Site, Cincinnati, Ohio)

A set of Pierces: 48 H.P. limousine and 36 H.P. landaulet. Capt. Butt and General Edwards negotiated a stupendous deal: $4,900 for the lot. (From *Automobile,* May, 1909)

could be mounted on the 48 H.P.'s chassis was thrown in at $400. The top of the line Pierce was a 60 H.P. that went for $7,100, so Clifton didn't give away the entire house, just the first two floors. These were serious discounts negotiated by Butt and Edwards. On top of it all, Clifton ensured that his company would maintain the cars through seasonal reconditioning and, for that most important feature of a 1909 luxury car, Pierce-Arrow would send a competent, company-trained chauffeur.

The Pierce was unusually smooth and quiet, and the transmission was seamless. Most cars by 1909 had moved from chain drive to drive shaft, but few had one as solid as the Pierce-Arrow. Properly worked, the chauffeur could shift this car through its four gears without a jolt, a capability for which the six-cylinder engine was designed. The big motor was good for any hill, and the factory built body was up to Pierce standards in every way, solid and tight.

While the Pierce-Arrow "six" renown would grow, the 1909 White steamer represented the apex of its kind.[20] The Stanley brothers who brought fame and speed records to their steamers had by 1909 dropped from racing, and their manufacturing business all but collapsed. The White was itself on this edge of the steam car's commercial acceptance. The following year the company gave in to Standard Oil and the rest of the automotive industry with introduction of its first gasoline model, based on a license from Delahaye of France. Steamers were soon abandoned. The company had already moved into the lucrative truck business. Come the American entry to war in 1917, regular production of automobiles halted. Albeit removed from a President's garage, the market for motor trucks was tremendous, and the White excellence in transportation continued.[21]

* * *

All the letters from the determined chauffeurs were for naught. Taft already

20. Pierce-Arrow later suffered from this reputation. The company kept loyal to the magnificent six well into the 1920s, long after Cadillac proved the eight-cylinder more popular. It is thought that Pierce's delay to move to eight or more cylinders led to the company's eventual collapse in the late 1930s, although that did not happen before the company fused two of them to create one of the greatest ever engines, the Pierce-Arrow Twelve.

21. In a 1914 venture outside of the White firm, Rollin turned his engineering skills to caterpillar-style "crawler tractors," which he called "Cletrak." The inspiration came of a fourth White brother who asked him for a vehicle that could get around his California orange groves without compacting the soil. The machines were useful for construction, road building, farming, military use, etc. The White Company supplied thousands of 1½ ton trucks to the U.S. and other Armies during WWI. The company produced trucks into the 1970s, when it was shut down. The assets were purchased by Volvo in 1981.

had his in George Robinson of the Quartermasters, and the Pierce company provided another with the limousine. Robinson was everything a chauffeur should be: humorless and beady-eyed intent upon his machine. Photographs depict him gripping the wheel and looking straight ahead without expression.

Abel Long, White House Chauffeur. Long arrived at the White House "highly recommended" by the Pierce-Arrow company. (From *American Motorist*, February, 1910)

Robinson told a reporter that he was "raised on steam."[22] As a boy he played with toy steam engines. His first job was with the Chesapeake Beach Railroad. He worked his way to fireman and engineer. He joined the Army in 1905, just in time to run General Bell's White steamer. With exaggerated stories of exploding boilers, a chauffeur of a steamer could be thought brave and skilled to manage the furnace and potential bomb. A chauffeur who drove a gasoline motor would generally have no experience with steam. Robinson was a creature apart from the rest.

In the early 1960s Robinson told a historian that he personally chose the Taft automobiles.[23] This was not the faulty memory of an old man. He was speaking the pride of a chauffeur. An automobile was a chauffeur's mount. His pride was in the mechanical beast he handled. He babied it, he cursed it, and he spent all day dealing with it. Chauffeurs loved to pose by their motor. Photographs invariably depict them either confidently at the wheel or standing proudly by the machine, a foot on the bumper or a hand on the bonnet, like a hunter by his prize. A chauffeur identified with his car to satisfy a marketer's wildest dreams. His relationship to the vehicle amounted to his entire self-image. Robinson was undoubtedly trained by the White company, either at its apprenticeship school in Cleveland or by the

22. "Taft's Daredevil Chauffeur," *NYT*, 8/15/09.
23. See Collins, p. 129. Robinson told Collins that he had been driving automobiles since 1899 and that his "first assignment" was a Washington to San Francisco cross-country motor trial in a 2-cylinder Winton that took 45 days. He also said that when Taft campaigned in 1912, he went to "all the states driving the President in the White steamer," which is untrue. Robinson was first employed by the Quartermasters in January, 1905, as a "laborer." He was dismissed from the White House in July of 1910 (his file is at NARA, QMG, RG92, Entry 89, box 6905). Another man, Edward "Doc" White claimed to have been the first presidential chauffeur. His obituary states that he was the "first auto mechanic at the White House and chauffeured five Presidents from 1909 to 1933," and that Taft "acquired a car and with it Mr. White" ("Edward P. White, First Chauffeur and Auto Mechanic for Presidents," *Washington Post*, 3/1/69). White was transferred to the White House from the Quartermasters in early 1913 (see "Is Minus a Garage," *Evening Star*, 3/4/13 and, for a list of early White House chauffeurs and hostlers, RG 130, entry 5, box 4, NARA, dated 1927, which puts White's entrance at 2/1/13, likely his first payroll appearance). Robinson also told the interviewer that there were but two other steamers in Washington. As of June, 1909, there were 76 steamers registered in the District ("Report of Commissioners of District of Columbia," 1909, p. 249).

dealer in Washington. The company insisted on this training to ensure the best possible performance and, thus, reputation, of its products. A well-kept steamer was a loving wife — although it required the same lubricated care as the in-laws. Robinson was wed to the White.

Along with an expertise in the automobile and driving, the other great asset of a chauffeur was spare time. Most chauffeurs spent their day waiting for the phone call at the garage. When not driving they were talking to whoever was around, usually other chauffeurs. Time not spent working on the car or poring through the owner's manual was dedicated to arguing over makes and designs with fellow professionals. Robinson was likely consulted by Captain Butt, earlier his superior at the Quartermasters, over the choice of automobiles. Had Butt asked, Robinson would have talked with great authority, explained the technical benefits of this or that car, and stood grandly for his beloved steamers with the conclusion, logically built, that there was but one choice, the White. Nevertheless, Robinson was far out of the loop on this purchase which was a government matter of the highest order.

The Pierce chauffeur, Abel E. Long, was cautious, polite, and trained to serve his gentleman and lady with smooth driving and manner. Long came out of military service in the Philippines and somehow ended up with the Buffalo company. He came "highly recommended" to the Tafts by the factory.[24] Along with the prestige of his diploma from the Pierce-Arrow chauffeurs school was a thorough training in the mechanics of that automobile. Long's limousine was world-class, and he knew it. The garage men were silenced by this machine. In such company, Long's chin could rise in accordance to his mount. The company ran colorful ads that depicted everything the car represented, minks, the opera, and town cars with tuxedoed gentlemen, ladies gracious and lithe, and always a chauffeur at the wheel. Taft's limousine was all the ads pretended — and the man trained to drive this car could but share the conceit.

24. An *Evening Star* article claimed that Long was "selected from among 5,000 employees ... as the best man for the position" ("Is Minus a Garage," *Evening Star*, 3/4/12 and "Taft's Daredevil Chauffeur," *NYT*, 8/15/09).

10

That New Car Smell and a Lady's Choice (or Just a Precocious Wife?)

Taft arrived in New Orleans from Panama on the 11th of February. That day he took care of the most pressing question, the disqualification of Senator Knox from the position of Secretary of State for having been in the Congress that voted a raise for the position he was to assume. There was no impropriety here, only a constitutional snag. Congress boosted the Cabinet salaries long before Knox could have known that he might be selected as Secretary of State. The handling of the affair was emblematic of Taft's manner. He appealed to Congress to rescind the previous measure, thereby annulling Knox's disqualification. Congress treated the request delicately. The Senate immediately heeded Taft's suggestion, while the House balked. A telegram to Speaker Cannon changed the sentiment. The Judiciary Committee announced the House's indisposition "to get into a controversy with the incoming administration...."[1] The honeymoon was still on.

Both Roosevelt and Taft worked to find a home for displaced or dissatisfied White House staff. They met specially to discuss the fate of Roosevelt's secretary William Loeb, a fine act of loyalty on Taft's part, for the position tendered, chief of Customs in New York, was a tremendous reward that Taft would better have given to his own rather than to a Roosevelt loyalist.[2] Those for whom Taft's plans left no place were rewarded with transfers to another department or given a pensioned retirement.

1. "Taft Expresses Wish," *Evening Star*, 2/12/09. Adams, of course, saw incompetence in Cincinnati and Ohio for it (*Henry Adams and His Friends*, p. 637).
2. There was some agitation that Loeb be given a Cabinet slot. Taft only went so far as to suggest it be done for a few months, which Roosevelt deemed unsuitable. Instead, and at Roosevelt's request, Taft gave him the Customs position (see Taft to Loeb, 1/7/09). New York political bosses were outraged. One of the highest possible political rewards was customs collector, especially at New York. The official salary was already as high as any government pay outside of the President himself. In 1909 the customs chief at the port of New York was paid $12,000, equal to the just then raised salary for his boss, the Secretary of the Treasury. The Vice President was paid only $12,000, as was the Chief of Staff of the Army. Filled by political appointees, customs officers managed the primary source of government revenue, import duties. From the beginning, customs officers were notoriously corrupt, tremendously powerful, and immune to scrutiny.

The big Taft heart assured a soft landing for all, even if they refused to see it.

From New Orleans, Mr. and Mrs. Taft ventured to Cincinnati, from where Taft took a two day trip to Washington to meet with Roosevelt and take callers from the third floor of the Boardman home. The press noted that Taft went to the White House in Senator Knox's automobile, along with Frank B. Kellogg, the "octopus hunter" of Roosevelt's anti-trust campaigns.[3] The visit was meant to shore up the final cabinet selections, and to quell speculation of a rift between Roosevelt and Taft. Taft was deferential to Roosevelt, and vice-versa, for complaints that Taft had ignored or not sought the advice of Roosevelt in the appointments had started already. Following Taft's "dear John" letters, sent just prior to the Panama trip to those of Roosevelt's Cabinet he declined to invite forward, rumors of a rift arose.[4]

While Taft was in Cincinnati being made a Mason, the word out was that he was purposefully avoiding Washington, especially since two Cabinet positions remained open. His next stop was Philadelphia for a speech, then to Washington for that quick visit, and back to New York with Mrs. Taft, until the formal entrance to the Capital on February 27. The New York visit drew criticism for his being in New York, i.e., with the financial "interests," as it was known the Treasury position was undecided. That Taft might choose a New Yorker was thought grievous.

Actually, Taft's hasty schedule had prevented completion of an obligation for magazine articles. He hoped that a little peace in his brother's home would allow some catch-up time. Not even seclusion there could keep Washington from intruding. New York was worse than Washington. Visitors gave him no peace, from General Horace Porter and Booker T. Washington to every port collector or postal clerk wanna-be in between. Meanwhile, Taft was tuning his all-important inaugural address. It was reported to be 5,000 words. "Better than 10,000," the Hartford *Times* noted, "but worse than 2,000."

The short, brutal life of a President-elect consists of throngs to bow to, mobs with hands to shake, job-asking, graft-quenching, autograph-craving, photograph-seeking petitioners, newspaper men, advisors, and local big guys looking to affirm ego and public image through access to the Man-to-be. Every supplicant who managed an audience with the President-elect was convinced of the urgency of his destination as Pheidippides on his run from Marathon. Taft's February escapes from Washington provided only a diversion in the territory, not the depth, of the intrusions.

By the time he reached Washington, Taft was exhausted. To make matters worse, his first destination upon arrival was the White House, and Roosevelt was again absent. Whether it was poor coordination, the early telephone age, press exaggeration, or a snub, Taft had much trouble hooking up with the President. Roosevelt's final acts were for himself, not his successor, including a last cut or two at Congress. Amidst his game of one-upmanship with the co-equal branch, Roosevelt couldn't let go either the Secret

3. "Meets on March 15," *Evening Star*, 2/17/09.

4. For the letters see reel 481, vol. 35, 1/22/09. For the rift and rumors thereof see "Taft and Roosevelt," *Evening Star*, 2/15/09. The article was all conjecture that added up to prescience: "Pessimists predict that it will be the beginning of a wide breach between the outgoing chief executive and the incoming.... They are sure that Mr. Taft has ignored his former chief ... in his cabinet selections ... and point out that Mr. Roosevelt's nature is such that he wants to have a hand in everything going on.... When he gets back from Africa the small breach will grow wider, and then the pyrotechnics will start. That is the way it is mapped out, anyhow." It didn't have to be that way, and only Roosevelt partisans saw it. They saw it because they caused it.

Service or Panama affairs. Additionally, he couldn't help but make political appointments, despite having earlier stated that he would leave further patronage to his successor.

While Taft roamed between Cincinnati, Philadelphia and New York, the biggest news out of Washington was that Roosevelt had quashed Taft's choice for the Secretary of Treasury. It was pointed out that the man, Senator James Hemenway of Indiana, had agitated for another candidate than Roosevelt's man at the 1908 convention. Taft didn't care, but he thought it prudent to test the choice against Roosevelt's ability to resurrect old slights. Forgiveness might have gone to the Senator but for the release of a report on the Secret Service matter from a committee Hemenway chaired. The conclusion was, of course, that Roosevelt was a scoundrel. "Consequently, it is reported," stated the *Times*, "the President brought the big stick into vigorous play on the instant and smashed Hemenway's chances."[5]

On that same day, another news item was that Taft purchased a saddle horse. "Tate," so named for the previous owner, was plenty big enough for his famously large new rider. At seventeen hands and 1,250 pounds, he was described as "an ideal weight-carrier with the best of manners."[6] Gossip was up to full gale over the changes coming at the White House and everything else Taft. Sunday newspapers ran full-page spreads on each of the family and the known cabinet nominees. The Taft genealogy was explored, and Mrs. Taft's dressing gowns were given a public fitting. Taft did little to spur this fascination. If a long walk with brother Charles made the papers it was not of his own doing or choice. If the reporters found it interesting that he played golf with his son, so be it. Nor did he try to stop it. He posed for their photographs, and he answered their questions.

The week of the 20th, the new automobiles rolled into town in anticipation of Taft's formal arrival on the 27th. News accounts turned to the automobiles themselves. "The color is a little unusual," wrote *Motor Age* of the steamer, "being a harmonious blend of subdued greens, with the United States coat-of-arms painted on each of the doors." White Company publicists let out the story of a man who saw the car at the factory and asked if it had any special features. "Yes," replied Rollin, "the special features which are found in every White car ... when we are making a car for the President of the United States, there is no way in which we can make it better than the car which you, or any one else, can purchase from us."[7]

The Pierce limousine was universally described as "big." In the catalog it was called a "suburban," to connote both city and country use. Beyond that, suburban implied large. It was painted dark blue with the door panels colored a "rich russet" (reddish-brown), with a narrow stripe of the same color that followed and accented the lines of the molding. The interior was upholstered in blue broadcloth, with the chauffeur's compartment done in leather, the appropriate layout for a limousine.[8]

5. "Roosevelt Keeps Foe Out of Cabinet," *NYT*, 2/20/09 and "Big Stick At Work," *Evening Star*, 2/20/09.
6. "Taft Gets a Saddle Horse," *NYT*, 2/20/09. During the 1908 campaign, the President of the Massachusetts Society for the Prevention to Cruelty to Animals declared, "It is outrageous cruelty to animals for a big 300-pound man like Taft to ride a horse ... I do not doubt the stories sent out from Hot Springs that the horse's legs have been wrenched and strained." In response, a Kansas admirer offered to send one "fit for him to ride." He wrote, "I have got one so big that I had to build a special stall to keep him in. He's twenty-five hands high and weighs 3,500 pounds stripped" ("Calls Taft Cruel to Horses," 8/17/08 and "Heavy Horse for Taft," 8/26/08, *NYT*).
7. "Two Motor Cars for Taft," *Motor Age*, 2/22/09 and *Vehicle Dealer*, March 1909, p. 249.
8. Leather was for utility and broadcloth for luxury.

* * *

Think of the thrill at the purchase of a new car. Magnify that by two of the finest cars in the world for the most important man in the country, and, on top of it all, this being the very first time it had ever been done. We can see how it was for everyone involved with these automobiles in early 1909. Congress held hearings on the cars. Top government officials managed their purchase. The factory workers knew exactly whose cars these were. The salesmen, the clerks, and the owners of the factories themselves were in on the excitement. The railroad men who handled them knew their destination.

New cars! The tourer's leather smelled of strap oil and saddle soap. The limousine's broadcloth was fresh and perfect. The woodwork on both was polished to a mirror. The brightwork sparkled. The white of the tires jumped and the paint blazed like — well, new. The tremendous headlamps, huge lanterns mounted before the front wheels and wrapped in brass, sparkled like flares to the day's light. Then there was that emblem, the Great Seal, affixed on both sides of each car that marked these as the most important motors of the land.

The White was shipped from Cleveland under the auspices of W.C. Sterling, the agent who handled the sale with Butt and Edwards. Sterling worked out of the White New York office and was in charge of Washington sales, which included that notable client, the War Department. Sterling personally met with the Tafts in December of 1908 when the motors were first discussed. The acquaintance was likely much older, at least as old as the White company's involvement with Taft's War Department. It all paid off for Sterling. Thanks to his good work and, "due in no small measure to the patronage of President Taft," the White Company opened a branch office in Washington over Summer of 1909.[9]

As a matter of propriety, the White and Pierce companies remained in possession of the cars upon their arrival to Washington. Taft's money wasn't due until March 4, so he had no authorization to use them on government time before then. The indiscretion was avoided by keeping the cars under the factory names until it could all be made official after the inauguration. The government paid for the steamer on April 7 against an invoice which dated the delivery as February 25, with a five day "storage" fee, as well as for costs of licensing in Maryland, Virginia, and the District.

Sometime before the Tafts' arrival, Butt gave the car a thorough trial. He probably did so right away. We can imagine that there was a first time it was brought over to the White House stables. We can imagine that as the steamer drew up, there gathered a crowd. To people of all stations of 1909, the running of an automobile was a mystery. Only the chauffeur knew what was really going on. The steamer would have rolled silently to a halt. The chauffeur, likely Robinson, would have, with the grand gestures of a pianist, turned the steering wheel-mounted throttle, depressed the brake and cut-off pedals, thrown the long shift into neutral, and pulled hard on the parking brake. Not a sound would have been heard from the engine which yet retained its full 600 psi of steam in tight suspension. He would have alighted to the left, the passenger side, and rounded the car to where the spare tires were mounted by the driver's seat, reached below the running board and adjusted a knob. The pilot light would have extinguished with the snuff of a candle.

9. "The White Company Open Branch Office in Washington, D.C.," *Vehicle Dealer*, July 1909, p. 230.

OUR ORDER NO. 704
712

YOUR ORDER NO. — Taft

The George N. Pierce Company.
Makers of
Pierce Great Arrow Cars.

The Pierce-Arrow Motor Car Co.

U.S. Gov
Sec LHG

Treasurer's Dept. 754 Main St. Buffalo, N.Y. April 13 1909

Sold to

Terms: Cash Shipped by NYC & PRR
By Car M.C. #95924 Frt Paid $49.00

NUMBER		
7101	— 48-6 cy Pierce Suburban equipped with Elect Lamps; Warner auto meter & clock; Prestolite Tank B; Argus Mirrors; Harrison Bumpers; Folding Robe Rails; La Crosse Toilet Case; and Reading Lamps and Spencer Air Pump; Cotton Cover; Net Hammock.	2500 00
30106	— 36-6 cy Pierce Landau with Extension Roof; Prestolite Gas Tank B; Electric Lamps; Extra Battery; Boquet Holder; Argus Mirrors; Reading Lamps; Toilet Case; Annunciator; 2 Extra Tires; 2 Covers; Tire chains; Net Hammock; Spencer Air Pump; Doors on Front Seats; Cotton Cover	2000 00
	Extra 7 P. Touring Body for #7101 equipped with Cape Top; Glass Front; Extra Folding seats; Extra Pullman Seats; Wired for Elect Lamps; Cotton Cover	400 00
		4900 00

PRICES AS PER CONTRACT provided
Charles Clifton Treas
L. H. Gardner Secy

COMPUTATION CORRECT
J. C. Mood Auditor.

Entered on P 148 I. B.

Certif # 1067 for 7101
" # 30106

Great deals! The Pierce-Arrow invoice. (Courtesy National Records and Archives Administration)

(Form approved by the Comptroller of the Treasury February 8, 1908.)

The Executive Office.

VOUCHER FOR PURCHASES, AND SERVICES OTHER THAN PERSONAL.

APPROPRIATION: "CONTINGENT EXPENSES, EXECUTIVE OFFICE."

THE UNITED STATES,

TO The White Company, DR.

ADDRESS: Broadway and 62nd street, New York, N.Y.

Date of Delivery or Service. 1909		Items.	Unit Price. Dolls.	Cts.	Per—	Amount. Dollars.	Cts.
Feb	25	1 automobile "White", 1909 Model "M", 40 H.P. seven passenger steam touring car, complete with top. Two brass acetylene headlights, two brass oil lights, one brass tail light, one Prest - O - lite tank, one Model "9" speedometer, clock and light, and one electric gauge light complete for				3000	00
		Total, - - - - - - - - - -				3000	00

MEMORANDUM DUPLICATE.

3000.00

3000.00

Paid by Check No. 709 216, dated April 7, 1909, on Treasurer of the United States,

The White House expense voucher for the White steamer. (Courtesy National Records and Archives Administration)

(Form approved by the Comptroller of the Treasury February 8, 1908.)

The Executive Office.

VOUCHER FOR PURCHASES, AND SERVICES OTHER THAN PERSONAL.

APPROPRIATION: "CONTINGENT EXPENSES, EXECUTIVE OFFICE."

THE UNITED STATES,

TO The Cook & Stoddard Company., DR.

ADDRESS: 22nd & P Sts., Washington, D. C.

Date of Delivery or Service. 1909		Items.	Unit Price. Dolls.	Cts.	Per—	Amount. Dollars.	Cts.
May	5	1-Baker Victoria #4102 as per agreement				1000	00
"	8	Installing charging station at the Executive Stables as per estimate				90	00
		Total,				1090	00

MEMORANDUM DUPLICATE.

1090.00

Paid by Check No. 1604, dated June 7, 1909, on Treasurer of the United States, in favor of the principal, for $1090.00

The White House expense voucher for the Baker electric victoria. (Courtesy National Records and Archives Administration)

Now, and exactly according to the White manual, the chauffeur would have prepared to twist the escape valve to bleed the hot coils of steam. He might have told those nearby to stand back, or he might have kept silent, smiling to himself at the jolt they were about to receive. When he turned the valve those six hundred–some pounds per square inch of vaporized water were unleashed. The onlookers would have been startled by the abrupt, harsh blow, like a veritable locomotive (to the modern ear, the wail of a jet engine, or, for the more cultivated out there, a cappuccino machine at peak eruption), as the coils let loose a tremendous spray of vapor. The crowds gasped and jumped back at the demonstration.[10]

Everyone knew the huge steamer was fast, and they knew Taft was sure to let it out once or twice. Robinson might have stood there bragging of just how fast he could take it — if he wanted to. He might have discussed the workings of the machine, the efficiency of the coil system, the ingenious "flow meter," the force of steam injected twofold into the cylinders. Or he might have bragged of the unique condenser system that separated lubricating oil from water to recycle it back into the boiler, giving the car more range than other steamers. He might have pointed to the knobs, the dials, and the multiple pedals, all of which must have reinforced the observer's conclusion that it was no small thing to manage. Maybe he scared them with stories of boilers blowing, then laughed it off as an impossibility with a White.

The Pierce-Arrow limousine arrived by train, as well. Abel Long must have been at the wheel as heads turned with it up Pennsylvania Avenue. This machine was magnificent. It stood almost eight feet high. Perched on a 130-inch wheelbase, it was fifteen feet long. It weighed almost 4,000 pounds.[11] With tall doors, extended driver's canopy top, and huge rear windows that revealed its immaculate interior, the Pierce was the very form of dignity and statehood. The enormous hood spoke of the motor beneath, which was oddly quiet. The tailpipes didn't belch or snort as we might think from an old car. No, the exhale was purposeful and even. The engine's famed smoothness came of its perfect balance. Its 4½ inch bore by 4¾ inch stroke cylinders were almost the size of coffee cans. And there were six of them. When automotive journalist spoke of six cylinders as motor perfection the Pierce six was the example.[12]

When the "48 H.P. Great Pierce-Arrow Suburban limousine" pulled in, the taut February ground would have crunched to its weight. But no one looked at the wheels. All eyes would have been on the chauffeur and the enormous carriage behind him, ears tuned to the firm beat of the great engine. Those filing in behind would have smelled the brittle exhaust that chugged rearward from the pipe. Eyes of those watching it pull towards them would have fixed upon the brightwork of the hood and lanterns and then, as it passed, upon the Great Seal and its eagle's extended wings.

10. Robinson told Collins that to scare away photographers, at the President's orders "he would simply put his foot on the valve of the steamer and let the steam come out around the car. This created a fog and foiled the photographers" (Collins, p. 133). Henry Merkel explains that by throttling hard in neutral the condenser would overload and go into "dump mode" and steam would be released through an undercarriage valve. "It does create quite the cloud," he says. Taft surely enjoyed the trick.

11. Specifications from the *Pierce-Arrow Passenger Car Production Specifications,* Pierce-Arrow Society website, www.pierce-arrow.org, 2001; the length of the 48 H.P. from "Automobiles May Solve the Traffic Problem," *Automobile*, 1/28/09, p. 196, per Pierce-Arrow.

12. For a 1909 look at the benefits of six-cylinders, see "How the 'Six' Gains Flexibility," *NYT*, 1/3/09, written by H.M. Sternbergh of the Acme company.

We can see the chauffeurs, the hostlers, the Secret Servicemen, and policemen circling the cars, trading compliments and wonder, shaking their heads in pride. Perhaps Loeb and Carpenter and others came running from their offices, dropping last minute preparations for the change of presidents to see what the Pierce and White companies had wrought. Butt, we know, was "trying" the machines, trying both their competence and his own pride in the them.[13] Would Roosevelt himself have come by, perhaps on the pretense to see his horses, and given the machines a brief, disinterested look?

* * *

Things were ready for the Tafts, who arrived on the 27th. On top of everything else, the Captain had become a Taft surrogate to the Inaugural Committee, which turned to him for loose ends during Taft's hideaway. The Chairman of the Inaugural Committee asked the Captain to meet with Taft right away to settle the most important question as to how Mrs. Taft intended to return from the Capitol to the White House.

Archie took one of the new motors to the Boardman house, where he found Mrs. Taft resting. He was pressed to settle these matters. "I sent word that I must see her," he wrote, "so I bolted to her room door and there had an interview with her partly hidden behind it." This remarkable discussion led to one of Mrs. Taft's most controversial acts, over which she was tried, sentenced, and executed in parlor chatter, on Capitol Hill, in the press, and by partisans everywhere. The complaint came from a combination of circumstance, her forthright self invention as First Lady, and a typical Roosevelt stunt. Amidst the complaints that the Tafts were disrupting tradition and Roosevelt's legacy, the outgoing President decided that he'd rather not stay around for the inaugural festivities. Butt's description continues:

> Occasionally she would get excited or greatly interested and appear to full view. She did not look bad, quite the contrary I thought, for she wore a richly colored Japanese kimono, which is very becoming, I think, to all women, and especially to her, for she knows how to tie them about her figure. It was at this interview that I asked her how she intended to come from the Capitol and she said in a motor, of course, and wanted to know why I asked. I then told her that the suggestion had been made for her to ride back from the Capitol with the newly inaugurated President, *which idea found lodgement in her mind at once.* I told her that the committee from the House and Senate had made different plans and had arranged to have only the President ride with a committee as had been the custom for the past century[14] [italics added].

This must not be discarded as a mere change in convention. It seems logical today that the incoming and outgoing Presidents ride to the inaugural together but not on the return to the new President's home. It was not of 1909 thinking, when democracy was yet an exception and the few republics of the world stood against history. America's unique quadrennial celebration was still part of a new age in the making and was barely four generations past the fourth and one of the most contentious elections in American history. In 1801 John Adams skipped town the night before Jefferson's inaug-uration. Eight years later, Jefferson told James Madison he wanted to ride back

13. He wrote of visiting Mrs. Taft at the Boardman house, "Fortunately I had one of the new White House motors which I was trying...." (Butt, *Letters*, 2/28/09, p. 362).

14. Butt, *Letters*, 2/28/09, p. 362 and unpublished passages, same date (the editors removed Archie's reference to her "becoming" kimono and "excited" demeanor).

to the White House with him, as a common citizen, to celebrate the new President.

The point was and remains that the presidency is an office and not a man. The miracle that is the peaceful transfer of power could be no better displayed than by the exchange of the throne from one President to the next and their cordial rides to and from the coronation. The king is dead, long live the king!— only the old one is still around to celebrate. Bill Clinton's 2001 post-inaugural exhibition upon his exit from Washington was nothing less than an attempt to elevate himself above the office he had just left and its new occupant. Roosevelt had the exact opposite in mind. Nevertheless, an important symbol was removed from the ritual, and by avoiding it Roosevelt achieved the same.

Archie's description continued:

> Since Mr. Roosevelt has seen fit to change the order of things," she said, "I see no reason why the President's wife may not now come into some rights on that day also. The reason that I do not enjoy accompanying Mr. Taft on trips is just for this reason. He is taken in charge by committees and escorted everywhere with honor, while I am usually sent with a lot of uninteresting women through some side street to wait for him at some tea or luncheon. When you come back tomorrow we will talk it over with him and see what can be done.

So Mrs. Taft decided to take the open seat. This lovely practice of President and spouse together passing the crowds up Pennsylvania Avenue was considered a sacrilege and for it Mrs. Taft a heretic. Butt wrote, "I telephoned to the joint committee of the House and Senate of her proposition to drive back with the President, and it was like an explosion in camp...." When the incredulous Inaugural Committee men asked the President-elect about it, he replied, "Why, certainly!"[15] The carriage ride back to their new home was the proudest moment of Mrs. Taft's life, "doing something which no woman had ever done before," she wrote in her memoirs.[16] As with many of Helen Taft's innovations, this one has endured.

* * *

The Tafts wasted no time in getting into their new car. The day they arrived to Washington they went for test drive. The *Times* announced, "The new automobile"— likely the steamer — "was tried by Mr. and Mrs. Taft this afternoon after their arrival here, and the new Potomac Park was explored."[17] Other reports noted that two cars had been purchased, although there was confusion on the details. The motoring section of the *Evening Star* announced that day the delivery of two motors, the White and a "36 horsepower suburban car" from Pierce-Arrow, a confusion over the limousine and the landaulet. A week later, the *Times* figured out there were two motors. "Two fine new automobiles already have been purchased with the $12,000 appropriated by Congress for this purpose and Mr. Taft has given them a thorough trial," wrote the paper.

> One is a good weather machine, a big touring car with detachable top, and painted in dark green of three shades. This will be the one most used by the President. The other car has a limousine body painted black,[18] and was purchased for the use of Mrs. Taft. Both bear on each door the official coat of arms of the United States.... The cars are in charge of men sent from the factories who will turn the machines over to the White House head

15. "Mrs. Taft Sets Suffrage Pace," St. Paul *Pioneer Press*, 3/2/09.
16. *Recollection of Full Years*, p. 332.
17. "Taft in Washington, Misses Roosevelt," *NYT*, 2/28/09.
18. It was blue.

> chauffeur, who will receive $100 a month. He will have one assistant.[19]

The *Evening Star* wasn't exactly sure what was going on either. On March 5, the paper announced,

> Mrs. Taft, wife of the President, will soon have her own touring car with a seating capacity of seven persons to cost, it is said, over five thousand dollars. It will not be delivered for several weeks. This, with the recent purchase of a car for the President, which he has used since coming to this city last week.... Mrs. Taft's chauffeur, it is said, has also been engaged. He is Abel Long of Buffalo, N.Y., formerly a soldier in the Philippines under Gen. Bell.[20]

The *Evening Star* learned about the landaulet but confused it with the limousine, which indicates that the decision on the landaulet was already made by this time. As for the factory chauffeurs mentioned in the *Times* article, the reference was to Long. The reported $100 a month salary was accurate for both Long and Robinson, and the latter was, indeed, the head chauffeur. Whatever the details, the Motor Age had finally arrived to Washington, D.C.

19. "Mrs. Taft to Make White House a Home," *NYT*, 3/8/09.
20. "Will Have an Auto," *Evening Star*, 3/5/09.

11

Portents

While the latest accusations rang of Mrs. Taft's violation of tradition and things Roosevelt, Taft set about some early spring golfing at the Chevy Chase links. He ran up to the club in one of the new motors the day before the inauguration. If anyone was looking for presentiments, this was it. The day before becoming the most important man in the nation he played golf. He didn't bother with his wife's schemes, and he left the inaugural plans entirely to others. After the initial shock and the how-dare-she's, the logic and dignity of Mrs. Taft's intended ride from the Capitol settled upon the reasonable.

Meanwhile, Roosevelt carried on his own little rebellions. Five days before leaving office, safe from elections or Congressional inquiry, he broke another presidential tradition. On the last day of February he was seen rolling up Connecticut Avenue in a carriage. With policemen hustling alongside on bicycles, the assemblage turned into the drive and under the porte-cochers of the Austro-Hungarian embassy. Across the street, the Brits took note. The news bolted to Roosevelt's friend, Ambassador Jusserand of France. And on a Sunday, no less. This trip onto foreign territory, although barely two miles from the White House, was leagues beyond his expedition to the Caribbean during which, although overseas, he never ventured beyond U.S.-occupied soil. It was a direct break of precedent. No American President had ever stepped on foreign land.[1]

Roosevelt again crossed convention and asked the Tafts to spend inaugural eve at the White House. It was a gracious act by the President for his old friend. Taft accepted the invitation with magnanimity. In a note to Roosevelt that contained a vigorous denial of "the slightest difference between us," Taft assured the President that rumors of a rift and Mabel Boardman's dictatorial calendar were not his doing. "I welcome the opportunity to stay the last night of your administration under the White House roof to make as sympathetic as possible the refutation of any such suggestion."[2] Much has been made of the dinner that night, how Mrs. Roosevelt and Mrs. Taft gave each other precise courtesy, how Roosevelt dominated the conversation, and how Taft slipped out to party with the Yale crowd at the Willard Hotel. Nerves over the dinner were for everyone

1. "Roosevelt Visits Austrian Embassy," *NYT*, 3/1/09. The reason for the choice of embassy was that the Austrian ambassador was the senior diplomat by length of service in Washington.
2. Taft to Roosevelt, 2/25/09.

but Taft and Roosevelt. Butt's assessment was that the evening went off "without a hitch." Although Taft later recalled it as a "funeral," after dinner the pair jovially discussed a treaty with Canada and cursed Congress. There was no immediate complaint that the dinner was strained.[3]

As of eight o'clock, the night of March 3, 1909, when Mr. and Mrs. Taft stepped from the great limousine through a driving, cold rain and into the White House, there was no resentment between Taft and Roosevelt. The good feelings carried past the inaugural. In late March, Taft wrote affectionately to the former President. In what has been seen as a demonstration of his listless state without a boss, Taft rather expressed his admiration for the man who had dominated his and the country's life for seven years: "If I followed my impulse, I should still say 'My dear Mr. President.' I cannot overcome the habit. When I am addressed as 'Mr. President,' I turn to see whether you are not at my elbow."[4]

Historians have taken literally Taft's tongue when firmly lodged in his cheek. First of all, as with all good humor, this was part truth and part jest. Taft had a week earlier said the same thing to Bourke Cockran, a Democrat who married the daughter of a close Taft friend.[5] He liked the line and repeated it in the letter to Roosevelt. It was not a signal of weakness or some kind of submission. It expressed Taft's dedication to Roosevelt and his legacy — Taft's unwritten platform, to which he pledged himself in his inaugural address— and did so in good humor.

At the Willard later that night Taft had a grand time. He hadn't wanted to go, for the last thing he needed was another speech to give and more hands to shake the night before the biggest day of his life. He was otherwise concerned about the Canadian treaty. That afternoon his Yale buddies showed up to the Boardmans' to convince him otherwise. "Say, Bill, do you remember that tug-of-war team? And that time Harvard beat the whey out of us playing base ball?" Taft started listening at that one. "Oh well, it isn't like it was in our day, Bill.... I was back at New Haven last Fall. You know they've taken down 'The Fence' and — Well, good bye, Bill." Now the man closed the deal. "I'm going to dinner and then have a look in at the smoker. Sorry you won't be there." Taft jumped. "Hold on," he cried. "Of course I've got to dine with Roosevelt, but let me see. Suppose I could drop in about 10:30. Do you think the boys would mind if I didn't stay long?"[6] Sold.

Taft showed up at 10:30 sharp, pretty timely for a man notorious for running late. To the Yalies who roared for their man, he gave a speech that has since confounded historians who mistake Taft's public introspection for fear. Nor have they shared his fine wit. He took the opportunity to express his gratitude to Yale and his faith in popular government:

> The spirit of Yale is the spirit of Democracy, every man doing his best. And if he does this, having the support of every other Yale man, that is all I ask for.... I am about to enter upon one of the most perilous journeys any man in our country can enter. Great obstacles can be met by obser-

3. Butt, *Letters*, 3/2/09, p. 378 and Pringle, p. 393. The dinner escaped Hoover's memoirs. On consideration of inviting the Wilsons to dinner the night before the 1913 inaugural, Taft wrote to Mabel, "Nellie is dead set against it, because of her memory of the Roosevelt dinner to me. You were at that funeral" (Taft to Mabel Boardman, 11/10/12).
4. Letter, Taft to Roosevelt, 3/23/09.
5. When Pringle quoted the line in his biography of Roosevelt, he wrote that Taft said it with "his chuckle faintly rueful" (p. 529). In his book on Taft, Pringle quotes the line without reference to any chuckles, rueful or otherwise (p. 399; citation here from Butt, 3/11/09, p. 9; Pringle misspelled the name as "Cochran").
6. "Taft Joins Eli Boys," *Evening Star*, 3/4/09.

> vance of common sense, courage, the sense of proportion and the absence of swell-headiness, which principles are inculcated at Yale.

Taft smiled broadly, then turned solemn for emphasis. His mates cheered this homage to democracy, Lincoln, and Yale. "You'll make good," shouted his brethren. He was thrilled. He shook every hand before leaving the room to another ovation. A reporter wrote, "Well, 'Big Bill' may have been happy when the election returns rolled in last November, but he could not have looked a bit happier than he did last night when the Yale gang got on its feet and cheered him."[7]

A month before he said to a Southern audience,

> The first thought that comes to me after hearing what I am quite free to admit is very sweet music to me, is a sort of trembling fear that, after four years, such a meeting as this and such expressions of good will may be impossible — that I shall be like the man who went into office with a majority and went out with an unanimity.[8]

Looked at backwards, Taft seems prescient of future troubles. He was cracking a joke. It was typical of his applause and laugh lines. Much of Taft's rhetorical style and humor either doesn't reinforce the perspective or simply escapes the historian. While Secretary of War, Taft's fine disposition was heralded. About to take office, he suddenly became fearful and disagreeable? This makes no sense, for no matter how painful the coming period, how disturbing the future break with Roosevelt, or how distressful the illness that was to strike his wife, the man kept his humor. Always. And all that came later.

* * *

The night of March 3, a southern-blown storm hurled snow and ice upon the city. The crack of frozen branches awoke Mrs. Taft. She couldn't sleep. Her dream was about to come true, and she was anxious. The champion of her dream slept through the night. He was sleeping off a year's worth of hassle, handshakes, and speeches that were to satisfy everyone but himself. This was duty to be fulfilled as much as ambition met. Taft was not to be uncomfortable being President, but he did not revel in the experience like his predecessor. He'd take it on and conquer it as he had everything else in life.

The next morning Taft and Roosevelt took breakfast together. The White House grounds were covered with snow and ice. The wind had not let up. "Even the elements protest," Taft joked. Roosevelt took the blame for himself. "I always knew there would be a blizzard right up to the end of my term," he said, both men laughing. Taft tossed the joke around all day. Greeting a reporter later that morning he said, "Ha, ha! I always knew it would be a cold day when I got to be President!"[9]

At ten o'clock a carriage and team of four horses waited near the North entrance. The coachman was known as the best in the city. Everyone was anxious about the weather. The chairman of the Inaugural Committee was asked if the parade would be held. He referred the question to General Bell, the Marshal of the parade,

7. "Taft Joins Eli Boys," *Evening Star*, 3/4/09. Wilson repeated the sentiments four years later to a similar audience. "Now I stand here upon the eve of attempting a great task — a profound and great one," he solemnly said at an inaugural-eve Princeton alumni dinner ("City Welcomes Him," *Evening Star*, 3/4/13).
8. Judith Icke Anderson, p. 117.
9. Except where noted, the following section taken from the accounts of March 4 and 5 by the *Evening Star* and the *Times*.

who said, "Of course it will. We won't be butted off the track by a little weather like this."

At 10:07, Sherman showed up, late. The carriages were called, and the parties stepped outside. With his trademark, "Good bye and good luck," Roosevelt bade farewell to the White House attendants who saw them off. Roosevelt entered first, then Taft. Senators Knox and Lodge followed and sat opposite the pair facing rearwards. The rest of the party joined their carriages according to rank, the Vice President, then Sherman, then the various Cabinet members, carefully by order of precedence, from Secretary of State on down. Accompanied by troopers from Ohio and scores of Civil and Spanish War veterans, the train left for the Capitol.

Ten minutes later Butt stepped to the front of the mansion and called for the limousine. The Pierce-Arrow pulled up and the Captain walked Mrs. Taft to the car. The automobile quickly caught the procession of police and military escorts and eight carriages. That morning Mrs. Roosevelt had given Archie a photograph and a note, "Goodbye, dear Archie. Thank you for everything." Butt wrote, "Can you wonder that my ride to the Capitol with Mrs. Taft seemed a little strained to me?" Mrs. Taft was a wreck of nerves, but "very happy," according to Butt.[10] Behind them the Roosevelt family prepared for their

The photograph here is of the carriage that drove Roosevelt and Taft to the Capitol for Taft's inauguration on March 4, 1909. The night before, a brutal ice storm struck the city. Historians have hooked onto the storm as a metaphor for the Taft presidency. Taft took on the job at a bizarre moment, and not just amidst a snow storm. Think of it as coming upon the crest of a hill. You're pushing hard, getting up to the top, and all of a sudden you're up and over, and careening wildly down the other side. Taft's countrymen frequently became dizzy on the way down. He kept order. (Courtesy Library of Congress)

10. Butt, unpublished letter, 3/5/09.

The outgoing President declined to "ride in the left seat" and skipped town after Taft's inaugural. Mrs. Taft took it for herself. It didn't go over well amongst the right-thinking in town, especially since there was already much discussion over the changes she might make at the White House. No matter, Mrs. Taft rode with her husband in the carriage from the Capitol right up Pennsylvania Avenue. The sun momentarily broke through the clouds to acknowledge it. And where were the motor cars? Not even Taft could change carriage for automobile at this most formal occasion, although one followed closely behind. Mrs. Taft took the Pierce-Arrow limousine to the Capitol that morning, and the couple rode in it together to the ball that night, the first official use of a White House automobile. (Courtesy Library of Congress)

own departure a short time later. As they pulled out in an automobile through the White House gates, Alice put on her best hippopotamus face. "This, darlings, is what is coming after you," she laughed.[11]

The carriages proceeded down Pennsylvania Avenue. Around the corner at the Willard the Yale boys were lined up. A huge blue flag hung from one of the windows with the taunt, "Yale '79," the class that followed Taft's, and by whom he had been kidded the night before for the hazing they received from the class of '78. They sang the Yale song, and Taft replied with a tremendous smile. The sun broke through the clouds for a moment and was just as quickly gone. The storm wasn't over. Those who lined the path did so with snow-blown faces. But there they were, yelling "Hurrah for Taft! Hurrah for Roosevelt!" From inside the carriage Taft and Roosevelt lifted their hats and bowed. "All the way to the Capitol," the *Evening Star* reported, "the cheering continued and showed that a mere matter of weather could not dampen American enthusiasm upon inauguration day."

That morning the House and Senate were wrapping up legislation for Roosevelt's signature. Outside the building angry rumors spread that the inauguration would be moved indoors. Inside, both houses prepared resolutions to move the ceremony to the Senate Chamber. Taft

11. "Mrs. L," p. 140.

reluctantly agreed. Waiting around, Taft and Roosevelt chatted with each other. "The room rang with the laughter of the two men," it was reported. Later, things calmed. At one point Taft and Roosevelt sat beside each other for ten minutes in silence. Then, while Taft relaxed with General Bell, Roosevelt hurried about the room chatting, even once calling to a friend who passed by outside the room. Meanwhile, the diplomatic corps, Cabinet officers, and members of Congress moved into the Senate chambers.

Mrs. Taft didn't let the weather deter her pride, which she carried high on her chin as Archie escorted her down the steps to the Senate chamber. "She was trembling all over," Butt wrote, "and only the prattle of Mrs. Sherman, which seemed to irritate her, brought her to a natural state of nerves." Neither did she become ruffled by the "wag" who whistled the wedding march as she and Archie descended into the room and which was taken up by a few others in the crowd. "I would have fought like a tiger to resent any insult to her then," Butt wrote. Mrs. Taft didn't care. "They're trying to guy us, you think!" she whispered.[12] Archie maintained his dignity, and Mrs. Taft kept her untouchable pride.

William Howard Taft spoke the oath. His mother had two years before warned him against this act. "Uneasy lies the head that wears the crown," she quoted to him. This warning to her son was based upon her insight that "Roosevelt is a good fighter and enjoys it, but the malice of politics would make you miserable. They do not want you as their leader, but cannot find anyone more available."[13] If Taft ever agreed it didn't matter anymore.

It was during this speech that a change was noted in the man. The genial smile went serious, just as the night before at the Yale dinner. During this speech he become presidential. "There was, indeed, an air about President Taft which even those who have known him well have never seen before," noted a reporter.[14] The Taft Smile had no place when swearing to uphold the Constitution. Rather, a "clear, keen voice" and a "serious and almost reverential manner" took hold. "There was no pretense, no humbug, nothing slipshod or ridiculous; the whole thing was so dignified, so effective, so impressive that it seemed not like an inauguration, but like something really important," wrote a surprised reporter. The audience reacted in kind. Taft's final "I do" set off a "spontaneous and enthusiastic" demonstration from the twelve hundred senators, representatives, judges, ambassadors and their wives.

While Taft finished his speech Archie led Mrs. Taft from the gallery to where she would meet her husband for the carriage ride to the White House. The weather calmed so the landau's top was brought down for the new President and First Lady to greet the crowds. Even better, as they started down Pennsylvania Avenue the sun pushed through, brightening the day like a Taft smile. The *Times* noted, "His carriage was open. He kept waving his hat to the thousands on both sides of him, and smiling — not with any large assumption of thick dignity, but very naturally and simply as if he and Mrs. Taft ... were having a good time, and she smiled happily." Were the warnings reported by the ice storm, history's agency for the Taft presidency, gone? Or was that sun-filled break the eye of the storm?

At their approach to the White House the crowds roared in approval. The day had only begun. Not a half hour after he

12. Butt, unpublished letter, 3/5/09.
13. Pringle, pp. 319–320.
14. "Taft Is Sworn In Senate Hall" *NYT*, 3/5/09. See William Manners, *TR and Will: A Friendship That Split the Republican Party*, pp. 72–76, for the view that Taft became a sourpuss upon his inauguration.

arrived to the mansion, at 2:25 Taft walked outside to preside over the parade. Up on the reviewing stand he turned to Sherman. "Put her there," he commanded triumphantly. Sherman clasped hands with the new President, and to great applause the parade began. "Relaxing for the first time since the ceremonies in the Senate chamber, Mr. Taft thus permitted his complete and wholesouled joy to bubble forth unrestrained," went one account. For the next four hours, amidst high winds which buffeted the standards and chilled the crowds, Taft watched more than 20,000 celebrants pass in his honor. Taft was especially proud of one set of marchers, a group of eighty-six musicians who called themselves "Taft's Own." The band had come to play in the cold Washington street all the way from Manila.

The celebration was not closed until after 8:00 to a tremendous fireworks and electric lights display that dazzled the President and First Lady, who watched from the South portico of the White House. At some point during this time, "upon his return to the White House from the reviewing stand," according to the usher Hoover, Taft threw himself into "a large comfortable chair, stretched out to his full length and prefaced his first order with the remark, 'I am President now, and tired of being kicked around.'"[15] Alas, Hoover doesn't tell us what constituted that "first order." Butt's letters mention no such event or mood in the President.

If he tried to relax it couldn't have been for very long. The day's schedule was rigorous. The First Couple were expected at the Pension Building at nine o'clock for the ball. Mrs. Taft's memoirs, written long before Hoover's, described the moment:

> Mr. Taft was reviewing the Inaugural Parade and the last of it did not pass the reviewing stand until after nightfall. He came in, however, in time to exchange greetings with old-time, enthusiastic friends, the members of the Yale class of '78.... When the last of them had wished us Godspeed and said goodbye, we stood, the five of us, — my husband, my three children and I, — alone in the big state dining-room, and tried to realize that, for the first time, the White House was really our Home.... We gazed at each other for a moment, with slightly lost expressions on our faces, and then nature asserted herself in the new President. "Let's go up stairs, my dears, and *sit down!*" said he.
>
> Poor man, he had not experienced the blissful sensation of sitting down since early that morning; so we proceeded out to the elevator, which Charlie, true to his boy nature, had, of course, already learned to operate.... But this time [Mr. Taft] was able, without delay, to reach the best easy-chair in the sitting-room where he remained until I prodded him once more into activity by reminding him that he must get into evening clothes else the Inaugural ball could not take place....[16]

If anyone wished to see Taft's dark side that day, they had to look hard. At the ball the Tafts were openly joyous. When an aide couldn't figure out how to work Mrs. Taft's train, she smiled and quietly told him to spread it widely. Taft laughed with her. Smiles and bows were the order for the rest of the evening, which wasn't over until after midnight, when the pair bade "good bye" to the happy crowd, ascended the big limousine, and returned to the White House.

That evening the first Presidential motorcade was witnessed by crowds of revelers, a mixture of tourists and soldiers who that evening turned Pennsylvania

15. Hoover, pp. 40–41.
16. *Recollections*, pp. 334–336. Mrs. Taft was too excited to be tired. "Not having been taxed so greatly, I was not yet ready to succumb to fatigue; besides I was now eager to roam around the house, to familiarize myself with the mysteries of my new home and to plan the assignment of rooms among various members of the family who were to come to us that very night."

Avenue into an impromptu block party. On the drive to the Pension building, Taft reflected with satisfaction on the long day and the ceremonies that were held in the Senate, which he felt was "more dignified." He told Butt, "I do not regret anything save the disappointment of the crowd."[17]

* * *

Whatever not "being kicked" around anymore meant, on March 5 it did not include playing golf. Taft would have to wait until the end of the month to make his way to the links. That March was crowded. Starting at 9:30 of his first morning in office, a crowd of congressmen and their guests awaited downstairs, each to show off to hometown supporters. At 10:30 Taft and Sherman stepped outside to review a New York regiment whose arrival was delayed by the weather. The review of troops might not have warranted the President's special attention except that Governor Hughes personally requested it.

Taft spent the day shaking some 4,000 hands. Crowds wandered outside the White House grounds, peering in through windows, and otherwise making a happy city. A President of 1909 was within the reach of the people. Up until an assassination attempt upon Truman and, later, Kennedy's murder, Presidents freely walked the streets, rode horses and otherwise mingled with the public. Things weren't quite as bad as during Washington's time when he complained of strangers looking into his wife's bedroom, but the president's mansion was still accessible to stray visitors. "No crowned ruler upon the earth is so much the victim of the inquisitive mob as is the President of the United States," wrote a 1909 commentator.[18]

The most important White House visitors of the day were Republican members of the House Ways and Means Committee, led by Chairman Sereno Payne, who extended an honest welcome to the new President with wishes for good relations and "harmony" between the two branches of the government.[19] Payne pledged to submit to the House a tariff bill as soon as the bell rang at the March 15 start to the special session called by Taft. The President thanked Payne and said he hoped the bill could be signed by June 1st at the latest, in order to have it in operation a good month before the July start of the new fiscal year.

17. Butt, unpublished letter, 3/5/09.
18. "The Fierce Light That Will Beat Upon Taft," *Evening Star*, 2/28/09.
19. "Taft Shakes Hands of 4,000 Callers," *Evening Star*, 3/5/09.

12

Motoring Manifest

In his 1908 speech to the Automobile Club of America, Ambassador Jusserand made space on history's shelf for the automobile. Locomotion, he explained, is the stuff of legend and history:

> This the men before us could do only in their imagination. The Orientals had King Solomon's carpet, Ruggiero had his hippogriff, Rabelais had his movable road, we have our automobiles, and we equal them all.

The members of the ACA needed no convincing. The automobilists knew they were onto something. They were making history and proud to be there. Automotive writers regularly turned to past dreams of rapid transportation for vindication of the automobile. One article on limousines traced the body style's origins from the Romans through to Napoleon and consecrated its motorized form as the apex of an ageless ambition.[1]

Washington's Union Station was inaugurated in 1907. It was not just the largest railroad station in the world. With its Diocletian interior, gold-plated ceiling, and seven hundred foot marble front, it was the most splendid. Architect Daniel Burnham aimed to "make no little plans." The front arches and grand interior was all Rome, the great civilization Americans had recreated in the New World. The Columbus Statue out front celebrated the hemisphere's first ambassador. The building itself was about the present.

Within the five score and seven years of the Capital City's presence the nation's map was much changed. With rail and telegraph spanning the continent, time itself succumbed to man's dominion. God's time, or that of the cows, no longer sufficed a people who could share a day's experience across 3,000 miles. Wall Street no longer slept alone. The people sensed this change. The law accommodated it. The railroads worked it. The telegraph and telephone brought it. Burnham set it in stone. Above Union Station's Roman arches and looking down upon the statue of Columbus were engraved words of faith in this extraordinary moment. The expression was self-awareness, not self-congratulation. Each declaration was followed by a biblical quotation to show that God himself willed it so: "Thou hast put all things under his feet" and "The desert shall rejoice and blossom as the rose."

> *Fire, greatest of discoveries,*
> *Enabling men to live in various climates,*

1. Cover story, *Automobile*, 1/5/11, pp. 3–7.

Use many foods, and compel the
forces of nature to do his work
Electricity, carrier of light and power,

Devourer of time and space, bearer
of human speech over land and sea,
Greatest servant of man, itself unknown...

The old mechanic arts, controlling new
Forces, build new highways for goods
and men, override the ocean, and make
the very ether carry human thought [2]

The celebration of the conquest of time and space — if without mention of those pesky automobiles, and the not-yet-famous Wright brothers. If the politics of 1907 disregarded those two innovations the references to "highways" and "new Forces" could not be misunderstood. Were Burnham's monument to human advance erected a few years hence, the automobile and its avian cousin would have played equal to the telegraph and the wireless.

* * *

Hardly two weeks into the new administration, the President's Aide-De-Camp was worn out. "In less than a week I have been to New York or vicinity twice," Archie complained on March 21, "and both trips have been nasty ones from the standpoint of fatigue." What prompted this observation was that the President had that evening unexpectedly and summarily announced another trip to New York leaving at eight the next morning. The Captain unhappily canceled his engagements and tried to find rest that night however he could. Of the President, he wrote, "He has marvelous powers of physical endurance."[3]

Butt's first notes on President Taft complain of his inability to keep appointments. "He moves very slowly, and I defy anyone in the world to hurry him. He makes engagements of which no one, not even his secretary, has any notion, and yet he expects everybody about him to be cognizant of the fact and to have everything in readiness for him." This clumsiness with conflicting schedules and late meetings had been overcome, in Butt's eyes, after only two weeks. The President now charged straight through his days. Archie wrote, "and he keeps one engagement after another with wonderful promptitude and with little evidence of wear on the nervous tissue."[4]

Butt's March 21 letter is the source of several Taft legends. Much misconstrued has been Taft's spontaneous napping, be it mid-conversation, at the opera, church, or over dinner. He is understood now to have suffered from a sleep disorder. Whatever the cause, his napping was, at worst, not detrimental, and at best, useful, to Taft. He otherwise ran his Presidency in high gear. His Congresses thrice worked long into the Summer. He entertained as much as any President before him. He was the most traveled executive up to his time. He certainly walked more golf courses than any, as well. This ability (or propensity) to sleep anytime, anywhere, especially on trains and motor rides, allowed the man to keep to a velocity that stranded those around him. Jack Hammond wrote of "his extraordinary ability to work long hours ... to finish a task. His power of concentration and of excluding the nonessentials was almost unique." Hammond attributed

2. One stanza, not reproduced here, is dedicated to the farmer, for whom apologies were ever requisite. Others are dedicated to women, philosophy, art, and politics. See Hofstadter, Chapter I, "The Agrarian Myth and Commercial Realities" for the period's political imagery of the farm.
3. Butt, 3/21/09, p. 17.
4. Butt, 3/10/ 09, p. 3 and 3/21/09, p. 17. Hammond wrote, "He was rarely on time for appointments, not because he meant to be late, but because he found himself interested in whatever he was doing at the moment and unable to break away" (Hammond, p. 547).

Taft's sleeping and eating habits to compensation for it. Hammond was dead-on that Taft exercised an uncommon ability to get work done, to meet the task at hand, be it rear platform greetings at "an unconscionable hour in the morning" followed by an early start "cheerfully" set upon the following day, to prepare a speech, or to manage a crisis.

When Taft spoke to his wife of himself as "Apollo-like," he was only half-jesting. His bulk belied a vital physique. In 1911, he descended 1,100 feet into a South Dakota goldmine where he was shown a stack of 125 pound gold bricks worth $30,000 each. "He picked up one of the precious bars with the greatest ease," wrote an amazed reporter. "Senator Gamble tried to do likewise, but was not so successful."[5] Taft took exercise deliberately for weight loss, and when he didn't he bloated. When he did it was vigorous. Butt was surprised after his first horseback ride with Taft. He wrote, "I must say I felt some disgust, for I had been accustomed to ride with Mr. Roosevelt, and I felt it to be a great comedown to jog along with Mr. Taft. I was mistaken in my man, however, for he was out for exercise, and he gave me as much as I wanted." A regular Taft habit was to motor a few miles somewhere and walk back. One trek caused Hammond, who was not accustomed to Taft's strong gate, to gaze "longingly at the street cars passing," Butt wrote. "The President had dropped into a long regular stride and Mr. Hammond had a hard time keeping his short little legs moving fast enough to keep up with the Chief."[6] Golfing in those unsedated days, too, was exertion, so that favorite indulgence kept him in shape. Additionally, and to the shock of unsuspecting hosts and the ladies of the ballroom, Taft was a superb dancer. In Panama, the girls were amazed and thrilled by his light feet. In Atlanta, Taft refused to leave the floor. "I can't leave now," he announced between dances, "please have the train held." He danced past midnight, leaving only after he had charmed all the wives of the local notables.[7]

Butt's March 21 letter also described a White House dinner that demonstrated Taft's earnestness, his levity, his politics, and his naps. Dinner was taken at seven-thirty with Taft, Butt, Edwards, and Cannon. The party rose from the table at nine and, as was the custom, took to another room for a cigar and a glass, neither of which the President indulged in. The dinner and conversation were pleasant, especially to Cannon, who enjoyed himself past the welcome hour. Not that it was getting late: Taft had a 10:00 appointment with a Senator. After that meeting, Taft returned to the others who were listening to *The Merry Widow* on the Victrola. "The President at once began to waltz around the room by himself," wrote Butt, "and I was astonished to see the ease and grace with

5. "President Taft Visits Gold Mine," *NYT*, 10/22/11. In late 1905 and pushing 320 lbs. on the scales, he wrote, "I am convinced that this undue drowsiness is due to the accumulation of flesh ... were I appointed to the bench I fear I could not keep awake in my present condition" (Taft to Helen Taft, 10/9/05, per Pringle, p. 286). The only relevant question is, did his weight and napping detract from his performance as President? The author thinks not. See "Taft and Pickwick: Sleep Apnea in the White House," by J.G. Sotos, Chest, in press 2003.

6. Butt, 3/7/09, p. 2 and unpublished passage, 2/27/10. Taft rode for exercise strictly. Hammond said he "never really enjoyed it" (Hammond, p. 540).

7. For dancing in Panama, see *Recollections of Full Years*, pp. 287–288 and in Atlanta, "Taft Kept On Dancing," *NYT*, 1/18/09. "The women were charmed with Judge Taft as a dancer. They say that he keeps perfect step, knows how to protect his partner, and is surprisingly nimble on his feet. 'To dance with him,' one partner said, 'you would never think he weighed so much.'" Taft wrote of the party, "The champagne flowed very freely and when I came away at half past twelve its effects were quite noticeable on some of the men, and, I am sorry to say, on some of the women" (Taft to Helen Taft, 1/17/09). 12:30? Was it a fib? Or did the papers exaggerate to say he danced past two A.M.?

The only other place President Taft spent more time than on trains, automobiles, and golf courses was the banquet table. Here he sits through somebody's speech. Taft could take in three, sometimes more banquets a day on his hectic New York trips. Butt said Taft perfected the banquet speech. It wasn't always easy for Butt. Of one banquet he complained, "Imagine presenting four hundred Austro Hungarians by name...." (Courtesy Library of Congress)

which he did it." Cannon jumped in, while Butt and Edwards sat watching, stunned by the outrageous scene of the two most powerful men in the country performing a midnight waltz, or, in Cannon's case, a "a sort of ragtime shuffle," right there in the House of Presidents.

Cannon finally laid into the purpose of his visit. "Now, Mr. President," he said, as they sat down, "let me look you straight in the eye and ask a favor." Taft knew what was coming. "Look me in the eye, always, for it makes it easier to deny you anything," he replied. Cannon leaned against the President's chair and laid out his plan on behalf of some man from Indiana. Taft refused because he already promised insurgent Senator Beveridge not to deal patronage in that particular direction. Beveridge had played that card quicker than Cannon. As Cannon made his case, Taft fell asleep. Butt did not record Cannon's reaction. Likely, as Butt described other similar scenes, Taft awoke momentarily and picked up the conversation exactly where he had left it. Taft would be recharged, and Butt and Edwards and whoever else was visiting would struggle to stay awake while the President carried on into the night, sometimes past two in the morning. Butt at first thought the President's naps were a result of a "phlegmatic temperament."[8] After a 14,000 mile train ride across the nation during which the

8. Butt, 3/21/09, p. 17.

President gave hundreds of speeches, shook thousands of hands, and woke up in a different place practically every day, Butt learned it was beyond lethargy. It was survival. Taft kept the pace for four years.

It was too much for Archie. "The President has a constitution of iron, apparently," he wrote in June 1911, following a series of New York trips, some of which included two lunches, three dinners, and more speeches and meetings in a single day. "When and where he will break down I do not know, but I do not see how he keeps up the pace as he does," he lamented. "Since returning I have been in a state of collapse, but that has not prevented him from calling upon me for golf every afternoon and dinner every evening. One evening I sent the motor car back, saying that I was ill and could not come to dinner."[9]

Butt's March 21, 1909, letter is also source of the legend that Taft shied from the public. Butt noted that the President didn't bother to wave to the crowds that gathered by his train, and that he went straight from the rail to the motor car. "What an opportunity he is missing!" complained Jimmy Sloan. "For God's sake, Captain, get him to lift his hat when the people yell, for if he don't they will stop yelling when he will want them most." Roosevelt was on both their minds. "It's alright, Jimmie [sic]," Butt said. "He will get shaken down after a while, and things will all come alright." "Never," Sloan said. "The other man has educated the public to know what to expect, and this one will be a dead card if he don't change." Butt wrote, "It was no use to argue with Jimmie [sic]. He, too, had been too long under the magic wand of Roosevelt to see things in any other way."[10]

Taft did learn to wave, to tip his hat. He learned to stand in the back of rail car, shake his fist, and spit out a stock speech. He learned that a president was better off in the grandstand than in a private box at the baseball stadium. He learned that a picture is worth a thousand words, including the moving ones. He learned that four thousand handshakes in a day were not just expected but necessary elements of the presidency. Butt frequently led the President through many of these acts of public relations, to which Taft was not otherwise inclined.

Another legend unfairly stuck to Taft is uncertainty. For every major decision in his life Taft convened his wife and his brothers, in person or by letter. He wrote each extensively, spilling complaint, plans, and the standing emotion. Mrs. Taft understood it. Of his letters she wrote, "I get the impression that I was made the victim of his thinking processes since he poured into them all the politics and the turmoil of the hour...." A 1910 news article described his thinking-out-loud style of correspondence: "It is to [his brother] Horace that the President directs his letters in times of stress and strain, and it is said that he emerges from composing such a letter with a smile and an expression of relief upon his face."[11]

Butt's job was similar. He was variously late night companion, social coordinator, press agent, military aide, golf partner, and sounding board. Butt was not a crutch — he was a walking stick. As with others around him, Taft used Butt for his own purposes. Taft could be brutally selfish this way, and Butt was among the victims. "I think he is a more selfish man than I had suspected," Archie wrote after a long trip, and, on another occasion, "He has very little consideration for those around him. He wants them to be comfortable and to enjoy themselves provided

9. Butt, 6/11/11, p. 675.
10. Butt, 3/21/09, pp. 18–19.
11. *Recollections*, p. 302 and "The Most Intimate Friends of President Taft," *NYT*, 5/29/10.

it does not upset his plans.... I don't suppose he is wrong in this, for a President cannot...."[12] A man does not become President — or, in the case of Taft, and Chief Justice — without the ego of the artist for whom the production is greater than the elements.

History has noted all the conflict and emotion of William Howard Taft. Rarely are we given so clear a look beneath the presidential armor. Not just in Taft's letters do we see his "thinking processes." Butt wrote his letters "for posterity," an historical record that would one day "be brought to light for the vindication of this good man whom I serve now."[13] Uniquely, the Butt letters give us a running view of the President's days. The only filter is Butt's own judgements and prejudices, principally of an ongoing comparison between Roosevelt and Taft and his conflicting loyalties to both. To read Butt's letters is to read the almost daily swings of his own and his subject's moods and utterances. Just as in his March 21 letter, in which Taft is in one paragraph phlegmatic and in the next a dervish, in a December 1911 letter, Taft goes from confidently predicting his reelection to being admonished by Mabel Boardman for "showing his depression" over it.[14]

Both emotions were real. We only know about them because they were recorded. We can take from it what we will, but were we to visit a newspaper the next day we would have no idea that the President was anything but on top. That December day in 1911, Taft dismissed five military officers and denied clemency to a convicted banker. Had he written his brothers or had Butt reported on some deep agony over those decisions it would have been added to the general catalog of a despairing, uncertain president. Taft's reputation has suffered from our proximity to him. Through Butt and his own revealing expressions, we are party to the naps, the gout of his ankle, and his so very human moods.

* * *

Archie and the Secret Service agents were not alone to suffer Taft's state of perpetual motion. Starting on the Fourth of March of 1909, things back at the White House stables got busy and would remain so for the next four years. Taft's incredible mobility came of a deliberate application of a new technology to serve his office and his people. This supposedly "conservative" and lethargic man made use of everything new, from a novel air conditioning system to radio, movies, telegraph, telephones, and the world's fastest ships, to airplanes and motor cars. He was unafraid of a new idea, yet he never allowed the new to detract from that which worked in the past. Tradition, too, had to make sense. Taft's management of White House etiquette was exemplary of his views towards the old and the new. He ignored protocol that diluted effective diplomacy and upheld that which leant to it.[15]

Roosevelt broke tradition. Taft amended it. Roosevelt broke rules. Taft

12. Butt, 11/14/09, p. 205, 7/11/11, p. 694.
13. This very quotation serves as an example of how Butt can be misconstrued. The fuller context regards the break with Roosevelt. Complaining about Taft, Butt wrote, "These letters are written for posterity, not for the President, and some day they will be brought to light for the vindication of this good man whom I serve now, but [Taft] does not mention the fact that all this could have been avoided by acknowledging openly and candidly the debt of gratitude he owed his predecessor." Butt wrote here in both praise and criticism of Taft — which at this time came of Butt's conflicting loyalties to Roosevelt and Taft (Butt, 9/17/10, p. 514). The published Butt papers have the additional filter of considerable editing.
14. Butt, 12/29/11, pp. 802–803.
15. See "Taft Tramples Formality: Makes the Simplest Kind of a Call on Justice Lurton," *NYT*, 1/3/10. Butt wrote that an unplanned presidential visit to the incoming Justice's hotel "took away the breath of some of the old-timers...." (Butt, 1/3/10, p. 249). Taft was out walking and suddenly recalled that the Justice

amended them. Taft disbanded Roosevelt's commissions for the very simple reason that a law required it. As the former members of the Fine Arts Council whined to the press, Taft went to work on Congress for a duly authorized commission.[16] Taft ordered his world by definitions of principle, law, and convenience. His insistence on this type of regularity led to trouble, of course. He sometimes confused the law with principle, or he betrayed a principle because of a law, but those instances were rare.[17] Taft's harshest critics accused him of betraying Roosevelt's conservation policies over legal technicalities. This talk was backwards, but in a day when constructionist courts were in bad favor with reformers, the charges that Taft favored the law over the people stuck. Taft could himself stretch a law or two. He beat upon Congress to create and fund his Tariff Board, for example, but Congress authorized it only to investigate the cost of labor and production overseas in order to identify unfair duties imposed on American exports.[18] In 1911, Taft went ahead and used the Board's findings to recommend Congressional action on the domestic tariff. The distinction between why the Board investigated and what Taft did with its findings was, indeed, extra-legal. He got away with it, although progressives never credited him for the artifice.

Taft's views of tradition fit into these categories in that general pattern: principle above all, so far as the law allows, but convenience first if legal and principled. His attitude towards automobiles is case in point. Taft used his cars for pleasure and convenience. Nevertheless, the motors also served the greater purposes of safety and efficiency, from which he took the fullest advantage. Safety came of the motor's agility, especially from a security point of view; efficiency was of its ability to devour the map. Just as importantly, *not* using automobiles would have violated these standards. When tradition called, such as at his and his successor's inauguration, it was carriages. Otherwise it was motors all the time, a break in tradition. And, quite frequently, it was at illegal speeds in those motors that Taft found joyfully convenient.

* * *

On March 14, 1909, newspapers picked up an enthusiastic wire story,

> The "White House Stable" is no more. The feed bins have given place to the gasoline tank. From the pegs which formerly supported the harness now hang

15. (*cont.*) had arrived: "There was a visible stir everywhere...." The *Times* report noted, "When the clerk had recovered from his surprise" he advised the President that Lurton was out. "Too Bad," said Taft calmly. "Please tell him that I called." Another example was the visit by the Duke of Connaught to New York. It was considered by all but the President a monumental slight that the Duke not only left Washington off the schedule, he invited the Secretary of State to New York. Unmoved by calls to anger, Taft stepped back and let the British ambassador manage a polite recovery. Taft was a gracious host to the King's uncle who went away thrilled by the reception. Another precedent was broken that day: the Duke, one of the highest ranking of England to visit the country, was greeted by the White House motor cars (See Butt, 1/23/1912, p. 814; greeting the Duke at Union Station was one of Archie's proudest moments).
16. Taft took the ire of interested parties, including architect Cass Gilbert, a close friend, to whom he replied that "the action of Congress made [Roosevelt's] order so nugatory that the only thing left to do was to revoke it.... I am strongly in favor of [the Fine Arts council's] existence and its exercising authority. I shall have to take my own way to bring this about, since it is a matter of considerable delicacy" (Taft to Gilbert, 6/25/09, Brown, Glenn, *1860–1930, Memories, by Glenn Brown*, W.F. Roberts Co., Washington, D.C., 1931; see also "Roosevelt Board Abolished," *NYT*, 5/26/09 and *Memories*, by Glen Brown, pp. 382–386).
17. Probably the worst was his decision to sign a bill providing for free passage of U.S. coastal ships through the Panama canal in violation of the Hay-Pauncefote treaty. Taft rationalized his decision with a bent legal interpretation that concluded that the treaty was not abridged. Elihu Root was astonished (see Pringle, pp. 646–653).
18. See "Mr. Taft's Tariff Board," *NYT* editorial, 9/17/09.

inner tubes and casings. Exit the coachman, enter the chauffeur. Ring out the "hay motor," ring in the steam engine.[19]

Sterling, of the White Company, according to the article, was "delegated" the task by the President himself. The thousand dollars a month forage and harness expenses that had kept Roosevelt's mounts and carriages in good order went now to gasoline, grease, and valves. Sterling didn't contain his efforts to the garage. The day of the inauguration, the local White dealer, Dewey Garage, ran ads in Washington newspapers. The copy was standard White material with Taft in mind. No advantage was going to be lost when there were 100,000 witnesses around to see that most famous large man riding around in their car. First came the usual jingle:

The White Steamer
Is the Most Desirable Car

All very well there. Now a little slice of Taft:

> *1.— Those in whose judgement the nation has the most confidence have selected the White Steamer for their personal use, thereby stamping it as the "correct car."*

Add a little patriotism to the mix....

> *2.— The White is the only car of distinctively American design. All other makes are copies or imitations of some foreign product. Who will say that the foreign designer is more capable than the American engineer of designing an automobile for use on American roads?*

...a nice jab at foreign competition, as well as at the ALAM, the Selden patent holders. Then on to explain why it's all a good thing....

> *3.— Steam is the world's standard motive power, and the steam engine, as especially developed by the White Company, is ideally adapted for automobile work. The White is the only car which is noiseless, odorless, smokeless, and free from vibration. All speeds are obtained without the shifting of gears, and the directions for operating it are summed up in the phrase: "Just open the throttle and steer."*

Now the sale:

> *4.— No matter where you use your White Car— in Europe, in our colonial possessions, or in any part of this country— you will find a branch office or an agency of the White Company ready to serve you.*[20]

A gentleman's agreement between the White House and the Pierce-Arrow and White companies disallowed direct application of what Butt had originally feared would be necessary, to "permit the makers to advertise the fact that their cars are being used for the White House." If residual benefit came of the general knowledge that the President used Pierce-Arrow and White automobiles, so be it. But there should be no direct manipulation of this endorsement. Needless to say, down to the speedometer, manufacturers latched on to the presidential automobiles.

One exploitation came in an advertisement by the Klaxon Company, makers of auto horns. Beneath a widely circulated photograph of the Taft family in the official White steamer, rang (honked?),

THE PRESIDENT OF THE UNITED STATES
USES THE KLAXON
ON HIS OFFICIAL WHITE STEAMER

The White House protested. F.H. Lovell of the company replied that Butt had reviewed the ad and had not objected to use of a "public photograph," that he had only asked that a letter he wrote not be published. "We will, of course, respect your wishes," Lovell wrote the Captain,

19. See "Motoring," *Evening Star*, 3/14/09 and "White House Stable Now a Garage," *NYT*, 3/14/09 and *Vehicle Dealer*, March 1909, p. 262.
20. Advertisement, *Evening Star*, 3/4/09.
21. Klaxon advertisement in *Life* magazine, per FH Lovell to FC Carpenter, 1/25/10, Series 5, case file 2071.

"although it is a matter of sincere regret that we cannot use the letter as it would make a very strong 'ad'; especially as it was so apparently unsolicited."[22] Lovell flatly told Taft's secretary that the company would run the ad once more.

At least one other Butt letter was circulated in proof of a product's superiority, one that made a fine display on the front window to the White Company's New York dealership. A certain W.R. Mason, who the previous November tried to sell an automobile to Taft, happened by the store in May and was "shocked" to find a letter from Captain Butt posted for all to see. Mason wrote the President,

> I have no earthly interest in the matter, but ... in passing the store of the Company I am obliged to say that I was rather shocked by seeing in the window the letter.... While reading the letter two gentlemen stopped and one of them said, "Well for God's sake look at that, Mr. Butt was probably paid well for that and I suppose he will be recommending some tailor or shoemaker and a lot of breakfast foods." ... I would hate to think that it is to be sent around the country. The "White" company is to be commended for using such letter as an advertisement, *but*, they must not make our President ridiculous."[23]

No reply seems to have come from the White House, nor further complaints from Mason. White, anyway, announced that its 1911 line of "M-M" steamers would include the "Presidential Pattern" touring car. Pierce-Arrow seems to have kept quiet on its White House cars, although certain of its elaborate, color ads depicted the automobiles in front of a mansion that looked curiously like 1600 Pennsylvania Avenue. Both companies otherwise let their famous Washington relations speak for themselves.[24]

The most egregious use of the President's image came from the makers of the Jones Speedometer. Atop a full-page ad in the May 1911, issue of *Motor Age*, and wrapped around an official portrait of Taft and facsimiles of the White House and the Capitol building, was the caption, "*President Taft Uses a Jones.... Naturally the Nation's Chief Executive wants the best speedometer that money can buy.... That is why President Taft uses the JONES— the National Speedometer.*"[25] Below was a copy of a famous portrait of the Taft family taken at Augusta in a loaned White steamer. Worst of all, the official presidential steamer did not employ the product. The company apologized to the White House:

> ...we regret very much that the President takes exception to the fact that his name and picture has been used in advertising the Jones Speedometer. We regret very much to learn that the President does not use the Jones Speedometer, for it is not our intention or practice to print misleading advertisements. We had presumed that our advertising agents were sure of the facts before stating that the President was using the Jones Speedometer. The inclosed photograph of the President in a car having on it a Jones Speedometer, and having hanging from the rear spring a Jones Speedometer police protection tag led our advertising agents to believe that Mr. Taft was a user of our product.[26]

22. FH Lovell to FC Carpenter, 1/25/10.
23. WR Mason to Taft, 5/20/09.
24. "White Steam and Gasoline Cars for 1911," *Horseless Age*, 5/11/10, pp. 730–732. Some years later Pierce-Arrow ran advertisements in France entitled, "La voiture des Présidents."
25. Jones Speedometer advertisement, *Motor Age*, May 1911, p. 51. The company also advertised that the Bureau of Standards had "indorsed" its product through tests of its accuracy. The White House cars used Warner speedometers, which may have been part of the frustration, for A.P. Warner was one of the greatest promoters around (for his wonderful story, see "The Man Who Invented MPH," by S.F. Welty, *Motor Guide*, Feb. 58, p. 45).
26. GL Holmes to CD Hilles, 6/1/11.

13

Tariff Soup

The tariff is an abomination, and if there is anything that makes a man feel in favor of free trade it is the attempt to secure the passage of a protected tariff bill.
—William Howard Taft[1]

Taft's first business was the tariff. He was pledged to it by the party platform of 1908:

> The Republican Party declares unequivocally for a revision of the tariff by a special session of Congress immediately following the inauguration of the next President, and commends the steps already taken to this end in the work assigned to the appropriate committees of Congress, which are now investigating the operation and effect of existing schedules.
>
> In all tariff legislation the true principle of protection is best maintained by the imposition of such duties as will equal the difference between the cost of production at home and abroad, together with a reasonable profit to American industries.

Taft was to insist upon that last sentence like a canon. Besides, he actually believed it. What was to be forgotten over the next four years, however, was what followed next.[2] Taft alone seemed to have remembered the text:

> We favor the establishment of maximum and minimum rates to be administered by the President under limitations fixed in the law, the maximum to be available to meet discriminations by foreign countries against American goods entering their markets and the minimum to represent the normal measure of protection at home; the aim and purpose of the Republican policy being not only to preserve, without excessive duties, that security against foreign competition to which American manufacturers, farmers, and producers are entitled, but also to maintain the high standard of living of the wage earners of this country who are the most direct beneficiaries of the protective system. Between the United States and the Philippines we believe in a free interchange of products with such limitations as to sugar and tobacco as will afford adequate protection to domestic interests.[3]

If that bores you, welcome to 1909. A strong majority of the population had voted for this language. The mandate was clear, or as clear as the 4,112 words of the Republican Platform, had anyone bothered

1. Taft to Mrs. Charles P. Taft, 7/18/09.
2. Later, the best critics could do was to complain that Taft kept his promises. "He is constantly talking of party pledges..." complained the *American Review of Reviews* in April 1910 (p. 396).
3. *National Party Platforms, 1840–1972*, p. 158.

to read it. Far more interesting to the popular press than to uphold the pledge upon which the President was elected was whether Nelson Aldrich or Joe Cannon had their dirty fingers in the mix. Forget that Taft and his party and its leaders won the election. What mattered, and what was interesting to reporters, was what "is is." Does "revision" mean up or down? Is the high price of eggs on the streets of New York because of the tariff? What evil lurks in the Congressional Record?

Taft went into the March special session of Congress with mandate ringing in his ears and "shoot" in his eyes. That January he wrote to Kansas City *Star* newsman Col. W.R. Nelson, "I believe the people are with me, and before I get through I think I will have downed Cannon, and Aldrich too, if Aldrich stands in the way, or else will have broken up the party and turned the matter over to the Democrats to make fools of themselves, as they doubtless would."[4] Nevertheless, Taft's overall strategy to tariff reform was normalcy. He knew the 1897 Dingley tariff to be excessive, yet he recognized how disruptive tariff making could be, to economics and, especially, to politics.

The tariff broke Grover Cleveland twice. With the exception of Dingley, which was handled magnificently by McKinley, the tariff ruined the Republican Party every time it messed with it. A decade later, Dingley, too, was tripping up its creators. William McKinley, whose 1896 election brought on Dingley, later hinted at reform but only after his 1900 re-election. Roosevelt had some ideas but was scared away. His re-election was more important, and after that there were other distractions and debts to pay by laying off the tariff. Taft went into it knowing the history and knowing there'd be hell to pay. Although he hadn't imagined the cost, he was committed to the reform. His condition was that the party's stand on the tariff plank mustn't bring down the rest of the platform. The price Taft paid for the tariff was adjusted for the rest of the platform.

* * *

Arkansas was one of the first states to adopt the 16th Amendment, under the theory, openly stated on the floor of its legislature, that the income tax would shift the burden to New Yorkers.[5] This was the general Democratic complaint against the tariff, that it punished consumers and protected producers. The party's mantra on tariffs was the "revenue basis," which translated politically into lower prices for consumers and markets abroad for farmers. Otherwise, particularly coming from William Jennings Bryan, the tariff benefited only the rich.[6] The party's solution was to pay for the government without taxing imports that competed with monopolies. The distinction between a "free trade" and a "revenue basis" tariff was impossibly obscure.

Republicans wanted protection, protection, protection, which stuck like a tattoo through the 1920s and led to the disastrous Hawley-Smoot Act of 1930. The great Republican illusion was that the protective tariff guarded prosperity. It's not easy to rid oneself of generations of self-delusion, starting, in this case, with Alexander Hamilton. The tariff they worshiped was a shadow thrown from the party's electoral success and the country's unrivaled growth. In a magnificently researched and brilliant refutation of protection, Democratic Senator Owen of Oklahoma laid it out plainly (and largely) in

4. Taft to WR Nelson, 1/5/09.
5. "The Income Tax," *NYT* editorial, 7/14/11.
6. See Democratic Platform of 1908.

the Congressional Record, "OUR NATIONAL PROSPERITY IS NOT DUE TO A PROHIBITIVE TARIFF, BUT IN SPITE OF IT."[7]

The Democrats tried to show that the "revenue basis" tariff would not, as Nelson Aldrich contended, increase foreign competition, and that reduced duties would cut into profits, not sales. Both sides pointed to the various 19th century tariffs to prove this or that. Each side desperately tried to link past economic patterns to the tariff, especially the depression of the 1890s. All that proved was that the economics of tariffs were disastrous when combined with the dumb monetary policy. The Panic of 1893 came not of the tariff but of the "Free Silver" movement, the intent of which was to lower the value of money, that is, to spread wealth through inflation (and literally turn the silver loads of Nevada and Colorado into gold). "Soft money" would kill an economy regardless of the tariff. Free Silver's victory came in 1890 with a Republican law that mandated government purchase of silver, which, of course, depleted the government's reserves of gold. Along with an excessive tariff, the economy was poisoned by the free flow of silver. The Republicans lost the election of 1892 to this combination, and the Democrats subsequently lost with Bryan over its threat. Bryan's political assent followed his "Cross of Gold" speech at the 1896 Democratic convention. While J.P. Morgan stabilized the economy by securing the country's reserves of yellow metal, Bryan screamed, "You shall not crucify mankind upon a cross of gold."[8]

Behind every tariff argument was an emotion. Protection meant the trusts, or free trade meant economic ruin. Tariff opponents were as guilty of believing in its magic powers as its supporters, in this case to enrich the rich and impoverish the poor. Low tariff partisans were joined by social reformers who condemned the wealthy classes. Insurgency in the Republican Party was propelled by the tariff, and it became the emotional line between the party's growing East-West divide. Although the progressives later stumbled on tariff reform, for them, in 1909, compassion was measured by one's tariff views: the lower the duties on milled cotton the more you cared for the farm and the masses. In today's language, the tariff killed babies and starved the elderly. Reflecting its odd conglomeration of Republicans, reformers, and the generally if unspecifically discontent, the best the Progressive Party of 1912 could manage on the issue was to call for the defense of the working man through a protective tariff, and in practically the same language as the Republican platform of 1908. Labor went both ways on the issue, calling for protection of jobs but taking offense at profits. Socialists wanted gobs of protection but only when "the people" owned business. A fine example of the mixed tariff lines was a march by 15,000 workers at Washington in April 1909 in support of higher duties on hosiery. The National Association of Manufacturers happily watched the spectacle while paying rail passage for the protestors.[9] The only consistent principle in tariff politics was hypocrisy.

What all factions failed to see was that it was liberty, justice, and equality that led to prosperity and the American dream, not high or low tariffs. While the tariff was a legitimate expression of self-government, it was the protection of property, the rights of man as administered in a fair and free system of laws and justice, and a union of states brokered by a central guiding

7. *CR*, 6/15/09, p. 3291. Owen's dissertation went 67 pages.
8. *Bryan*, by M.R. Werner, 1929, p. 75.
9. "Regiments of Women to Storm Congress," *NYT*, 4/9/09.

force upon which the nation was so successfully built. The tariff had its role in the development of the nation, but nothing to such extent as the one claimed for and the other against it. The tariff was a moderating, not a guiding force. It was, however, far and away the biggest issue of the day. Such were the very crossed lines on the politics of the tariff. When it came to actually making one it got real confusing.

* * *

Taft viewed the tariff as an equitable form of taxation. Grover Cleveland called it the "communism of pelf."[10] To Taft, Cleveland's talk of the tariff as a moral issue was the devil's tongue. The tariff— if reasonable, that oh-so-gray term — was just. Taft was a moderate protectionist who believed that the Dingley tariff had worked but now needed a mild laxative. He spoke of downward revision to reflect economic changes, but not a revision that would disrupt, or cause "embarrassment" of business.[11] He asked for revision, not revolution.

Here lies an important component to tariff revision that escapes the normal interpretations of tariffs as either high or low. The tariff operated laterally as well as vertically. Just as the automobile industry clamored for recognition with a duty of its own, the various tariff schedules represented distinct categories of the economy — or successful lobbies. Different duties could be placed on different grades of cotton, for example, with various effects upon industry, importers, and consumers, depending on how the item was categorized. When the Republicans of 1908, Taft included, spoke of the need for lateral revision to reflect changes in business "conditions," it was a legitimate claim.

Taft's error was that of his party, that the tariff alone defended prosperity. Taft knew, for example, that free trade was productive of international relations and peace. He also knew that the government needed funding, and to cut the tariff would lead to further deficits that were piling up following the 1907 panic. Taking the broad view to the issue, his solution was a mix of ideas and laws wrapped around a "scientific tariff," one to be based on facts and not politics. In his Inaugural Address, and as only he could say it, Taft explained his tariff intentions:

> A matter of most pressing importance is the revision of the tariff. In accordance with the promises of the platform upon which I was elected, I shall call Congress into extra session to meet on the 15th day of March, in order that consideration may be at once given to a bill revising the Dingley Act. This should secure an adequate revenue and adjust the duties in such a manner as to afford to labor and to all industries in this country, whether of the farm, mine or factory, protection by tariff equal to the difference between the cost of production abroad and the cost of production here.... It is thought that there has been such a change in conditions since the enactment of the Dingley Act, *drafted on a similarly protective principle*, that the measure of the tariff above stated will permit the reduction of rates in certain schedules and will require the advancement of few, if any[12] [italics added].

The language was precisely vague and unsurprising. But then Taft said something amazing. To the gathered national leaders, he flatly renounced Republican doctrine. Not a few heads must have snapped to attention at the words, "tariff" and "revenue" so ordered to sound as if a Democrat stood before them:

> In the making of a tariff bill the prime motive is taxation and the securing thereby of a revenue.

10. "Pelf" means riches and implies *stolen* riches.
11. Taft Inaugural Address, 3/4/09.
12. Taft Inaugural Address.

No clauses, no buts, and no neverthelesses. Only the unrepentantly dozing could have missed what followed. A government deficit was accumulating. "Should it be impossible to do so by import duties," Taft flatly stated, "new kinds of taxation must be adopted, and among these I recommend a graduated inheritance tax as correct in principle and as certain and easy of collection." Did he know what he was saying?

These were not new ideas, at least not for a radical, or the recently trounced William Jennings Bryan. Had not Roosevelt tossed about Congress the inheritance tax in a 1908 message? Everyone knew where that one would go. This time was different. And, yes, Taft knew exactly what he was saying. On that snowy day, Thursday, March 4, 1909, William Howard Taft shaped the next four years, and far beyond. Everything that followed in his Administration, the tariff fight, the misstatements of its effect, the insurgents, the corporation tax, the railroad bill, the 16th Amendment, Ballinger and Pinchot, trade reciprocity with Canada, the Postal banks, the Democratic takeover of the House, Roosevelt's bolt, and Woodrow Wilson's election ... all this was unleashed by that little line in the new President's first speech.

* * *

On March 15, Congress opened. The House Ways and Means Committee had been debating rates and costs and foreign competition and the American working man for months, investigating such things as automobile tires and the cost of flax. From Tawney's long letter to Taft pledging support of "a genuine tariff revision" to Cannon's assurances to redeem the platform, to Ways and Means Chairman Sereno Payne's genuine efforts, Taft was assured that the Republican party that had nominated and elected him was still behind him on this, his first initiative.[13] He prepared a message to be read to Congress the next day.

Curious House members gathered to listen to the President's message. Reporters accustomed to "an exodus to the cloakroom" during the reading of Roosevelt's missives were as stunned as the congressmen when after the three hundredth word the clerk pronounced, "Signed, William Howard Taft." The hilarity was spontaneous. Tawney pounded his desk in glee, and members hugged each other joyfully. At the Senate, where "applause ... is so unusual as to be startling," wrote a dispatch, even Senator Du Pont deigned to conjoin "the palms of his hands three or four times." Others laughed openly. One cried out, "That's bully!"[14]

Robert La Follette later recorded it as a dismal moment, Taft's first betrayal of the people. The account, from his autobiography, which was written after a four year gang fight with Taft and that was the equal to Roosevelt's own autobiography in its self-satisfaction, was flatly untrue. La Follette's memory brought back "a hush" and "a look of amazement ... on every face."[15] The shock was his alone. Taft's message was precise and his intent clear. The *Times* rather felt it a "model of direct-

13. Tawney to Taft, 11/25/08, "Taft and Cannon Meet," *NYT*, 12/10/08 and "Tariff Bill Ready For House To-Day," *NYT*, 3/17/09.

14. "Tariff Bill Ready For House To-Day," *NYT*, 3/17/09.

15. *La Follette's Autobiography*, p. 438. La Follette's version has infected the history of the moment; only the dismay of the insurgents has survived. Pringle called it a "disappointment" to advocates of low tariffs (p. 426). Beveridge's biographer, Claude Bowers, wrote that had Taft's message been a "militant call," it "might have been historic" (*Beveridge and The Progressive Era*, p. 334). Historian David Burton wrote, "A more politically attuned President, whether a Roosevelt or a Wilson, would have dramatized such an action and would have sought to rally public opinion" (*William Howard Taft: In the Public Service*, p. 62).

ness, brevity, and simplicity."[16] Taft set the special Congress to work with a reminder of the declarations of his inaugural address, all of two weeks old, to revise, revise downward, secure revenue, possibly with a new tax, disturb not business, and waste not time on other matters.

The *Times* feared "the only changes that can be made in the bill as reported ... will be in the direction of diminishing the reductions.... Washington is full of the representatives of the favored interests ... the shorter the session the less chance they will have to get in their fine work." So it was. The morning of Taft's message, the Payne Tariff Bill lay at the Government Printing Office, held in the utmost secrecy. The delay was due to last minute revisions insisted upon by a new member of Payne's Committee who held insufficient the bill's tribute to the board feet of the State of Washington.[17] His ideas on the lumber schedule were bolstered by the recent and incongruous testimony of the Chief Forester, Gifford Pinchot, that tariff protection would not save any trees. The lumber lobby scored an early victory.[18] Nevertheless, the reply of the full House came promptly. Uncle Joe's troops kept their promises. In less than a month Taft got exactly what he had asked, punctuated by a practically unanimous Republican vote.

An expression of the President's strength came from a Democrat, Francis Burton Harrison, who praised Taft's excursion into tariff reform. "Many schedules of the Payne bill offer ground for rejoicing among our partisans. I recognized in certain features of this bill a concession to public sentiment. It is impossible for us to fathom the sincerity of the promoters of the Republican tariff plank, but certain it is that their successful candidate for President was and is an honest man."[19] House insurgents agreed. With the exception of flare ups over the oil duty, which was said to be a concession to the Rockefeller interests, and crossed lines over the lumber duty, things remained quiet.

As the House rushed through the material, there had been some confusion over schedules and allotments for speeches. It was noted that one item contained a reduction in the duty on petroleum. To counter this sacrilege the leadership hastily struck a rule to allow for amendment of the clause before it went to a general vote. On April 7, regular Vreeland of New York offered a general substitution to the offending paragraph for one which resumed the Dingley rate of 25 percent on oil and allowed for a re-exportation drawback on duties paid. Only he blew it. Instead of referring back to the rule on the matter, Vreeland offered the change as an amendment, which opened the path for other amendments. Insurgent Norris of Nebraska immediately called for a change from 25 percent to 1 percent. The objection was raised that the rule allowed no amendments to Vreeland's amendment. Minority Leader Clark stood for a parliamentary inquiry. "Is the amendment so sacred that you can not touch it all?" he asked. Old

16. "President Taft's First Message," *NYT* editorial, 3/17/09.
17. "Tariff Bill Ready For House To-Day," *NYT*, 3/17/09.
18. Pinchot to Payne, 3/10/09, *CR*, 4/6/09, p. 1135. Pinchot violated common sense and the laws of economics with the conclusion that lower prices would lead to more destruction of forests. Higher tariffs that would raise prices would bring about less cutting, he unreasonably reasoned. What he was doing was reversing a cause and an effect in order to rationalize his agreement with the lumber industry over the tariff. In 1909, prices were high because of high demand and tariffs. His letter was published in the *CR* by Cushman of Washington as a justification for the duty. Tawney blasted Pinchot's testimony as "exalting himself" and intended as a means to impose his control upon all forests, public and private (p. 1132). Pinchot's foolish testimony killed the free listing of lumber.
19. "Cannon Fears Test on a Tariff Rule," *NYT*, 3/28/09.

Guardsman Dalzell replied with a smile, "I think that is the situation." Clark asked again if the rule was a "sacred thing that could not be touched?" Dalzell kept the smile. "That's about the size of it." This launched a mad volley of theories as to the history of the oil rule and rules in general. Such words as "germane" and "violence" were thrown as to a rule's effect and purpose. A reporter noted, "The fight after that was strictly parliamentary, the question being whether the amendment to the amendment provided in the rule was in order." Ah, yes, the People's House.

From the Chair, regular Olmsted settled it in favor of the rule as earlier set forth, that is with the 25 percent duty intact. This arose further indignation from the insurgents who joined the Democrats to vote down Olmsted by 136 to 168. The worst of it was that not a few regulars had wandered off the floor to hide themselves from the words "Standard Oil." Fitzgerald now stepped in. He had been ostracized by fellow Democrats for having offered a counter resolution to one by Clark on the Rules Committee that was favorable to Cannon. His theory was that by supporting Cannon, he and his allies were given key committee assignments.[20] Meanwhile, he had been slammed left and right, Democrat and Republican, for the act of treason. One of the charges held that he had acted on orders of Standard Oil. Fitzgerald punched back hard. "For three weeks I have stood silent while I have been accused of having been the subservient tool of this great corporation," he shouted. "I shall vote for [the amendment] and so fling back into their dirty mouths the charges brought by blackguarding persons and papers over this country."[21] The Norris amendment was needed, he said, to "cripple the abilities of this giant corporation to continue to fleece the American people."

This moved Cooper of Wisconsin into an animated attack on Standard Oil, ending with an applause-rousing conclusion that the 25 percent duty and the new drawback feature were intended to protect Standard Oil against competitors, while allowing the company to bring in Mexican oil free of taxes. In an unusual move, Cannon followed Cooper to the floor. As another Republican attempted to reply, Cannon gave forth an "emphatic gesture" to yield. He levied a damnation of advocates of free oil, who, he said, were acting against the interests of the 3,000 property owners in his Illinois district who received royalties from Standard Oil and other refiners. Cannon asked if the "demagogues," so apt to defame "the wicked Standard Oil," were not, "like old Samson [trying to] pull down the pillars and have the temple fall upon yourselves?" He further skewered Cooper's charge of an end-run via the drawback feature, pointing to the simple fact that the new law did not allow it, while the amendment, in effect, would. It "lets the Standard Oil, with their refineries in Mexico, ship not only the crude but the refined oil free into our market, with a nominal duty of 1 percent ad valorem. Still, the gentleman from Wisconsin [Cooper] and others flap their wings and crow, and crucify the people while they demagogue in denouncing this wicked Standard Oil. If the Standard Oil ... transgresses the law, the courts are open. If legislation in addition is needed, we are

20. The Gridiron lampooned the event. A pretend Rep. Clark called for a revision of the House rules but "Fitzgerald handed Champ Clark a lemon" ("Taft on Gridiron, Hugely Enjoys It," *NYT*, 4/18/09). For Fitzgerald's Rules maneuvers see "Bolting Democrats Get Choice Places," *NYT*, 3/17/09.

21. From "Oil Duty is Cut by Bolt in House," *NYT*, 4/8/09 and *CR*, 4/7/09, pp. 1170–1172. The *CR* had a softer version of Fitzgerald's attack, quoting him, "and so fling back at the foul calumnies and insinuations that have been thrown at me through discreditable prints...."

here to legislate....” But the Speaker himself was caught by a rule. Cooper rose to claim by point of order that Cannon had exceeded his time. The House broke into laughter. The objection was overruled by Chairman Olmsted, who didn't bother to look at his watch. To sighs and groans the Czar was given an additional thirty seconds.

There being little importation of crude oil, protecting or free listing it was meaningless. The fight was entirely symbolic: “the wicked Standard Oil,” the people, the rules, and the heated, dirty word, tariff. In the end the one percent duty was voted up, while an increase on the duty on coal was slipped in.[22] The next day Clark forced a formal “roll call” vote to place oil on the free list. A roll call meant an official accounting, so the defenders of the oil trust were to be put on the spot. Clark got his satisfaction. Only forty-six Republicans stood pat, including Cannon, Dalzell, and Vreeland. The rest ran for cover. The vote was followed by general agreement to add tea and coffee to the free list.

The last fight was over lumber. Here again the strange currents of the tariff prevailed. Midwesterners condemned rates that had once protected their now exhausted forests. Northwesterners demanded the opposite to protect their own industry, which included lumber companies recently moved there from Minnesota.[23] When Tawney proposed to return low quality lumber to the free list, where Payne's Committee had it before Pinchot's March 10 letter, representatives of lumber districts railed that Tawney had ceased to be a Republican.[24] Now we had fifty-seven Republican “lumber insurgents,” led, amazingly, by the Chairman of the Appropriations Committee, voted down by a coalition of regulars, some rules insurgents, and thirty-nine Democrats who bolted their free-trading brethren to stand pat with Cannon.

Finally, the evening of April 9, the Payne bill in its entirety came to a vote. In the gallery were Mrs. Taft, daughter Helen, and son Robert. Their joy and Mr. Taft's victory were made complete by a strong vote of 217 to 161. Four Democrats from Louisiana affirmed the measure, and only one Republican dissented. The revision was honest, and included a “new kind of taxation,” just as the President demanded in his inaugural address. Uncle Joe's House sent its considerable tariff reductions to the Senate along with an inheritance tax.

* * *

Government money can be raised in a lot of bad ways. The tariff is one of the worst. It is politically vexing and financially limited. For all the agitation over the tariff it paid for hardly half the government in 1908. Taxing luxuries and vice was all very well to make up the difference, only buy a couple battleships and there went upwards half the money taken in from all the tobacco smoked that year. Buy two more, as Roosevelt demanded every year, there went most of the other half.[25] In 1908 tariff revenue came to $268 million. That

22. The next morning it was discovered that the lower duty on oil “and its products” was countermanded by an amendment that specified “petroleum, crude and refined,” thus leaving the by-products unspecified, which meant that a 20 percent duty was automatically applied for items not listed specifically. Affected only were petroleum-based products such as cosmetics and “lubricating” oils which were minimally impacted by the duty. The insurgents and Democrats accused the leadership of deliberately slipping in a “joker.” It was an honest oversight and was fixed by a resolution to substitute “refined” with “a comma and the words ‘and the products thereof’” (*CR*, p. 1351).
23. See “The Waste of Minnesota Forests,” *Pioneer Press* editorial, 7/18/09.
24. See Fordney of Michigan, *CR*, 4/5/09, pp. 1115.
25. Battleships cost from five to ten million each.

covered the $154 million in military pensions, which left wanting any one of the budgets of the Army, Navy, or the federal bureaucracy, lightly called "Civil Establishment." With another $250 million in excise taxes on tobacco, spirits, and fermented liquors, and $70 million raised from various sources such as consular fees, "profits on coinage," land sales, etc., the government was still $60 million short of its total disbursements of $659,196,319.68, not including the self-financing Postal Service, itself bleeding from a subsidy of second class mail for periodicals and rural delivery.[26] Some other source of cash was the dire need.

Taft inherited a mess at the Treasury Department. He felt it a primary responsibility to good government to eliminate the deficit. Taft spoke of tariff reform in 1906, so his 1908 platform was not new. However, between 1906 and 1909 came changes that Taft could not ignore. On top of the annual extortion of Congress for higher pensions by the Union army veterans association, the Grand Army of the Republic (GAR), Roosevelt's Monroe Doctrine battleships, combined with the usual Congressional pork roast required federal dollar after dollar that taxed Dingley more than Dingley could tax imports, especially as imports fell with purchasing during the 1907 panic. Additionally, as the big dig in Panama moved forward, so did the dollar signs and the bonds needed to support it.

The excise tax on vice had its run. Liquor consumption, or taxable commerce in liquor, was on the wane as the Anti-Saloon League marched state-by-state towards the 18th Amendment. Taft estimated that the deficit would rise to $100,000,000 if new revenue was not found. Higher duties was not the answer. Economizing, which was to become a major initiative of his Administration, would help, but it could never account for a nine-digit deficit. To accommodate this situation Taft had to break free of the Republican philosophical box.

A Democratic Congress in 1894 attempted to buy off tariff cuts with an income tax. The tax was rejected by the Supreme Court in the controversial "Pollock" decision that relied upon the Constitutional distinction between a tax as "direct" or "indirect," the former being prohibited unless equally "apportioned" between the states and their populations.[27] Taft blew the whistle on this old game with his Inauguration Day call for an inheritance or other "new kinds of taxation."

The Senate dispatched the inheritance tax via express, return mail. It was bad enough that it was a Republican president's idea. Worse, it was already practiced by some states and would thereby constitute double taxation. If there was one thing the Senate could agree upon it was that the President mustn't interfere. When Taft called for the special session he pleaded that Congress limit itself to a revenue bill. It didn't. The reader must understand the importance of these things to the Senate of 1909. Congress felt that Roosevelt violated its powers and privileges. The same feelings were aroused whenever Taft told it what it ought do. Among the harshest criticisms thrown at Taft during his presidency was over his meddling in legislation. It started early.

The first Senate business was a Census bill that had been vetoed by Roosevelt.

26. "How It Happens That $600,000,000 Receipts Make a Deficit of $80,000,000," *NYT*, 5/2/09 and *CR*, pp. 1381–1383, 4/19/09. Democrats of 1909 liked to point to a total Federal budget that exceeded a billion dollars. To get there, the Post Office was included. The Department met its needs with its own revenues outside of general taxation. And "profits on coinage," you ask? That was in the days before a penny cost more to make than its worth. (Note that the *Times* and the *CR* had two digits reversed in the total for customs revenue, the former at $286 million, the other at $268 million.)

27. *Pollock vs. Farmers Loan & Trust Co.*, 158 U.S. 601(1895).

Senator Bailey took the occasion to fire a warning volley at the new President. Bailey let into the Congressional record an ugly, if somewhat prescient, analysis of Taft's presidential temperament:

> I hope that his Administration will be an unmixed blessing to all the people, but I do not hesitate to say that no man ever had a less desirable preparation for it than the present occupant of that high office. He went from the bench, where the tendency is toward a certain kind of tyranny ... arbitrary, irritable, and sometimes tyrannical. I do not mean that it will corrupt him in the sense that it will make him venal, but it will corrupt him in the sense that it teaches him to oppose his will against all obstacles and to insist upon the prevalence of his will even over the law itself upon occasion.[28]

Praying for the President's moral restraint, and speaking to ghosts of Roosevelt as much as to Taft, Bailey warned him against "sending messages to Congress, except in the ordinary and Constitutional way, and threatening us with his displeasure and his veto if we are to do what we think ought to be done and not what he wants us to do."

Nothing, not even committing the whole crew to the Ananias Club, could keep the Senate quiet. Its mandate is unique, as shown by the fight over Taft's autos. The body represents a division of power by geography, time — and personalities. The House must face the people's firing line every two years, the President every four. The Senate clock runs slow. Senators take the electoral examination every six years, one third at a time. Moreover, in the shrine to Calhoun, Clay and Webster, Rhode Island is the equal to New York and Illinois. In the Senate, it is truly one man, one vote. One Senator can make all the difference. Thus Senator Nelson A. Aldrich of "Little Rhody ... the High Priest and Keeper of the Sacred Tariff Cow," was, in 1909, the Master of the Universe.[29]

* * *

On April 10, the Clerk of the House delivered to the Senate H.R. 1438, "to provide revenue, equalize duties, and encourage the industries of the United States, and for other purposes." By unanimous consent, it was put to committee. News filtered from behind those closed doors that proved the Senate its own beast, especially in Aldrich's Finance Committee. Three days later, he reported his work to the Senate floor. "Back to Dingley Rates," lamented the *Times*.[30]

As part of the peace agreement with Tawney and Cannon, Taft played bystander during the House sessions, which consigned him to the same with the Senate.

28. *CR*, 4/10/09, p. 1314.
29. "Where Senator Aldrich Guards the Tariff," *NYT*, 4/11/09.
30. *NYT*, editorial, 4/13/09. In his autobiography, La Follette stated, "Aldrich kept the bill in possession of his committee for forty-eight hours. The corridors about his committee rooms were crowded with the representatives of the big protected interests... When Aldrich reported the bill he made a brief oral statement... [and] demanded immediate consideration of the bill... He was preparing, as usual, to drive roughshod over all opposition. I was not altogether unprepared for this action on the Senator's part, and, taking the floor, I protested... It was manifestly the purpose of Senator Aldrich to allow Senators no chance to prepare in advance to resist the sort of tariff legislation which the Payne-Aldrich bill provided" (La Follette, pp. 441–443). A couple things here. La Follette was referring to the moment Aldrich reported H.R. 1438 from his Committee. The *Congressional Record* disagrees with La Follette's account of himself (*CR* p. 1332, 4/12/09). If he said anything it went unrecorded. Instead, it was the Democrats, notably Senator Daniel, who took to immediate objection on the very grounds that La Follette claimed he spoke of. Next, Aldrich was plain and thorough in his presentation (see *CR*, pp. 1377–1383). When pressed by Democrats as to what had or had not happened in the Committee, he magnificently replied, "It might take a long time to tell things that did not transpire in the committee." He presented the sausage but not the ingredients. "The

He had a few plays, regardless. On the 15th, Taft broke the quiet from the White House and forwarded a message to Congress demanding free trade with the Philippines. He hadn't bothered the House with it, but now that Payne had gone to the Senate the President popped it on them both. At the same time insurgent Senators Beveridge and La Follette submitted to the Senate a measure that was to them, and later to Taft, almost a fetish, and over which they would fight with Taft and reality, like with everything else, for not having gone far enough. Their contribution was a bill "to create a tariff commission," a revision of a Beveridge bill from the previous year whose intent was create a "a body of experts" to assist Congress to formulate the tariff scientifically. These ideas were imbedded in Taft's 1908 platform, "*the difference between the cost of production at home and abroad, together with a reasonable profit to American industries.*"

Beveridge was further moving on an Indianapolis convention held that February to promote the tariff commission idea. By late April the various groups behind that meeting had grown to more than two hundred prominent business and trade associations. This lobby orchestrated sending of thousands of letters and telegrams that overwhelmed the White House and Capitol Hill mails with demands for "a competent tariff commission."[31] That business was behind the idea bothered no one. The idea was thought pure for it pretended to remove politics from the tariff, Taft's very ideal. Taft and the progressives parted ways on the issue because its proponents ultimately sought a commission not to advise Congress but to instruct it, an abdication of power unthinkable to a jealous Congress and, as Taft correctly and patiently explained to its fans, patently unconstitutional. Beveridge and La Follette didn't go that far, but their spirit of compromise didn't go very far, either.

Taft recognized both the futility and danger of a catch-all solution. In December of 1908, he wrote confidentially,

> The tariff commission business is of course one in which I sympathize with those who favor it, and yet it is impracticable, because Congress will never adopt it. For that reason, I hope that the movement in favor of tariff revision may not be hampered by such a suggestion.[32]

The following month, he realized the idea was becoming dangerous. In the much-quoted letter to Col. Nelson, in which Taft stated he would "down" Cannon and Aldrich, less frequently referred to is the preceding paragraph. Had Nelson and the progressives listened to this wisdom, their bitterness might have yielded to reason. Had they joined in Taft's careful moderation of such initiatives as the tariff commission, their glory might not have gone to Woodrow Wilson, who later seized many of theirs and Taft's measures. Taft wrote Nelson,

> I am very much afraid that the proposition to put in a tariff commission

30. (*cont.*) bill is here.... The Senate, the minority of the Senate and the majority of the Senate, have ample opportunity, without any limitation whatever, to read it, to consider it, to discuss it, and to amend it" (*CR*, p. 1333). La Follette was at this time more concerned with the Census bill, and into the tariff discussions, Cummin's income tax bill. La Follette became involved later on, and deeply so, as he dragged out the debates endlessly. That Aldrich did not fully report the bill was a reference to later complaints that the Finance Committee continually made changes to it, making it difficult to prepare in advance of floor votes. La Follette's history of the Payne bill is unjudicious, especially to the Democrats who managed their dissent brilliantly. And yes, Aldrich did "drive roughshod over all opposition." He had the votes to do it. More startling is the extent to which he compromised, large credit for which must be given to Taft.
31. "Tariff Tinkering at $10,000,000 a Day," *NYT*, 4/29/09.
32. Taft to JC Cobb, 12/28/08.

> would utterly fail. What I am hopeful of is that we may get a bill which will contain within itself a provision for a permanent tariff commission which could make its investigations and report each year the facts in respect to the matter ... I am not sure that we could do this, but that is the only practical result within reach, I believe.[33]

Soon after, Sereno Payne wrote the President, worried about the advance of the idea. In a reply intended for general consumption, Taft laid out his idea for "a permanent commission of tariff experts to keep themselves advised by all the means possible.... I should be the last to advocate a commission with any power to fix rates—if that were constitutional, as it would not be...."[34]

Beveridge had worked tirelessly for a commission. He kept faith after Roosevelt refused its public endorsement in 1908. He was willing to work with Aldrich on it. Between them, and although the pie was cut in half several times, following Taft's pressure on Aldrich it made it into the Senate version of the bill. At the Conference Committee, however, Cannon got the better of it. Taft salvaged what he could, a board, not a commission, but one empowered to investigate the cost of production overseas. Beveridge left bitter and hurt. The following year he cursed the results. "We asked for reality; they gave us a mockery."[35] Taft walked away with a tariff board which he used to beat upon standpatters and tariff reformers alike—and which was ultimately rendered feeble by the subversive efforts of the insurgents two years later.

Bailey used the general messiness that was tariff making to throw in the old income tax, so printed in the Congressional Record in its over 4,000 words and two and a half oversized pages of small print. Let's just say that every complication of the tax was exhibited, including double jeopardy, deductions and exemptions for charity, tangled definitions of what constitutes an expense and what a profit, a progression of rates over income, and methods of enforcement.

Albert Jeremiah Beveridge. The Indiana Senator was a leading "insurgent." Going into the presidency, Taft shared the essence of Beveridge's political ends, but differed on the means. When Beveridge found Taft would get there through the Republican leadership, he bolted leftward and opposed the Administration at every turn. Taft said of him, "Beveridge is such an honest and able man, I often wonder what makes him such a selfish pig. He never talks. He only preaches." In early 1910, as Taft watched the Senate insurgents condemn his legislation, he called Beveridge "the most sinister influence" in the break-up of the party. (Courtesy Library of Congress)

Aldrich struck first. "Can the Senator from Texas advise the Senate about the amount of revenue which would be derived from this amendment?" Bailey replied, "No more than the Senator from Rhode Island could now advise the Senate as to the amount of revenue that the tariff

33. Taft to WR Nelson, 1/5/09.
34. Taft to Payne, 1/18/09.
35. Bowers, p. 387. For Beveridge's 1908 efforts, see pp. 268–277.

bill itself will raise." Touché. He continued, "If the Senator's bill will raise $300,000,000 upon the consumption of this Republic, I would reduce that by $60,000,000, and conceding that $60,000,000 to the consumers of the land, I would lay it upon incomes exceeding $5,000." Lamenting taxes as "a necessary evil" and admitting the necessity to pay for government, Bailey excused his tax on incomes as a lesser evil than a tariff system built upon "the backs and appetites of people who, when doing their best, do none too well. I believe, myself, that there never was, and that there never will be, a juster or wiser tax devised than an income tax. I believe it is the only tax ever yet devised by the statesmen of the world that rises and falls with a man's ability to pay it."[36]

To manage railroad rates, Roosevelt lost out on the greatest change in American government in half a century, and the defining one for what followed. The railroads would practically die from excessive regulations and competition from automobiles and airplanes. Blinded by the politics of railroad reform, its populist proponents never figured that the automobile would do more to solve the farmer's problems than all the Inter-State Commerce regulations ever written. In 1910 a railroad man lectured Good Roaders, "No one factor is of more economic importance than the reduction of the cost of transportation between the farm and the railroad station. The country road makers have not kept up with the railroad makers." Before automobiles and roads built for them, it frequently cost more to ship produce a dozen miles to a railroad depot than from there onward to New York by rail. To get there, however, this man called for three hundred million Federal dollars a year, almost half the 1908 national budget and more than that year's tariff income.[37] The income tax laid the foundation for a government that would quickly move from the hundreds of millions to the billions and then trillions of dollars in revenue and expenses. William Howard Taft might today lament what was unleashed by his inaugural address. He would, however, freely admit the good that has come of a government able to lay asphalt across a continent, thrice (and more?) fund world salvation, administer to its poor and elderly, and step on the moon. None of that was possible with border and vice taxes. In the end, Bailey was right. But not yet. The Constitution needed a change to execute it.

* * *

The city of Washington is adorned with monuments to heroes. From Washington and Jackson, to Sherman, Grant, and Lincoln, to the victors history. It was a Republican Congress that drew plans for the Lincoln Memorial. Twenty years later, upon their seizure of the Congress, the Democrats built a monument to the founder of their party, Thomas Jefferson. Upon closer inspection one sees the footnote to District of Columbia memorials. It's all a matter of votes in Congress. Got a majority and you got a statue. Not until the 1910s was the Polish community able to exercise the political power to garner congressional votes for a memorial to their hero Pulaski, or the Swedes to their own, Ericsson. Here lies the key to the Taft presidency and the progressive, or any, era.

The age was at its core a transfer of power. The agitations of the period reflect not so much agitation itself but its empowerment. Historians ever argue the meaning of the period. It was a moral awakening or a middle class revolt; it was the growth of urban politics and the West;

36. *CR*, 4/15/09, p. 1351. Get it? April 15!
37. "Yoakum Shows Need of Country Roads," *NYT*, 7/29/10 and Nevins, p. 17.

it was this, that, and all things in between. Most fall back upon the "synthesis" theory that the reforms lacked cohesion and the various factions cumulatively accounted for "progressivism." There are fundamental realities in American life that no single theory can accommodate.[38] The 1910 Socialist triumph in Milwaukee was the victory of its appeal at that place and time. When its mayor was dumped the next election it was as much a victory of anti-socialism as a failure of the Socialists to get reelected. The voters turned on them, and the power was transferred elsewhere. The progressive age was— as any, but especially it — a conglomeration, sometimes coherent, mostly distinct, and ever confusing, of the exercise of political power, both for and against change.

Every element of the progressive era comes of the same formula. When Roosevelt got the votes he got the legislation. Congressmen were elected or not by constituents who approved or not. Debs and Bryan didn't win elections because they hadn't the votes. Roosevelt himself is case-in-point. During his first term, reelection guided him. The largest effect of his "no third term" pledge of 1904 was freedom from this political reality. It liberated the bully pulpit, but at the cost of the Executive Office. After the 1906 mid-term elections his mandate went lame, and the White House became a ceremonial office. Roosevelt stopped doing what brought his original success. Were he running for office in 1908 — or running the country according to his candidate's campaign (Hammond advised Roosevelt that "in his effort to help Taft he was keeping himself too much in the limelight"; Roosevelt replied, "I guess you're right, In the future I'll put on the soft pedal"[39]) — either Congress would have conformed to him or he to it in order to win the election. Instead, they warred on each other. With his instincts for agitation no longer tempered by elections and party, Roosevelt's politics and tongue freely wandered. He went every which way but to Congress. He peppered the legislature with recommendations, which it, owing him nothing, freely ignored.[40] The insurgents were likewise confined to this equation. With occasional alignment with Democrats they got occasional votes. If the home-district sentiment pointed to the regulars, the insurgents quietly voted the party way. When on their own, their rhetoric flew as wildly as they were voted down.

Fights over House rules started before Taft's tariff, but Cannonism meant little outside of Washington, the press, or the Democratic platform of 1908. Add tariff to the equation and Cannonism came alive. The rules insurgents' power grab was made possible by the tariff fight over which, finally, there was harmony. Cannon was severely bitten over the oil rate, but insurgency faded away with its free listing. Dissent only works when there is something to dissent. The regulars and the insurgents

38. For a stock review of the various elements that contributed to "progressivism," see "The Progressive Era: A Search for a Synthesis," by John D. Buenker, *Mid-America*, Vol. 51, No. 3, July 1969. See also the web publication *Progressivism* by Robert M. Crunden, www.myhistory.org, 2001. The classic interpretation of the "progressive movement" sees it as agrarian in origin, moved by middle-class reformers, and ultimately failing to the clash of interests and coalitions, such as urban vs. rural, labor vs. capital, native vs. immigrant, etc.

39. Hammond, pp. 537–538.

40. Taft recognized this dynamic. In 1910 he wrote, "It would seem as if the treatment that Congress gave him after my election, and before my inauguration, had made him deeply regret that he had not accepted another term, because then he found his power with Congress to have gone...." (Taft to Charles Taft, 9/10/10). Taft accomplished in law many of the final Roosevelt presidential suggestions, including federal workmen's compensation and an employers' liability bill, both of which Taft signed after Roosevelt's 1912 flight from his own legacy.

got along just fine in the House in April 1909. The insurgents voted for the Payne bill equally as the standpatters went along with the reform.

In 1912, academics reflected upon the turmoil that followed the Payne tariff. Cornell President Jacob Gould Schurman wrote that the agitation was a good sign, "the voice of discontent is very often, really, the voice of growing intelligence." The President of Columbia University, Dr. Nicholas Murray Butler, disagreed, pointing to "a discontent which the individuals affected have with and for themselves and which they treat as though it were a discontent with some prevailing condition in Government or in society ... the effect of half-education is not only to induce discontent, but to cause it to be directed against entirely innocent objects."[41] Actually, it wasn't half-education. Well it was, but it was more precisely half-education exercised in politics. As Dr. Butler wrote,

> Discontent of this kind is one of the chief forces making progress in the world, provided it is directed at a true cause ... it is safe to say that if every one of the revolutionary demands that are made regarding them was granted and satisfied, there would be just as much discontent as there is now. The nominal causes of that discontent would have been removed but the real causes would remain.

Those "nominal causes" had, in 1909, and following the model of Roosevelt's last two years, already turned into an effect. Reform became as often a means as an end. Meanwhile, where would discontent throw its votes?

* * *

Which brings us back to the Senate. The Old School and the Czars ran this shop, placed there in a solid majority by Republican legislatures. A bridge to change was erected by the House, but the Senate refused to try it. Nevertheless, the Senate had a few issues to meet, the first brought upon it by the President and his pesky tariff revision. Next was Bailey's income tax, empowered by Taft's Inaugural day hint. From there it was a matter of political deals, from the tariff commission to Taft's Philippines free trade bill, to Aldrich's rates.

Taft blew it all open by taking Bailey seriously. The Senate that squashed the inheritance tax would just as easily have sat upon Bailey's income tax. The President had other ideas. In mid–April he was riding high. Butt noted, "President Taft is a keen politician in his way and knows men and how to handle them for his own ends." Taft knew to hit hard when on top. For example, ever interested in the development of the Federal City, Taft demanded of standpat Senator Penrose $25,000 for Potomac Park and $5,000,000 for purchase of the land between the Senate-side of the Capitol and Union Station, the details to come later. Penrose pledged the cash.[42] Taft's next coup was over his traveling budget. Between the salary increase, the automobiles, and travel money, Taft squeezed $62,000 out of Congress for his personal use. Had Rep. Dwight's April 26 bill been adopted, it might have been double that. The New Yorker proposed that the national chief have his own train and $60,000 a year to pay for it. It might not seem a lot, but it was coming off a time Roosevelt couldn't get funding for an extra clerk, much less his precious commissions. Taft was getting all he asked, and more.

The principal objection to the income tax, voiced by Taft as well as in the Senate, was that the Supreme Court had already

41. "Dr. Butler Sees Hope for Republicans," *NYT*, 11/13/12.
42. Butt, 4/13/09, p. 52.

ruled it unconstitutional. Bailey said his bill overcame the conflict. Taft's additional objection was that of some very real consequence, the small matters of self-incrimination, perjury, and due process that would come of government meddling into the affairs of individuals. Throughout his presidency he maintained that the income tax ought be reserved for times of crisis. Nevertheless, the 16th Amendment would not have been enacted when and how it was were it not for him. It came of a much deeper game he played than Bailey, Aldrich, and La Follette.

In late April, Taft let it drop that "one form of income tax" would necessarily arise should revenue needs demand it. Aldrich replied that the new tariff would do just fine by itself. He spent the rest of the Spring denying the need for other taxes.[43] Cummins tried to organize the Western Senators to support an income tax, which the regulars adamantly refused. One organization man in April summed it up with, "No income tax, no inheritance tax, no stamp tax, and no corporation tax," while another crowed in late May, "The income tax is so far off that I have not thought of it. That is not worrying us at all."[44] Nevertheless, Aldrich was getting worried. With an alternative tax hanging over the Senate like the blade of a guillotine, and with Democratic and insurgent hands on the cord, the revenue imperative for high tariffs was being denied him.

Taft made it altogether more uncomfortable for Aldrich by playing coy. While the Senate debated and Aldrich turned Payne back into Dingley, Taft stayed cool.

43. "Aldrich Promises Plenty of Revenue," *NYT*, 4/20/09.
44. "Western Senators for an Income Tax," 4/19/09 and "Bailey Denounces Johnson on Tariff," 5/20/09, *NYT*.

14

Taft's Coup

The President made news not just over the tariff and his automobiles, but for his public ceremonies, the changed White House social scene, golf, and a new presidential pastime, trips to the ball park. Baseball was part of Archie's plan to initiate Taft to the ways of public relations. Taft had no problem with the suggestion, other than the game not get in the way of his afternoon exercise. This agreed, Butt snuck off to the stadium to arrange for a large chair to be placed in full public view. After a horseback ride, Taft and Butt headed out in the steamer. "No one in Washington could recall to-day just when it was that a President of the United States last attended a ball game in this city," wrote a reporter.[1] Taft loved it.

They arrived at the top of the second and took their seats with the Vice President and representatives Vreeland and Payne, who were in the President's favor for their "honest" work on the tariff. Butt managed to place the President six rows back from the first base line, as conspicuous as can be. With the President's entrance the home team pitcher caught stage fright and fielders bungled easy balls. They gave up two quick runs. Sherman and Butt educated Taft on the doings of the game, including the reason for a "frenzy" in the crowd over several close calls in the four-run Boston fourth, which much amused Taft. "No sir," Archie told him, "they never kill the umpires til the seventh inning." Butt left pleased at the "rousing reception" given the President.

Outside the Senate chamber a most pleasant spring continued. The House went into low gear while awaiting the return of H.R. 1438. All was joyous at the Taft home. Son Charlie played baseball on the White House lawn and tag on the roof. Workers next door were stunned to see Charlie and fifteen classmates sliding down the White House slants onto the balconies below.[2] Mrs. Taft's social plans went forward. For all the pre-inaugural speculation, her much derided schemes were accepted as the norm — and for the better. "The first direct evidence of Mrs. Taft's personal influence made its appearance several days ago," it was reported, "when two well-mannered butlers in livery appeared at the front door of the White House, in place of the tame policemen who for many years have performed a compromise service between a butler's duty and that of a private secretary."[3]

1. "Taft at Ball Game; No Hoodoo, He Hopes," *NYT*, 4/20/09 and Butt, 4/19/09, pp. 58–59.
2. "Tag on White House Roof," *NYT*, 4/4/09.
3. "The New Regime Within the White House," *NYT*, 3/14/09.

Capt. Butt took it upon himself to act as Taft's P.R. man. One of his first ruses was to get the President before a crowd at a baseball park. At his first game in 1909, Taft witnessed the home crowd's unfriendly reaction to a call. "No sir," Butt told him, "they never kill the umpires til the seventh inning." Speaking of the stretching in that inning, Taft did inaugurate that tradition, sort of, when he stood with the rest of the crowd in Chicago for the "Lucky Seventh," a common ritual in ballparks. He made the event famous. Taft is pictured here enjoying a ball game. Capt. Butt is just behind him, in all his military glitter. (Courtesy Library of Congress)

Another change was the appearance of a new piano with which Mrs. Taft demonstrated her high culture. Even Alice Longworth took to the new regime without criticism and appeared in good spirits at public functions at her father's old home.

While the President couldn't have been happier with the steamer, as Mrs. Taft awaited the jewel in her automotive crown, the landaulet, which arrived in mid–April, she further decided to extend her personal triumph over the automobile by taking the wheel herself. Butt was again assigned the duty, and he cut a lovely deal with the local Baker Motor Vehicle Co. dealer. For $1,000, Mrs. Taft eagerly grabbed the reigns of a little electric victoria and henceforth was seen in it running about the city. "No greater contrast can be found between the pomp and state of a European court and the democracy of America than to see the wife of the President driving her own automobile in the streets of Washington," it was reported.[4] Or his son. Young Charlie was spotted driving the electric, with instructor aboard, across the river to Fort Myer and back, "quick on both steering lever and brake."[5] His "chief

4. "Mrs. Taft Drives Her Own Car," *NYT*, 4/25/09. The *Evening Star* first saw her taking driving lessons on March 27 ("Mrs. Taft [*sic*] New Runabout") in what was probably the dealer's car. The invoice for the White House electric is dated May 5, from Cook & Stoddard Company of Washington. It was paid on June 7 (White House files, NARA, RG130). The White House Social Diary first notes Mrs. Taft's use of an electric on March 30.
5. "Charlie Taft a Chauffeur," *NYT*, 6/29/09.

Taft definitively started the presidential tradition to throw the first ball of the season, called "Strike One," starting, as pictured here, in 1910. As with automobiles and golf, Taft popularized baseball. Attendance surged during his presidency, and the game took on political and mainstream popularity. In 1912, the President of the Chicago Cubs wrote Taft, "All persons interested in baseball appreciate the many good things that come to the sport because of the recognition received from you as chief ruler of the nation." (Courtesy Library of Congress)

ambition" to drive the big cars, though, was denied him by his father.

The President set the pace. Of an April trip to New Haven, it was noted, "A novelty of the visit consisted in the use of automobiles. Carriages have heretofore been used."[6] Back home, he put the motors, golf clubs, and the horses to serious exercise. Meanwhile, Mrs. Taft set about refining Washington society. Along the Potomac River lay reclaimed land called Potomac Park. As the river was dredged and the Tidal Basin constructed, the "Speedway," a recreational drive that ran near the banks, became a popular see and be seen site amongst the social set.[7] The President frequently passed the area during his afternoon horseback rides. Mrs. Taft envisioned it as a springtime centerpiece.

She proposed that the Speedway be used like the Luneta, a park along Manila Bay, or London's Hyde Park along the Thames. Archie "ordered the automobile," and they drove along the pathway.[8] Mrs. Taft fixed upon a site for a bandstand, just South of the Washington Monument. The President gave the order for its placement and for concerts on Wednesdays and Saturdays. On April 17, the Tafts motored to the opening of the now-named Riverside Drive and the evening concerts, likely the first time the landaulet was officially graced by the President.[9] "I knew it would be a success," Butt wrote," but I did not anticipate the crush there would be. It was the result of her own idea and she has really provided a long-felt need here in the Capitol [*sic*] City."[10] From the landaulet, Mrs. Taft "waved a white-gloved hand" to the crowds, while "Taft's Own," still in town from the Inauguration, played its melodies to a gorgeous Virginia sunset over the river.

"It was a great day for society," noted the *Times*, and a notable one for the presence of automobiles. "For two hours the band played in the Esplanade, while auto-

6. "Taft Visits Yale, Attends a Play Here," *NYT*, 4/16/09.
7. The Tidal Basin is just that, a man-made basin to receive the flow of the Chesapeake Bay tide waters, thus allowing reclamation of the lands northward, including the later sites of the Lincoln and Jefferson memorials. The Speedway ran along the approximate path of today's Independence Avenue north of 14th Street.
8. Butt, 4/4/09, p. 39.
9. The White House Social Diary first mentions the landaulet on April 17, saying that Mrs. Taft and Capt. Butt took it out that morning, likely to review the preparations for the concert.
10. Butt, 4/17/09, p. 56.

mobiles chug-chugged around the driveway and carriages with merry occupants passed in review." An estimated 7,000 people gathered. "Everybody who had a carriage, a cart, or a motor car, push, electric or gasoline" showed up, wrote the *Evening Star*. "A Brilliant Event," the paper called it, "a decided success all around. Everybody said so."[11]

The landaulet was for show. Mrs. Taft loved hers. It was delivered in April of 1909, just in time for the launching of outdoor concerts in Potomac Park — the very site Mrs. Taft chose to plant the now world-famous Washington cherry trees. With the car's collapsible rear roof, the fashionable neighbors up Massachusetts Avenue were sure to know just who was riding behind those precious Great Seals on the doors. (Courtesy Library of Congress)

Another notable occurrence that day came with announcement of a gift of 1,000 flowering cherry trees from the mayor of Tokyo, another coup for Mrs. Taft, at whose suggestion the idea arose. She wanted Potomac Park to rival a Japanese Spring. With the help of a local botanist she arranged for the immediate planting of one hundred cherry trees in expectation of the arrival of the Japanese gift. Otherwise Mrs. Taft concerned herself with general management of the White House and the family's summer plans. She settled on a rented home in Beverly, Massachusetts, along the fashionable North Shore above Boston, and, in deference to her husband, near the famous Myopia golf club.

Taft dramatically changed Washington society through liberal use of his elevated salary and a wide open guest list. His truce with Congress went further than business. Butt was stunned to find Senator Bailey at the White House; stunned not just because of his recent, vicious speech against the President but because Bailey had not walked the White House gates since an episode during the McKinley days when he turned down an invitation on account of the lack of evening dress. Taft's harmony convinced him, and he showed up in proper attire and his wife in a properly huge set of pearls. Another reinstated to social graces was Senator Tillman, a principal of the Roosevelt "undesirables" and a charter member of the Ananias Club.[12] Gen. Miles and Tawney were also newly welcome. If the insurgents stayed away, it was on their own account. Taft hadn't yet discovered their bitter taste, although their snobbish refusal to mix with Cannon, Aldrich, and Bailey did not sit well with him. He was exercising clemency to all Roosevelt-era dissidents, from Southern Democrats to reactionaries such as Senator Hale of Maine. The insurgents were not excluded.[13]

One of the pardoned, Rep. Brownlow, "who has the same sort of affection for

11. "Washington Drive Opened," *NYT*, 4/18/09 and "Great Throng Out on Potomac Drive," *Evening Star*, 4/18/09.
12. See "The Difference," *NYT*, 4/25/09.
13. Bowers pointed to Butt's distinction between Roosevelt's dinner invitations being a "reward of merit" while Taft intended to use the White House "as a means to an end" (Butt, 4/27/09, p. 63; Bowers, p. 350). Bowers meant it as an example of Taft's blunt political skills. He took Butt's comment out of context. More

Here are the Tafts enjoying the landaulet. She enjoyed it more than he. When ordering a replacement in 1911, she wrote the factory, "The President has a great deal of trouble getting in and out of [it]. He is so big." Notice that Taft is sitting to the left — quite democratic, that. Capt. Butt wrote, "He always accords to a lady motoring with him the seat on the right of the vehicle, although custom has established the precedent that the President always takes the seat to the right.... President Roosevelt always took the right seat [in carriages or autos] ... but President Taft accorded this courtesy to his wife and now to every woman who happens to ride or drive with him." (Courtesy Library of Congress)

Theodore Roosevelt that is cherished by E.H. Harriman," wrote a columnist, had trouble finding the President's office, it had been so long since he stepped inside the building. The last time Taft met him, some time before, Brownlow was suffering an attack of blindness. Taft received him openly. After some chatter the Tennessean brought up his purpose. Taft told him to speak up. "Oh, Mr. President, I couldn't do it," replied an embarrassed Brownlow. "I am too modest." Taft stared at him. "Mr. Brownlow, gaze at me. Gaze at me hard. How do I look?" Brownlow replied, "You look disgusted." As he walked the man out the room, Taft said, "I am happy to see that your eyesight is fully restored."[14] The welcome was there for all Congressmen — if they dared.

Another big change was that Elihu Root took command of Washington political society. Lodge and Adams were handed their demotions. In the Senate, Root gave the best speeches, and at dinners he made the most appropriate toasts. Free of the Roosevelt shadow and now a Senator in his own right, he became the sage old man of the city. Taft would lean upon that broad presence throughout his four years.

* * *

Into May, and although the Senate

13. (*cont.*) fully: "President Roosevelt used [an invitation] entirely as a reward of merit and to pay for favors already performed and loyalty which had been proven. In fact, sometimes his invitations to dinner would follow so closely on a defense of him in the House as to shock the sensibilities of Mrs. Roosevelt." Same difference. The distinction was typical of Roosevelt's rationalization for his politics. Of the patronage he dealt to Taft delegates in 1908, he wrote, "I appointed no man for the purpose of creating Taft sentiment; but ... I have appointed men in recognition of the Taft sentiment already in existence" (Pringle, *Roosevelt*, p. 497). Most amusing here is that Butt claimed credit for Taft's idea, saying he first suggested it during his visit to Augusta in January. The most enlightening aspect of Taft's policy came in his comment to Butt, "The White House is a big political asset when used wisely," then, laughing, "I should like to hear the comments of some of these men when they receive their invitations ... I presume these people have never been invited to the White House before and seldom to a dinner anywhere. It is real joy to ask these. There is no motive behind their invitations save to give them pleasure, but that is what some of the others will not be able to comprehend, and in wondering how these simple people got here they will overlook the real reason which lies behind their own invitations" (Butt, 4/24/09, pp. 60–61). He cut back on the guest lists the following Winter, as the wide-open affairs became tedious and lost their allure.
14. "Heard and Seen Here and There," *Evening Star*, 4/3/09.

polarized between its Republican factions, Aldrich kept control. The insurgents were unable to gang up with the Democrats, for that side had problems of its own. Whenever the insurgents managed a strong bolt it was invariably matched by Democratic bolters who jumped to the other side of the room, assuring Aldrich his majority. Aldrich ran a masterful show, but it ultimately wasn't his show. Taft's shadow lay across the entire session. While smashing low-tariffs, Aldrich still had to answer to the President, something he was not used to. The pressure was yet subtle. On May 10, the insurgents complained that Taft was being unhelpful, saying the President should sway susceptible regulars to their insurgency, including Root. "There was talk among them last night of soliciting [Taft's] aid, but the plan was abandoned," recorded the *Times*. The next day's news carried a dispatch that Root had broken Aldrich on behalf of the President.[15]

The bizarre workings of the tariff were manifest in the attitude of standpat Senator Du Pont. Angered that sufficient protection was not graced upon blasting caps, he threatened to abandon the regulars and their own precious, high duties.[16] Another complexity in the tariff discussion was revealed in a debate on lead and carbon duties that centered on the difference in the cost of freight to New York from Utah and Mexico, which came of an attempt to apply the President's formulas of costs and reasonable profits. La Follette argued for lower duties because "the difference in the cost of production between this and foreign countries does not warrant this proposed duty...." There and everywhere, protectionists presented evidence of some industry in distress, be it due to "peon" miners in Mexico or insufficient duties which forced below-cost sale of some product.

Protection and revenue-only declarations got routinely mixed and the difference between them was frequently unclear. Whatever those differences, the debates on them were highly technical and often contradictory. Taft laughed it all off. When asked about the tariff he replied, "I'm not going to say that the tariff for revenue only and the tariff for the purposes of protection are one and the same thing when they both reach the same amount. But when a Congressman from Alabama favors a $2 tariff on lumber for revenue, and a Congressman from Washington or Oregon favors a $2 tariff on lumber for protection, they haven't any great amount of dispute between them."[17] The deliberations reminded him, Taft said, of his recent passage through Tennessee. To a local delegation that boarded his train he asked the name of a stream that ran along the line:

> The chairman mumbled something that was unintelligible. I asked him to repeat it. Again he mumbled so that I couldn't catch what he said. "I beg your pardon," I said, "but I didn't understand. Will you spell it?" "Waal, I don't reckon as how I kin," he replied. "Some folks spells it one way; other folks spells it different. In my pore jedgement, Jedge, they ain't no correct way to spell it."[18]

* * *

On May 21, the Senate turned its spurious attentions to the automobile. As with

15. "Aldrich Wins Fight on Lead, 44 to 35," 5/11/09 and "Aldrich Is Beaten; To Cut Tariff Rates," 5/12/09, *NYT*.
16. See "Aldrich Wins Fight on Lead, 44 to 35: Eleven Republicans Bolt, but Three Democrats Join with the Senate Organization," *NYT*, 5/11/09. An interesting aside from this article is that Aldrich referred, apparently for the first time, to Beveridge and Cummins as "progressives." Senator Newlands spoke of "progressionists" (see *CR*, p. 1885, 5/10/09).
17. "Taft Praises Valor of Virginia Troops," *NYT*, 5/20/09.
18. "Tariff Bill Puzzles Taft," *NYT*, 6/9/09. He used this story frequently.

every other of the thousands of items on the tariff schedules, here the gentlemen of the Senate were supposed experts on the subject. The Payne bill read:

> *140. Automobiles, bicycles, and motor cycles, and parts of any of the foregoing, including tires, axles, and ball bearings, 45 percent ad valorem.*[19]

The first question was if tires were rubber or automotive products. It was agreed that they might as well be of the automotive category, and axles, too, although the word "finished" would better define the parts as being intended for motors. It was so agreed until Senator Bailey interrupted, "I want to know if the automobile axle is susceptible of use for purposes other than that of automobiles." The question was if the word "axle" might find itself open to interpretation at customs, "because everybody will bring it in in the best way possible." It was agreed that "axle" meant automobile axle and thereby would be dutiable under the automobile category. Then Bailey said, "I wonder if the chairman of the committee is prepared to say whether this duty of 45 percent is the maximum revenue-producing duty or whether he thinks a higher duty would fetch more revenue?"

With this suggestion Bailey found himself an unlikely comrade in Senator Hale, a master protectionist and Aldrich's man on the floor. "I think I should agree with the Senator from Texas," Hale said with evident relish, "that any increase of the duty that could be afforded and could be paid by the owners of automobiles, which are not only a luxury but a nuisance, would be extremely proper for the Senate to consider...." Bailey offered, "We collected something more than $1,700,000 the last fiscal year from the importation of automobiles," to which Hale concluded, "Which is in itself a small mitigation for their presence." Bailey followed, "I thoroughly agree with the Senator, although he and I are probably the only ones not reconciled to those 'red devils.' Probably we may hereafter become reconciled ourselves." Hale replied, "I think the Senator and I are behind the times but I am very glad to have his company." Especially over a high duty.

"I would make people who import luxuries which are also nuisances pay for the privilege," continued Bailey, "and I would only be deterred by the fear that an increase in the duty might decrease the importations. In this, like in all other duties levied upon luxuries, I would stop only at the maximum revenue-producing point." This was populist nonsense mixed with sound economics. The Senate argued over silk, paintings, and china, and invariably levied as much "revenue-producing" duties as possible. Bailey here laid out a problem that would vex his own party's attempt at revision four years hence. What, exactly, is the ideal "revenue-producing" duty? Like "the difference between costs here and abroad," it was an abstraction that only practice, not theory, could reveal, if at all. These equations mattered little with the automobile "nuisances."

Of all the Senate defenders of the common man there was not a one who looked to the automobile as anything but a luxury. If the progressives felt differently they kept quiet. There was no free listing of motors on behalf of the farmer. Only two Senators had anything nice to say about the automobile, and one did so only haltingly. Michigan Senator Smith said that his state was "very proud" of its automobiles, but he went no further. Smith, a railroader, went both ways on autos. They are "destructive of roads," he declared.

The only champion of the automobile was none other than Nelson A. Aldrich,

19. This and the following quotations from *CR*, 5/21/09, pp. 2267–2270.

protector of interests, reformer of low tariffs, and owner of a fine Packard limousine. Here we see the earnestness with which Aldrich managed the tariff fight. "I have no question whatever that within a very few years the great mass of the automobiles that are used in this country will be made here. There can be no question about that. I think the American automobiles to-day are the best in the world." This, of course, due to the tariff. "But there are now, and will be for some time to come, a great many people, undoubtedly, who will buy some fancy makes of French or German automobiles, I am inclined to think that if we make the rate any higher we would in the end get less revenue." Quite an admission. For him a 50 percent rate was protection enough.

Senator Bacon took advantage of the discussion to go after Aldrich. He told of a friend who explained that "but one class of automobiles are imported at the present time. He gave me the name. It is a French machine. I do not remember it." What he was trying to remember was "limousine." Aldrich didn't catch this, and so corrected Bacon that there were "a dozen leading makes" that are imported. Thinking Aldrich cornered, Bailey offered that foreign autos ought have the name of the maker and country of origin engraved on them in plain view to "tell which Senators are riding in imported automobiles. I hope no Senator would ride in an imported automobile. I saw the Senator from Rhode Island riding in a very finely finished one, and I wondered if it was made in this country." Aldrich shot back, "It was made in this country. It was made in Detroit, Michigan," to which Smith threw in, "We are very proud of it."

Next, standpatter Heyburn laid in. Senate motorphobia was truly bipartisan. "I believe no greater imposition has entered this country at any time than these great snorting steam machines," he began. "Not only occupying, but destroying the roads," interjected Smith. Heyburn continued his condemnation:

> The roads were never made nor were the road laws of the country ever passed in contemplation of such a use. They are made throughout the country by the taxes and the labor of people who never can afford to own these machines, and they must stand off or flee to some place of safety as this great engine of destruction goes over the roads. I think I am not narrow in mind in regard to these things. I look at it from a practical standpoint. I have known, and every man in this room has known, of carriages driven by women being tossed aside and people injured or killed by these machines. I have in my mind more than one instance of the kind. They shout with glee as they see the farmer flying through the air, his horses in one direction and the farmer in another. Why, it is a subject of jest in the papers. The automobile goes along, and the farmer is distributed over the fence, perhaps into his own field. I had hoped that the committee would find that this tax upon pride might pay at least 100 percent, because that is all it is. No one ever bought a foreign automobile, except as instigated by the pride of ownership....

The President's modernity had not reached the leaders of the Senate. Such progressiveness was confined to the back seats of certain Peerless and Packard limousines belonging to the Senate's President and its reviled majority leader, the supposed leading antagonist of the people.

As for automobiles, the Senate insurgents had nothing to say. Beveridge followed Heyburn's soliloquy on road demons with an angry retort to previous accusations that Beveridge had wasted the Senate's time. He accused Hale of "jesting" about automobiles rather than seriously discussing the duties to be placed on them. Hale laughed at Beveridge, calling him "my young friend." Worse, Hale accused

Beveridge of playing politics. "I keep no account with the Committee on Finance, debt and credit, voting with them half the time and voting against them half the time."

"The Senate insurgents had more than enthusiasm," Pringle wrote, "they had a flair for hard, intelligent work. They divided the schedules amongst themselves, so that each would become a master of the cotton ... or other important rates. They made speeches or attended committee meetings in the daytime. At night they met at somebody's house — one feature was a case of beer supplied by the host — and pored over complicated statistics." Pringle's praise aside, the insurgents had a bad case of seriousness.[20] Progressive William Allen White carried it with him all the way to 1939, when he wrote to Pringle,

> My one quarrel with you is in your statement that the progressives were more emotional than the standpatters. Aldrich was just as emotional as Bristow. Aldrich's emotion was contempt born [of] hate and arrogance. Bristow's was righteous indignation and a zeal for good works.[21]

Quite a fence there the insurgents built. Taft, for example, wanted to get along with Beveridge. Prior to March, he received Beveridge to discuss Cabinet possibilities and afterwards invited him to the White House and on motor rides. But in the end Taft couldn't like the guy. "Beveridge is such an honest and able man," he told Archie. "I often wonder what makes him such a selfish pig. He never talks. He only preaches." To his wife Taft wrote, "He tires me awfully. He attitudinizes so much and is so self-centered and so self-absorbed."[22]

These were unforgivable sins, pride and poor company. Aldrich, especially, and even Cannon, were at least interesting in the dining room. Another insurgent, Clapp, Taft called "unstable, bitter and extreme." Beyond the personalities, Taft objected most to insurgent tactics and logics, which, he concluded, were the result of the personalities. "Mr. Clapp is a light-weight and has shown himself to be so in so many regards that I have no confidence in him," Taft wrote. "I was very much opposed to the Clapp amendment because it was unjust, and it was an altogether improper method of securing all for which he professed a desire."[23] For La Follette, Taft had no patience. Taft complained to his wife of an appearance, "where I shall have the pleasure of listening to Mr. La Follette, and somebody else equally objectionable."[24]

20. Pringle, p. 432. Cannon chocked it up to "exaggerated opinions of their own importance" (*The Memoirs of Joseph Gurney "Uncle Joe" Cannon*, p. 136). La Follette's autobiography complained that Aldrich "secured the adoption of an order that the Senate should meet ... at 10 o'clock in the morning, and that the sessions should continue without recess or adjournment until 11 o'clock at night ... [forcing] those Senators who were conscientiously investigating schedules either to abandon all of their efforts or to take the course pursued by our little group" (La Follette, pp. 442–443). Through to May, the Senate generally met between ten-thirty and noon and adjourned the afternoon sessions between four and six, taking weekends off. Little progress was made as the insurgents bottled up the debates. One June 1st, the Senate adopted a resolution to meet from 10:30 to 5:30, then from 8:00 to "no later" than 11:00. La Follette was absent, but his compatriot Beveridge said he "heartily" favored the resolution (*CR*, p. 2604–2607). A typical session that resulted was June 3. After listening to La Follette and Beveridge all day, the Senate reassembled at 8:00. Beveridge announced that La Follette was "ill, due to the great heat of the day and the prolonged and unusual exertion to which he was put in speaking for so many hours this afternoon" (which begs the question of who was put to what?). Even without him, the debate went until 11:00. They met at 10:30 the next day (*CR*, pp. 2678–2721).
21. White to Pringle, 9/7/39, Pringle Papers, Library of Congress.
22. Butt, 4/19/09, p. 58 and Taft to Helen Taft, 7/14/09.
23. Taft to EH Gary, 7/12/09. This letter is an interesting example of Taft's methods: it was written to Judge Gary, head of U.S. Steel, and in it Taft mentions speaking to Aldrich about Clapp's amendment to the corporation tax bill, which both Gary and Aldrich hated, and which Taft had proposed.
24. Taft to Helen Taft, 7/11/09.

Finally, Pringle misunderstood that it was Aldrich who mastered the schedules.[25] The insurgents learned a trick or two, notably the grand gesture, but they played defense, always in reply to their opponent's overpowering spin. Their ugly fate was to bounce between the regulars and the Democrats, who played them like poker chips.

Only La Follette said anything of relevance outside Aldrich's steamroller on the automobile duty. Before Aldrich raised the tariff to fifty percent, La Follette managed a sly condemnation of the entire tariff process. He asked that before the vote be taken he read from a private letter "with the sole purpose of securing information." It regarded an industry circular in praise the deft work of Henry B. Joy and Benjamin Briscoe to secure the Payne rate of 45 percent. The pamphlet bragged of the victory to exclude cylinder castings from the standard rate for metal products and its removal to the automobile category at a higher rate. La Follette's letter writer was in sympathy with the earlier testimony of W. C. Durant that this duty protected only profits and bad management. "In my judgement," La Follette's anonymous writer stated, "this is the kind of protectionism we curse.... No one has been so noisy and noisome as Henry B. Joy. We imported $3,000,000 of automobiles and exported $5,000,000 last year. A good many automobile manufacturers think no duty at all is needed. I, however, agree that the great majority of them need a considerable protection: whether so or not, I wholly disapprove of such efforts as are praised in the inclosed circular."

* * *

Nobody had any illusions that the President wanted "genuine" revision. The question was what he was going to get and would he sign it. Taft had a clear view of who was where. Cannon was cleanly reelected as Speaker. Aldrich proved his hold over the Senate resolute. Although Taft decided to work with, not against that power, he was hardly acquiescent. He held the veto sword high. He encouraged Beveridge in the fight.[26] He asked La Follette his thoughts. Meanwhile, the Senate insurgents ranted at Aldrich in the Congressional Record and their newspapers— and lost vote after vote.

Into June not much changed. Aldrich

25. Even Bowers admitted that Aldrich had, from his first days in the Senate, "studied the tariff, mastered its intricacies, and"—but of course—"acquainted himself with the wishes of the manufacturers of his State and New England" (p. 315). Bowers drew his description of Aldrich from N.W. Stephenson's biography, *Nelson W. Aldrich* (1930), and while he agreed with the detail, he sketched an opposite conclusion. Admitting that "Aldrich had a genius for leadership," Bowers only saw in it a "representative ... of Big Business" whose constituency was Pittsburgh and Zanesville, not "the masses of Rhode Island." (Hammond wrote, "Aldrich was an artist in steering legislation"; p. 552). Bowers' paranoiac praise of Aldrich is quite fun: "His mind was clear and powerful, and always he knew precisely what he wanted. Seldom was he caught unprepared with a plan. While others knew they were opposed to something pending, he always knew what to propose as a substitute while the others drifted in confusion. He had superior facilities for familiarizing himself with all the intricacies of any question...." Aldrich was "haughty, aristocratic ... at times arrogant...." and so on. Beveridge himself, it seems, understood the evil genius. "It is impossible to imagine anybody more charming than Senator Aldrich," he said. "He loved bright company, was fond of wit, jokes, repartee. He was one of the few leaders who had a bent for society; in this respect he resembled Alexander Hamilton, whom he admired more than any other character in history." What Bowers was about here was to build up his hero's glory in standing up to the "despot," especially in contrast to other "timid" Senators (Bowers, pp. 317–323).

26. For example, Beveridge wanted an increase in the tobacco tax. He felt himself a crusader against the tobacco trust, for when an emergency tax from the Spanish American War was rescinded the trust didn't pass the savings on to the consumer. Taft intervened and came away with a compromise with Aldrich that Beveridge considered treasonous. Such was the insurgent attitude towards any legislation that didn't go completely his way (see Bowers, p. 362).

raised insurgent ire for having sat upon unfriendly German labor reports that would have thrown the "difference between the cost of production at home and abroad" to a lower corollary. Bailey got into a fistfight with a reporter over revelations of certain unseemly business interests.[27] The other congressional relic, Cannon, made news for a boxing demonstration with "Philadelphia Jack" O'Brien. The Speaker's fighting reputation was furthered at the expense of the House Clerk. That man, Alexander McDowell, made the untimely suggestion that the 73-year old, cigar-chomping Speaker only knew how to fight "with a gavel." "Is that so?" Cannon replied without removing his cigar. "Put up your dukes right now and I'll show you a trick or two." McDowell gave an embarrassed, hesitant demonstration. Cannon insisted. "Oh, come, come. Get in proper position.... You look like an elderly lady trying to shoo chickens out of a garden path. Put your left foot forward and guard with your left arm. That's better. Now look out!" Cannon's moves "had the effect of completely demoralizing McDowell.... Sidestepping quickly he feinted wickedly with his left for the McDowell chin, and, as the Clerk threw up both guards, drove a hard one into the official's ribs." The clerk bent over in pain. Cannon walked away, muttering, "It was a shame to do it." When McDowell recovered, he protested, "Come back and make it a finish fight. I dare you." Cannon exhaled a thick smoke. "Aw, go and get a reputation first."[28]

One of Taft's most conspicuous events that spring was his very public presence at the Wright airship trials. "Aeronautics" was no new concept. George Washington presided over a balloon launch. Observers in balloons ringed the city of Washington during the Civil War. During Roosevelt's day daredevils dangled on trapezes and parachuted from balloons. The new word "dirigible" arrived along with automobiles, representing the application of light-weight automobile motors to lighter-than-air travel. Gliders had been around in fancy forever and in certain realities for some time, starting with Ben Franklin's kites and ending with Samuel Langley's much-ridiculed and not-so-flying machines. These machines heard from the Wright brothers starting in late 1905 were something else. Flight "without aid of balloon or gas bag" was an oddity, as if an automobile bastard had taken to air.[29] The motorists knew what was up. They pronounced their thrill and threw the Wright brothers a coming out party. The Aero Club of America, founded by the rich of the ACA, threw the spotlight on the amazing achievement at the January 1906 New York Automobile Show.[30]

Meanwhile, that land of a "frugal mind" was amidst negotiations for the European rights to the invention for $100,000, no skinny figure. As the Aero Club showed off the flying machine to the New York curious who tried with frustrated imaginations to equate kites, gliders, and automobile engines to birds and balloons, the French were getting busy with the Wrights.[31] The brothers had kept their secret for three years. What escaped notice for lunacy was dismissed as an evil

27. "Texas Tells Bailey Its Opinion of Him," *NYT*, 5/29/09.
28. "Cannon Lands with Fist," *NYT*, 6/2/09.
29. "Another Attempt to Solve Aerial Navigation," *NYT*, 1/7/06.
30. The Aero Club was formed in 1905 by seventy members of the ACA to solve the "problem of aerial navigation." While looking at the "immature" technology of "flying machines," the Club also sponsored traditional ballooning (see "News of the Clubs," *Automobile*, 11/9/05, p. 533 and "Balloons to Be Shown at Auto Show," *NYT*, 12/24/05).
31. "The New Flying Machines," *NYT* editorial, 3/2/06. The deal was not cut until 1908, after considerable demonstration.

Taft recognized the emerging airplane technology. His War Department in 1908 invited the Wright brothers to demonstrate their machines. The first trials ended in a crash and the death of an Army observer. Orville was back the next year — to President Taft's fullest endorsement, which included a government contract and a gold medal. Pictured here are the Signal Corps trials at which Orville set several world records. President Taft took the new White House automobiles to view the flying machine his government would soon purchase. Another notable event there occurred, the first tailgate party. Alice Longworth, Roosevelt's unruly, lively daughter, handed out "lemonade" from the back of her automobile during the tests. (Courtesy Library of Congress)

genius, which was fine with the brothers who were more concerned with perfecting their new art and protecting their patents than with publicity. Americans learned about the Wrights by osmosis. News leaked through the wires from Europe. Imitators got busy, such as the great Alexander Graham Bell, who teamed up with Glenn Curtiss. As the Wrights collected trophies in Europe, a test of Bell's "aerodrome," called the "Red Wing," was heralded as the first successful public demonstration of "heavier-than-air" flight in America. That was in 1908. The Wrights knew where to mine gold.

In 1907, Secretary of War Taft asked Congress for balloons for the Signal Corps. Europe's great advantage was cited as the exigence.[32] Later that month his Army decided to include the "aeroplane" in its investigation of the skies. The Wrights were invited to show off their wares.[33] The result was tests at Ft. Meyer, Virginia, in September, 1908. And it ended badly. News of

32. "May Ask Congress for Army Airship," *NYT*, 11/11/07.
33. "Army to Buy Aeroplane," *NYT*, 11/26/07.

world records for sustained flight were shattered along with a broken propeller that drifted like paper to the ground. Orville attempted to glide to safety, but he was too low for recovery. The crash killed his passenger, an Army observer, and landed himself in the hospital.[34]

Before the accident, speculation arose that Roosevelt would take a ride:

> The new sensation in the Government trials in aeronautics was furnished by a persistent report that President Roosevelt had announced his intention of going up with the aviator.... Mr. Roosevelt is given to the espousal of the unusual. He startled the country only a year or so ago by diving beneath the waters of Long Island Sound in a submarine boat. It is not illogical that he desires to invade another element.... Mr. Wright , however, is not enthusiastic over the matter.[35]

Roosevelt wasn't around for the tests, and he had already denied himself of "opportunities ... to show his prowess as a navigator of the atmosphere" with balloon rides. After his son took flight in Army balloons it was thought he might succumb to the temptation. His son's near crash landing ended the speculation.[36]

Roosevelt finally joined the matter when in December, 1908 he agreed to present a medal to the Wright brothers on behalf of the Aero Club. He refused to do it at the Club, instead offering up the White House, which the Club gladly accepted. Congress set to discussion of its own recognition of the now-famous Wrights.[37] These plans went nowhere for the rest of Roosevelt's term. Taft picked it up when Orville was back to redeem himself and the contract in June of 1909. Butt wrote of a Dayton man who told him that "for years, [the brothers] were considered to be half cracked, and it was not until of late, after Europe had crowned them as victors, that they were taken seriously. Indeed, the President referred to this himself, and wondered when the time would come when America would accept its own without waiting for the verdict of the rest of the world."[38] Taft was certain of their accomplishment. He made sure the city was prepared for the welcome. Although Butt felt the President's remarks at the presentation were "jocular" and "undignified," Taft took this flying business seriously.[39] He attended the Wright trials, and he ordered his Army to assist at other demonstrations.[40] With establishment of the Army flight school at nearby College, Park, Washington became one of the airplane centers of the nation.

When told that the Congressional medals would not be prepared in time, Taft was furious. He demanded a line to the Philadelphia mint. With the Superintendent on the phone, he said, "This is Mr. Taft. Why aren't the Wright medals to be ready...? What's that? W-e-l-l, I think I'm

34. "How Orville Wright's Aeroplane Fell," *Automobile*, 9/24/08.
35. "President May Go Up in Wright Airship," *NYT*, 9/15/08.
36. "Roosevelt Draws a Line," 2/11/08 and "Roosevelt Wants Air Trip," *NYT*, 4/24/08.
37. "Honor For Wrights," 12/17/08 and "Wright Gold Medal Plans," *NYT*, 12/22/08.
38. Butt, 6/11/09, p. 117.
39. Butt had a passion for airplanes, which colored his view of Taft's speech. "His remarks should have added another period, or at least a semicolon, to our history.... I did not think it was the time for jocularity, for the conquering of the air just at this time is the greatest problem before the world" (Butt, 6/11/09, p. 116). Later Butt became furious at the President for not letting him try one out. "I don't mind if Fitzgerald gets his neck broken," Taft told him, "but I can't afford to lose you" (Butt, 9/8/10, p. 507). Butt wrote, "I was sullen the rest of the afternoon.... I was never so keen to do a thing in my life before."
40. For example, see Hilles to RS Shaw, 7/13/11 (case file 1598) regarding Taft's orders for Army participation at a Chicago aviation meet, and "Needs of Aviation Confided to Taft," *NYT*, 1/28/12, for his attendance at an Aero Club banquet.

entitled to know. I'm rather interested. Oh, yes, I'm frequently guilty of taking an interest in the affairs of the Mint. No, I don't think it is unusual. You see, Representative Cox has just reported to me at the White House — why, yes, this is President Taft. You didn't know it? Now, tut-tut-tut, don't apologize. That's all right. You'll have them ready? Fine. Good-bye."[41]

At the award ceremony, Taft celebrated the new technology and spoke for its peaceful use. Rep. Parsons of New York noted that this was the first time a President had officially endorsed aeronautics since George Washington assisted a balloon launch. Taft demurred, saying that had his predecessor been there he would have honored the inventors with not just a medal but a ride. Taft's deferral to Roosevelt was sincere, but misplaced. That record-breaking President had ignored the technology along with the rest of the country for its association with automobiles and wealth.[42]

* * *

As Mr. Landis of the U.S. Mint learned the hard way, Taft would get what he wanted. And as the famous orator and demagogue "Justice" Stafford found when Taft's blood was up he was unconquerable. At a banquet in May of 1909, Stafford gave an hour-long speech on suffrage for the District of Columbia. Taft sat through it and the enthusiastic applause it aroused, showing only "that half-cynical smile which is indicative of good-natured disgust," wrote Butt, who was unsure how the President might react. Rather than acquiesce to the evening's enthusiasms Taft grabbed the reigns in defiance. "He not only declared against the franchise, but ridiculed Stafford and made him appear absolutely foolish," wrote Archie. "He belittled his judgement and denounced his entire theory of local government.... He gesticulated and his voice rose to great heights ... his whole judicial nature had been aroused...."[43]

Pringle wrote, "As president, Taft had often failed dismally in persuading the politicians to do his will or the public to support him." In 1910, Vice President Sherman had a different take. "Behind his pleasing exterior is a force of character which leads him always on the path of duty no matter what obstacle he encounters."[44] Sherman thus pointed to the up side of Bailey's admonition that Taft's judicial training "teaches him to oppose his will against all obstacles."[45] From his automobiles, to his tariff bills, to his renomination, Taft took what was his. What was beyond his reach he accepted and moved on. He signed Payne and pledged its modification. He was a realist, but he never surrendered. As Roosevelt would learn in the wild Republican nomination fight of 1912, Taft was a fighter to the bone.

All spring Bailey and Cummins kept up the income tax talk. Up to May, Aldrich managed to contain the talk to talk. By mid–June, he felt the noose tightening. While Senator Dolliver made a sarcastic pleading for a wool reduction that was "just enough to enable a man with a good conscience to defend the system before the country," Heyburn proved him right. "If it is necessary to keep out foreign compe-

41. "Taft Scares an Official," *NYT*, 6/8/09.
42. "Success Well Won, Taft Tells Wrights," *NYT*, 6/11/09. While he called for its use in peace, Taft admitted that the airplane would be developed for war.
43. Senator Tillman, himself a demagogue of some stature, afterwards told Taft, "Mr. President, I did not believe it was in you. I sat there astonished that you had the hardihood to hit them as you did. I think that speech of yours settles the question of franchise for all times in this self-centered community" (Butt, 5/10/09, pp. 79–81; for Taft's speech see Addresses, Reel 566, p. 42, LC).
44. Pringle, p. 994, "Ohio Sons Cheer Wrights and Taft," *NYT*, 1/11/10.
45. *CR*, 4/10/09, p. 1314.

tition, I would vote a rate of 1,000 percent." "Then where would our revenues come from?" inquired Senator Nelson. "Oh, we can always count on the vanity of people who would pay anything to have a foreign label or foreign coat of arms on their purchases," Heyburn replied. "You had better vote for the income tax," Nelson dead panned and sat down.

Confusion amongst its partisans kept an income tax resolution from a vote. Bailey wanted his 5 percent tax, Cummins wanted a sliding scale scheme, and Dixon argued for a corporation tax. Borah wanted his name on a bill of his own. The rest went this way or that over all the above or some other income, inheritance or — get this— stamp tax. The Democrats, meanwhile, could only agree on Bailey's tax and not on the tariff. Regional interests pulled at the opposition glue and weakened their ability to combine. Taft, who started it all, watched, waited. He split the Senate into breakfast meetings, golf rounds, motor car rides, and afternoon conferences. One by one, he laid his plan.

Everyone knew something was coming from the President, but no one knew exactly what or when. The insurgents, who had failed to force a vote on an income tax, were in mid–June about to strike. Taft knew this. He also knew that it was Aldrich's worst fear. Just as the insurgents gathered behind Bailey, Taft let it loose. The President's moment came precisely when Aldrich became most desperate and the insurgents were most confident. It broke them both. Aldrich got stuck with an income tax and the insurgents didn't get theirs. "He has pocketed every ball," Archie wrote.[46] Taft settled all questions about an alternative tax with a message to Congress on June 15:

> In my inaugural address.... I invited attention to the necessity for a revision of the tariff at this session, and stated the principles upon which I thought the revision should be effected. I referred to the then rapidly increasing deficit and pointed out the obligation on the part of the framers of the Tariff bill to arrange the duty so as to secure an adequate income, and suggested that if it was not possible to do so by import duties, new kinds of taxation must be adopted, and among them I recommended a graduated inheritance tax as correct in principle as certain and easy of collection.

Stop right there:

> ...new kinds of taxation must be adopted....

Wasn't anybody listening on March 4? This dagger had Aldrich's name on it:

> ...as correct in principle....

Then he continued with a lash upon the Democrats and the insurgents:

> ...I therefore recommend to the Congress that both houses, by two-thirds vote, shall propose an amendment to the Constitution conferring the power to levy an income tax upon the National Government without apportionment among the States in proportion to population.

Herein he both affirmed and answered the Pollock decision that annulled the income tax. To "re-enact" a law that was already declared unconstitutional, Taft said, was dangerous, as it "will not strengthen the popular confidence in the stability of judicial construction of the Constitution." A proper amendment would avoid the embarrassment, he explained. But he didn't ask for an income tax. To cover revenue deficiencies he instead suggested,

46. Butt, 6/20/09, p. 125.

> ...an amendment to the Tariff bill imposing upon all corporations and joint stock companies for profit, except National banks (otherwise taxed), savings banks, and building and loan associations, an excise tax measured by 2 percent on the net income of such corporations. This is an excise tax upon the privilege of doing business as an artificial entity and of freedom from a general partnership liability enjoyed by those who own the stock.[47]

Sound technical? It was. And, against the best hopes of the *Times* and business lobbies, it held up in court.[48] Aldrich was spared the personal income tax. Tariff opponents got new revenue to justify schedule reductions, and, with the additional regulatory powers over corporations, Roosevelt's legacy got a boost. Taft knew exactly what he was doing.

* * *

Taft ought to have felt a king's majesty at this time but for the deepest of personal tragedies. On May 17, his wife was felled by a stroke. Maybe it was the pressure of expectation or condemnations of her version of the First Lady. Maybe it was young Charlie's tonsillitis operation that day.[49] Maybe it was gravitational distress from spirited driving of the electric. (Sillier theories have been posited.) Whatever brings a stroke changes nothing of its effect. Mrs. Taft was hit amidst conversation with the Attorney General on a pleasant evening tour of the Potomac on the presidential yacht.

Butt ordered the vessel back to Washington. The President was in shock. "The trip back seemed interminable," Archie recalled, "and after reaching the dock we had to wait for the automobile. I practically carried her in my arms to the car. The ride home in the limousine was terrific." The President and Archie carried Mrs. Taft into the White House. "The President looked like a great stricken animal," wrote Archie. "I have never seen greater suffering or pain shown on a man's face."

That evening President Taft kept his schedule. He did not betray the horrible event of the day to his guests, who enjoyed themselves "to a special degree," Archie noted. "But what a dinner!" he lamented. "Every mouthful seemed to choke him, yet he never wavered in his duty...." Secrecy was called upon all involved. It made the papers the next day.[50] "He stands surrounded by sorrow now," wrote the Captain, "but it will not swerve him from his duty as he sees it." Taft kept to his schedule, which "has completely disarmed the sensationalists." Nevertheless, the President was entirely devoted to his wife's recovery. Everything that followed that summer was a backdrop to her illness.

Archie was amazed by the President's affections. "He seems to be thinking of her every second," he noted. Taft's desolation was never revealed to his wife, for whom he kept only smiles. He sat outside her room by himself, "looking into the distance." At golf, his usual enthusiasm was brief. Archie saw "a world of misery in his mind." The most Mrs. Taft could manage for the first weeks was a walk down the hall. One day the President and Butt set off for a horse ride. Helped by her nurse, Mrs. Taft came to the window to see her husband off. "She tried to smile," Archie

47. Taft long held that incorporation was a public grant, a privilege that was accountable to public purposes. See *The Conservative as Progressive*, by Stanley D. Solvick, *Northwest Ohio Quarterly*, Summer 1967, p. 39.
48. The *Times* called it, "the mark of a low depth of degradation in lawmaking ... a brat kidnapped out of the Denver platform of Bryan," and a Roosevelt law ("The Corporation Tax," editorial, 7/4/09).
49. "The operation was successful, but there was a good deal of blood, and the poor boy was hysterical when he came from under the ether," Butt noted (Butt, 5/17/09). See also "Mrs. Taft Stricken by Nervous Attack," *NYT*, 5/18/09.
50. When an usher told Butt the reporters learned of the attack, Taft prepared a statement.

wrote, "but it was only a ghost of her old smile." Still, Taft was encouraged. "On our return the President would not dismount until she had come to the window, and he threw her a kiss as he got off the saddle."

Shortly after the President launched his "bombshell in Congress," the Golf Cabinet, Archie, Edwards, and Senator Bourne, convened at the Chevy Chase links. The party returned to the White House and were informed that Mrs. Taft had taken a motor ride. The nurse said she was nervous "but once out of the White House she seemed to enjoy it." Her recovery henceforth would be measured by the regularity of her motor rides, marked particularly by her first trip in the Baker electric only a short time after her arrival to Beverly in July.[51]

51. From Butt, 5/17/09, 5/18/09, pp. 86–93, 5/27/09, p. 99, 6/22/09, p. 129, and the *Saturday Morning Citizen*, Beverly, MA, 7/17/09, as reproduced in the Beverly Historical Society website.

15

An Open House (Harmony Applied)

The day of the President's income tax message, Senator Owen presented his uppercased report on the tariff and its abominations. He presented table after table demonstrating the cost of labor, the friendly relationship between the tariff and the stock price of monopolies, the ruin it caused in the Panic of 1907, and the hypocrisy of its defenders. Right or wrong, his argument fell to a single thesis: "The bill should not pass, BECAUSE IT IS CONTRARY TO THE WILL OF THE AMERICAN PEOPLE."[1]

On July 8, the Senate came to its tariff conclusions, generally "contrary to the will" of the Democrats and insurgents, and specifically in disagreement with the House in 817 cases. With the standpat caucus intact, and Democratic and insurgent votes scattered to protect regional interests, Aldrich managed the outcome of almost every schedule, although not without compromise. Everyone took heat. The *Times* and its low-tariff editors skewered Taft for tactical error, capitulation, doing too little, and doing too much. Aldrich, of course, was blamed for it all, but even Democrats were attacked by Bryan, who caught them in that nebulous ceremony of lowering protective schedules while raising "revenue" duties—whatever that meant, and wherever that landed them, generally all over the place.

In Wallace Irwin's syndicated satire, *Hashimura Togo, the Japanese Schoolboy*, Togo's assignment was to report to his schoolmaster on the doings in Washington. There Togo discovered the official Senate reply to the Payne bill:

> From the House of Lords, Washington. To House of Commons, same place. Gentlemen and Insurgents: After so many useless months of dusty labor trying to Reform the Tariff without changing it in any way, we take pleasure in returning this depressing document with the assurance that we have accomplished almost nothing & hope you will do even less....[2]

On the editorial page, the *Times* laid it out plainly. The paper added up the electoral votes of the Midwest, subtracted them from the 1908 results, and concluded that the Republicans couldn't hold

1. *CR*, 6/15/09, p. 3252.
2. "Hashimura Togo, 'The Japanese Schoolboy,' Takes up the Tariff Question," *NYT*, 7/11/09.

a majority in the next election.[3] Taft wasn't running polls. Aside from quitting reading that paper, he was dealing with an altogether different reality. His strategy was paying off, and his conscience was clear. Despite all the criticism and confusion, throughout the 4,888 pages or 9,778,000 words of tariff debate in the Congressional Record, the Senate took its job seriously.[4] By the time the rates were printed every line of every schedule had been thoroughly raked. Every Aldrich victory came over a plainly presented, fully vetted argument on both sides. When the insurgents and Democrats won it was by force of argument. When they lost it was by votes, not ploys. Complaints of the muzzle, which arose from time to time during the debates, and vehemently afterwards, were not legitimate during the hearings. Though smashed by the votes, dissent was given its chance.

* * *

That was before the Conference Committee, which met to harmonize the differences between the House and Senate versions of the bill. With the exception of Payne, who went representing his own bill, the leadership of both houses sent men whose feet were stuck in protection. It was no longer philosophy, just politics and power.

Indignant at the show of bad faith with the choice of Conferees, and to preserve the original bill, Taft rolled up his sleeves. He believed in Sereno Payne, and he believed in his bill. "My impression is, from what I hear the country around, that the House bill, with a few exceptions, is regarded as a good bill," he wrote his wife. "The increases which have been made in the Senate have been exaggerated, so the public regard the Senate bill as a very bad bill, and the House bill, by contrast, as a good one."[5]

He declared that the Conference ought have "the reductions of both houses and increases of neither." He threatened the veto over a glove duty that was to reward a Cannon ally in the House, and when the Speaker menaced adjournment without a vote over a dispute on lumber rates, the President calmly advised him that Congress would be straightaway reconvened, Cannon's nightmare. As for Aldrich, Taft felt he was "sentimental" about his Senate work but willing to compromise. Aldrich worried that his troops would rebel against any downward revisions at Conference. "I told him he could use me as he pleases," Taft wrote his wife, "and that I would threaten him if he wished to, with a view to making some of these people come over."[6]

La Follette later claimed that before the Senate took up the bill Taft had promised to veto anything unreasonable that came out of it — a promise Taft did not make.[7] He couldn't have. La Follette's rear-view mirror image of a bill worth signing was one with duties lower than the original House bill, which, at the time, even La Follette had to know, was an impossibility. The House bill was wholly acceptable not only to Taft but to the entire Republican House caucus, save one, a Southerner. House insurgents to the man voted for it. Taft's strategy with the Senate and at Conference was to get a bill that the House would either accept or reject. He would let the House wield his veto pen. If

3. "A Matter of Votes," *NYT*, editorial, 6/17/09.
4. "9,776,000 Words on Tariff," *NYT,* 8/1/09. There were still five days of ranting to be added to this total.
5. Taft to Helen Taft, 7/11/09.
6. "Tariff Report In; Plan to Defeat It," *NYT*, 7/31/09, Pringle, pp. 439–440, and Taft to Helen Taft, 7/12/09.
7. La Follette, pp. 439–440. He reconstructed the history of the Payne bill to suit his opposition to Taft. For Taft's views, especially on the textile schedules, see Taft to Helen Taft, 7/11/09, 7/16/09, and 7/18/09.

the House accepted the final product, so would he. Purposefully or not, the Senate insurgents set up their own disappointment well in advance of the final outcome.

As the Conferees worked out the final increases and decreases, including a return to 45 percent on automobiles, the President reiterated what he meant by revision. Manufactures should be protected, but not so much as to promote monopoly. Raw materials should go with low or no rates of taxation. On July 16, twenty-three Republican regulars marched to the White House to protest the President's interference. He sent them packing with a statement that sparked headlines across the country. "President Taft is slow to wrath," wrote the *Pioneer Press* of St. Paul, which had already declared itself the eternal enemy of Taft should he not veto the bill, "but it is now disclosed that when once aroused he can be as strenuous as his distinguished predecessor." Over the next few days the *Times* ran articles on the President's strength.[8] Taft viewed it more simply. He wrote that night to his wife in Beverly,

> Some Congressmen and Senators came in today to talk to me about free raw materials, and to oppose it, but I spoke to them with considerable candor and I think they know generally that I am against their proposition. I want to get a bill that is substantially a downward revision, and if I don't get it out of the conference I shall not consent to have the bill passed at all. I shall not have to veto it. It will be sufficient to have it fail in the House, as it certainly will.[9]

The fight carried on through the next week. By the 25th, Taft had secured free hides, free oil, and a reduction in iron ore, and was on the way to smashing Cannon's gloves and the Senate's lumber duties. He was less sure of the insurgent attitude. "I don't know what the insurgents are going to do; whether Beveridge and his crowd are going to vote for the bill or to vote against it. It would be better for us, I think, if they were to vote for the bill, but I don't know how much better." On the 30th, the conferees again begged the President to lay off. "They have my last word," he told Archie. "And now I want to show my scorn for further negotiations by spending the afternoon on the golf links."[10]

That night the President and Captain Butt motored for an hour. Just minutes after they arrived at a dinner the message was received that the Conference was closed according to the President's latest demands. "Well, good friends," Taft announced, "this makes me very happy." Archie spoke first. "Mr. President, I have watched the struggle, and I congratulate you." Taft replied, "Did you expect me to weaken, Archie?" "Hardly that, sir, but I was afraid they might convince you." Alice Longworth "fairly danced in her delight," Archie wrote. Postmaster General Hitchcock, the most politically minded of the Taft Cabinet, arrived late with thoughts of compromise. He had met with some congressmen and wanted to impress upon the President the need for "harmony," which Taft's intervention at the Conference had threatened. Hitchcock was stunned when he heard the news. The President presided over a triumphant dinner. Motoring home, Taft told Archie, "I should not like my

8. "Taft Takes the Big Stick to the Aldrich Crowd," *Pioneer Press*, 7/17/09, "Taft Explains His Attitude on Tariff," 7/17/09, "The President's Laugh at its Fullest," "Tariff Bill to be As Taft Wants it" 7/18/09, "Taft Threat to Keep Congress in Session: Declares He Would Force Another Session If Senate Should Defeat Reductions" 7/20/09, and "Deadlock on Tariff, Payne Aiding Taft: Conference Is Halted and Aldrich and Canon Hasten to the White House," 7/21/09, *NYT*

9. Taft to Helen Taft, 7/16/09. The protest appears to have been a result the Taft deal with Aldrich, to "use me as he pleases...." If so it worked brilliantly.

10. Taft to Helen Taft, 7/25/09 and Butt, 7/30/09, pp. 163–164.

As the Payne tariff bill made its way through the special session of 1909, Taft laid low, playing golf, motoring, and attending the airplane trials — that is, keeping faithful to the promise for "harmony" between the executive and legislative branches. With "the Big Noise" gone off to Africa, Washington longed for consensus. Only, with tariff making, nobody would walk away happy. "Uncle Joe" and the House coughed up a reasonable tariff revision, but the Senate fight turned bitter between "standpatters" and "insurgents." The real game came from the White House when Taft dropped his "bombshell" proposal for an income tax amendment and a corporation income tax. The ploy disarmed insurgents and standpatters alike, and the tariff was kicked free of the Senate. Taft again squashed standpatter attempts to keep high duties at the joint Congressional Conference, and he signed his bill, the first major revenue bill in twelve years. *Judge* aptly portrayed a crippled but smiling tariff bill that the golfer President welcomed. (*Judge,* July 1909, Courtesy Library of Congress)

hostess to hear me say so, but the pleasantist thing about these dinners is the ride to and fro." Back at the White House the President asked for messages. There were none.

The next evening the President held a small dinner at the White House. The guests left at eleven, and the President had Archie call the steamer. A motor ride, Archie wrote, "always rests him and puts him in good condition for a healthful sleep." Before setting out, he spoke of the joys and the melancholies of the South Portico of the White House. "I remember once spending an hour here in the time of General Grant, and that evening still stands out more distinctly than any one evening in my life." He told Archie, "every President, since Monroe at least, has come here when worried and from this spot has renewed his courage for the fight — and most likely their best dreams were dreamed right here. I love to feel that Jackson must have been looking down this vista when he made up his mind to veto the bank bill … and that Lincoln's great soul was refreshed from this point.… I know that Theodore loved this spot … and his tempestuous nature would receive just that influence which made him one of the greatest figures the country has ever seen."[11]

Butt was amazed. "I have never seen him in just this

11. Butt, 8/1/09, pp. 165–167.

mood, and I felt that his soul was moved to great secret thoughts.... We got in the motor and never spoke, and we rode for nearly an hour without a word, and, stranger than all, he never slept, and when I glanced at him to see if he were asleep, he was looking hard into the fleeting darkness ahead. 'Good-night, old man,' was all he said as he got out of the motor and went indoors."

The President's final mood from the night before was with him still. When he had asked for his messages he was thinking of his wife.

* * *

In the end, Taft was pleased with the work of the Congress. He said much was accomplished although much needed to be done. Even the *Times* reported, "on the whole ... the reductions outnumber the increases, and therefore numerically it is a revision downward. And that is the fact on which the Republicans will place the greatest reliance in defending the measure before the people."[12] Leading progressive Albert Shaw had not yet discovered, as he would two years later, any betrayal by Taft and Payne. His monthly journal declared, "There have been many discouraging phases of this Congressional attempt to revise the tariff, but there have also been many things of a hopeful and promising kind; and especially toward the end there was a rapid clearing of the heavy atmosphere.... Speaking at large, however, it will be found that the new tariff is an improvement over the Dingley law in a great many important items...."[13]

Any disappointment the President may have had with the rates was hidden by his utter glee at what he called the "administrative features" of the bill, Philippines free trade, minimum and maximum rates, the corporation tax, the tariff board, and other side provisions.[14] He would not sacrifice those advances to please the insurgents or the *Times* and other newspapers. He would not ignore his party's will as expressed by its majority votes in Congress. He wrote his brother, "Of course, I could make a lot of cheap popularity for the time being by vetoing the bill, but it would leave the party in bad shape — it would leave us in a mess out of which I do not see how we could get, and the only person who would gain popularity would be your humble servant, and that at the expense of the party and men who have thus far stood with me loyally." Foremost on his mind were the "reforms of next year," he wrote, and for which he needed the Republican leadership, "so you see how much more hangs on the question than the mere subject of the rates in the tariff bill...."[15]

Following the Conference, House discontent splintered from the usual pattern over rules. Mann of Illinois swore eternal hostility to any paper bill written by the State of Maine. New Yorkers and other right-minded New Englanders condemned the corporation tax and threatened a bolt over that alone. Yet outside a small core, the rebels proved faithless mates. Twenty-

12. "Tariff Report In; Plan to Defeat It," *NYT*, 7/31/09.
13. *American Review of Reviews*, Aug. 1909, p. 131, 134. Though sympathetic to the insurgents, the article gives a fair summary of the events and situation. The latter quotation concluded that the most deficient aspects of the bill, the textile duties, would have to "await the more mature and scientific methods of study and treatment" of a "tariff commission or bureau" (p. 134), precisely Taft's strategy.
14. Taft to Helen Taft, 7/11/09. See glossary for minimum/maximum rates.
15. Taft to Horace Taft, 6/27/09. Pringle used the line as evidence that "Taft was almost always suspicious of any action likely to send a wave of popularity rolling toward him; he felt, possibly, that this, per se, proved that the action was unsound and demagogic" (p. 437). Taft was concerned, as he plainly told his brother, with his "reforms of next year" and with the state of the party. As for popularity, Taft enjoyed applause as much as any other politician; he didn't live for it. He had seen how far presidential popularity went in the 60th Congress.

eight insurgents could have thrown the bill the Democratic way. Only nineteen mustered the courage, most of whom, especially the Minnesota delegation, were on what became known as Taft's "reserve list" of emergency votes. Hiding behind the leadership's thin, but decisive majority, they were able to cast a negative vote for home consumption.

Taft's final work was to convince the Senate insurgents to vote quietly. He invited Dolliver, Beveridge, and Borah to lunch to plead if not their votes their silence. Taft wrote to Beveridge,

> I am very hopeful that the bill can be made such that even those who voted against it in the Senate, with one or two exceptions, will deem it their duty to vote for the bill when it comes out of conference ... and certainly this result would be very much better than such a confusion as would follow a veto, for it would make such a cleavage in the party that the hope of future legislation in the direction of reforms we all look to see made permanent, would be almost blasted.[16]

The examples Taft looked to were that of Borah and Nelson. Borah was angered by the rate on hides, but, as Taft told his wife, "I sent for Borah, of Idaho, and had a talk with him, and we made peace; for we had had somewhat of an issue before."[17] Nelson of Minnesota was compelled by local conditions to vote against the bill, but he didn't hold it against the President, which was fine by Taft. The rest simply couldn't keep their rebellion out of the Congressional Record. Amazingly, they were more unrepentant than the man they despised; Aldrich cooperated with the President, and the President covered his back for it.[18] The insurgents were too proud, prouder than even the Senate Czar. Taft was disgusted by the performance. Sure enough, as Carter blasted the corporation tax as too lenient, Dolliver hollered to posterity, "The American people are being duped with humbug and misrepresentation."[19]

On the closing day of the session Aldrich took the final word. He reviewed the accomplishments of the bill, thanked the Senators, and congratulated the American people "on the conclusion of a weary time, a weariness I share to the fullest extent." In summary he went straight to the criticism he knew would most bite: "Protection is not to protect or insure monopolies," he said. "No Senator can point out a single monopoly protected by this bill ... I can show that no increase has been made beyond a reasonable point." Then he confessed, "I could not get what I desired everywhere, but I want to say to the country that there has been devised no other bill so wise for the welfare of the country as this. I have no misgivings."

After final adjustments, the general bill was voted upon in the House and a resolution was made to adjourn along with the Senate at six o'clock. Twenty minutes before the hour, the Speaker ordered the hands of the clock advanced. Cannon then thanked the members. "Representing as we do in the aggregate of 90,000,000 people, producing as we do one-third of all the products of the civilized world, it is but natural when the chosen representatives ... should disagree.... Out of that disagreement comes compromises. Legislation is impossible except by the vote of a majority, and the majority cannot agree without compromise.... We have performed our duty to the best of our abil-

16. Taft to AJ Beveridge, 7/13/09.
17. Taft to Helen Taft, 7/22/09.
18. See Taft to Helen Taft, 7/12/09.
19. This quotation and the following section from "Whisky Decision Put Off" and "Taft Signs Bill; In Effect To-Day," *NYT*, 8/6/09.

ity." A reporter's description of the final scene noted, "The members appeared too tired to indulge in the usual hilarity which marks the close of a session, and they filed solemnly out, exchanging here and there a good-bye and best wishes for a pleasant vacation."

At three o'clock that afternoon, the White steamer was brought to the front of the White House. There it idled while awaiting word that the Government Printer had everything ready. The President and Captain Butt arrived to the Capitol at 4:45, his first visit since Inauguration. Taft was there to sign the most significant legislation in twelve years.[20] His entire Cabinet was beside him. Congressmen left the House and Senate chambers and lined the hallways to congratulate and shake the President's hand. To Heyburn, Taft said, "How are you, old high tariff?"

In the President's Room, Taft turned to Aldrich and smiled. "Well, I have not signed the bill yet. Do you think I ought to adjourn Congress before I sign it?" There would be no veto this day. "I certainly do not," Aldrich laughed. Payne walked in shortly thereafter with the document. At 5:07 of August 5, 1909, the President of the United States signed the Payne bill. Officially it was called the Payne Tariff bill. It would be called "Payne-Aldrich" by its enemies and by history. The President used the same pen as Cannon and Aldrich and handed it afterward to Payne, who grinned widely.

The only smile more broad that day came from the President. It was not over his signature of the general bill, which was executed with method. Taft's smile came earlier with the proud fixing of his name to the Philippines measure. To sign his name he used a pen of mother-of-pearl sent from the islands for the act. "I think he intends to send it to the Philippines," Butt wrote. "But he may retain it as an heirloom himself." Butt decided that the President was more pleased with the Philippine measure than the tariff bill itself. The President's official statement declared that he signed the bill,

> ...because I believe it to be the result of a sincere effort on the part of the Republican Party to make a downward revision, and to comply with the promises of the platform as they have been generally understood, and as I interpreted them in the campaign before the election. The bill is not a perfect tariff bill or a complete compliance with the promises made, strictly interpreted.... This is not a free trade bill. It was not intended to be. The Republican Party did not promise to make a free trade bill.[21]

He reviewed the various auxiliaries to the bill, including that which was most satisfying to him personally:

> The Philippine tariff section I have struggled to secure for ten years ... and it gratifies me exceedingly by my signature to give it the effect of law.

For those who look for portent from the clouds, the day of August 5 displayed all the significance of the ice storm of March 4. On Taft's motor ride up Pennsylvania Avenue the gods gave forth perfect golfing weather. No sooner had the President entered the Capitol than the skies blackened and were parted by lightning. Run that one by your Ouija board. The President was unmoved by the symbolism. As that March day before, he found only amusement in the weather. He told those gathered that they must be quite used to

20. The most significant legislation since 1897? Indeed. A revenue bill attends the most fundamental government issue, particularly one as far-reaching as the Payne tariff, which brought with it a dramatic change in the very form of government financing.
21. "President Taft's Message," *NYT*, 8/6/09.

the tumult. He left the building with the storm awash, disappointed only that the scheduled celebration dinner would be forced indoors.

The dinner that night was happy. Taft invited members of the Conference Committee, Democratic and Republican. A fine dinner was enjoyed by all, especially the President. This was the President's "Harmony Dinner." It is significant, that word, "harmony." Beveridge's biographer, Claude Bowers, called the dinner Taft's "moment of triumph — his last during the remainder of his term." That assessment is typical of the mindset: Bowers saw only Aldrich, Penrose, and Cannon drinking wine at the White House while "those whose names were the on the tongues of the people," the insurgents, were "speeding westward to arouse the people, already in revolt." Sanctimony flowed more freely on those trains than White House wine that night.[22] The Senate insurgents were high on dissent.

The President left the next morning for Massachusetts, happy with accomplishment, eager for golf and motoring, and anxious to be with his wife.

* * *

The Times grudgingly admitted the President's victory. "We do not say that Mr. Taft might reasonably have been expected to veto the bill he signed yesterday. It has been a long time in the making, and the revising of a tariff does in some measure disturb business.... Mr. Taft is a Republican. He might well have hesitated to veto a tariff bill enacted by a Republican Congress expressly summoned to meet for that purpose.... The country is probably fully aware neither of the vigor of his efforts nor of the resistance they encountered...." But, the paper concluded, "In signing the measure he confirms his minor triumphs, but accepts the major defeat."[23] The recommendation was that Taft ought have done as Grover Cleveland in 1894 and employed the pocket veto, letting the tariff in without a signature.

The problem was over the one schedule that marked the clear dividing line between protection and revision. The Old Guard would rather — and did — drink the poisoned glass than lose it. The Democrats would commit regicide with it three years later. Most of the final discussions in the Senate were over what was to become the most hated element of the Payne tariff, Schedule K, "Wool, and Manufactures of Wool." The rates went untouched in both houses from the beginning. At Conference, Taft was stuck with a wool schedule he knew to be unacceptable. Despite his declaration to seek further modification of the wool schedules, his pen was louder than his words that day.

Taft apologized for it thereafter as critics spun Schedule K into the Payne bill in its entirety. Nothing good in the bill the President could point to would placate them. By the time Taft escalated his rhetoric on Schedule K from distaste to condemnation, all associations between him and the words "genuine revision" were lost. Running on Schedule K, the Democrats in 1910 took the House. In 1912 they would get the whole farm, the Senate and the White House included.

22. Speaking of wine, Bowers accused Taft of serving cheap champagne at the Harmony Dinner to all but the evil standpat leaders who got the good stuff. Actually, Taft ordered the best champagne for the dinner, but Archie felt it would be "perfect nonsense to serve vintage wine to most of those people." Butt ordered that the good bottles be reserved for an important few. Bowers carefully worked his tale to imply that Butt acted on the President's orders. Taft had nothing to do with it (see Bowers, p. 365 and Butt, 8/6/09, pp. 171–172).
23. "The Tariff Revised by its Friends," *NYT*, editorial, 8/6/09.

Part Two
The Age of Hysteria

16

Civilizing the Savage: Motors, Roads and a Little Question of Money

While the tariff was still shaking loose, Taft escorted his wife to Beverly for the Fourth of July holidays. It was hoped that the "invigorating air of the sea" would restore her health."[1] The President kept by her side the whole way. He walked her from the train with great care to the White House landaulet that awaited at the station.

The entire town and thousands of visitors hoped to see the President. For his wife's sake, as well as to hide her condition, the President's train deliberately arrived earlier than the announced schedule. Nevertheless, the roads were crawling with the curious. The President's chauffeur was forced to a cautious pace. Later, from the lawn of his rented cottage, Taft gave a brief talk to the press who demanded to know all things tariff and Washington. He was in a fine mood, and unbothered by the legislative riot down South. He even consented to photographs, a hated ritual. He posed in an armchair on the lawn and told the reporters, "Now, gentlemen, shoot me full of holes, for this is your last opportunity this season."[2]

The weather, too, welcomed the President. He arrived that morning to clear skies. A storm threatened in the afternoon, but backed off, and it never rained. Fortune, it seems, smiled upon this venture and Mrs. Taft's recovery. She and the President took a motor ride under a tremendous and full rainbow that hung over the bay all the afternoon.

The *Times* ran a Sunday piece mocking little Beverly and the President's sly arrival, "like Peter Pan." There was "Archibald Willingham de Graffenried Clavering Butt," who arrived the day before to plan the President's deceit.[3] There was the Mayor, eager for attention and, surprise, surprise, showing up early with

1. "Rainbow for Taft in His Beverly Home," *NYT*, 7/5/09.
2. Butt, 7/4/09, pp. 134–135.
3. "Clavering," being the only addition to Butt's real name, is from the word, "claver," to gossip.

Celebrating the people. Celebrating the automobile. (Courtesy Library of Congress)

a prepared speech and copies for reporters, strangely found in his vest pocket. The city clerk and the postmaster stood nearby practicing their best "Hear! Hear!"s There were reporters earnestly trading rumors and making a story of the timing of the President's train. Photographers jostled for the best angle on the platform. When Taft arrived, "a wild excitement reigned supreme," wrote the satirist. "Even Capt. Butt yielded enough to the confusion of the moment to flick a bit of dust from his uniform." Before the Mayor could extract his speech, however, the President and Mrs. Taft were in the "big limousine" and away. And so it would go for Beverly, whose purpose for the President was escape from the masters and the parades of little towns like Beverly across the nation.[4]

Despite Beverly's disappointment with the President's search for peace, his association with the town was a happy one. Residents raked in the joys of high rents, full hotels, and the assorted business that follows a President.[5] The Tafts' choice of the North Shore reflected its social importance. Boston elites considered the area their own, but the exclusivity was long before broken when new money, such as Pittsburgh steeler Henry Clay Frick, put up palatial summer tents. Even the Brahmins were forced to pay their respects to Frick's very serious cash.

4. "How the President Arrived at Beverly Mass," *NYT*, 7/11/09.
5. See "Taft Starts Realty Boom," *NYT*, 4/19/09.

For the President, his Ohio friends were there, including the Andersons, the Boardmans, and the Longworths. "Cincinnati and Pittsburgh" had extended their hegemony to Henry Adams' home turf.

Frick was an interesting figure throughout the Taft period. He disliked publicity and politicians as much as politicians disliked the publicity of an association with him. Frick came up with Andrew Carnegie and made one of the world's great fortunes through development of coke furnaces. He spent his halcyon days buying art and watching politicians and old school Society grovel. Seeing the "best the North Shore had to offer" surrounding the man, Butt felt ashamed for them. "There are possibly a few who still hold out, but they will be there in time, just as that last Van Dyck ... finally found itself there."[6]

Butt was appalled at the President's relationship with Frick. During the following Summer of golfing at the Myopia club near Beverly, and ever playing the President's publicist, Butt appealed to the highest possible authority to keep him away from Frick. Mrs. Taft agreed. She had kept her husband out of a Rockefeller foursome at Augusta, but not even she was able to break the President's genuine enjoyment of Frick. The President played on. "We can't divorce them," Butt worried in July of 1910. All he could do was make fun of Frick's bad stroke.

The old man grew on him as Butt came to realize that Frick had supreme taste in art and company. "Nothing but the best satisfies him," Butt wrote,

> He wants everything about him on the same perfect scale. He told us, for instance, that his head chauffeur was taking lessons in aviation, and he had ordered him to pick out a good flying machine and buy it, for he wanted it especially to make his trips to the Myopia Club and return, as he was getting rather sick of the motor. The President asked him if he really intended to use the air for transportation. "Yes," said Frick, "just as soon as my man tells me he is satisfied that it is safe for me to try it. He is a splendid machinist, and it is his business to perfect himself in his trade. I have confidence that he will not take me in the air until he feels that he has mastered it.[7]

Whatever reservations Butt held were settled over a hand of poker. Getting there, he wrote, "the President and Norton [the President's secretary] and I slipped out of the house like criminals ... and stole past the secret service men and slipped as quietly into the Frick palace. In spite of the fact Norton and I highly disapproved of this latest move on the part of the President, we were quite keen for it and entered into the machinations of the President to deceive the secret service with more zest than we should have had." At the supreme summer home of "the steel magnate," surrounded by Rembrandts and Turners, the air cooled by Caruso and Melba on the phonograph, Norton and Butt sat by the President of the United States, the Secretary of State, and the owner of one of the world's greatest jackpots. Toking on a "delicious cigar," Butt wrote, "I was enjoying every minute I sat there. Every sense was being satisfied." Frick knew how to live. Norton, up and coming and full of himself, learned how the big boys play poker: poorly. He beat them all. As usual, the President enjoyed himself supremely, despite his horrible gambling. "How did you know I did not have four aces," he demanded of Butt, who held a straight over the President's bluff. "By your face, sir." Taft laughed, "Confound that face. I wish I had yours, Knox." Knox, who played a serious game, laughed back at him. "If you had, you might have more money. But you would not be President."

6. Butt, 9/3/09, p. 191 and 7/29/10, pp. 457–471.
7. Butt, 8/9/10, p. 468.

As always, Taft's diversions were golf, motoring, and wandering. The White House fleet was sent to accommodate these joys. For voyages up the coast, the Presidential yachts *Sylph* and *Mayflower* were moored in the harbor. For exercise, the President's horses were present. "We have all the motors with us, and still they are hardly sufficient to meet the demands of the family," Butt complained. "When I spoke of hiring another chauffeur to-day for the landaulet, Mrs. Taft objected, but the President thought it wise to get one." The President instructed her, "Let them have a good time while they can. In four years we may all have to become pedestrians again, and I want them each to look back upon this portion of their life with the keenest relish." Four automobiles weren't enough. Several cars were rented from the White Company, and when necessary, from a local agency. Archie concluded, "I have never seen anyone so keen about motoring as the President. He simply revels in it."[8]

* * *

Having been given a ride everywhere he went, Taft had probably ridden in more automobiles than any other person in the world. At the time, perhaps the only other person who tried out as many different cars in as many different places was Taft's 1908 rival, William Jennings Bryan. Then, Bryan's automobiling was part of campaigning, as he remained democratically "partial to horses." One of the earliest occasions of Bryan's motoring the author has identified came in January of 1908. In a side-line to a story of the evening's Gridiron Dinner, it was noted that the Perennial Contender was late. Delayed by his train just outside of town, Bryan rushed into the city by automobile. Motors otherwise stayed out of his campaign, with neither condemnation nor endorsement, but with a ride for the candidate in every town that wanted to show one off. Bryan learned the downside of motoring after the election. At Tampa his car hustled down a road. On the approach to a bridge a tire blew and Bryan was thrown, landing between the wrecked automobile and a bridge rail. His injuries were serious.[9]

Taft's own travels long brought him a certain intimacy with the laws of physics. In August 1907, his train derailed. He was unharmed and unfazed. "Secretary Taft aided in reassuring timid passengers," it was reported. Two months later in Manila, the horses pulling his carriage bolted. A bodyguard grabbed the reins and steered the team into a ditch. Just before the 1908 election, another train he was on derailed. By the time others reached the candidate, Taft was up, smiling, and asking what had happened. The more dangerous situation occurred that night—and he displayed even greater pluck—when he faced a crowd of steel workers in Cleveland. After speaking against their hero, the socialist Debs, Taft told the workers, "as this discussion seems to involve some issue as to whether I am a deep tyrant, deep at heart an oppressor of labor and otherwise, I have got to submit evidence that I do not eat a laborer every morning for breakfast; that I am not engaged in fighting that which is the backbone and sinew of the nation, the laboring classes."[10]

8. Butt, 8/10/09 and 8/15/09, pp.172–174.
9. "Bryan Is Injured in Auto Accident," *NYT*, 2/7/09. The earliest Bryan automobiling the author has found came in November, 1907, when Bryan visited New York. His hosts arranged to shuttle him between speeches in a "45" Premier automobile, with apologies: "Having several appointments ... scheduled at close intervals, it was determined by William Jennings Bryan that the automobile would be the most desirable conveyance" (*Automobile* photo caption, 11/7/07, p. 714).
10. "Taft in Railroad Wreck," 8/28/07, "Taft in a Runaway," 10/20/07, "Taft Shaken Up By Derailment of Car," 10/14/08, *NYT*. See also "Wreck Shocks President," *NYT*, 7/12/11, for worries over a deadly wreck of the "Federal Express" train that Taft frequently used.

The best-traveled War Secretary turned best-traveled President was to get used to these close calls, automotive and political. The first presidential motor accident almost occurred during the July 4th trip of 1909.[11] After a short stay at Beverly, Taft left for a joint British and French celebration of the discovery of Lake Champlain. There, he motored to Fort Ticonderoga to greet a crowd. It rained earlier in the day, perhaps in satisfaction of the desperate historical search for Taft's relationship to Thor. Whatever the mystical significance, the immediate result was wet earth. As the President's automobile took a hill, the wheels locked in the mud and the car slid sideways across the road. A "tense silence" overtook the crowd. Relief came as the chauffeur regained control. "The President was the least concerned of any person in the large throng," a reporter stated.[12] The ceremonies were followed by another rain storm which drenched the President and might give historians more cause for worry. Evidently at peace with his destiny, the President "seemed to rather enjoy the shower."

Another near miss came in Washington the following year. Pulling from the White House, the President jumped up from his seat and shouted at the chauffeur to watch out for a pedestrian. The driver veered and, in doing so, nearly rammed a trolley. A real and nearly serious accident occurred a week later in New York. This time the President's car actually collided with a trolley. His motor was second in a train of five cars running up Twenty-third Street led by a motorcycle policeman. At Eighth Avenue, a trolley that was stopped by the motorcyclist surged forward after the first car with policemen passed. The President's chauffeur deftly swerved to the left, but the car was caught and carried by the trolley a half-block down Eighth Avenue. No one was hurt. Taft smiled and waved the policemen forward, as he was hurrying to catch a midnight train for Washington.[13]

Taft was shaken. "It was the first time he has been away without me since he became President," Archie wrote. "And it was the first time he has had an accident ... the wonder is that he was not injured or killed, however he ... says I must not let [him] go alone again ... while it is very tiresome at times it is nice to feel that I am really of some use to him and that he misses me when I am not around."[14]

* * *

In August of 1909, the U.S. Army held maneuvers outside Boston that were to include a demonstration of the automobile as weapon of warfare. The Motor Age was held up by a Rhode Island cop. An Army automobile train was caught speeding and driving without licenses. It took seventeen hours to sort things out.[15] Must the U.S. Army obey state law? The Army was already at odds with various states over taxation of its properties. Now two dollar automobile licenses were the issue.

At Beverly was the entire White House garage, chauffeurs and all. It subjected Taft to one of the most vexing prob-

11. The first complaint against a presidential car came right away. That March, a man told the press the White House limousine carrying Mrs. Taft back from the Capitol caused his horse to bolt and his cart to be ruined. Captain Butt looked into it and concluded, "There is no foundation for the within claim, in as much as the horse was running away a square before the automobile got to him. I would recommend that no answer be sent at all, so as to avoid controversy and that letter be filed without answer" (Butt to FW Carpenter:, 3/26/09; see reel 348, case file 3573).
12. "Taft's Auto Skids on Dangerous Hill," *NYT*, 7/7/09.
13. "Taft Goes Westward to Greet Irishmen," 3/17/10 and "Street Car Grazes Taft's Automobile," 3/29/10, *NYT*.
14. Butt, 3/29/10, unpublished letter.
15. "Red Army Lands to Attack Boston," *NYT*, 8/15/09.

lems of early motoring, federalism. Not even the President of the United States could run his motors without permission of the locals. Or, could he? Or did his auto, like the English King's, "have more rights and privileges than a fire engine"?[16]

The White House avoided the matter in Beverly by registering its four and the two Secret Service autos locally. A Boston attorney was retained to register and pay for the plates and chauffeur licenses. The following summer Captain Butt had eight motors to register, the six from Washington plus two rented extras. The Massachusetts Highway Commission that year ruled that the President's automobiles need not sign up, in that the Commission was not entitled to charge a fee to the President. Problem: no fee, no license plate. Every cop on every road in the state would, and with joyful seriousness, halt any car that lacked plates. The matter was sent to the State Attorney General who ruled that the Commission could not issue plates without collecting fees. An appeal was made to the Governor who solved the matter by paying for the President's registrations. Seems silly, but it was a big deal. Wrote the *Times*, "The registration ... has brought the President and his military attache, Capt. Archie Butt, into a tangle with the red tape of Massachusetts officialdom, and it was only by the intervention of Gov. Eben S. Draper that it was straightened out."[17]

When Vice President Sherman took his government automobile to his Utica home in 1910, he caused another constitutional puzzle. The state demanded its indulgence. The President of the Senate refused. The situation arose in Maryland and Virginia in early 1911 when the White House asked for its permits for the year.[18] Taft's secretary, Norton, did not include payment with the registration requests. Both states took offense and refused to send the permits. "He's President, I know," said the Maryland State Motor Vehicle Commissioner, "but all automobilists look alike to me." Most democratic. The Commissioner further noted that he had advised the Sheriff of Montgomery County, Maryland, which borders the Federal city, to "let no man without a license escape." He was already angry that the Sheriff hadn't arrested the Vice President for not carrying a Maryland tag. "Princes, potentates, Presidents and Vice Presidents look alike to me in this automobile business," he stated.[19]

According to the Treasury Department, the U.S. Government owed no fees or taxes to either the District of Columbia or the states. More emphatically, the Quartermaster General, who was deeply involved in fights over state property tax assessments, declared, "By decision of the United States Supreme Court it is held to be settled law that the property of the United States and the instrumentalities whereby it performs its proper government functions cannot be taxed."[20] Taft ordered that the Attorney General give an opinion.

General Wickersham remitted a ten page analysis in which he concluded that automobile and driver licensing were

16. See "No Law for the King's Auto," *Automobile*, 4/11/07, p. 628.
17. "Taft's Vacation Delayed by Work," *NYT*, 7/3/10.
18. The White company arranged for the original Washington-area tags in 1909. A White House expense voucher to the White Company dated May 10, 1909, included $12.50 for "License and number pads Dist. Col., Va., & Md. For President's cars." Why the plural "cars" is unclear, unless White agents also registered the Pierce-Arrow (for Sherman's licenses see "Sherman Auto Exempt?" 9/8/10 and "Congress Provided Auto," *NYT*, 9/11/10). The 1911 Maryland fees were as follows: $2 per driver, $6 for autos of less than 20 horsepower, $12 for 20–40 horsepower, and $18 for over 40 horsepower (G Wickersham to Taft , 2/10/11).
19. "Demands Taft Auto Fee," 1/31/11 and "Taft Auto License Held Up," 2/1/11, *NYT*.
20. "Demands Taft Auto Fee."

established police powers to be exercised by states for the "conservation of the public safety." However, licensing fees were a tax and thereby "cannot be exacted" upon the federal government. He also noted that outside of regulating automobiles in the District of Columbia, Congress "has as yet passed no legislation" on interstate motoring.[21] In other words, states can regulate the President's automobiles and chauffeurs, including to require licensing but cannot charge a fee for it.

The issue was resolved by executive fiat, just as in Massachusetts earlier. The states, said the White House, reconsidered the matter." The Secretary of Virginia announced that "satisfactory arrangements" were discovered. What it was was peace with honor. The governors of Maryland and Virginia settled up without admitting defeat. "Regardless of the law," Crothers of Maryland said, "I have to-day directed that the tags be sent to President Taft for his four automobiles and that no charge be made for them. I think it is a courtesy due the Executive from a sovereign state that forms a part of the Commonwealth of the Nation."[22] Imagine that language today.

All the bother might have been avoided had in March of 1908 Congress enacted a bill introduced by Rep. Cocks of New York for national licensing of automobiles and drivers. The AAA, ALAM, and a chauffeurs' union testified to Congress as to the cruelty of the states. Motorists saw no difference between federal regulation of roads and that of rail and water routes. In February of 1910, AAA head Lewis R. Speare wrote in the group's magazine, "All automobilists who travel from one State to another are lawbreakers, simply because it is an impossibility for any human being to learn and remember all the diverse laws relating to automobiles.... If you blow your horn in one State, or city, you are arrested for disturbing the peace. If you do not blow your horn in another State you are arrested because you menace the life of citizens."

The President might well have chosen the North Shore for its roads. New York was at the fore of automobiling, but Massachusetts, led by a series of automobile-friendly governors, knew how to make a better road system. The difference was wholly political. Massachusetts politics were not nearly so complex as New York, where road building was impossibly braided through the state's maze of political factions and geographic power bases.

In New York, existing rules from a 1904 law and the State Highway Commission, consisting of "experts" appointed for six year terms in order to distance their work from politics, had escaped progress. Attempts to bring order to the state's road law and building went nowhere, including in 1909 when a reform bill was vetoed by Governor Hughes. The governor announced that the new bill failed to accommodate the "abuse of privilege" by and the "vexatious restraints" on motorists. The legislature went back to work, following the lead of a young state Senator, Albert Callan. Motorists fretted over a story of one of Callan's neighbors who told him, "Callan, I will vote for you, and I want you to pass a law so that I can stand out in my front yard and shoot every G — d motorist that passes my place." Against all worries, when Hughes signed the bill in June 1910 it was heralded as the first "scientific motor vehicle law" in the world. Speed was to be regulated by reasonableness, with police and courts empowered to decide between careful and negligent driving. Chauffeurs were to be licensed, joy-riding harshly

21. G Wickersham to Taft , 2/10/11.
22. Memorandum dated 2/15/11, BO James to Norton, 2/3/11, and "Free Auto Permits to Taft," *NYT*, 2/1/11.

punished, and auto registration more carefully and uniformly instituted.[23]

A crucial reform in Callan was that automobile fees and fines were to be applied to construction and maintenance of state highways. Here two vexing problems were faced, the one of revenue-hungry localities who looked to automobiles to pay the bills, and the other of automobiles destroying roads. Automobiles were a useful goat for so many ills as socialism and oppression. The more enduring charge was that the machines tore up the people's streets. Guilty as charged. That motorists ought pay for the roads was understood by all—except the motorists. The argument came down to whether the "vehicles should be made to fit the roads," as the New York Highway Commission reported in 1910, or, as motorists demanded, that the roads should fit the vehicles.[24]

That automobiles ruined the roads there was no doubt. "The latest charge against the automobile comes from New Jersey," wrote the *Automobile* in 1905, "where the farmers complain that the dust raised by passing machines drifts across the strawberry fields and settles upon the fruit, seriously affecting its market value."[25] As the cries grew, the Department of Agriculture's Office of Public Roads looked into it. In 1907 its chief, Logan Page, reported to Congress that automobiles were complicating the efforts of road builders. "Until the general introduction of automobiles, dust was considered as neither more nor less than a nuisance. The problem has, now, however, assumed a more serious aspect" (little spoken was that horse exhaust was a major contributor to the dust problem).[26] To his credit, Page kept to science, and his reports avoided condemnation of automobiles. He presented their effect as evidence without judgement. Out of office and free of politics, his predecessor, James W. Abbott, spoke directly to the problem. He called for autoists to "work openly for roads.... No one can say longer that the automobile interest should hold itself in the background lest it arouse antagonism." Except this: "Just how that should be undertaken, I am not yet prepared to say."[27]

The Roosevelt government's active ignorance of automobiles was fully manifested in the report of the Country Life Commission, Roosevelt's jewel. The Commission, Roosevelt bragged, held thirty public hearings and reviewed 120,000 farmer surveys. Its goal was "for better business and better living on the farm." The subject was so important he demanded Congress establish a Department of Country Life. Although quoting a farmer who stated what farmers needed most was good roads, the report dedicated all of three paragraphs to "Highways" and demanded only a "highway engineering service" to help the States "in working out effective and economical highway systems."[28] The word "automobile" didn't appear once.

23. From "Hughes Vetoes Proposed New York Law," 6/3/09, pp. 921–922 and "'Senator' Callan Plays Both Ends Against the Middle," 7/14/10, p. 64, *Automobile* and "Callan Bill Meets Many Requirements," *NYT*, 6/5/10. "Fictitious" tags were a problem. Habitual offenders and gangsters could speed away without worry of identification with fake license plates.

24. See "Motor Cars and Roads," *NYT* editorial, 1/13/10.

25. "Accused of Another Crime," *Automobile*, 6/22/05, p. 760.

26. "2,152,000 Miles of Public Road—7.14 percent. Improved," *Automobile*, 12/12/07, p. 898. See also, "Government Doing Little for Roads," *Automobile*, 3/7/07, p. 416. For horse dung and dust see "Looking Ahead in the Automobile Industry," *Automobile*, 3/3/10, p. 439.

27. "Time for Autoists to Work Openly For Roads," *Automobile*, 3/7/07, pp. 425–426. Abbott was a commissioner at the Office of Public Road Inquires, the predecessor to Page's office.

28. "Report of the Country Life Commission," U.S. Senate Document no. 705, 60th Congress, 2nd Session; pp. 5–7, 11, 36 (February 1909).

* * *

Things changed at the Office of Public Roads under Taft. The questions were the same, except with a new emphasis on automobiles. In May, 1909, Logan ran tests along Washington's Speedway.[29] The U.S. Army assisted, along with representatives of the AAA. The question at hand was the comparative effect of motor and horse traffic on macadam and dirt. With cameras capable of exposures of 1/2000 of a second, the "destructive effects" of automobiles were to be measured at speeds up to sixty-five miles an hour. One theory held that car bodies created a suction that lifted the earth as the vehicle passed. The AAA representative described how rubber tires kicked up dust which was then spread about by the wind of the car. Much thought was given to the differences between a carriage wheel, which was pulled from the front, and the rearward traction of automobiles. The most likely explanation was that the damage came of the combination of horses "cutting up the roads and automobiles stirring up and displacing the material thus cut up." Also came the simple observation that automobiles would do less damage than carriages were they run at a similar speeds.[30]

The Speedway had a macadam surface treated with petroleum as a coagulant to prevent dust. Macadam, named for its French inventor, was a century old road technology whose usefulness was challenged by the motor car. Macadam was crushed, layered rock held in place by a binding agent, usually sand or dirt. Rain, hooves, and slow-rolling iron wheels reinforced the surface, as stones were crushed and the binding agents impacted with use. Automobiles changed the formula by kicking up rather than pushing down the stones and filler.

Bituminous, asphaltic, and cement surfaces were the emerging technologies. With greater traffic, money, and urban politics, cities were the first to employ these surfaces. Statewide funds went to the political establishment which was yet weighted towards rural interests and where road builders knew only dirt and stone. Worse, the new hard surfaces were considered unsafe for horses; bad for horses meant bad for farmers, which meant too bad for automobiles. The public argument fell back from the new to the old, thus the New York Highway Commission's demand that automobiles pay for roads that could not support them. Motorists recoiled at the blame. To them, the roads were already bad, and the exigencies of automobiles would benefit all road users.

Whatever it was, it was expensive. In New York in 1910 there were 80,000 miles of state roads and another 10,000 miles built by towns. Of the state roads, about half were what the Highway Department bragged of as "improved." The remaining 40,000 miles were your basic mud trap in rain and dust bowl when dry.[31] The definition of "improved" meant crowned, grated, and with bridges. All were dirt. The best roads, of which about 4,000 miles were built or under construction, were of macadam. Across the nation, merely 2 percent of roads were "stone surfaced," and only 5 percent were graveled.[32]

In New York there was plenty of money for road building, what with commissions on bonds, profits on construction, and jobs to sell. That was the prob-

29. "Auto Tests on Macadam," *NYT*, 5/16/09.
30. "History of Good Roads Movement," *NYT*, 5/30/09, by Coker F. Clarkson of the ALAM.
31. "There are more than 40,000 miles of earth road, properly shaped and crowned, stones picked and removed, depressions filled, culverts and bridges repaired. Towns have constructed 8,000 miles of gravel roads, in first-class condition" ("Good Roads' Cost in New York State," *NYT*, 6/5/10).
32. "Road Situation in United States," *NYT*, 1/9/10.

lem. In 1912, the *Times* lamented, "The good roads of this State are not continuous. Because the $50,000,000 appropriated [in 1907] for their building was proportioned 'equitably' among the several counties, it was squandered on short stretches of highway that begin nowhere, end nowhere, and serve chiefly to line the pockets of local contractors who built them and are employed to keep them up."[33] A map of New York's roads matched one of its political structures.

In 1911, Democrat John Dix was made Governor. He proclaimed himself a "strenuous advocate of good roads." One of his first moves was to force through a bill to reconstitute the Highway Commission to be, shall we say, more amenable to politics. The money dispensing power was moved to the Public Works Office, and terms of the Commissioners were reduced to three years. What was at stake was not good roads but fifty million dollars and how, exactly, it might be split between Tammany and Albany. With their boys back in the saddle, it looked to go Tammany's way.[34]

Dix's legislation did much to redeem the New York highway system. The bill gave $2,000,000 for the completion of two existing "trunk lines" which were mere segments along the state's northern and southern borders. The "trunk" or "tree" form of road networks was the key to the Massachusetts example, in which the intra-state system was based upon core passages, with extensions following in importance and according to local initiatives. Good Roaders gloried in the New York plan and petitioned Washington and Ottawa to extend the northern road to Montreal. Taft replied to one advocate, "I have your letter in which you speak of an enterprise to build a broad highway of modern construction from New York City to Montreal. Of course I should like to see such an enterprise carried out. It would contribute to the social and business union of the two countries and cannot but be of benefit in many other ways."[35]

In a December 1910 report Agriculture Secretary Wilson stumbled into automotive revelation and spoke his department's first consent to the critical significance of automobiles to road building. Wilson, long a Good Roader and the farmer's best friend, reported to the President, "By reason of a rather remarkable combination of conditions, the immediate present may be considered the most important period in the history of road improvement in the United States." Wilson saw the moment as "transitional" from "extreme localization" of road manage-

33. Continuing ... "The American Association for Highway Improvement was born late, but not too late. Its mission since Nov. 22, 1910, has been to advocate the 'correlation of all road construction,' so that the important roads of each county shall connect with those of the adjoining counties, and those of each state with the roads of adjoining states" ("For Good Roads, Long Roads, "*NYT* editorial, 5/17/12; for the 1907 "Map Law" that allotted the $50,000,000 bond issues, see "Why New York Must Have a Second Bond Issue," *American Motorist*, Oct. 1912, p. 787).

34. Dix was also acting on a legitimate objection to government by commissions. The demise of the Highway Commission was a blessing to motorists, as the Commission proved itself backwards and unresponsive to their needs. In the New York Senate there was a sole Democratic dissenter to the move, a young politician by the name of Franklin Roosevelt, who was then commencing his crusade against Tammany. Dix was shortly thereafter accused of personally benefiting from the legislation, called the Emerson bill ("Dix Refutes 'Joker' Charge," *NYT* 2/21/11).

35. Taft to HD Hadley, 2/14/11. That August, a Louisiana Senator introduced a good roads bill that ended its long list of "whereas"-es with, "Whereas the President ... with wise patriotism, has publicly commended the enterprise for the construction of a highway from Montreal, Canada, to Miami, Florida, and also by open letter has endorsed the American Association for Highway Improvement...." (Senate Bill 3197, 8/0/11, *CR*). Another "whereas" complained that while this "white man's" government built no roads in the mainland, it made them for Eskimos, Puerto Ricans, Panamanians, and Filipinos.

ment to "the principle of centralization." He continued,

> It is a curious coincidence that the introduction of the motor vehicle at about the time when these changes in [road] administration began has brought about traffic conditions which have necessitated an equally radical departure from old methods of construction and maintenance. It will thus be seen that the entire subject of road improvement ... is passing through an exceedingly important period, in which the educational and scientific work of this branch of the service should prove of the greatest value.[36]

* * *

The 1909 Washington road tests were productive, although their most immediate result was that panicked locals complained to authorities that scorchers had usurped the Speedway. The Department of Agriculture's new attitude towards automobiles as expressed by Wilson came to fruition in another experiment during the summer of 1911. Acting on a $10,000 appropriation for the purpose, Page tested new technologies in "dust prevention," "road binders" and "methods of construction."[37] He selected Connecticut Avenue just north of Chevy Chase Circle at the Maryland boundary as a suitable location for its flatness and high traffic. A two-thirds of a mile stretch was divided into sections which were rebuilt with different surfaces, including "fill macadam," "modern pavement," "asphaltolene" and "asphalt binder." Standard Oil, Texas Co., the Good Roads Improvement Co. and others were invited to demonstrate, at their cost, the latest technologies. The greatest significance of the effort, however, was the specific Congressional endorsement of roads built to sustain automobile traffic. These materials were not needed for horses; they were detrimental to horses.

Again, the experiment caused some public outrage, this time directed at Taft. The following January an Ohio man wrote his Senator:

> At a Farmers Institute here yesterday afternoon, Mr. Jesse Taylor, speaking on the subject of Good Roads, made the statement that since 1851 no appropriation had been made by Congress for this purpose except in the Appropriation Bill of the last session of Congress, amounting to Ten Thousand Dollars, and that President Taft the day following its passage, had ordered the expenditure of the money in the building of a road to the Chevy Chase Golf Club Grounds, Washington, D.C. Mr. Taylor stated that the road had been built, as he had walked its entire length, ten miles, also saying "If Congress can build a road for Bill Taft to ride to the golf grounds, why can't something be done for the public?"[38]

Senator Burton wrote Taft, "Is this statement of Taylor's the truth, if not should it not be refuted, as you can imagine its effect upon an audience of Farmers interested in good roads."[39] Its effect upon Page was even greater. He fired off a letter to Taylor telling him to shut up. "I sincerely hope that you will desist from making such statements as this."[40] Taft

36. "Wilson Reports on National Highways," *Automobile*, 12/8/10, p. 977.

37. J Wilson to Taft, 1/26/12. The authorization read, "For conducting field experiments and various methods of road construction and maintenance, and investigations concerning various road materials and preparations; for investigating and developing equipment intended for the preparation and application of bituminous and other binders; for the purchase of materials and equipment; for the employment of assistants and labor; for the rental and erection of buildings; such experimental work to be confined as nearly as possible to one point during the fiscal year, ten thousand dollars" (T Burton to Taft, 1/2/12).

38. WB Bryson to T Burton, 1/19/12.

39. T Burton to Taft, 1/2/12.

40. LW Page to J Taylor, approx. Jan. 1912.

explained to Burton, "It constitutes a very small part of the road that I have to ride from the White House to the Chevy Chase Club in order to play a game of golf, constituting, as it does, just about one-tenth of the distance. I may add that I have been over the road very few times since its construction because I have not been able to play golf since August last."[41] That was the most scandalous aspect of it all to the President, as a gout of his ankle, the constant travel, and political agitations had kept him away from Chevy Chase for all too long.

41. Taft to T Burton, 1/26/12.

17

A Summer Scorching

"Oh yes, I passed through your town on our trip two years ago."
"Yes, you did, Mr. President. And the dust has not settled down yet."
—Taft greeting a visitor[1]

Flush with his tariff victory and anxious to see after his wife, Taft left Washington the afternoon of August 6, 1909. He received visitors from Congress and the Cabinet that morning, then calmly left town. "His departure to-day was in marked contrast to the dramatic leave-takings ... that marked the exits of former President Roosevelt. There were no Rough Riders and no crowds," noted the *Times*, just the President, Captain Butt, and secretary Carpenter, who "sped down Pennsylvania Avenue practically unnoticed."[2]

Mrs. Taft met the President at the sta tion the next morning. The locals had gathered, but, again, the President ignored them. He verily jumped off the train and ran down the steps to the "big touring car" where Mrs. Taft awaited. "The President's face lighted up with the keenest enjoyment when I told him that Mrs. Taft was in the motor outside," wrote Archie. The newspapers saw how he "embraced Mrs. Taft affectionately, and his beaming face showed his happiness at being freed from official cares and united with his family."[3] Mrs. Taft's "such improved health" was noted by all. That afternoon Taft played golf and took a ten mile motor ride with his wife.

Executive offices were set up in Beverly. The staff busied itself preparing the President's western tour for that Autumn. Various Cabinet members floated through town to discuss this issue or that, including currency reform, which put the reviled name "Aldrich" back in the news, removing politics from the census taking, i.e., being nice to Southern Democrats, and defining the Administration's position on anti-trust and interstate commerce law, Taft's engravings of the Roosevelt legacy to be put in the statutes. A few annoyances arose, including a barrage of anti-tariff editorials and a certain speech at Spokane that made the wires. Otherwise, Taft did his best not to let the world intrude. Outside of sporadic appearances at the office,

1. "Taft First to Like Motoring," *Cincinnati Enquirer*, 2/29/48.
2. "Taft on His Way to Summer Capital," *NYT*, 8/7/09.
3. Butt, 8/10/09, p. 173 and "President Greets Family at Beverly," *NYT*, 8/8/09.

it was all golf, even in the rain, all motoring, all dinner parties.

"Where is Taft?" ran a Sunday article in the *Times*. Reporters who were stuck in Beverly through the July tariff fight, "trying to convert into news the affairs of the President's family," were only further disappointed after the President's August arrival. "I only know one way of saying: 'Mr. Taft played golf to-day,'" moaned one desperate correspondent. "If I don't find a new way to say it before to-morrow morning I lose my job." Another agreed, "Just golf, golf, golf. No settling wars, or pitching hay, or electing new members to the club. Just a put [sic], or a stymie, or whatever it is, and back to the veranda. It's evil times we've fallen upon, boys."[4] The best the newsmen could do was to make fun of the "hoodoo" that vexed the President's game ("were it not for his figure, which unfortunately has a tendency to get in the way of his stroke....") and Archie's uniform ("that makes him the admired of all admirers"), and track the President's motor sprints around the North Shore ("Secretary Carpenter, hurrying down with the morning mail, has been greeted by a cloud of dust from a vanishing automobile"). When the President broke 100 at Myopia, the headlines rang. The reporters had to pass on the juicier news that more than a thousand dollars changed hands in the clubhouse over the President's 98. Butt came out five bucks on top.[5]

* * *

Two days into Taft's August vacation Gifford Pinchot went to work against him. Moving from trees to politics was easy for Pinchot, Roosevelt's sanctimonious Forestry Service creation, a man whom Roosevelt described as "a socialist but ... very useful as long as he was held down and not allowed to get away."[6] Pinchot was a key player in the "tennis cabinet," chief Incense Swinger, and a major cog in the Roosevelt publicity machine. He was one of the government untouchables who symbolized reform and the public trust. Pinchot's national fame started in 1908 when the President began preaching his usefulness.[7] Pinchot's Roosevelt was that of the 60th Congress. Pinchot's Congress was the 60th Congress. Of the Incense Swingers, Pinchot was the first to turn on Taft.

Taft considered the man "a crank" and "of a lunar character," but he was Roosevelt's crank and thereby Taft's to deal with. "But I am glad to have him in the government," Taft apologetically wrote, as it was almost obligatory when criticizing Pinchot to praise him.[8] Roosevelt made much display of Pinchot's value to the nation, and Taft had no intention of messing with the man. He promised Roosevelt that he would regard Pinchot "as a kind of conscience...." Well, sort of. Taft carefully qualified it to "in certain directions...."[9] Pinchot, however, had a problem with Taft, starting with Taft's decision not to

4. "Where Is Taft? Asks Beverly, Mass., in Vain," *NYT*, 8/22/09.
5. Butt, 8/24/09, p. 186.
6. Butt, unpublished passage, 1/7/10 (Butt's paraphrase of Roosevelt quotation).
7. Pinchot's popular unveiling came in November, 1907, with a report on the state of the nation's resources following a 5,000-mile inspection of the country and his placement on the Country Life Commission (see "The Prodigal Waste of Natural Resources," 11/10/07 and "Now the President Plans to Aid the Farmer,"5/24/08, *NYT*).
8. Taft to Horace Taft, 6/6/09 and Taft to FG Newlands, 9/9/09. See, for example, "Mr. Pinchot's Activities," *NYT* editorial, 3/17/09, which criticized him only after lauding his "invaluable services to this Nation," or "Commends Pinchot, But Asks New Law," *NYT*, 8/21/09, about a Denver congress that very carefully criticized Pinchot for "overlook[ing] technicalities in reserving forest lands," a.k.a. breaking the law.
9. Taft to Roosevelt, 12/24/08. This quotation has been misused. Anderson, for example, attributed Taft's pledge to follow Pinchot as a "conscience" in regard to "conservation policy" (Anderson, p. 73). Taft did

re-appoint Interior Secretary Garfield, and ending with the fact that Taft was not Roosevelt. In between were a few measures by Garfield's successor that sent Pinchot into a moral fit. Well, that was his side of things.

Pinchot's first assaults on the Taft presidency were inadvertent but, ultimately, no less damaging for it. As Taft walked on sticks between Cannon, Roosevelt, and the insurgents just prior to the special tariff session, Pinchot met with the "lumber lobby" at the Willard Hotel in Washington. The lumber men were most keen about word that Sereno Payne's committee had low grade lumber on the free list. Here the forester and the tree hackers joined in the view that the free listing would not "aid in the conservation of the American forests." Lumber protection now had the moral force of conservation. By a single vote, the committee added a fee. The lumber schedule became one of the most contentious matters in the tariff, the very subject of Tawney's brief insurgency.[10] Pinchot again interjected himself into Capital harmony by resurrecting a Roosevelt spat with Congress. He circulated a letter quoting Roosevelt's rationalization for signing the bill that banned his commissions, that they should continue regardless of the prohibitions.[11] Nothing came of the agitation except to remind everyone involved as to why they hated each other.

Pinchot's next move came five months later, and, although he publicly denied it, this one was purposefully aimed at the Administration. He and Interior Secretary Richard Ballinger were to speak to the National Irrigation Congress at Spokane, Washington. Behind the meeting was the crucial and long fight over the development of the West, the disposition of government lands. One such fight over coal reserves in Alaska is known to history as the "Ballinger-Pinchot Controversy," and is considered a crucial moment in the Taft Presidency. It was even more crucial to the careers of Theodore Roosevelt and Gifford Pinchot.

Larger than coal reserves and grazing sites was the singular concern of the West, water. The debate over who gets it, who doesn't, and how, where, and why water is divided, diverted, and drained away is yet today a tremendous concern. With emotions ever high over the matter, in 1909 the word of the day, "monopoly," was injected into it all. At Spokane, difficult questions over the public domain went from public policy debates to political hysteria. Panic over Standard Oil and "the trusts" infected the business of saving trees and streams. By the end of the year, George Westinghouse himself felt compelled to write the President to explain that his company had nothing whatsoever to do with "a supposed combination to control the water powers of the United States...."[12]

Taft was aware of the gulf between perception and reality in his role as Roosevelt's successor. Just into his Presidency

9. (*cont.*) not say this. The full passage is, "You can count on my continuing the movement as far as I can, and especially under the influence of Gifford Pinchot, whom I shall continue to regard as a kind of conscience in certain directions, to be followed when possible and to be ignored with a sense of wrong done to the best interests of the country." The "movement" was a reference from the previous paragraph on the "commission to make rural life more attractive." Even if taken in a general sense one must carefully note the disclaimer, "in certain directions...."

10. "Pinchot Is Blamed," *Pioneer Press*, 4/10/09 and Pinchot to Payne, 3/10/09, *CR*, 4/6/09, p. 1135. Pinchot's venture into tariff making lost him valuable support among certain regulars. Nicholas Longworth wrote, with the usual apology for the criticism, "I confess that I haven't such an abiding faith in Pinchot's judgement as I had before his testimony on the lumber duty but there is not doubt but that he has done some admirable work" (Longworth to Taft, 8/30/09).

11. "Mr. Pinchot's Activities," *NYT* editorial, 3/17/09.

12. G Westinghouse to Taft, 12/3/09.

he told the Golf Cabinet, "The fact is that while neither Root nor I even got the credit we were the most progressive members of the last Cabinet ... the two who usually aided and abetted President Roosevelt in what were called his radical policies." Taft was struck by how things had similarly fallen upon him as President. "If Roosevelt had taken a different way he would be further along in some of his reforms," he wrote to his brother in June of 1909.[13]

Among the first of his Administration's efforts to "legalize" the Roosevelt reforms regarded federal lands and water sites. Taft held that "withdrawals," or reservation of land from development, must accord to law. In June, he addressed the "necessity for a comprehensive and systematic improvement of our waterways, the preservation of our soil and of our forests, the securing from monopolistic private appropriation the power in navigable streams, the retention of the undisposed coal lands...."[14] Any arguments? Well, Taft believed in useful, careful development of natural resources and their preservation — according to law. His legalistic policies were hardly inspiring to excitable reformers.

During his final days in office, Roosevelt authorized withdrawal of a wide quantity of land for the protection of water power sites.[15] Secretary Ballinger restored 1,400,000 acres from that list, as he and Taft were convinced the withdrawals were illegal. Much of the designated land was already occupied by settlers, infringed upon existing townships, and contained good farmland. Ballinger instructed a survey of the water sites for future preservation outside of useful lands, and without compromising the intent of the indiscriminate withdrawals he cut the figure to 154,000 acres. The action was perceived by the Incense Swingers as a personal slap at Garfield.

Next came a hit on Pinchot directly. To protect against fires, the Forestry Service had been given oversight of power lines that crossed national forests. Pinchot granted permits only to companies that conformed to his idea of reasonable electric rates. Taft stopped the nonsense.[16] If that weren't enough to prick Pinchot's balloon, in July came reversal of another Garfield and Pinchot scheme. In January, Garfield had ceded to Pinchot jurisdiction over forests in Indian territories. Ballinger took it back. Indians were an Interior Department matter, trees or not, he said. Pinchot had to suck up and hand over not just his authority but all the files, maps, and other papers regarding the Indian lands. He gave objection, but in the quiet, bureaucratic language.[17] In August, he let his emotions express themselves more freely.

13. Butt, 6/29/09, p. 128 and Taft to Horace Taft, 6/6/09 (see also Pringle, p. 476). The comments were over the corporation tax and Roosevelt's conservation policies. A year later, when that gulf of perception had become an ocean, Taft told Archie that when Roosevelt "would get into hot water, he would send for the conservative members of the Cabinet and depend on us to get him out of it." Roosevelt, Taft said, "had a good deal of contempt for the judiciary. He did not like the delay of the law when he felt the public weal was to be served...." (Butt, 5/5/10, pp. 345–346).

14. "Taft for Conservation," *NYT*, 6/1/09.

15. "The Civil War in Taft's Official Family," *NYT*, 8/22/09. The report stated that the withdrawals were done "the night of March 3 last," although the information had been collected over the prior year. Pringle said it was "during 1908 and the closing weeks of his administration" (p. 481).

16. "Where Mr. Pinchot Stands," *NYT* editorial, 8/13/09 and Pringle, pp. 479–481.

17. "Ballinger Has His Way," *Evening Star*, 7/26/09. "This action settles a misunderstanding that was said to exist between Secretary Ballinger and Secretary Wilson regarding the interpretation of the law in reference to an agreement made last January between the Department of Agriculture and former Secretary Garfield of the Interior Department. This agreement gave the chief of the forest service jurisdiction over the Indian lands, which come strictly under the Interior Department, for the purpose of selling the timber, superintending the logging and protecting the forests generally."

"Legal technicalities seldom help people," Pinchot declared at Spokane. Behind the details, funding, and technology of forests and water use, here was the underlying theme to the Irrigation Congress. "Law is not absolute," Pinchot continued, "It needs to be construed.... Strict construction necessarily favors the great interests as against the people.... The great oppressive trusts exist because of the subservient law makers and adroit legal constructions." Against this kind of invective Ballinger presented Administration policy. He was immediately followed by a former Governor of California who set aside his prepared speech and went extemporaneously ballistic on the Administration. "Roosevelt was a President who did things first and talked about them afterward," he cried. "And that's the kind of men we should like to see in public office now."[18]

If Pinchot's speech wasn't enough to make the Judge President lose his lunch, it was thought sufficient cause to dump him. Taft wouldn't dare. Besides, Pinchot's immediate target was Ballinger, and Pinchot backed away from Taft. He wrote to the *Times* to deny that Taft was out of sympathy with Roosevelt's conservation policies.[19] Although it was well understood that the Spokane speech had "Roosevelt in 1912" written all over the margins, neither Pinchot nor Taft were ready for it. How this all intruded upon Taft's vacation was when Pinchot sent a General Land Office investigator, Louis Glavis, to Beverly to discuss the man's accusations of misconduct at the Department of Interior. Here came the Ballinger-Pinchot controversy.[20]

Interior Department field agents don't meet with Presidents. And certainly not during a President's vacation. For Taft to have considered Glavis at all, as he did on August 18, it was out of deference to Roosevelt. Were there no associations to Roosevelt, Taft would have put the whole set, Glavis, Pinchot, and all, to the lions long before. As it was, Glavis, a low subordinate to Ballinger, got a week in Beverly and a President's ear. Glavis spelled out his three year crusade to uncover corruption in the Department's handling of certain Alaska coal claims. The ultimate charge was that Ballinger was a pawn to a Morgan-Guggenheim syndicate. (No need to mention Aldrich with those names around.)

18. "The Civil War in Taft's Official Family," *NYT*, 8/22/09.

19. See "Pinchot In Danger of Losing His Place," 8/12/09, "Pinchot Denies He Attacked Taft," 8/13/09 and "The President's View // Mr. Pinchot's View," 8/13/09, editorial, *NYT*. The latter noted, "The present difference of opinion between Mr. Pinchot and President Taft is important, in that it indicated with clearness and precision the difference in methods between the present and the past administrations. It should never be forgotten that Mr. Taft was a judge before he became President. As the Nation's Chief Executive he still retains his respect for its laws."

20. See Pringle chapters 26 and 27. Pringle made an extensive study that not only exonerated Ballinger but led to a popular revisit of the controversy when his book was published. Then Interior Secretary Harold Ickes was so moved he completely and publicly reversed his views. See glossary under "Ballinger." Roosevelt historian George Mowry could not quite bring himself to acquit Ballinger, and he entirely exculpated Garfield. Mowry's case against Ballinger was that he was from the West and was associated with powers-that-be who distrusted Eastern reformers and federal interference with the development of the West. For Mowry's reluctant exoneration of Taft in the affair, see *The Era of Theodore Roosevelt*, pp. 250–257. For a contemporaneous reassessment of the Ballinger affair see "Roosevelt's Record in Conservation," *NYT*, 5/20/12, by W.D. Hulbert, letter to the editor. Hulbert explained that he visited Alaska in 1911 and wrote articles that were critical of Ballinger, but after further study, "I have learned a number of things I did not expect, and my views of the Taft and Roosevelt Administrations have been much altered." Hulbert particularly scored Garfield for having caused the very situation that Ballinger was thrown into over the coal claims. Of Ballinger, he wrote, "His conduct in connection with the Cunningham claims ... was rather entitled to praise ... the attack on him was unjust and undeserved." The letter went unheard during the 1912 election clamor. See also *American Review of Reviews*, Feb. 1910, pp. 131–138. With great elaboration of Pinchot's worth, Shaw's *Review* concluded that he blew it.

The specifics were less than clear. Glavis, with his "coal cases on the brain," as a Land Office commissioner said, made his case to Taft.[21]

The President ordered an investigation by the Attorney General and left it there, bothered, but not much concerned. On September 11, he wrote his brother,

> I am just now engaged in preparing a letter to Ballinger, passing on the issues which have been made at the instance of Pinchot and his followers, and ruling with Ballinger in every one of them. The cruel injustice which has been done to him makes me indignant. I shall, however, leave Pinchot out of the matter altogether, so that he will not have to break in unless he chooses to do so.[22]

Taft instructed Ballinger to fire Glavis for insubordination and false accusation. Glavis' charges were of "insinuation and innuendo," the President wrote, motivated by the zeal of pre-conviction. Taft was even less moved by the real power behind the whole deal. In the exoneration letter to Ballinger, Taft attacked the notion that he and Ballinger had betrayed Roosevelt and added to it a little brag: "There are now withheld from settlement awaiting the action of Congress, fifty percent more water-power sites than under previous withdrawals, and this has been effected by a withdrawal from settlement of only one-fifth of the amount of land."[23]

Pinchot's official involvement in a scandal over legal definitions and "construed" breaches of narrow law, irony of ironies, was through a legal technicality conjured by his departmental attorney that the contested coal claims were in a national forest. It was an Interior Department affair simply. But Pinchot didn't care about authority. Glavis was the Roosevelt bridge to get to Ballinger and, eventually, to Taft. Pinchot continued to meddle. His department lawyer and an aide leaked the Glavis report to the press and assisted Glavis in the writing of an article published in November in *Collier's Weekly*. The article was a sensation. Taft's opponents accepted the charges as gospel. Hearings were scheduled in Congress, where accusations flew, including one that Ballinger presided over "notorious land frauds." One of the Honorables railed,

> Rumors are even now current about the misuse of the million dollars appropriated to protect the public lands. I hear of thousands of dollars expended out of this fund for expensive furniture, of salaries of favorites that have been doubled ... with Ballinger returned to power as Secretary of the Interior, it was manipulated to assist land thieves in their depredations in the valuable coal lands in Alaska.[4]

Despite the conspiracy theories and party-line votes concerned with politics not truth, Ballinger was cleared by Congress. His reputation was not. Taft for a year refused to accept his resignation, feeling him unjustly persecuted. Pinchot, too, stood pat, and Taft refused to fire him.[25] Pinchot had to arrange his own lynching. This came in the form of a letter to Senator Dolliver in which he admitted his office's complicity in the *Collier's* article. It was pious rationalization, the motivation being the "saving of property of the pub-

21. Pringle, pp. 488–489.
22. Taft to Horace Taft, 9/11/09.
23. Taft to Ballinger, 9/13/09, per Pringle, pp. 495–496. Note Taft's "awaiting the action of Congress"—a stab at Pinchot's Spokane speech.
24. "Ballinger Accused," *Evening Star*, 12/16/09. This ballad was from Rep. Hitchcock, a Nebraska Democrat. Hammond wrote that Ballinger left office "practically without funds" (p.560).
25. Friendly with both, Jack Hammond tried to negotiate a peace between them. Pinchot wouldn't have it (see Hammond, pp. 556–560).

lic." It also violated an Executive Order that forbade extra-departmental communications. Taft fired him. "Your letter was in effect an improper appeal to Congress and the public to excuse in advance the guilt of your subordinates," Taft wrote. "By your conduct you have destroyed your usefulness as a helpful subordinate of the government, and it therefore now becomes my duty to direct the Secretary of Agriculture to remove you from your office as Forester."[26] The President otherwise filled the pink slip with the requisite praise for the man's service.

Taft fretted horribly, but not on account of Pinchot. His worry was that Roosevelt would take offense. He took the action only upon Root's encouragement. If Root saw fit, it had to be done. That day Taft summoned Archie and the White House motor. They drove five miles up Connecticut Avenue and dismissed the chauffeur. The President let it out on the long walk home. "He talked most freely about the matter," Archie wrote, "nothing had distressed him as much."[27] Taft hoped that his letter to Pinchot would speak for itself.

The whole thing was a power play, simply. The motives of *Collier's* are plain. The Glavis article was headlined, "Are the Guggenheim Interests in Charge of the Department of Interior?" The attacks on the "water trusts" and the "Morgan-Guggenheim syndicate" were both fanaticism and public relations, the business and politics of the anti-business movement.[28] The Democratic press followed the affair with glee, and Democrats voted against Ballinger in Congress, if only to damage the Administration. Worst of it all was Pinchot, whose involvement was laced with demagoguery, self-promotion, and untruths.[29]

26. "Pinchot Ousted," *NYT*, 1/8/10. "I would not have removed Pinchot if I could have helped it," Taft told a friend a few days later (Pringle, p. 509).
27. Butt, 1/9/10, p. 256.
28. In *The Era of Theodore Roosevelt*, Mowry did his best to establish a link between Ballinger and "a Morgan-Guggenheim Syndicate" (p. 253). If you get confused, go back to Pringle's study to sort it out.
29. The most damaging aspect to Taft personally was the revelation that he had ordered the back-dating of a document related to the internal investigations. This was neither unusual nor particularly unethical, but it didn't look good. Its revelation got great publicity for Glavis's attorney at the Congressional hearings, Louis Brandeis, who was to share the Supreme Court bench with Taft a decade afterwards. His and another attorney's considerable fees were picked up by *Collier's*. Some political traction was gained with the accusation. In June of 1910, Rep. Harrison said, "The scandalous fact that the President had sent to the Senate of the United States an official document ... of which the date had been willfully falsified by being predated...." Taft was so offended by this line of attack he refused to receive the congressman, one of the few who were unwelcome at his White House (see "Taft Bars Harrison from His Presence," *NYT*, 6/10/10). The charges otherwise did not stick and were little heard from afterwards. However, it all simmered within the progressives' rationalizations for so hating Taft. In 1913 Robert La Follette wrote a list of Taft sins, including "The subterfuges resorted to by his administration in defense of Ballinger" (La Follette, p. 477). Another flare up came in a 1916 article in the *New Republic*, which wrote that the predating was a deliberate deception. Taft considered a libel action, but Wickersham, who wrote the original memo, advised against it. "It remained for the sophistry of a Brandeis to put an immoral construction upon it," Wickersham wrote Taft. "I was pilloried in *Collier's*, the *New York Sun*, and a large variety of other publications ... and called by every vituperative epithet applicable to a liar and a forger" (Pringle, p. 513). Nevertheless, seven years later, he advised, it was not worth trying the matter all over again.

As with the tariff, Pringle asserted the "what if" Taft had not acted "until it was too late," saying that had Taft more actively defended Ballinger and had earlier fired Pinchot the public might have understood (Pringle pp. 504–505). The record disagrees. The September newspaper accounts were laden with Taft's defense of his Interior Secretary (for example, "Taft Takes Stand With Ballinger," *NYT*, 9/16/09). In Spokane Taft "took occasion to pay a tribute to Secretary Ballinger," wrote Butt in the official diary (Official Functions, 9/28/09, p. 177). As for firing Pinchot, Taft had no real cause until the Dolliver letter. His strategy was to let Pinchot hang himself. Taft wrote to Pinchot in September, before the *Collier's* article, "I must

The affair pushed Taft to further distrust of the progressives—not their cause, as the principles he shared with them as of March 4, 1909, he never changed—but their personalities and their tactics. He learned who his friends were not. During the scandal, Taft wrote his wife,

> I am in receipt of a letter and a screed written by Silas McBee of the Churchman in reference to Ballinger and Pinchot. McBee is one of those impressionist artists that are so often carried off of their feet by Roosevelt's sermons and preachments, and that have very little regard for the substantial methods of making progress through statutes and by lawful steps.... Pinchot has spread a virus against Ballinger widely, and has used the publicity department of his bureau for the purpose.... McBee, who has been attacking me in his paper, is anxious that I should ... appear before the Laymen's Missionary Society.... I shall go there and pour coals of fire on his head."[30]

* * *

Roosevelt had nothing whatsoever to do with the Ballinger episode. Archie noted that Taft was fastidious to avoid criticism of Roosevelt throughout.[31] The Incense Swingers and other political opportunists worked around them to engineer the break. "There are a good many political observers in Washington who regard the affair as the first definite movement in the splitting up of the Republican Party," noted the *Times* the day Pinchot was fired. Coincidently, that day House insurgents teamed up with Democrats to outvote Cannon on appointments to the joint committee of the Ballinger investigation. Pinchot was described as "smiling and good-humoredly" receiving visitors.[32]

Taft nullified the objections to his conservation policies with his legislation and the choice of Walter Fisher, a Pinchot associate—and a lawyer, to replace Ballinger in 1911.[33] Still, the "ultra-conservationists" wouldn't be satisfied. Their creed was populism wrapped in conservation. Taft stared them down. One occasion came in 1911 at Denver, a city gaga for Roosevelt. After a two-hour motor tour, the President told the 11,000 attendees of the Public Lands Convention that the "fetish" stage of the conservation movement had passed, and the nation ought now "settle

29. (*cont.*) bring public discussion between departments and bureaus to an end," in effect, a command to shut up (see Taft to Pinchot, 9/13/09). Pringle said this appeal came "almost pathetically." Hardly, for it was a direct order. Pinchot's actions are indefensible.

Another instance of Pinchot's deception, Taft explained to his brother: "[Pinchot] had allowed it to be known that he claimed that [Secretary of Agriculture] Uncle Jimmy Wilson had given him permission to send the Dolliver letter to Congress direct. Then when the question was asked him, he preferred not to answer unless the committee insisted; and then he did answer by evidence which was intended to convince the committee that Wilson knew the contents of the letter. Now, I happen to know that Wilson did not know the contents of the letter, though it is quite possible that he said things sufficient to enable Pinchot to state, that he had been given permission to send a letter to Dolliver. Wilson is very angry; his scotch is all aroused, and he denounces Pinchot as a liar and a deceiver, as he undoubtedly is showing himself to be. Pinchot does not lie outright, but he has the traits attributed to the Jesuits. He is cunningly misleading, and stands upon the letter of things when it suits his purpose, and insists on the spirit of them when that is helpful. I am quite sure that he has perfectly disgusted the committee, and while I do not know that we can prevent a partisan report by the Democrats, I know they feel in their hearts that the charges of Pinchot and of Glavis have fallen utterly flat and unproven" (Taft to Horace Taft, 3/5/10).

30. Taft to Helen Taft, 10/15/09.
31. Butt, 11/14/09, p. 203.
32. "Insurgents Defeat Cannon" and "Pinchot Ousted," 1/8/10, *NYT*.
33. Ballinger kept his dignity, if not his health, throughout. The appointment of Fisher, however, was unsettling. "The circumstance of the appointment of Mr. Fisher as my successor," he wrote Taft, "in view of his attitude toward your enemies and my enemies, was, I frankly confess, hard to bear, but notwithstanding this I credited you, as I do now, with absolute sincerity" (Ballinger to Taft, 7/28/11).

down to a calm consideration of what ought to be done in the preservation of our natural and our National resources and that steps ought to be taken which the mistakes of the past show to be wise." A man shouted, "Who owns the public domain, Mr. President?" Taft was unimpressed with the question, which came of the movement's hoarse mantra, "the people." He looked the man in the eye:

> The United States owns the public lands, and the United States is the people of the United States. I know how irritating it is to have somebody else lay down rules for your moral uplift, but you've got to stand a great deal in order to make progress. I will end as I began. I am not in agreement with your verdict.[34]

* * *

The irritations of the Pinchot business did not get in the way of Taft's 1909 summer vacation. And neither did the cops. The shrinkage of time and space that marveled the builders of Union Station had a baser, more human side to it, namely, scorching. The President was not only not immune to the speed disease, he was downright infected. But it was so infectious. Taft explained,

> There was a time in the use of the automobile — I shared it myself when I was plodding along with the tandem that nature gave me, as Holmes called it, when a spirit of intolerance was manifested against the horrible looking machine that the automobile then was to the ordinary eye. There was an intimation of "get-out-of-the-way or we will run you over," and a resentment against those who were using it until you yourself got into the automobile. Then human nature was shown in the quickness with which the attitude of mind can change, and you regarded as utterly unreasonable the slowness of the pedestrian and the idea that he had any right to any part of the street either for crossing or anything else. And then the utter outrage of having any dogs at all in any community that should get in the way of that magnificent instrument of travel and comfort![35]

The speed disease could not be helped, even in the face of horse-era laws and anti-automobile sensationalism. President Grant's admonition that the best way to deal with a bad law is to enforce it gave automobilists much occasion to reflect upon reasonable law. Our constitutionalist President avoided the theory while practicing the art. Between speeches on the sanctity of the law, he rushed about the countryside far in excess of the speeds allowed by law. Over his term of office the President's scorching was never held to account outside the editorial pages. He was stopped. And he was let off. The rights of kings prevented the embarrassment. The first incident was in September of the first Beverly Summer. Four magistrates from the town of Newbury were having a profitable time of it. The season was for motoring, and the surge in visitors that followed the Summer White House filled Massachusetts roads.

One afternoon, the President needed some down time. He earlier blew up at a man, "a reformer," according to Butt, who wanted to talk Pinchot. "Yes he is very angry," Mrs. Taft said. "When he raises his voice like that he is always mad." The calming effect of the ocean breeze and smooth North Side roads at thirty miles an hour were just the recipe. It was decided upon a visit to Justice Moody up in Haverhill, near the New Hampshire border. The route was leisurely, as the President's evening rides often made sixty miles. The

34. "Taft Seeks to Lure Back Party Voters," *NYT*, 10/4/11.
35. Taft speech to the ACA, 12/20/11, reel 580.

ACA journal had that August warned motorists that the usual 20 m.p.h. limit was recently changed in the town of Newbury to eight miles an hour, and a trap awaited just past a "double turn" leading to it. The President's car fell into it. At first, the constables didn't realize the size of their catch. At some point the Taft smile caught their eye and apologies were made. "President Taft expressed regret that his car had been traveling at a speed considered above the limit, and he instructed his chauffeur to drive more slowly for the rest of the trip," went a report. Butt's letter that day mentions the visit to Moody, not the speed trap. One of his only admissions to Taft's speeding came during a trip to Panama as the President's boat made a scalding eighteen knots through the Caribbean Sea. Archie wrote, "It is even more exhilarating than breaking the speed laws on the North Shore."[36]

Speed enforcement was also so very human. From the Providence policeman who held up the U.S. Army to the New York cop who ticketed a taxi in which the cop was riding, not just behavior and the law had yet to accommodate one another, its enforcement was an issue of deep query and often questionable practice. Our zealous New York speed enforcer jumped into the cab with the order to "Let her go lively!" Now, what's a cabby to do? He let her rip, which the cop timed at over twenty miles an hour. Magistrate O'Conner was incredulous. It became the first time he had ever let off a scorcher.[37]

When New York Governor Dix was caught doing 25 m.p.h., he protested "I'm the Governor; I'm in a hurry." The cop let him go. Other speeders weren't treated so delicately, including the Governor of Pennsylvania, whose tag was noted by a policeman that clocked his car at over 30 miles an hour. The fine was sent by mail. Normally the violator was brought before the local magistrate and given a hearing date. Bail would be set to ensure compliance. When the determined scorcher William K. Vanderbilt was caught at sixty-five miles an hour, he merely reached into his pocket for bail money. Another time he was short of cash. He had to put up his million dollar estate. "Is it worth $100?" the magistrate asked. One judge tired of the "speed maniacs" that were paraded before him. Announcing a "relentless crusade" against the disease he demanded $1,000 bail from offenders and threatened to jail owners as well as chauffeurs. And those stories of farmers and shotguns? Wilson's and Tillman's cure for motormania, the bullet, was employed by a New York policeman who fired a warning shot in the air and, unheeded, another into the tire of a fleeing chauffeur.[38]

In New York the serious side to scorching was in the news. The *Times* announced that one hundred persons were injured by automobiles in October of 1909. One incident involved a foot policeman who saw a car racing up Broadway. He jumped on a trolley and instructed the motorman to give it full speed. The speeders got away, but the policeman took down the tag numbers. It was the same car that earlier ran down and left a man and a little girl bleeding in the street.[39]

As result of the publicity, the Police Commissioner ordered a crackdown on

36. "Speed Traps," *Club Journal* (ACA), 8/7/09, p. 411, "Taft Auto in Speed Trap," *NYT*, 9/5/09 and Butt, 9/3/09, p. 192–193, 11/11/10, p. 557.

37. "Odd Charge of Speeding," *NYT*, 8/13/09. The cop threw his bicycle into the back of the cab and directed the chauffeur to a police station, whereupon he arrested the driver.

38. Farmers shot at automobiles less than policemen. "Gov. Dix Caught Speeding," 7/27/12, "Gov. Tener an Auto Speeder," 6/11/11, "Vanderbilt Caught Speeding," 4/22/09, "Warning By Courts to Auto Speeders," 4/6/09, and "Stopped Auto with Bullet," 11/13/09, *NYT*.

39. "Baker Transfers Auto Watchers," 11/10/09 and "Uses Car to Chase Speeding Autoists," 10/6/09, *NYT*.

speeding. Although he denied any actual corruption, he was aware that his bicycle force had developed a certain intimacy with chauffeurs. It was well known that some policemen and their families had full access to garages and free taxi fare. "Even wealthy owners of automobiles think it a high privilege to be on speaking terms with a policeman," said a deputy. Imagine the Commissioner's anger, though, when he learned that a copy of his order was posted in garages. Elsewhere, warnings went, "Sergt. Mallam and his men are out. Be careful." Arrests were down as a result. The Commissioner ordered policemen transferred and a special team to sweep the streets. That night the twenty-seven men and six automobiles of the "Traffic Squad" nabbed fifty-one speeders. Another forty were arrested the next day.

The *Times* was a good friend to the automobile. Outside a 1905 spat with the *Automobile*, which gleefully published an account of the arrest of the chauffeur of the editor of the *Times*, that daily promoted races, publicized shows, and gave copy and ad space to automobiles, including a weekly Sunday section.[40] Automobiles sold newspapers. The editors, however, would not stand for speeders, except in headlines that followed every accident. Monday papers had a regular summation of the weekend's carnage and the law's harvest of speeders. A President cruising New Hampshire roads at forty miles an hour was great news copy. The *Times*'s articles of the President's scorching went just beyond neutral, reaching, if not praise, then a lively story. Not so the editorial page, where the President's taste for speed was not excused:

> President Taft is not to be blamed for liking to go fast when he is out in an automobile. Therein he only shows a trait common to such part of humanity that is privileged to use this most delightful — barring aeroplanes, perhaps — of vehicles yet invented by man. When, however, he goes immoderately fast, as he seems to have done in the outskirts of Pittsburgh on Sunday, and, as according to report, he has often done before in other places, he sets a rather bad example for the people who lack his immunity from arrest. Some day he may run over somebody in one of these wild rides, and the somebody will be as dead, and remain dead as long, as if it had not been the Presidential car that killed him.[41]

The cause of the editorial fit came in May of 1910 during one of the President's trips. Outside of Pittsburgh he went for a motor ride. The *Times*'s news report was more sanguine than the editorial:

> He traveled sixty-five miles over typical Western Pennsylvania hills ... a smooth but dangerous highway, and covered the distance in two hours. The police cars, wrapped in a heavy blanket of white dust, were compelled to drop behind, and the Secret Service men were at times cut off. The President's car passed small hamlets, bowled over hills, swept through valleys, rounded sharp curves with the rear wheels sliding, and kept up such a hot speed that he was not recognized at all. The high-powered police cars were outdistanced and caught up only by driving recklessly down grades on which Mr. Taft's car slowed up a little. The President is said to have urged the speed..... After returning to Pittsburgh, the President drove in a circle, compelling the four cars which followed

40. "The 'Times' Still Unconverted," *Automobile*, 7/6/05. See also "Unfavorable Newspaper Influence and How to Counteract It," *Automobile*, 11/9/05, pp. 526–527.

41. "Setting a Bad Example," *NYT* editorial, 5/3/10. The attitude was consistent with the paper's position from the beginning of the Motor Age. See "Our 'Hostility' to the Automobile," *NYT* editorial, 6/26/05, which said the paper was "the relentless enemy of every automobilist who willfully violates the laws..." but not an enemy to automobiles, as the *Automobile* charged. The paper was friendly to motors, but harsh on scorchers.

> him to pass in review. He laughed long and heartily at the plight of the police and Secret Service men. All were white with dust from head to foot, and their faces were unrecognizable. "Took our dust," he cried between bursts of laughter.[42]

The notation of sixty-five miles in two hours is key here. An interested reader might hereby figure out how fast the President went—an average of 32.5 miles an hour. A few months later on the glorious country roads of New Hampshire, Taft outran the Secret Service men by clipping off 85 miles in 3 hours and 28 minutes, or just under 25 miles an hour average.[43] Thankfully, or, as the *Times* admitted, because he had good chauffeurs, the President never committed road murder, or was subjected to it himself.

Chief Wilkie of the Secret Service, too, was concerned. He scolded the President's secretary and his protective detail,

> It is not right to hurtle the President over country roads at forty or fifty miles an hour. Thirty miles an hour is the limit of safety for a conservative motorist; anything in excess of that simply invites disaster.... The speed with which the President's car has been driven at times ... has been the subject of much unfavorable comment.... I feel that if as a result of the bursting of a tire or the breaking of a steering connection or an axle, the President should be hurt, you would be censured for permitting fast driving....[44]

The best Wilkie could do was to ask his agents to please ask the boss to go easy on the chauffeurs' throttle.

42. "Baseball Placard Says 'Go See Taft,'" *NYT*, 5/2/10.
43. "Taft Enjoys Fast New Hampshire Trip," 8/28/10. Presidential scorching also came on the rails. On his return from the St. Louis tour, "with the proverbial smile working overtime," the President's train took the final forty-mile leg from Baltimore to Washington in thirty-seven minutes. Another of his trains hit 70 miles an hour on the way to Detroit (see "Taft Enjoys Fast Run," 5/31/10 and "Pass Railroad Bill in Senate," 6/4/10, *NYT*).
44. Wilkie to Norton, undated, Jan. 1911, marked "file carefully" (case file 41E, reel 361).

18

13,000 Miles on the Road to Winona

During his brief vacation at Beverly, the President prepared his moves for the regular Congress that Winter. If Congress objected, it would be cowed. The program was a full legislative invasion. The program was audacious; only, it was Grant's audacity and not Lee's— no swift end-runs, no feints and no toying. Taft's was a head-on charge. The platform would be fulfilled. First, to the people. That meant 13,000 miles over 56 days and through 33 states and territories, with a steamboat ride down the Mississippi from St. Louis to New Orleans.

By the start of the voyage, Taft's image was intact. *Togo, the Japanese Schoolboy* visited Beverly on the eve his departure. "That smile, Mr. Editor, are the most wonderful scenery I have seen in America. It are not so broad as Mrs. Sipi River nor so splashy as Niagars Falls ... Hon. Taft got a smile like a General Weather Condition.... It cost nothing to keep a smile. It are cheaper to give a friend a smile than a cigar." While Taft discussed with Togo how to launch a smile 13,000 miles across the nation, his secretary presented a package, labeled the Constitution. "'Pack it,' say Hon. Taft, 'in the most sacred & conspicuous place you can find—next to my toothbrush, if possible.'" Then Taft instructed "Capt. Archy Butt" to put the "golluf" sticks in the closet, as golf was a "Publik Duty," an arduous game like "Tariff Revision." Togo left the President pondering a few questions, including "If cotton cloth cost 10 cents before revision downward and 12 cents afterwards, how far down would it have to be revised before it cost 25 cents?" Taft's response was, "Such deep Problembs must be better answerred by some statesman who are intersted in Politicks."[1]

The press dubbed the trip, "The Swing Around the Circle." Taft called it a string of "one-night stands."[2] It was non-stop and the hours were full. He ascended the Great Divide, and there opened the gates to a vital $6,000,000 water works project, the largest of its kind. He descended 1,200 feet into a Montana copper mine. He explored Yosemite with John

1. "The Interviews of a Japanese Schoolboy," by Wallace Irwin, *NYT*, 9/5/09.
2. "How Mr. Taft Will 'Swing Around the Circle,'" *NYT*, 8/15/09 and Butt, 9/17/09, p. 197.

Taft is said to have been a boring speaker. Butt once complained that he droned on about policy and statistics. Less frequently noted, however, are those speeches Butt thought were home runs. Of a Taft confrontation with protesters, Butt wrote, "I have never seen the President so aroused." His speech to a group of attorneys was "splendid," and his speeches in the South were "impassioned." Of Taft's speech to New York automobilists, Butt noted, "When he gets started in a light vein he is always good." Taft could enrapture a crowd with his great wit and the famed "Taft smile," which he launched across America. He is pictured here at Augusta, Georgia, which he called his "Southern home." It was also Capt. Butt's hometown. The President stopped by Augusta on the final whirl of his 13,000 mile "Swing Around the Circle," a cross-country trip in the Autumn of 1909. (Courtesy Library of Congress)

Muir, catching the cheers of spectators below from a 3,000 foot cliff edge, and outpacing his escorts over the four-mile descent. In Chicago he viewed 150,000 children who lined the streets in welcome, and popularized the seventh inning stretch by standing with the fans at the top of the "lucky seventh." In Utah 20,000 schoolchildren received him, and a like number greeted him in Portland, Oregon, first in the formation a "living" American flag, then spelling "T-A-F-T" with placards. That demonstration moved the President to tears. "You call your city the 'City of Roses' because of the beautiful flower," he told the children, "but I look now upon 20,000 human roses."[3]

Taft wore his office clothes during the trip. It was a celebration of the people, not him. Aside from his famous comment that the role of the President was "to increase the gate receipts of expositions and fairs and bring tourists into the town," Taft meant to represent the people to themselves.[4] Sending him off, New York Governor Hughes bade him farewell. Hughes told an audience,

> He is going on a long journey so that the people may see him and hear his voice. It is an undertaking of difficulty and personal hardship, but it will be for the benefit of the people and will assist him also in the better discharge of his duties.[5]

This and subsequent "Western Tours" provoked criticism in Washington and the editorials. The attacks never stuck, even in

3. "Taft Opens Tunnel that Diverts River," 9/24/09, "Taft in Iron Cage, Goes Down in Mine," 9/28/09 and "Taft Deeply Moved by Children's Drill," 10/03/09, *NYT*. Butt's diary noted 5,000 children at Portland (Official Functions, 10/2/09, p. 183).
4. Butt, 6/1/09, p. 108. Taft liked the line and repeated it elsewhere.
5. "Taft and Hughes Praise Each Other," *NYT*, 9/16/12.

Congress, which caved whenever the President asked for more money after having exhausted his allowance. Taft was up front about the matter. "As you know, the people have voted me $25,000 for traveling expenses," he told his New York audience. "It is very hard to get anything from the Appropriations Committee unless you have a mighty good case." When his travel budget came up in Congress the following Spring, the headlines blasted Taft's expensive "wanderlust." The Democrats called him irresponsible. Once again, Tawney came to his defense. Tawney read off a list of Democratic governors and congressmen who invited or traveled with the President.[6]

The joke was that Taft ate his way across America, which had some truth to it. He was noticeably stouter upon his return to Washington in November. It was at more than banquets that the President met America. He faced his nation. He listened and he saw the great land and its people, and he was stirred to uphold them. And in that uniquely Taft way he confronted his foes directly. He was a friend to business, he told 5,000 trolley businessmen who were angry at the corporation tax. He was a friend to labor, he told workers in Chicago. And so on to skeptics in the South and the far West. Perhaps few were turned. Fewer went unimpressed. None got anything but an honest assessment of the President's thoughts and intentions.

When Taft saw Yosemite it was not just tourism, it was publicity for the National Park and conservation. When he descended the copper mine it was the important work and conditions of the miners and the industry on show. He called it "education." Near the end of the tour, he wrote his brother, "As I look back, I am not regretful in the slightest of having taken the trip. Whether it has done the people any good to see me is of course one question. That it has added to my information about the country and my understanding of the needs of the various sections, I have no doubt."[7]

At Natchez, Mississippi, he explained the usefulness of his river voyage. "After the beauty of the scene, I hate to come to commercial questions," he told a crowd from above the river, to where he arrived by auto:

> But we cannot get along without clothes and we cannot get along without bread and meat. While this trip, undertaken under the auspices of the Waterways Association, combines most of the beautiful, it has a deeper purpose and that is to draw to the attention of the country the need for some action in developing the utility of the great waterway that flows at the base of these bluffs. The problem is not solved, but I believe that it is in the process of solution. I believe it because we of the American Nation admit no obstacles that we cannot overcome.[8]

During the trip Taft called for good citizenship and patriotism. He spoke always for lawfulness and national unity. To a Houston audience he said, "President Roosevelt used to say that he had more friends and fewer votes in Texas than in any State of the Union, and I want to say that I am after your friendship, too. That's all I ask you for. The votes will come later." At Birmingham a voice called from the crowd, "We love you, Bill." Taft didn't hear, and asked for the person to repeat it. "We love you, Bill!" called several others in unison. Taft replied, "It might have been right to dissemble your love, but why did you kick me downstairs? The fact that you had so little to do with putting me where I

6. "Fails to Advance Taft Travel Money," *NYT*, 5/27/10.
7. Taft to Horace Taft, 10/28/09.
8. "Taft Profited Much by Tour of Nation," 11/14/09 and "Taft Near End of Trip on River," 10/30/09, *NYT*.

am makes me appreciate the warmth and sincerity of your reception all the more."[9]

In Minnesota he praised civic virtue, which, as he said in Sacramento, would bring material progress to all Americans. "Everywhere in this country I have found evidence of prosperity ... of course we want prosperity, but we wish prosperity ... so that everybody will get his share, and that it shall not be confined to a few who monopolize the means of production or the means of transportation...."[10] In Texas he lectured children on their citizenship and his role as President. Taft adored children. He was never happier in public than with them, be it halting his train to receive flowers from a little girl or writing a letter of absolution to another who spilled soup on the Presidential lap.[11] The Taft smile graced the youngsters of Terrell, Texas. "I am very glad to see the children here this Sunday morning. I am glad to see them with their [American] flags." One can just see the big man leaning toward the kids, his eyes alit. "Do you know the flag of Texas? Are you loyal to both flags? I bet you are. Now, my children, do you know who I am?" He continued in that unique Taft vein of acute self-awareness. His was not a pessimistic view—if it were he wouldn't have bothered. He was, perhaps, too aware of the limits of his office and his person, yet he was a realist. Had he never spoken of doubt, we wouldn't know; his actions did not betray it. Instead, he spoke candidly, as to the young Texans. What goes unrecorded is if they shared the President's irony:

> I rather think that you believe the President has more power that [*sic*] he really has. He is a sort of figurehead for the Nation for four years. He is a kind of man that they blame everything for, if it goes wrong, and if it goes right, he does not get any credit for it. But, my children ... why you are here this morning to see me is because, for four years, I am the Chief Executive of the United States, and as such for that time represent the sovereignty of the Nation, and am entitled to your respect as head of the Nation. In four years I shall step down and out, and I won't be entitled to your respect any more than any other citizen; but for the time being I am the head of the nation, and therefore regard you as loyal Texans and as loyal Americans. You come to see me on that account. I doubt if your fathers had much to do with my selection. But some times, in a republic, you have to submit to things you cannot help, and you have to get along the best you can with a bad job."[12]

Before heading west Taft confessed to Archie, "If it were not for the speeches, I should look forward with the greatest pleasure to this trip."[13] Starting out, Butt noticed his "labored efforts" at speaking. Taft disliked preparing speeches as much as giving them. When he had a major announcement to make he worked diligently. If it was not so important he procrastinated, often finishing on the train ride there. Early on, Archie noted, some chink in the schedule would cut into his time, and he would show up unprepared.[14] During the tour and into his Presidency Taft improved remarkably, especially at the extemporaneous remark. He memorized pat

9. "Blue and Gray Give Taft Greeting," *NYT*, 11/4/09 and Butt, 11/17/09, pp. 212–213.
10. "Taft Would Clinch Roosevelt Progress," *NYT*, 10/5/09. The *Times* replied, "would not Mr. Taft be well advised if he allowed the people to enjoy their prosperity...." (10/6/09).
11. "Child Stops Taft Car" 9/20/11 and "Master Berri Didn't Step in Taft's Soup," 7/02/11, *NYT*. Taft ordered the conductor to halt for a little girl who was jumping up and down with flowers for him by the tracks. He told her, "Thank you, my little maid."
12. "Taft Will Start River Tip To-day," *NYT*, 10/25/09.
13. Butt, 8/24/09, p. 185.
14. Butt, 3/21/09, p. 20. In May of 1908 candidate Taft visited Panama. He wrote his wife, "I reached here yesterday after an uneventful trip on the PRAIRIE.... They have a good library aboard, however, and I spent

phrases for different audiences and repeated them to different folks and places like a good politician. Mid-stream in the trip, Taft was, Butt wrote, "as felicitous as it is possible for a man to be, and instead of dreading to make a speech he delighted to make one and felt so certain of himself...."[15] The President hit his stride. Right into a mess.

To understand the developing hyper state of the national mind in the Autumn of 1909, one need only know that Taft was criticized during the trip for spending time with a member of his own cabinet and the Congressional leadership. It started in Boston with praise for the leader of the Senate, and a ride to Albany with one of his hosts, a Massachusetts Senator. Then on to Winona, Minnesota, where he paid a little back rent to the House Appropriations Chairman. Worse, Taft dared allow his own Interior Secretary to ride with him from Denver to Seattle, and he then took the Mississippi with the Speaker of the House. Associations with these "worst types" were so unfathomable that the President's own military aide fretted it would offend what he called "the best-minded people." Taft might have pulled a (late-term) Roosevelt and condemned as scoundrels the very men he needed to pass his legislation. Taft did the exact opposite, and precisely because he needed them for his legislation.

Neither his antagonists nor history had use for Taft's "rare good humor" that launched the trip. Or his 52nd birthday celebration with Governor Hughes.[16] Or his appearances with Democrats and insurgents, including La Follette. Forgotten is the President's manifest joy of the West, his sincere regard to the people of the South, and the countless rear-platform speeches at every train stop. Forgotten are the hundreds of thousands of plain Americans, Roosevelt's and Lincoln's folk, whom Taft touched with plain talk. Unnoticed, too, is the cold shoulder given Taft by insurgent elements in Iowa, Wisconsin, and Kansas.[17]

* * *

In his autobiography, La Follette characterized it all with horror:

> The President started on a tour across the country in September, 1909. At the outset in an address at Boston he lauded Aldrich as the greatest statesman of his time. Then followed his Winona speech in which he declared the Payne-Aldrich Bill to be the best tariff bill ever enacted, and in effect challenged the Progressives in Congress who had voted against the measure, and the progressive judgment of the country, which had already condemned it.[18]

Let's start with Aldrich. Togo called him the "High Chauffeur of the Golden Juggernaut." Before Boston's best at Mechanic's Hall, Taft declared the Senator sane. Not a good start in the eyes of Robert La Follette. Actually, Taft called Aldrich "one of the ablest statesmen." Oops?

This was the same Nelson W. Aldrich whose hands stank of a fortune made as a grocery wholesaler, who spent four months in Blue and the rest of the Civil War making money, and whose daughter

14. (*cont.*) most of my time reading.... I did not have the moral courage to tackle the speeches that I have to deliver on my return...." (Taft to Helen Taft, 5/7/08).
15. Butt, 11/14/09, pp. 200–201.
16. With the President's arm wrapped around his shoulder, Hughes declared, "You'll never call on me in vain." Over the years Hughes would make good the promise (from "Taft and Hughes Praise Each Other," *NYT*, 9/16/09).
17. See unsigned "Memorandum for the President," approx. Dec. 1909– (reel 124). "There was some coldness discernible in the Middle West," wrote Butt ("Official Functions," 11/14/09, p. 204).
18. La Follette, p. 477.

married John D. Rockefeller, Jr.[19] This was the same Nelson W. Aldrich whose very name, if attached to a tariff bill, could bring down a presidency. Pushing seventy years of age, Aldrich was now conspiring to dupe the people with a bank reserve system in order to preserve the nation's prosperity. Taft liked Aldrich.

Four days before the Boston speech Taft appointed the members of the Tariff Board, with a reformer at its head. Revision and his pledge for "the difference & etc." was still on his mind. The Board, although shy of his and Beveridge's tariff commission, would get him there. That, and other side-effects of Payne-Aldrich, such as the Philippine free list, the corporation tax, and the income tax amendment, were thanks to Aldrich as much as to any other. And Aldrich didn't like it any less than the insurgents, be it for opposite reasons. Taft didn't bother Aldrich with such matters in Boston.

In private, Taft defended his relationship to Aldrich. To Walter Fisher, later his Interior Secretary and a credentialed progressive, Taft wrote, "I am not afraid to refer to Senator Aldrich as a friend of mine, and as one of the most useful men in the Senate, a man with whom I don't always agree, but whose effectiveness, straightforwardness and clearheadedness, and whose command of men everybody ... must recognize."[20] Taft's public praise for Aldrich as "one of the ablest statesmen" was useful to critics only out of context. The larger phrase continued, "one of the ablest statesmen *in financial matters* in either house...."[21] [italics added].

That night in Boston, the President spoke of a drastically important reform. The 1908 Aldrich-Vreeland Act provided for extra currency during panics, and, more importantly, the National Monetary Commission which Aldrich headed. The project was huge and politically dangerous. Progressives and Bryan saw specters of Wall Street. Democrats saw ghosts of the Central Bank. Bankers saw government intrusion. The fearful everywhere saw only Aldrich. Meanwhile, the Senator kept low and worked hard to educate the public and herd the bankers.[22] At Boston, Taft wished Godspeed for Aldrich and currency reform. "I may have made a political mistake in doing it," Taft later said. "But I have the satisfaction of knowing that I said what I believed. The muckrakers think Aldrich has captured me, and I think I have captured Aldrich. The results will show which is right."[23]

Implicit to quarreling minds aroused by any tribute to Aldrich, regardless for what, was the "Aldrich" in the Payne bill. That alone was enough. But with some distinctly qualified praise for the tariff, the President made it easy for his critics at Winona, Minnesota. (Beware the sign that rhymes, the prophets ought have said; no word yet on the weather conditions.)

19. To describe Aldrich as a wholesaler was an out-and-out insult. Roosevelt, like other populists, blamed the middleman for looting farmers and hijacking consumers (see the Country Life Commission Report, p. 34). The various Taft biographers have skewered Aldrich with, "The American dream, to Nelson W. Aldrich, was of factories which blackened the sky and workmen who did not complain" (Pringle, p. 413), "Rather than representing people, he spoke for economic constituencies.... An aristocrat with luxurious tastes" (Coletta, p. 60), "cunning" (Burton, p. 63), and "icy, aristocratic, arrogant" (Manners, p. 67).
20. Taft to W L Fisher, 9/25/09, per Pringle, p. 414.
21. "Taft with Aldrich for a Central Bank," *NYT*, 9/15/09. La Follette hated Aldrich's Monetary Commission as much as Payne-Aldrich or Aldrich himself.
22. See *The Triumph of Conservatism*, by Gabriel Kolko, pp. 181–189. In this thoughtful reflection on the period, that left-leaning historian lamented that the leading characteristics of the progressive era, especially as regards business regulation and the monetary system, were shaped by business (whose interests Kolko confused with "Conservatism").
23. Butt, 11/25/09, p. 222.

There, he was to give a little public thanks to Jim Tawney for his whole lot of good work on the President's behalf. Taft's indebtedness to the House Appropriations Chairman went from the automobiles, salary increase, tariff board, and travel budget to a common dedication to budgetary reform and that refreshing harmony between Capitol Hill and the White House.[24] There was also to be at Winona a little praise for the new tariff, a little apology for the untouched wool rates, an outline of the work yet to be done to better it, and a forceful declaration of Republicanism as defined by Tawney's vote for the Payne bill.

But for a poor choice in modifiers the speech wouldn't have found its way into the Congressional Record as evidence against Taft in his own words.[25] But for sloppy use of the superlative instead of the comparative, as Taft explained two years later, the Governor of Minnesota wouldn't have clumsily endorsed Taft for 1912 by reminding people that Winona was forgotten.[26] On the up side, the President had stumbled upon a fine replacement for the mantra, "the difference & etc." Unfortunately, the substitute was that Payne-Aldrich was "the best tariff bill...." Big oops.

Taft's rationalization two years later was that "the comparative would have been a better description than the superlative," that is, "better," not "the best."[27] Certainly, and not just because Taft should have known better. In 1904 he wrote his brother, "I find the longer I live that the use of the superlative is either useless or dangerous, and that it is much better to have the hearers supply the superlative than to furnish it yourself."[28] He broke his own rule. His 1911 apology for it, however, was uncomely and atypically disingenuous— and would have been pretty good politics were it more timely: "I dictated that speech to a stenographer on the cars between two stations, and glanced through it only enough to straighten its grammar.... If I had prepared it two or three weeks before and revised it deliberately, as I ought to have done...." A lie, and a nice one, too. Two years too late.

* * *

Taft admitted to procrastination, but he was hardly lethargic, especially in regard to the Winona address. No, that speech was no small affair. Here was the President on tour to sell his agenda fresh off a hugely divisive tariff revision and facing a party split of which he was most aware. The real reason for Winona was not the tariff, it was Cannonism, insurgency, and the future of the Republican Party. Tawney represented everything Taft wanted of a fellow partisan: loyalty, integrity, and willingness to fall on the party sword. The Senate insurgents failed in two of these three, and some showed such poor faith as to lead Taft to doubt their integrity. Despite Cannon's underhanded Conference appointments and Aldrich's bulldozer, and despite Taft's sympathies for the rules insurgents, the leadership proved itself useful to the President. All Taft wanted to hear from Congress were the words "the platform."[29] His biggest fear

24. Butt figured Taft's Winona praise was repayment for the salary increase and traveling expenses (Butt, 11/14/09, pp. 200–202).
25. "Taft's Second Veto Kills Wool Bill," *NYT*, 8/18/11. During a fight over the Wool schedules in 1911, House Democrats voted the speech into the Congressional Record.
26. "Minnesota Favors Taft," *NYT*, 12/1/11.
27. "Taft Makes Clear His Tariff Views," *NYT*, 12/1/11, excerpted from "President Taft's Own View, An Authorized Interview," *Outlook*, Dec., 1911.
28. Taft to Horace Taft, 8/4/04.
29. See "William Howard Taft and Cannonism," by Stanley D. Solvick, *Wisconsin Magazine of History*, Vol. 48, 1964–1965, p. 57. In this interesting article, Solvick discusses the process by which Taft turned to the

going into the presidency was that the Old Guard would rebel—and it tried. Taft conquered it. When he yelled, "jump," the question was no longer if, but how high. He would squeeze reforms from the regulars they couldn't have imagined were within themselves—and that Roosevelt failed to uncover. The Senate insurgents became the unstable quantity. During the tariff session the power of their votes proved as limited as their voices were shrill afterwards. Their loyalties were more than questionable.

In Boston, Taft declined to discuss the tariff, saying he would address it out West. As with a conservation speech to be given at Spokane, Taft deliberately planned his target. The Spokane speech was worked on the night before, but it was long in creation and meticulously prepared and reviewed. Plans for the Winona address reached back to the final days of the tariff battle in July. As Taft beat upon the conferees to lower duties, especially Pinchot's lumber tariff, Jim Tawney faced an unpleasant consequence no matter what resulted. If he voted against the tariff he would lose his Chairmanship and the eventual and very real possibility to become Speaker. Yet, his home state sentiment was anti-tariff, and, above all, anti–Cannon.

Tawney's considerable usefulness to Minnesota was acknowledged without endorsement by his opponents.[30] His free lumber fight was applauded without warmth. Outside his district, where he controlled the press, he was frequently vilified for his fights with Roosevelt and his proximity to Cannon. The *Pioneer Press* of St. Paul, an insurgent Republican organ, especially, moaned about Cannon, Aldrich, and all things un–Roosevelt. For example, even before Pinchot's Spokane speech, even before Glavis's fakery hit the newsstands, the *Pioneer Press* ran an editorial excoriating Ballinger, and Taft for supporting him:

> Ballinger remains in the cabinet at Washington, not to forward, but to antagonize "the Roosevelt policies...." Especially offensive to Roosevelt Republicans has been Mr. Ballinger's obstructive and personally aggressive attitude toward Forester Pinchot [7/27/09].

As with Ballinger, the self-described "Roosevelt Republican" press concluded that the tariff was a failure long before the evidence was in.

Tawney knew the howls that would follow a vote for Payne, including those of the Twin Cities flour millers who were upset at not enough protection for themselves.[31] He took the dive. Doing so, he gave cover for the rest of the Minnesota delegation, which kept mum on the direction of its votes until the last moment. When the bill arrived from Conference, the House leadership counted votes. In the end, the margin was sufficient to allow some dissatisfaction to be expressed. Taft wrote his brother,

29. (*cont.*) regulars for the tariff fight and Taft's views on party and party loyalty. Notable is Solvick's conclusion, "In the last analysis, the only question for Taft was how best to utilize the available instruments of power in order to achieve the program of his administration" (p. 56). That insight aside, Solvick remained sympathetic to the insurgents. For example, he called "petulant" Taft's admonition to William Allen White that the concerns of the program were greater than those of the insurgents (p. 57).
30. See "Insurgency in Minnesota: The Defeat of James A. Tawney in 1910," by Roger E. Wyman, Minnesota History, Vol. 40. No. 7, Fall, 1967.
31. See "Vote Against Tariff Bill," *Pioneer Press*, 7/31/09. Tawney was credited for having raised duties on barley. The duty was opposed by representatives of brewery districts from Michigan, Missouri, and New York. Mixing it up more came a Kansas representative who wanted higher duties on barley to satisfy prohibitionists (see "Free Lumber is Beaten in First Round," *Pioneer Press*, 4/7/09).

> Yesterday's vote in the House was uncomfortably close ... but the truth is, there were quite a number of men who felt that for home consumption they would have to vote against the bill, but who would have voted for the bill if the danger would have been greater. This was the case with the Minnesota representatives."[32]

When Taft's wife expressed concern at the close margin, he assured her, "There were a good many who would have voted for the bill if we needed them."[33] Taft's visit to Minnesota was an implicit part of the deal. Speculation about it commenced in early July. The vote in August made it a certainty.[34] Tawney wrote to the President:

> After speaking to you yesterday.... I saw and talked with Mr. Stevens, my colleague. He says, and I agree with him, that the only hope of getting other Republicans of Minnesota into line is through your influence and the effect of your visit to the State. He heartily approves of your making the strongest possible tariff speech in Winona. Mr. Stevens says that if this is done it will force all Republicans to get behind you and line up the party all over the State.[35]

Meanwhile, everyone went on vacation, Taft to Beverly, and Tawney to the Minnesota lakes. There, and resting under what was left of the now protected Minnesota stumpage, Tawney was amazed to read an announcement that the St. Paul papers *Pioneer Press* and *Dispatch* were organizing a public "ratification" of the votes against Payne. All the Minnesota congressional delegation were to be invited except Tawney. He shot off a telegram "to give them something to think about," and which "created consternation in the ranks of the democrats and mugwump protectionists in St. Paul." He wrote,

> Before completing your arrangements to especially honor the Republicans and the one Democrat from our state who voted against the final passage of the Payne bill, I would suggest that you ascertain how many of them pledged the president of the United States to vote for the bill if their votes were necessary to pass it.[36]

The movement continued, but without the support of other newspapers and any of the Minnesota Republican congressmen who recognized their debt to Tawney or, in the case of the state's leading insurgent, Senator Clapp, figured the meeting would only strengthen Tawney. The St. Paul papers, which Tawney called "no longer republican," were further humiliated when they were caught publishing a faked telegram from Taft in support of the ratification meeting.[37] The event was canceled.

The situation amplified the importance of Taft's visit. "As you will see," Tawney wrote in mid–August, "considerable importance will be attached to your utterances at Winona regarding the Payne

32. Taft to Charles Taft, 8/1/09.
33. Taft to Helen Taft, 8/4/09.
34. See "Taft Coming Here," 7/11/09, "President to Laud Tawny," 8/5/09 and "Taft Courts Strife," 8/6/09, *Pioneer Press.* The paper said that Taft would give another tariff speech in Iowa in rebuke to Cummins.
35. Tawney to Taft, 8/6/09. Tawney was particularly concerned that the *Minneapolis Tribune*, a more regular newspaper, had come out against him over the vote. Tawney took it in the chest for the other Minnesota congressmen, especially Stevens.
36. Tawney to ES Warner, from "Suggests a Pledge Probe," *Pioneer Press*, 8/16/09
37. From Tawney to Taft, 8/18/09 and "Taft's Name Forged to Aid Cannon Man," *NYT*, 9/3/09 (the *Times* got the story backward, and blamed it on Tawney). The St. Paul group tried to bring La Follette, Cummins, and other Senate insurgents to give national prominence to the ratification. The *Pioneer Press* lamented that their schedules never seemed to match. The insurgents purposefully stayed away (see Bowers, p. 369).

tariff law in our state." He recommended that "for the good of the party as well as for the future success of my colleagues," the President not focus on Tawney's solitary vote:

> Were you to make any reference to me and my vote ... it would undoubtedly be construed, inferentially at least, as a criticism on the votes of my colleagues.... But any reference you might make to my efforts ... and in support of your own efforts in favor of downward revision could not be so construed.[38]

Having thus advised Taft of the minefield in which he found himself, Tawney urged the President to join him, and fully armed:

> I sincerely hope that you have not abandoned your intention to deliver your first speech in defense of the Payne tariff bill in my home city. There is nothing that I could suggest that would, in my judgement, contribute more to the alignment of the republicans of Minnesota in support of that law than a strong, forceful statement from you on that occasion. We will give you a rousing meeting and reception at Winona.

Three days before departing Beverly, Taft wrote his brother, "I start out on my western trip with a great deal of concern, because I do not know exactly what to talk about, and I shall be expected to make long speeches at each of the important places where I stop. I shall talk about the tariff when I get to Minnesota, but not, I think, before that."[39]

* * *

At Winona, on September 17, Taft carefully reviewed his longstanding position for a downward revision, the hard work through 1908 by Payne and his Ways and Means Committee to review the tariff schedules and costs here and abroad, and, in numbers such as $106,000,000 and $579,000,000, the ultimate effect of the final revisions. A lot of homework went into the speech. "Experts of the Treasury Department," Taft said, provided the numbers. Upward revisions were confined to luxuries, he explained, and cotton was divided between various grades, thus allowing for lower duties on some qualities and needed protections on others. He concluded that a "substantial revision" had occurred, although problems remained, particularly with the wool rates. Only after a thorough, precisely prepared review of the bill did Taft conclude,

> But, as I have already said, I am quite willing to admit that allowing the woolen schedule to remain where it is is probably not a compliance with the terms of the platform as I interpret it, and as it is generally understood. On the whole, however, I am bound to say that I think the Payne tariff bill is the best tariff bill that the Republican Party has ever passed; that in it the party has conceded the necessity for following the changed conditions and

38. Tawney to Taft, 8/18/09.

39. Pringle notes that Taft considered Winona as the locale for a tariff speech as early as August 23, but the biographer then points to a Taft telegram to his wife just before the speech to show that it was carelessly written. Dated September 16, it read, "Tomorrow Milwaukee and Winona. Hope to be able to deliver a tariff speech at Winona but it will be a close shave." That was the day after his birthday celebration with Hughes and two days after the Boston speech. He was working on it already—and worried about it. The 16th, Taft spent a busy day at Chicago, so time was tight. The 17th, the day of the speech, he cabled his wife, "Speech hastily prepared, but I hope it may do some good." On the 20th, he told her, "I said what I thought and there is that satisfaction." In October, he wrote his son that the speech "is the best thing I have done.... It is a truthful statement of what I think..." and again, in November, he wrote, "I meant every word of my Winona speech." Taft handled the speech deliberately, his last minute work, day-before jitters, and 1911 apology notwithstanding (see Taft to Horace Taft, 9/11/09, Taft to Charles Taft, 8/23/09, Taft to Helen Taft, 9/18/09, Pringle, pp. 452–456, and Taft to WD Foulke, 11/18/09).

> tariff rates accordingly. This is a substantial achievement in the direction of lower tariffs and downward revision, and it ought to be accepted as such.

That judgement rendered, the speech was only half done. "And now the question arises," the President continued, "What was the duty of a member of Congress who believed in a downward revision greater" than the bill provided? "I am here to justify those who answer this question in the negative." Here was the point of his speech. "Mr. Tawney was a downward revisionist, like myself. He is a low tariff man...." and, listen up you insurgents, "He is a prominent Republican." Had Tawney and others voted down the bill or had the President vetoed it, "we would have left the party in a condition of demoralization that would have prevented the accomplishment to its purpose and a fulfillment of other promises which we had made just as solemnly as we had entered into that with respect to the tariff."[40]

Telling Republican opponents of the tariff to carry forth in opposition to it, as "their right" and their "duty," but "within the lines of the party," Taft warned,

> It is vastly better that they should seek action of the party than that they should break off from it and seek to organize another party, which would probably not result in accomplishing anything more than merely in defeating our party and inviting in the opposition party....

The furor over "the best tariff" failed to blunt the speech. That's because the hyperbolic criticism entirely missed Taft's point. The distinction between dissent within or without was his query, not the wool rates. Winona was about insurgency, and Taft struck it hard. Shortly afterwards, he wrote his wife, "I see that Cummins and La Follette and the rest of them propose to fight, but I anticipated this, and I am ready to stand with the party and see who comes out best."[41]

* * *

Within two months of Winona, the *Times* would lament the betrayal of the tariff fight by the insurgents. Was Cannon right that those "sensitive gentlemen" had gone wobbly?[42]

Insurgent discontent was not caused by the Payne tariff. La Follette went into the tariff fight already upset with Taft's 1908 platform. In the tariff, the Senate insurgents had more than anything else found an issue over which to preach their, what a commentator called, "doctrines of dissatisfaction." Good political noise came not from iron schedules but the "interests" (capital "I"), Aldrich, and any combination thereof that might make a melody. The principle was dissent. Objection to the

40. "Taft Lauds Tariff as Nation's Best," *NYT*, 9/18/09. The logic to Taft's statement was clear and perhaps implied, but he did not say it. Initial reports of the speech did not make the extrapolation that if it was, as Taft said, the "best tariff bill that the Republican Party has ever passed," it was "therefore the best tariff bill ever," which he did not say. The *Pioneer Press* version stuck to Taft's text ("Tawney Right on Tariff Says President," 9/18/09), as did the *Times*, although not in the headlines ("Taft Lauds Tariff as Nation's Best," 9/18/09). The *Chicago Tribune* kept to the text, but its sub-headline strayed into "*President Declares Aldrich-Payne Bill Best Which Ever Was Passed by Congress*" ("Taft Upholds the New Tariff," 9/18/09). The *Evening Star*'s account was completely re-worded and included "and therefore the best tariff bill that has been passed at all...." ("Why He Signed Bill," 9/18/09). The paper's editorial proved more exact, calling the speech a "challenge to all its opponents.... In his opinion the new measure is the best of its kind his party has ever framed, and he expects it to meet the full requirements of the case. Still he does not consider the tariff question closed ("The President on the Tariff," editorial, 9/18/09). Your author concludes that none of it would have mattered. Even if Taft used the mere comparative, "better," opponents would have screamed. Payne was a necessary convulsion, which would have been made far worse with a veto.
41. Taft to Helen Taft, 10/3/09.
42. "Winona and Washington," *NYT* Editorial, 12/7/09.

Payne bill was a vehicle, not a destination. La Follette, particularly, needed an issue. In early 1909, his popularity was fading. He rode the Payne bill straight back into Wisconsin politics.[43] When Cummins announced, "The Fight will go on, and, if anything, it probably will be a broader and hotter fight in the future," his talk was on the tariff. The *Times* correctly figured he meant 1912.[44]

Taft measured insurgency not by its committee votes, but by its floor votes, which Tawney, from his free lumber insurgency to his final vote, embodied. Taft encouraged and helped the Senate insurgents—during the hearings. Their final vote against Payne was a vote against the party as much as against the tariff. When asked if he would be "read out" of the party, insurgent Dolliver stumbled into just such an admission. "It depends on whether the Republican Party consists of the people or a sub-committee of the Senate. If it is the latter, we can't be read out of the party, for we were never in it."[45] The sincere example of tariff insurgency was that of Minnesota Senator Nelson, an old hand who voted against Payne. He kept quiet about it and remained in the caucus.

Cannon was invigorated by the President's challenge. The upcoming session would be his last ride as Speaker, and he took it at full speed. Cannon was himself one of the biggest victims of Taft's insistence upon regularity. For all his bluster, Cannon had twisted to Taft's song as much as any other. Now that the President rewarded regularity at Winona, Cannon turned up the volume. "Senators and Representatives ... who voted against the enactment of the Payne bill," he said, "voted to increase or maintain the duties on industries and products of their own States and sections. They were protectionists for their own people, but they were opposed to protection for other people in other sections." If the insurgents were unhappy, he said, it was their problem. "Senator Cummins complains that I have read him out of the Republican Party.... The Senator does me too much honor. I have not the authority to read any man out, nor have I the disposition.... I have never known of any man or group of men being read out of any party except by themselves."[46]

* * *

At Winona, Taft praised a representative who stood for downward revision and his party both, however convoluted the mix. The circle was closed the following year when Tawney was rejected in a Republican primary by the force of crossover Democratic votes.[47] While insurgent Republicans dropped the tariff, the Democratic party won a House majority in 1910 on the very issue. The circle was made utterly vicious, however, when during that election Tawney was made the subject of another speech by a national figure at Rochester, Minnesota, next door to Winona. In the speech, Gifford Pinchot discarded the tariff:

43. "Taft Stirred Anger of Anti-Cannon Men," *NYT*, 10/10/09. The point of the article was that mid-western dissatisfaction was not over the tariff, it was of republican insurgency. "Nothing Mr. Taft could say in defense of the bill would count very much with most of these people against the doctrines of dissatisfaction preached so steadily to them by La Follette, Cummins, Bristow, and Beveridge." See also an undated, unsigned political memorandum to the White House, approx. 12/27/09 (Taft Papers, reel 124) that reviewed the political scene and demonstrated that the tariff was less an issue than insurgency. The author wrote, "La Follette has recovered, through his attitude with respect to the tariff, the popularity he had lost. Prior to the tariff, he was on the down grade."
44. "The Insurgents," *NYT* editorial, 9/28/09.
45. "Taft Stirred Anger of Anti-Cannon Men," *NYT*, 10/10/09.
46. "Cannon Is for War on the Insurgents," *NYT*, 11/27/09.
47. "It was simply the vote of the Democrats in counties where there was no Democratic contest...." Tawney explained ("Tawney on Defeat," *Pioneer Press*, 9/22/10). Historian Roger Wyman agreed (pp. 326–328).

> I notice an effort to get my position on the lumber tariff involved in this campaign. My position on that subject was taken in good faith, wholly with reference to the perpetuation of our forests. I believed I was right, and I do not propose now to make either apology, retraction, explanation or excuse. The question of my stand on the lumber tariff has no more to do with the fitness of Mr. Tawney to represent the First Minnesota district *than it has with the price of butter*. I came here to discuss questions which have"[48] [italics added].

Had Tawney voted against Pinchot's lumber tariff, Pinchot would never have showed up to excoriate him for having voted with his party. Pinchot didn't care about the tariff. He only mentioned it in his own defense. Instead, he spoke about Roosevelt's commissions. And, he actually said this: "Mr. Tawney is the most dangerous opponent of the public welfare in the United States."[49]

That was certainly true if one owned an oleomargarine factory. You see, Tawney's diary farmer constituents wholly agreed with Senator Nelson's praise for Tawney's energetic fight against that product — which they were certain threatened the very price of butter.[50]

* * *

Maybe, as history has it, Taft dug his grave in Boston, tossed dirt on it in Winona, and held his own wake on the Mississippi. But he got there in the fastest trains and the hottest cars. For modernists the trip was a celebration of the horseless age. If it escaped anyone in the heartland that the President rode about Washington in automobiles, the trip brought it to their home town. With rare exceptions, such as in San Francisco and New Orleans where he was greeted with carriages, everywhere he went the President was run about in automobiles.[51]

Starting with the seventeen mile motor ride from Beverly to Boston that launched the trip, Taft kept automobiles in the news. The review of Chicago

48. "Tawney Scored by Gifford Pinchot," *Pioneer Press*, 9/6/10.

49. The charge was aired by all the usual suspects, including *Collier's Weekly*. California reformer and future Bull Mooser Francis Heney also made an appearance in Tawney's district and repeated the slander, as well as reading from Roosevelt's "Secret Service" message from January of 1909 ("Heney Replies to Tawney's Speech, *Pioneer Press*, 9/18/10). Tawney's reply included, "I am not here tonight to misrepresent any one; nor am I here to denounce any one as an enemy of public welfare.... In no district in the United States is the subject of the duty on lumber better understood and in no district is the sentiment of the people now more in favor of free lumber than in this district.... I need not say to you that on the floor of the House I opposed the organization of the House in fighting for free lumber and for a reduction of duties generally all along the line. That fact is established and my most bitter enemy does not deny it ... my failure may be attributed to several causes, but primarily it was due to the influence and action of Gifford Pinchot" ("Tawney Answers Pinchot in Kind," *Pioneer Press*, 9/14/10).

50. "Insurgency in Minnesota," pp. 323–324. Nelson also defended Tawney's fight against Roosevelt's commissions and called Tawney "one of the ablest most industrious, and most energetic" of congressmen. Taft was pained by Tawney's defeat (see Butt, 9/23/10, p. 527).

51. From White House records and news accounts, it appears that the White House motors were not shipped with the President on these trips. Chauffeur George Robinson recalled in the 1960s that the White steamer made the trip down the Mississippi. Unlikely. The author has encountered no transit expenses for the President's cars, or the chauffeurs, except to and from Beverly. Robinson and Long stayed with Mrs. Taft in Beverly while the President roamed the country. A passenger list from the 1911 tour contains none of the chauffeurs ("Western Trip of the President, case file 2374, reel 430). Taft relied on motors provided by hosts or rented locally during his trips (see Secret Service telegram, Wheeler to Sloan, 3/8/11: "Impossible to rent automobiles here but feel certain I can secure two in Atlanta which can be driven over here tomorrow"). The White Company freely offered cars for the President and the Secret Service in New York and elsewhere (see WC Sterling to FW Carpenter, 3/16/10, 3/28/10, and 5/18/10). By existing photographs, Robinson seems to have been sent once to Augusta, Georgia, as an undated photograph depicts him there in a White steamer — not the White House steamer, most likely in December of 1909.

Taft's version of politics was to meet the people. And he did it with gusto, wearing out his aides, the Secret Servicemen, and the press corps. "The President has a constitution of iron, apparently," wrote Capt. Butt. Taft's four years were spent traveling at an unrelenting pace. He toured the nation twice. He went to Panama as presidential candidate, President-elect and twice as President. He was practically a fixture at New York and New Haven. He tore up the roads at Augusta, Georgia, for his winter time-off, and his summer vacations were spent exploring New England. All told, it was estimated he put in 114,559 miles during his four years in office. Pictured here, he greets a crowd from the rear platform of his train. (c. 1909, Courtesy Library of Congress)

children was by motor, as was the entrance to the baseball game. After the Winona speech Taft was off by motor to deliver a series of speeches on his Postal savings banks plan. He bounced between the Twin Cities in automobiles while laying out his foreign policy. In Des Moines it was more autos and a speech on railroad reforms and the Inter-State Commerce Commission. In Denver the President motored to speeches on income taxes and praise for the women's suffrage in Colorado. Then he was driven about Colorado Springs to enjoy its wondrous view of the Rocky Mountains. At Pueblo he was honored with a flag-covered ride in a Stoddard-Dayton car.

At Salt Lake it was a motor ride to the Tabernacle. From Montana was reported "an exciting automobile ride over the mountains from Butte to the mouth of the Leonard Mine. The grades are steep and winding, but the chauffeurs were experienced men, and, while there was apparently no threat of danger at any stage of the trip, there was a sigh of relief when Mr. Taft was placed safely aboard the Mayflower" [rail car].[52] At Spokane it was an hour's motor ride before a major address on conservation, land reclamation,

52. "Taft in Iron Cage, Goes Down in Mine," *NYT*, 9/28/09.

A rare inside view of Taft's rail car. Everywhere he went, local politicians, Democrats and Republicans, jumped in to steal a little shine from the presidential spotlight. (Courtesy Denver Public Library, Western History Collection, by Harry M. Rhoads, RH-864)

and, with Ballinger and Pinchot as the backdrop, a dedication to the Roosevelt legacy. He motored into Idaho for more speeches and a dinner of game (beats 'possum). To 20,000 in a Seattle auditorium it was ship subsidies and Alaska followed by a motor ride to greet children, veterans, Eskimos, Malay Indians, and Hawaiians.[53]

More praise for Roosevelt came in Sacramento, along with more automobiling, as in Fresno where Taft spoke to preachers on the virtues of restraint. Good citizenship, he told them, was in the Bible: "He that ruleth his spirit is greater than he who taketh the city." Then it was to the city of trolleys, Los Angeles, where the President was greeted by the mayor and led on a twenty-five car automobile parade, his machine decorated in chrysanthemums. Pasadena and the orange groves of Riverside were other automobile destinations.

Onward to the territories of Arizona and New Mexico, where the President spoke for statehood and simple, rational constitutions, that is, unlike Oklahoma's, which he called "a zoological garden of cranks." Meanwhile, the Secret Service prepared this precedent-setting visit with Mexican President Porfirio Diaz. Saloons on the Mexican side were closed, and in El Paso suspicious types were jailed. The meeting itself went according to Old World rules of carriages and military escorts. Diaz started it off with an entrance to El Paso in an elaborate carriage of gold-plated hubs and doors. Taft responded in carriage kind in Juarez, Mexico, only in a "hired livery rig" that the Mexican press found distasteful.[54]

Automobiles were used throughout Texas, including in San Antonio where the President halted his motorcade to listen to the singing of "America" by 14,000 school children. After a stop at brother Charles' ranch and relaxing motor rides over the property, Corpus Christi brought a talk on railroads and river and harbor improvements and a sore throat which Taft's doctor blamed on the two day's rest at the ranch. In Dallas the President was saluted by rebel yells. At Houston the crowds filled the downtown. At each the President went by motor.

53. "Taft Makes a Plea for Ship Subsidies," *NYT*, 10/1/09. William was a popular baby's name amongst the "Igorrote" tribe (Malay Igorots, from the Philippines). They were a popular attraction in the U.S., making appearances at the 1904 St. Louis Fair, for example, where they danced and boiled dogs for dinner.

54. "Taft and Diaz Meet; Talk of Friendship," 10/17/09 and "Taft Profited Much by Tour of Nation," 11/14/09, *NYT*. During the initial negotiations for the meeting, it was felt that neither leader should leave his own territory. The meeting was originally set for the center of the bridge! (See "Taft-Diaz Meeting," *Evening Star*, 8/2/09). See Butt's extensive account in "Official Functions," pp. 208–219, reel 599.

Next, he ascended by rail through Arkansas, notorious for poor roads which the schedule precluded his sampling. His bad throat kept him off the platform all the way to St. Louis, from where he launched the river flotilla down the Mississippi. No matter that he traded train for steamboat, at every stop down the river came motor rides to local sights. Aside from the bad throat, the worst of it came at Cairo, Illinois, where opossum was sent aboard. Taft admitted he "doesn't hanker for it." The only other excitement came when Postmaster Hitchcock arrived late to a sunrise speech and found his path obliterated by the cruising automobile train of the President on his way back to the river. Otherwise, the partying moved to the Congressional boat with the loading of nine poker tables. "If you catch anybody bluffing, Uncle Joe," Taft yelled from his own boat, "take the money."[55]

Although greeted at New Orleans by carriages, the President took a motor tour of the city. There, he insisted on attending two football games for the simple reason that tickets had been purchased with the promise of his attendance. The Secret Service had some reason to fear "anarchistic attacks." "Oh, fiddlesticks," Taft replied. He enjoyed the games. The next stop, at Jackson, Mississippi, brought an hour's motor ride, as well. In Birmingham he motored, of course, in addition to preaching suffrage for women — if they wanted it. "I am not a rabid suffragist. The truth is I am not in favor of suffrage for women until I can be convinced that all the women desire it. When they desire it I am in favor of giving it to them, and when they desire it they will get it, too."[56] At Columbus he told the crowd, "You are not in favor of war and I am not in favor of war, and we will never seek it if we can in any honorable way avoid it. But in the history of nations, when war becomes inevitable and puts to trial the manhood, the courage, the self-sacrifice of a nation, hard and hellish as war is, the test is one to which a people may look back with pride and with thanks to God that they survived the test and showed themselves worthy of enjoying the blessings of such a Government as ours."[57]

Into Georgia the President discussed the nature of citizenship, the presidency, and the law. Roosevelt ought to have taken notes, for Taft would throw his way in 1912 what he said in Georgia in 1909: "I know that sometimes in the zest and enthusiasm of reform there is an impatience with legal limitations and statutes that seem to be directed against that reform ... such as to lead us to disregard or ignore it. I do not think ... that that is the best way of getting rid of legal limitation that interferes with progress." Then, to Pinchot and the Roosevelt loyalists, Taft said plainly, "The first thing that we have got to do after arousing the people to the necessity of change, is to change the law and not rely upon the Executive himself to ignore the statutes and follow a law unto himself because it is supposed to be the law of higher morality."[58] Taft here defined his role in the Roosevelt legacy — and called upon Congress to assist by putting into law those "good many measures" of reform he spoke of during the Tour.

He refused a mint julep in Savannah, but accepted a motor ride, his fastest yet. Mayor Tiedeman showed off his awesome Packard "30" touring car, with the President, Archie, and Jimmy Sloan along to speed across the route of the city's 25-mile Grand Prize race course(the site of the 1911 Vanderbilt Cup). The *Times* reported that

55. "Waterway Problem Expounded to Taft," *NYT*, 10/27/09.
56. "Taft for Suffrage If Women Want It," *NYT*, 11/3/09.
57. "Taft for Suffrage If Women Want It."
58. "Don't Override Law, Taft Tells Georgia," *NYT*, 11/5/09.

"with his gray automobile cap pulled well down on his head" the President hit 52 miles an hour and "seemed to enjoy the ride immensely." You bet he did. The *Automobile* proudly quoted the President, "This is the finest course that I have ever laid eyes upon, and you shouldn't let it be idle. Why, if we had it in Washington, we would have Grand Prize races every six months."[59]

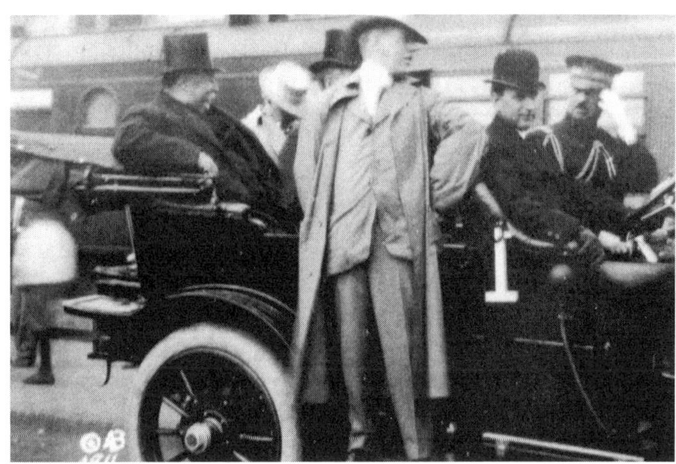

Top: **Backseat triumphant. Capt. Butt, as ever, in position.** ***Bottom:*** **Taft's protective detail worked overtime, the officer in charge, Secret Serviceman Jimmy Sloan, especially. During Taft's 1910 visit, the St. Paul** ***Pioneer Press*** **watched Sloan at work, calling him "one of the cleverest men that ever looked for the suspicious, bulging side pocket. It is his business to suspect everybody.... It might also be mentioned that Sloan's right hand never came out of his right side pocket, where his fingers were closed on the butt of his revolver.... He carries himself with a don't-tread-on-me air that is convincing." (Both photographs Courtesy Library of Congress)**

At Charleston there were more automobiles, as well as a man blown into the air by a premature cannon salute. From there it was a visit to the state capital and a review of the old and the new South. Between motor rides past antebellum homes and new "skyscrapers" that marked Columbia's recovery from Sherman's march, Taft spoke fervently of "the passing of all sectional feeling." Finally it was a peaceful return to Washington through beloved Augusta, which Taft declared, to his hosts' enthusiasm, his Southern home. On to Richmond where the President summed up "the Programme." He spoke of careful use of public domain resources, postal banks, reform of the interstate commerce laws, antitrust enforcement, monetary reform, judicial procedures reform, a Lee memorial, and a Federal Health Bureau for the investigation of disease. "That is a pretty long list of things to do," he admitted, "but if we set our shoulders together we can do a lot in one session or two sessions of Congress." At Washington's Union Station he pronounced to an awaiting crowd, "I'm glad to get back. Let

59. They averaged 40 m.p.h. over 25 miles. From "Taft Auto Speeds Over Record Track," *NYT*, 11/6/09, "President Taft O.K.'s the Savannah Course," *Automobile*, 11/18/09.

me see—I left here August 6—well, I'm back again feeling just as well as when I went away—or even feeling better."

The President was the only person on the trip to speak that way. The reporters were exhausted. Butt was near dead. And another 2,000 miles were to start the next day. "He stood the trip remarkably well," Archie wrote during the grueling tour, "for two reasons chiefly: he has no nerves, and he really sincerely likes people." For the Captain a hundred mile horse ride through an ice storm was easy compared to two months and 13,000 miles of nonstop railroad, motor car and boat travel. The President's mood was fine throughout.

Not just the tour, but talk of the Programme wore out all but Taft. Congressmen who dared listen must have felt tired already. In Taft's ambition discontent was easy to find. His monstrous agenda presented an easy target, be it for socialists or bankers, and upon Congress he threw the burden to sort it out. The question for Taft was not whom to please, but who would enact his bills. As he did during the tariff fight, Taft would turn to those in power for redemption. In early December, the *Times* announced, "Speaker Says Congress Will Heed President's Recommendations for New Legislation."[60] Before the trip, Cannon's support was not a given. Winona made it sure.

Most importantly, one small joy found its way to the President during the trip. At Vicksburg he received good news of Mrs. Taft's health. He wrote her, "I read it over again and again and it made my day happy."[61]

60. "President Returns to Home in South," 11/7/09 (quotation from reporter's paraphrase) and "Taft at Capital; Long Trip Ended," 11/11/09, *NYT*, Butt, 11/14/09, p. 205, and "Cannon Declares He Will Aid Taft," *NYT*, 12/2/09.
61. Taft to Helen Taft, 10/28/09.

19

Road Blocks

We live in the Age of the Automobile.
—William Howard Taft, 1910[1]

Attendance at the January, 1909 New York automobile shows was the highest ever. Sales were tremendous. The industry was amazed at its progress. The previous year's production, estimated at some fifty or sixty thousand cars, was stupefying.[2] It was thought that the rapid growth would continue and an incredible 75,000 automobiles might be pushed into the great American market in 1909. Henry Ford spoke of 25,000 cars from his factory alone. "After an interview with Henry Ford," wrote the *Automobile*, "one expects to see automobiles as common as paving blocks upon getting out into the street...."[3]

Had the common man's car, so much talked about, so little discovered, finally arrived? All these expectations, all the discussion, and all the drooling envy of some one million horse-drawn buggies a year tempted the makers of automobiles to think of—75,000 cars for 1909. But what a number—75,000 new automobiles! Then something happened, something amazing. And nobody saw it coming. And despite Henry Ford's huge, but not up to brag 20,000 cars, over 125,000 automobiles were manufactured and sold in the United States of America in 1909. Nobody saw it coming.

Prosperity could now be openly measured by automobiles. In Racine, Wisconsin, it was reported in October of 1909, concern over the tariff was overwhelmed by the economics of automobiles. Tariff discontent gave way to $8,000,000 in new orders for the town's auto maker. Payne? Aldrich? The 45 percent added to the sticker price of foreign competition seemed just fine to workers getting work and owners getting rich. Gasoline, previously thought a waste product of petroleum distillation, useful only as a solvent, was pushing twenty cents a gallon. "Glove cleaner" was suddenly good for more than removing stains and running stationary utility engines. It was now a staple retail

1. "The Age of the Automobile," *Vehicle Dealer*," Feb. 1910, p. 250.
2. Contemporaneous estimates of 1908 production varied from 35,000 to 60,000 cars. The historical number reads 63,500. See Appendix D for annual predictions and production.
3. "How Detroit Will Build 50,000 Autos in 1909" *Automobile*, 12/17/08, p. 867.

product, right there next to hay and whiskey. Just as farmers learned the benefits of the rich man's car, Yankee fishermen freely adopted motor boats for safety and profit. In politics, the lexicon of the automobile was no longer a pejorative. Speaker Cannon defended the tariff by pointing to rich farmers, "stepping high and some of them ... riding in automobiles." Women drivers were no longer *enfants terribles* and suffragettes, and now included the President's wife and daughter, who made the news photos at the wheel of the Baker electric. Women strikers in New York were assisted by J.P. Morgan's daughter who arranged for automobiles to rush picketers across the city. For the rest of New Yorkers, gasoline-powered taxis, buses and mail carts carried them into the Motor Age. The motoring President's countrymen were convinced.[4]

Amidst the auctioning at the Autumn 1909 Horse Show in Madison Square Garden an automobile was put into the ring and paraded like a horse. The auctioneer read off the machine's "pedigree, dam and sire, age and mark." The audience caught the joke, and amidst the hoots came a bid of five dollars. Senator Bailey, a major horse breeder, joined in with a dollar raise, which launched a raucous bidding that settled at $1,000. The price was among the highest paid for horses that day.[5]

The changed acceptance of the automobile into Taft's presidency was evident in the new AAA magazine, *American Motorist*. The magazine started out in early 1909 with automotive fiction and articles on how doctors found motor cars useful. Like other automobile journals, there was also discussion over the cost and practicality of motoring, with an eye towards ridding the sport of the stigma of wealth. Into Taft's first year, however, the joys of motoring were joined by darker issues of law and, of real impact, roads. Automobiles were politics now. The magazine henceforth focused on national financing of roads, known as "Federal Aid," and federal licensing for motorists and their cars.

By the end of 1909, motoring was synonomous with the nation's President. Dailies pictured him in automobiles throughout the Western Tour. The following February, *American Motorist* featured a cover photograph of the President and Mrs. Taft alighting from the Pierce-Arrow limousine and the headline, "National Autoists: President and Mrs. Taft." Meanwhile, "Sunny Jim" Sherman was busy exercising his Vice Presidential spare time around automobiles. Following his inauguration he posed for photographs in the Studebaker electric "tube car" that ran along the underground "motor car line" between the Capitol and the new Senate Office Building. That summer he handed out prizes at a Hill Climb near his Utica home and graced with his presence the races at Syracuse that featured Barney Oldfield, the inveterate holder of world records and equally proficient murderer of spectators. "Never before, in these United States, has one high in the councils of the nation favored an automobile event with his presence," cooed the *Automobile*.[6]

Back in Washington General Miles was thrown from his horse on the Speedway. As he was sped to the hospital in the automobile of the Assistant Librarian of

4. "Taft Stirred Anger of Anti-Cannon Men," 10/10/09, "Gasoline's Part in the Progress of the World," 10/10/09, "Cannon Is for War on the Insurgents," 11/27/09, "Miss Helen Taft Driving a Baker Electric," 10/31/09 and "Autos for Strikers In Shirtwaist War," 12/21/09, *NYT*. The Racine factory had to be the Mitchell Motor Car Co., the city's largest, which produced almost 3,000 autos in 1909 (with thanks to historian Beverly Rae Kimes).
5. "Horsemen Jeer Auto in Old Glory Ring," *NYT*, 11/25/09.
6. "Features of This Unique Office Building," 3/14/09, "Sociability Run for Motor Owners," 6/19/10, *NYT*, and "Vice-President Honors Richfield Climb," cover story, 8/12/09 and "U.S. Has Vice-President at New York

Congress, he could thank his strong efforts to bring about the acceptance of automobiles. For its motoring president, generals, librarians, and congressmen, as well as for its broad, paved roads, Washington, D.C., was proclaimed "The American City of the Automobile." Declared the AAA magazine, "President and Mrs. Taft have given a great impetus to motoring in that very large section of officialdom which, even in minor matters, takes its cue from the occupants of the White House." The motorphobic Capital City that issued the lowly license plate number 2549 on January 1, 1909 had by 1912 the most automobiles per capita in the United States. Following Taft, new registrations skyrocketed. Burnt gasoline filled the Washington air.[7]

If the President's motoring statement required punctuation, Taft implanted a big fat exclamation point on the *City of the Automobile* by attending its automobile show in January of 1910. "He is the first President of the United States to visit an

"Good roads, good laws, and good behavior" was the call of early motorists. They were creating a whole new way of life — and trying to figure it out at the same time. That is to say, they were learning how to drive. These images from the first issues of the AAA's magazine, *American Motorist,* discussed road hazards and safe driving. Efforts towards "good roads" and "good laws," however, were severely limited by the political liability that was the automobile. (From *American Motorist*, April, 1909)

6. (*cont.*) State Fair Races," 9/23/09, *Automobile*. Of the Senate machine, a reporter said, "I hope I'll be here when two automobiles meet each other coming around a curve. The air will be full of smashed Senators." For a catalog of Oldfield's destruction, see "Oldfield's Accidents," 9/25/10, *NYT*.
7. "Gen. Miles is Injured," *NYT*, 4/28/10, "Prominent People Who Use the Automobile," *American Motorist*, Feb. 1910, pp. 65–67 and "Wonderful Growth of the Industry," *Automobile*, 7/25/12, p. 164. Great thanks to Mr. Stephen Raiche for information on DC registrations. Following the District in highest automobiles per capita in 1912 were Nebraska, South Dakota, Indiana, Iowa, and Maine. California and New York had the most cars.

When Taft showed up with his presidential endorsement of automobiles, political questions about motoring suddenly found voice. The AAA lauded Mr. and Mrs. Taft as the "National Autoists." Within two years, the AAA set up offices in Washington, and Congress finally took seriously its legislation. (Reproduction of *American Motorist* cover, February 1910) The blemish in the photograph on Taft's face is from a surviving original at the Library of Congress.

automobile show," noted the Washington *Post*. Dealers had been pleased with the results of the 1906 show, especially with the press treatment; the papers that before showed a "pronounced antagonism to the automobile" began to "sit up and take notice."[8] In 1907 it was noted that "Washingtonians are getting automobile wise" and not asking "a lot of fool questions, as at previous shows...."[9] These were dealer events mostly held at local garages. So when a full-blown exhibition arrived in 1910 it was called, inaccurately, the first exhibition in years.[10] The show was a complete affair, with an orchestra, society night, aviation exhibit, and a McKinley "carnation day" in honor of the martyred President and his favorite flower.[11] Held at the city's Convention Hall, the *Evening Star* bragged that it was "the finest show of a similar character ever given south of New York...." More than 40,000 visitors walked the gates, an unheard number previously.

Taft's arrival was announced with eager toots of horns across the floor. He wandered the exhibits, joked with salesmen, and studied the aviation exhibit, accompanied, all noticed, by Sterling of the White Company. "I suppose that the more perfect the automobile becomes, the better will be the aeroplanes," he said, "for, as I understand, the motor is the vital principal [sic] of both." Afterwards, Taft and Captain Butt motored about the city before retiring to the White House.[12]

8. "Washington Show Results," *Automobile*, 2/15/06, p. 395.
9. "Washington's Auto Show is Open," *Automobile*, 1/31/07, p. 216.
10. "National Automobile Show," *Evening Star*, 1/23/10.
11. "Show Ends Tonight," *Evening Star*, 1/29/10. Each lady was given a carnation, McKinley's good luck charm. The story is that McKinley gave his flower off his lapel to a little girl at a receiving line in Buffalo in 1901. The man next in line shot him.
12. "Fine Display Made," 1/24/10, "Great Day at Show," 1/28/10, "Motoring," 1/30/10, *Evening Star*, "Taft at Auto Show," *Washington Post*, 1/30/10 and "Taft Goes to Auto Show," *NYT*, 1/30/10.

Taft launched a motoring nation, sometimes literally. In 1910, he posed with a group of Virginia motorists in front of the White House mansion and its new West Wing, which he helped to design. He wished them and the motoring nation Godspeed. (From ***American Motorist,*** May 1910)

After his return from Africa in 1910, Roosevelt bought a Haynes automobile. Into 1912, he was seen at the wheel. Had the Colonel conquered the car, or did the car conquer the Colonel? (From *American Motorist*, March 1912)

highest social honor one can have is a raid from the Night Riders led by the intrepid Alice." During the Wright airplane trials she held perhaps the first ever tailgate party. "She invites those who visit her in her motor car to have tea and lemonade," Archie wrote, "and if they accept the latter they are agreeably surprised to find a delicious gin fizz...."[14]

Her father, the country's most prominent motoring holdout, was soon turned, as well.

By then, Ambassadors freely called by motor. The social set, led by Larz Anderson's $25,000 garage and seven cars, was beset with out-doing. Thomas F. Walsh, the city's richest man, and who had already lost his son to an auto accident, switched his considerable stables to a garage. Mrs. Pullman, Mrs. Townsend, Mrs. Hanna, and others of the "professional widows" crowd treated their automobiles as "show objects."[13] In her electric, Alice Longworth sped about to poke convention or to erupt a midnight party. Her "Night Riders" raids, named after infamous Tennessee vigilantes, became legend. Alice's version consisted of rousing a social posse to deliver "howls and cat calls" outside respectable residences until the owner joined the party, which moved on by motor car to the next victim. Archie wrote, "Now the

Roosevelt's motorphobia went into a permanent lapse upon his return to New York from the Africa trip in June of 1910. A Naval flotilla greeted his vessel and crowds cheered his five-mile carriage ride through the streets. Although the Reception Committee earlier turned down an offer by a dealers' association of sixty motors for use in the parade, when it was over, Roosevelt was taken away by automobile.[15] Back at Oyster Bay, where he declared himself closed up "like a native clam," the silence was broken by the roar of the family's new auto, a Haynes, a 4-cylinder, mid-priced, respectable car. Roosevelt remained at least romantically opposed to the Motor Age. That October he wrote that motors were "distinct additions to the discomfort of living." Concerns over discomfort, however, went to the steep drive to his house, which

13. "Prominent People Who Use the Automobile," *American Motorist*, Feb. 1910, pp. 65–67 and *Walking Tours of Old Washington and Alexandria*, by Paul Hogarth, EPM Publications, McLean, Virginia, 1985; p. 73. Taft joked about the "professional type of widows" of Washington who lived socially off the renown of their dead husbands. He compared them most unfavorably to the quiet dignity of Mrs. Thomas "Stonewall" Jackson (Butt, 5/21/09, p. 94).
14. Butt, 5/15/09, p. 83, 7/28/09, p. 159.
15. "No Autos in Roosevelt Parade," *Automobile*, 6/9/10, p. 1057.

he had macadamized so motors could make the grade rather than slip in the mud. Into the Winter of 1911, he was seen at the wheel himself.[16]

The automobile now fit nicely into his headlines, such as "Roosevelt Puts In a Strenuous Day: Makes an Auto Record, Holds Conferences, Talks on Nature Faking, and Receives Friends."[17] In addition to all that, he declared himself not opposed to Governor Hughes, lunched with the Camp-Fire Club, met with Booker T. Washington, Col. Lyon of Texas, members of Chicago's politically powerful Hamilton Club, the manager of *Collier's*, two Englishmen, various reporters, and dined with Robert Collier of the magazine. The automobile bit came of his besting the Long Island Railroad train to Manhattan by five minutes. When Robert La Follette tried to sneak into Oyster Bay to clandestinely meet with Roosevelt, he was caught by reporters who recognized the family car and chauffeur.[18]

Who could argue anymore?

* * *

There were still a couple of lingering problems, a few road blocks to the proper development of the Automobile Century. Congress, Speaker Cannon found, was still not altogether friendly to motors. Although he got an official automobile in the summer of 1909, his timing was off again. Taft's cars were wedding gifts from Congress. Cannon asked for his during a divorce. Amidst the tariff discussions, the Senate voted $12,000 for automobiles for both the Speaker and the Vice President. Cannon's House balked. Outrage! Sims cried. This time he dropped the horse defense. Why, Civil War widows had to survive on $6 pensions while generals and politicians rode in government automobiles that cost thousands of dollars.... Clayton of Alabama questioned why the Vice President's appropriation included the word "automobile," and it was "other vehicles" for the Speaker. "Does this mean that we are to provide an aeroplane for the Speaker? Or does this mean that the Speaker is to ride around on a motor cycle like the policemen use?" Tawney sent it back to the Senate for clarification. The explanation was made, and in the haste to rid themselves of the tariff and everything else,

Uncle Joe and Senator Nelson of Minnesota pose here by the Speaker's official automobile, a 40 H.P. Studebaker-Garford touring car. Following Taft's appropriation, the Speaker and the President of the Senate, Vice President Sherman, demanded their own cars. They were given $6,000 apiece, making the Congress co-equal to Taft's $12,000 garage. (From *American Motorist*, February 1910).

16. "Million Join in Welcome to Roosevelt," *NYT*, 6/19/10, *Harper's Weekly*, 6/25/10, p. 10, Brands, p. 686, and "Roosevelt Runs an Auto," *NYT*, 1/20/12.
17. *NYT*, 6/23/10.
18. "Roosevelt Talks with La Follette," *NYT*, 6/28/10.

$6,000 each was voted in for "automobiles" for the Speaker and the President of the Senate. Cannon's official automobile arrived in December of 1909, just in time to help him taunt the insurgents at the short Winter session. His was a 1910 four-cylinder, 40-horsepower "Studebaker-Garford" touring car, done up in maroon.[19]

The following year the subject of Cannon's automobiles ignited the final battle over his power in the House. In what was a test vote for the real amputation the next day, the House insurgents teamed up with the Democrats on March 15, 1910, to rob the Speaker of his automobile and chauffeur. "Our 'Uncle Joe' is dangerous enough when he is sitting still," an insurgent told a reporter. A month later Cannon got his gasoline allowance, but only after appealing to the jealousy of the House. "I believe that the Speaker of the House of Representatives, whoever he may be, should in all matters be of the same dignity as the Vice President, who presides over the co-ordinate branch."

The matter was not finally settled until the following year when a new Congress and a new Speaker took it up. This time it was Champ Clark, defender of mules. Clark's Democrats won a majority in the mid-term elections of 1910. In his party's tradition, he eschewed Whig elitism. He might have known that Jefferson rode a horse to his inauguration because his carriage was late to arrive, but no matter, for Clark declared himself of the Horse Age and talked of riding a mule into the Speakership in April of 1911. That election also brought to Congress its first Socialist, Victor Berger of Milwaukee. After watching Clark take the trolley to work, Berger suggested the Speaker's $6,000 automobile be used by Congressmen to go "slumming" to witness poverty in their host city.[20] Not for another year did Clark fully settle into the back seat.

Another road block to the Automobile Century was potentially grave, although largely unknown outside the industry. An innocuous news item appeared in the papers on September 16, 1909. "Motor Car Patents Upheld By Court." A lawsuit by the ALAM to enforce its Selden patent against Ford had been simmering in court several years. Ford's attorney warned, "Few people realize how much is at stake in this Selden litigation. ...This growing industry ... would be jeopardized should the original contention of the licensed association be sustained."[21] The Federal Circuit Court granted the patent rights to anything akin to "The combination with road locomotive, provided with a suitable running gear and including a propelling wheel and steering mechanism, of a liquid hydrocarbon engine of the compression type, comprising one or more cylinders...." Among automobiles, steamers and electrics were exempt from the definition. Anyone building, importing or selling a gasoline car would have to pay homage to the ALAM.

It was a good year for the Association. First, Congress administered the 45 percent tariff inoculation against imports and granted the industry its own category. Now the Selden patent was endowed with the force of law with which to crush domestic competition—but for one man who would not back down. This was the man

19. *CR*, 8/4/09, p. 118, "No Auto for the Speaker," 8/3/09, "Cannon gets the $2,500" 4/9/10, "No Auto for Cannon," 3/16/10, and "House Won't Give Speaker an Auto," 4/12/10, *NYT* and "Motoring," *Evening Star*, 12/5/09.

20. *NYT* photo caption, 3/12/11 and "Berger Wants Clark's Auto," *NYT*, 5/19/11. Berger's real reason for wanting to use the car was that he had spent good money on trolleys and hired motors in order to acquaint himself with the city, as was his duty as a member of the House District Committee. Berger's request had less to do with the extravagance of the Speaker's automobile than his own pocket change.

21. *NYT*, 9/16/09 and "A Statement by Ford's Attorney," *Automobile*, 1/31/07, p. 254.

who built his first car in a shed and had to take down a wall in order to remove it, only to be jeered by the neighbors—"It made me mad to see those boys demonstrate their supremacy over Detroit's first automobile," he said.[22] This man who thrice started over in business was equally undaunted by the most powerful element in the industry, the ALAM. In January of 1911, the U.S. Court of Appeals overruled the lower court decision. Henry Ford had won. He was lauded at the New York auto shows. With great magnanimity, Ford avoided public comment. With equal grace, the ALAM invited Ford and his partner, James Couzens, as guests of honor to its annual banquet. Col. Clifton lit a long pipe and passed it to Ford, who puffed a cloud of blue smoke. Shortly after, the ALAM was shut down.[23]

Now, to fully launch the Automobile Century, a final issue remained unresolved. Building and buying automobiles was one thing. Finding a suitable place to drive them was another. Good Roads posed not just technical difficulties, but perplexing legal and political problems.

22. "Ford Tells of Trials," *NYT*, 1/14/12. Ford's was not the first automobile in Detroit (see "The Legend of Henry Ford," by Keith Sward, 1948, p. 12).

23. "Smoke Peace Pipe at A.L.A.M. Banquet," *Automobile*, 1/19/11, p. 232. It has been pointed out that the Selden patent would expire in 1912, anyway, and besides, Ford could easily afford the 1¼ percent licensing fee (over list price). However, the ALAM represented more than just the patent. It was legitimacy in the business. Ford became a hero because he won. Without the court victory, subversive ALAM advertising to the effect of "don't buy a lawsuit with your car" might have had its intended effect upon Ford and others (see *The American Automobile*, by John B. Rae, pp. 33–38). Following the 1909 decision, Ford's comrades in the anti–Selden industry group, the AMCMA, ran for cover. Eight members, including three of the most important, Maxwell-Briscoe, Mitchell, and Reo, took on ALAM licenses, and the association collapsed. Even industry rebel Durant made up with the ALAM, with whom he previously jostled over Buick and Olds royalties (Nevins, pp. 426–428). Then again, were the ALAM successful it is not inconceivable that the Taft administration would have challenged it as a "combination in restraint of trade." Attorney General Wickersham prosecuted the "bathtub trust" based upon monopolistic use of an enamel patent (see "Auto Prices Kept Up By Trusts, He Says" *NYT*, 11/28/08 and "Government Wins the Bathtub Suit," *NYT*, 10/14/11). Nevins overstates the general effect of Ford's court victory, with, "psychologically at least, [it] was like a chisel blow snapping the fetters which had hobbled a large part of the automotive industry" (p. 457). Nevins saw that something had changed in 1911 and attributed it to the Selden case.

20

Taft Settles It

I have pleasure in saying that there is no movement that I know of that will have a more direct effect to alleviate the difficulties and burdens of the farmer's life, will stimulate the traffic, and add to the general happiness of the people more than the establishment of good roads throughout the country. I do not think that because this may have been stimulated by people using automobiles it is to be frowned upon, for while persons using automobiles are by no means the most important in the community, the fact that their sharp interest has focused the attention of the public on the movement entitles them to credit.

—William Howard Taft, August, 1909,
to Richmond, Virginia, motorists[1]

As the modern reader will note, road surfaces often change crossing state lines. The great historical accident of American federalism evades even today's national bureaucracy. Federalism was the fundamental question of the Good Roads movement of 1909. The Judge President answered it.

Taft's letter to the Richmond Good Roaders was laced with apologies for motorists. The man had just rammed through Congress a $12,000 sanction of automobiles and would for four years personally demonstrate their usefulness and push his government to assist in their development and that of roads for them. Even he was careful with his words. In August of 1909, a time when he was ripping up Washington, D.C., and Massachusetts roads in some of the greatest motors in the world, he felt the need to rationalize it as friendly to the farmer. It didn't matter that it was true. He had to say it.

Two years later Taft could more freely praise motorists. To the Automobile Club of America on December 20, 1911, he announced, "the working out of the automobile is a wonderful development."[2] In this radical speech Taft pointed to the automobile's role in the era's shrinkage of time and space. "As you look back as far as I can look back, to 1876 ... the changes are marvelous," he told the very exclusive, very rich ACA members and guests that included Governor Dix, several ambassadors, and a host of America's richest,

1. "Taft Advocates Good Roads," *NYT*, 8/4/09.
2. This section from Taft speech, 12/20/11 (reel 580), "Taft Says States Should Build Roads," *NYT*, 12/21/11, and "The Twelfth Annual Banquet," *Club Journal*, 1/6/12, pp. 601–606.

including Henry Frick, William K. Vanderbilt, John Archbold, John Flagler, John Jacob Astor, Elbert Gary, and J.P. Morgan. "Most of them were millionaires," Butt noted.[3] Taft's words were for all Americans: "The telephone, the electric railway, all the electrical devices for the reproduction of the human voice, and the automobile — what could we do without them now?"

Taft commenced his speech with the requisite apology for his presence among the privileged. "I never belonged to what I always used to call the 'carriage class,'" he told the carriage class. "I walked, or rode in street cars.... It is true that the accident of office and the generosity of a Republican Congress gave me for a time the privilege of understanding the fascination of traveling by this new method, but there is no permanency of tenure in the machine or in the office. Therefore, I beg of you to understand that I appear here only in a temporarily representative capacity."

The joke worked on an audience that knew everything about the President's $12,000 garage. They knew that his brother Henry rode around New York in a Fiat limousine, one of the best and most expensive cars of 1911.[4] They knew that brother Charles, who recently added a Rembrandt to his art collection, traded automobiles like horses. The President's modesty was the repentance they all had to make for their motoring. Knowing that the speech would be reprinted across the land,

Taft said, "If you had traveled as much as I have, if you had been met in every town of five or ten thousand people in every State, with a hundred automobiles, in order to demonstrate the prosperity of that particular town, you would understand that the use of the automobile has gone quite beyond that class which I aspired to and never acquired membership in." Everywhere Taft went he went about in automobiles. He rode in more different cars in more different places than any other person of his day. At every stop he was greeted by townspeople who knew of his love for motoring and who wanted to demonstrate their prosperity and modernity. Taft is pictured here in a Cole automobile in Concord, New Hampshire, March 1912. (Courtesy Leroy D. Cole)

3. Butt, 12/21/11, p. 799.
4. "Auto Notes," *NYT*, 4/18/09. Taft certainly knew this car.

knowing that an election was less than a year away, the President of the United States had made his apologies and could now focus on what he really thought. He could now congratulate "those gentlemen who are making it an industry that contributes greatly to the wealth of this country, and adds much to its manufacturing product." Due praise, that. But wait—

> How rapidly we adapt ourselves to the absolute necessity of those improvements of which we knew and imagined nothing fifty years ago! I am sure that of all of them the automobile coming in as a toy of the wealthier classes is going to prove the most useful of them all to all classes, rich and poor.

No more alibis to the farmers, no more excuses for privilege. A nation frightened of itself, cowered by its own success, shackled in its own grandeur, whose beacon was dimmed in shame, was then and there acquitted of its self-indictment. Its people had been scolded to repentance, told again and again their offenses, that their joys were abuse, their progress was pain. Taft overturned the ruling. He annulled the verdict. He cast the plaintiffs abroad, back to where discontent was never free, to where no Vanderbilts, no Morgans, and no Harrimans built no things and frightened no one, to where no Durants, no Dodges, no Fords would ever democratize space and time. The gentry of the ACA and the great American multitudes Taft rendered equals again. He made those millionaires the equals of those who feared, of those who envied; he made them the equals of everyone, including those who would punish, not uphold, who would tear, not sew, the great American fabric—in all its crazy threads. The nation would no longer have to look away; Democracy in America was affirmed.

Doing it, Taft condemned his audience that night to obscurity. He opened the ballroom doors, shattering their exclusivity. The ACA's hard work for the automobile was no longer needed. The Club would be forgotten by history. In declaring the automobile the poor man's toy, Taft rendered the Automobile Club of America irrelevant:

> If you had traveled as much as I have, if you had been met in every town of five or ten thousand people in every state, with one hundred automobiles, in order to demonstrate the prosperity of that particular town, you would understand that the use of the automobile has gone quite beyond that class which I aspired to and never acquired membership in. It means that the automobile has come here for use.

Saying it, William Howard Taft changed the world. Roosevelt's and Ford's beloved farmers were safe to ride in automobiles now:

> It is contributing, like the telephone, like the suburban railway, like the rural delivery of the post office, to the possibility of comfortable life on the farm, and it is tending, together with high prices of farm products, to turn back again those who seek the city and professional life to a place where they have an assured income and are not troubled with suits or litigation or chase by the Government.

Taft hit a number of themes here. Abandonment of the farm and the cost of living were perceived at the time to be national crises. He poked fun at rich farmers, while praising the great benefit of the automobile to the farmer's life. And he couldn't resist a jab at his own anti-trust actions, especially in front of Morgan, whose steel trust was just then taking a Justice Department broadside. Now he addressed the issue of federal licensing, which, despite the defeat of the 1908 Cocks bill, was still at the fore of motorists' political crusades. Taft said,

> You might set up some theory of yourself being an unopened and complete package sent from Connecticut into New Jersey, through New York, that can not be opened until you reach the point of your destination, and in some way or other call upon the Federal Court to protect you in that transportation, whether you escape the tax and the license, and all that sort of thing, for the grooves that your automobile makes in the roads of your state, I am unable to say, because those who are charged with the responsibility of keeping up the roads know that while the automobile owners have promoted the question and the pursuit of good roads, they have very largely contributed to the difficulty of building and maintaining them.

After this spanking came an explanation of his efforts on behalf of better roads. "The experiments made as to what may avoid the influence of those great big rubber tires upon macadam roads are proceeding, and I hope something will come of them," he explained. Taft well knew reformers, and he well knew their enthusiasms for results yesterday. His solutions were always methodical. To the impatient, he told a little story:

> I speak with considerable deference, because I find that gentlemen who study good roads as a diversion, as an avocation, have such decided views that one who is just charged with the good old governmental way of building a road finds some difficulty in appreciating, and also finds that he is not regarded as an authority in any respect. I had a call from a gentleman who is an automobilist and also a good roads man, and eats, sleeps and drinks good roads. He came to me and said: "Mr. President, I desire that you appoint delegates to a good roads convention — a national good roads convention." I said, "I will be very glad to do it, sir. We have two departments in which there are road experts." "Which are they," said he. Said I, "We have the Agricultural Department, where we have a Bureau devoted to experts who are laying experimental roads for the country, for the farmers." Said he, "I have had occasion to know how much they know. I have looked into it, and they don't know anything about it at all. They have not the first principles at hand." I said, "Then we will go into the War Department, and we will take the army engineers, and I will send you some of them. They have been building roads in the Philippines, in every State in the Union, in Cuba, on the Isthmus, and elsewhere." Said he, "If my boy did not know more about the real principles of building roads than they do, I would not allow him to continue the study of it." I said, "Good morning, sir, I am not in the road business, and I have no delegates worthy of being sent there."

The story was all about the impertinence of the Good Roaders. As the insurgents, they had a friend in Taft, but one who tired of their constant demonstrations. "The question of good roads, as I say, is a difficult one, not only because of the perfection of the road for resisting this much heavier travel, but also because of the question who is to pay for the roads. Are they to be built by the State? Are they to be built by the county? Whoever builds them, who is to take care of them? This is a much more important question." Again, as with the insurgents, Taft told the motorists, your goal is noble, but your compass is askew:

> But I hear the earnest patriot — and it does not make any difference how he construes the Constitution — if there is any plan of running a national road near his farm, I hear the earnest patriot say, "it is the business of the general government to build its roads. Let us have a national road running from New York to San Francisco, to teach the world what a model road is." What will it cost? "Ah, what difference does it make what it costs, you can strive and hunt ways of saving $100,000 in the matter of employees at Washington; but when it comes to building roads what is $100,000,000 between friends?"

This was Taft at his best. Here was the man who stood before steel workers in Cleveland and asked for their vote while admonishing the excesses of their demands. Here was the man who stood down his own party, regulars and insurgents, who told off the National Grange to its face, their votes be damned. Here was the man who shook his finger at magazine publishers and told them he would yank their postal subsidies regardless of their editorial content. To the gentlemen of the ACA, whose touring cars and limousines were too often jolted by ruined macadam and whose chauffeurs too often required bail, Taft told it straight. The man whose income tax amendment made it all possible declared,

> And there is the difficulty, gentlemen. I admit that the general Government has the power to build roads for the purpose of promoting interstate commerce. It has done it already. But I venture to question the wisdom of opening that method of spending the Federal Government money.... If we could confine it to two or three roads, I would not object, but we have forty-eight different states, and every state is as anxious to share in the common funds at Washington as every other state ... the stopping of which will never end.

There you have it, a marvelous summary of and answer to the fundamental automotive issues of the day. Taft's synthesis was prescient, comprehensive, and correct. The man was no idle passenger. His time in the back seat was not wasted. The speech came of three years upon roads across the land. He had motored in California, New Hampshire, and Colorado. He knew the good and the bad roads of Pennsylvania, Texas, and Oregon. He directed his government to explore their improvement. And here he announced a major shift in government policy. Perhaps the gentlemen of the ACA felt too scolded to notice. If they did, they might have understood that the government would soon enough pave their way. As with many other issues, Taft anticipated and helped to launch a different world, even if it was one he did not like. Did you, dear reader, notice?

> I admit that the general Government has the power to build roads for the purpose of promoting interstate commerce.[5]

It wasn't just "post roads" anymore. It was no longer federal "aid" or military roads or a Lincoln memorial road, or any number of backward schemes to get the Feds into road making. National road building was now a full-blown part of the powers of Congress, Article I, Section 8's ever elastic "commerce clause." From this simple, sweeping admission Taft decreed the legality and inevitability of the Federal Aid Road Act of 1916, the Federal Highway Act of 1921, the 1956 Interstate and Defense Highways Acts, and the ultimate paving of America.

* * *

The month after Taft's speech, January of 1912, the AAA held a convention a block from the White House and prepared to move its headquarters to the city. The group had become a major lobby.[6] Its legislation found sponsorship, and its affairs made the news. Although upset that Taft told the ACA that the central government ought stay out of the road building

5. In the *NYT*, ACA, and AAA reprints of the speech, the word "national" was inserted before "roads." It doesn't change the meaning, import, or impact of the utterance. The shock came of the words "general Government."
6. "AAA Will Soon Open Washington Headquarters," *NYT*, 12/15/12. The group's first convention in Washington came in 1910 and was called "the first legislative convention of its kind ever held in this country" ("Motoring," *Evening Star*, 11/21/09).

business, the big news at the convention was the President's admission that federal expenditures on roads was constitutional. The *American Motorist* reprinted excerpts from Taft's ACA speech beginning with, in bold type, "I admit that the general Government has the power for the purpose of promoting inter–State commerce to build National roads."[7] The editors reveled in the admission. "To have the President of the United States unhesitatingly say that the Government has the right, is most important at this time, even though he places himself on record as against the proposition, because of the enormous amount which might be expended."

Then there was Taft's joke that to qualify for federal licensing, motorists must profess to be "an unopened and complete package" sent over state lines.[8] The humor was lost on these frustrated interstate motorists. Wrote the *American Motorist*, "It must be frankly confessed that apparently he has not yet given the subject the most thorough study...." Actually, the AAA ought to have more carefully heeded the President's judicial experience. Their impatience with constitutional limitations was exactly the kind of "zest and enthusiasm of reform" that Taft said led to disregard of existing law and the creation of worse.

In 1908, the AAA sponsored a court challenge to state motor laws. A New York resident in a New York–licensed car was sent into New Jersey on the way to Pennsylvania with the intent to be arrested for the absence of local tags. He was. The defendant's case was based upon the interstate commerce and equal protection clauses of the Constitution. Almost nine years later the Supreme Court found that the motorist was not equal to Taft's joke. The Court ruled that the individual states had power to regulate and tax automobile use within their boundaries and that the Constitution was in no way offended by the New Jersey arrest.[9]

Taft's ACA speech acted like a king's proclamation. Had he endorsed federal licensing, the AAA's court challenge wouldn't have been so imperative to the cause. With his denial it was their only hope. Were national licensing invoked, automotive law would have developed far differently over the century.[10] Likewise, after that speech, the constitutional objections to federal road building dissolved. The AAA turned its energies almost wholly to Federal Aid.[11]

Democrats and Progressives both

7. "Taft Says Federal Aid Constitutional, But—," *American Motorist*, Jan. 1912
8. This section of the speech was omitted in the ACA's reprint.
9. "A.A.A. Appeal to U.S. Supreme Court," *American Motorist*, June 1914 and "Adverse Decision by the Supreme Court," *American Motorist*, Jan. 1917. See also "Concerning Pending Federal Legislation," *Automobile*, 4/7/10, p. 684.
10. Federal licensing and licenses would mean Federal courts. Anyone who has been caught speeding on Federal property will know what it could have been like, universally, had Congress usurped States of these policing and regulatory powers. As bad as are State traffic courts and fines, imagine the joy if the Federal government ran the show.
11. See *Federal Aid Road Act of 1916*, by Richard F. Weingroff, Public Roads On-Line, website, Summer 1996, Federal Highway Administration. Weingroff points to a 1907 Supreme Court ruling that "settled the constitutional question." In that case the Court ruled favorably on the constitutionality of the Panama Canal. Rather fed up with plaintiff's arguments, the Court made the caustic reply that every kind of interstate construction, such as rails, bridges, canals, and roads, were among the powers of Congress. Since the specific instance regarded a territory, *A fortiori*— lawyer-speak for "duh"— the Government could build roads, railroads and a canal in Panama. Nevertheless, the Court flatly stated that Congress has "the power ... to authorize the construction of a public highway connecting several states" (*Wilson v. Shaw*, 204 U.S. 24). The author has not encountered mention of the *Shaw* case by 1910s Good Roaders. Their opponents still looked to the Constitution as the principal obstacle to Federal Aid. Had the Court been appealed to, *Shaw* might have been the guide, but, of course, there was no law to sue against. The issue in 1912 was not legal but political, thus the importance of Taft's ACA "ruling." (With dear thanks to James F. Bromley, Esq for legal

sponsored road building in their 1912 platforms, although the Democratic plank called for "Post Roads" only, as it had in 1908, and the Progressives called for "National highways," walking around the key words, "Federal Aid." The 1908 Republican plank had vaguely stated, "We recognize the social and economical advantages of good country roads, maintained more and more largely at public expense...."[12] The party's 1912 plank didn't mention roads at all.

Like the income tax, Taft passed on the revolution he personally launched. During the 1912 election year, he refused to attend a Good Roads convention in Atlantic City. He told his secretary, "I am not going ... for the reason that I would make more enemies if I went than if I stayed away because I would have to tell the truth. I do not believe in involving the Federal treasury in a weight of obligation to build roads that the States ought to build."[13]

Road building was an agreed-to necessity. The problem was politics and money, ever one in the same. The various states spent $200,000,000 in road building and maintenance in 1913, the vast majority by republican states. Many of the democratic states had no highway departments or organized road building efforts. How would the federal government apportion the funds? New Yorkers correctly figured that their tax dollars would go to roads elsewhere. The AAA kept a nonpartisan stance on the issue. Its position was that even if the state-to-state and urban-to-rural account balance between tax income and expenditures were skewed, the ultimate benefits to commerce, travel, and safety were for all Americans.

Counting the zeroes, John A. Stewart, President of the International League for Highway Improvement, endorsed Taft's sentiments on road building. "It is estimated by engineers of high standing," he said, "that for the Government to build even 10 percent of the roads ... would cost over $2,500,000,000. To build an adequate system of roads ... would cost at least $25,000,000,000. There can be no doubt whatever that a direct tax would be necessary in order to carry out any scheme of Government aid, nor is there doubt that such direct tax would have to be levied at a constantly increasing ratio."[14]

River and harbor projects, which Taft was up against every session, were dowries to the era's marriage of national and sectional politics. Add to it road building, and the bride's father woud go broke. What changed the equation was the income tax. Stewart prophesied that an initial $25,000,000 appropriation would turn to 250 millions every year, numbers that were fantastic to a people and a time whose entire federal budget was just over a billion dollars. And if so, Stewart asked, would apportioning the work amongst the states follow the apportionment of the taxation? Not likely, he knew, for like all federal programs, and especially one of this size, appropriations would follow "political pull and exigency." Answering his own question, he asked, "What scheme is it possible to present that will be fair to all the states and which will satisfy all?"

Stewart's solution was a National Highways Commission, "whose duty," a reporter explained, "was to co-ordinate

11. (*cont.*) research; of the attitude of Justice Brewer in the *Shaw* opinion, while Mr. Bromley will not go so far as your author in calling it "caustic," he admits, "He was startled at the enormity of plantiff's argument...!"

12. Roosevelt wanted something on farmers, a request Taft combined with that of the Good Roads Commission for a statement in favor of the "extension of the free rural [postal] delivery." Taft told the Platform Committee to "get in a plank on farmers in reference to the movement in favor of good roads by state aid and such incidental national aid as may be constitutional" (Taft to W Ellis, 6/9/08).

13. Taft to Hilles, 9/21/12.

14. "Uncle Sam Too Poor to Build the Roads," *NYT*, 1/28/12.

and plan the inter–State roads to be built by the States, and as far as possible bring about uniform traffic and road regulation among the several states, as well as report to Congress a feasible plan for inter–State registration of motor vehicles." "This," said Stewart, "is as far as the Government should go...."

Like Taft, Speaker Cannon was a modernist on the roads but ever a constructionist when it came to the central government. Cannon leant his powerful presence to the National Good Roads Association in Baltimore in May of 1909, but not his votes in Congress. "I hope you'll keep on in your good work, and in the fullness of time, at the expense of counties and States, we'll construct good roads," he told them. In reply, it was stated that the government ought economize in shipbuilding in order to address the need for good roads. "It is impossible that an apostle of republicanism should oppose this," said a Good Roader. Still, in 1912 there was old Uncle Joe seen turning the first spade of a major Illinois— state funded — road project.

In addition to straight-out appropriations, the movement counted on at least one back-door federal entry to the business of road building. As of January of 1912, already three years past the centennial celebration of Lincoln's birth, Congress had yet to settle upon a memorial plan. What better way to honor the martyred President, it was argued, than with a "living" memorial? The Lincoln Memorial Highway from Washington to Gettysburg would represent the practical Lincoln. The great man would want a useful monument upon which the nation he saved would grow into the future he hoped. In early 1909, then–Senator Knox compared the idea to the Appian Way, named for a Roman emperor.[15] Opponents saw through the rhetoric: it was a "wedge for the establishment of a fixed policy of granting Federal appropriations for the construction of public highways," explained a Congressman.[16]

In 1910, Senator Taylor of Tennessee told the AAA, "I am a States' rights Democrat, so cannot say how far I can go on the Federal registration idea, but I am heartily in favor of anything that will help the good roads movement, and hope some day to be able to step into my automobile here and drive to my home in Tennessee in a single day." The following year Senator Williams of Mississippi said, "There is no doubt of the constitutional right of the Federal Government to establish post roads. If the end, to wit, the establishment of post roads, is constitutional, then, in the language of Chief Justice Marshall, any means necessary or appropriate to the end is constitutional."[17]

These were isolated comments prior to December 20, 1911. Within a week of the ACA speech, Taft was presented with a petition from his own city's Chamber of Commerce. "WHEREAS, the internal development of our country for the good and uplift of all of our people throughout the United States and Territories is the first duty of Congress; AND WHEREAS the first material step of civilization is to provide highways...." Pointing to "thousands of millions of dollars" in land grants for railroads, "one thousand millions" appropriated for river and harbor improvement, "many hundreds of millions" spent on the

15. "Senate Clash Over Lincoln," *NYT*, 1/22/09.
16. "Sentiment Favors Lincoln Highway," *NYT*, 4/2/12. Cannon had a few thoughts on the matter: "Speaking respectfully, to my mind it is the prostitution of that great man's name when you speak of using it as an argument for the promotion and construction of good roads" ("Cannon Explains List of Great Men," *NYT*, 1/26/13).
17. "Legislative Convention at Washington," *American Motorist*, Feb. 1910, p. 61 and "Federal Support for Good Highways," *NYT*, 12/17/11.

Panama Canal ... the petition demanded quick passage of Senate Bill no. 3197, "calling for one million dollars for preliminary surveys for seven national highways...."[18]

Previous to Taft, automobiles undermined the Good Roads movement. No federal dollars would go towards a subsidy of motorists. Federal Aid bills, like SR 3197, were stillborn in congressional committees. Through Taft's action, example, and words, automobiles were accepted by his government and by his people. Col. Albert Pope, the man who put a motor and two extra wheels on the bicycle industry, Henry Ford, who brought the automobile to everyone, and all the others in the business and the clubs and their luxury cars, were stranded without political legitimacy. Starting with the National Seal he put on the doors of his cars, Taft gave it to them.

A few weeks after the ACA speech, the *Times* reported, "A surprisingly large proportion of the members of Congress and others in public life have placed themselves on record in favor of Federal Aid."[19] Even Champ Clark put down the reigns long enough to show a kindly face to automobilists. He surprised the AAA with an unscheduled appearance at its January 1912 convention. After delegates applauded madly, chairman Diehl called for three more rounds of cheers. Clark lectured the group on the difficulties to get anything through Congress and pledged his favor for the Lincoln Memorial Highway. A month later, a photographer couldn't believe his eyes, but there right in front of the Capitol and the whole world was Speaker Clark sitting in an automobile.[20] That Spring Clark's House was peppered with road building legislation. One of the most active proponents, Rep. Shackleford, launched at least three road bills. He succeeded two years later with a bill to provide to states $25,000,000 annually. Although the Senate didn't concur, it was the first modern large-scale Federal Aid act to make it through a house of Congress.[21]

Taft, too, gave in to this monster of his own creation. In 1912 he signed an appropriation that allocated $500,000 in direct federal grants for "experimental" post roads. More importantly, it funded a Congressional Committee, headed by Taft's old golf and motoring partner, Senator Bourne, to study the road building issue and attempt to balance the disparities and concerns of Federal Aid.[22] Even Cannon

18. T Grant to Taft, 12/26/11. SR 3197 was introduced on August 10, 1911. It called for $1,000,000 for preliminary surveys of seven national highways that would connect the four corner points of the Continental United States, Portland, Maine, Seattle, Los Angeles, and Miami. The last of its resolutions was, "Whereas the President of the United States, with wise patriotism, has publicly commended the enterprise for the construction of a highway from Montreal, Canada, to Miami, Florida, and also by open letter has indorsed the American Association for Highway Improvement: Therefore, Be it enacted...."

19. "Federal Aid for Highways Favored," *NYT*, 1/14/12.

20. "National Roads a National Need," Feb. 1912, p. 107 and "Speaker Clark Uses an Automobile," May 1912, p. 362, *American Motorist*. The car was not the Speaker's official motor, but a National "40" coupe, known as a fast car. "The interesting and important fact still remains that Speaker Clark, like former President Roosevelt, as noted in the March *Motorist*, has revised his ideas as to the utility of the motor car."

21. Nelson Aldrich's Senate beat Shackleford to the honors, although on a smaller scale. In early 1909, the Senate allotted $50,000 for survey of the proposed Lincoln Highway. Knox was the foremost promoter of it. Uncle Joe's House didn't agree, and the project died (see "Provide For Lincoln Way: Senate Allows $50,000 For Survey of Great Road to Gettysburg," *NYT* 1/23/09). Shackleford's $25,000,000 Federal Aid bill (H.R. 11686, 2/10/14) combined direct federal payments with an old finance scheme he introduced previously that, through a twisted leasing scheme, the government would "rent" roads from localities for mail delivery (see also "Good Roads," *American Motorist*, Feb. 1914, p. 119; note that the article, "Federal Aid Road Act of 1916," Public Roads On-Line, incorrectly lists the date of the Shackleford Bill as 1912—the author was likely referring to other bills introduced by Shackleford that did not pass).

22. For Bourne's ideas see "Practical Plan to Spend $3,000,000,000 For Public Roads," *NYT*, 5/11/13 and "National Aid to Good Roads," *North American Review*, Sept. 1913.

now supported it. In 1913, the former Speaker declared, "I am willing to assist and have the Federal Treasury assist properly toward their construction as post roads, or in aid of their construction."[23] That year, Bourne presented the Committee's findings. These initiatives came to fruition a few years later in the form of the "Federal Road Aid Act." The federal government would provide $75,000,000 to be matched by an equal amount from the states for the building of rural post roads.[24] The pen President Wilson used to sign the bill was given to the president of the AAA.

23. "Cannon Explains List of Great Men," *NYT*, 1/26/13. Previously, Clark and other Democratic anti-automobilists had no problem with Federal Aid; they just didn't want it to benefit motorists. Cannon loved motoring but hated the idea of Federal Aid.
24. Another $10,000,000 in federal money went to building roads in national forests. However, the Act provided only $5,000,000 for the first year. The in-fighting among the states commenced immediately after passage of the bill. Florida complained of its comparative lack of "post" roads and demanded federal dollars for the building of other important avenues that might be of "military importance." The rest of the state legislatures tripped over themselves to meet the federal requirements, including eleven states that had no highway departments at all. States with advanced road systems, such as New York and Connecticut, got busy meeting the rules for maintenance funds (see *American Motorist*, July 1917). The program was lost to world war and subsequent economic distress, despite 1919 legislation that added more funds. The federal government was heavily in debt and states could not afford their share of the expenditures, anyway. In 1921, Warren Harding, a motoring enthusiast who drove his Locomobile from Ohio to Washington while a Senator and was the first President to ride a motorcar at his inauguration, signed the Federal Highway Act, the first successful federal road building program.

21

The Moody Blues: Taft Triumphant and a Democratic November

I had a letter the other day from a man who said: "I don't like the tariff bill which was passed and which you signed. I don't like your association with Joe Cannon. I don't like your association with Aldrich. I don't like what you are doing with respect to the magazines and the periodicals and suppressing free speech. I don't like anything about your administration." Well, I sat down and dictated the following: "My dear Sir: You are in a bad way."

—William Howard Taft, January 29, 1910,
from a speech to magazine editors[1]

During the 1909 Tour, Taft wrote his wife that he tired of the newspaper clippings his secretary forwarded. The *Times* was the most annoying, with its attitude of such a "wild and infuriated nature."

> With the "Times" the wish is father to the thought, and they have me defeated at every turn long in advance of the event; and they are so wild that nobody thinks it worth while when the event happens to point out how lacking in sense they have been in their prophecies. They are especially determined to show that this trip has done me and the party no good. But as that can hardly be determined short of the regular session of Congress, and the campaign that follows it, I don't feel particularly troubled by their present diagnosis.[2]

At his return to Washington, the only place Taft found anything but despair was at the reporters' off-the-record Gridiron dinner. "The fact that the cackling of geese saved Rome does not justify the insurgents

1. "Magazine Men Dine," *Washington Post*, 1/29/10. The reference to "free speech" was over Administration efforts to bring balance to the Post Office budget by increasing rates on second class mail. Taft announced the problem to Congress in a December 1909 message that explained that second class mail, by which magazines and newspapers were shipped, cost $63,000,000 more than it took in. Magazines and newspapers found no hypocrisy in their status as a protected interest, subsidized by the people, that is, by first class mail users and taxpayers (see Pringle, p. 566).
2. Taft to Helen Taft, 10/24/09.

in making such a racket," laughed the satirists. "Things are different now."[3] In print, reporters otherwise went after Taft with Pinchot this, Ballinger that, with the tariff and Roosevelt mixed in. Taft remained defiant. During the trip, he wrote his wife of the newspapers, "I think they will find that I am stronger than they suppose. This disposition to use Roosevelt's reputation and popularity as a club to beat me is not of course very agreeable, but it is something which I might have expected and did expect, but I hope to be able to demonstrate to the country that I am consistent in the course that I am following...."[4] Back home on a motor ride to a round of Autumn golf, he declared,

> Well, I find on my return everybody full of despair and predicting all sorts of evil. One member of the Cabinet tells me that there is a cabal of the Roosevelts' friends to force an issue between us and another that Pinchot has got to be dismissed. Still another tells me that the reformers don't believe that I intend to push any of the reform measures instituted by Roosevelt and that hell is to pay everywhere. The trouble is that they don't believe me when I say a thing once.... I think the next Congress will show my sincerity....[5]

The situation that Winter seemed hopeless to all but the President. His humor was in fine form. He didn't even get angry when his military aide slammed the limousine door on his fingers.[6] Instead, the next day the pair plotted cutting back on guest lists for receptions, and, over Mrs. Taft's objections, extending the invitations to dinner. They relished the effect. It would, Archie wrote, "cause as much consternation in Washington as the revision of the tariff...." Between motor trips in which Taft discussed religion and joked about the funniest incidents of the Western Tour, he walked down Pennsylvania Avenue with only the Captain, gave a rousing, heartfelt speech to the homeless at a mission in New York's Bowery, and, on Christmas Eve, wandered through Washington stores for some shopping. He greeted everyone he met, including a group of drunken revelers who were embarrassed to find the President of the country staring at them as they walked out of a saloon. "Merry, Merry Christmas," Taft yelled out, and raised his hat. "Merry Christmas, Missure President," they replied. Taft cheerfully asked store clerks, "Do you know who I am?" "Is my credit good?" "Do you know where I live?" Archie found it all "quite exhilarating and joyous." That night fell a quiet, happy snow. It was a beautiful first Christmas at the Taft White House.[7]

During the President's two-month chat with America, his legislative plans

3. "An Evening with the Gridiron," *NYT*, 12/19/09.
4. Taft to Helen Taft, 10/28/09.
5. Butt, 11/14/09 p. 208. Continuing, Taft said, "I have told the Cabinet that if I had done anything to be ashamed of or had said anything which might have brought on them all this gloom, then I would feel some regrets possibly. But I have done nothing that I would not do over again, and therefore I must feel that their troubles are either imaginary or else someone else is to blame."
6. Butt wrote, "We had a rather jolly evening until the last moment, when in getting out of the limousine I mashed the President's fingers in the door and he yelled out in pain. I know how it hurts, and I felt terribly sorry, but it was really his fault, for while I got out of the wrong side of the machine in order to help out the women, he reached over and took hold of the encasement in order to pull himself up, and so when I slammed the door it caught his fingers. He said nothing, but hurried upstairs to put his hand in hot water, and when I saw him this morning he did not feel much the worse, though the ends of his fingers on his right hand were swollen and blue and the nails had already begun to discolor" (Butt, 11/17/09, p. 209).
7. Butt, 11/17/09, p. 213, 11/25/09, p. 221, undated letter, pp. 233–234 (the Bowery visit was on 12/14/09), and 12/25/09, pp. 239–243. Taft bought gifts for the Secret Servicemen and books for Edwards and Butt, which Butt treasured. See also "Washington Enjoys White Christmas," *NYT*, 12/26/09.

were discussed to acclaim. Business had taken the Payne tariff in peace; other than juggled cargo schedules according to the rise or fall in rates on August 6, the transition was smooth, just as Taft had promised.[8] In December, Taft formally submitted his first State paper to Congress. The message was lauded for its focus and tone, especially as compared to those of his predecessor.[9]

Yet into the new year all was gloom. Even Wall Street got moody and staged a tantrum. Panic struck, including a seventeen-year-old investor who shot himself over the market shakes. Taft refused to give a stock downturn presidential attentions which, he felt, would cause more panic. He stayed cool. "They don't frighten me at all with the cry of panic," he said when the panicked, such as the ever-panicked railroader J.J. Hill, begged him to do something. The market soon got over the burst of a late 1909 bubble that was caused, in part, by overconfidence in the side-effects of the Payne tariff. Easy money had bet on higher corporate profits, which were to come, but not at the expected pace.[10]

The press treated the President as beaten. Sunday morning readers were shown on the front page of the *Times* contrasting images of a smiling Taft from the year before and a downtrodden Taft of that March. He was treading down stairs, actually—most disingenuous of the editors. Worse, the paper noted, "Mr. Taft has recently been described as the James Buchanan of the Republican party."[11] The moment was not so small as to be thought comparable to the eve of civil war.

At least one contemporary saw through the hysteria. J.W. Foley perfectly framed the situation in a satire aimed at the man who would soon be comparing himself to Abraham Lincoln. In "An Open Letter to T.R.," Foley had some fun with the false drama of early 1910:

> My Dear Theodore.... I am not an alarmist, but ... things are going from bad to worse in this country. Some of the outrages committed are so villainous that I shudder to relate them. For example, have you heard what they have done to "Giff" Pinchot? ...You remember how he used to slide into the executive office with a bunch of tree seedlings and some moist earth and make forests rise before our very eyes? ...On a chill day in January, when he was engaged among the limbs of one of the trees he loved so well, he was pierced with a letter from the White House, laden with adjectives, encomiums, and tributes to his fealty to the public, and came down bleeding and mortally wounded, to the ground.... Think of it Theodore. Pinchot canned, and for so small a crime as insubordination.[12]

Foley further skewered Pinchot's dressed up resignation, then laid into Roosevelt himself:

> But that is not all.... Do you know that a delegation of railroad Presidents sat for hours in the ... White House? ... [and] not a message of hot words was sent hurtling in their direction.... Is not that a sorry tale? ...The whole country is either conserving or insurging. Uncle Joe Cannon is still smoking and belching forth lava. Pinchot and Glavis are in violent eruption. Kenesaw Landis shows signs of recurring activity. Nels Aldrich is still at

8. See "Rush to Escape New Tariff: Steamship Captains Told by Wireless to Hurry in with Cargoes," *NYT*, 8/5/09.
9. See "Taft's Message In; Trade His Theme," *NYT* 12/8/09.
10. "A Billion Loss in Stock Values," 2/5/10 and "Boy Speculator Shoots Himself," 4/25/10, *NYT*, and Butt, 1/27/10, p. 265.
11. "Contrasting Photographs of President Taft," 3/6/10 and "What are Mr. Taft's policies?" editorial, 3/24/10, *NYT*. Taft was not unaffected by it all. In March, Butt noted the strain (3/28/10, p. 312).
12. "An Open Letter to T.R.," *NYT*, 2/20/10.

> liberty. Bob La Follette is hoarse and worn from upholding the Constitution. Cummins is nearly all in. Business is overflowing the whole country. Eggs are 60 cents a dozen. Uncle Jim Hill is shooing the people back to the farms. Pierpoint Morgan is negotiating for the National Library. The gap eaten by the President over 13,000 miles of this country refuses to close. Bryan has opened his presidential campaign for 1912, and, Heaven knows, the country is in need of him. Come home, Theodore, come home.

It got so bad that rumors of Cabinet defections made headlines in April. Nothing could be more politically embarrassing than to deny a negative. When Secretary of State Knox made it plain he was going nowhere, reporters were unfazed by the non-news. It was treated as "an expected denial."[13]

* * *.

What it was was Joseph G. Cannon. All politics were "Cannonism" now, and one's decency was measured by proximity to Uncle Joe. Cannonism marked one of those brief explosions of hysteria that rake American politics and the press and disappear at the next outrage. Cannon was no more reviled than before. The President had done nothing different in relation to Cannon than his predecessor. Taft got as much or more from Cannon as Roosevelt, who cut deals with the Speaker freely. What Taft could not coax from Cannon as an ally he squeezed by sitting on him. The Old Guard was on Taft's side, not other way around, as the insurgents complained.

The legislative record of William Howard Taft is unusually productive. Throughout his term he wielded congressional interest to his own ends, unafraid of ungainly political alliances so long as the result fit. First it was with the regulars on the tariff. Then in 1910 he turned the insurgents upon themselves and the standpatters upside down with his postal banks and railroad bills. Then vice-versa, while using the Democrats on each with the Canadian free trade "Reciprocity" bill in 1911. The reason is that he was unafraid to change or adapt to a situation. Taft wasn't going to let either radical or reactionary mangle his Programme.

Criticisms, then and now, that Taft didn't steamroll Congress in the making of the tariff fail to recognize that Taft's adoption of Cannon and Aldrich neutralized their power. In opposing the President, there was no political downside for the Senate insurgents. If they poisoned Taft's agenda, as La Follette tried with railroad reform, it was "for the people."[14] If they successfully impregnated a bill with their terms, they could claim the victory. If they failed either way, they could blame Taft, and die martyrs. The problem with the strategy is that the insurgents, La Follette especially, divorced themselves of constructive statesmanship. They consigned themselves thereafter to wearing fringe.

Taft explained it to his brother:

> That was the [insurgents'] purpose ... as soon as it turned out that I got this legislation through then they claimed they had done everything to defeat it, and that the really useful features of the legislation had been secured by these same Insurgents. Although that view has prevailed in Iowa, and possibly Wisconsin and in Kansas, I think, generally, the country has given me credit for what was done.[15]

Had Taft challenged the Old Guard, 1910, the year of the insurgents, would have been theirs in which, as Foley put it, to

13. "Five Men May Quit the Taft Cabinet," *NYT*, 4/9/10 and Butt, 4/5/10, p. 319.
14. See "Taft Legislation in Insurgent Hands," *NYT*, 5/4/10.
15. Taft to Charles Taft, 9/10/10.

conserve. Instead, the insurgents insurged. Cannon and Aldrich pledged support for the Programme, including the postal banks which they detested. "I think it a decided step toward populism," Cannon told Taft. "But it was put in the platform and therefore I am willing to aid you to carry out the party's pledges in the matter."[16] When Cannon joined the minority in 1911, that is, when he was freed of the responsibility of power, he turned hostile. In 1910, the Speaker did as the President told.

* * *

Taft learned that the power of his constitution combined with a good early March wind at twenty miles an hour could illicit agreement even from Cannon. The Speaker promised to support the postal banks bill from the back of the White steamer. A few days earlier, Aldrich was subjected to this unique torture by touring car. Knowing the President's intentions, Butt instructed the chauffeur to take the long way about. The wind rose to a chill. Archie described the moment:

> It had turned very cold, and the wind was very high and the Chairman of the Finance Committee of the Senate was almost frozen and asked if the top could not be put up as he was not accustomed, as we were, to these open-air rides. I fished him out a sweater from under the seat, one belonging to the President, and the President made him put it on. It would have encircled his body twice. With this compromise we went on with the top down, but owing to the wind it was disagreeable to all except myself, who took off my hat and let the cold wind do as it might with my hair.[17]

"I do not disguise from myself," Taft told Aldrich, "that the so-called insurgent movement is getting a strong hold within the party. If not checked the Republican party will be as fragmentary as the Democratic and I feel that it is my duty to hold the party together as much as possible. If I should recognize the insurgents I could split it wide open as Cleveland did the Democratic party."[18]

The hiss of the burner and the chug of the cylinders of the steam car were familiar to Aldrich. He and other Senators, insurgents and regulars alike, had roamed Washington in the President's car to discuss the tariff. This ride was not to forge compromise. This time, with the brutal cold and running side streets to avoid being seen, it was utter politics. Taft said, "The dissatisfaction has got too great a hold on certain sections to hope to do anything by compromise. It must be cut out like you would cut out a cancer and we will go far to doing this— if we can defeat the Dolliver [and] Cummins faction at the next election." Taft was particularly concerned with Beveridge, whom he said "was the most sinister influence...." Taft's friend Bourne had already succumbed to insurgent pressure over the postal banks measure.[19] Now, Taft and Aldrich agreed to fight, although not openly. Aldrich suggested that rather than oppose insurgent appointments, the President ought instead allow current appointees remain in place, thus keeping the insurgents on edge and cutting into their influence back home.

That settled, Taft then laid it down for Aldrich. "He is not without political

16. Butt, 3/9/10, p. 303.
17. Butt, 3/7/10, pp. 299–300.
18. Woodrow Wilson refused to refer to the Cleveland administration as Democratic.
19. Butt wrote of Bourne's vote against the administration, "For Bourne is personally devoted to the President and it must be some very strong motive which brought about his separation." Their break was bitter and fought out over patronage, which Taft denied Bourne through 1912 (see Bourne to Taft, 5/2/12; Taft drafted a sarcastic reply but decided against sending it). It was one of the sadder casualties of the party split.

sagacity," Archie wrote of what Taft next told the shivering Senator:

> I want to say this to you Aldrich, that it is a matter of humiliation to me after the way I have fought Uncle Joe to come to rely upon him as my chief support in the House. I don't know that I thought much better of you at one time, but it has come down to this, that I am forced to rely upon you and the Speaker to put through the very measures which you are popularly supposed to be opposed and to receive no assistance at all from those men who have for years spoken in favor of the measures I now advocate."[20]

* * *

Following the March 15 defeat of the Speaker's automobile funds that paired insurgents with Democrats, Cannon was struck again by a deadly combination of insurgent wrath, Democratic discipline, and apathetic regulars. It was a minor point of order but huge in effect. Regular Crumpacker proposed a routine amendment to a Census bill. Democrat Fitzgerald, shrewd always, appealed to the rules that no amendments could be considered on that day. Cannon allowed it to go forward, saying the census was privileged as a Constitutional issue. Crumpacker saw what was up and moved to retract his amendment. He was overruled 153 to 121. Fitzgerald then demanded another vote directly on his appeal. Cannon intervened with a tremendous speech on the need for order and precedent, which, if overruled through "pique or otherwise ... may come to plague the House in the future." He declared himself uninterested in his personal role and obedient to the majority vote, whatever the result. The vote went 163 to 111 and included 42 Republican insurgents, the most yet put together by that coalition.[21]

The insurgents went to work the next day on the larger issue of the Speaker's hold over the Rules Committee. A resolution was drawn by insurgent Norris to remove appointments to the House as a whole. Frantic, the leadership called in absent regulars, some from as far as Chicago. The debate carried into the night. At 2:30 in the morning a group of regulars broke quorum and headed for bed, but Champ Clark happily conjured the Constitutional prerogative by minority vote "to compel the Attendance of absent Members."[22] The Sergeant at Arms was ordered by the Chair to round up the absentees. This was done without enthusiasm, also at the Chair's order. Only one representative was brought in. He was indignant. "I want to know who made the motion on which I was arrested," he demanded. His impressment was argued with laughter for a half hour, generally over the right of a Republican to sleep in an expensive hotel.

Cannon returned at six o'clock on an hour's sleep and presided over what one Democrat called "a state of anarchy" until noon. The ordeal lasted 28 hours and ended at an impasse based upon the Speaker's prerogative to consider rules for an unlimited time. Throughout, several adjournments were taken for conferences between insurgents and regulars. The hope was that the Speaker would resign from the Rules Committee in exchange for which the insurgents would not attempt to break his power of appointment to it. Both Cannon

20. Butt, 3/7/10, unpublished passage (grammatical corrections here). The published version of this letter (p. 299–301) omitted the "sinister influence" reference to Beveridge, and otherwise skipped an entire page that included the Taft quotation here. The President and the Senate Czar also agreed to privately raise funds to support Administration-friendly opponents to insurgents in their home States.
21. "Cannon Defeated in Vote on Rules," *NYT*, 3/17/10.
22. Article I, Section 5.

and the "ultra insurgents" refused the compromise.[23]

The "anarchy" continued for two days to full galleries, so full that on the final day of the battle spectators broke windows and pushed through the main door to the House floor. More conferences failed, and the votes went forward. At noon on the 19th, the Speaker entered the House to a tremendous, but one-sided applause. He discarded a motion for adjournment that was intended to salvage him, and read a detailed speech on his position. He explored the constitutionality of the Speaker's powers and reviewed the history of its precedent, which included a ruling from an equally autocratic Speaker, Democrat Samuel J. Randall, from 1878 that, as Cannon explained, a "proposition to amend the rules was not a case of Constitutional privilege."

After he lost a series of votes to table the Norris motion, Cannon put forth a straight-out question: "Shall the decision of the Chair stand as the judgement of the House?" There it was. At the firing line, Cannon removed his blindfold. As the various questions were alternately to deny or affirm a motion, many members shouted "Nay ... no, Yea," in confusion. It took the intervention of the Sergeant at Arms to bring order and a final tally. By 160 to 182 the Speaker's judgement was denied. From there it was a matter of procedure. The insurgents held their numbers at around 35 to 40 throughout the votes.

Norris then offered an amended version of his motion, which provoked a three hour debate along the lines of Clark's statement, "This is not a personal fight against Joseph G. Cannon of Illinois." Oscar Underwood most aptly stated the combined Democratic and insurgent case. "We are fighting a system to-day which enables the Speaker of this House to wield such a power as to overthrow the will of the majority of this House." Regular McCall replied with straight politics. "I do not propose to vote to deliver the Speaker, bound hand and foot, over to the minority party, although I know that if you do that he will go with head unbowed and erect, in the simple majesty of American manhood. This proposition does not emanate from the House of Representatives. I do not condemn a whole class, but you are doing the behest of literary highwaymen, who are entirely willing to assassinate a reputation if they can only sell a magazine." McCall ended with a hyperbolic appeal to Cannon's likeness to Ulysses:

> Pull on, and in regular order strike
> the sounding billows, for my purpose
> holds to sail beyond the sunset and the
> baths of all the western stars until I die.[24]

Norris replied, "We represent a principle far beyond any man or set of men. There is no feeling here unless it is brought in by the Speaker or his friends." His motion then prevailed 193 to 153, including 45 Republican yeas. A vote to remove Cannon from the Rules Committee immediately followed, going 191 to 155. The Speaker seized the floor to give his own requiem. "The country believes that the Republican Party has a majority of forty-four in the House...." he declared, "yet this is not the case."

So ended Cannonism. The day's final act was a motion by the "ultra-insurgents" to remove Cannon from the Speaker's office. Revolution quelled with this vote. Only eight Republicans voted to twist the knife. Cannon was essentially re-elected Speaker by ten more votes than the year

23. "Cannon Beaten, Friends Admit," *NYT*, 3/19/10.
24. "Cannon, Shorn of His Power Keeps Office," *NYT*, 3/20/10.

before. Regulars "whooped and howled ... two enthusiasts hauled out a great big Stars and Stripes and waved it frantically...." The hard-core insurgents moped and cursed the "cold feet" of their fellow rebels. A Democrat picked up "Auld Lang Syne," which was countered by Tawney and other regulars singing, "Oh he's the boy to know, our dear old Uncle Joe." Clark wept at the final show of personal support for the Speaker.[25] Nevertheless, Clark was the biggest winner that day. And he knew it. Democrats were pleased by all outcomes, especially the failure to remove Cannon. "They regard him as their best asset, and propose to make the utmost of it," the *Times* noted.

Taft was traveling at the time and refused to be involved, anyway. He read the news from Rochester. Looking up, he laughed "rather roguishly," Butt wrote, and declared, "Well, Archie, I think they have got the old fox this time. It would be funny, if he got the best of them after all, but Crane's last dispatch would indicate that the regulars had given up hope.... But it is fine to see how he is fighting ... he does put up a good fight."[26]

* * *

Winter turned to Spring, and Taft's politics bloomed with the season. Cannon's defeat assisted the President enormously. During the 1909 Mississippi River trip, Taft floated the idea to send Cannon to pasture. He wrote his wife, "if so, we shall have a much easier sledding than with him as an incubus to carry." At the least, Taft hoped for some compromise over the Rules that would "keep a Republican majority sufficiently loyal and disciplined to pass the legislation which we promised. Cannon would feel himself vindicated by a failure to do so."[27] It worked out better than Taft could have hoped. With rules insurgency satisfied he found a more uniform Republican caucus. Only in the Senate was heard the word insurgent, and there Taft's Boston embrace of Aldrich truly paid off. The Senate Czar granted Taft his legislative indulgence. And where Aldrich was absent due to his health and the Monetary Commission, the junior Senator from New York stepped in. That Elihu Root declined to stay in the Cabinet proved fortuitous.

The President's agenda wore down Congress despite La Follette's best efforts to beat him to it. One La Follette speech went five hours and had to be carried on the next day. The Senator had been plotting his statements for some time, it was noted, for many of his complaints had already been remedied in the bill he was discussing.[28] The regulars had no such invigorating interest in the session. To most, fulfilling the platform was a bore. To the rest, it was radical. To the insurgents it was never enough. A March headline spoke wonders for the situation: "Taft Railroad Bill Has No Defenders."[29]

Taft's bills were sent up, progressives spun them their way, regulars volleyed back, and the President signed his legislation. And so it went through the extended regular session from December to June. Taft had almost no defeats. The Democrats played their usual role as the minority. Only this time they did it right. Between the rhetoric, contrary votes, and timely points of order, the party exercised uncommon discipline.

First came the Postal Savings bill, which the Old Guard despised. When

25. Pringle, *Roosevelt* p. 529.
26. Butt, 3/19/10, pp. 307–308.
27. Taft to Helen Taft, 10/28/09 and 3/19/10.
28. "How Senators Cut Taft Railway Bill," *NYT*, 5/25/10.
29. *NYT*, 3/16/10.

Robert Marion La Follette. "Fighting Bob" was the period's leading "progressive." La Follette was as earnest a speaker as he was reformer, frequently overzealous on both counts. He could lecture the Congressional Record for hours, often to a near empty chamber. Of his performances on the floor of the Senate, Elihu Root said, "When doughty Bob is speaking and he hears any whispering ... he turns round and glares at the offenders until they cease to speak. He never makes a speech that he does not once or twice go through this dramatic performance for the benefit of [Senator] Bacon ... [who] can whisper louder and talk lower than any man I ever met." The *Times* felt that these performances, such as one five hour tirade, were for the best: "It would be cruel to expect any man to carry such a head of steam as that without relief at the safety valve, and nobody could wish that the Senator should explode as the result of suppression of language and ideas." La Follette is pictured here in 1905 doing the Chautauqua pose. (Courtesy Library of Congress)

Aldrich and Cummins faced off over it, Taft alone could win. To the one it was government intrusion; to the other it was Wall Street forced upon Main Street. In what may be seen as a metaphor for the entire Taft administration, both reactionary and radical came away piqued, and the President signed his bill.[30] The railroad bill was next. The now more regular House affirmed the President's recommendations in the form of the Mann bill in early May.[31]

The Senate, much as during the tariff fight, got bogged down in insurgent and Democratic opposition, only this time without Old Guard enthusiasm for obstruction. The issue was La Follette's baby. His fame in Wisconsin came of his fight with the railroads. Now in the Senate, he was going to fix the railroads for the entire nation. The insurgents so loaded the debate with amendments and poison pills, the bill almost died—until Taft pulled another audacious move, akin to his tax amendment "bombshell." An association of western roads announced in late May a rate increase, Congress be damned. Taft set his bulldog Attorney General on them: submit to the rules of the bill—as yet not

30. Republicans reluctantly endorsed the concept as an alternative to bank deposit guarantees demanded by Democrats. Mowry unfairly held that Aldrich only went along with it because he used it as a way to dump on the government hundreds of millions in low yielding notes held by commercial banks (p. 261). In fact, the insurgents succeeded in barring investment in those bonds in the Senate version of the bill, and in the final bill the ability of the government to invest in commercial bonds was severely restricted (see "Postal Bank Bill Passed in New Form," 3/6/10 and "Postal Bank Bill Accepted by Senate," 6/23/10, *NYT*). Besides, the dollar values of the Postal banks never reached such levels. It took Taft's intervention to pass the bill. As Taft wrote to Otto Bannard about the postal banks and railroad bills, "The truth is that the leaders of the House and the Senate did not intend to pass either bill, and would not have done so if I had not made a fuss about it and insisted ... they will admit—certainly Aldrich does—that they were not in favor of either bill and only passed them because I urged it upon them" (6/11/10).

31. "Railway Bill Passed" *NYT*, 5/11/10.

passed, he told them, or submit to the Sherman Act. The railroads backed off. The President's popularity spiked. The *American Review of Reviews* noted, "Thus the bold step of the roads, met by the equally bold action of the Administration, created a situation that practically compelled Congress to give the pending bill its final touches...."[32] A few days later the Senate shook itself free of the insurgent choke hold. The bill then went to Conference where Aldrich's cool hand bent the House bill more to his shape, making it somewhat less offensive to him and the *Times*. On June 19, Taft signed it into law.[33]

The final disposition of the land withdrawals that had so excited Pinchot and the *Pioneer Press* was settled quietly and without applause. And typically it was thanks to the regulars whom the President sat upon to force his plan. In April, Taft pushed the Senate to "legalize" the withdrawals with appropriate legislation. Western Senators were furious. Exasperated, Borah of Idaho said, "Then, Mr. President, as we are to understand it, you are going to do as you damn please without consulting the interests of those states mostly affected." Taft just smiled, with "that little glint" in his eyes that Archie knew meant anger. Chuckling, Taft told the story of a schoolteacher who chose the son of a "cantankerous farmer" for punishment as an example to the rest. The farmer came to the teacher and was rebuffed. "It appears to me that you expect to run this school as you damn please," said the farmer. Taft described the teacher's reply. "The old pedagogue fixed his eyeglasses and looking calmly into the face of the irate father, said, 'Your language is coarse, your manner offensive, but you have grasped my idea.'"[34]

Between the extremes, Taft reeled in his legislation. Again, he stepped in at the Conference sessions. He killed a House provision to exempt unions from antitrust laws, and he generally kept order by waving about a pork River and Harbors bill like a ten dollar bill. In an article entitled, "Reluctant Congress Bent to Taft's Will," the *Times* reported, "It is a personal record for the President not equaled by a Chief Executive in a great many years, and it has been accomplished by methods utterly unlike those used by the White House in the preceding seven years." Another report declared, "Not in many years has there been a President who has impressed his will so strongly upon Congress."[35]

On June 25, Congress adjourned to the sound of the President's busy pen. Taft went away without a labor-friendly reform bill on court injunctions, but he otherwise completely had his way. With a threat next to adopt national incorporation of businesses, currency reform, and other measures, the President left town happy. Taft's biggest regret was the $52,000,000 River and Harbors bill which he signed with a warning to Congress to lay off the candy the next time. He could hardly veto it after the Mississippi trip, even though it threatened to throw the federal books off balance.

Cannon declared that the 61st Congress had "accomplished more and done better work than any other Congress of which I

32. Jul/1910, p. 7. The *Times* felt the bill "sacrificed" investors ("Unconvincing Witnesses," editorial, 6/15/10).
33. "Taft Halts Rise in Rail Rates," 6/1/10, "Pass Railroad Bill in Senate," 6/4/10 and "Taft Quickly Signs the Railroad Bill," 6/19/10, *NYT*. Mowry credits the passage with a diabolical deal between Aldrich and Democrats that traded the railroad bill for Arizona and New Mexico statehood (p. 260). Once again, Mowry discredits Taft's role. The statehood bills were in Taft's platform, so the Democrats weren't getting much in return, if that is why they voted for the railroad bill. Taft's action on the rates shook it all loose.
34. Butt, 4/5/10, p. 321. Archie said Taft's use of story telling was reminiscent of Lincoln.
35. "Taft Smashes Plan to Permit Boycotts," 6/24/10, "Reluctant Congress Bent to Taft's Will," 6/21/10 and "Congress Adjourns," 6/26/10, *NYT*.

During the 1910 legislative session, Taft bombarded Congress with proposals to put the Roosevelt moral awakening into law. As he had with the tariff, Taft split the difference between conservatives and insurgents and signed his legislation. The standpatters were the more forgiving, as they held the responsibilities of power; free of it, the insurgents railed that Taft had betrayed the Roosevelt legacy, and lost vote after vote. In the unusually successful legislative session of 1910, Taft signed a number of important reform bills, including the Mann-Elkins Act, conservation and labor bills, and the enactment the Postal Savings banks system — all right out of the 1908 platform and the Roosevelt legacy book. (Clifford Berryman cartoon, c. 1910, Courtesy Library of Congress)

have been a member...."[36] Taft got his two battleships, the Railroad bill, of which he was most proud, the postal banks, a worker-friendly Bureau of Mines, new railroad safety rules, Arizona and New Mexico statehood authorization, the Fine Arts Commission, a tariff system for the Philippines, renewed funding for the Tariff Board, and a campaign publicity bill, among measures, practically the 1908 platform itself. A signal accomplishment was Taft's insistence on the budgeting method for appropriations. Without Congressional invitation, Taft instructed his Cabinets to report their money needs to the legislature. He would fight throughout his term for this executive branch heist, which would later make its way into the appropriations mix. The President could also point to the encouraging state of the public finances. The Payne bill and the corporation tax proved effective revenue tools, and Taft's war on waste kept Congress in line. The books officially turned from red to black in March, and by the end of the year, the deficits were entirely trounced.[37]

36. "Cannon Lauds Congress," *NYT*, 6/26/10. Significantly for Congress, the Secret Service scandal was put to rest in the Mann White Slavery Act, which, over the issue of prostitution, clarified federal jurisdiction for certain crimes and led to the formation two years later of the Bureau of Investigations, known today as the FBI.

37. Taft wrote his wife, "The session on the whole has been a good deal of triumph for me in the way of legislation.... Crane and Aldrich and Custis of the Senate, Cannon, Mann, Tawney, and Weeks of the House were of great assistance" (6/26/10). Tawney, especially, paved the President's road in the House, even for the battleships. His support for the postal banks and the Tariff Board funding were crucial, and he welcomed the President's budgets. He also helped direct $100,000 towards a formal inquiry into government efficiencies, formalized the following year as the Commission on Efficiency and Economy (see Pringle, pp. 604–605). See also "Federal Surplus in March," 4/2/10, "Taft Declares War on 'Pork Barrel,'" 9/22/10, "Taft Cuts Deeper into Estimates," 11/30/10, "Taft Is Setting up His Own Policies," 12/29/10, and "Billion Dollar Session of Congress," 3/11/11 *NYT*.

* * *

So who was complaining? Insurgency in the Senate lost its urgency as Taft's Programme was defined in legislation. The fine print of the postal banks and railroad laws gave outrage a headache. The tariff kept its zebra coat of black and white, but only the Democrats made an issue of it, as ever.[38]

Cannonism was the glue that bonded the House insurgents, and with the Speaker's defeat rebellion there lost meaning. Taft was making firm the Roosevelt legacy and the 1908 platform. Yet the "Roosevelt Republicans" were unhappy. Their dissatisfaction over the tariff was not unavoidable, it was purposeful. Besides, had Taft done all that they asked their displeasure would have been the same. Despite Taft's 1910 success, Garfield ran in the Ohio gubernatorial primary on an anti–Taft plank. The "progressive" wing of the party, well on the way to changing the word from an adjective to a noun, remained discontent. What was it about?

The *Times* nailed it when the editors wrote, "Garfield is so progressive that he fairly shoots ahead. He preaches all the new doctrines, and he really seems to believe in them."[39] Whatever those doctrines were. The *Times* thought that progressivism and Bryanism ought, as Cummins suggested, join forces. "There will be no lack of slogans."[40] Indeed, progressivism was coalescing into its three-part chant, "initiative, referendum, and recall," the movement's catch-all solution to all ills by subjecting government, including lawmaking and judicial review, to majority votes of the people. Before raising that flag what the movement represented most was contrarian dissent.

While loaded with voter anxiety, the Republican progressives overshot the public mood. Recall that "standpat" and "insurgency" were the vocabulary of the tariff and Cannonism. Cannon was beaten and Taft proved an illusive target. There was nothing of his legislation outside of Payne that the insurgents could point to with the force of popular opinion. Their largest problem with the tariff was that Aldrich had his name on it, and all they could say about the 1910 session was the same old, same old that Taft's victories came of Aldrich and Cannon. The insurgents failed to beat Taft, and they failed to carry the nation with them. It took Roosevelt to concentrate their discontent into a viable force. And not even the great Theodore Roosevelt could throw the Big Guy.

Meanwhile, the Democrats played straight, keeping the tariff tight in their hand. The voters rewarded them for it in three special elections. In the Spring a House election in a New York district went from a 1908 Republican majority of 10,000 to defeat by 6,000 votes. Another Republican district in Massachusetts similarly fell. The entire State of Maine went awry that September. The Democratic candidates won on tariff discontent, a pattern repeated in the Democratic November.

* * *

38. Clarke offered to support a revision of the wool tariff, with the promise "not open other schedules" ("Dares Taft to Act on the Wool Tariff," *NYT*, 5/22/10). Although this incites a huge "what if," Taft was in no position to force a tariff revision on the Republican regulars on whom his success during the session entirely relied.

39. "The Progressive Garfield," *NYT* editorial, 7/26/10. The editors told a story Garfield's enthusiasms when, during the Roosevelt administration, he "rushed up to the Capitol with a bill ... modifying the use of the injunction. He showed it to one or two Senators, who had the audacity to gasp. They explained to him that his bill would demolish the principles of Anglo-Saxon equity jurisprudence that have prevailed for centuries."

40. "The New Party," *NYT* editorial, 7/22/10.

The 1910 New York governor's race was cut open by Taft's appointment of Governor Hughes to the Supreme Court. Hughes was an interesting political creature, perhaps all that was Taft in 1908, a moderate progressive and untouchable. Like Taft, he befuddled liberals and conservatives alike. He challenged the Republican machine yet found his way within it. Hughes' acceptance of the appointment split the New York Republican Party. On the one side was Vice President Sherman. Roosevelt became the other side. This, his first re-entry to politics, ended in disaster.

"IS THAT THE BEST CARE YOU COULD TAKE OF MY CAT?"

A significant moment in 1910 came with Roosevelt's Napoleonic "return from Elba" that June. He tried to stay clear of the growing rift in the Republican party, but in a series of speeches over the summer he launched his "New Nationalism" that marked a significant departure from Taft Republicanism and Roosevelt's own legacy. Taft tried to remain loyal, but with "New Nationalism" what the legacy meant was no longer clear. This cartoon depicted what Roosevelt loyalists thought of Taft's caretaking of his legacy, whatever it was now supposed to be. (*Puck*, 1912, Courtesy Library of Congress)

The game played out at the state Republican convention at Saratoga. At issue was who would hold the temporary and permanent chairs. Roosevelt was there against his better judgement. He avoided all attempts to draw him into the Ohio campaign which pitted Garfield against regular Warren Harding.[41] But New York was different. The Republican machine was entrenched and unfriendly to the former President. They'd been through Roosevelt convulsions and preferred his absence. Besides, they were having enough problems with Hughes and his annoying plan to institute primaries. It was at the Governor's request, Roosevelt later said, that he went political on behalf of the primary law. The regulars saw it as unwelcome meddling. The bill was defeated at the Assembly and Roosevelt was accused of "interference." The fight was all too tempting for everyone.[42]

Sherman challenged Roosevelt, and all he accomplished was to bring Taft into the mess with the intimation that Taft was behind the Vice President's maneuver to oust Roosevelt from Saratoga. Sherman was voted Temporary Chairman. Party leader Timothy Woodruff gleefully announced, "We have exchanged the steam roller for the locomotive" and the headlines rang, "Beat Roosevelt for Chairman." Roosevelt was furious, and not just because Taft

41. Harding and the regulars of Ohio won the party in-fighting and were smeared in the Fall by the Democrats. Complicating Roosevelt's loyalties to Garfield was his son-in-law, Nicholas Longworth, who led the Ohio regulars.

42. "Defy Roosevelt in Both Houses," *NYT*, 7/1/10. They might have accused Taft of the same thing, for he spent the Spring urging Hughes' electoral reform. See Taft to WL Ward, 6/30/10, "I wish you would go to Albany at once and straighten out the primary tangle. You are the man to do it. The Hughes compromise ought to go through for the good of the party and all concerned." He sent similar letters to others, such as Griscom, Greiner, Kraske, and Woodruff.

had met with Woodruff the week before.[43]

Roosevelt much preferred newspaper stories such as "Roosevelt Won't Dip into Politics," "Roosevelt On Exploring Trip," or even better, "$20 to See Roosevelt," that about a speeding ticket given a chauffeur who hurried to make a Roosevelt speech: "All right. $20 for the glance," the judge told him.[44] Roosevelt's anger turned to wrath when he saw the headlines two days after the Sherman endorsement, "Taft May Side With Regulars." It was one of the era's typical non-stories that went something like this: Sherman beat Roosevelt. Taft met with Sherman. Taft "may" side with Sherman. Whatever the truth to the story, to political boss Lloyd Griscom, by mid–September it created a dire need for news of a meeting between the former and current presidents. Taft had received Roosevelt at Beverly earlier that summer. Other than it happened and was cordial and strictly social, the meeting was kept private. The news effect was the correct one: "Roosevelt and Taft in a Warm Embrace: 'Just Like Old Times'" Now politics was the sole reason.[45]

This cartoon represents the Taft view of the situation. Prometheus was punished by Zeus for stealing fire from Olympus. The Taft Prometheus, here bound by "gratitude, loyalty, admiration, allegiance, devotion, regard, and obligation," is being picked at by the Roosevelt vulture. (1910, *New York Times,* September 11, 1910)

This next meeting was surrounded by a rather cantankerous circumstance out-

43. "Beat Roosevelt for Chairman," 8/17/10 and "Woodruff and Taft Talk Local Politics," 8/9/10, *NYT*. Woodruff, a former Lt. Governor of the state, would betray Taft for Roosevelt in 1912.

44. *NYT*, 6/24/10, 8/12/10, and 7/24/10.

45. Headlines from *NYT*, 8/18/10 and 7/1/10. Taft smashed all criticism with public release of a letter to Griscom that defined his position. He blamed the press for stirring up rumors and cast responsibility upon both Sherman and Roosevelt equally for not having followed his previous advice to settle their differences in a conference (Taft to Griscom, 8/20/10 and "Taft Denies He Aided Sherman," 8/23/10) *NYT*. The affair salvaged the Beverly newsmen from stories about golf and motoring. Butt was surprised at how much inside information they dug up. Butt was angry at Taft, thinking that he had betrayed Roosevelt by allowing his new secretary, Charles Norton, to conspire with Sherman and the Old Guard to attack Roosevelt. He was further annoyed at Taft's enjoyment of Roosevelt's defeat (see Butt, chapters LIV-LV). Pringle wrote that Taft ought to have defended Roosevelt more strenuously, and that his denials of culpability were rendered "pathetically" (p. 577). Taft didn't defend anyone, nor should he have. His position from beginning to end was one of neutrality, despite his private sentiments towards Roosevelt to which Butt was overly sensitive. Butt was told by "correspondents stationed at Oyster Bay" that Roosevelt felt Taft "had been trying to double cross him ever since he left the United States." The cause of Roosevelt's anger, the reporters said, was not that Taft had not endorsed Roosevelt's policies but that Taft "had turned even them over to the enemies of the people to carry out" (Butt, 9/20/10, p. 519).

Butt wrote two asides to his sister-in-law, Clara, about his own comments on the situation. The first followed a talk with Taft in which Taft applauded his demeanor. Taft told him, "I know how it distresses you side the thoroughly cantankerous New York situation. In early September, both Taft and Roosevelt addressed the St. Paul, Minnesota, Conservation Convention. Taft went first. He praised Roosevelt's legacy, but stood decidedly against Roosevelt's latest calls for stronger federal intervention.[46] The speech was huge for Taft, despite its being crowded from the headlines coming from Fargo, "Roosevelt Seizes Crank on Platform."[47] Even the *Pioneer Press* was struck by Taft's forcefulness. The best the paper could do in complaint was to say that he was hard to hear. Notably absent was any criticism of the content of his speech, particularly as compared to Roosevelt's talk the next day.[48] The differences were exactly and forever that line between Taft and Roosevelt. The *Times* wrote that Taft "submits to the Congress a careful and orderly statement ... with a succinct and intelligent account...." while "Mr. Roosevelt approaches the subject in the mood, if we may be pardoned the simile of a pugilist, 'looking for trouble'...."[49]

What Taft provoked at St. Paul was a badly needed silence. Pinchot was shut down. Roosevelt backed off. Taft "delivered a most masterly address," wrote Butt, "and while his reception ... was not as demonstrative as that accorded to Mr. Roosevelt ... his speech was much better...."[50] Word came privately that Roosevelt was bothered by Taft's speech, as he might well have been, for Taft carefully but clearly walked around Roosevelt's increasingly radical rhetoric.[51] In his own speech, Roosevelt kept quiet on Taft, but he let slip a dig at Tawney, which meant Taft's Winona.

Two weeks later, they met at New Haven, to Taft's convenience.[52] Strain was apparent to the reporters who sent back stories that the men "seemed more serious than usual." Following protocol, the host was the President. Taft waited for Roosevelt at a private luncheon. Afterwards, Taft offered Roosevelt an automobile ride to the train station. The President climbed in first. Taft was mindful of formality, but not usually so much as to force his guest to crawl over him for the left seat, as was noted by the

45. (*cont.*) ... I know how you feel, for I know how it distresses me ... I have watched the dignified silence which you maintain when [Roosevelt] is under discussion, and I admire you for it ... you will never have to explain yourself to me." This caused some reflection in Butt. He wrote to Clara, "What a fortunate thing it is I have had you to pour out my feelings to, else I might have been led to express my pent-up indignation to people at random. But after I write it all to you, I get it off my mind and start each succeeding day with my conscience clear and allegiance pure" (Butt, undated letter, Sept. 1909, pp. 529–530). The next month he wrote, "The President is a high-minded and lofty judge, and a pure and spotless man. I sometimes wonder, Clara, if I have done him any injustice in my letters during this past summer. I have thought over every word I have written and I am convinced that I have not been hypercritical on account of my great admiration for Colonel Roosevelt" (10/18/10, pp. 546–547).

46. "Taft Is Cheered Praising Roosevelt," *NYT*, 9/6/10.

47. *NYT*, 9/6/10. See the editorial, "More Roosevelt Luck" (9/7/10). "Monday was President Taft's day.... Yet Roosevelt loomed largely on the first pages.... An accommodating and unaccountable crank interrupted his speech at Fargo...."

48. "Taft Makes Two Speeches and Smiles on Thousands," *Pioneer Press*, 9/6/10. "Reading a rather stern lesson to the delegates to the National Conservation congress...." The spin came in another article, "Crowds Did Not Warm to Taft," (9/6/10). For reaction to Roosevelt's speech, see "'Great Speech,' Say Politicians.... Some Prefer President's," *Pioneer Press*, 9/7/10.

49. "A Striking Contrast," *NYT* editorial, 9/7/10.

50. Butt, 9/7/10, p. 504.

51. See JH Harding to HC Frick, 9/15/10 (Taft Papers), on Roosevelt's attitude towards Taft's conservation speech.

52. This section from "Roosevelt Has Talk with Taft," 9/20/10 and "Roosevelt Didn't Seek Taft Meeting," 9/21/10 *NYT*, Brands, p. 677, Butt, 9/20/10, pp. 518–526 and Taft to Helen Taft, 9/25/10.

press. Proper and presidential, but hardly warm.

Automobiles peppered the stories of the meeting. First, Roosevelt was late to arrive to the luncheon because of car troubles. Griscom's car blew a tire upon arrival to pick up Roosevelt, so the party took Roosevelt's hired motor which subsequently lost "part of its gearing." That was the transmission. The chauffeur fixed it in half an hour. The ride to the train station was also very public. The people of New Haven were treated to a view of the first automobile ride by successive presidents of the United States. Crowds lined the streets "agape" at the sight of the pair "in animated conversation" in the back seat. Some saw the motor car skid slightly on the rainy streets.

The whole affair did Taft no good. Rather than pointing to Republican joy in New York, the President was forced to deny he had anything to do with the disaster. Then the meeting with Roosevelt turned into an absolute circus when the next day Roosevelt hollered at reports that the meeting came at his request. The rumors were started on "the President's train," it was said. Passing on a great opportunity to make Taft look good, Roosevelt proclaimed himself innocent of coveting the President's attentions. Griscom took the blame. "It was perfectly characteristic that after having sought the interview, as he undoubtedly did," Taft wrote his wife, "our friend should at once advertise that it was not at his instance, but at Griscom's, or wearing around to the point of showing that it was at my instance."

Finally, the Saratoga convention ended acceptably for Taft. He recused himself from Sherman and the State machine, and Roosevelt took hold as Temporary Chairman. Root sat in the permanent chair, and Henry Stimson was nominated for Governor. The *Buffalo Commercial* flipped over Roosevelt's involvement in the campaign. "It is a pity, for Mr. Stimson deserves a better fate than to be sacrificed upon the altar of Roosevelt's egotism and ambitions," wrote the editors.[53] Roosevelt's ambitions were yet vague, but it was true that Stimson could hardly be seen past the Roosevelt headlines. His presence meant fireworks. Sparks flew when Root suggested that if Stimson lost, radicals would take over in two years. Roosevelt blew his hat at the inference. Root confirmed his distaste for campaigning. None of it mattered, for the election was a repudiation of Republicans all, Taft, Roosevelt, and the party's twelve year dominance, an outcome hastened by insurgency. Like Harding in Ohio, Stimson fell to the Democratic landslide that November. Taft's consolation was that, although he lost Ohio, Roosevelt lost New York.[54]

* * *

Roosevelt otherwise spent the summer in the headlines with such names as Beveridge, Dolliver, Pinchot, and La Follette. Privately, he concluded that Taft was guilty by association with the such names

53. "1884 and 1910," *NYT* editorial 10/19/10; quoting from the *Buffalo Commercial*. See also, "Roosevelt Angry Over Root's Speech," 10/30/10, and "Roosevelt and Other Radicals," *NYT* editorial, 11/1/10.

54. See Taft to Charles Taft, 10/18/10: "I don't know really how important it will prove, but it would seem rather embarrassing if Roosevelt carried New York and I lost Ohio. I am anxious to do what I can to bring about success in Ohio." They both ended up looking bad. Root credited Taft with salvaging the New York situation, and asked Roosevelt to reciprocate in Ohio. "Taft did help very materially in the Saratoga Convention," he wrote, "and your help in Ohio would be generally regarded as a fair and manly thing" (Jessup, p. 165, letter dated 10/19/10). Roosevelt didn't oblige, and he would soon make excuses for Saratoga, saying he was there because Hughes needed his help. "All I did was to try to help them out..." he said in April, 1911. He also disavowed himself from the Saratoga tariff endorsement, blaming it on Root and Payne ("Where Roosevelt Stands," *NYT*, 4/21/11).

as Crane, Aldrich, and Cannon. Roosevelt rediscovered his old theme, "the bosses." Along the way he did little for Taft. The applause for Washington from Oyster Bay was just polite. In Iowa, the best Roosevelt could say for the Administration was that the Tariff Board was a good idea. Mention of the word "tariff" drew cold stares from that audience. Requisite praise for Taft in the Saratoga speech was tempered, especially as compared to his celebration of Stimson; that is, hardly unqualified. The *Times* identified it as damnation by "faint praise." Of that performance, Taft wrote his wife, "I hope you saw the proceedings of the Saratoga Convention and the very satisfactory resolutions endorsing your husband. Roosevelt made a speech praising me also, which must have gone a little hard with him, but which indicated that he found it necessary."[55]

As in New York, although without their specific involvement, the competition between the men permeated practically all the Republican campaigns. The Taft-Roosevelt line between Harding and Garfield was definitive. At the Iowa convention portraits of Taft and Roosevelt were faced off as in a duel. The enthusiasm was for the Roosevelt picture; Taft's was displayed with defiance. Kansas succumbed entirely to insurgency and the Roosevelt cult: "We send our greeting to Theodore Roosevelt, and, as Republicans, we stand ready to enlist him in the fight for human rights." Even without that flighty salute, the platform said it all by saying nothing of Taft. Visiting Denver, Roosevelt was greeted with calls for 1912.[56]

Roosevelt always found himself in the West. The Denver speech, arranged by Pinchot, was originally intended to trash Ballinger. By the time Roosevelt got there his mind had wandered to larger issues. Everyone knew where he stood on Ballinger. Instead he confessed his feelings for the courts. The sentiments were not new. As President he displayed impatience for judges, particularly those who put the law over the people, as he saw it. In Denver he spoke of good judges and bad judges. One, a local activist for whom Roosevelt halted his first speech until he was allowed in the door, was of the good sort. Later, to the Colorado legislature, he spoke of the bad ones. By certain decisions, he declared, the Supreme Court had created a "neutral ground in which neither State nor Nation can exercise authority, and which would become a place of refuge for men who wish to act criminally, and especially for the very rich men who wish to act against the interests of the community as a whole." ("He is the judge of judges," replied the *Times* in a caustic editorial the next day.)[57]

In Kansas he hit the flip side of what would be his 1912 campaign. At a John Brown "Bloody Kansas" battle site, Roosevelt resurrected the square deal. Surprise — he found himself standing on the right side of it with Abraham Lincoln himself. This was the "Osawatomie" speech and "New Nationalism." With the exception of a little noted paragraph in which Roosevelt again struck for the tariff commission idea, the speech was an embarrassment for Taft. Asked about it a few days later, the most innocuous thing the President could come up with was that

55. "Roosevelt Praises Taft on the Tariff," 9/04/10 and "Taft and Roosevelt," editorial, 9/13/10, *NYT*, and Taft to Helen Taft, 9/28/10. In Iowa, Roosevelt gave a positive review of the President's efforts to secure the Tariff Board and its re-funding. Even that was a bit of a slight, for Taft had a board and not a commission, the progressive nickname for a solution. Roosevelt was never able reach to his usual enthusiasms when discussing the tariff.

56. "Rout for Taft Men in Iowa Convention," 8/4/10, "Kansas Cold to Taft and with Roosevelt," 8/31/10, and "Roosevelt in 1912, the Cry in Denver," 8/30/10, *NYT*.

57. "Mr. Roosevelt's Attack on the Courts," *NYT* editorial, 8/31/10.

"ALL ALONE! ALL ALONE! NOBODY HERE BUT ME!"

Into 1911, Taft went his own way. He launched a dramatic initiative, a free trade agreement with Canada known as "Reciprocity." It took another long, special session and a lot of Democratic votes to get it, but Taft signed his bill. Standpatters and insurgents were thrown into unusual coalitions of insurgents voting against low duties and standpatters voting for free trade. This *Puck* cartoon depicts Taft in 1911 with "dear John" letters from insurgents and standpatters alike. "Farewell, you are too conservative for me," wrote the radical Republicans, while the conservative Republicans wrote, "Farewell, you are too radical for me." Notably, standpatter Senators Aldrich and Penrose were Taft's successful generals during the session. Meanwhile, Republican insurgency turned into the "National Republican Progressive League," headed by La Follette, who had 1912 ambitions. Note in the cartoon the La Follette portrait on the desk and another of Roosevelt on the wall. The election of 1912 was on the way. (Courtesy Library of Congress)

Roosevelt's program would require a new constitution.[58]

The speech, given to Civil War veterans and since enshrined in textbooks, was a typical Roosevelt production, a Wizard of Oz Technicolor morality lesson framed by the black and white of a Kansas farm. Taft called Roosevelt's speeches of that summer, "the same old kind—attacking corporations, corruption in politics, and setting forth his own views and his own actions as instances of proper conduct with reference to the wicked powers of evil in the Republic." What changed, Taft noted, was that "the speeches are fuller of the ego now than they ever were, and he allows himself to fall into a style that makes one think he considers himself still the President of the United States."[59] Or someone who wanted to be President. The Osawatomie address ran like a campaign speech.

Roosevelt outlined his platform, starting back where he left off in his 1907 and 1908 messages that went unheeded and unread in Congress: the direct primary, physical valuation of railroads, corporate and labor regulations, income and inheritance taxes, a tariff commission, & etc. Even the Navy made the list. With the exception of the tarriff commission, it was old hat, the same sundries he shoveled upon Congress in his second term. The rhetorical mood was what shocked. In 1908, Dr. Butler advised President Roosevelt, "The specific recommendations contained in [your] message are, for the most part, very generally approved by intelligent people.... The feeling of sorrow ... is due chiefly to the form in which you have couched the message.... My point is that you are not making any headway...."[60]

58. "Taft is Not Pleased by Roosevelt Plan," *NYT*, 9/3/10.
59. Taft to Charles Taft, 9/10/10.
60. Butler to Roosevelt, 2/4/08 and 2/6/08, per Pringle, *Roosevelt*, pp. 480–481.

The Republican Party was thrown into factions, as depicted by this Joseph Keppler cartoon of November 1911. Two of the faces in the clouds are the Taft "conservatism" and Roosevelt "New Nationalism." The "demoralized weather vane" pleads, "will somebody please tell me where I'm supposed to point?" In the end, it went Taft's way. (Courtesy Library of Congress)

The atmosphere at Osawatomie was just as cloudy—only cirrus clouds, and sky high. Roosevelt always stood sideways when going radical.[61] The clauses and exceptions drawn around the platitudes are dizzying. Bold statements such as, "This New Nationalism ... demands of the judiciary that it shall be interested primarily in human welfare rather than in property..." and "I am for men and not for property, as you were in the Civil War" were great stage material—property is slavery, he was saying. Well, sort of. The qualification:

> I am far from underestimating the importance of dividends; but I rank dividends below human character. Again, I do not have any sympathy with the reformer who says he does not care for dividends.... I know well that the reformers must not bring upon the people economic ruin, or the reforms themselves will go down in the ruin.[62]

Where Roosevelt lost track, and he would remain on this false course, was when he compared his age and his imperatives to those of Abraham Lincoln.[63]

Soon after, Taft wrote to Elihu Root,

61. Hofstadter called it "vigorously equivocal rhetoric" (p. 235, footnote 9).
62. *The New Nationalism*, pp. 36–37.
63. And John Brown, perhaps more accurately. He said, "It is half melancholy and half amusing to see the way in which well-meaning people gather to do honor to the man who, in company with John Brown, and under the lead of Abraham Lincoln, faced and solved the great problems of the nineteenth century, while, at the same time, these same good people nervously shrink from, or frantically denounce, those who are trying to meet the problems of the twentieth century in the spirit which was accountable for the successful solution of the problems of Lincoln's time." In 1912, Robert Todd Lincoln denounced Roosevelt's self-comparisons to his father (see "Roosevelt Assailed by Robert Lincoln: Protests at the Perversions of His Father's Words to Support the Colonel's Doctrines," *NYT*, 4/29/12).

"I am the last one to withhold criticism from Supreme Court decisions.... The whole difficulty about the business is that there is throughout the West, and especially in the Insurgent ranks to which Theodore was appealing, a bitterness of feeling against the Federal Courts that this attitude of his was calculated to stir up, and the regret which he certainly expressed that courts had the power to set aside statutes was an attack upon our system at the very point where I think it is the strongest." But it was worse than that. "Indeed, my fear is that in this regard he simply spoke the truth as to his own views."[64] At Osawatomie the Constitution was mentioned once, and critically.

That Roosevelt at this point intended to run for President in 1912 there is no conclusion. At moments, Taft thought so. "The fact of the matter is if you were to remove Roosevelt's skull now, you would find written on his brain '1912,'" he told Archie just after the New Haven encounter. "But he is so purely an opportunist that should he find conditions changed ... [he] would deny it was ever there."[65] That decision evolved, and came and went, as Taft said it would. Roosevelt may have been one of the last to recognize it. Osawatomie made it inevitable.

As difficult as it was for Roosevelt to place laurels on another man's White House, Taft found nothing but pain in Roosevelt's ex-Presidency. With the exception of that minor business of the tariff upon which the Democrats— empowered by the insurgents— would trounce the Republicans in 1910, and again in 1912, the most popular figure of the time and fellow Republican gave nothing for Taft to uphold. Taft continued to speak of Roosevelt's legacy, which Roosevelt, himself, abandoned with his leftward bolt.

* * *

In the Autumn election the House of Representatives was turned upside down. Slower to change, the Senate remained nominally Republican, although with a tight balance should insurgents join Democrats. Taft was undisturbed. He considered the loss a deserved lesson to the insurgents, even if it came almost entirely at the expense of regulars. The election was a lesson for him, as well. Taft learned that the patronage club must be swung fiercely or not at all (and that one must not get caught either way).[66] He learned that legislation does not necessarily translate into votes, except in the negative. Politics, he learned, was attitude. Above all else he learned to keep moving.

The curious evolution of the Taft-Roosevelt relationship seemed settled over the Winter of 1910. Following the disaster in New York, Roosevelt kept quiet. On top of Stimson's loss, the mix-up with the Old

64. Taft to Root, 10/15/10.

65. Butt, 9/20/10, p. 524.

66. Taft's patronage play failed to advance regulars, but it succeeded to confine insurgency. Furthermore, the loyalties he reinforced in the State machines proved most useful during the next election. Had Taft backed the insurgents, he would have lost control of the party entirely. One instance of success came in Indiana. With Taft's backing regulars pulled the rug from under Beveridge. Beveridge was furious. Taft said it was Beveridge's own fault for opposing the Administration. As Indiana regulars praised the Payne tariff, Beveridge's Democratic opponent John Kern said that the Senator's commitment to tariff reduction was "here and there," a truly devastating and largely true criticism. For all the complaints about Payne-Aldrich, the differences between insurgents and regulars on the tariff was one of degree, whereas the differences of both with the Democrats was of kind. Beveridge, Kern said, "would only regulate the amount of plunder ... in particular and isolated cases" (Bowers, pp. 396–397). Kern won on the double influence of absenting regulars and tariff discontent, which Beveridge had done so much to arouse. A few other instances of Administration interference in local politics worked exactly as the insurgents did in general, as the agitation split the party and the Democrats walked away with the cup (see "Beveridge and the Election of 1912," by James R. Parker, *Indiana Magazine of History*, June 1967, pp. 104–107).

Guard brought trouble from both sides. He tasted what Taft got every day from the insurgents. Where Roosevelt felt he bested the New York machine, the insurgents saw betrayal. Cummins was shocked that Roosevelt backed Root for the Saratoga chair. He announced that the insurgent cause had "fared better with Roosevelt in Africa." Taft, of course, was highly amused. Earlier that summer he wrote, "The sage at Oyster Bay is keeping the public in doubt as to just what he proposes to do and is arousing the curiosity to an intense point by a promise to support Beveridge in Indiana and Lodge in Massachusetts." New Nationalism went only so far, especially since its author spoke one way out West and another back East. Between Cummins's offer for return fare to Africa and vicious censure from the likes of General Miles, Roosevelt went back to the original plan to clam up, voicing himself only in articles in the *Outlook*. It was said that even Gifford Pinchot was upset with Roosevelt. "I hope this is true," wrote Butt, who was coming to understand Roosevelt's complicity in the split, "for be it so, a great obstacle is removed from the path of reconciliation."[67]

In private, Taft and Roosevelt renewed their familiarity. Taft forwarded his message to Congress for Roosevelt's opinion. Knox ventured to Oyster Bay to discuss a Japanese treaty.[68] Roosevelt endorsed Taft's Canadian Reciprocity plan. It was a noble pursuit, he declared at a February 1911 Republican Club love-fest with Saratoga enemies Barnes and Woodruff.[69] As an animated Mexican border dominated headlines that Spring, Roosevelt elicited a promise from Taft to send him in should it come to war. In a pathological letter that underscored Taft's later view that Roosevelt was "obsessed with his love of war," Roosevelt laid out in precise detail the conditions under which he would enlist—no "profitless police duty" would do, the numbers of troops he would require—"The division would consist of three brigades of three regiments each," and the officers who would serve him—"I have my brigade commanders, colonels, and in many cases majors and captains already in mind...."[70] Taft deferred on the war, but said he would call should it come to that. On June 6, 1911, Taft met with Roosevelt at a gathering in Baltimore. Roosevelt was seen heartily shaking hands with Cannon, Sherman, Root, Lodge, and Penrose, the Old Guard itself. "Hello, Mr. President," he said to Taft, who replied with his heartiest, "Hello, Theodore!" Taft and Roosevelt sat by each other during the proceedings and whispered jokes about the speakers.[71]

Roosevelt was otherwise chased by

67. "Insurgents Bar Roosevelt," *NYT*, 9/30/10, Taft to Edwards, 7/27/10, "Calls Roosevelt Traitor," *NYT*, 10/4/10, and Butt, 11/25/10, p. 564. Miles demonstrated some mighty good outrage: "Look at his political tracks since he returned from the African wilds. It is a trail of discontent, bombast, disaffection, and even treason. And without one word of commendation for the existing Administration, which in my opinion, has been eminently proper and dignified and a great improvement ... this politician starts on a one-man tour, a personal political campaign, haranguing the people, inciting discontent, mixing with malcontents, embarrassing those in authority and power without an excuse or reason.... It is disgusting ... this constant vulgar exhibition of a former President running loose over the country surrounded by newspaper men for whose edification he walks, talks, acts and sleeps, hungrily swallowing calcium at its strongest pressure and reveling in the concentrated rays of the light of what should be to a sane man undesirable publicity."
68. Roosevelt to Taft, 12/8/10.
69. "Roosevelt and Old Guard Make Peace," *NYT*, 2/14/11.
70. Discussing Roosevelt's later attack against Taft's peace treaties, Taft wrote, "That is the secret of his present attitude. He has the spirit of the old Bersekers [*sic*] and he would think it a real injury to mankind if we did not have war...." (Taft to Bannard, 9/10/11). Roosevelt's war-envy letter makes it clear. Your author recommends this letter to Roosevelt biographers and psychiatrists alike (Roosevelt to Taft, 3/14/11).
71. Butt, 6/7/11, pp. 670–674.

journalists and partisans who demanded his views on politics, Taft, and his own future. He stuck to the game, denying everything and damning the rest. A reporter from the *Times* asked him for clarification on an article the paper had run on his support of Taft. A friend of both had let it out that Roosevelt not only declined to be a candidate for 1912 and would not only stay out of Taft's way, he might endorse Taft on the stump. Roosevelt's practiced reply was, "You know I never give interviews. But any statement purporting to come from me to the effect you have just mentioned is an unqualified falsehood." It was a sublime non-denial denial. A few days later, Roosevelt affirmed another friend's statement that he "emphatically would not be, that he would regard it as a calamity, if he were nominated...." He told a reporter, "Every word there is correct."[72]

72. "Roosevelt to Aid Taft in 1912 Fight?" 6/7/11 and "Roosevelt Won't Run," 6/9/11 *NYT*.

22

All Upside Down

I find that most of the world wake up with surprise and indignation to find me attempting to keep my promises.....

—William Howard Taft[1]

When Taft believed, really believed that he was in the right, he could target an issue like a sniper. With the tariff, Taft shot his mark, but it was for a resolution within politics. Even for Roosevelt, whose secret was to treat everything as a crusade, the tariff was too muddled for righteousness. The Payne bill came of legislative babysitting, not generalship, as was necessary at the time. Taft displayed an energetic leadership in the 1910 sessions akin to his intervention during the tariff Conference, but it was politics again, not morals. It was during the fights for Canadian free trade "Reciprocity," the "Arbitration" peace treaties, and the 1912 Republican nomination that in moral righteousness the Taft giant arose.

Taft worked his Congresses like few previous Presidents. The four sessions that spanned Roosevelt's two terms met for a total of 1,135 days. Taft called two special sessions, and overall Congressmen toiled 935 days during his four years.[2] Taft was unafraid of the neighbors down Pennsylvania Avenue who were, themselves, ever wary of his hospitality. Taft spent the 1911 sessions hammering two themes that would prove unsuccessful then and crucial to the future. The first, international arbitration treaties, was a tremendous diplomatic victory that the Senate passed like a kidney stone; Taft refused the product. The next, reciprocal free trade with Canada, would mark a great Taft victory in Congress that voters in Canada chose not to affirm.[3]

1. Taft to Otto Bannard, 9/10/11.
2. Wilson choked 654 days out of the 63rd Congress—a friendly Congress. The 64th Congress got off easy with only 368 days of work. Taft's legislative partners were incoherent from day one, and his second Congress was split between parties (from "The Office of the Clerk, Historical Highlights," House of Representatives website www.clerkweb.house.gov, Oct., 2001). A Congress is under a President's control only insofar as calling special sessions. However, the length of a Congress is a reflection of a period's political activity, which a President, of course, can greatly influence, as did Taft. A long Congress may not be productive, such as the second session of the 62nd Congress, but a long Congress will usually mean that Washington is sorting something out. In Taft's case, that meant his legislative program, which was hugely ambitious.
3. Historians have blamed comments by Taft and Champ Clark for the failure. Taft said that Canada was "coming to the parting of the ways," a mild reference to its strict trade relationship with England. On the House

Various arbitration treaties were already operative at the Hague courts. This was all very well, Taft noted, but those treaties were useless for ensuring peace, for "We leave out the questions which when they arise are likely to lead to war. If arbitration is worth anything it is an instrumentality for avoiding war. But, it is asked, would you arbitrate a question of national honor? I am not afraid of that question. Of course I would."[4] Taft knew it was revolutionary. He knew Andrew Carnegie would laud him for it. What would Roosevelt think?

It is easy to dismiss these peace advocates whose greatest accomplishment, the French and English Arbitration treaties of August 1911, came just a few years before world war. There was nothing naive in Taft's treaties. Peace with strength, yes, but strength untempered by principle or law leads to war. The absurdity of European war would confirm in Taft's mind the dire need for binding, meaningful arbitration of differences between nations. Taft developed this view in addresses to peace societies, which were something of a fashion in New York. In an unprepared speech in March 1910, Taft announced at a peace dinner that although "the Lord looks after fools, drunken men, and the United States," right thinking men ought seek some other recourse than war.[5] Into 1911, he converted the issue from banquet tables to serious diplomacy.

In May, Roosevelt responded in the *Outlook*. It became their first public feud since the silly Griscom affair the year before. Roosevelt's side of things was all too easy. While the President would spend the year declaring the United States the world's hope for peace, Roosevelt took the low road with, "Among private individuals the man who, if his wife is assaulted and has her face slapped, will go to law about it, instead of forthwith punishing the offender, would be regarded with derision. In just the same way, the United States ought never specifically to bind itself to arbitrate questions respecting its honor, independence and integrity."[6] Privately, Taft wished that Roosevelt would lay off. "I am sorry that Theodore thought it necessary to come out in advance of a definite knowledge of what we are trying to do," he told Carnegie.[7] In public, Taft pointed to the example of Roosevelt's arbitration of the Russo-Japanese war.

The volleys that started calmly in May grew riotous by Autumn, when the language tracked precisely the coming fight between the two men. In September, Roosevelt punched lower with, "There are other persons whose ingrained personal timidity is such that they are more afraid of war than of any dishonor,

3. (*cont.*) floor, Clark stuck his nationalist foot in his mouth with, "I hope to see the day when the American flag will float over every square foot of the British North American possessions clear to the North Pole" (Pringle, p. 585). As dumb as it was for Clark to say it, it changed nothing of the outcome. British agitation, all the way to the apostle of British superiority, Rudyard Kipling, created a hysterical backlash against the agreement (see "Kipling's Warning Against Reciprocity," *NYT*, 9/8/11). The comments by Taft and Clark were merely useful for opponents, not defining of the events. London papers even made a scandal out of the presence of U.S. Naval maneuvers on Lake Michigan (see *London Post*, 4/29/11, per case file 1140, reel 412). In the end, Taft was more correct than he knew about the "parting of the ways." Canada was as yet represented in Washington by the British Ambassador. Taft negotiated directly with the Canadians, and thus hastened its more formal independence from Britain in the 1930s.
4. Taft to Carnegie, 3/20/11, per Pringle, p. 737.
5. And, he told the peace advocates, the two battleships he wanted from Congress would go a long way towards peace. During the 1912 debate over the ships, Tillman mocked Taft with a proposal to build the largest battleship in the world. "Let such vessel be named 'Terror' and become the peacemaker of the world" (from "Taft Is for Peace with Reservations," 3/23/10 and "Tillman's Poor Joke," editorial, 7/12/12, *NYT*).
6. "Roosevelt on Arbitration," *NYT*, 5/19/11. Taft never put "independence" and "integrity" on the table.
7. Taft to Carnegie, 3/20/11, quoted from Pringle, p. 743.

personal or natural." To this, Taft sublimely retorted,

> We are not looking for insults from other nations, and we don't fear insults from other nations. We are big enough even if we should be insulted by anybody to just do what a great strong man does when he is insulted under conditions where he can restrain himself at all. He holds himself in and says, "I am a greater man because I resist the temptation to lick your pusillanimous little body."[8]

To the appeals for male chivalry, Taft spoke of another aspect of a woman's dignity. "No pension compensates for the loss of husband, son, or father. The glory of death in battle does not feed the orphaned children nor does the pomp and circumstance of war clothe them. The voice of the women of America should speak for peace."[9]

* * *

Canadians resented the Payne tariff. Citing the huge trade imbalance with the United States, Canadian industry pushed its government to avenge the U.S. tariff fence. At the same time, Payne's much misconstrued "maximum and minimum rates" clause required the President to spank foreign vagrants who discriminated against the United States, which included Canada for its asymmetrical trade agreements. These conflicts met in March of 1910. The last thing the Administration wanted was a trade war with Canada. Negotiations were tight, but Taft and Knox pulled it off, and the punitive rates were untouched. The experience resurrected the McKinley free trade dream and various reciprocity deals of the past, including one with Canada in the 1850s. Taft put Knox to the scent. Knox bagged the deal.

Taft sent the treaty to Congress in late January of 1911, re-framed as a revenue bill in order to avoid the two-thirds Senate vote necessary for treaties. As such, it started in the House. Whatever it was, Republicans didn't much know what to do with it. The coalitions that had lined up for and against Payne were reversed. Although the trade agreement covered mostly "natural" products, manufacturers salivated over greater access to the Canadian market. The printing industry, as in editorial boards of every newspaper and magazine in the country, went delirious at the prospect of cheap Canadian pulp. Farmers reacted according to the competition in Canada, such as wheat growers who suddenly found solace in the philosophy of Payne and Aldrich. "Reciprocity" became a stock word. Taft named a new horse for it. The gateway city of Buffalo named its auto show for it. The "Reciprocity Tour" was planned as the year's Glidden Tour theme to highlight the problem of motoring across state lines.[10]

"I think it may break the Republican Party for a while," Taft wrote to Roosevelt during the calm of early 1911. "At least it will show the hypocrisy of some people." Indeed, Cummins was tripped up when his floor speech against Reciprocity was interrupted with quotations from an old Cummins speech. Seems that Governor Cummins of Iowa once spoke in "vigorous

8. "Roosevelt Assails the Taft Treaties," 9/8/11 and "Bryan Toasts Taft as Highest Official," 10/3/11, *NYT*.
9. "Taft Urges Women to Work for Peace," *NYT*, 10/18/11.
10. "Among the Motorists," *Evening Star*, 3/12/11, "Buffalo Reciprocity Show," *Automobile*, cover story, 2/9/22, and Glidden to Taft, 4/5/11. Glidden wrote the President, "The annual tour of the American Automobile Association for the Glidden Trophy, leaving Washington June 19th for Ottawa, is this year to be called 'THE GLIDDEN RECIPROCITY TOUR.' I hope the Reciprocity measure will have passed Congress by that time so that our pilot car may have the honor of carrying an Official Copy for the Canadian Capital." The official name was the "National Reliability Contest of the American Automobile Association," although it was "generally known as the 'Reciprocity Tour'" (*American Motorist*, June, 1911).

defense" of free trade with Canada. La Follette called Reciprocity the "little brother of the Payne-Aldrich Act, the greatest legislative wrong inflicted upon the American people." The slander was all very well and typical, but La Follette got his lines crossed, for he was defending tariffs now. Worse, his conspiracy theories started to sound like Cannon. He accused the press of supporting Reciprocity solely for cheap paper. As for the Old Guard, it didn't know what to do. Cannon screamed bloody hell. Senate regulars were dazed and confused.[11]

It was a perfect Taft situation. Old coalitions were so twisted that Democrats and Republicans, insurgents and standpatters couldn't be recognized one from the other. Insurgents joined up with the Old Guard in protest. Horace Taft wrote his brother President,

> I am still chuckling over the Canadian reciprocity agreement and enjoying the situation of the Insurgent friends of the poor. They are like my friend, Mrs. Wiggin, of whom her son said, "Oh yes, Mother wants us all to get married, as long as we don't marry anybody in particular."[12]

A Grange representative interrupted a White House reception for children with a biting speech against Reciprocity in front of the President. Taft listened politely, then told the man to keep his votes to himself. "I never saw the old man so mad. He was hopping, and he gave them hell," said Jimmy Sloan. Taft told Archie, "Their daring to come to me and threaten me with their miserable votes! I want this country to know that I will do nothing I do not think to be right if my reelection depends on it." Archie wrote, "He is always at his best when he gets angry, and whenever he gets that way he makes a hit with the public."[13]

At first the House leadership sat on the bill in committee. Taft came down hard and the bill got unstuck. The lame duck House tossed it over to the Senate in less than twenty days. The night Reciprocity was voted up in the House, Taft held the annual dinner in honor of the Speaker. Cannon hardly said a word. Rep. Dalzell told the President, "I only hope you have not killed the Republican party." Taft replied, "It will be stronger than ever.... You must remember there are other things besides high protection for which the party stands." Cannon snubbed Taft at social affairs over the next months. When the President encountered Cannon at a country restaurant, a favorite D.C. motoring destination, all greeted him except Cannon. Later that evening, Cannon approached the President and made an exaggerated bow. The President looked up with complete disinterest, paused, then continued his conversation with his guests. Cannon left humiliated. "When the President cuts anybody, that body is cut," wrote Butt, "and there is no explanation to make. That ends it."[14]

The Senate balked, even over the endorsement of the High Priest of tariffs, Aldrich.[15] Taft warned that it would be done now or it would be done in a special

11. Taft to Roosevelt, 1/10/11, "Taunts Cummins with Old Speech," 6/30/11, "La Follette Severe on Taft's Record," 7/14/11 and "Senate Rejects the Root Plan," 6/27/11, *NYT*.
12. Horace Taft to Taft, 2/2/11.
13. Butt, 5/8/11, pp. 643–644.
14. "Reciprocity Passes House, 221 to 92," *NYT*, 2/15/11 and Butt, 2/14/11, p. 599 and 8/20/11, p. 745.
15. See "Aldrich Favors Reciprocity Bill," *NYT*, 2/21/11. Pringle called Aldrich's endorsement "less than ... [Taft] must have desired" (p. 590). Whatever Taft's expectations, it shocked the Old Guard. Standpatter Penrose was for it from the beginning. As Congress freaked over Reciprocity, Taft wrote to Aldrich who was convalescing. In this six page letter, Taft outlined his thoughts on Aldrich's currency plan and described the Reciprocity reasons and doings. Then he wrote, "I sincerely hope that your rest is doing you good....

session. To one of the rousing Senate complaints that followed, the President declared, "Senator Depew has sung his song with great beauty.... It's a little bit like the husband who had an invalid wife, and who wished she'd get well—or something."[16]

The last day of the Congress, March 3, 1911, the President sat in the Capitol. In full dress, Archie stood behind him and watched "Senator after Senator come in and protest against the extra session." Butt was stunned by the display. He watched Taft break up a filibuster. He watched him receive the offending Senator, who stalked in, Butt wrote, "looking like a fighting Indian.... I saw the President smile and thank him when he felt like killing him.... I saw the President sign bills and hold conferences at the same time, never losing his temper once and keeping his head when all those around him were losing theirs...."[17] Finally, the clock was set back in order to pass a final Deficiencies bill, and the Congress adjourned without Reciprocity. The 62nd Congress was opened a month later by the President's call.

The Reciprocity bill expired with the change in sessions. The now minority-party House regulars were free to oppose the measure. The now barest minority of a minority House insurgents joined with border-state regulars to condemn it. The Democrats announced their joy that the President had joined their party and passed the measure with ease. Half the Republicans, mostly regulars, gave it their votes.

The Senate was again the battleground, although the lines were as crossed as in the House in January. Each faction stuck a fork in the bill. The worst of it, however, fell upon the Senate insurgents who traded the righteousness of their 1909 stand against Payne for spite against Taft. When La Follette was caught denouncing both a Root amendment for duties on print paper and Reciprocity for liberating it, all he could say was that the news industry would, like the railroads, big business, etc., etc., "Obtain advantages through the passage of the bill."[18] In the end, and thanks largely to Aldrich, Penrose, Root, and sixteen standpatters who voted for it, the President got his bill.

Taft put into the fight the full force of his office. From the joint celebrations of Champlain, his 1910 visit to the Canadian border at Maine, to his endorsement of a highway to be built from Montreal to Florida, and the highly publicized negotiations themselves, Taft constructed the issue. He deftly turned a problem into a solution, and gave it the force of a moral imperative. Calling a special session for the deal was a daring move, and he thereby made Reciprocity the dominant headline of 1911. The *Times* was ecstatic over his victory. "As high politics this was masterly.

15. (*cont.*) I long for your presence. I feel about you, as Scott said of Rhoderick Dhu. A blast upon your bugle horn were worth a thousand men" (Taft to Aldrich, 1/29/11). Pringle used this quotation as evidence of Taft's dependency upon Aldrich; only he employed it without context to Reciprocity (p. 411). That was most unfair, especially since Pringle cited the same letter during his discussion of Reciprocity (without the "bugle") and called it a "shrewd appeal to the high priest of protection" (p. 590). Pringle would surely have recognized that were Aldrich and his vile bugle more available to Taft during early 1911, Taft could have passed the measure without going into a special session. It was not the first time Taft talked about bugles. In 1908 he defended one of Roosevelt's Messages to Congress as a "bugle call" ("Taft Says Message was a Bugle Call," *NYT*, 2/11/08).
16. "Taft Laughs at Senators," *NYT*, 2/28/11.
17. Butt, 3/8/11, p. 600.
18. "Senate Rejects the Root Plan," *NYT*, 6/27/11. The best he could do in his autobiography was to condemn Taft's "attempt to foist upon the country a sham reciprocity measure" (La Follette, p. 477). Root's amendment was concerned with a loophole that would allow duty free pulp from other countries as well as Canada, a concern that proved prescient. It caused an uproar. Newspapers damned Root. His amendment didn't pass. (See Jessup, pp. 222–223.)

As statesmanship, it is unexampled in our history.... The president has literally tried his case before the people, and, by the force of the conviction he has implanted in the public mind, he has won."[19]

* * *

Taft won, but at the price of reviving Payne-Aldrich. Penrose helped Taft keep the Reciprocity bill clean of tariff amendments, a great victory, for there would be no distasteful riders to swallow to get it.[20] But in shedding reciprocity of that baggage, the tariff checked in by itself. Taft knew it and was ready for it. "After the reciprocity bill passes I presume a vote will be had on the farmers' free list and on the wool bill. I do not think that either will pass. If it is, I shall veto it," he wrote his brother.[21]

The Democrats who delivered Reciprocity made squirmy bedfellows. Taft got more than he asked. At every turn the word "schedule" rumpled the sheets. To get Reciprocity, Taft got an entire session dedicated to the tariff. Taking advantage of all the talk about duties, House Democrats pushed out revisions on the pulp, wool, steel, and cotton schedules. In the Senate, insurgents and Democrats likewise teamed up. Taft's position was that he called Congress to consider Reciprocity and only that. He vetoed any tariff bill that slipped through the divided Senate.

Taft held that revisions presented prior to the Tariff Board's reports were illegitimate and politics. The Board was created to remove politics from funding considerations, and he wouldn't compromise it to please Democrats and insurgents. He wrote that June,

> I am going to veto any tariff revision bill that comes up to me at this extra session except reciprocity. I don't see why I should not cultivate the pleasure of being consistent even if my friends the progressives find it necessary to be inconsistent at every turn. They are shooting their heads off in favor of the tariff commission be-

In July, 1910, the presidential party explored the most easterly point in the country. At Eastport, Maine, near the Canadian border, the President declared his "hopes for closer trade relations with [our] Northern neighbor." The dream nearly came true with his 1911 Reciprocity measure. Unfortunately, Canadian voters, still more British than American, rejected the agreement. (Courtesy Library of Congress)

19. "Reciprocity Passes Senate, 53 to 27," and "Mr. Taft's Triumph," editorial, 7/23/11, *NYT*. The *American Review of Reviews* was opposed to the measure from beginning to end, as the journal had turned on Taft in late 1910. The only good the *Review* could find in it was the opening of a new relationship with Canada, which was admitted to be unto itself "worthy of great consideration" (July, 1911, p. 4). That's called praise by faint damnation.
20. See Taft to Robert Taft, 8/27/11.
21. Taft to Charles Taft, 7/13/11.

cause they wished a scientific revision of the tariff, and now they are talking of a general revision without any report from the Tariff Board simply to defeat reciprocity."[22]

This was noble and true. If he signed a wool revision, which he admitted was necessary, he would undercut the Board which was to announce its findings in three months. He told Archie, "They think I will be afraid to veto a free wool bill, but I will show them I don't propose to be bulldozed by them. If they want to remain in Washington all summer I am willing to do so. If it becomes a game of bluff I can keep my cards off the table as long as they can."[23] With that kind of conviction, and a slash of his veto pen, on August 17, 1911, Taft deliberately, knowingly committed the sole enduring mistake of his presidency.

Taft was fully aware of the political costs of his defense of the Tariff Board over the Wool revision. To his wife, he wrote,

> I am inclined to think that this is a clever move both on the part of the Insurgents and the Democrats and that it will involve me in a loss of prestige which I gained in the reciprocity fight. It will be said that I criticized the wool schedule in my Winona speech and yet when an opportunity is presented to modify it I veto it.[24]

The veto is a tricky power. Once threatened, a President must use it. Congress is a wolf. It can smell a weak President. Taft knew this. He also knew that the threat of a veto can be just as effective when signing legislation. Congress heeded his warning the year before not to send another pork bill like the River and Harbors measure. He might have done the same with the Wool bill. Congress sent him enough veto fodder in the Statehood, Farmers' Free List, and Cotton bills which he dispatched triumphantly and for good reason. He dispatched those hastily written, stupidly political measures with vigor and effective indignance. His reasons for not signing the wool revision, carefully laid out in a major speech in September, were philosophical, not technical, sound, but dry.[25]

He could have accepted the Wool bill as not his responsibility. With a warning to await the Tariff Board for the other revisions, he might have put an end to the gratuitous tariff attacks. This would have disarmed the Democrats of the issue that gave them the House majority. Instead, the vetoes allowed the Democrats to ignore the Tariff Board altogether and continue to pepper Taft with revisions through 1912. Signing the Wool bill would have killed all lingering complaints about the tariff and

22. Taft to Hubert Taft, 6/28/11.
23. Butt, 6/22/11 pp. 684–685. Butt suggested to the President to veto the wool bill and sign the Farmers' Free List, explaining that it would deflect the Democrats. Taft laughed off the suggestion with "Archie, you are a free trade Democrat, and you can't change." Taft was aware of the danger of the Farmers' Free List, particularly as named. "The name does make it harder to veto, but it won't deter me from what I see to be my duty" (Butt, 8/3/11, p. 725). Taft's brother Horace also wanted the President to sign the tariff bills. The President was furious at the suggestion. The *Times* deplored the vetoes but acknowledged the President's consistency to await the Tariff Board, which the President worked so hard to create. For a good review of the political reasons to accept the wool bill, see memo to Taft from Senator Brown (7/29/11), whose most compelling argument was that Taft's pledge to revise Schedule K was the greater obligation than that owed the Tariff Board. For Taft's fullest defense of his position see Taft to Henry Taft, 8/3/11. The Farmers' Free List was all politics, and Taft would have nothing to do with it. In addition to being a wholesale revision of duties, it arbitrarily revised classifications and thereby would have caused a mess of conflicts in the schedules. Worse, the bill "purported to put agricultural instruments on the free list," which, Taft explained, were already free, as provided by a clause in Payne that allowed reciprocal free trade in farm implements (see Taft to Robert Taft, 8/27/11).
24. Taft to Helen Taft, 7/28/11.
25. "The Vetoes of the Woolen, Free List and Cotton Bills," Addresses, reel 576.

the cost of living. Signing the Wool bill would have restored to Sereno Payne his good name. Signing the Wool bill would have called the Democratic bluff. Instead, the veto kept Payne and Aldrich on angry lips through 1912. Winona stood.

The Payne bill was a necessary convulsion, and Taft handled it magnificently, especially if viewed through the Reciprocity fight. In 1911, Taft got barely half the regulars to go along with him, and that after two years of beating them into shape. That number would have been less in 1909 when there were fewer Democrats to pair up with for a majority. Both insurgents and regulars proved promiscuous when free of the responsibilities of power. Even if Taft did force the regulars into deeper revisions, he would have done so at the absolute cost of his 1910 legislation, as well as the all important side-deals of Payne. Taft's achievements in 1909 crystallize if viewed through Reciprocity.[26]

* * *

Another of Taft's 1911 triumphs came of a brief, violent, and wholly fabricated scandal that he shot dead. Though silenced by Taft's 1910 St. Paul conservation speech, the fanatics had not given up their hatred for him. One, M.F. Abbott, published the contents of a letter that implicated Taft, his brother Charles, and former Interior Secretary Ballinger in a scheme to profit from opening railway access to a harbor along the Chugach National Forest in Alaska. Abbott wrote that in reviewing Interior Department files she discovered a sinister reference in the postscript to a routine note. Known subsequently as the "Dick to Dick letter," being from Richard Ryan to Richard Ballinger, it revealed Ryan's connection to Charles P. Taft, through whose influence Ryan's Controller Railway, a front for the "Morgan-Guggenheim syndicate," was given exclusive rights to the harbor. The words "monopoly," "conservation," and "Ballinger" again collided and looked to bring down a President.[27]

Pinchot went ape. La Follette angrily demanded an explanation. Testimony from Charles Taft, Daniel Guggenheim, and Secretaries Hitchcock and Fisher was ordered to hear their version of "the curious story told by Miss M.F. Abbott about the mysterious 'Dick to Dick letter.'" The hysteria happened to coincide with the final debates on Reciprocity. "The insurgents have been hammered so because of their attitude in respect to reciprocity, that they are getting very desperate," Taft explained to his brother, Charles, who had never heard of any Dick Ryan, "and this Controller Bay business is one of the instruments that they hope to use to attack me and produce a counter-effect."

What occurred was that in 1910 Ryan's appeal for harbor rights to Controller Bay was met at Taft's order with a general opening of the area to give the same opportunity to others. A year later, the new Interior Secretary, Walter Fisher, gave Abbott access to Department files, and she concocted the postscript to an existing letter. Opponents used the accusation as an excuse to resurrect the Ballinger-Pinchot affair. Once more, progressives cried, the Administration favored a special interest over the people. Roosevelt chimed in with

26. For the opposite view, see *American Review of Reviews*, Sept. 1911, p. 289 and March 1912, p. 261. The editors held that had Taft only asserted the same leadership over Payne as he did over Reciprocity, the tariff problem would have been resolved. This conclusion came of the usual slander that the Payne tariff ended up "a very little higher rather than a very little lower" than the previous tariff. Wrong on all counts, especially in contrast to the *Review*'s own opinions on it in 1909, which defended Payne.

27. This section from Taft to Charles Taft, 7/13/11, W Fisher to Taft, 7/19/11, Ballinger to Taft, 7/28/11, "Fight to Involve Taft in Scandal," 7/12/11, "Taft Refutes Alaska Charges," 7/27/11, and "Would Hold Alaska Wealth, 12/10/11, *NYT*.

Over the summer of 1909, Chief Forester Gifford Pinchot launched the "Ballinger-Pinchot" affair, an attempt to lay upon the Taft Administration charges of corruption in the handling of Alaskan coal fields. It went nowhere, except to divide the party. Pinchot became a singular force in the split of the Republican party, especially after he and La Follette succeeded to drag Roosevelt into it all. The fanaticism that possessed the anti–Taft extremists of the Pinchot school was never more evident than in the Summer of 1911, when an "ultra-conservationist" muckraker concocted fake evidence of corruption by Taft. The "Dick to Dick" letter claimed that Taft had betrayed the people in favor of the "interests." Pinchot hollered and La Follette demanded an investigation. Taft "nailed" it with a devastating reply that called it all, as shown here, a "malicious falsehood." (Clifford Berryman cartoon, 1911, Courtesy Library of Congress)

an article on the general subject in the *Outlook.*

Taft lobbed another bomb at Congress, a devastating denial that condemned the Abbott charge as a "bogus ... wicked fabrication." More importantly, he affirmed that the action on Controller Bay was done not just openly and legally, but wholly in the public interest. Taft cut back at Roosevelt by pointing out that Ryan was not connected to the Morgan-Guggenheim group, especially since that syndicate had already been given similar access to the harbor by Roosevelt in 1907—at the recommendation of Pinchot. Taft's enemies had moved to such ludicrous extremes that, outside of continued Pinchot "frothings," as Ballinger called it, there was no reply. The scandal was stillborn. Roosevelt turned instead to the idea of government ownership of the coalfields railroad.[28] That December, at the advice of Ballinger's old foe, Louis Brandeis, and Pinchot's brother Amos, the Democratic House dropped the matter. Secretary Fisher, who was a Pinchot friend, thus learned firsthand the "desperate methods" employed against the President in the Ballinger-Pinchot affair.[29]

* * *

28. For some Pinchot "frothings," see "Pinchot Says Taft Dodges Alaska Issue," *NYT*, 7/28/11. Roosevelt's opinion on the railway from "Defends Alaska Policy," *NYT*, 8/11/11.
29. House Democrats blocked Republican attempts to hold Abbott to account for her duplicity. Although the affair occupied much space in the press and Taft's personal letters that summer, Pringle did not discuss it. Two other scandals made a try at Taft that summer. The first came over alleged improprieties of an Army officer and Taft friend, Major Ray, involving somebody's wife. That somebody, a government clerk, threatened to blackmail Ray, and the whole thing turned into a Congressional investigation that threatened to draw Charles Taft back into the news. "We have not done anything dishonorable in the matter," Taft wrote to Charles, "and while it is not pleasant to have your intimate relations disclosed to the public, we will have to stand it...." (Taft to Charles Taft, 7/13/11). The other scandal, which was politically dangerous, involved Dr. Harvey Wiley of the Agricultural Dept. who feuded with his boss, Secretary Wilson. Nothing came of either affair. For the Wiley business, see Pringle, pp.728–731.

Following Taft's July victory with Reciprocity and his spanking of the Abbott charges, La Follette turned his anti-administration crusade back to the tariff. "La Follette is anxious to rehabilitate himself and it is with him anything to beat me," wrote Taft. "It has become an obsession with him ... but I don't think that even if the bills pass and I veto them, I shall be put in such as hole as my insurgent friends think."[30] He was right, in the immediate, anyway, for Reciprocity's passage raised his esteem in the public despite the tariff vetoes. The vetoes would not have been necessary were it not for the insurgents, whose votes gave the Senate Democrats their majority. But the insurgent band, whom Taft called "the black flags," scored no points that summer.[31]

Within the precarious marriages of necessity between regulars and Democrats over Reciprocity, and between insurgents and Democrats on subsequent tariff bills, the Capitol domestic scenes were frequently complicated. The insurgent scheme was to let the Old Guard vote down a Democratic bill, then jump in to salvage it with its own versions. The Democrats joined votes with the insurgents, but they wanted no other associations. They preferred that the victories be theirs, not La Follette's, whose dictates made for much discomfort. In August, when La Follette planned to hyphenate his name to a House Cotton bill and Cummins and Bristow added iron and sugar amendments to it, the Old Guard teamed up with the Democrats and gleefully watched the insurgents trip.

It started when Penrose stuck his thumb in the wind and discovered that North Carolina Democrats were none pleased with reductions in the cotton schedule. Attempts were made to placate them with revisions in textile, chemical and machinery rates, which caused Cummins and Bristow to withdraw their own amendments, as they expected a defeat of the whole thing. Penrose told Democrats that the regulars would step aside, thus allowing the House bill to pass without the insurgent amendments. When the bill came up, some regulars literally bolted: they ran from the chamber, much to the amusement of the galleries. Those who remained sat with their arms folded, "shaking with laughter at the obvious distress of the La Follette wing," and enjoyed the spectacle. Cummins invoked a rule to require a vote and was overruled 36 to 15. La Follette demanded the same again of Penrose, to which only a few hands were raised. Mightily frustrated, La Follette yelled out that the Vice President had not counted some hands. Standpatter Oliver interjected with the point of order that La Follette had not risen to address the President of the Senate, to which Vice President Sherman, "with malice in his voice" and a huge smile, replied, "The Chair sustains the order." La Follette "threw up his hands in the gesture of a drowning man and sank back in his seat." The House bill was voted up. Next, Democrats proposed amendments identical to those of Cummins and Bristow, who then furiously rejected them. The record now showed insurgents voting against themselves and tariff reduction. When it was over, and with a snicker in his eye, Penrose somberly declared, "It was a spontaneous uprising of the people."[32]

As Taft described it, "The result was a complete collapse of the coalition between the insurgents and the Democrats, a

30. Taft to Helen Taft, 7/27/11.
31. Taft to Charles Taft, 9/10/10.
32. "Senate Democrats Rout La Follette," *NYT*, 8/18/11.

great bitterness of feeling, and a very great humiliation to La Follette who in the wool bill and in the free list bill had been striding like a colossus from one House to another in laying down the law as to what compromise could be adopted. This subjected La Follette and his associates to ridicule the country over."[33] It was more than an embarrassment for La Follette, who had been enjoying his fast ride as Senate Czar. It clobbered his presidential ambitions. There would be no Taft veto of another La Follette bill for him to rant about in his newspaper.

33. Taft to Robert Taft, 8/27/11. This 16-page letter gives an absolutely hilarious description of the Old Guard trick on the insurgents. "The crowning piece of the comedy," Taft wrote, came of an amendment to the chemicals schedule by a North Carolina Democrat, which the House adopted without study. Afterwards it was discovered that the amendment was based on a flawed investigation that had confused ad valorem and fixed duties, and ended up raising duties on certain products.

23

Automaniacs

In June, 1910, the Society of Automobile Engineers (SAE) announced it was completing a list of specifications for automobile construction.[1] SAE's crucial work was to set standards for an industry of manufacturers that had hardly a bolt size in common. Notice of the standardization of automobiles in society came at the same time from Chancellor Day of Syracuse University. Day warned graduates that "young business men were becoming so infatuated with the motor car that they were losing their business positions."[2] As had motorists in response to Wilson's "nothing has spread Socialistic feeling" accusation of 1906, manufacturer Benjamin Briscoe pointed to the gross benefits of the automobile for the common man. Unlike 1906, however, Briscoe might have applauded the Chancellor, for implicit in this latest censure was a recognition of the ascendancy of the automobile.

It was said that auto envy and the speed disease drove men to mortgage the house and lose their jobs. J.J. Hill, not surprisingly, blamed the high cost of living on the auto craze. Bankers worried that loans were surreptitiously diverted into automobiles. Keepers of America's youth warned that auto temptation was too great for a young man's restraint. The concerns were not without foundation. A New York banker was indicted for a $25,000 stock fraud which counsel claimed was the result of the "speed mania." The judge ordered a lunacy hearing. The banker's mother testified that as a child his "headaches and nervousness" abated only to the Coney Island "Witching Wave" ride. A taximan told of $3,500 spent on some 900 wandering motor drives over three years in which the banker cared only for fast and faster, regardless of direction.[3]

Another man discovered himself hopelessly $200 short of auto satisfaction, a "victim of an unconquerable passion to possess a motor car." He invented a desperate, ingenious ploy. To protect the guilty he was described in the news as "Junket," a clerk. The dealer was the "Hustleup Automobile Company." Seeing the machine in the shop window every day was too much for Junket. He gathered all his money and walked into the store. "No use beating around the bush," he started. "I'll put my proposition right up to you,

1. "Use of Materials in Motor Car Work," *NYT*, 6/26/10. This is the "SAE" on your can of oil.
2. "Auto's Economic Value," *NYT*, 6/26/10.
3. "Motor Car Extravagance," letter, 5/5/10, "Belling Had Speed Mania," 1/21/11, *NYT*. See also the 6/23/10 issue of the *Automobile* for a full reply to the criticism by various experts (pp. 1146–1151).

and you can give me your answer right off the bat." Seems that Junket knew someone who "might be persuaded to buy a car like that one in the window." Would a $250 commission reward the deal? The manager agreed but wanted proof. "His name is Junket," said Junket. "Frederick K. Junket—and he's a clerk in an office up here in the Highstory Building." The manager was incredulous. A clerk? Counting off his money—exactly $250 short of the price, Junket said, "I never heard of any better proof than money. I'm Junket." The manager was furious, but kept the deal. "Now if you knew what a time I had selling myself that car you wouldn't say a word about the $250," said Junket. "I earned that commission." Junket's remaining $50 was spent on a garage.[4]

Other than a fistfight at an Albany auto club banquet that was embarrassing but unrelated, motorists defended themselves magnificently against this latest anti-automobile hysteria. They seized Briscoe's arguments and pointed to the economic benefits of the automobile. Former ALAM executive Coker Clarkson declared that automobiles solved the problems of city congestion (!) and "added new hours of opportunity to every business man's day."[5] Clarkson turned outrage against itself with, "The outcry against the automobile lately voiced by certain financiers and educators of National prominence ... is the old cry against progress." K.P. Drysdale further explained,

> The wiseacres, the would-be philosophers, and the self-appointed guardians of other people's affairs have proclaimed the widespread purchase of automobiles to be an economic waste which, if not checked, is going to cause the ruination of the country and other kinds of calamities. All of which can be classified as nothing more than "rot."[6]

Drysdale declared that auto purchases promoted the "free and rapid circulation of money" and provided "livelihood for a million people." The industry produced "skilled artisans" and created an "endless" chain of economic and social benefit. That farmers were "the subject of severe criticism for their extravagance in buying automobiles" was a criticism of prosperity itself.

Other claims of auto benefit were less credible. Motoring was a "cure for throat trouble" and useful to prevent "nervous affections" and insomnia. "French scientists," it was said, "have discovered that motoring tends to increase the red blood corpuscles and that the vibration of the automobile stirs up the sluggish blood current, thereby bringing more blood to rejuvenate and nourish the starved tissues." Others weren't so sure. While one tailor claimed that motoring "develops the chest," another disagreed; the clearer result in his clients of backseat riding was an increased waistline. Finally, there came the new diseases, "auto foot" and "chauffeur's fracture." The first was due, simply, to "too little walking." Chauffeurs' wrists were done in by engine backfires during cranking. The other dangers of automobiling were well understood and documented in the headlines. But no one could have foreseen the near-death of a chauffeur who

4. "How to Buy a Motor Car," *NYT*, 3/2/13.
5. "Fight at Auto Banquet," 4/24/11 and "Economic Value of the Motor Car," 7/3/10, *NYT*. In 1909, the Pierce-Arrow Company measured the length of its cars, compared them to a team of horses, and announced that the automobile would free space in city streets ("Automobiles May Solve the Traffic Problem," *Automobile*, 1/28/09, p. 196). The company should have pointed out that the greatest savings in city space, from the shrinkage of time: faster moving, automobiles could fit into more space than horse-drawn vehicles. This was pointed out by an Army Captain in 1901 regarding use of motors at Army depots (See "The Use of the Motor Vehicle in the United States Army, 1899–1939," p. 16).
6. "Auto Responsible for Present Prosperity," *NYT*, 10/2/10.

was almost taken out by a suicide jumper. The 365 foot fall concluded on the hood against which the chauffeur leaned while reading a newspaper.[7]

A terrifically shocking development in automobiling came when a series of chauffeur elopements hit the news. More than a few of the daring, the manly, and the dangerous automobile pilots ran off with the boss's daughter, or wife, even. How more to outrage society than a wild, romantic descent into steerage? One perfectly outraged mother of an eloped daughter found the offending chauffeur outside the St. Regis Hotel in New York and beat him with a strap. The usual conclusion was a quiet return home by the girl and an unspecified "settlement" for the chauffeur.[8]

A more general outrage followed when criminals discovered the great economic and other benefits of automobiles. The getaway car, the drive-by shooting, the carjacking, and the fence resulted. Rival gangs carried a gunfight up Broadway. Thieves held up a car outside of Rye, New York. The heist failed, however, when the car wouldn't start. They ran off on foot. A girl was beaten or worse after being lured into a car with the enticing offer of a motor ride. Bank robbers escaped in "black" cars. The "motor bandit" joined the new lexicon as newspapers tracked outrageous stories from France of an anarchist gang that robbed banks and escaped in stolen motors. In America, motor bandits robbed payroll clerks, banks, and cars.[9]

The need for stricter chauffeur licensing was highlighted by these stories. It was thought that in New York City hundreds of chauffeurs were ex-convicts. There was always the mundane but equally drastic need to filter out bad drivers. One student of an automobile school managed to convince his teacher to give him a chance in a runabout. All was well until a grocery wagon horse bolted as the new driver came upon an intersection. He panicked, threw the wheel sharply and sent the car into three men who crossed the street. He desperately dropped into reverse and right into a little girl. One of the men was knocked senseless and the girl "lay screaming in the sidewalk."[10]

Chauffeur testing under the Callan law went into effect on August 1, 1910. That July the first batch of four hundred chauffeurs were subjected to an hour long written examination, and deep questioning as to their "character and habits" and experience at the wheel. In or out of Fifth Amendment protections against self-incrimination, the chauffeurs were quizzed as to their reputations for intemperance, scorching, and criminal past. Then they were required to demonstrate driving ability. The next group arrived for testing primed by the earlier class. The commissioners popped a new set of questions and fifteen very surprised chauffeurs failed the exams. And so went the most thorough and largest licensing program in the country. The task was enormous. In New York City there were 30,000 chauffeurs to be tested.[11] It worked for the most part,

7. "Auto as Cure for Throat Trouble," 5/1/10, "Motor Car Riding an Aid to Health," 7/10/10, "Automobile as a 'Cure,'" 9/17/11, "Differ on Auto as a Means to Health," 4/4/12, "Auto Foot the Latest," 12/27/12, "Plunges 365 Feet from World Dome," 12/7/11, *NYT*.

8. "Beat Chauffeur at St. Regis," *NYT*, 8/1/11. The chauffeur's reputation was long set. A 1909 automobile journal stated, "White's Restaurant wishes to announce that hereafter when any chauffeurs borrow girls and do not return the same within a reasonable length of time, they should either notify the management or furnish substitutes" ("Ohio Automobile Notes," *Auto News*, April 1909, p. 31).

9. "Fight Pistol Battle in Speeding Autos," 9/29/10, "Highwaymen Hold up Three in Auto," 8/9/10, and "Lured Away in Auto and Left Senseless," 3/20/10, *NYT*.

10. "Runs down Four in Auto," *NYT*, 3/12/11.

11. "Test for 400 chauffeurs," 7/15/10 and "Examiners Drop Many Chauffeurs," 7/19/10, *NYT*.

excepting one man, "Kansas City Riley, who took the examination for the whole gang and is doing pretty well now selling them," wrote a satirist.[12]

"The average chauffeur thinks the average owner is full of liquor, incompetent, and near-sighted," said engineer Frank B. Gilbert, "and the owner thinks the chauffeur is a man just out of jail." Between them deaths by automobile increased every year, as did outrage in the press. The *Times* declared, "Speed cranks take more lives than murderers," and ran headlines such as "Automobile Death Harvest Doubled in Three Years." The National Highways Protective Society got busy with a drive to halt the "speed mania." C.H. Parkhurst wrote a letter describing the death of a little girl who was "confused by the dazzle of the headlights" and run down. "If this is what democracy means, give us oligarchy, monarchy, despotism, anything that will hold down the regardless insolence of the few under the pressure of some irresistible authority," he pleaded. He demanded that reckless autoists be charged with attempted murder, even if no injury resulted. Soon enough New York decided to license owners, too, as was already the case in Massachusetts.[13]

Satirist J.W. Foley got into things with the adventures of "Pliny The Youngest." On a visit to 1911 from ancient Rome, Pliny II was already much amazed by the "first principle that all men are created equal, a declaration that the philosopher would successfully controvert were he minded to do so." But this matter of conveyance in fast chariots, called "autocars," was beyond him. In the "joy wagons" he saw no joy. "The chariot in which it befell me to journey was driven by the power, so I learned, of some forty horses, and to this I might add by the power of one ass, who sat with a circular device of wood ... which he turned alternately to the right and left, as it was his fancy, to overturn some pedestrian...." Those that escaped screamed, "Fool!" to which the chariot driver deftly replied, "Fool!" In front of this "chuffer" was a crystal square that if gazed into fills even calm men "with contempt and loathing for all creatures." Pliny II noted that in back of the chariot were plaques which "indicate the number of victims the chariot hath slain." His ride terminated in a demonstration of the "metamorphosis ... discoursed of so charmingly by Herodotus," by which the chariot was "transmogrified" into a turtle.[14]

* * *

The dangers of motoring came home to the White House in June of 1910, when Taft's son, Robert, ran down an Italian laborer outside of Beverly. It was thought that the man would die. The President and his advisors seriously worried over the consequences come November. It marked one of the few times the name "Taft" crowded "Roosevelt" from the headlines. The news billed opposite to "Roosevelt Talks with La Follette."[15] It was also one of the few things of Taft's presidency, the weather included, to interfere with his golfing. That afternoon he played horribly. It turned out that Robert had driven slowly past a group of workers who were oiling the roads. This one man failed to make way and was tossed to the gutter and into the hospital. The President telegraphed the man and instructed that the best surgeons attend him. He instructed his son, "You would better not leave Beverly or appear in

12. "Bateye as Chauffeur," *Automobile*, 11/3/10.
13. "Automobile Owners Oppose Amendments," 2/5/13, editorials of 4/14/12 and 2/2/03, and "Slaughter in the Streets," letter, 12/22/12, *NYT*.
14. "Pliny the Youngest Philosophizes on Joy Wagons," *NYT*, 8/27/11.
15. *NYT*, 6/28/10.

the machine for the next day or two." An investigation exonerated Robert, although it was discovered that he was driving on an expired license.[16] The worker was compensated by the President with $500 cash (more than the man's annual salary), paid hospital bills, and a trip to Italy to visit his family. The honor of being run down by a presidential motor car was soon again extended to a Salem, Massachusetts, child. This time White House chauffeur Abel Long was driving Mrs. Taft and her sisters. A boy jumped into the road from behind another auto and was hit by the car's broad front fender. Long was commended for a quick reaction that avoided worse injury to the child.[17]

Whatever outrage might have followed the news of Mrs. Taft's accident was drowned by the headlines from St. Louis. Aeroplane pilot Arch Hoxsey there captured two firsts, the American long distance record for sustained flight and getting Roosevelt up in the air, which had become something of a race among aviators. The flight was not planned. Roosevelt was there to praise Taft's tariff position. Hoxsey met him at the field and invited him up. Nobody remembers the speech. "By George, it was fine!" Roosevelt proclaimed after the four minute flight. Up in the air Hoxsey's passenger screamed, "War, army, aeroplane, bomb!" as he pretended to attack a Signal Corps installation below.[18]

* * *

The summer of 1910 was almost relaxing for the President. Congress finished up at the end of June, the earliest summer closing during Taft's four years. The disturbances of the coming mid-term elections, Roosevelt's ongoing Return from Elba, and the ensuing political circus in New York were the only shadows cast upon a pleasant vacation. From the Summer White House Taft ran the government and otherwise enjoyed golf, motoring, and boat rides up the coast. During a visit to Maine, Mrs. Taft became the first First Lady to visit another country when she spent an afternoon in Campobello, Canada.[19] For his autumn plans, Taft set aside a planned continental tour to visit the Canal Zone and Guantanamo Bay, Cuba.

The following Summer of 1911 was shorter, but more notable. The season opened with the First Baseball thrown before 16,000 in April (the home team lost), peaked with the Taft wedding anniversary party in June, and culminated with another huge Western Tour which all but killed Archie. It was a hot summer. Hundreds died as temperatures hit three digits across the country. Reporters marveled at the President's endurance. On his return from a trip to Indianapolis it was noted, "Mr. Taft showed the effects of the heat less than any other member of his party. Major Butt, his military aide, and Secretary Hilles were bedraggled and spent, but the President swung down from his car smiling and walked with almost a jaunty step to the automobile that was awaiting to convey him to the White House." Horace Taft publicly wondered how his brother could take the heat. Taft had one trick to

16. The law requiring annual renewal changed shortly after he received his license, and he was excused.

17. Butt, 6/27/10, unpublished passage and "Robert Taft in Auto Runs Over Laborer," 6/28/10, "Robert Taft Exonerated," 7/7/10, "Taft Rewards Gregorio," 8/14/10, and "President Here Again Next Week," 10/12/10, *NYT*, and Taft to R Taft, 6/27/10. Only two other incidents seem to have involved the White House autos, both the following summer. In August 1911, Taft's motorcar collided and locked with another car coming around a corner in Salem, Massachusetts. No one was hurt, and Butt told the man to send the repair bill to the White House (*NYT*, 8/14/11).

18. "Roosevelt up in Aeroplane," *NYT*, 10/12/10.

19. "Taft Spends Night on Canadian Border," *NYT*, 7/20/10.

keep cool. A ton of ice was daily placed below the newly opened Oval Office, and fans blew air over the ice and into the room. Congressmen who suffered through the 100-degree and Reciprocity heat at the Capitol were dismayed to find the President smiling behind his White House desk to a cool 80 degrees.[20]

Mrs. Taft's health remained shaky through the Spring of 1911. "How Mrs. Taft stands the strain is more than I can see," wrote Archie. (Of the President, he "has a constitution of iron.") Nevertheless, she visited the Capitol to see the Reciprocity debates and joined the President on his crazed New York banquet tours. These left everyone but the President "perfectly bedraggled and worn." In New York, Archie ordered the photographers away from her. "I asked them to go away and they informed me that they had been sent there and could not leave. I told them how nervous she was and again asked them to withdraw and they declined. I then lost my temper and said rather roughly, 'If you had a God damned bit of decency you would go and the first one of you who attempts to take a photograph will get punched in the head.'" They backed off. At Washington the train stopped short of the station so that Mrs. Taft could step directly to the limousine. That evening Taft and Archie motored for more than an hour. "I went where the spirit moved me," wrote Archie, "for the President went fast asleep and never woke up until we got back to the White House."[21]

Despite the heat wave, our prognosticators of the weather, doom, and fate would be dismayed at the downright perfect weather that attended the Taft Silver Wedding Anniversary celebration. Showers were predicted. Beautiful weather broke out. There was not a hint of 1912. For this we must look to a bizarre June demonstration at Times Square. Maybe the *Times* was headed for trouble or Oyster Bay was forewarned. Whatever it meant, it was sure strange to see mid–Summer snowflakes tossed about the city along with a 19-degree temperature drop.[22]

Mrs. Taft stoutly prepared perhaps the most extravagant party ever held at the White House. Drawing on a Venetian costume ball she invented at the Governor's palace in Manila, this was her crowning affair. Tycoons, generals, kings, emperors, the Congress and the Pope chipped in with every possible object made of the silver anniversary metal. Although not motivated by politics the generosity was certainly enhanced by an avoidance of politics; none dared neglect an offering, not even Roosevelt. He sent an antique silver bowl. "It is hideous to see such profligacy," went a since much-repeated Butt note. Less frequently quoted is his assessment of the party itself. "I believe it was the most brilliant function ever held in that historic mansion."[23]

The party was as much a celebration of Edison as the Tafts. Colored electric lights were strung in the White House, around the White House, and all over the White House, including the grounds and the fountains. What electric lamps couldn't reach, paper lanterns and flowers covered. Even the Washington Monument was lit up. To Mendelssohn's "Wedding

20. "Taft Back at Capital," "Brother Pities Taft," 7/6/11, and "How Taft Keeps Cool," 5/21/11, *NYT*. For a history of the Oval Office, see Seale, p. 756–760. It came of the extension Taft added to Roosevelt's "temporary" office building built just to the west of the White House. Roosevelt's tennis court gave way for it (the author hasn't seen that named as a cause of the breakup....)
21. Butt, 4/20/11, p. 613, 6/11/11, p. 675, and 4/28/11, p. 623, and 5/18/11, unpublished letter.
22. "72-mile Gale Brings a June Snowstorm," *NYT*, 6/17/11.
23. Butt's complaint was at the giving, not the receiving, which critical historians have turned into a slant on the Tafts. As for the word "profligacy," he used it frequently (Butt, undated letter, approx. 6/15/11, p. 679).

March" the President and Mrs. Taft descended the South steps to greet the more than 5,000 guests. "Most democratic," wrote the *Times*. Most gratifying it was for the Tafts. For Helen Taft, it couldn't have been finer.[24]

* * *

In August of 1910, the White House inquired of the White Company if a new steamer might be made available at a "fixed expense," maintenance included. The original plan from January of 1909 to lease a new car every year had suddenly taken a certain attraction. The President's travel budget had barely limped into the new fiscal year, and House Democrats nearly succeeded in curtailing it. The White company replied that for a $3,500 annual fee, it would provide a new car every year and "keep [it] in good working order."[25]

Taft had a new secretary. The first, Fred Carpenter, was loyal and efficient but, like his boss, not politically minded. He was shipped off to Morocco to tend to his keener instincts in diplomacy. He was replaced by Charles D. Norton, a Republican operative who came to the job through the Treasury Department. Norton was ambitious, wired, and appropriately scheming for the position of the President's secretary. (Butt thought that Norton always had a scheme going.) To match his new office, Norton wanted a car. Pierce-Arrow proved, as ever, beyond accommodating with a new 36 H.P. landaulet leased for $500 per year.[26]

Needless to say, and as great a car and as beloved to the President as it was, a White was not seven times a Pierce-Arrow. Likewise, a Pierce was not one-seventh a White; Clifton's deal was unbeatable.[27] Butt and Norton insisted on a better price for a steamer. Walter White got involved in October. He refused to budge. Instead, he told Norton that a new car was unnecessary. "Our cars are well built and we have always considered that they should last several seasons. The President has had his car now for two seasons and unless it has been badly abused by the driver it hardly seems to us that it should be necessary to make an exchange for a complete new car." White offered to overhaul the car as had been done the previous October. "It is a fad with some people to have a new car every year," he advised, "but we have never found that necessary and it has always seem[ed] to us that where a manufacturer advises a new car every year he shows lack

24. Mrs. Taft was defensive in her memoirs: "I have a right to be enthusiastic in my memory of that party because without enthusiasm it could not have been given at all. And why should not one be frankly grateful for success?" ("Recollections," p. 392, Butt, 6/20/11, p. 681 and "Tafts Receive 5,000 on Lawn," *NYT*, 6/20/11). See also Seale, pp. 760–763. Seale noted that it was probably the first time the White House had been fully illuminated, and that, so impressive was the production, "a scene beautiful beyond description," according to one account, Taft ordered the lights and the music repeated a second night for the public.
25. RH Johnston to CD Norton, 8/26/10 and 9/14/10.
26. The author has not found the original contract for the landaulet. A 1913 expense report notes a lease contract date of 9/29/10 (expense voucher, 6/19/13, NARA). See also a White House memo, 4/15/11 on insurance for the Pierce-Arrows: "2 cars were purchased by the government two years ago; one is the President's car with an extra touring body, and the other is Mrs. Taft's landaulet. These cost approximately $4,000 in the aggregate. In addition, one car is consigned for the use of the secretary. The government owns the two cars, and the Pierce-Arrow company owns the one that is used by the secretary. There is an agreement that these three cars will be replaced annually with new cars. This agreement provides that the annual rental for each car shall be $500, and that this will cover the cost of tires, oil, grease, repair parts, rebuilding in case of accident, overhauling and the maintenance of fire insurance. The government must furnish gasolene, and maintain liability insurance in case there is such insurance" (case file 755, reel 405). An invoice from the local Pierce dealer, dated 11/29/10 for a "D.C. license number" may have been for the Secretary's new car.
27. "Clifton was cagey!" writes Bernie Weis of the Pierce-Arrow Society (Weis to author, 3/16/02).

of confidence in his product." Nevertheless, White wrote, and without budging on the lease offer,

> If you believe that the car the President now has should be exchanged on account of abuse that you know of which it has been subjected, or because of some unusual or excessive strains such as arise from accidents which you are afraid have weakened the car and on that account you believe it is advisable that he should have a new car, we would be willing to make an exchange by taking in the old car and giving him a new one for $2800.00[28]

Evidently the White House felt that the "unusual and excessive strains" had been too much. Walter White might not have been aware of the kinds of trips the car suffered, such as when Mrs. Taft insisted, over her husband's amused objection, on taking a Maryland route up the Potomac River. "The President enjoyed her discomfortiture [*sic*] every time we got bumped," Archie wrote, "for she insisted that she knew all the good roads, whereas in fact she picked out all the bad ones." Or perhaps White didn't know how Taft regularly put all of his 300-plus pounds into the car with senators and congressmen to negotiate national affairs on joy rides through Rock Creek Park or "humming" through the Soldier's Home, a favorite Taft destination. Perhaps it was the political dead weight of all those standpatters whom the President shuffled about that strained the car's integrity, or the moral burden of his insurgent guests. Perhaps White didn't understand the extent of the strenuous and illegal scorching the President so enjoyed in the wonderful steamer. Or that when the President didn't use the car his military aide did. Archie snuck off with it whenever he could.[29] Or, perhaps, White knew all that and was therefore unwilling to lower the lease price. Nothing came of the offer until the following summer, when Walter White gave his final offer of a $2,000 credit on the old steamer towards a new one.[30] By then it was too late. As Archie wrote:

> The only question which arises as regards the purchase of a new car is the funds on hand.... The President unquestionably prefers to retain a steamer, but we have had such advantageous offers from other companies that from a purely business point of view it is hard to turn them down.[31]

On August 9, 1911, a 66 H.P. Pierce-Arrow 7-passenger touring car was delivered to Beverly. The invoice came to $6,278.50. The bill was rendered with "credit by car #7101 [the 1909 48 H.P. limousine]—in exchange: 6,278.50." Clifton explained, "The figures which we use are the list price figures of the new car, and to make an even exchange you will observe we have credited your car at the same price. That, of course, is simply a method of book-keeping necessary to complete our records." Clifton also noted that at the request of Major Butt the old car was to be kept for a time by the White House, the billing to be "based upon the pro rata of its time on the basis of five hundred dollars per year." A very, very sweet deal. The Tafts were most pleased. An exact duplicate of the 66 H.P. was ordered that November.

Norton, who had instigated the arrangement, was gone by then. He man-

28. Walter White to Norton, 10/26/10.
29. Butt, unpublished passages, 1/30/10, 4/9/11, and 6/26/10, pp. 413–414.
30. WC White to Butt, 7/28/11.
31. Butt to WC White, 8/1/11. Butt begged White to give him a good deal on a lease. He also complained that the car was still in good condition and ought be valued higher. There is no reply from White in the existing papers.

aged politics and publicity better than his predecessor, at times too much better. In September of 1910 he let it out to the press that insurgents would no longer be denied patronage.[32] What that meant was that they were previously being denied patronage. Good politics to do, but horrible to admit. Taft could only keep quiet about it rather than admit that he had no control over his Secretary. The next February, Norton threatened a special session just at the wrong time. The President's chances of running the Reciprocity bill through the Senate were rendered more difficult. Enraged Senators demanded a retraction and sat on the bill. Norton had to go.[33] In March, Archie learned Norton's final little game.

Norton ever tried to ingratiate himself to Butt. He was jealous of Archie's proximity to the President. Archie knew what was up. "I know him so thoroughly and having taken his measure as the most slippery dishonest man I have ever come into close contact ... he no longer annoys me and I find some pleasure in being with him, hearing him lie in every sentence and wondering what quirk his mind will take next." The comment followed an offer by Norton to help Archie double dip his expense reimbursements from the White House and the War Department. It is unclear what Norton was trying to gain from this, or if it was altogether improper, as Norton sought legal recommendations from the War Department. There was more to it. Butt continued,

> Then here is what he actually had the gall to say to me. "The only thing which stands in the way of doing this is a crippled condition of our finances, but if I carry out my plan and get the President's permission to sell the White Steamer and substitute it with Pierce Arrow cars I will have plenty of funds to do all this with and more. Now if you could say to the President as I have tried to explain to him that the White Steamer should be discarded I am sure he would consent for me to make the change before I go."
>
> I did not pretend to answer his offer to bribe me.... The entire matter above is summed up in the statement that Norton hopes by establishing only Pierce Arrow cars in the White House to get a Pierce Arrow for nothing for himself when he moves to New York. He has been trying to work it ever since he came to the President and Sloan tells me that he has been open in his demand for a car provided he could put through this deal. This is not suspicion but actual facts. I could prove it before a judge, but I merely want to place this here as one evidence of the man's character....[34]

The White House did not move to Pierce-Arrows through Norton's design. The White Company refused to lower the price, and its offers were rejected. The steamer was repaired instead of replaced. Negotiations moved to new Pierce-Arrows. Perhaps when Norton found himself being shoved out the door, he conspired to ride away from the White House

32. This letter was used extensively against the President, for without it there was no real evidence of his use of patronage. Norton stated that patronage was withheld against Republicans who "seemed to be in opposition to the administration's efforts to carry out the promises of the party platform." This was true, but it ought not have been admitted. The letter empowered critics of the Administration, such as the *American Review of Reviews*, which used it as an excuse for its about-face on the Administration (see Oct. 1910, pp. 388–389). The journal that was initially friendly towards Taft henceforth cloaked him in Norton's letter.
33. See "Taft Willing to Step Aside," 9/16/10 and "Deny Taft Threat and Blame Norton," 2/10/11, *NYT*, for two Norton gaffes. Pringle pointed to Taft's loose collar on Norton as a major cause of the President's difficulties, as Pringle saw them. Hammond wrote that Taft finally dumped Norton after his own personal intervention, coming at the insistence of Cabinet members and the press (Hammond, p. 551).
34. Butt, unpublished passage, 3/25/11 (edited here; Butt spelled gall "gaul").

(Form approved by the Comptroller of the Treasury February 8, 1908.)

The Executive Office.

VOUCHER FOR PURCHASES, AND SERVICES OTHER THAN PERSONAL.

APPROPRIATION: "CONTINGENT EXPENSES, EXECUTIVE OFFICE."

THE UNITED STATES,

TO The Pierce-Arrow Motor Car Company, DR.

ADDRESS: 1695 Elmwood Avenue, Buffalo, N. Y.

Date of Delivery or Service, 1911	Items.	Unit Price. Dolls.	Cts.	Per—	Amount. Dollars.	Cts.
	For repair and upkeep of three automobiles from September 1, to October 31, 1911,				500	00
	For repair and upkeep of one automobile from August 12, 1911, to October 27, 1911,				104	17
	Total,				604	17

MEMORANDUM DUPLICATE.

604. 17

604.17

604.17

Paid by Check No. 532615, dated Nov 16, 1911, on Treasurer of the United States, in favor of the principal, for $604.17

"For repair and upkeep of three automobiles." In 1910, the President's new secretary wanted a motor car. His wildest dreams were satisfied with a 36 H.P. Pierce-Arrow landaulet rented by the White House for $500 a year. The President got in on the deal the following year with an even exchange of his old car for a new one, a 66 H.P. also leased for $500 a year. The entire fleet was updated on the same terms. The Wilson administration quickly renewed the contract on March 22, 1913. (Courtesy National Archives and Records Administration) in one.[35] Just before leaving Washington, Norton tried to arrange a meeting with Clifton, who wired back, "Dispatch 22nd received too late to be in Washington today. Your existing arrangement elastic enough to provide for another car if desired on same terms as last one. Can come to Washington this week if you will name

In 1911, the White House ordered new sets of wheels from Pierce-Arrow. The 48 H.P. limousine was replaced by two 66 H.P. touring cars, and Mrs. Taft renewed her faith in the 36 H.P. landualet with a 1911 replacement. Here President Taft stands in the back of one of the 66 H.P's. (c. 1912, Courtesy Library of Congress)

35. Butt's views of Norton were severely colored by Norton's anti–Roosevelt machinations. However, Butt was not a liar. At best, there was a misunderstanding; at worst the accusation was true. Norton did request a ruling from the Army on the subject of Butt's expenses (see CH Whipple to Norton, 3/28/11 and memorandum dated 3/29/11, case file 1158, reel 412). Whatever happened, the author is unaware that Norton drove to his job as President of the First National Bank in New York in a gratis Pierce-Arrow (it was of Norton that the usher Hoover complained that a Taft secretary left for a position "with financial interests in New York"). That position elevated him far above an automobile freebie; then again, maybe that's why he so badly wanted one, to have a car to match the job.... There seem to have been three 36 H.P. landaulets delivered to the White House between 1910 and 1911, but only two were ever listed at any time in existing records. Perhaps Norton escaped in one after all. If he did, it was likely done properly, for, without judgment on Norton's character, graft was not in Col. Clifton's vocabulary. The author doubts a bribe was made, even if demanded. Clifton was a scrupulous manager. A 1913 sketch of him joked, "As you go down the hall to slip the purchasing agent a bit of graft the Colonel sticks his head in and catches you" (from *Hoo's Hoo and Wat's Wat in Gasolene*, by Henry Caldwell, p. 11). White House Historian William Seale wrote that Norton "convinced Taft that it was absurd to use a car [the steamer] that had to be driven to one of

day."[36] That Norton met with Clifton is uncertain. The import of Clifton's message was the "existing arrangement"—the lease for Norton's landaulet. Clifton thus, and ever adroitly, cut the deal for a new car—for Mrs. Taft. Now she took over. On April 29, Mrs. Taft wrote to Clifton,

> I received your notice about the cars, and am very much pleased at your doing so much more than you intended. The limousine I will have just as the other one was, '48 horse power, six cylinder Pierce-Arrow Limousine; But the landaulet which we take with the Touring Car to our Summer Cottage, the President has a great deal of trouble getting in and out of. *He is so big*. I think if you would give us the one which Mr. Hilles has now, it would be very much better for the President—*that is an inch and a half wider in the door, two inches would be better*, but I presume you make them of a certain size. I want the top to lower, as the Landau does. The Touring Car will be just as the old one was. I want very much to have a 66 Horse Power Touring Car, but I must wait for that. Send samples of cloth to put in the landaulet. I have not altogether decided upon the color yet. Thanking you ... for doing so much to please us.[37]

Mrs. Taft wanted the same pattern as the old landaulet. The fabric was unavailable. The local Pierce dealer, Cook & Stoddard, worked with her to choose another. In May she wrote Clifton to correct the shade of brown, "not tan," that she wanted for the landaulet. "I am extremely sorry that we could not come nearer to Mrs. Taft's views," wrote Clifton, "but we exhausted all the stocks available and certainly have shown due diligence." On July 12, Clifton wrote to Charles Hilles, Taft's new secretary, "I trust you will pardon my bothering you in the matter, but I wanted to be sure that it was being handled in a way that would meet with your entire approval." Oh, and by the way, he closed the letter, "Another thing I would like to bother you with is this: We have not rendered our bill for the current year—that is, on the arrangement from October to October [the lease for the secretary's car]. I would like to know your wishes concerning that, and would also like to know just what form you would like to have it put in."[38] Directly subtle, or vice versa, and either way superb.

The rejuvenation of the White House garage was made complete with a new Baker electric the next year. For $809.50 and the old car, a new $2,000 victoria was sent over. By the end of the year the fleet consisted of two 66 H.P.'s, two 36 H.P. landaulets, one of which was used by Hilles, the new Baker victoria and a Baker baggage car.[39]

* * *

35. (*cont.*) Washington's circles to be turned around. When Taft reluctantly agreed to auction it off in 1911, Norton was the winning bidder!" (p. 765; from conversation with Garrison Norton, 1982). Did Norton end up with the steamer instead of a Pierce? Perhaps, but the turning radius was not the reason why the steamer was shelved, and not just because it turned as well or better than other large cars of the day. Norton was no longer at the White House when that decision was made.
36. Clifton to Norton, 3/27/11
37. Mrs. Taft's reference to a 48 H.P. limousine was before it was decided to have 66 H.P.'s, the first of which was delivered to Beverly with a touring body. The limousine body was later placed on it for winter use (Helen Taft to C Clifton, as reprinted in "Helen Herron Taft: Influence and Automobiles," pp. 221–223; this letter does not appear in the Taft Papers).
38. Clifton to Hilles, 6/30/11 and 7/12/11.
39. Other sources here: White House memorandum by Charles Hilles, 11/29/11, Clifton to Hilles, 8/11/11 and 11/27/11, White House expense voucher, 9/7/12, NARA, and "Is Minus a Garage," *Evening Star*, 3/4/13. The new Baker survives in the Henry Ford Museum in Dearborn, Michigan. The previous November the dealer offered to lease the car for $600 a year—if he knew about the Pierce-Arrow arrangement, he certainly hadn't a clue of the price.

The original steamer chauffeur, George Robinson, was dismissed at the President's request in July of 1910. He was transferred back to the Quartermaster, which employed him as an automobile repairman and chauffeur. His replacement was Francis Robinson, who came to the Tafts in Massachusetts at the recommendation of the White Company.[40] Long was promoted to head chauffeur. One of his first tasks was to find someone to wash the cars at night. The Army night watchman refused, saying his orders prohibited it. Long turned to the Executive Office for help. "I want a man that will take the place of the night watchman and wash cars. The other night both cars were out and had to be left until next day to be washed. This will eventually ruin them." He also demanded that the watchman keep the stove burning "in order that the automobiles may not freeze up." The office wrote back, "Where did night watchman get his orders not to wash cars at night?" This led to a shake-up at the garage, and the watchman was replaced.[41]

Long took ill in June 1911, and Francis Robinson was promoted to head chauffeur. One of his first acts was to ask for a raise. Butt intervened and a raise was granted — to the two assistant chauffeurs. The head chauffeurs had already been given a $25 raise before Robinson's arrival. He and Long were kept at $125 a month. The second chauffeurs were given a ten dollar raise to $90. A more dramatic change occurred that year when the Quartermaster received authorization from Congress to demolish the stables and build a garage with chauffeurs' living quarters. The stables were torn down, and the horses, including the President's three and Archie's two saddle horses and the cow, were moved to a nearby Quartermasters stable. The garage was never built, possibly because the chauffeurs expressed no desire to live at the office. The automobiles were henceforth housed at a Quartermasters garage a few blocks away. The chauffeurs complained of the location for its distance from the White House and its unpaved driveway, which dirtied the cars.[42]

* * *

Ever looking to demonstrate the end of the sectional divide, Taft planned to attend the fifty-year anniversary of the Battle of Bull Run at Manassas, Virginia, on July, 21, 1911. The President chose the event to announce that the arbitration treaty with France was all but formally concluded. He would also engage in a little motoring politics, as it was on the eve of the Senate Reciprocity vote. Getting there he celebrated the automobile, the steamer in particular.

Taft was enjoying his evening motor rides as an escape from the heat, the "stuffy house," and politics. Archie suggested they drive to Manassas. He wrote, "Tomorrow we are going to motor to Manassas and while it will be rough [going] it will take his mind off Congress and his troubles and give him corduroy roads and bumps to

40. There was no reason given for George Robinson's dismissal. His transfer back to the Quartermasters was done at the request of the White House. He eventually wound up working as an Army chauffeur in San Francisco and Hawaii. He was discharged in 1913 after taking a leave of absence to be with his ill mother in Virginia. The Taft White House sent a letter recommending "sympathetic consideration" of one of his requests, so his favor remained there (R Forster to WR Pedigo, 3/1/13). Additionally, Gen. Edwards wrote, "He is a tip-top man, as far as I know, and any consideration you can show him...." (Edwards to JB Aleshire, 9/4/12, National Archives, QMG, RG92, Entry 89, box 6905). For Francis Robinson's recommendation by the White Company and Long's promotion, see Butt to Norton, undated, July, 1910 (case file 335, reel 330) and Norton to AE Long, 12/9/10 (case file 502B, reel 397).

41. White House memorandums, 11/30/10 and undated (case file 502B, reel 397).

42. "Is Minus a Garage," *Evening Star*, 3/4/13. It was later called the "Army Motor Service Garage" ("The President's Car," *American Motorist*, March, 1925, p. 20).

think about instead of Schedule K and what other pieces of deviltry La Follette is planning."[43]

Afterwards, Archie wrote to Clara, "Of course you have read the absurd accounts of our trip to Manassas. Ridiculous as it all sounds I fear it is not exaggerated, for a more novel day I have never had in all my varied experiences with Presidents." Archie laughed at the press accounts of the amazing day. The press men had gathered at the Willard Hotel that night to put together their stories:

> Of course they put phrases into the mouths of all of us, had the President doing things which he never did, gave accounts of me swimming the fords and rescuing Senators which I did not do, and even rescuing young women in runaways which also formed a part of their imaginative accounts of the day. The President was in fine feather and did say and do many things which were far better than were attributed to him in the press, I did forge two streams one time up to my armpits ... and three times I did get out of the motor bare legged to lead frightened horses by the automobiles.[44]

It all started at the White House at half-past noon with a train of four cars, the President in the lead in the steamer with his Virginia hosts, Rep. Carlin and Senator Martin. In the second car ran the White House publicist and other aides, and the last two cars consisted of Secret Servicemen and reporters. It was a perfect day. (No portents.) Without incident the President made it to Falls Church, Virginia, although the reporters' car "came to grief" before crossing the river. They hired another, smaller car and hustled to catch up.

At this first stop Taft took lemonade and made a speech to three hundred in praise of Carlin, their representative. Heading next to Fairfax City they drove towards a storm front. (Finally, a sign.) The Quartermasters' chauffeur James Rundle let out the throttle for "some swift and dangerous running," Butt wrote, which undoubtedly thrilled the President.[45] The lead car made Fairfax just ahead of the downpour, which the others, unable to keep pace, took fully.

Taft jumped from the car into the cover of the Fairfax courthouse. The mayor welcomed him and insisted he review the town's proudest possession, George Washington's will. The President appropriately marveled at the document and commented on the general perfection of Washington's character. He also greeted a party of Senators, including Bacon of Georgia and Nelson of Minnesota, who had fifty years before faced off on opposite sides of the war, Bacon having fought at Manassas. They arrived earlier in Senator Brandegee's personal motor, a "big" car. Then the President slipped away for a lunch at Senator Thornton's house that delighted Archie. "A perfect Virginia midday meal ... overflowing with fried chicken ...

43. Butt, unpublished passage, 7/20/11 (edited here for spelling and grammar).

44. From Butt, 7/22/11, pp. 702–710, "Has Strenuous Trip," *Evening Star*, 7/22/11, and "Taft at Bull Run," *NYT*, 7/22/11. The accounts of the *Evening Star* and the *Times* kept to Butt's stories. For a look at the road conditions Taft encountered see "Auto Trip to Warrenton, VA., Via Manassas and Bull Run," *Evening Star*, 11/28/09. "The earth is of such a character that in wet weather it would be almost impassable.... On numerous occasions Bull Run creek would become a raging torrent...."

45. Rundle managed the steamer in Washington while the other chauffeurs were at Beverly. Quartermaster General Aleshire recommended him to the White House: "We have in our employment a most excellent chauffeur, Mr. Rundell [*sic*], who was recommended to us by the White Steamer Company. Mr. Rundell has had four years experience in the shops of the White Steamer Company. He is a man of excellent habits; does not smoke or drink; is of good appearance; quiet; neat; an expert chauffeur in every respect; and in my opinion possesses every qualification that a chauffeur for the White House should have" (JB Aleshire to CD Norton, 7/19/10; Butt and the White House payroll spell his name "Rundle"). Butt liked Rundle.

Virginia ham ... real corn bread hot and crisp ... which melts away in the mouth and tastes of the meal of which it is made."

They left at 2:45 to clear skies (now what?)— and horrible roads, "the worst road I have ever seen," Archie wrote. The already bad Warrenton pike was rendered "terrific" by the storm, "the worst stretch of road President Taft's big steamer had ever encountered," wrote a reporter, with ruts and puddles that re-

In July 1911, Taft made a remarkable automobile journey from Washington to Manassas, Virginia, to celebrate the anniversary of the Battle of Bull Run. Major Butt wrote, "Ridiculous as it all sounds I fear it is not exaggerated, for a more novel day I have never had in all my varied experiences with Presidents." The President's beloved, although now rickety, 1909 White steamer proved itself magnificent that day. A thunderstorm made the normally sedate Virginia streams rage, but the President wouldn't be held back. Approaching one, his party encountered a group of Senators stuck mid-stream. Taft ordered Butt to test the water, which came to above his waist. The President ordered the car ahead, anyway. The chauffeur raised the steamer to full power, and it pushed through. Passing the Senators, Taft called, "Oh you old Standpatters!" To the Major, Taft said, "What would you have done if you had brought that old gas car which you wanted to bring?" (These photos depicting a similar scene are taken from a White "Pathfinder" expedition near Roanoke, Virginia, of May–June 1909; Courtesy Henry Merkel)

sembled "hog ponds." The road was the least of it. The thunderstorm had endowed the "peaceful little" Virginia streams with torrents. When the President's train approached one they discovered Senator Brandegee's car stranded mid-stream.

"Much to the enjoyment of the onlookers," Archie kicked off his boots and waded in to gauge the depth. Here the steamer proved its worth. "His pride in this old rickety car knows no bounds," wrote Archie, "and he would willingly have gone through double the hardships ... to tell Mrs. Taft what his motor can do in a pinch." With Butt up to his waist in water and "frantic" Senators warning them not to cross, Taft ordered the car forward. Rundle, "our game little chauffeur," increased the pressure, knowing the burner would be doused but counting on the built-up steam to carry through. As the steamer forged sixty feet of water the President stood in back and laughed at the Senators. "Oh you old Standpatters," he yelled. The *Evening Star* noted, "It was a sickly sort of a smile the President received in turn." To Archie, Taft said, "what would you have done if you had brought that old gas car which you wanted to bring?" Hilles winked at Butt. "It's lucky for us we got his old car repaired in time for this trip, isn't it?"

Two other cars made it through, and the President insisted the passengers give their seats to the Senators who were rescued by a wagon. Taft joked, "It is hard to choose but I feel that I must save old Nelson's vote to the insurgents tomorrow so we will just take him in." To Nelson, who was intractably against Reciprocity, Taft said, "This is not a bribe, old man. La Follette will need your vote more than I do, so bury your consciences and come in." Nelson sat uncomfortably between the President and Senator Martin, "who is no sylph," noted the *Times*. The reporters were left on the opposite bank. Their car was smaller and the driver didn't dare. Their distress was relieved when a local man told them, "You fellers needn't worry. Them cars won't git nowhar. Two miles further on Willow Spring run empties into Rocky run and there ain't no automobiles built that can cross it after this storm."

Indeed. A few miles later the steamer approached Rocky Run. Taft ordered Archie to test it. The water was chest-high. "Manassas or bust," the President cried. Butt ordered the Secret Service car in first, since it was a hired car and "would make no difference if it was stranded." It stuck half-way. Seniority again weeded out the troops, and the Senators piled into the two remaining cars. They backtracked to the first crossing which had risen another foot, as Archie discovered the hard way. The second car tried it and stuck. Butt ordered Rundle to pay it no mind. The steamer pushed through and up the bank. They left the Senators behind. The rest of the trip was marked by several frightened horses, which Butt walked past the steamer, the odd view of his socks draped over the windshield, and horrific dust near Manassas, which hadn't a drop of rain. The President's steamer and the reporters' car were the only to arrive. It was now quarter to six, almost two hours late.

The old veterans gave the President "a rousing welcome." He meant to give two speeches, one at the battlefield in honor of the soldiers and the other on arbitration in town. In what Butt called a "flub-dubb speech ... which brought tears to the eyes of the veterans of both sides" he deftly joined both themes into a review of the battle, the bravery of the soldiers, and an appeal for the cause of peace. He drew laughter and applause by noting that the pace of the Congressmen to arrive for the day's celebration was much slower than the

Only two cars of the presidential procession made it to Manassas, the White and that of a group of journalists who found a drier route. Taft is pictured here speaking at Manassas, telling the Civil War veterans and locals, "Virginia is a hospitable State. Its soil and its stream gather about you and cling to you." (Courtesy Library of Congress)

Shortly after the Manassas trip, Taft again put the White steamer to some vigorous use. On a whim, he decided to run up to Baltimore, leaving the Secret Service agents behind. He made it there in two hours, including twenty minutes spent repairing a tire. As the steamer pulled up to a service station for fuel, a crowd gathered, which made Butt nervous. "Speech, speech!" yelled the onlookers to the amused President. He bowed and smiled, but otherwise kept quiet. A newspaper reported, "The last the spectators saw was the big form of the President, shrouded in the clouds of dust which the machine left behind, waving farewell." The trip home was scorching at its best. "Coming back," Butt wrote, "we made the machine sing.... The wood work of the car caught fire from the heat generated by the speed we were traveling." They made it in one hour, twenty-five minutes, "no fudging," wrote Butt proudly. "Of course the Secret Service men will be furious and they ought to be but there is no managing the President when he takes it in his head to go somewhere.... Some day he will get left at this game when he finds himself spilled on the roadside or huddled in some corner by a jam of people." After their return to Washington, Butt asked the President if he could send the car back to the garage. Taft told him to keep it prepared for an after-dinner ride. Rundle, the chauffeur, "rolled his eyes to heaven ... but this only shows how mad he is about motoring and the faster he goes the happier he is." One of Butt's last letters from February of 1912 noted, "My trouble is auto-intoxication...." Pictured here is a modern photograph of the original 1909 White Steamer, the first Presidential automobile, which today resides in the great automotive collection at the Heritage Museum, Sandwich, Massachusetts, not far from the North Shore roads Taft tore up in the great car. (Courtesy Heritage Museums & Gardens, Sandwich, Cape Cod, Massachusetts).

departure of northern Congressmen fifty years before, who scurried back to Washington when their army fell apart. "A visit to Virginia conjures up sweet reminiscences—reminiscences of Virginia beauty, chivalry, and hospitality. I am glad to be on the soil of Virginia—some of it has adhered to me," the President laughed. "I am sorry to be late, but Virginia is a hospitable State. Its soil and its stream gather about you and cling to you."

Another important event that day

came of a promise extracted somewhere along the bouncing roads or crossing swollen streams that only three Democratic Senators would vote against Reciprocity. The truth to the President's cutting joke that Nelson's vote was more important to La Follette than to him was assured.

24

Progressively Unhappy and a Happy Discontent

It was in 1911 that progressivism replaced insurgency. Insurgency was dissent, a turning away. Progressive meant action, forward movement. The terminology was important. "Progressive" meant any number of things, but mostly the badge endowed the bearer with the magical properties of righteousness, "politically correct" to the modern ear. Nevertheless, the progressive express, which Roosevelt earlier set running and later grabbed a hold like a late-running passenger, ran on discontent.[1]

"We wish the progressive would be a little more definite and specific," the *Times* complained following a Woodrow Wilson speech. Dr. Syntax was only then learning the gospel. "Our laws lag almost a generation behind our business conditions and our political exigencies," he stated.[2] The progressive faith was as short on specifics in its solutions as it was on defining the problems. The problems were the "interests"; the solutions were "direct" everything.

In early 1911, La Follette organized the National Republican Progressive League. Its "Declaration of Principles"—a hyped appeal to Jefferson's Declaration, mimicking even its structure of a complaint and a resolution—cited the crimes against the people that added up to very little other than that in the Payne tariff and the 1910 session "the public interest has been baffled and defeated." It committed the "undersigned" to the proposition that "popular government is fundamental to all other questions." The first three "principles" demanded "direct" elections of Senators, "elective officials," and convention delegates. The last two went to "the Initiative, Referendum and Recall" and a "corrupt practices act."[3] That was all very well, but how exactly it would bring about railroad reform was left unclear, other than that progressives should win at the polls, as

1. The normal story is that the intellectual force behind the movement was Herbert Croly's 1909 book, *The Promise of American Life*, a progressive anthem that turned Theodore Roosevelt into a rabid liberal. Rather, Croly appealed to Roosevelt's innate spirit of rebellion. Croly provided fuel but did not set the fire. Croly's work was itself a synthesis and "derivative" of larger, older doctrines (see *The Lost Promise of Progressivism*, by Eldon J. Eisenach, University of Kansas Press, 1994; p. 39).
2. "The Progressive Gospel," *NYT* editorial, 1/19/12.
3. La Follette, pp. 495–496.

Roosevelt concluded in the New Nationalism speech. On Roosevelt's other hand, his excuse for not enlisting in La Follette's League was that the progressives should be concerned with more concrete issues.[4] The *Times*, too, wondered, "If they abandon to the States the various whimsies which make up the doctrine of direct government by the people, what is left? Nothing we can see, save a bald, undisguised, old-fashioned hunt for offices. Greed for power remains their only discoverable principle."

At the December 1911 Gridiron dinner, the progressives were on the menu. The satire was vicious and precise. "Attracted by agitation," Dante came to visit. He was treated to a parade of the latest political fads. Marguerite Democracy flirted with the Progressive Faust. Miss Prohibition and Miss Socialism, "who wanted not dynamite but beer"—a dig at socialists in Milwaukee—cavorted with "Miss Populist" and "Miss Greenback ... whose blond wig and pink tights had been stolen by Miss Free Silver." Progressive Faust was treated to a rendition from the Stand-Pat Mephisto:

When new parties bid defiance to my glorious past,
I predict that each alliance I will rule at last,
At their wooing and their chaffing,
How can I refrain from laughing,
I will rule at last.

Marguerite Democracy protested. "You've had your day, Stand-Pat. Your ways we shun." Stand-pat Mephisto replied,

I'll gather you all in ere I have done;
for every party, as it starts in life,
Is led by a reformer, brave in strife;
And when his cause is won he does his best
To firmly hold it safe 'gainst every test,
Defending each assault with all his powers.
We're all stand-patters — after we get ours.[5]

The Gridiron the next February hit again. The progressive candidate for President of the Club was accused of "stealing all the planks in Bryan's platform." The candidate, a Rough Rider, replied, "That is real progressiveness. Progressives take anything they can find. All we want is something to divert the people until we get the jobs."[6]

* * *

In June of 1911, the *Times* declared "Mr. Taft's Progressiveness." Understanding that this was a conservative paper in matters of business and law, although non-partisan, it was quite an admission. Except in the company of "tariff reduction," the word "progressive" was not often used as a compliment on those pages. The *Times* fretted all of 1910 that Taft was a legislative busybody who would bury the nation in new laws. Suddenly the paper discovered in Taft a progressive it could like. What had changed was not just the paper's elation over Reciprocity.

4. See Roosevelt to J Bourne, 1/2/11 ("The Letters of Theodore Roosevelt," Harvard University Press, 1954, Vol. VII, pp. 196–198) and Anderson, p. 181. The New Nationalism speech ended with an appeal "to get the right type of good citizenship, and, to get it, we must have progress, and our public men must be genuinely progressive." In declining to join the League, Roosevelt wrote that direct primaries and Senate elections were "merely means to ends." The progressives should stick to "physical valuation of railroads" and "workmen's compensation," which were "ends." He emphasized that they mustn't become "a small knot of men ... trying to dictate popular polices instead of rallying the people to their support."
5. "Peace Dove a Goose at Gridiron Dinner," *NYT*, 12/10/11.
6. "Roast Candidates At Gridiron Feast," *NYT*, 2/18/12. Taft didn't escape the grilling. When the standing President of the Gridiron was asked why he should be re-elected, the reply was that "his best qualification is that he [already] has the job." See Hofstadter, pp. 132–133, for a discussion of Roosevelt's absorption of Bryan's radicalism.

What makes Taft so illusive to history was equally confusing to his contemporaries. The confusion comes of the impression that Taft juggled through his moment. To appreciate him took a lucidity that was rare in an age of hysteria when change became its own cause. So it was that the newspaper that in early 1910 portrayed Taft as weakly appeasing both liberal and conservative came to the conclusion the following year that the man was in the driver's seat after all:

> The President's hand on the steering wheel is as calm and sure as that of the motorist who takes a long look down the road, while some of the zealous reformers are as unsteady and insecure as the driver who looks a yard or two ahead and tries to dodge all the little stones.... There is indeed need for Republicans who shall be sanely progressive, and for Democrats who shall be conservative.... Day by day the President is revealing himself as the Progressive on the old issues, rather than as the inventor of new issues. Of issues we have too many, and of leaders who are safe to follow there is a painful deficiency.[7]

Dr. Schurman of Cornell concurred with the definition. "The reactionary worships the past, the radical flouts the past, but the Progressive, while retaining all that is sound and valuable in the past, also vitalizes it with the living ideas of the present and creates new institutions for our day and generation."[8] He was talking about Taft.

So what was progressive, and what was radical? At Peoria in September of 1911, Taft explained:

> I have been charged with not being progressive, and therefore to be condemned. What one does, this man thinks is progressive, another man thinks is retrograde. There are, however, two great schools—one which believes that the present is not perfect perhaps, but that changes from it would be dangerous. They are the strictly conservative, and perhaps are known as the reactionary. Then there is another class at the other end which is extreme in its view that the whole present condition is wrong, and there must be radical changes if we live at all. Now, I think—perhaps I am wrong about it—but I think I am going along in the middle of the road between those two; at least that is what I am trying to do, and I believe the legislation of this Administration has been along that line.[9]

Taft accused the peddlers of reform "nostrums" of selling to a demand of their own creation. This talk followed almost a year to the day Roosevelt's New Nationalism address, also given to Civil War veterans. Taft replied:

> Higher aims for the betterment of society ... have invited from the active minded of to-day suggestions of remedies that are so extreme that the medicine to many of us seems worse than the disease. Those who are charged with the responsibility and sobered with the difficulties, find ourselves in the middle of the road, resisting the tendency to Socialism on the one hand and the inertia of reactionary contentment with present evils and ambitions for greater concentration of financial power on the other: but we are gradually solving the problem."[10]

He next gave it a perspective that would be lost on the Bull Moose crusaders to Armageddon during the Apocalypse of

7. "Mr. Taft's Progressiveness," *NYT* editorial, 6/24/11. The occasion was a Taft speech on the currency reform.
8. "Schurman Predicts Roosevelt's Defeat," *NYT*, 3/20/12.
9. "Trusts, Taft Says, Must Obey the Law," *NYT*, 9/23/11. For the specifics all anybody had to do was go back to Taft's inaugural address, by which he stayed course.
10. "Taft Warns Against Extremist Methods," *NYT*, 8/24/11. Please note the sarcasm in the "active minded" reference.

1912. "The present does not bring difficulties so great as you had to meet and overcome in '61," he said to Roosevelt as much as to the old soldiers. Those present difficulties will be met by the

> level-headed, the practical, and the courageous among us, and by reducing the influence of the demagogue and the theoretical extremists on the one hand, and the reactionary influence of combinations of wealth on politics and progress on the other. Its solution will be consistent with the preservation of our ancient institutions of personal liberty and private property under the Constitution.

So here was the President, stuck between the extremes, hands firmly on the wheel, intent upon the great American middle road. If it was his self-appointed role to mediate his age, he also took it upon himself to ensure that 1789 remained intact, for which a good many had little nostalgia. Maybe he didn't win many votes with that speech in August of 1911, but he set the rules for the contest of 1912 and the progressive era itself. "My own forecast of the coming campaign," Taft wrote his friend and most astute political adviser, Otto Bannard, "is that it will veer from the tariff round to an issue between extreme radicalism and moderate conservatism."[11]

* * *

If they wished, Americans of 1911 could look upon their day as the best of times. The country was never more prosperous, and that prosperity had never reached more Americans.[12] Strikes were numerous but comparatively peaceful and contained to local issues and places. While Paris was shuttered by turmoil, labor strife was not part of the American national dialogue. The spell of anarchy that claimed McKinley was left to the foreigners. The riots were in Budapest, not New York. The 1912 elections in Germany foretold the disorder: the Reichstag was split among seven factions, with socialists taking the largest single slice.[13] Even Merrie England was beset by tumult. While suffragettes threw rocks through the P.M.'s windows, George Bernard Shaw declared Jesus a failure.[14] Was the U.S. immune?

Twenty-one lives proved to Americans the seriousness of radical words when a bomb tore through the offices of the Los

11. Taft to Bannard, 9/10/11.
12. Without apologies to the Howard Zinn school of populist history: workers were better off in 1911 than at any time before in American history. And things were getting better. Sanitation, health, salary, working conditions and hours, housing, and recreation were in improvement, and not just as a result of agitation — or automobiles. Prosperity brought it. On December, 25, 1911, the *Times* took an amazed look around and found that "Wage-earners as well as holders of securities have reason for joy this Christmas. Not since 1907 have there been better times for the good workman ... the cost of living has fallen in proportion that wages will buy more...." Not only that, productivity was such that labor's "improving condition is not due to greater effort, but the reverse" (editorial, 12/25/11). For modern analysis, see "Historical Statistics of the United States," by the Bureau of the Census, 1976, pp. 322 for "Consumption Expenditures of City Wage- and Clerical-Worker Families of 2 or More Persons: 1888–91 to 1960–61." These statistics are as nebulous as any, but the upward trend in household income is clear, rising from an average income in 1888–91 of $573 to $651 in 1901, then jumping to $1505 for 1917–1919. The Taft period of 1909–1913 marked the period of highest income growth, which occurred between the Panic of 1907 and Wilson's war economy. Hofstadter notes that those on fixed salaries lost ground during the price increases of the 1897–1914 period (p. 170). Your author agrees that the cost of living was a "dominant motif in American life" (p. 171) but disagrees that it outpaced the rise in incomes and general wealth. The perception was strong enough for Democrats to make it an issue in the 1912 campaign and, as Hofstadter wrote, give "mass appeal and political force to many Progressive issues...." (p. 173). Taft countered with frequent talks, messages to Congress, and government studies on the subject. He ran in 1912 on "prosperity"— a legitimate defense against complaints of the cost of living.
13. "The Results in Germany," *NYT* editorial, 1/27/12.
14. See "G.B. Shaw's View of Christ," *NYT*, 5/30/11.

Angeles *Times* in 1911.[15] Accused were the brothers McNamara. The leftist world came to their defense. When the brothers confessed, Gompers wept. Their counsel, Clarence Darrow, found himself in the awkward position of being himself a lawyer's client over accusations of an aggressive outreach to the jury.[16] A sweep of New York and Indianapolis found that the McNamaras were not lone players. The terror went away. Of greater concern to Americans was the rising cost of eggs.

The agitation that plagued the world was not demonstrative in American culture. It infected political leaders, reformers, and their press, but it was not manifest in daily life. Good Americans were too busy mortgaging the house to buy automobiles to worry about Congressman Victor Berger's calls for the abolishment of the Senate, Eugene Debs' scheme to discard the Supreme Court, or La Follette's plan for federal ownership of Alaskan railroads and coal mines.[17] Progressive Walter Weyl complained that "an increasing bitterness is felt by a majority which is no worse but better off than before." Huh? He fretted that the sky-high bank accounts of the "plutocracy" made the professional and middle classes jealous. So we have the "income gap," the worst crisis Weyl could conjure.[18]

The 1910 election, presumably over Republican insurgency, was more about cleaning house than anything else. Using a broom called tariff the Democrats ran the cyclical shakeup that necessarily follows lengthy incumbency. Most Republican insurgents survived the election, only the noise was greater than their numbers. The Democrats swept. The only vital national issue was the tariff—a local issue made national by the insurgents, thus empowering Democracy. Where local representatives were out of step they lost, as Tawney learned the hard way.[19] The political trend was change. New blood won, including socialists in Milwaukee, their first try to govern a major city. (It didn't work.) In 1911, Woodrow Wilson toured Nebraska. At one stop he was introduced to the mayor, a socialist. "Are there that many socialists in your town?" Wilson asked. "Oh, no," replied the mayor. "My vote was 20 percent socialist and 80 percent protest."[20] Political philosophy didn't matter to the voters. They voted for change, not socialism, for insurgency, not progressivism.

Taft saw it coming. In 1910 he wrote,

> The present political situation is a curious one. Indeed, the condition of public opinion is curious. It seems to be feeling

15. The incident is infrequently mentioned in histories which otherwise point to the Triangle Shirtwaist Company fire of 1911 as the most significant social disturbance of the Taft era. That fire was indeed horrible and the carnage far worse, with 146 dead, than the Los Angeles bombing. However, altogether the "dynamite outrages" claimed over five years upwards one hundred lives and millions in property. James McNamara confessed and was sentenced to life for the *L.A. Times* attack; his brother, John, confessed to another bombing and was sentenced to fifteen years. The McNamaras held leadership positions in the Structural Ironworkers Association, based in Indianapolis, and were associated with the Samuel Gompers's American Federation of Labor. Gompers, who abhorred violence, was not involved in the bombings. For more on the "dynamite" outrages, see the *American Review of Reviews*, Jan. 1912, pp. 8–12 and March, 1912, p. 275; the former article correctly pointed to the particularly insidious aspect of the *L.A. Times* bombing in that it was an attack on the freedom of expression.
16. "Darrow Indicted on Bribe Charges," *NYT*, 1/30/12.
17. "Wants Senate Abolished," 4/28/11, "Debs Cries Against the Supreme Court," 1/14/11 (in the name of Abraham Lincoln....), and "La Follette Cure for Alaska's Ills," 8/22/11, *NYT*.
18. From Weyl's "The New Democracy," 1914, pp. 242–243, per Hofstadter, p. 147.
19. One of the complaints against Tawney was that he cared more for national than local politics (see "The Power of the People," *Pioneer Press* editorial, 9/22/10).
20. "Rush to See Wilson on Washington Visit," *NYT*, 6/5/11. Hofstadter counted 1,039 socialists elected to local offices, including 56 mayors, across the country by mid–1912 (footnote 7, p. 239).

> the effect of the flood of misrepresentation which manifests itself in a protest against everything and everybody who is not in the forefront crying "Stop thief!" It is not a natural condition, however, and we people of America are so sane on the whole that I look for a change, not rapid, but sufficiently marked in the course of three or four years to give those of us that have not been carried off our feet hope of the Republic. With such a tremendous cry and so little wool I think the people will realize it after a while and give credit to those of us who are trying to make progress by legislation and by things done.[21]

Agitation devolved into a hundred different movements, which cumulatively added to change, but a change without coherence. The change was from, not to. Liquor moved politics in Kansas, Maine, Texas, and Kentucky. California fretted over Japanese immigration, the politics of dynamite, and corrupt local politics and overzealous fights against it. New York was busy as always trying to figure out which machine, Democratic Tammany or Republican Albany, should snag the most booty. The Midwest was caught up in the "local option," a reform to provide home rule to municipalities that were run by statewide legislatures. The region was defining insurgency as normalcy, or going Democratic. The far West was beyond definition: half wanted Roosevelt back, half wanted tariff reform, while another half wanted protection; half again wanted conservation, and the final half wanted to expel the federal government from its borders. More than any other state, Ohio reflected the situation. The 1910 census showed that the Buckeyes were half urban. Yet between Cleveland, Cincinnati, Columbus, Dayton, Toledo, and Akron not one city or any combination dominated state politics, which were fractured like the rest of the country. Taft's homeland was completely unmanageable.

"Kansas is practically all insurgent," wrote one wry commentator. Yet "Kansas doesn't care much about the tariff because it is thickly populated with farmers who do their haying in automobiles ... it is hardly worth while to start a discussion with a Kansas farmer about Schedule 18 of the Payne bill. He will look at you with a fishy eye and change the subject to the question of the relative merits of Panhards and Packards ... nevertheless Kansas is a red hot insurgent state." Of its neighbor, "You have to be an insurgent to be a regular in Nebraska."[22]

Reform was everywhere. The country had become dissatisfied with itself, although the problems it saw in the mirror were cosmetic. The justly upset — miners in Colorado, textile workers in Massachusetts, and others of no voice — would vent outrage more explicitly and remain more unheard than the growing American middle class, whose unrest was a new-found luxury. Like the Edwardians who reached into their boudoirs for social reform, Americans of 1910 couldn't distinguish between the annoyances of daily life and true suffering. As a result, hysteria turned petty or just plain bizarre.

The cumulative outlook was summed up by a drunken man whom Taft watched stagger along a Washington street. Muttering to himself about a debt he felt Congress ought pay for him, the old man said, "And this man Taft, I don't like him neither. He don't do nothin', they say, but travel and spend money. I won't take off my hat to him. They say they will have me 'rested if I doesn't, but I don't care.

21. Taft to W D Evans, 9/12/10.
22. "Nationwide Split of Republicans," *NYT*, 1/30/10, by "a Washington observer." A great article, very insightful and very funny.

Roosevelt—well, I don't think much of him nuther, but they say he knows more 'an old Taft." Laughing with the President, Archie rather keenly observed, "I think he is monopolizing the air of the nation."[23]

Railroader turned social critic J.J. Hill barely survived his own hysteria. His various predictions included that the automobile craze would bankrupt the country, massive unemployment would beset 1911, and the world would soon starve from overpopulation.[24] Waiters in New York staged dinner-hour strikes by blowing whistles in the dining room and bursting into the streets, which prompted one diner in evening dress to ask, "Good heavens, are we going to have this sort of thing on this side of the pond also? I thought I had fled all that when I left England."[25]

The Detroit Tigers joined the fun with a strike in protest of the suspension of Ty Cobb for beating a fan. Future Supreme Court Justice Louis Brandeis told Congress the "dynamite outrages" were the result of despair of the laboring classes at the "great controlling trusts." If there was any truth to Brandeis's assertion, the list of evil doers included the ice trust, the paper trust, the bathtub trust, the baseball trust, the whiskey trust, the movie trust, the electric trust, the magazine trust, the cereal trust, the wire trust, & etc. Hardly an industry was left to serve the outrage of the Attorney General. One of Roosevelt's hysterias was over ethnicity; a white woman who gave birth to quadruplets won his congratulations for her "anti-race suicide accomplishment." He also became the first male "Spug," a group dedicated to the "prevention of useless giving" of Christmas presents. Samuel Gompers demonstrated his contempt for the times by trampling an American flag, as did a group of socialists at Union Square in New York. At that city's meat markets, angry women poured kerosene and set steaks afire in protest of the "high cost of living," a crisis that was ridiculed as the "cost of high living." Discontent got truly outrageous when a robber complained that he hit "every house in Richmond Hill" and came up with only twenty-five cents.

It was a wacky time. And there were wacky solutions about. One, in response to the hysteria over automobile accidents, was an inverted cowcatcher made of a web of rope that was to be mounted on the front of automobiles to spare pedestrians. A St. Louis woman sought to "regenerate" poor girls by placing them in a "refined" home once a week. Another woman's solution to socialism was to divorce her husband, as he had turned violent after taking up the red flag. Sinclair Lewis, the Marxist writer, had it worse. His nasty and very public divorce proceedings gave him a very personal take on the socialist demand to end the institution of marriage. His wife ran off with Harry Kemp, the "hobo poet." Her discontent must have been marvelous.

Outrage came cheap in the early 1910s. Even the vintage year 1776 was in liquidation. An abolitionist called the

23. Butt, 2/9/12, pp. 839–840.

24. Taft responded to Hill's starvation theories by telling farmers in Kansas City that the American farmer could feed 200 million ("Taft Says 200,000,000 Can Be Fed Here," 9/26/11, *NYT*). One of the few predictions this Cassandra got right was that the Republicans would lose in 1910 if the tariff were not revised sufficiently downward ("J.J. Hill Says Tariff Must Come Down or Republicans Go Out," *NYT* 4/16/09).

25. This section from "Vanderbilt Guests See Waiters Go Out," 5/16/12, "Detroit Baseball Club on Strike," 5/18/12, "Brandeis Denies Economies of Trusts," 12/15/11, "4 Births Please Colonel," 10/13/10, "Enroll Roosevelt as First Man Spug," 12/14/12, "Gompers Trampled on American Flag," 1/02/11, "The Insult to the Flag," editorial, 5/3/12, "Rioting Women Put Kerosene on Meats," 6/8/12, "Burglar Caught, Disgusted," 7/16/11, "Novel Auto Invention to Lessen Street Dangers," 6/25/11, "To Regenerate Slum Girls," 5/12/12, "Wife Blames Socialism," 4/23/11, "No Divorce for Sinclair," 12/21/11, "Constitution Out of Date," 12/27/11, and "Denounces Our Forefathers," 2/23/10, *NYT*. "Cost of high living" from Hammond, p. 554.

Founders drunkards who "would not be tolerated today." A labor attorney declared the Constitution was drafted by witch burners. Historian Charles Beard's career was launched in 1913 with publication of his "Economic Interpretation of the Constitution of the United States," which, to the mind set of the day, equated Washington with Rockefeller. (Taft despised the book.) Serious people were taken by silly ideas.

One doom booster that Taft found particularly grating was the normally sane Senator Borah, who had lately succumbed to the national distemper. Following Taft's emphatic ACA speech, the President joined a Republican Club banquet just in time to hear Borah say, "I am in full sympathy with those who are at war with present conditions." Calling America the most "lawless" of civilized countries, the Senator compared the McNamara brothers to Standard Oil. He ended with an almost biblical appeal for justice and security, "for all, rich and poor." Taft was tired and his voice was gone from non-stop speeches. Calmly, he replied to Borah with the force of being right. "It is hard to follow such a stirring appeal," he started. He admitted that the nation faced troubles. But it was a trial of temptation, not distress. "I believe it is true that we do not hold the law as sacred as we should.... Think of using the broom to sweep back the ocean. No matter how careful we may be we do not have the support of the public in many of our best endeavors nor of the newspapers that love to make heroes of murderers." The audience broke into huge applause. The President stared "quizzically" at Borah, which aroused yet more cheering.[26]

* * *

It was a strange climate for a leader. The easy thing would be to take the panic joy ride. Or add the prefix "new" to his philosophy. Taft had use for neither revolution nor slogans. His summation came in the comment, "If there is anything that arouses disgust in me it is the calamity howler...."[27] He held in contempt groundless change. He would, however, as much as any other formulate what the changes of the era would be. His participation was to stare down radicalism from all politics, right and left.

Tops on Taft's don't list were the attacks on the courts. At the base of it all was a contempt for the law manifested in the "recall," the third and most radical stanza of the progressive theme song, "initiative, referendum and...." When applied to judicial decisions, the recall provided that by majority vote the people were to have the veto power over the courts. It was repugnant to Taft. The fight against it would be his Thermopylae.

"With respect to much of what has been discussed as to being progressive...." Taft told an audience, "Occasionally, however, there crops out something extreme in the form of a judicial recall in a Constitution tendered to the Federal Government for approval." The reference was to the Arizona constitutional provision providing for recall of judges and that Congress approved. When advised to expect the bill,

26. "Taft Hears Borah Call US Lawless," *NYT*, 12/21/11. Borah had earlier come out against the judicial recall in defense of Taft's veto of the Arizona statehood bill. "A feeble, a timid, an obedient judiciary," he said with a comparison to the chaos that preceded the Glorious Revolution in England in 1688, "has always in the end proved to be an incompetent, a cruel, or a corrupt judiciary" ("Borah and Root See Peril in the Recall," *NYT*, 8/07/11). By December he was taken by the moment's hysteria. The following year he announced support for the recall.

27. "Taft Will Enforce Law to the Letter," *NYT*, 10/28/11. Pringle rather pathetically lamented that Taft had no slogans. "Taft's tragedy was that he had no comparable label of his own," he wrote. "So he was branded, in a measure unfairly, the guardian of the Old Regime" (p. 569). He couldn't have meant that Wilson and Roosevelt succeeded because they had slogans?

Taft knocked his fist into his hand and announced,

> By George, I am ready for them. I rejoice in the chance to give this Recall business a blow. What a lot of cowards they are in the Senate! There is not a handful of men there, either Democrats or Republicans, who believe in the Recall of the Judiciary, and yet they send me the Constitution of Arizona with this provision in it. I believe I can give this Recall business such a blow as to set the American people to thinking.[28]

Taft marked it return to sender. "I wrote my heart into that veto," he said defiantly.[29] The progressives went looney. Senator Clapp of Minnesota, evidently forgetting the Payne-Aldrich atrocity, called the veto "the blackest act of tyranny ever committed on a free people." Taft could only laugh. "I knew I was guilty of a good deal," he said. "But I never knew I was guilty of conduct that could be described by such lurid terms."[30]

Indiana Governor Thomas Marshall, the "progressive with a brake on" and Wilson's Vice President, described the judicial recall in brilliantly simple terms: "Lincoln held it to be the inalienable right of an unsuccessful litigant to go down to the tavern and cuss the court. It is the theory of Roosevelt that it is the right of an unsuccessful litigant to go down to the tavern and overrule the court."[31] House rules insurgent Augustus Gardner turned on fellow progressives as they bounded leftward to avoid Taft's missiles. "One of the leaders of the Progressive Republican League has said a firm belief in the recall of Judges by the people is the true acid test of a Progressive," Gardner declared. "I dispute an analysis determined by any such chemistry. I deny the application of the epigram and in its place I offer a truer maxim. A firm belief in the foundations of our Federal Constitution is the rock from which the liberal reformer defies the radical destroyer."[32]

* * *

Next on Taft's list of no-no's was socialism. He opened the 1911 Western Tour with a duet for the collectivists and the nationalists. To farmers at Syracuse, he said,

> You are rich. And you are able to do a lot of things in order that by example you may show what can be done to aid the people by a friendly, but an earnest Government. Observe that I say "aid the people," and by that I do not mean that the State shall take the place of individual effort, but I mean that the aid which the State gives should be limited to the impulse, to the assistance and encouragement of the stimulus of individual effort. For I am an individualist first, last and all the time, and I am bitterly opposed to the theory of Socialism —that is— to transfer the object of individual effort to State control and State supervision.[33]

Was the socialist movement an innocuous agitation? Was the proposition of that party's 1912 vice presidential candidate a joke? Or was he serious when he declared,

> We will take all the farming land in the country and place it under the control of the Government. We will either confiscate all the land or we will tax it to its full

28. Butt, 8/9/11, p. 742.
29. "Trusts, Taft Says, Must Obey the Law," *NYT*, 9/23/11.
30. "Taft May Lose Vote; Registered Too Late" *NYT*, 10/29/11.
31. "Thomas R. Marshall," *NYT* editorial, 7/4/12. Root used the expression in 1910 to defend Roosevelt's *New Nationalism* speech, saying that Roosevelt was merely cursing the courts, not trying to overthrow them (Jessup, p. 169). That was 1910.
32. "In House by Gardner," *NYT*, 4/5/12.
33. "Taft Has New Plan to Save Treaties," *NYT*, 9/17/11. The specific reference was to charity.

rental value, and thus force the owner to turn his acres over to the State. Every dollar of unearned increment belongs to the State.[34]

His ticket polled almost nine hundred thousand votes, and took the highest slice of the popular vote of any straight socialist ticket in American history.

The socialist and the progressive met at the intersection of the courts and Wall Street, where they found a common outrage. At Osawatomie, Roosevelt made the almost Marxist statement, "Combinations in industry are the result of an imperative economic law which cannot be repealed by political legislation."[35] After the 1911 Supreme Court decision on the Standard Oil case, which broke up the trust, and launch of the government dissolution suit against U.S. Steel, the progressives turned on the Sherman Anti-Trust Act. Ostensibly, the Standard Oil busting was a failure because the company's broken pieces remained under the same ownership, and the pieces were worth more than the whole — a fine testament to competition. Roosevelt would later call his own Standard Oil and Taft's other anti-trust cases "fake prosecutions."[36]

George Perkins, a former Morgan syndicate partner, who, like many a good Old Guardsman, bought his way into the national town hall, declared, "What has given us sweatshops? Competition. What has given us child labor? Competition." This type of thinking evolved into Roosevelt's "industrial democracy" of the 1912 campaign, which the *Times* figured "not one in a hundred" Bull Moosers understood. Enlightenment, wrote the editors, could be found from "any intelligent Socialist," such as the Mayor of Schenectady, who half agreed with Perkins: "The only thing necessary is to change the ownership," he said in defense of the trusts. The *Times* understood an outcome that mattered little to ownership, "control of business by the Government would mean the control of Government by business."[37]

At a 1911 banquet for Taft, Democratic congressman Martin Littleton complained that the Sherman law was inadequate to control renegade wealth, that more regulation of business was needed. The President stood in reply. For twenty years, he expostulated with the patience of a schoolteacher, the Sherman Act has been "construed, and construed, and construed, and finally by the Supreme Court.... But what has my dear friend Littleton to offer? Only one course is open. Either we will have individualism or we will have combinations in restraint of trade going to that point where the people will demand that the power of men engaged in such corporations be transferred to the Government. And then we will have State Socialism."[38]

34. "Action and Reaction," *NYT* editorial, 2/3/13. No mention of punishment for those who would refuse.
35. "The New Nationalism," p. 29. Would "Hegelian" or "dialectical materialism" be more palatable?
36. "Roosevelt Charges Untruths to Taft," *NYT*, 5/6/12. Kolko agreed. "The component companies remained near monopolies in their respective territories and did not compete with one another. The competition that eventually returned to the industry was due to factors ... that had nothing to do with the Court's decision" (p. 167). Those factors, Kolko argued, were "the shift in the oil-producing areas from the East to the West" and "the radical transformation of the uses for oil" (gasoline), which heralded new competitors such as the Texas Company and Gulf Oil (pp. 40–42). Kolko failed to consider what would have happened had Standard Oil won the case. Kolko admits this: "The dissolution decree of 1911 tended to knock Standard out of its lethargy...."
37. "Congress Lashed by G. W. Perkins," 8/7/11, "Socialist Assails Taft," 1/28/12 and "Industrial Despotism," editorial, 8/31/12, *NYT*.
38. "Taft Defends Act to Control Trusts," *NYT*, 11/1/11. Taft so blew away Littleton he felt compelled to apologize. He wrote that he simply could not have let Littleton's remarks stand in the presence of the Chief Executive (Taft to MW Littleton, 11/4/11 and Taft to Horace Taft, 11/5/11).

That's called closing the circle. Taft's vision was exact:

> The court has exhibited a courage in facing the necessary results in enforcing the [Sherman] statute that, instead of promoting an attack on it, ought to make every American proud that we have such a tribunal.... We did get along with competition; we can get along with it. We did get along without monopoly; we can get along without it; and the business men of this country must square themselves to that necessity. Either that, or we must proceed to State Socialism and vest the Government with power to run every business.[39]

Business, of course, was as outraged at Taft as Littleton. Attorney General Wickersham was "tyrannical," Otto Bannard complained in a scalding letter. Taft replied,

> The whole trouble with you, and with everybody else engaged in the matter, is that you are not willing to come up and face the music and agree that the methods of business ought not to include combination for the purpose of suppressing competition and driving other people out of business by methods akin to duress. In other words, you seem to think that unfair competition is essential to progress in business and I deny it, and I am strongly in sympathy with the principle of the anti-trust law that denies it.[40]

* * *

It had been a long time coming, but as Taft watched the sticky details tapped from New Nationalism, Theodore Roosevelt came to embody for Taft the potential evils of "state socialism" and the destruction of the courts. In February of 1912, Taft measured the Era of Discontent. "Such extremists are not progressives—they are political emotionalists or neurotics, who have lost that sense of proportion." The *Times* concurred. "President Taft's diagnosis of the case of the Progressives seems to be pretty sound," wrote the editors. "We think it will be confirmed by the autopsy."[41]

Taft further said that the politics of hysteria would bring about the conditions of the French Revolution or turn the country into a banana republic. Everyone, especially Roosevelt, knew of whom he spoke. The insults thrown during the Arbitration spat were just practice. The battle would go from theory to the ugly politics of the Republican nomination. The war was for the nation's identity. Taft went to war.

39. "Trust Decisions Defended by Taft," *NYT*, 9/19/11.
40. Bannard to Taft, 6/24/12 and Taft to Bannard, 6/29/12. Bannard hit one undeniably true complaint, right or wrong, that Wickersham "acts without regard to political considerations...." Butt wrote that Wickersham "has about as much political judgement as an ox...." (7/13/11, p. 696; see also the Wiley affair for an example of Wickersham's disregard for political consequence). Pringle agreed with Bannard and, for opposite reasons, with Roosevelt. After reviewing Pringle's manuscript, Taft's son, Senator Robert Taft, wrote a strong objection to the characterization of his father's anti-trust enforcement as immoderate and, in the U.S. Steel case, unfair. He pointed out that the greatest achievement of his father's vigorous anti-trust enforcement was not just to attack existing ones but to halt further combinations. That is, had Taft *not* enforced the Act the outcome would have been far worse, and, your author adds, "national socialism" would have been a large step closer (Robert Taft to Pringle, 8/31/39, Pringle Papers, Library of Congress).
41. "Taft Fires on His Opponents," 2/13/12 and "The Pathology of the Progressives," editorial, 2/15/12, *NYT*.

Part Three
The Third American Revolution (that almost was)

25

The Third Rail and the Cowcatcher

I am particularly anxious that in the progressive movement we shall not find ourselves landed where so many other movements have landed when they have allowed enthusiasm to conquer reason.

—Theodore Roosevelt, January, 1911[1]

The 1912 Republican primary was officially opened during the Senate debates on Reciprocity. The candidates were La Follette, Cummins, Roosevelt, and Taft. La Follette coveted it. Cummins lusted for it. Roosevelt disavowed it. Taft asserted it.

To a barely populated Senate chamber on July 13, 1911, La Follette confessed the country's need for himself. He had been rehearsing all summer to unhappy Senate audiences, said the *Times*, for the Chautauqua. This time he chose the wrong day to lecture the Congressional Record. Members were far more interested in the fantastic arrival of aviator Harry Atwood, who circled the Capitol in celebration of his triumphant flights from Boston. During his three hour speech dedicated to Taft's betrayal of the people, La Follette was neither interrupted nor insulted once.[2] Not good.

Cummins revealed himself in September with an eight-count indictment of the President, headed, of course, by the Payne-Aldrich conspiracy. The charges were a stunning admission of the vast difference between appearance and reality in 1911. The best Cummins could do was to complain that the President hung out with standpatters. Most ironic, for based upon much of Cummins's evidence the standpatters would have hung Taft for being a progressive.[3]

1. Roosevelt to J Bourne, 1/2/11 ("The Letters of Theodore Roosevelt," Vol. VII, p. 197).
2. "Mr. Taft's Usurpation," editorial, 7/10/11, "La Follette Severe on Taft's Record," 7/14/11 and "Atwood in Flight Calls on Congress," 7/14/11, *NYT*. The editorial abusing La Follette is funny.
3. "Cummins Attacks President's Record," 9/6/11, "Iowa Prepares for Taft" 9/19/11, "Not 'Progressive,'" editorial, 9/7/11, *NYT*. According to the Senator, Taft had sabotaged his own legislation, including the interstate commerce, postal savings, and statehood bills. Otherwise, Cummins fretted over free trade with Canada, peace treaties with France and England, and that Taft harbored an unfriendly "attitude" towards public lands. The only consistency Cummins displayed was over the wool schedule and the income tax, and he very easily could have sided with the President on both. Taft gave him the 16th Amendment, and had the insurgents stood behind the Tariff Board the wool schedules could have been revised by its findings.

Above: To the Aeronautical Society in 1911, Taft praised the "courage and zeal" of aviators whose sacrifices, including that of life by some, were for progress and improvement for all. He declared his government dedicated to the "development of aerial navigation." His Army purchased airplanes and set up a pilots school. His Postal Department experimented with airmail delivery, tested personally by the Postmaster General. Taft invited to the White House the winner of the "The *New York Times* Cup," where he congratulated the pilot, Harry Atwood. Taft's lofty enthusiasms remained on the ground, however: he declined offers for rides on account of his "***unaerodynamic***" shape. (Courtesy Library of Congress; for a biography of Atwood, who was quite the character, see ***Skylark: The Life, Lies, and Inventions of Harry Atwood*** by Howard Mansfield, 1999) ***Left:*** In celebration of his tapered flights from Boston to Washington, aviator Harry Atwood buzzed the Capitol, the Washington Monument, and the White House. Amazed and frequently panicked spectators, including Congressmen who poured out of the Capitol, watched him dive to within yards of the Monument. Atwood followed his spectacular performance the next day by zooming across the Mall, circling the Monument, and landing on the South Lawn of the White House. The plane stopped thirty feet from where the President awaited to present him with a gold medal. "He took off his hat and walked as calmly up the steps and spoke to the President as if he had arrived by motor or carriage," Butt wrote. (From *New York Times,* July 23, 1911)

The complaint wasn't that Taft was not a progressive, which to Cummins's mind meant one who opposed the President, but that the President didn't follow the demands of five Senators over the majority of the party. "Again the President was found in the company of reactionaries and not with the progressives," went the explanation of the Taft crime in the Postal banks bill. Guilt-by-association was also the charge over the income tax amendment and corporation tax, perpetrated "through the instrumentality of the most pronounced reactionaries of Congress," i.e., the majority vote. The rest of the complaints were peppered with either, "I am in hearty sympathy with the President but...," or, "he seems to be out of harmony with...."

His case was weak. This Senator who dissed White House social affairs, who refused to receive the President when he visited Iowa, and who turned on Administration bills like a revolving door, unfurled in this speech a stunning admission of pettiness. Ah, the tyranny of the minority, whose dissent overrules a majority and boycotts dinner parties! The *Times* answered for the President. "We observe with satisfaction, however, that Senator Cummins rings against the President no charge of insincerity, no imputation of those failings or derelictions which involve reproach on moral grounds." The editors let slip the usual jab at the President over the tariff, although the hypocrisy was all Cummins's. "He has for many years done lip service to the cause of tariff revision, but somehow his votes are generally cast on the other side." More damning was, "No two progressives would altogether agree as to what progressivism is." In the indictment of the President, Cummins proved what Taft said, "progressive is that which progressive does." The *Times* pointed out,

> Perhaps the absurdity of their whole body of doctrine has been no where so completely demonstrated as by Senator Bourne, when he invoked the support of the big business interests for the most advanced of all the Progressives, Senator La Follette. The progressive mind is distinctly not in harmony with itself, and its state is subject to instantaneous changes without notice. A ferment of that kind may be lasting and violent enough to destroy a party, it can never bring one into being.

Behind Cummins's and La Follette's rhetoric was panic. Taft's estimates of the 1910 election were prescient. His strong hand in 1910 elevated him above his party and the insurgents. His patronage scheme strengthened his hold of the party base. In the Reciprocity fight and the "Dick to Dick" affair the public rediscovered the Fighting Taft of the Payne conference and the Railroad bill. As he beat upon Congress and turned up the presidential volume, the voters and, more importantly, the party machine, smelled success. Progressive Frank Munsey wrote to Beveridge in July of 1911, "the political situation is still badly mixed, but Taft has his renomination well in hand." Even Roosevelt was convinced that Taft was "stronger than he was." Taft wrote his wife that July, "Sometimes I think I am going to be reelected but generally the conditions ... are not very favorable — I am stronger than my party and I am not strong enough."[4] A month later, although still doubtful about the final results, he felt certain to hold the renomination. He wrote his son, "In politics, so far as the National Convention is concerned, things look fairly favorable." Into the Autumn and following the latest monster Western Tour, his hold on the party became only stronger.[5]

4. Taft was similarly wary during the 1908 election. He was always cautious with his optimism.
5. Section from Bowers, p. 412, Brands, pp. 688–689, Taft to Helen Taft, 7/28/11 and Taft to Robert Taft,

The progressives could not rebuild the party in their image. Not even the one man who possessed the power, access to money, and hold on the public to make a new political party could take over the existing Republican party. He failed to do it over his seven years at its head. Although he was the only man in American history to mount a third-party presidential run that outpolled a major party, it was a fall back plan after he was unable to crash that party. And even he couldn't sustain the fever required for permanent delirium. If there is any confusion as to whether the Bull Moose consisted of a personality or a political movement, let it be here dispelled. Roosevelt's take was that the movement needed the force of his personality, not the other way around. "I am fighting for the people and not for myself," he would protest throughout the 1912 campaign. He otherwise conducted it in the first person pronoun.[6]

In January of 1912, Cummins announced that his own candidacy was merely in support of La Follette, the accepted leader of the progressive movement. However, the La Follette boom collapsed to Taft's strength and an odd performance by the Senator in Philadelphia in early February. Friends said La Follette was worn by a strenuous speaking tour and worried over the health of his daughter. Whatever it was, it was mostly the shadow of Roosevelt that chased La Follette everywhere. The man was campaigning against an undeclared candidate whom even his closest backers preferred. La Follette may have gotten the progressives' first kiss, but true love was elsewhere. The frustrations showed up at the Philadelphia banquet as a two hour, incoherent, repetitious rant that ended with calls to sit down and shut up. Taft told Butt the previous November, "the trouble is, Archie, that the Colonel, I fear, is encouraging this talk [of his candidacy]. I wonder what La Follette thinks of it. As Bob's stock goes down, Roosevelt's goes up. The Progressives see that it is impossible to nominate La Follette, so they turn to Roosevelt."[7]

Roosevelt sat tight, as he had all summer. A British journalist and Roosevelt friend, Sydney Brooks, revealed the Roosevelt attitude in an article in August 1911. "Mr. Roosevelt is still frankly disappointed in Mr. Taft. He chose him for the Presidency, not as the ideally best man, but as the best man available." Taft was "a perplexing failure," nevertheless Roosevelt "is not to be reckoned an anti–Taft man."[8] Not just fence sitting: that's straddling both sides. The word into the Autumn was that Roosevelt was not a candidate unless the people insisted. He wouldn't promise

5. (*cont.*) 8/27/11. Anderson wrote, "By calling the disastrous special session of Congress in 1911 and pushing reciprocity, Taft had risked his stature as party leader for economic union with Canada" (p. 179). Taft feared it might, and he was willing to risk it, but Reciprocity did not break the party. By the end of the year the regulars were lined up behind Taft, even those who opposed Reciprocity. And the case for a "disastrous" session is dubious, although one might view the wool veto in that light, and that alone. Taft achieved his objectives, and without compromise. Hardly disastrous. Anderson was making the case that Taft failed as a party leader, so he discounts the strong political advantage the reciprocity fight brought. On top of it, Taft's general popularity was enhanced by the Arbitration treaties, despite Roosevelt's derision of them, the failed "Dick to Dick" scandal, and his constant talk on anti-trust.
6. This one from "Taft Snows Colonel Under," *NYT*, 3/27/12. It was a theme all year long.
7. "Cummins Openly After Presidency," 1/21/12 and "La Follette Ill; Makes No Excuses," 2/3/12, *NYT*, and Butt, 11/24/11, p. 767. In his autobiography La Follette described "the decline of the Taft strength and the astonishing progress of my candidacy" (p. 537). His theory was that Roosevelt stayed out of the race until La Follette had weakened Taft. La Follette grossly overestimated himself. Even the sympathetic *American Review of Reviews* doubted that La Follette could ever take the Republican nomination (Feb. 1912, p. 141).
8. From the Return from Elba on through to his autobiography, Roosevelt's rearview mirror became ever fuzzier concerning his enthusiastic attitude towards and warm relationship with Taft in 1908 ("Some Talks

that he wouldn't accept the nomination. That's what "friends" said, anyway. It was all quite absurd, best summed up by a cartoon of Roosevelt in a waiter's uniform holding a tray, "presidential nomination," before a mirror. "I decline," he said to his image.[9] But it worked. Indeed, no one ever boomed himself so effectively as Roosevelt. The *Times* was dismayed. The paper complained that while La Follette, Taft, Wilson, and Clark underwent the expense of campaign offices and mailings, every Roosevelt "no comment" was dispersed across the nation at no charge.

The Brooks article noted one other factor in the equation, the wild cards. "Mr. Roosevelt's friends ... are less committed by past responsibilities, are freer to do as they think best," wrote the Englishman. Pinchot, Garfield, Munsey, and others worked the La Follette boom with all the enthusiasm displayed in Pinchot's remark, "since Col. Roosevelt has eliminated himself Senator La Follette is his logical successor."[10] The Incense Swingers were busy as elves, throwing powders here and there between Oyster Bay and Madison, Wisconsin.

The only person who gave open fight to Roosevelt was his home-state nemesis and fellow Harvard alumnus, William Barnes, Jr., who, with his huge presence and booming voice, would bedevil Roosevelt's delegates at the party convention in 1912. Barnes was already scuffling with Taft over the Administration's lack of conservatism. His solution was active standpattism. He advised Taft to avoid "a destructive policy." Otherwise he poured gasoline on the Roosevelt fire, accusing the Colonel of wanting a dictatorship. In mid–December this became known as the "Barnes-Taft-Roosevelt complication." If anyone could tweak Roosevelt it was Barnes. "I firmly believe that any man who is a candidate for nomination for President of the United States should say so," Barnes challenged.[11]

You can't "smoke out" someone who breathes smoke, wrote the *Times*. "A process of disclosure is, nevertheless, in progress, but it is not so much a 'smoking out' as a tearing off of disguises.... The observant have long been aware that Mr. Roosevelt intends by fair means or foul to secure the Republican nomination....

8. (*cont.*) with Mr. Roosevelt," *The Fortnightly Review*, by Sydney Brooks, quoted from *NYT* editorial, 8/20/11).
9. Cartoon from *NYT*, 8/27/11. Regarding Roosevelt's refusal to publicly support Taft or his "Insurgent critics," Anderson wrote, "In his own inimitable manner, Roosevelt chose to do neither" (p. 176). Interestingly, Anderson then wrote that Taft was "too stubborn to make way for his predecessor" (p. 178). Which is it? Like Pringle's take on the 1910 New York situation, Anderson would have preferred that Taft step down for Roosevelt with a bow and a thankee 'marm. The problem with such views is that they find no fault in Roosevelt's antics. For example, when Anderson described Taft's description of Roosevelt's "New Nationalism" speech as containing "wild ideas," the historian qualified Taft's comment with the prefix "allegedly" (p. 178; Taft quoted from letter to Horace Taft, 9/16/10). The attitude that Taft's opponents did no wrong has wrongly created the attitude that Taft did wrong. See Anderson's article, "The Legacy of William Howard Taft," *Presidential Studies Quarterly*, Vol. XII, No. 1, Winter, 1982. While Anderson defended Taft as a progressive, he refused to condemn the progressives for their extremes that divorced themselves from Taft. The explaining needed was from the progressives, not Taft. The essay gives an admirable defense of Taft, but defensively (see p. 31, however, for one of the better offenses for the Taft legacy).
10. "Pinchot Comes out for La Follette," *NYT*, 11/28/11.
11. "Speak Up, Says Barnes," *NYT*, 1/5/12. The December Gridiron dinner made fun of Roosevelt and Barnes. A peace dove appeared that turned out to be a goose ("the dove of peace is always a goose," was the explanation) with a message from Oyster Bay. "I am always for peace. I'd cut off both arms to get it — both of Bill Barnes' arms. — Theodore Roosevelt." ("Peace Dove a Goose at Gridiron Dinner," *NYT*, 12/10/11). Roosevelt took his revenge on Barnes in 1915 when Barnes sued him for libel. Roosevelt ruined Barnes in court. When asked what damages he received, Roosevelt laughed, "My dear fellow! I was the de-fen-dant!" (Pringle, *Roosevelt*, p. 577).

Towering ambition cannot long be dissembled."[12] All the pressure of Barnes, the press and the Incense Swingers couldn't force a word from Roosevelt. The best they got was a January declaration at a banquet that he would run "If the nomination is forced upon me."[13] Deniability was maintained by Roosevelt's insistence that the dinner was off-record. Anyone quoting him was a "liar," he told reporters as he left the club. Walking out behind him was the entire Ananias Club, as lying tongues spoke freely of the revelation.

The advantage to not being a declared candidate was that Roosevelt didn't have to take a position on anything. He submitted articles to the *Outlook* with nothing due to a voting public. The disadvantage was that he was not campaigning. Ideally, he would await a convention stampede, bow to duty, and gracefully accept the nomination like a crowned prince. But Taft was no fool. His first move was to wrap up the National Committee, which set the rules of the convention, most importantly those concerning the appointment of delegates. Roosevelt would have to storm the castle.

Roosevelt's drama may have deceived popular history, but his contemporaries were not duped. The famed "my hat's in the ring" statement never was. When it was first relayed to the press it was like every other non-comment he let slip through "friends," then either denied or confirmed, or both, with a "no comment." It was only later, after his official announcement, that he took it up, another slogan etched onto the big stick. The actual declaration came in late February through a reply to an orchestrated letter from eight governors who declared the world ready for his salvation.[14] His "I will accept the nomination if it is tendered me" brought yawns, not surprise. The Roosevelt campaign office was already open in New York. His name was already on ballots. The Gridiron was already making fun of his candidacy. The Taft campaign correctly noted that the Roosevelt boom was hardly "spontaneous."[15]

Months before, Roosevelt warned friends in the Taft Administration to pack their bags. He sent one such message in early December, long before any hats were tossed about. "Alice," he told his daughter who was relishing all the intrigue and outrage, "when you get the opportunity, tell Archie from me to get out of his present job. And not to wait for the convention or election, but do it soon."[16] The plot was to include the defection of the President's own personal aide.

12. "Smoking Out the Colonel," *NYT* editorial, 1/5/12.

13. "'I Will Run,' Says Roosevelt," *NYT*, 1/10/12.

14. See "Roosevelt Says He Will Accept Nomination," *NYT*, 2/26/12. The "hat in the ring" came out a few days earlier, and Roosevelt gave the standard non-denial denial to it. The *Times* reported that in "an *alleged* conversation with W.F. Elrick, a Cleveland politician.... Elrick, *according to the dispatch*, asked the Colonel for a direct answer concerning his position. 'My hat's in the ring. You will have my answer on Monday,' the Colonel *is said to* have replied. Col. Roosevelt did not either affirm or deny the story ... 'I tell you I have absolutely nothing to say,' he burst out shortly" [italics added] ("Roosevelt Back to Storm Boston," *NYT*, 2/23/12).

15. "Money and Skill in Roosevelt Boom," *NYT*, 1/22/12. At the February Gridiron the Rough Rider interrupted the inauguration of the Club's new president. "If a progressive President is to be inaugurated, I am here," he announced. "But you said you were not a candidate." "Maybe so, maybe so. But I have always found it convenient to have a string to every declaration." A skit on Robin Hood's band lampooned the Incense Swingers, "Friar Pinchot" and "Little Jim Garfield," and their fellow outlaw, "Will Scarlette La Follette" ("Roast Candidates at Gridiron Feast," *NYT*, 2/18/12).

16. Butt, 12/4/11, p. 776. In January Butt mentioned this to Taft's secretary, Hilles, who heard the same from others "closely associated" with the ex–President (Butt, 1/13/12, pp. 811–812). Navy Secretary Meyers was said to have been told, as was, likely, Stimson (see "Meyer Quits Taft, Washington Hears," *NYT*, 6/18/12).

Probably the only surprise that followed the February announcement was that Roosevelt promised not to bolt if he lost the nomination. Taft's reaction? It was nothing new. He flatly told reporters that he would win the nomination.[17] And what of the Democrats? Champ Clark said it best:

> Many persons were amazed when the Republican National Committee fixed their convention for June 18, the anniversary of Waterloo. Now comes Col. Roosevelt on Feb. 26, the anniversary of the day when Napoleon escaped from Elba. No doubt the result of the November election will complete the historic parallel by sending not only the Colonel, but the whole Republican Party to Helena — a consummation devoutly to be wished. This year all things work together for the success of the Democrats and the good of the country.[18]

A few days later, Roosevelt passed through Boston, "fairly bubbling over with vitality and enthusiasm."[19] The novelty of the situation was his alone. Back at Washington, Taft set about the hard work of the responsibility he faced. Roosevelt's candidacy was no longer inevitable. It was no longer a threat. The rumors that attended Taft's 1909 entry to Washington and that overshadowed his term of office were at last confirmed. At least now he wouldn't have to pretend or hope or not know what it all meant. The break was ugly, but it was official. Newsmen compared notes and concocted theories. It started at the nomination in 1908 when Taft refused Beveridge as the keynote speaker. It was the Cabinet selections. It was the treatment of Roosevelt relatives in Washington. It was the U.S. Steel suit. (It was everything but the tariff.) Taft no longer had to care.

Roosevelt's delay tactics, or his reticence, or whatever, played out too long. Though his boom "was like pushing a street car down a hill," a supporter said, while denials were sent out from Oyster Bay Taft collected delegates at the state conventions. "Taft Steam Roller in Working Order," declared the *Times* in December. The January Oklahoma convention was full of Rough Riders and featured a fifteen minute pro–Roosevelt riot and 500 pounds of explosives blown in testament to their undeclared candidate. Surrounded by worried Taft men, party boss Jim Harris "quietly smoked his cigar through it all." Then he named the delegates for Taft.[20]

* * *

The short session of the 62nd Congress opened in early December. The President sent his greetings in the form of a 6,000 word message dedicated to a single topic, the trusts. Once again, Taft pushed the progressives to the left. They could only complain that his plan didn't go far enough. Taft framed his proposals with recent Supreme Court anti-trust decisions. The Court, he said, made good on the Sherman law, and all that was needed was statutory clarification for the courts and for business. He did not propose more regulation, as the progressives demanded, but an adjustment of existing rules and the availability of federal incorporation, should interstate companies choose it. That Taft dedicated his first message to the trusts is significant. Like the tariff, emotions and demagoguery led this one. Most importantly, Taft needed it put to bed for the acute reason that the previous October the issue became most intimate for Roosevelt.

17. "Taft is Confident," *NYT*, 2/26/12.
18. "Driven By Roosevelt into the Taft Camp," *NYT*, 2/27/12.
19. "Roosevelt is Back, Eager for the Fray," *NYT*, 2/29/12.
20. "Roosevelt a Very Busy Man," 1/25/12, "Taft Steam Roller in Working Order," 12/10/11, "Dynamite Fails in Roosevelt Boom," 1/24/12, *NYT*.

Things started that June when House Democrat Stanley got himself a committee to avenge the Roosevelt years. The Democrats knew the smite, and with the majority control of the House they were learning how much better it felt to give than to receive. One among numerous House investigations was the Stanley Select Committee which brought back to Washington in a public parade the leading characters of a much quieter pilgrimage to the city in 1907. The Wicked Henry Clay Frick. The Devious Elbert Gary. The Overlord J.P. Morgan. Those first two had slipped into Washington as quietly as Steel Giants can on the morning of November 4, 1907 to meet the President of the United States. It was the Panic of 1907. Wall Street trembled, and the President hadn't a thing to do. What with markets strangled by a taut currency, bank credits buried in farm mortgages and a bungled stock speculation that sucked mercury from Wall Street thermometers, the nation turned its lonely eyes once again to Morgan. On top of the government deposits into banks, President Roosevelt was told, a steely $20 million to salvage the investors in the Tennessee Coal and Iron Company would help restore the calm. This was done, and by some coincidence or other, Stanley wanted to know, up until 1911 the Department of Justice hadn't bothered the United States Steel Company, the trust of trusts. What it all meant to Roosevelt is that he had to admit stupidity to escape charges of corruption.[21]

It's a bit more complicated, of course, what with the President of 1911 playing golf with Frick and the former President planning a coup of the Republican party with Frick's former associate. Add to it an Attorney General, locked and loaded, and, Stanley said, with all the noise of his Committee it was only a matter of time before the government heard the call. The hearings went all summer. Morgan testified. Roosevelt testified. His working excuse was that he had acted for the good of the people. He handled the questions deftly, although no minds were changed. The issue

21. The charges and the investigations were not new. In February of 1909 a Senate committee similarly concluded that Roosevelt erred in his acquiescence of the deal. The *Evening Star* reported, "The conclusion reached by Senator Kittredge, who has prepared a report of the investigation of the Tennessee Coal and Iron Company's absorption by the United States Steel Corporation is that the merger forms a combination in restraint of trade, and that President Roosevelt had no authority of law to sanction the deal.... If adopted [the report] may form the basis of an order to the Department of Justice to bring action against the steel corporation under the Sherman anti-trust law" ("President Found at Fault," *Evening Star*, 2/20/09; see also, "Accuses President of Countenancing Violation of Law," *Evening Star*, 2/21/09). This conclusion was actually far more damaging than that of the Stanley Committee, which lost to its heaving outrage the deal's subtler stench. Roosevelt had no more authority to promise *not* to do anything about the Tennessee Coal deal than he had to any promise *to* oppose it. It was legal advice the Executive Office had no business giving, even for the public good. At the time, in what Pringle called one of his "posterity letters," Roosevelt wrote of the meeting with Frick and Gary, "I answered that, while of course I could not advise them to take the action proposed, I felt it no public duty of mine to interpose any objections." Gary's recollection, confirmed by Root, was that he said, "I would not feel like objecting to the purchase under the circumstance" (Pringle, *Roosevelt*, pp. 442–443). The latter was probably more accurate, but it's the same, either way. The more correct answer would have been, nothing has yet happened, therefore the Government has no opinion. Instead, he gave the Government's opinion in advance of the fact, thereby making it a sanction. History has generally accepted Roosevelt's view. Even as President, Roosevelt based his industrial philosophy entirely upon a distinction between "good" and "bad" trusts. The "good" ones were those that cooperated with the Government. Aside from its "bad" rebating practices, Standard Oil was particularly "bad" to Roosevelt because it refused to fully cooperate with his Bureau of Corporations, headed at the time by Garfield (see Kolko, pp. 82–83). This attitude grew to absurd proportions when in 1906 the Mellon company announced that an oil pipeline project had been declared "good, clean" by the Secretary of Interior. Department clearance was required for it involved Indian lands, and such was the specific reference. However, seizing Roosevelt's rhetoric, Mellon compared the statement to the Government's attitude toward Standard Oil. ("Government Indorses Standard Oil Rival," *NYT*, 11/21/06.)

became Taft's political problem when his government sued U.S. Steel in late October for violation of the Sherman Act. From the embarrassment of the filing Roosevelt found opportunity. First, the soft tones. It was "not one word" in response to the inquiring minds of the press.[22]

It is thought that the suit brought the final break, that it was just one thing too many for Roosevelt to put up with. Perhaps. More importantly is that the simmering philosophical differences therein converged. Before the Steel suit was filed, Taft's strong public defense of the Sherman Act and his jackhammer attack on socialism were already stirring things up.[23] Taft deliberately framed his argument around the alternative to the Sherman law, "state socialism," to which he said the progressives would take the country. Roosevelt came back with the trademark hand-in-fist, teeth-clicking dismissal of evil. "Socialism — the cure-all Socialism is a quack remedy," he protested. "I'm saying just what I mean. It is a quack remedy, I want you to understand that. I don't mean there are no dangers in capitalism. I mean we cannot afford to rely on one set of virtues or charge all our troubles to one set of ills."[24] The Steel suit forced a confrontation of political views, not personalities.[25]

* * *

In December, Taft and the Cabinet laid out his Programme in a series of talks and messages to Congress. It was full-blown electioneering. Postmaster Hitchcock reported on the need for a parcels service and the use of airplanes for mail delivery. Secretary of State Knox declared that "Dollar Diplomacy," a name started as a pejorative, was a good description for an effective policy. Treasury Secretary MacVeagh announced expected surpluses and proclaimed the Administration in favor of the Aldrich Plan for currency reform. In his formal messages, Taft vehemently endorsed and expanded upon these statements. His greatest efforts, however, went towards Senate confirmation of the Arbitration treaties and the findings of the Tariff Board. Schedule K was beaten, he declared.

It was a magnificent show. The President was in the news constantly, crowding, if not pushing La Follette and Roosevelt from page one. By the end of the year Taft's constant release of new proposals buried La Follette, who was forced into defending against charges of radicalism, not a good political position.[26] The air was getting thicker at Oyster Bay, too. In response, Roosevelt stepped up his "no news" campaign. Vile rumors circulated and old letters resurfaced by odd coincidences, and there was plenty to say. He resurrected

22. "'Not a Word,'— Roosevelt," *NYT*, 10/28/11. See also "To Dissolve the Steel Trust," *NYT* editorial, 10/27/11. The *Times* was horrified by the suit, but not in defense of Roosevelt.
23. See "Taft Has New Plan to Save Treaties," *NYT*, 9/17/11.
24. "Roosevelt Unafraid of Judges," *NYT*, 10/21/11.
25. Unless Roosevelt really was so petty as to rupture a political party over a third party's lawsuit? That can be the only conclusion of the view that the U.S. Steel suit was a personal attack on Roosevelt. Your author won't go there. Others have.
26. See "La Follette Scores Trust Decisions," *NYT*, 12/30/11. Like Roosevelt, La Follette was made uncomfortable by Taft's push from the right, especially as socialists pushed them back hard from the left. La Follette was compelled to defend against Taft's charges that the progressives and their "direct democracy" would destroy representative government. "The progressive movement has no motive toward changing the present form of government," he said. "It is not the idea to abolish the Legislatures or Houses of Representatives [which nobody called for — he was being careful here not to associate himself with socialists cries for the end of the Senate] but to abolish the political machinery and to bring the citizen in touch with the man who is transacting his business by establishing the direct vote, from President down to coroner. That is bringing government right up to the people."

Harriman. He brought out the Ananias Club and the expletive. "Infamous" were the falsehoods, "unpardonable" the lies, and "mendacious" the obliquities.[27]

Taft watched with varied emotions. His December predictions of certain victory at the Convention turned to pessimism into February as the reality of Roosevelt's game descended upon the White House.[28] Both he and Archie still suffered from exhaustion from the latest and hugest Western Tour. The physical strain turned mental into the new year. Mabel Boardman, dear and faithful Mabel, told the President to keep his chin up and not to show his depression in public.

All told, Taft's strain showed more in Archie's letters than elsewhere. Taft could hit the on-switch as easily as take a nap at mass. The morning after another crazed New York night of banquets a visitor awaited Taft for a nine o'clock appointment at Henry Taft's home. The man had seen the performance the night before and was amazed to hear from the breakfast table in the next room the enormous Taft chuckle. "Butt," the visitor said, "I would give all the wealth of the Rockefellers and the Vanderbilts if I could laugh like that after such a night as we had last night."[29]

27. "Roosevelt Adds to Ananias Club," 12/24/11 and "A Charter Member of the Ananias Club," 12/28/11, *NYT*.
28. See Butt, 2/21/12, pp. 845–847, the day of Roosevelt's Columbus speech. "I never saw him so pessimistic before."
29. Butt, 12/29/11, p. 803 and 12/20/11, p. 798.

26

Outed

Following Roosevelt's feigned submission to duty and what were to be called the "little Governors" and their prefabricated entreaty, echoes of George Washington reluctantly putting down the plow to save the nation were resoundingly brief. Roosevelt was out, simply, and with the smoke more or less cleared, he picked up the sword and hit the campaign trail. Actually, he was already on the road, having just given the "Charter of Democracy" speech in Ohio a few days before. Of his own performance there, he declared, "Big business always shudders slightly when I speak of it."[1] Business was not the only thing to shudder, slightly or otherwise. Roosevelt outed himself completely on the question of the recall of judges—and added judicial decisions to the public review.

Now he was off to Boston and shades of Patrick Henry. Wrong state, perhaps, but enjoyable to partisans and infuriating to enemies. "If recall of Judicial decisions be revolution, make the most of it," he twitted. And then to Lincoln, with the promise "to keep the Government of this country genuinely a Government of, by and for the people." Even the ancient world was stirred. A letter writer to the *Times* declared that judicial recall had been tried 1,900 years before in the form of a mob veto of Pilate's finding the Son of God innocent. Schurman of Cornell warned against "Caesarism."[2]

The uncertainty of Roosevelt's course had been a chain upon Taft. "But I can't get into public rows with him," he explained to Archie in December. "He knows that, and he has me at a disadvantage." The day of Roosevelt's Columbus speech, which Taft knew to be the real declaration of candidacy, Taft still felt constrained by

1. One wonders at the choice of the word "slightly." He wanted business to shudder but not too much. As La Follette complained, Roosevelt was always careful to temper his populism. "While Roosevelt was President, his public utterances through state papers, addresses, and the press were highly colored with rhetorical radicalism. His administrative policies as set forth in his recommendations to Congress were vigorously and picturesquely presented, but characterized by an absence of definite economic conception. One trait was always pronounced. His most savage assault upon special interests was invariably offset with an equally drastic attack upon those who were seeking to reform abuses. These were indiscriminately classed as demagogues and dangerous persons. In this way he sought to win approval, both from the radicals and the conservatives. This cannonading, first in one direction and then in another, filled the air with noise and smoke, which confused and obscured the line of action, but, when the battle cloud drifted by and quiet was restored, it was always a matter of surprise that so little had really been accomplished" (La Follette, pp. 478–479).
2. "Roosevelt Indorses Recall of Judges," 2/22/12, "Roosevelt Answers Cry of Revolution," 2/27/12, "Pontius Pilate's Decision Reversed," letter, 3/3/12, and "Schurman Predicts Roosevelt's Defeat," 3/20/12, *NYT*.

their old friendship. "He has drawn the line now," he told Archie, "and I hope we can keep the fight from becoming personal."[3]

The comment came during a two hour walk. Taft was somber and hardly spoke. His first words were, "Well, Archie, what do you think of the Recall of Judges as announced by the Colonel to-day?" The Major's loyalties were on the line here, but not because Taft distrusted him. The question was rhetorical. Taft knew the struggle Archie endured, for they all suffered it. He wanted to make it clear that the fight was about ideas, not personal loyalties. The jealousies and intrigues of 1910 were over. "I have always been opposed to the Recall of the Judiciary, Mr. President," the Major replied smartly.

Nearing the White House, Taft stopped. "Archie, I am going to say something which may surprise you, and therefore you must not say anything about it.... Well, I have a strong presentiment that the Colonel is going to beat me at the Convention. It is almost a conviction with me." Here Taft spoke the defiance that historians generally attribute to stubbornness. Taft knew the fight was coming. He watched it build for two years. He saw his political mentor and dear friend turn not just against him but against his core values. He knew the force of the man and his words upon the populace. And with his fullest conviction he believed that his old friend was dead wrong. "But don't think me capable of quitting," he said to Archie. "I can fight just as well when losing as when certain of victory...."

Archie wrote to Clara on the eve of Roosevelt's announcement,

> The President is going to fling his hat into the ring in Ohio the first part of next month.... He is always at his best when fighting, and I am glad he feels aroused to the necessity of a fight at last. He is too easy-going and kindly to contend with the political elements, but once aroused he becomes dynamic. You may get a different view of him when he enters for the death grip.[4]

On February 28, Taft announced that he, too, would campaign. Although he deplored the spectacle of a President on the stump, the apologies were for Roosevelt. Taft would respond only to the text of Roosevelt's "Charter of Democracy" speech. But he would do it in Ohio, the scene of the crime. He would avenge the slap delivered by Roosevelt in launching his campaign from Taft's home state. Now decided to openly fight, his blood was up.

* * *

Roosevelt's extended courtship was a trial balloon. La Follette, anyway, felt like he was strung up in the air. There was much for Roosevelt to figure, from Taft's strength to the strength of the reaction for and against himself. The flirting was meant to stir the people to an unrelenting call for salvation. In January, another of his legionnaires rode off from Oyster Bay, blessed with inside information: "He expressed great doubt, however, as to whether any man has a right to decline to serve the people."[5] While Roosevelt blamed Taft for making him answer the people's call, he set about finding a way around his 1904 declaration not to seek office again — this small business of a third term. Whether of some great moral struggle within the man or of unscrupulous design, these statements served their purpose to give emotional legitimacy to a profound political issue. Washington and Jackson declined it. Grant was denied it. McKinley

3. Butt, 12/31/11, p. 804 and 2/21/12, pp. 845–847.
4. Butt, 2/23/12, pp. 848–849.
5. "Roosevelt in Doubt, So Colby Reports," *NYT*, 1/21/12.

swore from it. The best Roosevelt could do, straight-faced and convinced, was to say that what he meant in 1904 was three *consecutive* terms. Get it?

You could if you were convinced that everything you did was novel and brilliant. In March, Roosevelt's automobile sank into the mud. Reporters chasing behind pulled up to the sight of the ex–President standing in back, arms flying, and exhorting the chauffeur to pull this lever or try that way. The car dug further in. A reporter ran off to retrieve a rope to extract it. "Bully!" Roosevelt cried, "I was in a hole that time!" With such enthusiasm he declared — not himself — his ideas essential to the survival of the nation. After a stage from which he spoke collapsed, Roosevelt, unhurt, declared, "It was the weight of intellect that caused the platform to break down. Our platform won't break down." Great joke, but it was preface to the hyperbole: "In the end the servants of the people will have to stand on that platform or the American democracy will be a confessed failure." This kind of talk prompted, perhaps for the first time in American politics, and unfortunately not the last, the commentary of the shrinks. Neurologist Morton Prince told Americans to relax, the storm from Oyster Bay was the product of the "distortion of conscious mental processes through the force of subconscious wishes," that's all.[6]

Despite the contention, into the Autumn of 1911, Taft was in firm control of the Republican Party. La Follette's presidential ambitions fell to Taft's renewed popularity that came of his Reciprocity and other legislative successes, his "Arbitration" peace treaties, and his firm stand in the "Dick to Dick" scandal. The wild card was the Bull Moose. What would Roosevelt do? (Clifford Berryman cartoon, 1912, Courtesy Library of Congress)

Roosevelt's strategy was to force a popularity contest. "And because I believe in genuine popular rule," he said, "I favor direct nominations, direct primaries, including direct preferential Presidential primaries...." Taft took him on. "I favor it, and welcome it," he announced.[7] By a delicious irony the first primary went for La Follette. Even though the Senator had dropped an active campaign in early February, Roosevelt polled just over half of La Follette's votes in North Dakota. The President took only a few hundred votes,

6. "Roosevelt Thrown as Platform Falls," 3/24/12 and "Roosevelt as Analyzed by the New Psychology," 3/24/12, *NYT*.
7. "Roosevelt Answers Cry of Revolution," 2/27/12 and "Taft for Primary with Safeguards," 3/19/12, *NYT*.

probably the sum of all federal appointments there. In even sweeter irony, the Roosevelt campaign cried foul, saying Democrats voted for La Follette. "If the Democrats had stayed out of the Republican primary there is no question that Roosevelt would have won," complained a manager.[8]

Throughout March, Taft rolled through state conventions and two more primaries: Indiana went Taft, as did New York, significantly, for it was Roosevelt's home state. Roosevelt supporters in Indiana refused to accept the results and appointed their own delegation for the nominating convention, which forced Roosevelt to deny rumors of a general bolt. The momentum was Taft's. His declarations against the recall and the third term had put Roosevelt on the defensive, not a comfortable position for the man. Declaring the fight to the end, Roosevelt kept up the attack, which included an invasion by a flag-speckled automobile on a Minnesota auditorium. "My hat is in the ring, and it is going to stay in the ring," he declared. Behind the scenes his forces laid out Plan B. The campaign found fraud everywhere. As Taft piled up delegates, the Roosevelt managers prepared contesting delegations. Publicly, their candidate accused Taft of election fraud and abuse of patronage.[9]

The flow shifted back to Roosevelt following primary victories in Illinois and Pennsylvania, the latter at the hands of William Flinn over Senator Penrose. Watching Roosevelt claim his victories those of the people over the bosses made it all the more frustrating for Taft, as Pennsylvania was delivered to Roosevelt by a boss. Roosevelt's explanation was that virtue was defined by whose side the boss was on. The Illinois defeat was attributed to anti-boss sentiment, as well. There, Taft took a beating on behalf of Senator Lorimer, who was under investigation in the Senate for bribery and whose supposed alliance with Taft was the basis of the Roosevelt campaign in the state. Roosevelt knew that Taft had no relation to Lorimer. It didn't matter. Taftism meant bossism. Roosevelt was for the people.[10]

Taft took the losses calmly. On April 15, he wrote Mabel,

> We must accept defeat as it is, close up our ranks and fight on. Of course, it is difficult to tell where our lines may falter in view of these heavy defeats, but I believe we can still hold them so as to secure the nomination. Then we'll buckle on our armor and fight for our institution. We may be beaten, but "When the forts of folly fall, They'll find our bodies near the wall"[11]

Less sanguine, the *Times* lost blood over Taft's reverses. Calling Roosevelt an "ambitious, plausible, selfish, and conscienceless demagogue," the editors lamented the Taft managers' tactical mistake to leave the Illinois fight up to the regular machine, a.k.a. Lorimer. As for Pennsylvania, "Mr. Roosevelt's instant profiting by the labor troubles in the anthracite region points with unmistakable directness to the quarter where the peril lies....

8. "Beat Roosevelt in North Dakota," *NYT*, 3/20/12.
9. "Roosevelt Rides into Hall in Auto," 3/30/12, "Roosevelt to Try Again If Defeated," 4/9/12, and "Roosevelt Charges Taft With 'Frauds,'" 4/10/12, *NYT*.
10. There was also a sly, if unintentional, attitude towards Lorimer that worked against Taft and that bolstered the charges of a supposed association with Lorimer: Lorimer was a Catholic. While Taft took heat from Catholics for coming out against Lorimer (see Taft to FC Kelley, 1/30/11), by accusing Taft of defending him Roosevelt gained support from anti–Catholics who were ever prepared to accuse Taft of collusion with the Pope.
11. Taft to Mabel Boardman, 4/15/12. The lines, into which Taft injected the first person, were from Mathew Arnold's "The Last Word."

The sentiment against [Taft] has been artificially engendered by Theodore Roosevelt and his band of sycophants and place-hunters, and by the ignorant, deluded phantom-chasers of the Populistic school...." Want hysteria? A few days later, apparently sobered, the editors noted, "Mr. Roosevelt has seized on the factional fights in the Republican Party with his usual skill and rather less than his usual scrupulousness.... It is a pity that so good a man as Mr. Taft should be involved in their punishment...."[12]

While Taft declared the fight already won, Nebraska, then Oregon, fell to Roosevelt. The President picked up New Hampshire and Rhode Island and made a surprisingly strong showing at Iowa, where he campaigned hard. At the end of April, Taft still led the count with just a few major states to go, Massachusetts, California, Ohio, Maryland and New Jersey.

In these first-ever presidential primaries immediately evident were voter apathy and cross-over party votes, problems that have plagued primaries since. Only the most motivated bothered. In the New Jersey primary, only 41 percent of the Republican votes of 1908 were scared up. "The advocates of the direct primary have told us times without number that if the people could only have a chance to name their own candidates," scolded the *Times*. "The theory that the people demanded the direct primary as a means of escaping the thralldom of the bosses breaks down at the first test."[13]

Worse, these first primaries demonstrated that money is quicker than reform. Stories of black Roosevelt supporters in new clothes came out of the Maryland primary. If true, that was old-time politics. The change was that with low turnout the primaries proved efficient buys. Later, when Congress held hearings on campaign money, it became evident that early charges of the effect of Roosevelt cash were not altogether unfair. Taft managers decried opposition money spent in Massachusetts that came to five dollars a vote. The accusation of three hundred thousand in Roosevelt money in Ohio was mightily exaggerated, but with the kind of money being thrown around it seemed not inconceivable. All told, and depending on who did the telling, anywhere from $350,000 to over $800,000 was spent directly on Roosevelt's behalf before the convention doors opened.[14]

* * *

Into April, Taft spoke obliquely of Roosevelt. He avoided name calling and direct reference. After the Pennsylvania and Illinois primaries, it became apparent that voters needed more than political theory. To the imploring of his campaign managers, Taft admitted that the Roosevelt grenades would do less damage if he tossed a few back out the window. Otto Bannard advised that Roosevelt "is not nearly so effective on the defense, and he should be held up to ridicule...." Taft replied,

> My dear old Ban:
>
> Thank you for your letter of the 18th. I am afraid it will be necessary to reply to Roosevelt's attacks, but I am very sorry it is so.
>
> We will win![15]

12. "To Mr. Taft's Managers," editorial, 4/15/12 and "Home to Roost," editorial, 4/17/12, *NYT*.
13. "The Primary Myth," *NYT* editorial, 6/9/12.
14. "$200,000 Roosevelt Fund," *NYT*, 6/7/12. Pringle totaled Roosevelt's pre-convention money at $338,000 (p. 789). A figure floated in Congressional hearings later that year had it at $836,005 (see "Campaign Expenses Low," *NYT*, 10/26/12). During the Ohio primary La Follette challenged Roosevelt to name his backers and their sums, saying he had a campaign fund of $1,000,000 ("Challenges Colonel to Name Backers," *NYT*, 5/18/12).
15. Bannard to Taft, 4/18/12 and Taft to Bannard 4/19/12. Bannard also wrote, "I suppose Nebraska and Oregon

Roosevelt's start in late February was slowed by the need to justify himself and the third term. He slung the usual themes of the privilege, human rights and "social and industrial justice," but Taft's March sweep kept him on guard.[16] In April, with the volume up, he found traction in Illinois and Pennsylvania through the guilt-by-association charges against Taft. "The chief present adherents of the President, gentlemen like Senator Penrose, Senator Gallinger, Mr. Barnes, Mr. McKinley, Mr. Tawney, and their associates…" he clamored.[17] The hypocrisy was marvelous, and Taft's replies to the theory, not the insult, went nowhere. The demagogue is unstained by argument; the disciples let the criticism fall like leaflets handed out on the street. What Taft needed was something to give his own supporters to uphold. The only effective retort, Taft found, was to load up with mud, too.

On April 25, Taft opened the Massachusetts campaign with a vicious, direct, and very personal assault on Roosevelt. "Taft Scores Roosevelt; Thousands Cheer Him," blared the Boston *Globe* the next morning. "Boston Crowd of 12,000 Hears Him Answer Colonel's Charges in Speech Bristling With Defiance."[18] The vague references now had a clear target. The tit now had a tat.

It was a bittersweet day for the President. In the morning the distaste of his mission was given a reprieve by the joy of a little girl's sweet endorsement. "I am your little cousin, Betty B. Higgins," she wrote in a letter she presented that morning. "Your sixth grandfather, Deacon Samuel Chapin, was my seventh great-grandfather, so one-ninth of you and one-tenth of me are alike, but ten-tenths of me hopes that nine-ninths of you will be President again." That afternoon, Taft went to work.

"This wrenches my soul," he told his Boston audience, as his three years of private consternation were finally given a public vent. "I am extremely sorry my mission to Massachusetts is unpleasant. I am here to reply to an old and dear friend of mine, Theodore Roosevelt, who has made many charges against me. I deny those charges. I deny all of them. I do not want to fight Theodore Roosevelt, but then sometimes a man in a corner fights. I am going to fight." While he felt the burden of loyalty had driven him to this ugly extreme, as he poured into his speech he lost his three years of hesitation and denial. He was finally and thoroughly freed of the Roosevelt leash, and, more importantly, the betrayed friendship that had him cornered. His gestures grew in volume, and his speech, despite a bad throat, rose in emphasis. "His whole nature revolts against unjust attacks," Archie once wrote. Now counsel for his own defense, Taft threw his every ounce of outrage at Roosevelt.[19]

Taft laid out the Roosevelt charges and a cogent defense against them. The accusations he faced were bold. There were misquotations, hypocrisies, and outright lies. There was Lorimer, Reciprocity, Standard Oil, and the tariff. There were false charges of stolen delegates. Was it, the President asked his audience, "a square deal?" The most biting of all was the accusation of disloyalty. "Neither in thought, nor in word nor action have I been disloyal to the friendship I owe Theodore Roosevelt."

15. (*cont.*) are barren soil, but it will come out all right in the end unless Roosevelt buys a lot of southern delegates with Perkins' money. He would stop at nothing."
16. See "Roosevelt Denies Third Party Report," *NYT*, 3/29/12.
17. "Roosevelt Thrown as Platform Falls," *NYT*, 3/24/12.
18. Boston *Globe*, 4/26/12.
19. "Taft Opens Fire on Roosevelt," *NYT*, 4/26/12 and Butt, 7/12/11, p. 694.

The night of the Boston speech Taft sat in his train as if alone in the world. He wept. A reporter saw him. The President looked up. "Roosevelt was my closest friend." Although "visibly shaken" on the way to that train, the night was a catharsis. Just after the speech, Taft gave an upbeat talk to an Associated Press banquet in New York — by telephone. Rediscovering his humor, he spoke to five hundred diners from two hundred miles away:

> I shall not weight my message to you with an expression of my respect for the concentrated power in this country that you gentlemen represent. The safety of the country lies in the fact that you neutralize each other, and in the growing conviction of the country that the truth is not in you, but that it lies between you … I am not thereby consigning you all to an Ananias club, however strong your desire for close association under some banner, but I am explaining to you how each one of you saves the country from the rest.[20]

A few days later, as he boarded his train for Washington, the President was downright enthused. "His face beaming," to a reporter he declared, "I am told that no such crowds ever turned out before, and that greater approval was never before shown to any candidate in this State."[21] He never campaigned so enthusiastically. Massachusetts went Taft's way by a small but decisive margin that, due to some 15,000 corrupted ballots, might have been huge. Either way, it was a crucial victory. Both he and Roosevelt outpolled the leading standpatter, Senator Crane, which means that Taft won with more than a straight-line vote. Without Massachusetts, Taft would have lost the nomination no matter how many delegates were stamped out by the party machinery.

Biographer Pringle wrote that the Boston speech was delivered "soberly and convincingly, but without great brilliance."[22] Pringle did note that one segment was "effective and moving." It was much more than that. The speech turned the race around. The momentum of the Roosevelt victories in Pennsylvania and Illinois was halted just enough for Taft to keep in control. The end game was set.

* * *

Pringle also criticized Taft for speaking of himself in Massachusetts as a "man of straw." What the President said was, "No man has the right to misrepresent another to get himself up in office no matter how humble that man is. Condemn me if you will but condemn me by other witnesses than Theodore Roosevelt. I was a man of straw, but I have been a man of straw long enough. Every man who has blood in his body, and who has been misrepresented as I have been is forced to fight. I appeal to my friends in Massachusetts, who, I think, believe in the square deal." Taft's audience knew what it meant:

20. Pringle, pp. 781–782 and "Taft 'phones Speech Here from Boston," *NYT*, 4/26/12.
21. "500,000 Turn Out to Cheer Taft On," *NYT*, 4/30/12. To Mabel, Taft wrote, "I am glad that you liked the speech. It was not a pleasant thing to do but there seemed no other way and the response has been very flattering. We are hoping for results in Massachusetts. The people there are very enthusiastic and I think the State is aroused." A postscript, evidently written after the returns came in, was less joyous. "Mass. was not all we could wish but it will steady our horses some" (Taft to Mabel Boardman, 4/30/12).
22. Pringle, p. 777. For a contemporaneous reaction, see Nicholas Murray Butler to Taft (4/26/12): "Permit me to congratulate you most sincerely upon your notable and statesmanlike speech at Boston last evening. I know better than most others how much it cost you to speak out frankly as you did, and under what compulsion of conscience and of principle you were acting. The tone and temper of the speech are as splendid as its content is convincing."

Roosevelt was a liar. The crowd replied enthusiastically, "go to it, Bill!"[23]

Taft declared himself a representative of a cause, not ambition. This was both a sincere assessment and a deliberate mockery of Roosevelt's own lavish protests of disinterestedness. Here was the most important effect of Taft's Boston speech, moving or not: Roosevelt became the issue. Although Roosevelt's reply was quick and vicious, the criticism of Taft suddenly lost its edge, as the axe swung both ways now. Taft pounded and pounded on Roosevelt. As absurd as were allusions to Louis XIV and the L'Etat, c'est Roosevelt, it was unusually good material for his partisans to enjoy. Taft even took up a chant or two, such as to detail a Roosevelt accusation then ask his audience, "Is that giving me a square deal?" "No!" they shouted back. In Ohio, Taft said, "Four years ago Theodore Roosevelt painted me in such glowing language to the American people that I blushed. Now he is using about me language equally strenuous and equally inaptable. Has he changed or have I?" "Roosevelt has," came the cry.[24]

In going personal, things got very personal. Roosevelt called Taft "fathead," "puzzlewit," and "honeyfugler."[25] While avoiding the direct insult, Taft sarcastically discussed Roosevelt's "courage" to lie about Taft's record, and wondered what would become of the nation were Roosevelt to die. Roosevelt compared himself to Lincoln. Taft compared himself to a rat.[26] More old correspondence was dug out by both sides to prove this hypocrisy or that. An international incident was nearly started when Taft published private letters in proof of Roosevelt's previous support for Reciprocity. It got so zany that the *Times* defended both Taft and Roosevelt, the one for having nothing to do with a Roosevelt Administration decision not to prosecute the Harvester Trust, and the other for not having prosecuted the trust. Roosevelt said of Taft, "It is a bad trait to bite the hand that feeds you." Finley Peter Dunne's character Mr. Dooley answered for him: "His hand was in me face whin I bit it."[27]

Otto Bannard wrote Taft to encourage the attacks:

> ...you should not step back into the defensive. It is a weak up hill position to be explaining why you have to fight and complaining of T.R.'s treatment. You are better on the attack and he is at quite a disadvantage on the defensive. Show him up for a pretentious, insincere, seeker after a permanent dictatorship — advocating anything to get votes, secretly flirting with any trusts that will put up money and using any boss who would help him. It seems to me you struck better notes in Maryland than you did in Ohio.... Soak him as a dangerous radical, who stops at nothing and is a preacher without sincerity. Don't flatter. Don't listen to compromise. There is no opportunity for a second ballot and you will surely get it on the first. Keep up your courage.[28]

23. "500,000 Turn Out to Cheer Taft On," *NYT*, 4/30/12.
24. "Taft Drives Home Roosevelt Attack," 4/27/12 and "Taft Keeps Up Attacks," 5/16/12, *NYT*. For a Louis XIV remark, see "20,000 Cheer Taft in Last Ohio Appeal," *NYT*, 5/21/12.
25. Brands, p. 712.
26. "Taft in Maryland Trails Roosevelt," *NYT*, 5/5/12. There, Taft repeated the "in a corner line," only he replaced "man" with "rat." At Hyattsville he shouted, "I'm a man of peace, and I don't want to fight. But when I do fight I want to hit hard. Even a rat in a corner will fight." Pringle called it "tragic." The author here is unconvinced. Taft's audience knew exactly what he was talking about. A President was not to campaign, much less in a primary and in Hyattsville, Maryland. It was a constant theme of Taft's that he had no interest in the shouting match, but Roosevelt forced it upon him and, more importantly, the office.
27. "Roosevelt Held Back Trust Suit," 4/25/12, "Colonel Says Taft is the Disloyal One," 4/27/12 and "Mr. Dooley Philosophizes on the Campaign," 5/19/12, *NYT*.
28. Bannard to Taft, 5/10/12. Taft replied, "Thank you for your encouraging note of May 10th. I recognize the force and wisdom of your suggestions and will endeavor to carry them out" (Taft to Bannard, 5/12/12).

* * *

Taft never let up. He couldn't, for he was on his own. The Republican establishment stayed away. Where local candidates were on the ballot they joined the President's campaign. The rest played the waiting game, especially national figures. Even the New York Old Guard kept an open stance by not formally "instructing" its delegates to Taft.[29] Root agreed with the urgency of the President's campaign but refused to enlist, telling Taft that since Roosevelt hadn't named him directly he had no business there. Even some of the Cabinet hesitated, notably Hitchcock, Taft's 1908 campaign manager. "Frank!" Taft screamed at a Cabinet meeting, "Are you for me or against me?"[30] Additionally, Roosevelt tore away large chunks of the party machinery. Every boss defection stole with it the patronage, the money, and the indispensable local influence. Meanwhile, if he relied on a boss such as Cox of Cincinnati, Taft was skewered for it by Roosevelt; without the help of those organizations, Taft had no delegates.

With the May loss of his home state, Ohio, Taft's viability was put to its worst test. He had already locked up the needed delegates, but the late primaries swung completely to Roosevelt. There was talk of a third party ticket — a conservative party to counter a Republican Roosevelt run — or a compromise candidate, such as Hughes. To that idea Roosevelt replied, "I'll name the compromise candidate. He'll be me." Taft was equally defiant. On the eve of the Ohio vote he declared the election over. He congratulated the nation for having avoided the ruin that would follow a Roosevelt third term. When the losing returns followed, Taft pointed to seventeen Ohio delegates he could add to his total count, and pronounced, "This will constitute a clear majority in the national convention."[31] He left for the East Coast buoyant and smiling.

Into New Jersey, Taft kept up the scorching attacks, and with a new emphasis. "Few more enthusiastic welcomes have ever been accorded to a candidate than he received in the course of a wild automobile tour yesterday," wrote the *Times*. "It was a spectacular and interesting trip. Those who had charged the President with being 'settled' in his habits should have seen him tearing over the road at a speed varying from forty to seventy miles an hour." It started at Jersey City with a party of fourteen motors. After a speech at nearby Bayonne, Taft was joined by another twenty-two cars. He then led this unique, flag-flying motorcade on an amazing and wild parade. Between speeches and bows at Newark, the Oranges, Passaic, and Montclair, Taft blew across the Meadowlands, ending up that night at Englewood, overlooking the Hudson from the Jersey cliffs. Did he really hit seventy miles an hour? Probably not, but the speeds literally made the President's hat fly. His military aide did the honors of collecting it twice. Whatever the truth to the reports of scorching, it was enough to scare some of the chauffeurs. "What can we do?" complained one. "It is our business to stick to the President and the President set the pace."[32]

That morning Taft passed within view of the Statue of Liberty and the towers of Manhattan from across the Hudson where America was asserting itself with construction of the world's tallest building, the Woolworth tower, just then reach-

29. See "New York Won't Instruct for Taft," *NYT*, 4/10/12.
30. Pringle, p. 764.
31. "'I'll Name Myself,' Says Roosevelt," 5/21/12, "Taft Declares Colonel Beaten," 5/20/12 and "Taft to Fight On; Claims Victory," 5/23/12, *NYT*.
32. "Wild Auto Ride for Taft," *NYT*, 5/26/12.

ing its almost sixty stories. Taft had a mood to match it. Despite a bad throat, his speeches were vigorous and fun. Laughing with a crowd at Arlington, he joked, "Col. Roosevelt says he will be the candidate. But that is only another one of the unnecessaries which he has made us familiar with." Then he went serious. "This man is intoxicated with the love of power. When the time comes that one man's life is essential to this government as a republic, then it ought to go out of business." It came down to just that for Taft. At Orange, he declared, "Theodore Roosevelt is a dangerous man, and when he asks for a third term I consider it my highest duty, higher than the Presidency of the United States, to come out and utter a solemn warning to the people."

The night before the vote, Taft walked the boardwalk of Atlantic City, enjoying the ocean winds, and mingling with some of the 10,000 who gathered to hear him. A crescent moon hung low in the sky. His train pulled out at 7:15 the next morning. The exhausted press corps couldn't believe the President's stamina. He made eight speeches on the way, including stops in towns along the Delaware River. He was especially gratified to see the farmers who arrived at the stations in automobiles. At Woodbury, where he declared "Delicious!" the strawberries presented him by a little boy, he lectured the town's girls: "I have no doubt that when these young ladies grow to womanhood they will have the ballot, but whether you do or not you ought to make preparation to understand your country and to know the gratitude you ought to offer to God for being Americans." Despite all the present carping, he told them, "This is the best country and the best Government that ever was." The day ended at 1:00 that night in Washington.[33]

Roosevelt swept the New Jersey vote. He won the open primaries, proving the obvious, that he was the better campaigner, the more attractive personality. He was, as La Follette put it, "the keenest and ablest living interpreter of what I could call the superficial public sentiment of a given time, and he is spontaneous in response to it."[34] But, as Roosevelt already knew, it wasn't enough. Taft won the delegate race by taking just enough popular votes to add to his machine totals. In doing so, he stood against the greatest assault upon an opponent of Roosevelt's career.

Taft told his audiences why he made the fight. "If I consulted my own wish, I would be silent under Mr. Roosevelt's attack, and trust to the future to vindicate me." Then, walking the platform, hitting the rail, and red with anger, he continued,

> But I represent a cause. I represent the Republican Party that stands for wise progress under the Constitution, and stands for liberty regulated by law. I must do my duty, and answer the charges of Col. Roosevelt.... But I am forced against the wall with my back to it, and I'm bound, if I have any manhood, to fight.[35]

Bannard congratulated Taft for hanging tough. "You fought nobly to the finish, but those who vote in the direct primaries

33. "Taft Winds up Campaign," *NYT*, 5/29/12, from reporter's paraphrase.
34. La Follette's view mirrored Taft's own expressed a year before the election. During the calm of February 1911, Taft told Archie of Roosevelt's peculiar fancy of himself as Lincoln. Taft rather compared him to Jackson: "Between him and Lincoln there is nothing in common.... Roosevelt was a great President, but not in the way he thinks he was great. He got a great hold on the public mind and used it" (from "As La Follette Sees Roosevelt," *NYT*, 5/20/12 and Butt, 2/12/11, p. 593).
35. "Taft Drives Home Roosevelt Attack," *NYT*, 4/27/12.

prefer the man of war who boasts of his prowess and commits depredations on his neighbor's lands. All the world loves a fighter. It still remains to count the delegates and whatever the result, the Democrats cannot fail to win and will always be under obligations to that extraordinary free booter and pirate T.R."[36]

36. Bannard to Taft, 5/29/12.

27

"With a heart full of love and gratitude..."[1]

The most traumatic event of 1912 was not the Republican nomination. Nor was it the November election. That moment which most occupied the headlines had nothing to do with politics. It may have been the only thing to keep Roosevelt out of the headlines. The night of April 14, 1912, the *Titanic* sank, and with it Major Archibald Willingham Butt.

A much smaller news item lay on page two of the *Times* on March 1st. "Major Butt On Sick Leave: President's Aid Going Abroad to Recuperate His Health." It was noted that Butt never recovered from the fatigue that followed the last Western Tour and that he hadn't a vacation in four years. The day before Archie walked the plank onto the *Titanic* there appeared another news item with his name: "Why Major Butt, the President's Aid, Went to Rome."[2] The author was "a Veteran Diplomat," one of the anonymous bylines used for the *Sunday Times*' Washington commentary. "Ostensibly he was worn out by his arduous duties at the White House, but really he visited the Pope to discuss the question of Precedence of American Cardinals at our official functions."

Archie was certainly a leading expert at diplomatic etiquette. Social precedence meant more to him than anyone short of those with or just beyond it. The man who announced several hundreds of callers at a White House reception, who manhandled the "handshakers" and the ingrates at the President's endless banquets and receptions, and whose erect, perfect salute had greeted the Duke of Connaught at Washington's Union Station, indeed visited the Vatican. He went because he wanted to meet the Pope. There was no secret mission, one way or another.[3] In this, the

1. Butt to Taft, 3/9/12, written from Gibraltar, aboard the steamer *Berlin* (Taft Papers).
2. *NYT*, 3/1/12 and 4/14/12.
3. Archie carried a letter of introduction from the President. The news of his visit to Rome provoked bitter outrage from anti–Catholics groups. Taft was used to the vitriol, as he had been subjected to it ever since he negotiated purchase from the Vatican of its Philippine properties in 1902. Also, as a Unitarian, Taft empathized with his fellow Catholic Americans for the abuse they received on account of their religion. Following the stories of Archie's trip, Taft issued a statement denying any secret missions. "Among the insidious methods of attack pursued by some against me is the attempt to arouse religious prejudice on the charge that I am in some manner unduly favoring the Roman Catholic Church" (Taft Papers, reel 460, case file 316, 5/12/12). Butt's description of his audience with the Pope is marvelous. He told the Holy Father

first report was exact: Archie needed a break.

Archie's close friend and sometime boarder, the painter and journalist Francis Millet, saw his condition and pleaded that Butt join him in Italy where Millet had business. Archie fretted over abandoning the President. Millet begged Taft to intervene for Archie's sake. "I am completely tuckered out, and the doctor advises me to take a rest," Archie confessed to Clara.

> I hate to leave the Big White Chief just at this time, though I will be back before the middle of April. I have come to the conclusion that if I am to go through this frightful summer I must have a rest now. I drive myself like a steam engine and feel tired all the time. I shall do little in the way of sightseeing. In fact, I think the sight of a train makes me sick.[4]

The Roosevelt spat fell upon Butt as much as any other. There was Alice, of course, and her edge. "Isn't it the most wonderful thing in the world, Butt?" she said of her father in November. "Of course he would not have the nomination this time, but it just shows what is in people's hearts." There was Corrine Robinson, one of the Roosevelt sisters who recognized the wedge of jealousy driven between the Tafts and the Roosevelts back in 1909. She remained, like Alice, fond of Taft. "When I think of the old days at the White House, and how these two men seemed to love one another, it makes me very unhappy to think of the great chasm which lies between them now. How they would get together and talk and discuss matters! And I remember the way their laughs would mingle and reverberate through the corridors and rooms, and Edith would say: 'It is always that way when they are together.'"[5]

At the invitation of Mrs. Roosevelt, Archie visited Oyster Bay in late January. Taft encouraged the trip, and the Roosevelts were delighted to see Archie. Roosevelt was exactly as Archie remembered him, such as to hold a two hour soliloquy. Mrs. Roosevelt, whom Archie adored, sent kind words to the President. Roosevelt didn't mention Taft's name. Evidently worried about what Roosevelt might say, just before the visit Archie wrote, "I would not ask to be relieved from the President now if my whole life was at stake. My devotion to the Colonel is as strong as it was the day he left, but this man has been too fond of me for the past three years to be thrown over at this time and having it sent all over the country that another Roosevelt man reads the handwriting on the wall and gets out of the sinking ship, or some other such mixed metaphor."[6] Afterwards, his loyalty to the President hardened:

> I lay awake a long time last night, trying to make up my mind as to what my duty was in regard to this trip to Italy. I seem to have been dragged into it by force of circumstances. It seems to me that the

3. (*cont.*) that the President kept a photograph of the Pope on which the Pope had inscribed something in Latin, and that none of the Cabinet could figure it out without a dictionary. The Pope was delighted and laughed, Butt was told, "the heartiest laugh ... since he was made Pope." He then asked if Taft could read it. Archie wrote to Taft, "I promptly said yes, that it would have been very difficult Latin indeed for you not to be able to read it at sight. I hope this is the truth, for I should hate to have a lie checked up against me later on by Pius X, but I had no idea of admitting that you had any defects after all he had said." Archie wrote that when a Cardinal asked if he was Catholic, he replied that "if he wanted some men to fight under him, I would gladly enlist, but as a Spiritual force I was afraid I was a failure" (Butt to Taft, 3/23/12, Taft Papers; see this delightful letter and the last of Butt's letters from Europe in case file 209, reel 457).
4. Butt, 2/23/12, p. 847.
5. Butt, 11/27/11, p. 771 and 1/15/12, pp. 812–813.
6. Butt, 1/29/12, pp. 832–834, 1/13/12, p. 812.

> President will need every *intime* near at hand now. If we are ever to be of any real comfort to him, this is the time. I am hesitating about the wisdom of going, but I will think it over and try to reach some decision to-morrow. I really can't bear to leave him just now. I can see he hates to see me go, and I feel like a quitter in going.[7]

The next day Archie canceled his passage. The President and Millet insisted he go. Finally, on February 27, he prepared to leave. To the White House he sent careful instructions on how to care for the President. "My only anxiety is that the President may need someone to walk with him when you cannot walk," he wrote to Hilles, "or whom he can take out to the golf links and play with, without being bothered by officials. Rockwell plays an excellent game of golf and knows just what to do to make himself of use and yet not be a nuisance."[8] To an Aunt, he wrote:

> I received your letter this morning and greatly enjoyed the reference to the malady from which we are both suffering. While my trouble is auto-intoxication, yours is too much automobiling. Strange to say, I first suffered from too much automobiling, and I think the auto-intoxication originated there, so you see that you don't get the last auto-trouble! ...Well, good-bye, dear Aunt. Keep yourself from worry, and when I come back we will get together somewhere and talk over the various phases of auto disease. Love to Kate and the pretty granddaughter. I did get her photo, and have had it framed, but it seems to me that I have got beyond acknowledging anything except that which calls for an imperative answer. Your affectionate nephew, Archie.[9]

On March 2nd, Archie left for Naples on the steamer *Berlin*.

The first news from the *Titanic* came just before the Pennsylvania primary. Leaving port the great ship nearly collided with another boat. The *Times*'s report of the incident noted, "Major Archibald Butt is also a passenger. He spent last week with his brother, who lives in Chester, and says he had a very pleasant holiday, but is glad to be getting home again."[10] Four days later the afternoon papers said that the *Titanic* had encountered an iceberg, but the passengers were on the *Carpathia*, and the *Titanic* was on its way to Halifax for repairs. The President went to the theater that night without worry. The next day, Americans awoke to the biggest headline of the year.

The primaries, the delegate count, the initiative, referendum and recall, and all other troubles were lost to the President's distress. When he returned from the theater that night, the real story was all over the White House telegraph office. The President was frantic. He ordered all information forwarded to him. A personal telegraph went to the White Star Line, "Have you any information concerning Major Butt? If you communicate at once, I will greatly appreciate."[11] He ordered Navy cruisers and revenue cutters to the search and recovery.

Over the next days, Taft and his brother, Harry, pestered the White Star office for news of Archie. He refused to believe the Major was lost. He wired the Butt family at Augusta with his faith that Archie would come out all right. With the news sorted by the survivor count and their stories, the President consoled himself with pride in his aide. "I never had any idea that

7. Butt, 2/26/12, p. 851.
8. Butt to CD Hilles, 2/27/12.
9. Butt, 2/27/12, pp. 851–852.
10. "Titanic in Peril on Leaving Port," *NYT*, 4/11/12.
11. "President Taft Stunned," *NYT*, 4/16/12.

Archie was saved at all. As soon I heard that 1,200 people went down I knew he went down, too. He was a soldier, and was on deck, where he belonged."[12]

The Senate opened hearings on the disaster. At Wall Street, the panic over the shipping line was offset by a run on Marconi stocks. The kings of England and Spain and other leaders telegraphed their sympathy at the loss. The Pope, the Duke of Connaught, and the President of France mentioned Archie by name. From Nebraska, Roosevelt telegraphed the Army General Staff asking for news of Archie and released a statement that the Major had "met his end as an officer and gentleman should, giving up his own life that others might be saved. I and my family loved him sincerely."[13]

The *Carpathia* arrived the 18th. That evening there was a race like no other in the history of the automobile:

> By 8:15 o'clock a procession of automobiles, limousines, touring cars, and taxicabs had started south on Seventh avenue, the most direct route from uptown to the pier. Over the wet asphalt they sped at racing speed, their headlights brilliantly illumining the otherwise dark street. They tore along sometimes three and four abreast, ignoring all traffic rules, and the police stood aside and watched them.... The racing chauffeurs, their cars massed close together and filling Seventh Avenue almost from curb to curb as the Jericho Turnpike was filled in the first days of the famous Vanderbilt Cup race, paid no heed to the rules of the road, which would have caused them to stop at the main cross-streets—thirty-fourth, twenty-third, and streets in which there are fire apparatus.[14]

More than five hundred automobiles crowded the pier.

The survivors came ashore with incredible stories of J.J. Astor, who calmly waved goodbye to his bride as he lit a cigarette, Benjamin Guggenheim, who stated, "We've dressed up in our best and are prepared to go down like gentlemen," the orchestra playing on the way down, which one story claimed was at Archie's order, and of gunshots and panic. The stories of Archie were that he took authority over the mad scene by the lifeboats. His strong hand more than once was laid upon the shoulder of panicked men who tried to force their way into the lifeboats, including at least one youth whom he told it was a privilege to die like a man. One story was that he lifted a Miss Marie Young into a lifeboat, gently wrapped her shoulders with a scarf, and stepped out. "Good-bye, Miss Young," he said. "Luck is with you. Will you kindly remember me to all the folks back home?"[15]

That last was a great story, but it was not true. Young wrote the President, "Although a Washingtonian, I did not know Major Butt, having been in deep mourning for several years. The alleged 'interview' is entirely an invention by some officious reporter, who thereby brought much distress to many of Major Butt's near relatives and friends, for when they wrote me, of what a comfort the story was to them, I had to tell them it was untrue...."[16] One young girl, however, likely did owe her deliverance to the Major. A 14-year-old Syrian who spoke no English arrived to New York on the *Carpathia*. Through a translator she told a reporter of how "a tall man ... picked me up in his arms...." As she told her story, the reporter concluded she was speaking of Archie Butt. "As he carried me I noticed he was weak and I

12. "Taft Despairs of Butt," *NYT*, 4/19/12.
13. "Roosevelt's Praise for Butt," *NYT*, 4/20/12.
14. "Carpathia Here with the Rescued," *NYT*, 4/19/12.
15. See "Butt Was Tireless in Helping Women," *NYT*, 4/20/12.
16. M Young to Taft, 5/10/12. Taft replied on 5/12/12, "You are entirely right in stating the matter as you have."

could understand he was praying for strength to get me to the lifeboat. I was praying for him and for myself, and that my prayers were partially answered is shown by my presence here."[17]

* * *

On the 1st of May the President returned to Washington from the vigorous Massachusetts campaign in order to attend the unveiling of a Rodin statue given by France. After only five hours in the city, he left for Georgia to attend memorial services for Archie. "I couldn't prepare anything in advance to say here," he told the 1,500 mourners at Augusta. "I tried, but couldn't. He was too near me. He was loyal to my predecessor, Mr. Roosevelt, who selected him to be military aid, and to me he had become as a son or a brother." A few days later Taft presided over another service at Washington. "I cannot go into a box at a theater; I cannot turn around in my room; I can't go anywhere without expecting to see his smiling face or to hear his cheerful voice in greeting." Then he said what was obvious to all, "it is difficult to speak on such an occasion." The President was in tears.

> He was on the deck of the *Titanic* exactly what he was everywhere. He leaves a void with those who loved him, but the circumstances of his going are all what we would have had, and, while the tears fill the eyes and the voice is choked, we are felicitated by the memory of what he was.[18]

Taft campaigned all the way to and from Augusta. Heart-wrenching memorials to Archie came at the time of the Boston and Maryland speeches in which he attacked Roosevelt directly for the first time. Was Archie part of the corner the President felt himself backed into? The emotions he felt the night of his Boston speech were full of Archie. With the Major and all his companionship and common sense gone, so, too, was the daily connection to Roosevelt the Major represented. Taft made the decision to attack Roosevelt directly only after the *Titanic* sank. He had been considering it, lamenting it a few days before. He hardened to it afterwards. Pringle called that decision "one of the hardest ever faced by Taft."[19] Archie would have been too proud.

17. "To Archie Butt Little Syrian Girl Owes Life," Jacksonville *Times Union*, 5/25/12.
18. "Taft in Tears as He Lauds Major Butt," *NYT*, 5/6/12.
19. Pringle, p. 774.

28

Outrage Denied

The party that nearly abandoned its President during the primaries vindicated itself to him during the Chicago National Convention in late June. Taft stayed home while the leadership led a steadfast army of party regulars to humiliate Roosevelt and his insurgents. The enduring metaphor is the steamroller. Going in Taft had no such assurance. The Roosevelt contests to state delegations that dominated pre–Convention activity were not the core issue. The protests, the demonstrations, and the accusations of fraud were not a goal unto themselves. Nobody expected the National Committee to do anything but what it did in rejecting most of the contests. The real purpose of the outrage was to loosen the Committee's hold and turn the delegates to a Roosevelt stampede. This was still an old-time convention. The steamroller was at work; unclear was who would drive away with it.[1]

Even with late wins at Ohio and New Jersey, Roosevelt was running out of room. His first step was to fight for "contested" delegates, which came of split conventions and conflicting claims that resulted. The contests were reviewed by a special committee that met for two weeks before the full convention opened on June 18. At the President's insistence, the committee took the time — an enormous and often tedious amount of time — to review every contest and hear every objection.[2]

While the National Committee generally gift-wrapped Taft delegates, even Roosevelt managers Borah and Kellogg admitted most of them duty-free. Their compatriot, Governor Hadley, probably the only man besides Elihu Root who left the Chicago circus with his reputation intact, walked out of the Missouri hearings with only a few delegates and fair praise for the proceedings. "I will say for the National Committee that in dealing with Missouri it has acted fairly," he announced.[3] Those were not words Roosevelt wanted to hear. Any legitimacy to the proceedings

1. On the first day of the convention Taft wrote, "The result is still quite doubtful, but I am very hopeful that one thing will be accomplished and that is that Mr. Roosevelt can not be made the regular nominee of the Republican party. If that hopefulness is justified, I shall be content" (Taft to Delia Torrey, 6/19/12). Taft was thinking here of a third candidate. His own success was uncertain in his mind.
2. For a case study of the Texas disputes, see "Theodore Roosevelt, William Howard Taft, and the Disputed Delegates in 1912: Texas as a Test Case," by Lewis L. Gould, *Southwestern Historical Quarterly*, Vol. LXXX No. 1, July 1976. Gould concluded, "In this contest to see who was the better practitioner of the legal piracy called Republican politics in the South, Taft had outstolen Roosevelt" (p. 55).
3. "Divides Missouri on Taft's Advice," *NYT*, 6/14/12.

would rob him of the outrage he needed to steal the Convention.

In a year of exaggerations, the sublime in absurdity was finally achieved when a North Carolina contest came down to a decision not between Taft and Roosevelt delegations but between rival Roosevelt factions. The sublime in the outrage metaphor was a Roosevelt manager's complaint that the National Committee was "a bunch of crooks joy riding on a steam roller." Roosevelt man Col. Lyon, the boss of Texas, matched up with the year's historical parallels. "I have heard much recently of the '100 days' and the 'return from Elba,'" he said. "I give you fair warning that if you persist in the way you are going there will be a repetition of another historic incident — the Commune." The analogies ran dry as the outrage turned stale. At the contest hearings, it came down to this exchange between Roosevelt supporter Francis Heney and National Committeeman Kennedy of North Dakota. "You lie," shouted Heney. "You lie," shouted Kennedy.[4]

Roosevelt backed off earlier threats to invade Chicago. From Oyster Bay he told reporters, "You see I am here. I am not on my special train." Nobody was fooled. "We are told that Mr. Roosevelt will go to Chicago in person at the first indication that he is not getting 'fair play,' a 'square deal,'" wrote the *Times*. "We may assume that Mr. Roosevelt will certainly go to Chicago."[5] And so it was. For all the theft, thievery, and thieving, Roosevelt boarded his "special train." The ride was disturbed only by a large rock on the tracks put there by boys. The train's modern air-brakes averted a crash. The rest of the way was uneventful, which is not always a good thing in the Rooseveltian way of publicity.[6]

Despite the staged hesitation, Roosevelt was so quick to Chicago that he beat there the man who was at that moment the object of his outrage. Roosevelt's train passed near the very town where that man was happily celebrating the centennial of his alma mater, Hamilton College, as if unaware of the storms out West.[7] The man was for two weeks the most powerful in the country, Senator Elihu Root. His refusal to campaign for Taft would pay off now. There were no flies on Root. His hands were clean of the primary rat fight, and even Roosevelt avoided attacks on Root for fear of offending his own delegates. Elihu Root was one of those remarkable characters in American politics who transcend an age, not because he would fit any period, which he might, but because he was an untouchable amidst his own.

When Roosevelt hit Root, it was with apology, declaring that it wasn't so much the Senator "personally as his representation of Barnes and the rest of the privileges."[8] Say what? Was not guilt by association the worst crime of the day? Even if the President of the country was not, the former Secretary of State and preeminent force in the Senate was beyond Roosevelt's demagoguery. As for Taft, he could count on Root. The two men were convinced of the extreme situation. Root called the role of Temporary Chairman "too difficult and too unpleasant a post" to refuse. "To me the welfare of the party is of much more importance than the welfare of either the two candidates. The scrap of these two men is comparatively insignificant. Its effect upon the party and

4. "Divides Missouri on Taft's Advice," 6/14/12, "Contests Bitterly Fought to the End," 6/16/12, *NYT*.
5. "The Colonel at Chicago," *NYT* editorial, 6/4/12.
6. "Small Crowds Greet Colonel on Journey," *NYT*, 6/16/12.
7. "Root's Alma Mater Vied With Chicago," *NYT*, 6/24/12.
8. "Roosevelt Again Turns on Root," 6/4/12, *NYT*. See also "Roosevelt Drops Fight on Root," *NYT*, 6/1/12.

the party's future must be regarded as important."[9]

* * *

Once at Chicago, Roosevelt found a chaos more to his liking. He shook hands and clicked his teeth as he made his way from his train, then paused with satisfaction atop the steps to review the pushing crowd. He motored to his hotel, where another demonstration greeted him inside. His bodyguards, "every one six-footers and built proportionally," practically carried him to his suite using "the most approved football tactics." The five men were part protective service, part rabble rousers, and part ornaments. The group consisted of a former Secret Service agent, a cow puncher, a sheriff, an adjunct officer, and a man nicknamed "Fighting Pat." Awaiting him were the Incense Swingers and the money men, Chicago press mogul Medill McCormick, trust builder George Perkins, and newspaper financier Frank Munsey.[10]

The Roosevelt delegates, the "Theodores," surrounded the hotel and shouted for their man. Roosevelt climbed out his second floor window to the top of the hotel entrance and waved his "campaign" hat. Practically confirming Taft's warnings of a return of the Sun King, Roosevelt proceeded heartily in the first person. "Chicago is a mighty poor place in which to try and steal anything," he started. "California's twenty-six votes are mine. They are mine, and they will be counted for me." He then shouted defiance to "the politicians" who "dead or alive, will be made to understand that they are the servants and not the masters of the rank and file, of the plain citizens of the Republican Party."

The noise contrasted with the reality that forced Roosevelt to Chicago. His arrival there was surrender. The delegate contests did not advance. Particularly ominous were the outrageous admissions by some of his managers of the fairness of the proceedings. The pre–Convention quiet meant that the hoped for stampede was not to materialize spontaneously. Roosevelt would have to conjure the outrage himself. Thus his arrival on the scene. Plan C.

Edging toward the opening of the Convention the Roosevelt camp played directly to the delegates. First was the announcement of defectors from the Taft side. It was conducted as tightly as the "little Governors" orchestra. Each defector had a timetable and a prepared statement. It was embarrassingly un-spontaneous.[11] Most of the bolters were Southerners, black and white, although the list included two important New Yorkers, one of whom was already known as a Roosevelt booster. The next day the second New Yorker recanted, as did most of the blacks who said they were misled by the Theodores.

The next publicity blitz was over the content of a possible Roosevelt plank that would be acceptable to regulars. Although a product of the feverish minds of Pinchot, Garfield, and Munsey, "the amateur liberators," it was let out that the initiative, referendum, and recall would be dropped. Typical of their efforts was Munsey's piece on the tariff which set out the origins of labor and capital and ended with a conclusion on the tariff which Roosevelt refused to embrace. Protection stood. It was to be a Republican document.[12]

The final piece to Roosevelt's maneuvering was a Convention-eve speech to give one more kick to shake loose the next day's proceedings. Baring his soul, apparently, or his best theatrical skills, he ex-

9. "Root, Full of Fight, Fears for His Party," *NYT*, 6/17/12.
10. "Roosevelt Gets Chicago Cheers," *NYT*, 6/16/12.
11. "Roosevelt Captures 12 Bolters," *NYT*, 6/17/12.
12. "Colonel No Radical If He's Nominated," *NYT*, 6/18/12.

plained just why he was there. From the drop of his hat in February, to a Chicago June, fighting "in honorable fashion for the good of mankind," he proclaimed, "we stand at Armageddon and we battle for the Lord."[13] It was an astonishing speech, and desperate. Comparing Chicago to Armageddon might not to some seem an exaggeration, but invoking the Lord for his candidacy was truly, as the *Times* said, "grotesque." What is most amazing is that on the eve of the Convention, Roosevelt lobbed a Hail Mary pass.

He started out with the same, self-congratulatory rationalizations he made all season,

> When in February last I made up my mind that it was my duty to enter this fight, it was after long and careful deliberation. I had become convinced that Mr. Taft had definitely and completely abandoned the cause of the people and had surrendered himself wholly to the biddings of the professional political bosses and to the great privileged interests standing behind them.

And to La Follette, he continued, "I had also become convinced that unless I did make the fight it could not be made at all, and that Mr. Taft's nomination would come to him without serious opposition."

Then onward it was to the fine print of the usual complaints, all laid out marvelously in 9,000 words, practically a Taft message to Congress. Yet the final question betrayed his fear: which side of the Lord are you on? Whatever the Almighty's feelings, the weather was "fair and cool" with "moderate variable winds...."[14]

The opening day of the convention was wild, a tumult. Watching from the press box William Jennings Bryan laughed, "If you didn't know where you were you might think you were in a Democratic convention."[15] On the floor, the respective bosses, Flinn and Barnes, went to work, which went like this: when a Theodore seconded Governor Hadley for Temporary Chair, Barnes punctuated the speaker's points with a wild laugh, a cue to the "Tafters" to join in, most of whom hadn't a clue as to what was being said. A reporter noted, the "speech was utterly ruined." Things got truly fun when the Tafters screamed "Bryan! Bryan! Speech!" while the Theodore, Heney, went on about Taft and theft and other offenses against Roosevelt and the Lord.[16]

Following Heney was a Tafter, Senator Bradley. Safely back among his California delegation, Heney tossed a bomb Bradley's way. "Did you vote for Lorimer?" Bradley stalked across the platform, pointed his finger at Heney, and shouted, "Yes, I voted for Lorimer, and when I did I voted for a man ten thousand times better than you." A report noted, "All the uproar that had preceded this looked like a prayer meeting compared with what followed. When Bradley could be heard again he waved his fist at the Californian and roared, 'And the time shall never come when the great State of Kentucky will fall so low as to take moral advice from Francis J. Heney.'"[17] Ten minutes passed before calm was restored.

To get to the vote on Temporary Chairman there followed a series of par-

13. "Roosevelt Speaks to a Great Throng," *NYT*, 6/18/12.
14. Chicago *Tribune*, 6/17/12 and 6/18/12.
15. "Roosevelt Gets Chicago Cheers," *NYT*, 6/16/12.
16. "Taft Victory in the First Clash," *NYT*, 6/19/12.
17. Heney was famous for his anti-corruption investigations in San Francisco. However, like many of the period's crusaders, Heney fell overboard in prosecutorial zeal. He overreached, like Pinchot, by going national. Heney's attacks on Lorimer were responsible for much of the Senate defense of Lorimer. Certain Senators who wanted Lorimer out were unwilling to do so at Heney's profit. The Illinois Senator's most effective defense was his prosecution, which included Heney, McCormick, and other hyperactives.

liamentary motions and points of order presented by both sides. The motions were prepared the day before, as were the objections and rulings. It was a careful dance whose object was to make the partner trip. And for everyone to yell a lot. The Roosevelt side kicked off with Hadley's declaration that the National Committee was illegitimate. Committee Chairman Rosewater overruled him. Next business.

The only serious play — and it was brutal — was by the La Follettes, of all people. "Battle Bob" was still in it, and his Wisconsin team was as loyal as any. The Theodores hoped to join with the La Follettes to outvote the regulars and direct the steamroller their way. Roosevelt's managers went into the convention with the understanding that the Wisconsin Badgers were behind them. Henry Cochems, who had nominated La Follette for President in 1908, nominated Wisconsin Governor Francis McGovern. Unnoticed by the Theodores was that Cochems spoke "as an individual member of the Wisconsin delegation."

Governor Johnson of California, "with a paunch and a punch," the man who would be the Bull Moose vice presidential candidate, took the stand for McGovern. While Johnson railed, "We deny the right of any set of men to Mexicanize the Republican Party," the Badgers quietly watched him fall into their trap. It was not until later that anyone realized that the cheering for McGovern came from the Theodores, not the La Follettes. The trap was sprung when La Follette's manager, Walter Houser, declared that La Follette refused to enter into "combinations." The Wisconsin caucus had earlier that day voted 14 to 11 against supporting McGovern along with the Theodores. Although two more joined Cochems to vote for McGovern, the rest spread their votes amongst other candidates. The blow was decisive.

The La Follette votes alone would not have been enough to put McGovern, and thus Roosevelt, on top, but any momentum in that direction was halted. As the votes went state-by-state, including two by Californian women, the first at a national convention, the pressure was on for a display of final loyalties. A number of the Southern bolters stayed bolted, as did twelve New Yorkers. The rest stuck hard to Taft. Root was elected by a margin of fifty-six. Significantly, at least thirty Roosevelt delegates voted for Root over McGovern.

There was as yet no certainty that Taft would prevail. On the Democratic side, the winner of the primaries, Champ Clark, lost the nomination through typical convention intrigue, side-deals, and the general flow of enthusiasms. Likewise, neither the primaries nor the National Committee could alone determine the outcome at Chicago. Told that the Roosevelt delegates really wanted "to be regular," Root replied, "The only way for them to do that is for them to get Mr. Roosevelt a majority of the delegates in the convention on the formal balloting." He wasn't stonewalling. That was the way it happened. The convention was not predetermined. Roosevelt used the rudimentary primary system and appeals to "the people" as his wedge. At Chicago, he punched it too hard. The delegates reacted to the shocks by firming up for Taft.

Day two was as unruly as the first. A woman, "extraordinarily pretty ... a wild Roosevelt enthusiast," led a thirty-five minute Roosevelt demonstration. The night before she held a similar rally from atop a table at Roosevelt's hotel. The stampede failed. Several demonstrations for Hadley, which included cheers from Taft delegates, were more successful for their greater spontaneity. Bryan was impressed by the show for Hadley. Most distressing for the Theodores was the rejection by the floor of a compromise over the contested delegates. The vote was won by six more votes than Root had taken the day before.

Through it all Root kept a firm hold. "He conducted himself with ... impartiality ... a resolution that nothing could daunt, and with a stern dedication that checked and intimidated even such unterrified strong- arm men as Flinn of Pennsylvania," wrote the *Times*'s dispatcher.[18] Flinn could spark a riot by standing up. Root stopped one such uproar by calmly laying his hand on the shoulder of a Taft speaker whom Flinn was taunting. The speaker and all the delegates stopped cold to see what Root would do. He demanded "reasonable and decent debate." The calm lasted but a few minutes before Flinn stood again as an order for chaos. "Sit down," Root screamed. Flinn ignored the glaring Chairman and lifted a megaphone to shout insults at the Taft speaker. Root stood firm, and Flinn finally sat down. And so it went all day, including a threat by Root to evict a man, "delegate or not." All day Barnes kept his troops in perfect line. They stood quiet during the Roosevelt demonstrations and hooted with their floor leader on cue. Above all, they kept their votes intact.

A high-octane performance by Roosevelt backfired that evening during the final meetings of the Credentials Committee. Around ten o'clock word went to the Roosevelt hotel that the Committee had voted down all further contests and placed a gag on debate at the next day's general convention. Furious, Roosevelt telephoned the committee room and ordered a bolt. His man on the line, George Record, tried to explain that no such vote had been taken, but Roosevelt couldn't hear over his own rage. Record ordered the Theodores out. After bolting, the Roosevelt managers huddled, returned, and then finally stomped out around midnight. That night Roosevelt declared himself "through."[19] Roosevelt was already upset with his lieutenants for not pressing hard enough. They had accepted too many decisions with too little outrage. Once, when told that twenty-eight seats were indisputably stolen, Roosevelt screamed, "Twenty-eight? Twenty-eight! Why, if you got the whole lot, it wouldn't change the result or give you control of the convention. You must make it at least a hundred. Contest at least a hundred seats!"[20]

The next day's headlines were all about the Credentials Committee and the bolt, over which Roosevelt men lined up on opposite sides. Discord struck the Theodores. The hotheads such as Johnson demanded redemption. Another manager said, "We have made a great mistake. Heretofore our record has been clean and straightforward." The next day they had no fight left, their energies spent on caucus votes on whether to bolt and over failed compromises. Roosevelt's overreaching put Taft in control. There was no longer talk of a third candidate, which may well have been Hadley. "The Roosevelt bands have all gone out of business," wrote the *Times*. That was literal; all the musical groups were quiet after the wild second day. At some point, Roosevelt was privately asked why he bothered to stay around. "I intend to see that Mr. Taft is nominated," he replied.[21]

Into the week, as the test votes at the Convention racked up larger Taft majorities, the Credentials Committee gave a full hearing to the final protests. From the dais,

18. "Roosevelt, Beaten, To Bolt To-day," *NYT*, 6/20/12.
19. "Roosevelt Misled Ordering a Bolt," 6/21/12 and "Roosevelt, Beaten, to Bolt To-day," 6/20/12, *NYT*.
20. Nicholas Murray Butler to Pringle, 11/12/15, Pringle Papers (see also, Pringle, pp. 806–807).
21. "Roosevelt Misled Ordering a Bolt," 6/21/12, "Convention Will Nominate Taft," 6/21/12, *NYT* and Pringle, p. 805, from Arthur Crock to Pringle, 7/19/30.

Root announced, "by unanimous consent the views of the minority can be expressed." This brought cheers from the Theodores. When Taft delegates objected, Root declared, "The Chair hears no objection." This went on as the Roosevelt men offered their side, with the applause growing each time the speakers opened with, "Mr. Chairman." Over the antics of Heney and Johnson and a Theodore who refused to vote until his name was correctly pronounced ("Wyzer ... Weezer ... Wayzer," screamed the Secretary), the seating of the delegates proceeded for two days. The steamroller joke was all the Theodores had left the final two days. "All aboard!" "Let her rip," "Where is the traffic cop?" and "The steam roller is exceeding the speed limit," were greeted with a laugh from Root, who replied to that one, "the chair sustains the point of order."[22]

The whole thing was a humiliation. Roosevelt ordered his name removed from nomination. All he could do was to repeat his primaries chant, "My hat is in the ring, and it's going to stay there more than ever." Taft's nomination was met with confusion among the Theodores. To a rump convention that followed, Roosevelt gave a sober reply, asking the delegates to return home and gauge public sentiment. He declared himself ready to support any candidate who properly represented "a progressive platform."[23] Actually, he needed to see what came out of Baltimore, where the Democrats were sorting out his future. Back at the hotel, the largest ques-

As Taft collected convention delegates, Roosevelt maintained that he would not be a candidate — unless the people demanded it. Roosevelt's ambitions were made clear in early 1912. Everybody knew the announcement would come, and it did finally in February. La Follette was not pleased when the insurgents abandoned him wholesale for the far stronger Roosevelt personality. It was now Taft against Roosevelt, old friends in the pit against each other. The question would be decided at the party convention in June. Who would have — and hold — the most delegates? With his late start, Roosevelt lagged behind. So instead of fighting within the party, which Taft held firmly, Roosevelt challenged Taft to an open primary. Let the people decide. Roosevelt took most of the primaries, the nation's first, but Taft held more delegates. This cartoon depicts Roosevelt's attempts to "contest" those delegates at the Convention. (Clifford Berryman cartoon, 1912, Courtesy Library of Congress)

22. "Plan is to Nominate Taft To-Night," *NYT*, 6/22/12.
23. "Roosevelt Named by Rump Convention," *NYT*, 6/23/12.

tion was answered by Perkins and Munsey, "Cash at Armageddon," as the *Times* called them.[24] The money bags awaited. Munsey announced plans for a third party.

From the winner's circle, Otto Bannard wrote the President:

> We held on the 10 yard line and did not fumble the ball. I take my hat off to Wm. Barnes, Jr. He was a great field marshal and we are all under obligations to him, the ex-wicked one. If Hughes had yielded to temptation, the line would have weakened, provided the enemy accepted him, but T.R. wanted the office and had no other interest. I thank you for saving the party and the country from that intolerably selfish imposter. We hold the fort, and he is the guerilla. We have the conservative party and he cannot be President again.[25]

At Washington, Taft listened to reports from Chicago, went motoring, and played golf with his son, Robert. Business as usual, that is. When it was all over, he issued the statement,

> Never before in the history of the country was such a pre-convention campaign fought. Precedents of propriety were broken in a President's taking the stump, much to the pain and discomfort of many patriotic, high-minded citizens, but the emergency was great and the course thus taken was necessary to avert a National calamity, and in view of the result, it was justified.[26]

24. "Cash at Armageddon," *NYT* editorial, 6/20/12.
25. Bannard to Taft, 6/24/12.
26. "Taft Renominated by the Republican Convention," *NYT*, 6/23/12.

29

Behind the Roar — Taft's Quiet Game

A platform is thought meaningless. It states one thing and the candidate another. Yet a platform is an insight to the sincerity of a campaign's rhetoric, especially when the candidate, as did Roosevelt, calls the platform a covenant to the people. Between promises and obligations, it represents the extent that a party contracts itself to reality, the reason why in platforms radicalism is perfumed and policy is whispered. Platforms carry precise, crafted distinctions between what the campaign pours and what it is willing to drink. In the 1912 platforms what was viable was meticulously construed. By that definition, that is, excepting rhetorical flights, the platforms were embarrassingly similar.[1]

In attitude and rhetoric the Progressive platform ran like Beveridge's keynote address to the party's convention in which the platitudes were barely tethered to the ground.[2] Like its candidate, the platform was all mood. It loudly splashed muddied details. That platform, it is said, has been justified by history. Some of it. Equally interesting is what did *not* come from it and what went missing in the first place. The platform was a retreat, Bull Moose *Lite*. After all the sermons on Taft's anti-trust suits, the Progressives actually called for *strengthening* the Sherman Act. At least

1. For example, the Republican platform magnificently defended the Courts then feebly called for easier impeachment of judges. On the biggest issue of all, the tariff, the Republicans stood for revision with protection, the Bull Moose wanted revision with protection for labor, and the Democrats called for "revenue only" without harming business. (See also *The Triumph of Conservation*, by Gabriel Kolko, pp. 197–199.)
2. Beveridge screamed, "We stand for the rule of the people as a practical truth instead of a meaningless pretense." Another gem went, "We stand for intelligent cooperation instead of reckless competition." With the tariff, "scientific" of course, it came down to "A tariff high enough to give American producers the American market when they make honest goods and sell them at honest prices, but low enough that when they sell dishonest goods at dishonest prices, foreign competition can correct both evils" (Bowers, pp. 426–430). Try getting that one through Congress. Among the few specifics Beveridge landed upon was the recall of legislators and referendums upon laws passed by them. Beveridge hesitated until the last moment to join the Bull Moose, as he correctly understood it to be a one-man movement. His language at the convention and in his announcement to support it, in a letter to the Indianapolis *Star*, were, historian James Parker wrote, political cover ("Beveridge and the Election of 1912," by James R. Parker, *Indiana Magazine of History*, June 1967, pp. 113–114).

that's what the plank said when read to the convention. A shocked George Perkins "slammed his chair back" and pulled off a "one-man bolt." The press ran the platform without the blasphemy. Wilson derided it as the "missing plank."[3] On the tariff, the party stepped sideways and renamed protection's dependents labor. The call for Good Roads paved all of one sentence. The platform's demand for easier revision of the Constitution was distinctly unspecific, and one had to look closely to get to the party's most famous slogan, the "initiative, referendum and recall." Its formulation was almost apologetic:

> The National Progressive Party, committed to the principles of government by a self-controlled democracy expressing its will through representatives of the people, pledges itself to secure such alterations in the fundamental law of the several States and of the United States as shall insure the representative character of the Government.
>
> In particular, the party declares for direct primaries for nomination of State and National officers, for nation-wide preferential primaries for candidates for the presidency; for the direct election of the United States Senators by the people; and we urge on the States the policy of the short ballot, with responsibility to the people secured by the initiative, referendum and recall.[4]

This was an about-face, runaway retreat from the rhetoric of the movement. Indeed, many of its more concrete ideas were already included in the Republican and Democratic platforms of 1908 and 1912, and Taft signed or would sign legislation that achieved it.[5] All these questions of labor reform, business regulation, water sites, and "social and industrial justice" presented the standard challenges to the scope of federal powers, and would be sorted by Congress and the courts, as ever. The "initiative, referendum and recall" represented a dramatic change in the very form of government. The three distinct federal powers that schoolchildren learn by rote were to have a fourth appendage, which by majority vote of the electorate would enact laws, veto judicial decisions, and remove public officials. What Borah called "the court of last resort," especially if imposed at the national level, meant revolution.[6] Yet the Progressive platform hid its most dramatic proposal as a prepositional phrase at the tail end of a list of unrelated demands, merely "urged" upon the states.

The campaign held up the recall as a superhero; the platform treated it as a technicality. With this equivocal sentence construction the Progressive party hid its radicalism beneath upturned lapels. And the recall itself was hosed down. The platform further limited it to a referendum on judicial review of state police powers.[7]

3. "The Autobiography of William Allen White," p. 486 and "Panaceas Offered by the New Party," *NYT*, 8/8/12. Modern versions contain the missing phrase.
4. Platform of the Progressive Party, per *History of American Presidential Elections: 1789–1968*, Vol. VI, by Arthur M. Schlesinger, Jr., p. 2186.
5. The short list includes: a Department of Labor, regulation of child labor, worker health and safety laws, the eight hour day (the larger question, left untouched by the Progressives, being the extent of the Commerce Clause), a parcel post, Federal employee pensions, and a Health Bureau. Other demands that Taft was already working on or Wilson would enact included currency reform, revised court injunction rules, and civil service reform.
6. "Will Get the Sword, Col. Roosevelt Says," *NYT*, 6/18/12.
7. The recall was subsequently defined as a popular review of state court decisions that invalidated "an act, passed under the police power of the state." "Police powers" were State regulations of industry, particularly, that which conflicted with court protections of contracts and private property over such issues as minimum wages and work schedules. Roosevelt drew this language from the Dean of the University of Pennsylvania Law School, William Draper Lewis, who later argued at a seminar on the topic, "What is needed

Additionally, the Party's pledge to "self-controlled democracy," a lovely phrase to beautify what it really meant, namely, "direct democracy," was proclaimed to "insure the representative character of Government," the plain opposite of the "initiative, referendum and recall." Why the retreat?[8]

Taft was responsible for this underwhelming, self-conscious rhetoric. During the primaries Taft's vigorous discussion on the nature of government cut "direct democracy" at its philosophic knees. Taft championed the American Founding and representative government. While Roosevelt screamed for the blood of the corrupt — he did say in Chicago they were wanted "dead or alive" — Taft put his more concrete ideas to the test.

Here the author shall borrow of the hysteria. The Republican primaries meant far more than the split between the candidates and the general circus surrounding it. During those crazed months, the two largest men in America fought out the meaning of their political nation. Although the President effectively turned the nomination into a referendum on Roosevelt, both men seized the day to lay out crucial visions of popular government. It was Publius and Cato, Lincoln and Douglas.[9]

Roosevelt smelled political opportunity in popular agitation, and he was uniquely able to give it a name. He also knew that the people wanted affirmation of their own goodness. He did so by attacking privilege, an easy amorphism. Some of these definitions are today in place. Principally, the American people have a more direct relationship to Washington. Just as importantly, some of Roosevelt's elixirs required a new kind of government. Taft cornered the extremes of his progressivism by pointing to its ultimate conclusion, direct democracy and the dismantling of the Constitution and the courts by subjecting them to majority enthusiasms. At the same time, he challenged state socialism and socialism in general, two of the more dangerous corollaries of the movement. Roosevelt was no socialist, although many of his ideas crossed their path.[10]

At a banquet in March of 1912, Taft shook his fist at discontent and the extreme solutions proffered it. He said the agitation wrongly "attacked our present institutions, as the basis of all injustice and inequality...." He explained the futility of the socialist destruction of private property. He pointed to the dangers of unchecked majority rule. Taft wondered,

7. (*cont.*) is the power to declare certain classes of laws free from restriction against arbitrary legislation, as is done under the process of orderly amendment ... the so-called 'recall of decisions' is an attempt to provide a means of exercising such power; it is essentially conservative of the power of the courts." The Dean of New York University Law School disagreed. Judicial recall is a "symptom of a general wave of dissatisfaction ... [a] sop to the people," he said ("Political Scientists Afraid of Recall," *NYT*, 10/27/12). The only other specific judicial reforms demanded by the platform regarded injunctions and judicial review, the latter being a misguided and happily unfulfilled demand that every state court ruling that invalidated state law, based on the federal Constitution, be subject to Supreme Court review.

8. Where the Progressives got stage fright the Socialists were fearless in their demands: the recall stood for itself and was demanded at the national level; amendment of the Constitution was to be by a "majority of the voters in a majority of the States" and a call for a Constitutional convention to immediately revise it; the attack upon the courts was frantic.

9. You decide who was who. For the uninitiated, Publius and Cato were two of the pen names used in the Federalist and Antifederalist pamphlets that debated the enactment of the Constitution.

10. Debs gave himself credit for much of the Progressive platform, and the socialist Bruere reviewed Roosevelt's nomination acceptance speech. The Bruere disclosure upset not the Progressives but the socialists who called Bruere a traitor ("Debs on Roosevelt," editorial, 8/14/12 and "Colonel's Platform Edited by Socialist," 9/5/12, *NYT*). Hofstadter wrote, "The growth of Socialist sentiment ... enabled men like T.R. to argue more plausibly that the sort of moderate and gradual reform he stood for was urgently needed, over the long run, to stave off more drastic forms of protest" (p. 240).

if "Government is framed for the greatest good of the greatest number and also for the greatest good of the individual," how, then, to balance between those goals "that both may proceed side by side"?

He recognized the imperative of reformers. He admitted the inadequacies of the "Jeffersonian idea" that the "least government is best" to meet present conditions. He acknowledged the necessity for statutory response to those demands. He conceded the need for change, but he would not yield to impatience, for no solution was adequate that did not enforce "as the highest ideal in society ... equality of opportunity for every member born into it." That meant that change must—and could—come "without destroying the present structure of our Government and without affecting the guarantees of life, liberty, and property...."

> The most abiding compliment that can be paid to the American people is to point to the fact that in the Constitution which they framed and have maintained they have recognized the danger of hasty action by themselves, and have, in its checks and balances, voluntarily maintained a protection against it. The trust is that in this last century we have vindicated popular government in a way that it has never been vindicated before.

Cut! Imagine an American President having to defend in public the very form of government he heads! Taft continued,

> Distrust of popular government! The pride that I have that this is a popular Government, and that it has shown itself the strongest in history, is as deeply embedded as any feeling that is in me. I would be the last man to exclude from the direction of the ship of state the will of the American people. That is the ultimate source of authority, and it does not in any way minimize my faith and my love of popular government that I insist that the expression of that popular will shall be with the deliberation to make it sound and safe.[11]

Taft continued his defense of Constitutional government into the national campaign. He spoke of the dangers of radicalism, socialism, and "instantaneous" government. "What then?" he asked in August:

> Votes are not bread, constitutional amendments are not work, referendums do not pay rent or furnish houses, recalls do not furnish clothing, initiatives do not supply employment or relieve inequalities of condition or of opportunity. We still ought to have set before us the definite plans to bring on complete equality of opportunity, and to abolish hardship and evil for humanity. We listen for them in vain.[12]

No, it would not be too much to say that William Howard Taft proactively construed a great transition in American history. The initiative, the referendum and, less frequently, the recall found a place in various states and in various combinations, but they failed to disrupt the "representative character of the Government" that the progressives of 1912 so apologetically affirmed in their platform.[13] Monopolies did not prove to be an "imperative economic law," as Roosevelt warned at

11. "Taft For Popular Rule With Reason," *NYT*, 3/10/12. Taft was both defending representative government and responding to Roosevelt's suggestion that he distrusted the people.
12. "Taft and Root Assail Radicals," *NYT*, 8/2/12.
13. In Kansas, home of insurgency, the legislators decided that recall of "public officers," i.e. themselves, was too much. Ohio, inspired by Roosevelt's "Charter of Democracy" speech, experimented with fine print and sent forty-two constitutional amendments, practically a small book, to the people who underwhelmingly affirmed thirty-two amendments by a vote of less than half the 1908 electorate. Direct democracy and the rule of a majority of a minority championed the initiative and the referendum by 311,188 to 220,184 (from "Action and Reaction," editorial, 2/3/13 and "Progress In Ohio," editorial, 9/30/12, *NYT*).

Osawatomie. The Electoral College escaped unbruised. The Constitution kept its spine, all the while proving itself an effective instrument of the popular will, as demonstrated by the period's four Constitutional amendments. And the Presidency, over Roosevelt's declarations, was not subjected to the recall.[14]

* * *

The former Roosevelt presidency meant nothing to the Progressive campaign of 1912. A Progressive Club banquet in 1913 discussed the "records of the achievements of Theodore Roosevelt ... in the past year."[15] The sole reference to anything of the larger past was as a comparison to the new Roosevelt. If "the records of the achievements of Theodore Roosevelt *in the past year* was [*sic*] written by the impartial historian it would be seen that never in his illustrious career had he soared so high, battled so well, or achieved so much" (italics added). The Bull Moose campaigned in the future tense.

Not so the Democrats who, aided by an unlikely alliance of Senators La Follette and Penrose, gleefully poured the old Roosevelt legacy through a sieve. These were the Clapp Committee hearings, and were not altogether pleasant for Roosevelt. Not a few ghosts had yet to find closure. Roosevelt managed the nostalgia in unadulterated Rooseveltian hyperbole, that is, by condemnation. The specific distress came of the long past 1904 campaign and the unseemly dollar sign that served as a doormat to the Republican campaign headquarters. The only reason anybody cared was because that old doormat was back at the entrance to Progressive Central.

Penrose confessed to a Standard Oil conspiracy to assist the 1904 effort that one way or another involved Roosevelt and likely he himself in $100,000 of smelly Rockefeller money. Innocent! shouted the Colonel as he produced — from Wilkes-Barre, Pennsylvania — a letter, voilà, of absolution that proved that he had nothing to do with it.

The *Times* was amazed. "If any one should produce an affidavit from twenty eminently respectable gentlemen, declaring that they had personally seen Mr. Roosevelt boil and eat his aged grandmother in the cellar of his Oyster Bay residence on a given day in June, 1905, he would produce from the inner right-hand pocket of his coat a certificate showing that his lamented grandmother died and was buried in November, 1887."[16]

One John D. Archbold of one Standard Oil Company, it was learned at the hearings, donated to a certain political party $125,000 upon the condition that its head, one Theodore Roosevelt, be made aware. That the chief was told was never established. Likely, he was not. Roosevelt presumably learned of it when a journalist made it public during the campaign, at which time he ordered the money returned. It never was. That Archbold was trying to buy influence, and that Roosevelt was trying to avoid that influence yet keep the money, was self-evident. In 1912, Archbold said it was so and left for vacation in Europe. Roosevelt said no way and sue me. A confusion as to who used the money, the state or national committees, left the issue unsettled.

"I thought by their underhand methods that they might do some harm to the Progressive Party, but I have them on the hip," declared Roosevelt righteously. "They are now in the open. The Lord has delivered them into my hands, and I'll hew

14. "Roosevelt Favors Recall of President," *NYT*, 9/20/12
15. "Roosevelt Named as 1916 Candidate," *NYT*, 2/13/13.
16. "The Colonel and His Pursuers," *NYT* editorial, 8/24/12.

them as Israel hewed Ammon, hip and thigh." Nevertheless, it was made quite clear that if not the Lord or Standard Oil, Morgan and his U.S. Steel partners had been very much on Roosevelt's side in 1904. Roosevelt admitted to knowing of contributions from Frick and McCall of the steel trust. Morgan testified to his own generosity. Roosevelt's reply was that no favors were delivered. Wilson got the best of it all with his slashing comment, "I understand from the newspaper reports that Mr. Roosevelt was distressed by my suggestion the other day that the United States Steel Corporation was back of his plan for controlling the trusts. He interpreted my remark to mean that they were supporting him with money. I was not thinking about money." As for Frick, his affection remained with his golfing partner. "No, I'm not going to support Roosevelt this time," he said, smiling. "I am going to remain in the Republican Party."[17]

There was no smoke from the Taft camp, for the tank was empty. Taft's campaign was near broke the entire way. Brother Charles bailed him out. To his some $200,000 that financed the primary went another $150,000 toward a total fund of $905,000. Wilson broke the million dollar barrier, mostly spent in the general campaign. Roosevelt's IPO was floated by some three-quarters a million in pre-convention money, and at least that again to get him through November.[18]

On the Democratic side, Bryan raised the roof at the Baltimore convention. From demanding to be Temporary Chairman (he lost to Judge Parker, Champ Clark's man), condemning Tammany (which provoked fist fights on the floor; "I knew I had them," he later said), threatening a bolt (which brought rumors of a Bryan deal with Roosevelt), and finally throwing his considerable influence to Wilson, who was nominated on the 46th ballot (now there's an old time convention!), Bryan controlled the headlines, if not the convention.

Wilson's nomination ended Roosevelt's chances. Had Parker or Clark been nominated, Roosevelt might have been able to claim the left of both parties. Unthinkable collusions with Bryan, which some progressives actively sought, may then have brought about real Armageddon, one way or another. On his way to congratulate Wilson, Franklin D. Roosevelt ran across Theodore Roosevelt's son Kermit. Franklin informed Wilson, "I met Kermit on my way here, and he told me about his father. He said, 'Pop's been praying for Clark.'"[19]

The Democratic convention was strike two, the second-in-a-row devastating breaking ball taken by Roosevelt. For his supporters, the great national struggle suddenly went local. As soon as the Democrats left Baltimore the Bull Moose desertions commenced. The practical-minded left to shore up their Republican homes.

17. "How Women Won Roosevelt to Them," 8/31/12, "Roosevelt Says Big Gifts Didn't Purchase Favor," 10/5/12, "Wilson Promptly Answers Roosevelt," 10/9/12 and "Frick for Taft Now," *NYT*, 10/5/12.

18. The Roosevelt expenditures were skewed to different values before and after the conventions but generally added up to between $1.3 and $1.5 million. It was a ton of cash, one way or another, and by far the highest amount of all three candidates. Certainly the Progressives were starting from scratch, although that problem was offset by the free press generated by the sheer outrageousness of the situation and the large chunks of the Republican machinery they carried off. (See "Taft Fund was $904,828," 12/03/12, "Rival Republican Funds $1,110,000," 10/10/12, "Raised $1,500,000 to Aid Roosevelt," 10/26/12, and "Funds for Wilson Total $678,364," 10/26/12, "91,000 Gave to Wilson Fund," 11/16/12, *NYT*. The $678,364 for Wilson quoted in the 10/26 article did not include $215,000 in pre-convention funds. His total fund was $1,100,000. It is important to note that these numbers account only for the National campaigns.)

19. "Convention Beats Bryan," 6/26/12, "Bryan Spared Mrs. Taft," 7/11/12, and "Bryan Threatens to Bolt the Ticket if Named by Aid of Tammany Votes," 6/30/12, "A Roosevelt-Bryan Party," 7/21/10, "The Bull Moose Prayer," 7/4/12, *NYT*.

The Progressive party that ran ads, "Men and Women of the New Order: Your Country Calls You," couldn't keep the troops in line. Three of the "little Governors" dodged the draft, Hadley most importantly. He declared himself content with the regular platform and pledged to fight the progressive cause from within. Another, Osborn of Michigan, told his followers to vote for Wilson in November. Most of the insurgent Senators stayed regular, including Borah, who was up for reelection. He needed the organization. La Follette became one of the few notable Republicans to campaign actively for the party outside his own state.[20] Added to the confusion were conservative Democrats who pronounced themselves favorable to Taft. "I was never so near being Republican as I am to-day," said a Southern Democrat, "and if I had the casting ballot in the Presidential election this year, I think I should cast it for Mr. Taft." Even the Socialists were splitting up as the bomb-now-talk-later Industrial Workers of the World (IWW) radicals took offense at the party's declaration for peaceful action.[21] Otherwise, fences around the country practically collapsed from the weight of the undecided. Taft joked about a man "who has been mildly for me for President, but has hunted for the highest place on the fence...."[22]

As during the evenly split 2000 election, the press treated the public to an elaborate discussion of what might occur should no candidate win a majority in the Electoral College. The more serious questions arose when Roosevelt plotted contests in the states where his presence was weak. Charles Taft announced that Roosevelt's resignation from a Republican Club was a good start "for a man who is no longer a Republican," but he might also renege his claims on Republican electors.[23]

Taft's managers implored him to fight fire with fire, turn the magical phrase, to pump his fists, and attack as he had done during the primary. Taft declined. He would not go on the road. Instead, he apologized for having stumped at all. With Roosevelt defeated at the convention, Taft wanted no further indignities to stain his White House.[24] He spent the summer declaring himself the November victor and doing little to that end. Officially, the campaign was conducted from the Beverly front porch through statements issued by mail and telegraph. It turned into perhaps the first and last golf-course campaign in history. With few exceptions, the Cabinet was even less inspired and generally refused to campaign. With vice presidential candidate James S. Sherman silenced by illness and, shortly before the election, death, the President had no front-line counter to the active Roosevelt and Wilson speech making. It didn't matter. Taft was running to a different goal line. During the primaries he fought for his country. During the election he fought for his party.

The day of his official "notification" as nominee, Taft teamed up with Root at the White House to denounce Roosevelt,

20. "Bull Moose 'Ad' Asks Funds" 8/21/12, "Hadley Won't Join Bolters," 6/24/12, "La Follette Joins Taft," 8/25/12, *NYT*. Hadley lost in November. His promising career was cut short by the party split.

21. "Iowa Republicans Reject Taft Ticket," 7/11/12, "See a Chance for Taft in Three-Cornered Fight," 7/9/12, and "Socialists Also Face Party Split," 6/30/12, *NYT*.

22. Taft to Helen Taft, 7/22/12.

23. "A Roosevelt Menace," editorial, 7/17/12, "Colonel May Yield to Flinn's Method," 7/23/12, and "Charles P. Taft Advises the Colonel," 7/20/12, *NYT*. Roosevelt and Flinn tried to keep the same electors on both Republican and Progressive ballots and let the popular vote decide their loyalties. This would ensure at the minimum a pretext for a dispute. Anderson wrote, "Much of the initial energy of the Republican campaign was diverted from electioneering toward the elimination of Bull Moosers disguised as Republican electors...." (p. 198).

24. "Taft Not to Stump for Votes this Fall," *NYT*, 7/14/12.

Wilson, socialism, and all things not or no longer Republican. A steamroller drove nearby. "The campaign has begun," a man shouted.[25] Indeed, the President brought back the tactic that worked so well in June. Again it was to maintain order among the regulars. He pulled out the patronage club and swung it rightward. Deserters were kicked out. A postmaster in Kentucky printed an editorial lambasting Taft for, among things, being "the recipient of stolen goods [the delegates].... A man who denies the divinity of Jesus Christ [his Unitarianism]...." Taft instructed the Postmaster General to dismiss him "for vilification of the President of the United States."[26]

Taft became all law and order and things Republican magnified by hyperbole. He became an outright demagogue. He stood pat upon protection. He said a victory by either of his opponents would lead to panics and reversal of all the good brought by the Republican Party over its fifty years. He blasphemed the 1894 tariff reduction, which left Wilson and the *Times* amazed at the suggestion that a panic was started by a law that came a year later. Taft was all protection, prosperity, and an independent judiciary, issues guaranteed to rouse only the Republican choir.

The *Times* lamented Taft's political shift, particularly when he equated Wilson to Roosevelt. The editors failed to recognize the President's purpose. Taft's aim was to steer the party through a crisis. He let Roosevelt soak up discontent, maybe even to split it with Wilson so that Taft could step between. (Wilson played a fine game of being both conservative and progressive.) Whatever happened, Taft would salvage the Republican Party. If the Party was finished, it was because it accepted its own death.

Taft wouldn't let it die. He kept up the public front of confidence, and perhaps even believed it at times, especially in the late summer when the Progressives faltered. Special elections in Maine and Vermont went Republican. Allusions to Benedict Arnold were taking a toll.[27] This confidence became the collateral damage of the Roosevelt shooting in Milwaukee in mid–October. The deranged assassination attempt and Roosevelt's speech with a bullet in the chest ended Taft's campaign. Shocked and sympathetic, both Taft and Wilson immediately stopped attacking Roosevelt, and an amazed public moved its sympathy to the injured candidate.

The bookies had it right from the beginning. Just after the Republican convention, one man put 10 to 1 that Taft wouldn't receive a single electoral vote. Close. Taft took eight from the two safest Republican states, Utah and Vermont. Days before the election Wilson was the 4 to 1 favorite, with Roosevelt leading Taft at 10 to 7, up from even odds before the shooting. Those who put up 1 to 3 that Wilson would outpoll the other candidates combined were cleaned up. Another loser, the owner of a Taft bet, leapt from his roof. To one hundred witnesses he kept his promise to jump off a house should Taft lose.[28]

Journalists were amazed by Taft's good humor. With a smile, he pointed to the party's almost four million votes and declared that its "cardinal doctrines are safe." The post-election debates that Wilson and Taft represented a rejection of Roosevelt, or that Roosevelt and Wilson were a rejection of Taft, or whatever,

25. "Taft and Root Assail Radicals," *NYT*, 8/2/12.
26. Taft to Hitchcock, 7/3/12.
27. "President Cites Benedict Arnold," *NYT*, 9/7/12.
28. "Bets Taft Will Lose All," 6/27/12, "Wilson Odds Up, 4 to 1," 10/8/12, and "Lofty Leap For Taft Man," 11/08/12, *NYT*.

mattered nothing.[29] Taft found more relief at Roosevelt's loss than consternation at his own defeat. He would enjoy that ride with Wilson up Pennsylvania Avenue. "It wouldn't have been so easy if things had been different..." he said, "but I would have taken the ride just the same." Another Inaugural day ride with Roosevelt would have been, for Taft and his party, a funeral procession. Instead, and thanks to Taft's inward-focused campaign, Sereno Payne could declare the party "a very lively corpse."[30]

29. Nicholas Murray Butler, who later joined Taft on his eight electoral votes as the Vice Presidential candidate of record, declared that the Wilson-Taft combination meant that the "revolutionaries are outnumbered" ("Dr. Butler Sees Hope for Republicans," *NYT*, 11/13/12). Popular history has concluded that the election was a progressive victory, in that Wilson and Roosevelt together badly outpolled Taft. This view is ignorant of Democratic politics, as it assumes that Wilson's progressivism was the party's and that Wilson's progressivism is what elected him. Rather, the most cogent explanation of the election was provided contemporaneously by Irving Fisher, who charted the respective votes per state to show that the 1912 results were eerily similar to 1908: Wilson failed to expand the Democratic base, and Roosevelt failed to attract progressive Democrats ("Roosevelt Failed To Get Radical Democratic Vote," *NYT*, 1/7/13). Furthermore, and amazingly, there were fewer total votes in 1912 than 1908, and that includes new women votes in several states. The missing voters were uninterested Republican and Democratic conservatives.

30. "Taft Plans to Keep the Old Party Alive," 11/7/12 and "What the President sees in the future," 11/19/12, *NYT*.

30

Motoring into the Sunset

In January of 1913, Taft was celebrated by various Republican clubs at a dinner in New York. He was amused and proud of the odd gathering. "It is not usual for the deceased to give very full expression to his feelings at the wake," he started, "but I remember that in one of Boucicault's Irish dramas the corpse was sufficiently revived to partake of the liquid refreshment and became the chief participant in the festivities." Never was a loser so confident. "We were beaten in the last election. We ran third in the race. Why is it that we gather here with so much spirit, and with so little of the disappointment and humiliation supposed to accompany political disaster?" he asked. "The fact that brings us here is that in the late election there were 3,500,000 voters, an irreducible minimum of the Republican Party, who were determined to remain a force in the community to prevent any constitutional amendment and legislation of a revolutionary programme announced by the so-called Progressive Party."

Taft reminded his fellows why they fought, that direct democracy was an attack on 1789 and Madison himself:

> A popular government is a government by the people — that is, by a majority of the people, who under the law are given the right to exercise the electoral franchise, and constitutional limitations are imposed to prevent the misuse of the power of the majority, so that the individual or the minority may not suffer injustice through the action of the majority.... Thus it is easily seen that under the Progressive programme the whole machinery that has been so carefully built up by the old statesmen of this country and England, to save to the individual and to the minority freedom, equality before the law, the right of property and the right to pursue happiness, is to be taken apart and thrown into a junk heap.

These protections were salvaged by the Republican party, he declared, a party that would remain fast in their defense. He thus closed the long drama of the primaries. The victory was of Republican principles — his principles, that he would not compromise, not even to electoral defeat. He closed the speech with a call for reunion — on his terms, although without bitterness. "Let us invite those Republicans who left us under an impulse that calmer consideration shows to have been unwise to return and stand again shoulder to shoulder with us in this critical time in our country's history."[1]

1. To bolters who demanded a change in the party's delegate and other convention procedures as a condition of return, Taft replied, "I haven't any objection to any method which shall be fair. That is not a reason for

So who were these felled trees that gathered at the Waldorf-Astoria on January 4, 1913, with the noisy pickets of striking waiters scuffling with detectives outside? The ghosts of Roosevelt past gathered that night: Archbold of Standard Oil and questionable 1904 campaign donations; Morgan as in J.P. and Tennessee Coal; and Parsons, Odell, and Depew, former Roosevelt associates and bossism itself. If that wasn't enough to make a good progressive shake, in plain view were Penrose, Crane, Butler, Choate, and Barnes, and a roomful of the privileged, the malefactors, the undesirables. Every one of them rose and applauded when the President arrived. Taft's calls for the survival of the republic and republicanism drew wild ovations. Why would they listen to the man who couldn't keep their party intact? That alone is remarkable. More so, however, is the vision rewarded them by their prophet in defeat: stick with my losing ways and ye shall prevail.

Elsewhere, the newspapers were full of the incoming President and the latest Roosevelt call to admit no compromise. Two weeks later and not far from the Waldorf, the Madison Square Garden and the Grand Central Palace would open their doors to the largest automobile shows yet.

* * *

The Congress that started in December of 1911 lasted until late August of 1912. Along with the Mexican situation and other such worries, Taft had Congress to manage throughout the primaries and into the national campaign. This longest session since 1894 was literally a joke. "Riders" and "jokers" were inserted in appropriation bills and with in-fighting, grandstanding, and Taft veto threats, the government was almost shut down. In late June, Taft wanted nothing more than to get to Beverly. He was forced to hold his train to sign a rushed compromise bill to fund the government an extra month.[2]

For Taft, one of the few satisfactions of that Congress came when he learned that La Follette had again found himself perplexed by the tariff. As part of Taft's rightward bolt during the national campaign, he vetoed all tariff bills, including another wool revision. La Follette, of course, would condemn the President, but, as Taft explained to his wife, "He was afraid he might hurt me against Roosevelt and he hated Roosevelt so he did not want to help him. This is rather a funny situation, but I think he will probably hit me notwithstanding."[3]

One of the few sane voices during the mixed up session was that of the old fox, former Speaker Cannon. Stirred, but not shaken by the turmoil, he admonished his classmates:

> Why do we orate and tear passion to tatters about general legislation on appropriation bills. Leather and prunella what for? To try to inflame public sentiment for use in September and October in order that we may appeal to the people? For what? That a wicked Senate or a wicked President did wrong in not yielding to the representatives of the people, who are just going back to get their power of attorney renewed! ...Thank God, I am optimistic. I believe the country, with 99,00,000 people is better than it has ever been. Sometimes people who are pessimistic are going to abolish the whole shooting match so that — presto! change! Hop, skip and a jump! — an appeal might be taken to the people and the Supreme Court reversed and the Constitution rendered null and void. Thank God, that Constitution, while

1. (*cont.*) joining or giving up the party. It is the principle that the party advocates that should control one in its support" ("Taft Invites All Bolters to Return," *NYT*, 1/5/13).
2. "Congress Provides $75,000,000 for July," *NYT*, 7/2/12.
3. Taft to Helen Taft, 8/15/12.

> it may hide, here and there, some thief, some monopolist, is yet the great charter of security and freedom![4]

On the productive side, the nine-month session produced the eight-hour federal work day, dumped Lorimer, protected seals, coughed up a battleship, spanked Russia for mistreating American Jews, regulated "radio-telegraphy," created a child labor bureau and a federal pension program, split the Commerce and Labor Department in two, started the parcel post system, sent the 17th Amendment (establishing the direct election of Senators) to the states, and authorized a memorial fountain to Major Archibald W. Butt, among other things. Of the 26,392 bills introduced in the House, 1,237 were reported by committees, and 358 became law. On August 25, the President again missed his Beverly train — three times. He stayed at the Capitol until 4:15 that morning. The blessed end finally arrived twelve hours later. Taft made the next day's five o'clock train.[5]

On his Fourth of July getaway ten thousand people received the President at Beverly. He was thrilled. He thanked the crowd and declared himself and the First Lady "happy to be here ... to renew our claim to be Yankees."[6] The smile and the humor were in fine shape. He waved to the crowds that lined the streets all the way to the Summer White House. There he spoke again, then went inside to put on his golf outfit. It was a perfect summer day, a happy, if hot, premonition.

Taft left the next day and ended up spending most of July and August at Washington coping with the unruly Congress. Mrs. Taft's summer was interrupted by the death of her beloved father in August. She canceled her social calendar and went into mourning. The Taft children romped about as usual. Out West, Robert declined the gift of a cub bear from the Blackfeet tribe. "I don't think I dare take this thing home in the face of the strained relationship between my father and one of his old friends," he joked. His sister Helen made the news for hitting all bullseyes at 200 and 500 yards at a government rifle range in Gloucester. The Navy boys were impressed.[7]

After Congress finally adjourned, the President looked to his kind of relaxation. Unfortunately, his bad ankle again flared, as did rumors and his doctor's confirmation of the gout. He was sidelined from the links. So he chose to recuperate in the back of the awesome Pierce 66 H.P. tourer. In early October, the President and Mrs. Taft escaped by motor with their guest, Mabel Boardman, to explore western Massachusetts, Vermont, and New Hampshire. While Roosevelt and Wilson fought the campaign in the headlines, Taft's version went, "President Enjoys a Real Vacation."[8]

The weather turned to a perfect New England Autumn, crisp and with the trees afire in color. From Beverly the route was that of today's I-90, westward from Boston through Worcester to Springfield, passing through the great Massachusetts mill towns of the original American industrial revolution. Onward to Lenox, Taft ordered

4. "When Cannon Needs Pluck," *NYT*, 8/16/12.
5. The Senate saw 7,474 bills introduced and 1,062 reported. From "Deadlock Keeps Congress Sitting," 8/25/12 and "Senate Surrenders, Congress Adjourns," 8/27/12, *NYT*.
6. "Crowds Cheer Taft in Beverly Parade," *NYT*, 7/5/12.
7. "Mrs. Taft's Father Dead," 8/6/12, "Young Taft Gets a Bear," 8/7/12, "Miss Taft a Good Shot," 10/6/12, *NYT*.
8. This section from "Taft Completes Tour," 10/13/13, "Taft at Williams," 10/13/12, "Taft visits MacVeagh," 10/11/12, "Autos in White Mountains," 9/16/12 and "Taft Visits Homes of His Ancestors," 8/20/10, *NYT*, and "President Enjoys a Real Vacation," *New York Tribune*, 10/5/12 (reprinted in *American Motorist*, Nov. 1912, p. 882).

a halt to enjoy the views from "Jacob's Ladder," a highlight on motorists' maps. From Lenox they crossed Pittsfield to spend the night at Dalton with Senator Crane. A remarkable 182 miles was made that first day, and, the press noted, there was "not even a puncture to mar his progress."

They next headed north along the present Route 7 and the Taconic Mountains to Williamstown. There, and with heartfelt expression, the President told the students of Williams College of the "value of college friendships." They headed eastward for a luncheon at Brattleboro, along the Connecticut River, and then made it across the Green Mountains for dinner with Robert Todd Lincoln in Manchester. Along the way they stopped at Townshend, the birthplace of Taft's father, then passed through today's ski country to Montpelier. Driving through a land rich in history, they passed the graves of settlers and patriots, which they may have stopped to read and honor, as Taft had done on a motor trip with Massachusetts Governor Draper in 1910. To the candidate who called upon its spirit in the now distant election campaign, 1776 and 1789 were manifest.

Next it was eastward to Bretton Woods, at the base of the White Mountains, already a famous automobile destination. The area was enjoying a tourism boom brought about by motorists who could now wander off the normal railroad routes. Its newly built resorts were graced that August alone by more than 2,500 motorists. Exercising his automobile-rested ankle at Bretton Woods, Taft caught a round of golf. Next was southward to Dublin for a visit to the home of Secretary MacVeagh, then to the familiar ground of coastal New Hampshire and Massachusetts and on down to Beverly. It was an incredible trip for a President, the first of such distance and time wholly removed of water, rail, or horse. The Touring Club of America was done justice by its most famous member.

Although dodging the campaign, Taft wouldn't be kept from the baseball scores. On the way down the coast in the presidential yacht to New York harbor for a review of the fleet, he insisted on hearing news of the World Series. The scores were relayed to his boat by wireless. The Red Sox beat the Giants. (The progressive era came and went with the Sox, or vice versa.) It was in New York that Taft received the shocking news that Roosevelt was shot. He immediately sent private sympathies and condemnation of the act to the press.[9]

The Summer White House was kept open until late October. Taft kept pace receiving delegations and issuing bulletins from Beverly, but was ever in hotter pursuit of Myopia golf, when his ankle allowed it, and motoring. He ran off on day trips, such as one 150-mile motor ride through the rain to Poland Springs, Maine, where he greeted schoolchildren and reviewed an artillery detail. It was perhaps the most peculiar election campaign by a sitting President. Measured by the results, it was the worst ever. By its methods, it was the first modern campaign. The President used the telephone, the wireless radio, the automobile, and, if the new Post Office machine carried any of his dispatches, the aeroplane, to spread his message. He reached the voters through instant communication, fast travel — and motion pictures. Taft was filmed from the front porch, and his image set upon the political trail.[10]

At least one set of voters embraced the President's unique campaign. On his return to Beverly in late October, among the

9. "Taft Gets Details of Game," *NYT*, 10/13/12.
10. See "Pictures to Boom Mr. Taft," *NYT*, 9/1/12.

The Congenial President — and a very modern one. Taft embraced new technology and applied it to his fullest benefit. Trains, automobiles, telephones, and the telegraph shrank space and time, allowing the President to squeeze more from his four years in office than any other President before him. In addition to endorsing the airplane, he used motion pictures in his 1912 campaign, enjoyed a novel air conditioning system at the White House, gave a speech over the telephone from Boston to a banquet in New York, and addressed Boy Scouts by wireless from hundreds of miles away — probably the first presidential radio address. He also received wireless updates on the 1912 World Series from his boat as he traveled down the Eastern seaboard. (Courtesy Library of Congress)

pile of letters, telegrams, and requests was one from the Republican National Committee asking Taft to sign forty photographs.[11] A national club wanted to distribute pictures of the President to its local organizations, with the thought that its 38,000 members would be flattered to the point of voting for him. Jack Hammond thought it was a great idea. The historian can only hope that Taft signed the photos, and that the group's members gave him their heartiest vote that November. They had been mightily led by the President, and he, brilliantly served by their kind. Taft was, in fact, a member of the club. Back in April, during the hectic primary campaign, Taft's initiation into the Professional Chauffeurs Club of America was held at the White House. They told him,

> We come, Sir, to ask you, Mr. President, to become one of us by accepting this little Membership Card, and as a token of their confidence and respect for

11. WC Webster to R Forster, 10/16/12.

the real Chauffeur of this great touring car and ship of State — Our Country.[12]

Not two weeks after the 1912 election Taft was in a distinctly good mood. On a visit to New York, the President and Major Rhoads, Archie's replacement and long Taft's personal physician, motored to the Juvenile Asylum at Chauncey. Five hundred boys lined up to receive the President as he alighted from the automobile. Inside, he told the story of a boy who overcame his weaknesses by focussing on his strengths. "You started out handicapped," he explained to the orphans, "but follow the lesson I have told you and you will finish first and become good patriotic citizens when you grow up to be men." The man who turned the spade for countless YMCA, orphan, and library building inaugurations and who could never turn from a child's smile was truly satisfied this day. He joined the orphans to whistle and sing "Jolly Boys" and "The Star-Spangled Banner." As his party moved away, a "curly-headed youngster" shouted, "Good bye." Taft turned and smiled. He shook the boy's hand.[13]

That night at a banquet of the Lotos Club, a sort of optimists' society "in the habit of entertaining famous men," its leader explained, the President displayed every bit of what the *Times* called "The Unconquerable Mr. Taft."[14] This was the occasion of his most celebrated speech. After much applause and repeated bows, he began. "The legend of the lotos eaters was that if they partook of the fruit of the lotos they forgot what had happened in their country and were left in a state of philosophic calm, in which they had no desire to return to it." Ever walking the historically-confused path of the half-serious, half-jest, he continued,

> I do not know what was in the mind of your distinguished Invitation Committee when I was asked to attend this banquet.... I knew that generally on an occasion of this sort the motive of the diners was to have a guest whose society should bring them more closely into contact with the great present and future, and not be merely a reminder of what has been. But after further consideration, I saw in the name of your club the possibility that you were not merely cold, selfish seekers after pleasures of your own, and that perhaps you were organized to furnish consolation to those who mourn, oblivion to those who would forget, an opportunity for a swan song to those about to disappear.[15]

Around jokes about "what are we to do with our ex-presidents?" he examined the presidency itself. As for ex–Presidents, he felt himself a bit of an expert on the topic. Following "Dr. Osler's method," Taft suggested "the proper and scientific administration of a dose of chloroform, or of the fruit of the lotos tree ... the funeral pyre ... might make a fitting end to the life of one who has held the highest office, and at the same time would secure the country from the troublesome fear that the occupant could ever come back." There was more to it than ridicule of Roosevelt, although that, too.

Taft had been doing some thinking. The title of his speech was "The President." The speech was the foundation to theories he later more completely explained in the lectures, "Our Chief Magistrate and His

12. RE Shadel to Taft, 4/15/12 (see reel 459, case file 301). The meeting was held on April 19, and the President inscribed a photograph and presented it to the Club. The same inscription was asked that October for the forty photographs.
13. "Taft Whistles with the Boys," *NYT*, 11/17/12.
14. *NYT* editorial, 11/18/12.
15. "Taft Comes Out for Single Term," *NYT*, 11/17/12.

Powers."[16] Taft discussed the nature of the office he held. First, he reviewed that pesky question he frequented while there: what are the limitations of its powers? "It is said that the office of President is the most powerful in the world" and that it "can exercise more discretion than an Emperor or King...." Taft was as bemused by this as ever. He construed the executive power as enumerated, not extrinsic, as Roosevelt later romanticized of his own presidency. "Of course there are happy individuals who are able entirely to ignore those limitations," Taft said without subtlety. Still, he had a few suggestions. "It is contrary to my own love for the dear old Constitution..." but, "yielding to the modern habit, and just to show that though I am a conservative I am not a reactionary or a trilobite," he offered a fundamental change. He thought the presidency would better serve the public interest were it limited to a single, six-year term.[17]

A mark of the Taft presidency was his attempt to remove politics from government functions. He believed the President would better serve the people if freed of electoral pursuit. Following the theme, he next suggested that Cabinet members be provided floor space in Congress where policy and executive matters could be discussed freely with lawmakers — and insults and politics could be answered more directly. He was not, however, suggesting the parliamentary system, he assured. Taft also declared the era of muckraking closed, managed a jab at Wilson with his amusement over talk of an "open" White House, said his greatest disappointment in office was the failure of the Arbitration treaties, thanked Congress for his salary, reminded its members that their many intemperate remarks against him were yet in the Congressional Record, and thanked the American people for the "honor" of high office. He assured the country that despite its "very emphatic verdict," he left with only gratitude and the hope that "real good has been accomplished" during his term. He closed with a toast, "To the next President of the United States!" The speech was magnanimous, gracious, wholly appropriate, and fine leadership. The reception was tremendous.

Other speakers predicted a repeat of the "practical joke" played on Cleveland of two, non-consecutive terms. One noted that Taft's presidency was not "touched by even the suggestion of scandal." Andrew Carnegie lauded the Arbitration treaties for having "spanned the hitherto impassable gulf" of questions of "national honor," which he said would secure Taft's fame. Elihu Root, as always, was precise: "We need not wait for history to do justice to a man like President Taft. With him when he goes back to private life will go the honor and the esteem of the American people whom he has served so well."

* * *

> I shall turn over the affairs of the Government with all its departments in excellent running order, with the economic policies I have introduced that have proved to be of the greatest practical value, with the public credit unimpaired and with the country enjoying unprecedented prosperity....
>
> — William Howard Taft[18]

16. Reprinted as "The President and His Powers," by Columbia University Press, 1967
17. An old Democratic idea, championed as recently as 1911 by Champ Clark ("For Six-Year Presidents," *NYT*, 1/4/11) and vaguely in the 1912 Democratic platform. Taft's views of the powers of the President are broader than normally thought. For a good review, see "William Howard Taft: A Constitutionalist's View of the Presidency," by L. Peter Schultz, *Presidential Studies Quarterly*, Vol. IX, No. 4, Fall 1979. Schultz wrote, "Taft criticized Roosevelt's stewardship theory as overly broad and even as unlimited.... But, contrary to the common understanding, Taft did not interpret presidential power in a way which stringently limits that power, or even in a way that subordinates the President to Congress" (p. 403).
18. "What the President Sees in the Future," *NYT*, 11/19/12.

Wilson was learning the joys of the presidency-elect. Cabinet intrigue, photographers, and offensive petitioners trespassed his Bermuda retreat. As he came to terms with Taft's Pinchot affair nemesis, Louis Brandeis, Wilson largely ignored Taft, although they privately corresponded regarding domestic White House concerns, advice for which the Wilsons were grateful. The President-elect avoided Taft's invitations to meet, or to use a government boat to visit Panama. Wilson's arrogance outpaced his electoral count, it seemed to Taft, who urged moderation. Taft hoped Wilson would not try to "out–Herod Herod."[19]

Unlike the previous boarder, Taft cleaned up after himself. The government Taft bequeathed his successor was in supreme condition. Taft's economizing and tax reforms left a $40,000,000 surplus. Alternative revenues, so important to Wilson's only clear mandate, the tariff, were in place. The 16th Amendment was ratified, and the corporation tax, fully inspected by court challenges, was constitutionally clean. The economy was humming. Taft could celebrate a strong Navy and herald the progress of the Canal, two crucial pieces of the Roosevelt legacy he nailed to the floor. Since Wilson refused, and to publicize its progress, Taft visited the Canal in December. He planned a civil government for the American Zone and danced with the wife of the President of Panama in Panama itself, stepping again upon foreign territory. Taft returned full of praise for Colonel Goethals and his amazing accomplishments.

Additionally, Taft left Wilson with a secure border. Mexican troubles were kept in Mexico. Foreign trade was higher than ever. Embassies and missions were shored up, and the all-important Foreign Service was delivered from politics to the merit system. The issue of a new national anthem,"O Glorious Land of Liberty," the President wrote its author, must await the incoming Administration.[20]

The hurricane passed. The expected calm of March 4, 1909, finally arrived. Though littered with debris, the political scene was clearer than it had been in years. Roosevelt was beaten, his electoral coat permanently shorn. Oyster Bay relinquished the correspondents and the intrigue to Washington. The Republican Party rediscovered its old, steady temper, if in opposition. Senate Republican insurgents were a minority of a minority, and they and the regulars were freed of each other. The Democratic leadership, particularly that of Fitzgerald and Underwood in the House, was vigorous and reasoned.

Payne, Winona, Reciprocity, and the 16th Amendment radically eased Wilson's tariff reforming. Had he to bake a tariff from scratch, the history of Wilson's presidency would have been very different. Another major Wilson-era reform was also set by Taft. Aldrich's 1912 currency bill never escaped the Senate, but in presentation of his Commission's report, its foundations were handed to a new Congress whose job was to create a consensus and not to argue the politics of monetary reform. Pringle wrote that Taft failed to place the Federal Reserve in his legacy book by leaving its creation to Aldrich's Commission. Pringle errs in that the Commission's work was only just being finished by 1912. Going back to 1907 and through his term, Taft pursued and promoted the idea and necessity of currency reform.[21] From the inaugural

19. "Taft Warns Wilson," *NYT*, 1/18/13.
20. "Taft Dodges an Anthem," *NYT*, 12/4/12.
21. See "Taft Defends the President," 12/31/07, "Mr. Taft's Progressiveness," editorial, 6/24/11, and "Taft Asks Congress to Aid His Policies," 12/07/12, *NYT*, as well as Taft's annual messages to Congress of

address, the praise for Aldrich in Boston, to messages to Congress every year, Taft stoked the issue and provided legitimacy and political cover for Aldrich to pursue his work. Although none of the 1912 presidential candidates dared touch currency reform with anything less blunt than platitudes, whoever won would finish the job. As with the tariff and the income tax, Taft did the bleeding for Wilson.[22] It was up to the Democrats now. The desk was clean, and if they chose to act like Democrats it was all theirs to do, Secretary of State Bryan and all.

The final, Winter session of the 62nd Congress was ugly as ever. The Democrats were content to await their new majority, the Republican condemned sat on their hands, and the insurgents insurged. Taft's veto broke the rest. Nothing without unanimity got by. Roosevelt's influence came in a Senate vote, acting on Taft's Lotos Club advice, to limit the Presidency to one six-year term. The House rejected it, as well as Taft's non-voting seats for Cabinet members. The most notable event was a Taft speech in the Senate, the first there since John Adams. Taft was invited to a joint Session, also a first outside of inaugurals, to eulogize Sherman. Although this robbed Wilson of the innovation, Taft there avoided politics. Nevertheless, Taft's mixing with Congress, a subject of criticism through his term, habituated the body to the active presence of the Executive and left an open door for Wilson to use or abuse it at his own peril.

* * *

The transition at the White House itself was orderly. The staff was professional, and the air clean of the jealousies that defined the Roosevelt exit. Taft wrote recommendation letters and wished his staff success in the political afterlife. He begged the Wilsons to keep Mrs. Jaffray and his steward, Arthur Brooks. The lease arrangement with Pierce-Arrow was satisfactory to all parties. Wilson renewed it immediately. To the chauffeurs, the outgoing President wrote kindly notes, such as to, "My Dear Long,"

> Before I get out of office I want to record Mrs. Taft's and my satisfaction with your service as chauffeur during the past four years. We have found you to be an expert driver and a courteous and willing employee, and I am glad to commend you to all with whom you may seek employment.[23]

Chauffeur Francis Robinson would stay at the White House through the 1920s and become a living emblem of the White House garage. Abel Long resigned on June 15, 1913, and the author is unaware of his destination. He may have returned to Pierce-Arrow, as Col. Clifton had earlier offered to find him a place "that will not be lacking in self-respect."[24] The highest praise for the chauffeurs was from this one

21. (*cont.*) 1909 and 1911, and his important speech to the New York State Bankers Association of June 22, 1911 ("Addresses," reel 576).
22. In 1913 Aldrich watched from retirement as his plan twisted through the Democratic Congress. In the end, he and the Old Guard opposed what was largely his own plan. Had Roosevelt managed the reform a more centralized version tuned to his "New Nationalism" would have emerged. Had Taft managed it, Aldrich's more independent formula likely would have prevailed. As it happened under Wilson, the differences were mostly in degree, not kind, between Taft's 1911 recommendation, Aldrich's bill, and the ultimate formulation. In 1913, Republican pressure in the Senate, notably from Elihu Root, salvaged what Aldrich should have recognized as largely his own work. (Hatch wrote that it looked more like a bill offered in 1908 by Rep. Charles Fowler; p. 48.) Although his bill was dead-on-arrival, Aldrich's accomplishment came in presenting the "Report of the National Monetary Commission" on January 9, 1912.
23. Taft to AE Long, 2/28/13.
24. Clifton to Hilles, 6/19/11.

who knew. After the factory refurbished one of the 66 H.P.'s, Clifton wrote that the car's condition was a "a very great tribute to Long and to the care that has been given by the White House staff...."[25]

The only negative account Taft left his successor was somehow appropriate. During his term, the matter was ever one of chiding and legislative maneuvering by the Democrats. Taft delivered the problem wholesale to Wilson. By January of 1913, that year's White House travel budget was shot.[26] Wilson would have to come in as did Taft, asking Congress for spare change. Then there was another item Taft refused to leave for Wilson. The occasion of Clifton's praise for Long regarded the 66 H.P. Taft wanted the car.

Thanks to Long's superb treatment, the car needed no repairs outside of new brake linings and repainting. Only to be determined was the design of a monogram that would replace the Official Seal. Clifton forwarded a set of suggestions. The car was fixed and prepped with a summer touring body. As usual, Clifton's service was superb and his terms generous. A New Haven Pierce dealer received and delivered the car to Hotel Taft, where its new owner stayed in a special suite. On May 28, Taft wrote Mabel, "We are going to have an automobile as long as the money lasts. I am not an able financier, at least my wife thinks I am not." The next day he wrote a thank you note. "My dear Colonel Clifton: The automobile arrived here in good condition, and I have placed it in Mr. Wuestefeld's garage ... I am greatly indebted to you for your promptness and kindness in this matter."[27]

Taft wrote to Hilles:

> The automobile arrived safely and we took our first trip in it yesterday. It seemed like old times to go over the ground as smoothly as it carried us. I shall go out to golf to-day in it and feel as if for a moment I had resumed the luxurious life of long ago. Mrs. Taft says we will not be able to afford it, and perhaps that is true. At least we will afford it until we can not afford it, and then we will hang up the machine.[28]

Whether he could afford it or not, Taft overruled his wife in the matter.

Clifton had not asked for payment until the limousine body was placed on the chassis in the Fall by the local dealer. Only then, when professor Taft inquired, did he discover the bill was already paid. Brother Charles had picked up the check. The professor was angry. He assumed that Hilles, who made the arrangements, asked Charles for the money. Hilles explained he indeed had asked the President's brother for some money, but only as one among various friends who were to "chip in" for the automobile and a fund for a chauffeur. Charles insisted to pay it all himself, which went on top of three other Pierce-Arrows he bought that season.[29]

25. Clifton to Taft, 5/2/13.
26. "Wilson May Lack Fare," *NYT*, 1/22/13.
27. Taft to Mabel Boardman, 5/27/13 and Taft to Clifton, 5/28/13. The only complication was over the chauffeur. Due to insurance policy concerns over the arrangements with the factory to hold title until the Autumn, Taft had to release the man he hired, Frank Brecht, and use a man from the local Pierce-Arrow garage (see Taft to GR Wuestefeld and Taft to F Brecht, 5/28/13).
28. Taft to Hilles, 5/28/13.
29. Hilles to Taft, 11/5/13.

31

The Automobile Triumphant

Yet we Bull Moosers ... were fat and saucy in our attack upon aggrandized capital, were almost alone in our charge upon the citadel of privilege ... the whole cause and justification of our attack upon the established order was paling. And the injustices of the distributive system were being corrected, not by laws but by speeding up the wheels of industry in the United States and to an extent around the world.... In our own country a new element had come into the industrial and commercial picture. The automobile age had arrived. Ford's assembly belt was turning out Model T's. A kind of democracy was coming into the world and not through the ballot box, not by marching cohorts in the streets carrying banners, not even out of Congress nor its laws. The thing which was changing our world was the democratization of transportation.

— Former Bull Mooser
William Allen White, 1946[1]

As 1912 closed and President Taft prepared for his future, the automobile was triumphant. The *Times* declared it, "The All-Conquering Automobile."[2] This declaration came not just from Henry Ford's stunning goal to produce 200,000 automobiles in 1913, or the prediction that 600,000 cars would be built by the entire industry. It was not just from the even more stunning thought that many people would or could buy automobiles. It was not even the more than $50,000,000 indebtedness in road bonds that New Yorkers voted upon themselves for the sake of smoother roads and smoother rides—for automobiles.

The final ascent of the automobile was marked by the return of the horse. The one and only Newport affirmed what was true ten years before: there was nothing new in horses. Back to the past again, and the resurgence of polo. (This had nothing to do with the legal squabble between Mrs. Belmont, owner of the Newport mansion, the "Marble House," and a grocer; her automobile was seized upon attachment for a $400 grocery bill she disputed.) Newport revisited the horse as the speed disease was

1. "The Autobiography of William Allen White," p. 499.
2. *NYT* editorial, 10/20/12.

freed of its wealthy quarantine. A pandemic broke.[3]

New York's fashionable couldn't have been happy to learn that one of its street's finest limousines, a French import, was owned by the doorman of a Central Park hotel. "He requests that his name be not mentioned," went the report, "lest dimes be handed to him instead of dollars when he whistles to the chauffeurs of waiting limousines to pull up to the awninged entrance."[4] Over Taft's four years the exclusivity of the automobile was ruined. After telling the ACA that his motoring was on loan from the government and elsewhere joking that in leaving Washington he was exchanging social status from "that of the automobile to that of the pedestrian class," Taft literally took it with him.[5]

To prove itself smart, the counter-counterculture set returned to the horse. Neglected Westchester and Newport hostlers must have wondered at their luck. Taste and exclusivity were lost to the utter utility of automobiles. With roads crowded by the underclass, those too mindful of gravity to fly aeroplanes decided it prudent not to "throw away the old thing in enjoying their taste for the new."[6] The "vogue of the horse" became the rich man's rage just as the automobile had been only a few years before.

Nevertheless, garages weren't reconverted to stables. While Ford pumped out the common man's car, the wealthy sank their money into ever more expensive automobiles. Dealers along New York's "Automobile Row" booked record orders for limousines. For the rich, "the big, beautiful limousine is ... a utility car," it was noted. Auto shows were short on "freak cars"—luxury, not speed, was the theme. The words "comfort" and "a lady's" were more important than "magneto" and "carburetor." Saks & Co. introduced $22 "black seal limousine cases" in the ladies' section. The latest in cars was now writing pads, footrests, portable desks, and an "automobile bridge set." The most stunning car of the Autumn season was a "triple-berline" displayed at the London show. It was essentially three carriages melded into one huge automobile that was "luxurious in the extreme." The radical change was the enclosed front seat. The chauffeur was now inside the car.[7]

This setup, along with the introduction of useful self-starters, marked a major social change in automobiling, the demise of the chauffeur. With Cadillac's hugely successful electric starter, introduced in the 1912 model year, the crank was no longer an impediment to driving. Why, even a woman could start a car now, it was said.[8] "Self-drive" hit the automotive lexicon. Design and law set about accommodating it. There arose an urgency for licensing all drivers, and a new limousine style emerged to satisfy an owner's wishes to drive or be driven. As the roof and side walls grew around the front seats, the forward passenger window was made to retract fully, equalizing either the driver to

3. "600,000 Autos Next Year's Crop," 11/13/12, "The Horse Has Come Back to its Own Again," 11/17/12 and "Seize Mrs. Belmont's Auto," 9/8/12, *NYT*.
4. To affirm an old legend, the article mentions a waiter who overhead a conversation and took a stock short with all of his $2,500. It turned into $18,000 in two days. That became $50,000 which went towards putting his son through MIT ("All Things Come Around to Him Who Will but Wait," *NYT*, 6/30/12).
5. Taft to Mrs. William Hooper, 2/3/13, per Pringle, p. 848.
6. "The Horse Has Come Back to its Own Again," *NYT*, 11/17/12.
7. "Selling Season for Motor Cars," 11/3/12, Saks & Co. advertisement, 6/23/12, "Novelties for the Motorists' Comfort," 1/7/12, and "Last Word in Motor Car Luxury," 11/24/12, *NYT*. The Saks limousine case included "White Persian ivory hair and cloth brush, mirror, soap, cream, tooth powder and talcum boxes, tooth brush holder, comb, scissors, nail file, button hook, corn knife, orange stick, buffer, and rubber-lined pocket for wash cloth."
8. See "Self-starter Brings out Women Drivers," *NYT*, 1/12/13.

the passengers or the passengers to the driver.[9] American builders next took the limousine's form and gave it to everyone. Development in steel body construction made enclosed cars feasible on the assembly line and put cheaper closed cars on the market. Here was the birth of the sedan car. These technologies dramatically changed the convenience of the automobile, but they were not the cause of the social advance. The demand for it came first.

The Taft period marked the normalization of the automobile. With its general acceptance, the industry turned nostalgic. Before, rearward looks to the past were intended to establish the automobile within the history of transportation, the latest cog in the story of the wheel. Now the introspection was to view the early days of motoring as history itself. Stories abounded of the earliest races, the first auto shows, and the primitive days of a decade before. It was accepted in 1912 that automotive technology and design were mature, and advance would come in variant, not revolution.

The final tap on the nail that killed the Horse Age came with the release of the last horse-drawn trolley cars in New York. New York led the nation in the motorization of municipal services. The Cleaning Commissioner in 1912 requested $210,000 to purchase forty motors for refuse and street watering and another $200,000 for "motor street sweeping machines." Most other cities had already exchanged horse-drawn for electric trolleys. In New York, the horse trolleys were tourist attractions.[10] Their demise just happened to coincide with another event, the Horse Age's equivalent to John Henry's final, fatal victory over steam. Well, sort of.

It started slowly, out West. Amidst the September campaign, a small notice appeared in the *Times*. "A novelty was recently witnessed at Wichita, Kan., when a motor polo game was played, the teams being mounted on four stripped motor cars, each carrying two men." Being what they are, New York promoters didn't let this one go. Soon enough, first, the American League ballpark, then, Madison Square Garden, were filled with crowds who watched the "thrills" and "spills"— no kidding — of Automobile Polo. There on Christmas Eve were "King and Ferriter snatching a double victory off Sterling and Jackson," 7–4 and 12–10. King was the "expert" driver and Ferriter the mallet man. They won despite "a sensational spill" which left Ferriter "helpless," precisely what the audience came for. The mounts were Model T's, for the car's sturdiness and planetary transmission that allowed forward and reverse gear changes in full motion. They were equipped with roll bars should they "turn turtle." Although Vincent Astor made an appearance in the stands, Auto Polo didn't last.[11] The game was ceded back to the horse. Automobilists kept the roads.

* * *

It wasn't all safe for motoring in 1912. During a 150-mile September automobile

9. "Great Progress in Car Building," *NYT*, 6/30/12. One of the first of these "dual-use" limousines was displayed in June of 1912 in Europe. With the division window lowered, the owner could share the "saloon" with the passengers without feeling like a servant. With the window up, the chauffeur was appropriately in a separate compartment. For full discussion of the social change from chauffeured to self-drive, see *Stretching It: The Story of the Limousine*, by Michael L. Bromley and Tom Mazza, 2002.
10. "Horse Fast Gives Way to Motor," 1/19/13 and "Driving out the Horse," 11/3/12, *NYT*.
11. "Play Polo with Motor Cars," 9/1/12, "Thrills in Auto Polo," 12/25/12, "Autos Smash Head-on," 12/4/12, *NYT*. In London in 1907 a strong man circus act used a Ford Model N in a stunt, "owing to its lightness in proportion to power and size...." ("A Ford Car in the London Hippodrome," *Automobile*, photo caption, 5/16/07, p. 838).

campaign around beautiful Vermont, Roosevelt descended from his machine to enlist the lovely village of Morrisville into his political storm. His entrance was by eighteen oxen and a hay wagon. After this bizarre display he explained to the gathered farmers the glories of the Progressive party, its special relationship to Lincoln, and, to this border state, the viciousness of Reciprocity. He claimed his kind of progress would also benefit their wives. A man shouted, "What's the matter with the farmer's wife?" The reply might have been to Aldrich, Miles, or Taft. "You automobile man over there who asked that question," he railed, "if you were a farmer you wouldn't ask it." Later, Roosevelt declared that managers of the nation's capital, i.e., the President, had abused the public trust by building "boulevards for the benefit of the wealthy people in the suburbs and especially for the benefit of real estate speculators."[12] Never mind his platform's declarations for Good Roads. No, motoring wasn't yet safe from demagoguery.

Whatever the import of oxen in Morrisville, Roosevelt admitted to his own automobiling, or its usefulness, anyway. To that audience he explained, "We've got to get the truth to you despite the newspapers and that's why I'm traveling about Vermont in automobiles and an ox wagon." Ox wagons were fine for Morrisville, perhaps, but throughout the rest of Vermont automobiles served him far better. Automobiles allowed him to hit more towns, see more crowds, and spread more demagoguery than ever before. It was not by oxen that Roosevelt raced at 45 m.p.h. to catch a scheduled automobile parade in his honor. From the parade's lead car, a man sang "Onward Christian Soldiers." Behind was one of the campaign's "Flying Squadron" motors, circus cars done up as roving Rough Rider-mobiles, complete with bandanas, murals of Roosevelt, and American flags.[13] In what was one their most productive counterpunches, New York Republicans held their own auto campaign. Every day at noon from the headquarters at the Vanderbilt Hotel, a "string of gaudily bedecked automobiles" called the "Prosperity Special," including one with a band, headed out for political excursions across the countryside.[14]

Wilson found himself on both sides of the automobile. To the good, he got around in motors just like Taft and Roosevelt. To the bad, just before the election he took a nasty head wound from the roof of a limousine when he was bounced on a bad road in New Jersey. In October, he addressed an Atlantic City Good Roads conference at which he must have been pleased to see the Grange represented. He started with the obligatory apology for his own automobiling. "I tell you frankly my interests in good roads is not merely an interest in the pleasure of riding in autos," he said. He next took his rhetoric a step further to where it belonged, to where Taft launched the movement, beyond the apologies and class warfare. Taft had told the ACA that the automobile contributed to "increasing ... the intercourse between all the people." The professor politician, too, saw beyond its immediate role as a conveyance. "It is not merely an interest in the much more important matter of affording farmers ... and residents in villages means of ready access to such neighboring markets as they need for economic benefit," Wilson declared, "but it is also the interest in weaving as complicated and elaborate a net of neigh-

12. "Fooling the Farmers," 9/3/12 and "Roosevelt Pledges Quick Extra Session," 9/18/12, *NYT*.
13. "Colonel's Last Word an Attack on Root," 11/5/12 and "Circus Cars for Roosevelt," 8/31/12, *NYT*.
14. Similarly named railroad trains with Republican speakers chased Roosevelt in the Midwest ("Taft Men Working to Save Onandaga," *NYT*, 10/29/12).

borhood and State and National opinion together as it is possible to weave."[15]

Previously, the Grange and the AAA were lions walking in circles around the prize (a prize bagged by the automobilists). They agreed on the fundamental need for better roads, but they weren't ready to hold hands. A 1908 meeting between a New Jersey auto club and the State Grange was the exception that proved the rule that farmers and motorists still had issues. That a granger declared, "When the motor car becomes cheaper ... the farmer will be the first to adopt it for business and pleasure," meant that even in enlightened New Jersey the contradistinction was louder than the protest.[16] Eastern Grangers were learning a lesson yet unheard in the West and that should have been learned years before. As late as the 1910 AAA convention in Washington the group felt obligated to speak to the farm.[17] It took a former Master of the National Grange to explain it for them. Only then could the *Automobile* declare that the farmer is "awakening to his opportunity [for good roads] now that the automobile is backing him up; it is a common cause." As the statement was being won, the question moved from farmer to worker. "Is it a breach of citizenship in America for a workman to purchase and use an automobile?" asked the *Automobile* in 1911.[18]

Although he had come a long way from accusing automobiles of fomenting socialism, Wilson couldn't let go the auto-demagoguery. Bad motoring remained a useful political tool. "I have no objection," he said, saying what he ought have said in 1906, "to the ordinary automobile, properly handled by a man of conscience who is also a gentleman. Many of the people I see handling automobiles handle them as if they had neither conscience or learning. You know what men do when they have a joyride; they sometimes have the time of their lives, and sometimes, fortunately, the last time of their lives." All very well, and a good line. But Wilson's point was that bad motorists were like bad businessmen. "Now," he continued, "these wretched things— the lawless corporations— are taking joyrides in which they don't kill the people that are riding with them, but they kill the people they run over."[19] Oh, well, that one would never go away. Some motorists were acceptable.

The triumph of the automobile was set in law the following year. Four years before, the Senate argued what duties on imported automobiles would produce the most revenue. Aldrich wanted 50 percent. Heyburn wanted one hundred. The Democratic Congress of 1913 concurred that Payne's 45 percent was the appropriate "maximum revenue-producing point," as Bailey called it in 1909. Only this time the duty was split. Automobiles with a value under $2,000 were allowed in at a discounted 30 percent. If it was for the people, it was no longer a "nuisance" and a "privilege." Cheap cars were for the people.[20]

The crucial affirmation came a year later. With the assent of the farmer, the politician, the working man, and the public at large, the automobile passed the checkered flag when the demagogue waved it. In his 1914 study of the plutocracy,

15. "Gov. Wilson's Head Cut in Auto Shake-up," 11/4/12 and "Wilson for Good Roads," 10/1/12, *NYT*.
16. "Jersey Grangers and Autoists Talk of Good Roads," *Automobile*, 10/1/08, p. 483.
17. See "National Legislative Convention at Washington," *Automobile*, 2/17/10, p. 365.
18. Editorial, 6/9/10, p. 1058 and "Resume of the Year's Work, 1/26/11, p. 250, *Automobile*.
19. "The Real Wilson Revealed on Stump," *NYT*, 10/6/12.
20. "The Tariff and the Industry," *American Motorist*, Nov. 1913, p. 1012. The most radical and meaningful reduction was on tires, going from 35 percent to 10 percent, again, a recognition that automobiles were a consumable.

Walter Weyl complained, "Our jogging horses are passed by their high-power [sic] automobiles. We are obliged to take their dust...." Wait—Weyl's abused didn't suffer from automobiles; they suffered from not having one: "We are creating new types of destitutes—the automobile-less...."[21]

21. From "The new Democracy," pp. 242–243, quoted by Hofstadter, p. 147.

32

"Whatever we have thought of you, we love you"

I don't like to be uncharitable, and I wish to retain my patriotism generally, but your letter, in which you express the hope that I am having a good time, and the view that I am out of all that you are in, and which you would like to be out of, suggests one or two remarks.... It is a little bit like that old sailor who had been a mate for forty years, and who hired a man to come to his house every morning at six o'clock and knock on the door, and say, "Mate, the Captain orders you on deck to furl sail," to which the Mate replied, "Tell the Captain to go to hell!"

—William Howard Taft
to Elihu Root, May 5, 1913

By March 5, 1913, there were at least two contented men in the country. Woodrow Wilson was more happy, perhaps, than content, so it was not he. The first days at the White House are necessarily dizzy for all but the most maniacal of occupants. Contentment ought not be the emotion of an incoming President. No, contentment was elsewhere. One to feel it was Joseph G. Cannon. "I haven't built an air castle for thirty years," declared the former congressman. "But as we grow older we grow more content with the present."[1] He had made his peace. The other was William Howard Taft.

Roosevelt once called Taft a good "hater." He was a magnanimous former President. Neither resentment nor bitterness were to be found in ex-President Taft. Just after the 1912 election, Taft wrote J.W. Hill,

> I could not truthfully say that I do not regret the inability to carry out some plans that I think I might have matured and made useful to the nation in the next four years. But of personal disappointment, I know you will believe me when I say there is none. ...I harbor no ill will against anybody, even Beveridge—could I put it more strongly?

He fought his fight and moved on. Yale and teaching the beloved Constitution were his destination. "In my small way, I

1. "Uncle Joe Cannon's First Talk as a Private Citizen," *NYT*, 3/9/13. Cannon lost in 1912. All his long life Cannon would collect no moss. He was back two years later, and served until 1923.

want to contribute to the upbringing of undergraduates of one institution to the realization of the benefits of being Americans," he told Yale alumni.[2]

Taft had good reason for his satisfaction that "a great deal was accomplished which will be useful to the people in the future...."[3] There was another thing, though, something of which few were aware, and to which he allowed himself conceit. "I have succeeded in securing the adoption of a new set of rules for equity proceedings in the United States courts," he bragged. "I hope to be able to secure new rules to govern proceedings at common law and if I succeed in my efforts in that direction I shall have accomplished more for so-called social justice than all the hollering and hysteria of the professional reformers could achieve in a thousand years." In March he told correspondents, "The thing that is mentioned least is the thing in which I take the most pride.... Six of the nine Justices, including the Chief Justice, to-day bear my commission. And I have said to them, Damn you, if any of you die, I'll disown you."[4]

Taft kept busy up to the last moment of his tenure, signing bills, autographs, even answering the demands of a little girl from Wyoming who refused to leave town without a kiss from the President. Her desperate mother wrote the White House. Soon thereafter, the President found on his appointment calendar, "Phyllis Westrand, Lander, Wyo., (to be kissed)." He told her, "So you want to be kissed by the President.... Well, I hope you will remember that." When it made the news, the White House was inundated with callers and their daughters to be kissed.[5]

Taft's final visit to New York as President came in late February. The occasion was his receiving the Carnegie Gold Medal for "peace work." The dinner was warm, and not a touch bittersweet. Taft closed his speech with, "Good-night, my friends—good-bye. I am going back to Washington to lay down such power as I have had — a power which I have been glad to exercise wherever I could in the cause of peace. And I leave you with the most cordial expressions of thanks for your appreciation of what I have done and for your kindness in taking the will for the deed." A standing ovation replied. Job Hedges, the failed Republican candidate for Governor, summed up the evening's—and, at last, the country's—sentiments toward Taft the man:

> To you, Mr. President, and to the exquisite lady who is your helpmeet in the White House we reserve the tribute of unselfish personal love. Whatever we have thought of you, we love you.[6]

Taft made one last appearance at a police dinner that followed. The policemen blew their whistles and cheered him a full five minutes. His appreciation for them was earnest. He praised their work to protect him and act as his guides through New York streets. "I feel that I am speaking to men who have been through

2. "Keep Your Feet on the Ground," *NYT* editorial, 2/1/13.
3. Taft to Bannard, 11/10/12.
4. "What the President Sees in the Future," 11/19/12 and "Taft in Cheery Vein Reviews His Record," 3/4/13, *NYT*. The *Times* used "darn you." Pringle quoted from the same source and substituted what was likely the actual quotation, "damn you" (p. 854). For Taft's efforts as President on court reform, a good start is "White Will Reform Equity Court Rules," *NYT*, 6/4/11.
5. "Insisted on a Taft Kiss," *NYT*, 1/12/13.
6. "No Intervention Is Taft's Decision," *NYT*, 2/23/13. In Taft's obituary, the *Times* noted, "Taft left the White House with his Administration discredited, although personally he had lost little of the esteem in which he had been held by his fellow countrymen" (3/9/30). The article called his ascension to the Supreme Court "a 'come-back' unprecedented in American political annals."

very much the same experience that I have." The cops again cheered when he called them patriots, "ready to stand up" for their country.[7]

Earlier in the day he tended to another of his New York occupations with a visit to the "Blind Lighthouse," a charity and home for the blind. To an audience that included Helen Keller, who beforehand sat in the President's chair and declared, "I am the first woman to be President of the United States," Taft reflected on what it meant in those very human terms before him, this political idea of "equality of opportunity":

> I have often wondered, when I have read the Declaration of Independence ... what the blind must think about the statement that all men are born free and equal. Behind those eyes that do not see there must be a good deal of question. We are not equal in opportunity or environment. What is meant is that it is the aspiration of a popular Government to bring about as near equality of opportunity as possible. That is why we are here.[8]

In these words proof could be no clearer of what Joseph Choate said of Taft in his welcome. "Here is one who is as good as he is great — President Taft." Taft again marked out one of the political boundaries of the modern world that he helped to launch. "We who have sight feel that those who have not have not had quite a square deal. We want to help them, and we find that the best way is to help them to help themselves."

* * *

Two stories surrounding the Wilson inaugural have been wrongly affixed to Taft. The first was Taft's speech to the National Press Club, his final official address. To a body of men with whom the President had found little satisfaction, he mentioned a few of his shortcomings as President. It was the standard Taft self-deprecating half-joke that has been taken wholly seriously by history. He reviewed his long public career, attributing his stunning advancements to there never having been "a time that I did not have my 'plate' up at the right time." Of his Presidency, he admitted, "My sin is an indisposition to labor as hard as I might; a disposition to procrastinate and a disposition to enjoy the fellowship of others more than I ought." Those words have been taken as a confessional, the definitive Taft.[9]

Taft was after a few things here. Of his career and his upright "plate" he concluded, "Now, gentlemen, after that record, still in health, do you suppose that I regret anything; that I have an occasion for kicking and squealing? What kind of man would I be if I did, with the measure all on my side?" He had administered a presidency through strife and endured one of the nation's most contentious elections, both made difficult, in part, by the men before him. He had no regrets, he was bragging. "It is difficult for me not to feel very grateful for what has happened to me. When I look back over my fifty-five years of life and see how every good thing has come to me and very little bad, it seems to me that I ought to brace myself against what might come in the future to offset the good luck that has attended me before." We must take him at his word. There was no regret, not even for a little pro-

7. "Taft Praises Police at Their Big Dinner," *NYT*, 2/23/13.
8. "President Opens 'Blind Lighthouse,'" *NYT*, 2/23/13.
9. "Taft Is Grateful for All He Has Had," *NYT*, 3/2/13. Horace Taft was furious at the "indisposition to labor" remark. "I was sorry that you put into your *familiar* talk with the reporters what was kind of a confession of laziness. This is so untrue, judging you by any ordinary standard of vigor and diligence, that it gives an entirely wrong impression and yet one that has already had some acceptance. I got into some hot words with George Seymour on the subject a few months ago" [italics added] (Horace Taft to Taft, 3/7/13). Taft's reply didn't mention it.

crastination and socializing. His pride was well earned, and his humor as strong as ever.

Sadly, these jokes have stuck. Claude Bowers, Beveridge's biographer, derided Taft's career, attributing it wholly to chance. "Fate had taken a kindly man of judicial temperament and thrust him into a position of political leadership for which he was singularly unfit ... the child of fortune; Fate had lifted him from one appointive office to another...."[10] Pringle did little to defend Taft against the charges. Upon reviewing Pringle's manuscript, Horace Taft protested. Of his brother's fortitude, he wrote,

> I kept thinking of the impression, which I think you give, of a rather lazy man who ambled along from one promotion to another without much reason for it. This makes me bear down on his energy and success....[11]

The next mistake of history comes to us of our bitter little man at the White House, the usher Hoover. He wrote that upon return to the White House from the Capitol with the new President, Taft lingered around and made a general embarrassment of himself. He said Wilson invited Taft to lunch, but expected him to decline. "It was really sad to observe Mr. Taft ... he was practically dragged from the scene..." wrote Hoover.[12] The usher's skirt shows again. For the record, Taft and Wilson arrived to the White House just after 2:00. Taft walked out the back door at 2:53. That short time was spent at a luncheon that Mr. and Mrs. Taft had prepared for the Wilsons and for the outgoing and incoming Cabinets. According to another account, Taft's welcome was "more than

The author's favorite photo of Taft. (Courtesy Library of Congress)

10. Bowers, p. 336.
11. This inspired Horace to include a strong defense of his brother in his own memoirs (Horace Taft to Pringle, 5/11/42, Henry F. Pringle Papers; see Horace Taft's autobiography, "Memories and Opinions," Chapter 10).
12. Hoover, p. 56–57. See Pringle for a refutation of Hoover's account of the day (pp. 854–855). The Hoover

Next time you cross the old Million Dollar Bridge that spans Connecticut Avenue over Rock Creek Park in Washington, D.C., think of Taft, for whom it was renamed following his death. In his day as President it was his bridge to a round of golf. He probably took it at 40 miles an hour, telling the chauffeur to get it up. (Courtesy Library of Congress)

kindly." He showed the President and his family around their new home.[13] Finally, any lingering by Taft was because of a late ride.

The original plan was that after the White House luncheon Taft would be driven to a friend's residence, where his family awaited, then to the station for a 3:15 train to Augusta. Since the luncheon had a late start due to delays at the Capitol, two White House motors were dispatched to take Mrs. Taft and her party to the station. There, in a black "traveling" dress and carrying a bouquet of violets, she waited for her husband. Meanwhile, Taft's limousine had been sent to fetch two of Wilson's infant grandchildren from the Shoreham Hotel. Taft awaited its return. At 2:53 he stepped into the limousine. Two motorcycle policemen guided the car as they rushed to catch the train. The chauffeur was Abe Long, who had driven President-elect and Mrs. Taft to the White House the night of March 3, four years before.[14]

On the way to Union Station, Long guided the limousine across the foot of the Capitol where crowds awaited the inaugural parade just then to commence. The ex–President was recognized with "a mighty ovation" that followed his car down the street. He smiled and tipped his hat, much pleased with the spontaneous demonstration from the Democratic gathering. At the train station a farewell party of fifty awaited Taft in the presidential suite. "I am now retiring to a pedestrian life," he

12. (*cont.*) papers at the Library of Congress include notes for his book. In his notes, Hoover said that Hilles arranged a scheme to force Taft to leave before the luncheon, but that Taft avoided all the efforts. Hoover wrote, "Not a moment passed but what those who had Mr. Taft's interest most at heart were trying in some way to get him to leave the room and retire from the assembled throng, apparently so indifferent to his every consideration. Word finally came that Mrs. Taft would not wait for Mr. Taft any longer at the place of meeting but would continue on to the station. This was not told to Mr. Taft but instead he was again reminded by me that the time was so short he would not have time to carry out the plans to go by for Mrs. T[aft] and to the station unless he left at once. This had the desired effect and he was practically dragged away from the scene of his former achievements, for it was in the dining room where he was shown to the best advantage the car in waiting in the South grounds. His goodbye and last trip to this automobile was not one of a great deal consequence [*sic*]. Time was short and those with him so insistent he hardly had the opportunity to bid adieu to his successor" (Hoover papers, Reel no. 9, "Inaugural 1913" section).

13. *White House Profile*, by Bess Furman, p. 287.

14. "Crowds Cheer Taft as He Leaves City," *NYT*, 3/5/13 and "Wilson Pleased With Inaugural," *Evening Star*, 3/5/13.

laughed. "Don't forget me." When he and his family walked through the concourse, cheers again arose, which Taft recognized. Among the onlookers who pushed against the ropes were three little girls who had come to wish goodbye to their leader. Miss Helen Taft kissed the Camp Fire girls and promised to visit soon.

* * *

A warm greeting at Augusta, the largest ever for him there, brought not memories of 1909 but the satisfactions of 1913. To 1,000 schoolchildren, each with an American flag, Taft arrived to Archie's hometown as one of its own. The mayor accompanied him to his hotel. Not a half hour later Taft was headed for the country club. That afternoon, he and Mrs. Taft went motoring. The greeting at New Haven a month later was even more enthusiastic. The town's new citizen, professor Taft, smiled upon the scene before him. Of his month's stay in Augusta, he said, "It felt fine to be free."[15]

Back in Washington on the afternoon of the 5th of March, President Wilson snuck away from the hand-shakers and office-seekers who inundated the newly "open" White House. He escaped through the back door for a motor ride with his wife.

15. "Augusta Welcomes Taft," 3/6/13 and "Taft Back, Ruddy and Ready to Work," 4/1/13, *NYT*.

Appendix A

Letters and Documents

Taft's Speech to the Automobile Club of America

On December 20, President Taft addressed the Twelfth Annual Banquet of the Automobile Club of America at the Grand Ballroom of the Waldorf-Astoria hotel in New York City. Started in 1899, the ACA was the most important motoring club in the nation. The ACA's membership was privilege itself. The Governor of New York answered its mail. The State legislature enacted its laws. The Club sponsored races, assisted tours and touring, lobbied governments, and generally promoted automobiling, motor boating, and aeroplaning. It was one of early motoring's most important assets.

In 1911 the Club's agitation forced the city of New York to rebuild its worst roads. That same year it successfully lobbied Albany for laws against outdoor advertisements (early billboards) and sent out parties of "sign smashers" in trucks to remove unsightly advertisements. The ACA was especially successful in its work with overseas clubs to promote automobile-friendly laws for tourists to bring in-transit automobiles across borders duty-free. The Club also sponsored technological development with a world-class "automobile laboratory" to test motors. The Club owned two Manhattan buildings, one twelve stories high, with social, meeting and hotel rooms, a chauffeur's club, fuel storage, mechanical supplies department, administrative facilities, and a 130,000 square foot garage. There were almost 3,000 members. Taft held an honorary membership.

After a year's campaign, in September of 1911, Taft accepted the invitation from ACA president Henry Anderson to speak at the annual banquet. "We wish to make this dinner an occasion of international importance," Anderson wrote. "We urge you to give by your presence the support to the automobile industry which it deserves, an industry in which hundred of millions of dollars are invested and hundreds of thousands of men are working."[1]

At the banquet Anderson introduced Taft. Bragging of the ACA's "passport," which allowed entry through customs of personal automobiles for tourism in many countries, Anderson joked that it was as

1. H Sanderson to Taft, telegram, 9/29/11. Sanderson had been bugging Harry Taft to get his brother to the annual banquet since at least that January. Harry forwarded one letter, saying, "Here is another gentleman who thinks that by making me a conduit force will be added to the consideration which he thinks should lead the President to attend the annual banquet of the Automobile Club of America. I have said that I would see that the letter got to the President"(Henry Taft to CD Norton, 1/20/11).

great a power as the American passport itself. The Club "can give ... a slip of paper that, in a practical sense, throws down almost every customs barrier in the civilized world, and permits him to pass from one country to another, unmolested by the customs regulations of boundaries and frontiers." It was a lead to Anderson's real point. He continued, "I wish I could announce to you that we had been as successful in our own country, in obliterating States lines [laughter], and annoying, conflicting and oppressive State regulations, and license requirements. I hope the day is not far off when the policy of our States will be governed rather by considerations of hospitality and courtesy than by considerations of tribute."

Taft knew the complaint. He had suffered its consequences. In his speech he marvelously answered the usual solution, federal licensing, with a joke. He also knew the sensitivities of the ACA members towards federal aid in road building. This he answered with a clever, mocking, anecdote (which the ACA magazine omitted in its reprint of the speech), and settled it with an almost judicial ruling. The speech settled the most important legal issues of the Motor Age: licensing, which Taft declared would remain with the states, and road building, which he said was within the powers of the federal government. The speech was otherwise peppered with bright references to the political issues of the day, Reciprocity, anti-trust, and the high cost of living. Taft made fun of himself and his audience, sometimes with brutal sarcasm. It was a model speech, not just of Taft, but for any President. To "prolonged cheers and applause," President Taft rose to speak:

Mr. President, Gentlemen of the Automobile
Club, Ladies and Gentlemen:

I have never quite understood the kindly persistence that your president and his associates showed in inviting me to this festal occasion. I never belonged to what I always used to call "carriage class." [Laughter]. I walked, or rode in street cars. When the automobile took the place of that more dignified procedure, I am sure Judge Moore will agree with me in that—I transferred the carriage class to the automobile class, and considered myself still excluded.

It is true that the accident of office and the generosity of a Republican Congress [laughter] gave me for a time [laughter] the privilege of understanding the fascination of traveling by this new method, but it is only a loan. There is no permanency of tenure in the machine or in the office [laughter], and, therefore, I beg of you to understand that I appear here only in a temporarily representative capacity. [Laughter.]

I am told that automobile clubs in Europe are headed by the Dukes and the Grand Dukes, and those who occupy places of near royalty, and that by way of a somewhat forced analogy it was deemed wise to have the temporary Executive of this government present at one automobile dinner in order to show that there was some "pull" at Washington.[2]

I am glad to be here in any capacity; glad to learn of how much the automobile and its uses have contributed to international friendship among those who can afford to carry automobiles through a custom house. [Laughter]. Reference has been made to the limi-

2. This section omitted in the ACA reprint of the speech, therefore any applause, shock, or laughter that followed is unrecorded. Someone at the ACA either felt, or thought someone else might feel, offended by the President's joke about royal motorists.

Taft's speech to the American Automobile Club annual banquet, December 20, 1911, at the Waldorf-Astoria, in New York City. (From *Club Journal,* January 6, 1912). At the President's table identified from left to right: Mr. F.M. Schmolck, Mr. Patrick Francis Murphy, Hon. E.H. Gary, Lt. Gen. Nelson O. Miles, Hon. John A. Dix, Gen. Horace Porter, Hon. William H. Taft, Mr. Henry Sanderson, Count J.H. von Bernstorff, Senor Don Juan Riano y Gayangos, Mr. Melville E. Stone, Mr. John G. Milburn, The Duke of Newcastle, Mr. Henry W. Taft, Hon. William Barnes, Jr., Hon. Victor J. Dowling, Hon. Chauncey M. Depew, Mr. F.A. Vanderlip.

tation on my power. The truth is that in the performance of my official duties, I don't meet anything but limitation [great laughter and applause]. Your presiding officer has said to you that his power, in certain regards, was much longer than mine. I have no doubt of it, and if he can get, as he says, by issuing a mere yellow a ticket, so much of value through Loeb and the custom house here, he can exceed any power that I have. [Laughter.]

I am glad to know that I am having the pleasure of addressing not only those who use the automobile, who really form that class that I dare call, in the presence of a brother of mine who teaches the classics, fruges consumere nati,[3] but also those gentlemen who are making it an industry that contributes so greatly to the wealth of this country, and adds so much to its manufacturing product. I tried to help them out by getting the duties lowered into Canada. [Applause.] Once in a while I do something for somebody that ought to make them grateful [laughter and applause], but even that seems to be broken up by a slowness on the part of Canada to appreciate a good thing when she sees it.

Seriously speaking, my friends, the working out of the automobile is a wonderful development. As you look back as far as I can look back — at least with any sense of eco-

3. From Horace, the expression means "born to reap its rewards" or "born to consume the fruits of the earth." While Horace liked *carpe diem* and that sort of thing, Franklin used it in contrast to Yankee industriousness, and Henry George, Jr., used it in his *The Menace of Privilege* (1905) to slam the plutocracy. Taft used it to make fun of his audience. How many of them caught it?

The audience included: J.P. Morgan, Henry Clay Frick, William K. Vanderbilt, John Archbold, and John Flagler. "Most of them were millionaires," Major Butt wrote. (From *Club Journal,* January 6, 1912)

nomic changes— to 1876, and think of what has happened in that period in the promotion of the comfort of the human race, the changes are marvelous. The telephone, the electric railway, all the electrical devices for the reproduction of the human voice, and the automobile — what could we do without them now? How rapidly we adapt ourselves to the absolute necessity of those improvements of which we knew and imagined nothing fifty years ago! I am sure that of all of them the automobile coming in as a toy of the wealthier classes is going to prove the most useful of them all to all classes, rich and poor [applause].

There was a time in the use of the automobile — I shared it myself when I was plodding along with the tandem that nature gave me, as Holmes called it [laughter], when a spirit of intolerance was manifested against the horrible looking machine that the automobile then was to the ordinary eye. There was an intimation of "get-out-of-the-way or we will run you over," and a resentment against those who were using it until you yourself got into the automobile. Then human nature was shown in the quickness with which the attitude of mind can change, and you regarded as utterly unreasonable the slowness of the pedestrian and the idea that he had any right to any part of the street [laughter], either for crossing or anything else. And then the utter outrage of having any dogs at all in any community that should get in the way of that magnificent instrument of travel and comfort!

If you had traveled as much as I have [laughter and applause], if you had been met in every town of five or ten thousand people in every State, with a hundred automobiles, in order to demonstrate the prosperity of that particular town, you would understand that the use of the automobile has gone quite beyond that class which I aspired to and never acquired membership in. [Laughter]. It means that the automobile has come here for use. It is contributing, like the telephone, like the suburban railway, like the rural delivery of the Post Office, to the possibility of a comfortable life on the farm, and it is tending, together with high prices of farm products, to turn back again those who seek the city and professional life, to a place where they have an assured income and are not troubled with suits or litigation, or chased by the government. [Laughter and applause].

Many serious problems are going to be presented, and you are having them now, with these State lines, and these authorities, of whom you can have three in a very short automobile ride just in this neighborhood. I do not know how you are going to get rid of them. You might set some theory of yourself being an unopened and complete package, sent from Connecticut into New Jersey, through New York, that can not be opened until you reach the point of your destination, and in some way or other, call upon the Federal Court to protect you in that transportation. [Laughter]. Whether you escape the tax and the license and all that sort of thing, for the grooves that your automobile makes in the roads of your State, I am unable to say, because those charged with the responsibility of keeping up the roads know that while the automobile owners have promoted the question and the pursuit of good roads, they have very largely contributed to the difficulty of building and maintaining them. The experiments made as to what may avoid the influence of those great big rubber tires upon macadam roads are proceeding, and I hope something will come of them.

I speak with considerable deference, because I find that gentlemen who study good roads as a diversion, as an avocation, have such decided views that one who is just charged with the good old governmental way of building a road finds some difficulty in appreciating, and also finds that he is not regarded as an authority in any respect. I had a call from a gentleman who is an automobilist and also a good roads man, and eats, sleeps and drinks good roads. He came to me and said: "Mr. President, I desire that you appoint delegates to a good roads convention — a national good roads convention." I said, "I will be very glad to do it, sir. We have two departments in which there are road experts." "Which are they," said he. Said I, "We have the Agricultural Department, where we have a Bureau devoted to experts who are laying experimental roads for the country, for the farmers." Said he, "I have had occasion to know how much they know. I have looked into it, and they don't know anything about it at all. They have not the first principles at hand." I said, "Then we will go into the War Department, and we will take the army engineers, and I will send you some of them. They have been building roads in the Philippines, in every State in the Union, in Cuba, on the Isthmus, and elsewhere." Said he, "If my boy did not know more about the real principles of building roads than they do, I would not allow him to continue the study of it." I said, "Good morning, sir, I am not in the road business, and I have no delegates worthy of being sent there."[4]

The question of good roads, as I say, is a difficult one, not only because of the perfection of the road for the purpose of resisting this much heavier travel, but also because of the question who is to pay for the roads. Are they to be built by the State? Are they to be built by the county? And whoever builds them, who is to take care of them? This is a much more important question. But I hear the earnest patriot — and it does not make any difference how he construes the constitution — if there is any plan of running a national road near his farm, I hear the earnest patriot say, "it is the business of the general Government to build its roads." [Laughter.] Says he, "let us have a national road running from New York to San Francisco to teach the world what a model road is." "What will it cost?"

4. This section was omitted in the ACA reprint of the speech.

Ah,“ what difference does it make what it costs? You can strive and hunt ways of saving $100,000 in the matter of employees at Washington; but when it comes to building roads, what is $100,000,000 between friends?” [Laughter.] And there is the difficulty, gentlemen. I admit that the general Government has the power to build roads for the purpose of promoting interstate commerce.[5] It has done it already, but I venture to question the wisdom of opening that method of spending Federal Government money. I think it is much better to have the neighborhood and the State, as a large unit, expend its money in the construction of roads across the State, of aiding the counties to keep the roads in repair, because, if you once set out upon a plan of national roads, in addition to the plan of national waterways, I don't know how great the expenditure will amount to. If we could confine it to two or three roads, I would not object, but we have forty-eight different States and every State is as anxious to share in the common funds at Washington as every other State. [Laughter.] It is a dangerous experiment that I would suggest great delay and deliberation before you undertake so great an expenditure, the stopping of which will have no end. We have had some experience in that in Washington, and we are looking forward now to large expenditures. If you are going to add roads, and you are going to run your automobiles through them and over them and into them, and are going to promote the cost of them as you will, increasing, of course, the intercourse between all the people, creating a benefit which I do not minimize, nevertheless I say to you that if you can reach that benefit without opening the national treasury, I think it will be the wiser and more statesmanlike course. [Applause.]

I did not intend to talk so long gentlemen, but when you get into a governmental discussion on the subject of economy, the mind runs on to a Congress that is striving to save money [laughter], and I am anxious to express the sympathy that we all feel in that effort. I thank you sincerely for your kind attention.

—William Howard Taft,
December 20, 1911,
New York City

Adapted from text of speech, Taft Papers, Library of Congress (reel 580) and *Club Journal* of the Automobile Club of America, January 6, 1912, pp. 601–606.

5. The White House text lacked the word “National,” which was included in the ACA version, and in those printed elsewhere.

Appendix B

Inventory of White House Transportation

The White House Garage

Make	*Type / Color*	*Model Year*	*Date delivered*	*Cost/ Terms*	*Serial/Tag #*	*Purpose*	*Disposition / Notes*
White Model "M" 40 H.P. seven passenger steam touring car	Tourer w/ extra closed body — Green	1909	Feb. 25, 1909 approx.	$3,000 cash	6971	Touring — Taft loved this car.	Dropped in late 1911; Survives at the Heritage Plantation Museum, Sandwich, Mass.
Pierce-Arrow 48. H.P.	Limousine w/ extra open body — Blue	1909	Feb. 25, 1909 approx.	$2,500 cash	7101	Formal car	$400 for touring body; exchanged for 1911 66 H.P. #66306
Pierce-Arrow 36 H.P.	Landaulet — Blue	1909	April 15, 1909 approx.	$2,000 cash	30106 DC tag 3710	Mrs. Taft's car	
Baker	Electric Victoria	1909	April 25, 1909 approx.	$1,000 cash	4102	Mrs. Taft self-driver	$90 for charging station
Baker	1,000 lb. electric delivery wagon	1909	June 1909	$1,400 cash	161		First White House utility automobile
Pierce-Arrow 36 H.P.	Landaulet	1911	Aug/Sept. 1910	$500 lease	31340 DC tag 7747	Secretary's Car	*First leased car; replaced in 1911 under lease terms (contract dated 9/29/10)
Pierce-Arrow 36 H.P.	Landaulet	1912	Autumn 1911?	leased for $500 / year	32637	Secretary's Car*	replacement for 31340? Resold by Pierce-Arrow in 1914
Pierce-Arrow 36 H.P.	Landaulet	1912	Oct. 1911		32345	Mrs. Taft	Resold by Pierce-Arrow in 1914
Pierce-Arrow 66 H.P.	Touring body w/ limousine body placed for Winter — Blue	1912	Aug. 1911 shipped to Beverly	$6,278.50 credited by exchange of #7101	66306		Purchased by Charles Taft for the ex–President, who took it to New Haven, Connecticut, in 1913.
Pierce-Arrow 66 H.P.	Touring body — Blue	1912	Dec. 1911		66458		Ordered in Nov. 1911 as a duplicate of No. 66306
Pierce-Arrow 36 H.P.	Landaulet	1912	mid–1911		32623	Secretary's Car*	A late 1911 garage inventory lists #32623 amongst the 1911 deliveries, excepting #32637; This car seems to have been delivered after #32637.

Baker	Electric victoria — Blue	1912	Aug. 3, 1912	$809.50 cash	7816	Replacement for 1909 electric	Survives at the Henry Ford Museum at Greenfield Village, Michigan
Rentals *(incomplete list)*							
White steam tourer	model M?		1910	$250 rental / season $22.50 / day			"Rented for season of 1910" and "use of automobile," New Haven and New York, Sept. 1910
White steam tourer	model M?		March 1911	$200 rental			Rented $20/day in Augusta, Georgia; another rental was for New York City on 11/2/11 at $7.50
Harper Garage, Beverly, MA	rentals	various		$5.00, $3.00			occasional rentals during the Summer at Beverly
J. B. Hayes, Wash., D.C.	rentals	various		$20, $30			Rental cars, including May to June 1912 and Jan. to March, 1913; the White House also hired extra chauffeurs in D.C. and Beverly
Barnette Bros., Wash., D.C.	rental		July 1911	$68.50			Rental car used on the Manassas trip (Butt sent it to test the stream first because it was a rental)
Carriages & Other							
Coupe, Rockaway, Brougham, and buggy carriages	per repair receipts						Mrs. Jaffray refused to ride in the motors, although there was talk of her using the electric in 1911
Various bicycles	per repair receipts						

* Secretary's cars: In August or September of 1910, Pierce-Arrow delivered a 36 H.P. landaulet to the White House under lease terms of $500 per year. There seems to have been some turnover in these cars, possibly because the Secretaries kept them, under arrangements with Pierce-Arrow, after they left the White House. Charles Norton left in March of 1911, and we know from the Butt letters that he was attempting to arrange for a Pierce for himself. It is unlikely that Pierce-Arrow gave him one, but it is very likely that he was sold the car at generous terms. The next Secretary, Charles Hilles, arranged the purchase of Taft's 66 H.P. after he left office, so it is possible that he, too, took one of the White House motors with him.

The White House Stables

(incomplete; from inventory of Dec. 1910 & other)

Name	*Type*	*Owner/Rider*	*Notes*
127, 702, & 281	saddle horses	Quartermaster	for Butt & Sergt. McDermott
Arcealus	saddle horse	Miss Helen Taft	
Greenbriar	saddle horse	Taft	
Tate	saddle horse	Taft	
Starlight	saddle horse	Quartermaster	for Taft
Drum	carriage horse	Quartermaster	for Taft's Secretary
Crook	carriage horse	Quartermaster	for Taft's Secretary
Raymond	carriage horse	White House	for the "messenger"
Prince	carriage horse	Quartermaster	for the "messenger"
Bush	carriage horse	White House	for Mrs. Jaffray
Larry	saddle horse	Butt	personal horse
Reciprocity	saddle horse	Taft	named for the Reciprocity trade agreement; sold to a Senator in early 1913
Chinkapin	saddle horse	Helen Taft	Bolted with a friend of Helen's riding & was killed in a collision with a trolley in Jan. 1913
Mooley*	cow	Taft	died in Spring of 1910
Pauline*	cow	Taft	gift from Wisconsin Sen. Isaac Stephenson

* There were two cows. The first was named "Mooley" and was installed at the White House stables in March of 1909. It died the next Spring. In October, 1910, Wisconsin Senator Isaac Stephenson, through his farm manager, Jim Torrey, a distant Taft cousin, presented Taft with the 1,500 pound "Pauline," a prize Holstein that could produce up to 25 pounds of butter a week. Pauline spent the latter part of the Summer of 1911 at a Milwaukee dairy exhibition where she was a big hit. Her daily 16 gallons of milk was sold in fifty-cent souvenir bottles that netted up to $80 a day for the President. She was shipped back to Stephenson's farm after Taft left office.[2]

2. "Will Take Cow to Taft," 9/25/10, "Taft's Cow Worth $80 a Day," 8/10/11, and "Taft Cow on Retired List," 2/2/13, NYT.

The White House Garage and Stables Employees

(salaries as of December 1910; incomplete list)

Name	*Position*	*Automobile/Duty*	*Salary*	*Notes*
Robinson, George	chauffeur	White steamer	$100	dismissed back to the Army in July 1910
Long, Abel	chauffeur	Pierce limousine	$125	started at $100 / month left June 1913 recommended by Pierce-Arrow
Robinson, F.H.	chauffeur	White steamer/ Pierces	$125	stayed through 1920s recommended by White Co.
Rundle (last name)	Quartermasters chauffeur	Ran the steamer when the other chauffeurs were at Beverly, likely starting in 1910	N/A	Rundle was Butt's favorite chauffeur. He came to the Army at the recommendation of the White Company
Ramsey, H.L.	asst. chauffeur	rented White steamer at Beverly & other cars	$80	salary later raised to $90 left prior to Dec. 1910;
Jackson, W.L.	asst. chauffeur	Baker wagon	$80	salary later raised to $90
Strauss, Wm. F.	cleaned automobiles	"day duty"	$50	
Wagstaff, Walter	secretary's chauffeur		$80	
Scott, John	cleaned stables	took care of cow	$55	
Burlesque, Richard	drove housekeeper	also 2nd footman	$65	
Diggs, George	hostler	also 2nd footman	$60	
Davidge, Richard	hostler for saddle horses		$75	left in 1910?
Night watchman			$60	
McDermott, Sgt. Cornelius	in charge of stables	on Quartermaster payroll	N/A	
Eugene Davis, Ambrose Brown	Policemen, Third Precinct, motorcycle escorts	drove "Reading Standard motorcycles" (rode bicycles during Roosevelt admin.)	N/A	

Two Letters from the Life of a White House Chauffeur

February 1st, 1911
Hon. C. Norton
Sec. to the President

Dear Sir—

Answering your note of the 31st inst., would say that on Monday night after leaving the President and Party at the new Willard was ordered back at 10:45 PM. While waiting at the Garage, I received an order from Mr. Sloan [Secret Serviceman] to be back at 10:15 PM and then at 9:55 PM I received an order from Mr. Sloan to be back at 10:00 PM sharp. I was there at exactly 10:00 PM. I waited there until 11:25 pm before they came out and then carried the party to the German Ambassay [*sic*]. I received orders to wait. It has always been customary for the President to stay at least one half hour on similar occasions. I told the footman to watch the car and that I was going inside to get thawed out and to notify me when wanted. I was inside less than 5 minutes when notified, and am willing to swear that it was not over 45 seconds before I was in front of the door, which as yet had not been opened, and it is my belief there was no delay whatever. If there was it is the first time in nearly two years of service.

I would request that the Secretary make a set of rules by which we are to go by, and I feel sure that they will be obeyed and do away with this anonymous* reporting.

Yours Obediant [*sic*]
A.E. Long

June 24, 1911
Mr. Chas. D. Hillis [*sic*]
Secretary to the President

Dear Sir,

I take this opportunity in asking you for an increase in salaries for the men connected with the automobiles at the White House Garage. Most of them have worked for the same salary they got when they first started. We all work late hours† and I think that you will do what is right by them. I suggest you give Jackson $100 per month, Wagstaff $100 per month, Burlesque $70 per month and Robinson $150 per month. Hoping you may pass-on the above favorably and thanking you for past favors,

I remain,

Very Truly Yours
F. H. Robinson
White House Garage

* What do you suppose that was about!

† Taft kept them out late. As the motorcycle policemen were not to report to the garage until noon, it seems that the chauffeurs didn't usually have to get an early start, anyway. The head chauffeurs were not given raises, as their salary was already elevated from the original $100 a month. The assistant chauffeurs were given an increase.

A Most Important Endorsement

On April 12, 1912, R.E. Shadel of the Professional Chauffeurs Club of America wrote to Charles "Hillard," the Secretary of the President. No offense seems to have been taken by Charles Hilles, for the group's request was granted:

> By unanimous vote of the Professional Chauffeurs Club of America we have been instructed to present His Honor Pres Taft with an Honorary Membership Card in our organization which numbers 38000 men in the United States of America.

A few days later, the meeting was accepted and set for the April 19. On the 15th, the Club wrote the President:

Sir:-

Probably one of the finest bodies of men in the world, who are holding their watchful care by day and night the lives of our Presidents, public men, the kings of commerce, down to the humblest citizen of the Nation, their mothers, wives, children and sweethearts, are the Locomotive Engineers.

Twenty-three thousand useful, grand, real men — the servants of the people that have held the respect and confidence of all classes of our citizens since the steam engine made the railroad locomotive a possibility.

Comparatively few people perhaps have a clear conception and fully realize the fact that the recent discovery, wonderful and rapid development of the gasoline engine has made it the twin brother or sister ship of the most powerful and fleetest locomotive ever manned by the courageous engineer with his hand on the throttle guarding the lives of our millions.

This "silent" little wonder has made possible the great commercial trucks, the little runabout for the masses and the luxurious six cylinder palatial touring cars unequaled by the finest Pullman cars that were ever created. In fact they are truly private overland trains, and today they are daily carrying more passengers than the combined ocean grey hounds and the railroads.

Manned by the active, clear-headed, skillful and trustworthy army of men which we represent.

Thirty-eight thousand of them, with a waiting list that will by January 1st, 1913, have a membership of fifty thousand — one-third as many men as Uncle Sam employs in the Army and Navy combined.

From this seasoned army of men "fine and fit," with clear active brains and clear visions should be made the nations [*sic*] body guard.

These men when the call to arms is sounded will man the artillery, ammunition supply wagons and gasoline trucks. They are the men that will rush the dead and dying in the auto ambulances to the hospitals and Red Cross Tents, and when the peace is restored they will become the people's messengers in conveying secret and confidential dispatches and the mails, daily papers and magazines throughout the land; thus putting to its most useful calling, that wonderful little silent motive power — the gasoline engine.

Right here the question is suggested — should not the Government lend a helping hand in the education and preparation of this state and National Organization, by supplying them with useful literature, and when desired by the majority of the State Club, provide military instructions.

We do not ask for this; we merely raise the question now for the thoughtful consideration of the Nation.

These young men are today solving the problems of cheaper living by taking the gasoline commercial trucks to the farmer's doors and the market places, bringing food to the people cheaper and better than the steam roads can do it.

They are giving pleasure, happiness and prolonging the lives of millions of our people who take to the valleys and hills with their touring cars throughout the length and breadth of the land today.

This band of men today are the equal of the Railroad Engineer, and to be a member of this fine organization, just in its infancy for usefulness, the men must pass a more rigid examination than the Locomotive and Steamship Engineers, and like them, they are the cream of the profession.

These men, Sir, have delegated us to journey from the great city of Baltimore, the Home of the Railroad, Telegraph and Steamship, to the Capitol [sic] of the Nation, and how fitting it is that Baltimore City should have been selected as the starting point.

We come, Sir, to ask you, Mr. President, to become one of us by accepting this little Membership Card, and as a token of their confidence and respect for the real Chauffeur of this great touring car and ship of State — Our Country.[3]

3. RE Shadel to Taft, 4/15/12 (see reel 459, case file 301)

Appendix C

Chronologies

Chronology of Presidents (1869–1929)

1869–1877	Ulysses S. Grant	(Republican)
1877–1881	Rutherford B. Hayes	(Republican)
1881	James A. Garfield	(Republican — assassinated)
1881–1885	Chester A. Arthur	(Republican)
1885–1889	Grover Cleveland	(Democratic)
1889–1893	Benjamin Harrison	(Republican)
1893–1897	Grover Cleveland	(Democratic)
1897–1901	William McKinley	(Republican — assassinated)
1901–1909	Theodore Roosevelt	(Republican)
1909–1913	William H. Taft	(Republican)
1913–1921	Woodrow Wilson	(Democratic)
1921–1923	Warren G. Harding	(Republican — died in office)
1923–1929	Calvin Coolidge	(Republican)

Chronology of Speakers of the House (1869–1931)

James G. Blaine	Republican	1869–1875	Grant Administration
Michael C. Kerr	Democratic	1875–1876	Grant
Samuel J. Randall	Democratic	1876–1881	Grant/Hayes
Joseph W. Keifer	Republican	1881–1883	Garfield/Arthur
John G. Carlisle	Democratic	1883–1889	Arthur/Cleveland
Thomas B. Reed	Republican	1889–1891	Harrison
Charles F. Crisp	Democratic	1891–1895	Harrison/Cleveland
Thomas B. Reed	Republican	1895–1899	Cleveland/McKinley
David B. Henderson	Republican	1899–1903	McKinley/Roosevelt
Joseph G. Cannon	Republican	1903–1911	Roosevelt/Taft
Champ Clark	Democratic	1911–1919	Taft/Wilson
Frederick H. Gillett	Republican	1919–1925	Wilson/Harding/Coolidge
Nicholas Longworth	Republican	1925–1931	Coolidge/Hoover

Chronology of Major U.S. Tariff Laws, 1872–1930

1872 High Civil War–era tariffs reduced, but reset higher again in 1875 (Republican)

1883 The "Mongrel Tariff"—passed by a lame duck Congress with few reductions (Republican)

1887 Allison bill—fails in Congress and Grover Cleveland loses next election (Democratic House, Republican Senate)

1890 McKinley Tariff—high duties for protection and to reduce revenue surplus (Republican)
1894 Wilson–Gorman Tariff—compromise of low duties in House and high duties in Senate that was enacted without Cleveland's signature (Democratic)
1897 Dingley Tariff—protectionist bill (Republican)
1909 Payne–Aldrich Tariff—moderately reduced duties and increased "free lists" (Republican)
1911 Reciprocity bill—free trade agreement with Canada passed by a split Congress (Democratic House, Republican Senate) and nullified by the failure of a similar law in Canada
1913 Underwood Tariff—reduced duties (Democratic)
1922 Fordney–McCumber Tariff—raised duties (Republican)
1930 Smoot–Hawley Tariff—raised duties (Republican)

Appendix D

Statistics

Annual Automobile Production, 1901–1913

Year	*Production*	*Increase*	*Registrations**	*Increase*	*Rural/ Farm Autos*	*% of Autos Rural/ Farm*	*Average Sales Price*	*Notes*
1901	7,000	—	14,800	—	—	—		
1902	9,000	29%	23,000	55%	—	—	—	
1903	11,235	25%	32,920	43%	—	—	$1,133.37	
1904	22,419	100%	54,590	66%	—	—	$1,351.45	
1905	24,550	10%	77,400	42%	—	—	$1,609.79	
1906	33,500	36%	105,900	37%	—	—	$1,853.93	
1907	43,300	29%	140,300	32%	—	—	$2,137.56	†
1908	63,500	47%	194,400	39%	—	—	$1,926.94	
1909	127,731	101%	305,950	57%	—	—	$1,719.93	§**
1910	181,000	42%	458,500	50%	50,000	11%	$1,482.96	††
1911	199,319	10%	619,500	35%	100,000	16%	$1,245.99	§§
1912	356,000	79%	902,600	46%	175,000	19%	$1,083.10	
1913	461,500	30%	1,194,262	32%	258,000	22%		
1914	543,679	18%	1,625,739	36%	343,000	21%		
1915	895,930	65%	2,309,666	42%	472,000	20%		
1916	1,525,578	70%	3,297,996	43%	687,000	21%		

* Registrations are problematic in that early autoists frequently registered their cars in multiple states. As a comparative between years, however, the numbers are revealing.

† Contemporaneous accounts listed 1907 production at 52,302 (47,302 gasoline and 5,000 steam and electric "pleasure automobiles," from *Automobile*, 2/13/1908, pg. 219, citing figures from the ALAM).

§ This production figure corresponds with that cited by the *Times* on 11/13/1912, citing "government figures."

** Production numbers represent the highest increases in the chart. In early 1909, the industry estimated production that year would total 75,000. Had Ford been able to meet demand the numbers would have been higher.

†† Rural/ Farm numbers can only be rough estimates. Still, it demonstrates how few automobiles were bought by farmers, particularly given that half the entire population was rural (not all on farms). Automobile consumption remained urban/suburban. The dramatic increases in production represents entry of the middle classes, not the "masses."

§§ In 1911 the industry stumbled over itself due to undercapitalization and inventory problems, especially General Motors. Additionally, weather conditions and generally high levels of economic activity in all sectors created a shortage of rail cars for transporting automobiles, thus depressing production.

Source: "Motor Vehicle Facts and Figures," Automobile Manufacturers Association, 1968 (numbers include overseas assembly of U.S. made automobiles, which, along with exports, only became significant after 1914 and which likely accounts for the jump in 1916 production). Source for average sales price is the *Automobile*, 7/25/12, pg.165. Numbers of farm automobiles is from "Historical Statistics of the United States" U.S. Department of Commerce, 1976 (that publication and the "Automobile Facts and Figures," National Automobile Chamber of Commerce, 1934, offer slightly different annual production numbers, including 1909 which both list as 123,900).

Contemporaneous Data and Estimates vs. Historical Data, 1905–1911

Year	*1912 Estimates**	*Annual Increase*	*Expected Production†*	*Increase vs. Expected††*	*Increase vs. Known§*	*Historical Estimates*	*Increase vs. Actual*
1905	25,000	—	28,000	—	—	24,550	—
1906	34,000	36%	50,000	79%	100%	33,500	36%
1907	44,000	29%	45,000	-10%	32%	43,300	29%
1908	56,000	27%	55,000	22%	25%	63,500	47%
1909	120,000	114%	75,000	36%	34%	127,731	101%**
1910	187,000	56%	280,000	273%	133%	181,000	42%
1911	210,000	12%	200,000	-29%	7%	199,319	10%

In 1906 and 1910 enthusiasm outran reality, while more sober estimates were made for 1908 and 1911. Nobody saw 1909 coming, either as against the previous year's enthusiasms or its known production. In March of 1910, the *Automobile* talked of one million cars to be built in 1913, guessing that 1909's dramatic growth would continue at pace ("Looking Ahead in the Automobile Industry," *Automobile*, 3/1/10, pg. 438).

* From the *Automobile*, 1/4/12, pg. 13. Prior to the 1911 dismantling of the ALAM, the industry counted production in categories of "definitive" and "maximum" numbers to differentiate between licensed and unlicensed production. Figures here are from the "maximum" lists and differ somewhat from the historical figures.

† Contemporaneous estimates of a new year's expected production. Sources are:

—1905: "Twenty-Eight Thousand Cars," *Automobile*, 1/14/05, letter, pg. 44
—1906: "Review of the Automobile Situation," *Automobile*, 1/11/06, pg. 97
—1907: "Big Year for Autos, Early Show Features," *NYT*, 11/25/06
—1908: "Some Figures on America's Record Output," *Automobile*, 10/17/07, pg. 545
—1909: "America's Position in the Motor World," *NYT*, 3/7/09 (This number was repeated elsewhere, including in *Automobile*, which at one point also guessed 80,000; see "Outlook in the American Automobile Industry," 1/14/09, pg. 99)
—1910: "Some Statistics of the Cars," *Automobile*, 2/3/10. In another article, the magazine guessed at 300,00 for 1910 ("Looking Ahead in the Automobile Industry," *Automobile*, 3/1/10, pg. 438).
—1911: From "Statistics," *Automobile*, 1/5/11, pg. 16. This number was from an estimate of the necessary activities of the machine tool industry in order to produce 200,000 automobiles. The industry was wary of declaring itself for 1911, as estimates from early 1910 far exceeded actual output. The next January an evidently chastised *Automobile* made fun of "prognosticators" ("Resume of the Year's Work," 1/26/11, pg. 253). Still, it was understood that a good 400,000 cars were in use in the country that would need to be replaced eventually, and that general growth would continue, so the industry was optimistic. However, there was less talk of those one million buggies sold in 1905.

†† This column represents the percentage increase of existing year's expectations versus the previous year's expectations, a vague comparative indicator of industry mood.

§ This column represents the percentage increase of existing year's expectations versus the previous known production, another vague indicator of mood versus reality.

** Nobody saw 1909's huge increases coming. Taft was the reason for it.

Production per Price Category, 1910

Price Range	*Production*	*Notes*
$485–750	16000	
751–1,000	49000	*
1,001–1,250	58000	†
1,250–1,600	22000	†
1,601–2,000	8000	
2,001–3,000	15000	
Over $3,000	12000	

Source: *Automobile*, 6/23/10

* Model T category, 32,053 cars
† Buick categories, 30,525 cars

(Source: "The American Car Since 1775," by *Automobile Quarterly*)

Washington, D.C. New Registrations Per Year

(per motor vehicle category)

Year	*Gas*	*Steam*	*Electric*	*Government*	*New Auto Registrations*	*Motorcycles*	*Tag No.'s Issued*	*Est. Autos in Use†*
1906	342	28	125	0	**495**	40	n/a	~1,000
1907	n/a	n/a	n/a	0	**500***	92	100–1541	~1,400
1908	795	98	108	5	**1,006**	296	1542–2548	<2,500
1909	1,370	71	180	14	**1,635**	355	2549–4343	~4,000
1910	1,812	44	170	18	**2,044**	472	4344–6272	6,030
1911	2,650	46	158	44	**2,898**	548	6273–9289	8,322
1912	2,887	30	189	77	**3,183**	695	9290–12868	~12,000

Source: "Report of Commissioners of District of Columbia," 1906–1913

* 1907 numbers are offset by a new registration rule, as per below. Before that rule, there were about 50–60 Spring and 25–30 Autumn registrations per month, which would bring the annual total to about 500–600 new automobiles.
† Author guesstimates. 1910 and 1911 numbers are from contemporaneous reports.

These numbers reflect *new* vehicle tags issued per year, as owners were not required to register annually. [Note: Commissioner reports followed fiscal years ending June 30; the author has divided numbers into calendar years, based upon six-month reports.] On September 15, 1907, a rule was invoked to require standard plates, as before motorists made their own. Therefore, the Commissioners' Reports of October and November, 1907 registrations reflect a total census, not just new registrations. Those numbers were 885 gasoline, 347 electrics, 119 steamers and for a total of 1,377 automobiles (plus 26 motorcycles). A 1905 article in the *Automobile* stated there were "nearly" 2,000 cars in the city (9/14/05, pg. 297). This seems unlikely and it is not reflected in the Commissioners' reports.

There were more about 30% more registrations in the second half of 1908 than the first half, which would normally be the opposite, as the buying season was from December to April. This indicates a heightened interest in automobiles in the city in late 1908. Note also that the 1906 and 1908 figures show higher proportions of electric and steam car registrations, which indicates a slow acceptance of gasoline cars in the city. The reader may conclude whether or not it had anything to do with the incoming President's well-known motoring enthusiasms and his preference for White steamers.

Government registrations in 1908 were probably military cars and the sole official motor on Capitol Hill that was used by the superintendent of the building. Into 1909 and following the White House's example, the municipal government began to use automobiles. The *Evening Star* wrote in late 1909, "The necessity for motor vehicles for the various branches of the District government is becoming, it is conceded, more and more apparent every day. The water, sewer, engineer and police departments have made a start in this direction, and now comes Chief Wagner of the fire department, who will urge Congress ... to provide him with a motor." The article described how, in responding to an alarm, horses pulling fire trucks "were practically overcome" by the distance and hills and barely arrived in time to prevent a suburban fire from spreading. The fire chief's own horse couldn't make the ride; he found an automobile that took him to the scene in time. He said, "had the fire occurred in the summer time none of the horses could have made the run" ("Motoring," *Evening Star*, 12/5/09).

Additional Notes

—"Government" registrations include Federal and municipal governments.

—Tag numbers do not necessarily reflect total number of automobiles, nor new registrations, as certain numbers were reserved for different types of automobiles, motorcycles and other vehicles. Also, many cars from other states were registered in the District for temporary use there, especially from residents of Maryland and Virginia.

—Many thanks to Stephen Raiche for sharing his research on DC licenses.

Glossary of Terms

AAA—American Automobile Association. Started in 1902 as a conglomerate of independent motor clubs to promote automobiles, oversee racing contests, provide touring information, and champion good automobiling, good roads, and good road law. By 1912 the AAA had become a major Washington lobby. Its efforts to push federal funding for road building were rewarded in the 1916 Federal Aid Road Act.

ACA—Automobile Club of America. The oldest and most important independent automobile club. It was based in New York and had an A-list membership. The Club owned two large buildings at 54th and 55th Streets. Taft's 1911 speech to the ACA was seminal to automobiling, its industry, road building and the future. The ACA and its rich members contributed to early motoring as much as any other organization or figure. They are to be applauded, as Taft did in his speech. Their demise also came with that speech. The Club would last through to the Depression, but its mission was fulfilled when Taft announced that its motoring exclusivity was over.

ALAM—Association of Licensed Automobile Manufacturers. Formed in 1903 as a settlement over lawsuits to enforce the Selden Patent, the ALAM was the chief industry representative through 1911, when it was disbanded after the Selden Patent was held inapplicable to 4-stroke engines. The ALAM selectively administered licenses for the Selden Patent, and thereby attempted to restrict competition. The ALAM also sponsored the largest annual trade show in New York and served as a clearinghouse for automotive standards and information. It was looked upon by non-members and importers as an unfair trust or monopoly, and was opposed by the AMCMA (see below). The other industry group, the National Association of Automobile Manufacturers (NAAM), remained neutral. (Contrary to appearances here, the Selden fight was not over acronyms.)

AMCMA—The American Motor Car Manufacturers Association, the anti–ALAM, anti–Selden patent organization, consisting of Ford, Maxwell-Briscoe and others. Called the "unlicensed association" it held its own shows. It fell apart after the Selden patent was upheld in 1909 and most members fled to the ALAM.

American Association for Highway Improvement—Started in November 1910, its goals were "to arouse and stimulate sentiment for road improvement throughout the country; to cooperate with local organizations working for good roads; to aid in bringing about efficient road administration in the States; to seek a continuous and systematic maintenance of roads; and to aid, as far as we properly may, in securing the enactment in the several States of good road laws." Its President was Logan W. Page, Chief of the U.S. Office of Public Roads. Other important government officials involved were James Harlan of the Interstate Commerce Commission and Lee McClung, Treasurer of the United States. Taft endorsed the organization. He was also its most prominent member. He was to attend the group's first annual Congress as the keynote speaker, but missed it due to illness.

Ananias Club—The place to where Roosevelt sent liars, accusers, and assorted enemies. It was effective during Roosevelt's first years in office, but by 1909 it had become a joke and a mark of prestige among his enemies.

Anti-automobile—A few derogatory terms for motors, motorists and motoring were: begoggled ruffians, autocrats, automobile insanity, motor intoxication, the obnoxious class, engine of destruction, red devils, and joy wagons.

Arbitration—Taft's 1911 treaties with England and France to arbitrate certain international disputes. The treaties greatly expanded the existing types of disputes that would be submitted for arbitration at international courts. Supporters lauded them as a great advance towards world peace. The Senate weakened the core elements to the treaties, and Taft dropped the matter.

Atmospheric champagne—Taft's description of the joy of open air motor touring.

Auto Polo—Just what it says: cars, drivers, and mallet men chasing a ball around an arena. More significantly, it was the definitive transformation of the Horse Age to the Motor Age—and an equally so *not* definitive transformation of the Motor Age back to the Horse Age. This late 1912 craze didn't last long, but it was a great try and otherwise validated the automobile in mainstream culture. It was the first of the automobile sideshows that still enrapture audiences and advertisers.

Autoist—Motorist, including riders and drivers, but not chauffers.

Automobile—By 1909, the standard automobile was a 4-cylinder gasoline-powered open car. Luxury was defined by the size of the engine and the chassis. The primary social use of automobiles was "touring," generally weekend runs or, for the wealthy, tours in Europe. Automobile touring revolutionized the tourism industry, as tourists were no longer confined to ports and train stations. Automobile commuting was just coming into common practice with the development of closed, all-weather cars that could be used all year. In 1909, the "Big Four" of the automobile industry were Ford, Maxwell-Briscoe, Reo, and Buick, along with Cadillac and Studebaker-EMF. The top domestic luxury cars of 1909 were Locomobile, Packard, Peerless, Pierce-Arrow, and Stevens-Duryea.

Ballinger-Pinchot Affair—The name for the sum of events that started in August of 1909 and ended in congressional hearings through the following Winter. Secretary of the Interior Richard Ballinger was accused by a government Land Office Investigator, Louis Glavis, of having abetted the supposedly illegal "Cunningham" coal claims in Alaska. The issues were: (1) were the claims valid? (2) did Ballinger violate ethics rules by having had acted, less than a year out of public service, as a private attorney for the Cunningham group? and (3) was a syndicate behind the claims? It all became an "affair" because of the publicity given it by Gifford Pinchot, who trumpeted Glavis's cause and whose Forestry Service office assisted Glavis to publish his accusations in an article in *Collier's* magazine. Pinchot used the affair to go after Ballinger and Taft, and to leverage his own political power. The Congressional hearings went nowhere. Glavis and Pinchot were fired by Taft, and Ballinger resigned a year after the hearings. He was innocent.

Beverly, Massachusetts—Location of the Taft "Summer White House." Beverly lies across from Salem, along the North Shore of Massachusetts. The choice of the house at Beverly satisfied Mrs. Taft's views on sophistication and economy and her husband's demand for a nearby golf course. The first house there was rented for two summers, but the owner refused to renew for 1911 because of the complications of a presidential tenant. The Tafts found another house nearby for the next two seasons.

Brownsville affair—A race riot in 1906 that turned into one of the most contentious issues of Roosevelt's presidency. Black troops stationed at Brownsville, Texas, either attacked, were attacked, or were falsely accused of attacking local whites, most likely all three. Whatever happened, when pressed for details, the soldiers refused to testify against one another. Roosevelt fired them all, including a Civil War hero. Senator Foraker used the issue as a platform to fight Roosevelt. Taft's involvement came of his role in it as War Secretary. He had serious reservations and felt that Roosevelt overreacted but did as told to fire the soldiers. It cost him support from black voters in 1908. Roosevelt somehow managed the claim that critics of the affair were acting for the trusts. It was not an exemplary episode for anyone.

Bull Moose—The nickname for Roosevelt's third-party candidacy of 1912. The party was officially called the "Progressive Party." The "bull moose" comes from a Roosevelt letter of 1900 in which he declared himself ready to campaign for President McKinley and his own vice presidential run, "I am as strong as a bull moose and you can use me to the limit."

Bullet head—As opposed to Mush Head. "I did not come here to be abused by a bullet head," declared an attorney during a trial of a chauffeur for theft. "A bullet head is much better than a mush head," retorted the other attorney. The judge called for order.

'bus—Short for "omnibus"

Cabinet—For those hunting for issues, Taft's Cabinet choices were the starting point of discontent even before Taft became President. Not since Van Buren took over from fellow Democrat Jackson had a newly elected President kept any of his predecessor's Cabinet. Since Taft, it has happened only twice, from Coolidge to Hoover and Reagan to Bush, and with only three positions each time. Additionally, Presidents of non-elective successions regularly replaced the Cabinets they inherited, especially into their second terms, as did Roosevelt himself, whose 1905 Cabinet was almost entirely new from the one he inherited.

Campaign publicity—Campaign Finance Reform in the modern tongue. During the 1908 election, Bryan challenged Taft on the issue. Taft surprised Bryan by whole-heartedly supporting a law for the public naming of financial backers. The result was a 1910 bill that required their publication, although not until after an election.

Canada—Not a sovereign nation in 1909. This is an important distinction to understand Taft's Reciprocity treaty. Although the treaty failed in Canada, it hastened the country's independence from the United Kingdom. Even today, the Queen is Canada's titular head.

Cannonism—A derogatory term to describe the hold of Speaker Cannon over the House Republican leadership. To the hard-core insurgents and their press, Cannonism came to embody everything that was wrong in the nation.

Car—The modern term for an automobile originally was a reference to a train or trolley car. In 1909 automobiles were referred to as "motor cars."

Chautauqua—What started as a training camp for Sunday school teachers at Lake Chautauqua in New York in 1874 became, by 1909, the "Circuit Chautauqua." Politicians, preachers, and performers used the roving, circus-like lectures for fun, profit, and political advancement. Undertones were generally moral and religious. William Jennings Bryan and Robert La Follette were among the star performers. Even though the Chautauqua was yet popular, it had become something of a joke by 1909, used as a derogatory reference to a bad speech or speaker.

Chief Magistrate—The President.

Cigarette fiends—Nick and Alice Longworth were heavily criticized for Alice's smoking, especially in Longworth's home district in Cincinnati. Ladies did not smoke. Alice used smoking for its enjoyment and shock value. Taft allowed her to smoke in the White House, which amazed the guests.

Commission—The progressive cure-all for government or social problems. Commissions were thought to operate outside of politics. To some extent and in some places this was true; largely it was politics by another means.

Conference Committee—The joint committee of Senate and House representatives to reconcile different versions of a bill.

Conservation—The movement for the conservation of natural resources. "Conservation" in 1909 included the use of public lands, not just the preservation of park land. The chief angles of conservation were: 1) to remove public lands from exploitation altogether, generally through creation of parks; 2) to make public lands available to farmers and ranchers; and 3) anti-business sentiment that feared corporate exploitation of public lands and waterways. Taft was accused by the "ultra conservationists" of abusing the Roosevelt conservation legacy. Actually, Taft worked hard to put it into law. Taft protected vast amounts of public land during his four years and was a careful and fair administrator of it. He did not treat it as a political issue, which allowed opponents to use it against him.

Cost of Living—Starting during the Roosevelt days, and accelerated by the anti–Payne bill rhetoric of the Democratic party during the 1910 and 1912 elections, inflation was a thematic background to the Era of Discontent. The "high cost of living" occupied much press and the pages of Congressional investigations. Taft's party responded by pointing to rising prices overseas, an indication that the tariff was not responsible for high prices, and general prosperity. Progressive historians have pointed to it as a substantive crisis of the age. The period was marked by a rise in prices, but not by monetary inflation. On the whole, the "crisis" was rhetorical, as increases in wages and credit outpaced prices, particularly to the benefit of the growing middle classes. A comparison to the 1990s ought be explored. Both periods showed an increase in the cost of commodities and basic consumables and a decrease in the cost of manufactures and a dramatic increase in productivity.

Country Life Commission—Roosevelt's 1908 commission to study the conditions of rural life and make recommendations for its improvement. The Commission mailed questionnaires to farmers and held public meetings in various states with farmers and experts (see "uplifters"). Roosevelt submitted the report to Congress in February, 1909. He asked Congress to fund the Commission $25,000 to complete its work and to create a new executive branch, the Department of Country Life. Congress ignored both requests. A "Country Life Convention" that met during the November 1909 "Second National Apple Show," sponsored by the Spokane Chamber of Congress asked President Taft to reprint the report for free distribution, to which Taft complied. Although Taft had little interest in the Commission, he did not drop the subject, preferring that the mission be ministered by the Department of Agriculture. Outside of the Department's activities, Taft aimed to assist farmers with his Postal Banks and, in 1912, with his recommendation for "co-operative agricultural banks."

Cut and Dried—Something already fixed.

Dick to Dick letter—A letter from Richard Ryan of the Controller Railway of Alaska to Richard Ballinger that was said by a muckraking journalist to have contained a postscript that revealed the corruption of Ballinger, Taft, and Charles Taft. The accuser was M.F. Abbott. Her charges were published in newspapers in mid–1911, and hearings were set in Congress. Taft ended it with a searing letter of denial to Congress. It was a scandalous attempt to revive the Ballinger-Pinchot affair.

Direct Democracy—Government by majority vote. Taft accused the progressives of abandoning representative democracy for direct democracy, which others pointed out had failed in Athens some 2,500 years before.

Elba—The island to which Napoleon was first exiled and from which he returned triumphantly to France in 1814. The island of St. Helena was where he was sent after Waterloo. During Roosevelt's Africa trip of 1909–1910, there was much talk of the "Return from Elba." During the 1912 campaign the Democrats had fun with the analogies of Elba, Waterloo, and St. Helena.

Era of Discontent—A side-term your author suggests for the "progressive era."

Executive Automobiles—The White House automobile fleet.

Federal Aid—Federal funding for road building.

Federal Licensing—Motorists demanded federal driver's licenses and car registrations to avoid local licensing required to drive in each state.

Freak—A car of unusual design, look, or capability, especially popular in 1904–1906.

One "freak" look followed the shape of a capsized rowboat, which was more aerodynamic than other designs. "Freak" automobiles were becoming less common by 1909, although an occasional mutation would appear, such as the "Automobile Wind Wagon" (powered by a propeller) and the "Gyroscope Car" (something about a flywheel to avoid tipping over) which both appeared in 1909.

Free List—Or "free listing." Duty-free imports.

Free Silver—A populist, agrarian, and Western movement from the 1880s that demanded silver coinage. It was the successor "soft money" movement to the "greenbacks" (paper money and a political party). The goal was "cheaper" money with which to pay down debt. The core motivations of the movement were anti–Easterners, anti-business, especially New York banks and railroads, somewhat anti–Semitic, and anti-establishment Republicanism. The culmination of the movement came with the 1890 Sherman Silver Purchase Act. Greenbacks and Treasury notes poured in and gold flowed out. Free Silver, along with a new and very high tariff, depressed agricultural prices and the general downside of the 1880s business expansions, all combined in the Panic of 1893.

Glidden Reliability Tour—A long distance reliability competition sponsored by the AAA that was inspired by the group's 1904 automobile tours to the St. Louis Fair. The following year, "The King of Touring," amateur motorist Charles Glidden, offered a trophy for a similar tour. Winners were decided by timing, sportsmanship and vehicle performance. Pierce-Arrow won the first events and was said to have "hypnotized" the trophy. Glidden Tours served to publicize the usefulness of automobiles and the horrid conditions of the roads.

Golf Cabinet—Taft's golf buddies, principally Capt. Butt, Gen. Edwards, Senator Bourne, and Vice President Sherman. Meetings were convened at the Chevy Chase club.

Good Roads—The movement for the building of roads. There were various and sometimes conflicting motivations behind Good Roads. It was a farmers' movement, a bicyclists' movement, and finally, by 1909, an automobile movement. Motorists complicated the Good Roads issue by demanding roads suitable for automobiles.

Grange, the National—"The Patrons of Husbandry," a fraternal order of farmers started in 1867 with the goal to educate and empower farmers, especially in the marketplace. It was an anti-railroad force in the 1870s and 1880s, fighting for low rates. The Grange was a strong Washington lobby. It opposed Taft's Reciprocity bill. On the up-side, its long-held support for Good Roads was, by 1912, modified to include good roads for automobiles, not just hay wagons.

Hoodoo—Bad luck or a bad luck charm. Used frequently in reference to Taft's golf.

Incense Swingers—Roosevelt loyalists, who, Gen. Edwards explained, were "largely of the New England element, possibly more the Harvard type, who are supposed to stand around the President as acolytes do about a priest and swing incense at him and about him, while the center figure stands with this skirts outspread to receive the adulation ... and who never think the President makes a mistake."

Initiative, referendum and recall—The progressive theme song for "popular" democracy. The initiative allowed citizens to submit a law to legislative or popular vote. The referendum submitted existing law to voter approval. The recall removed public officials and/or overturned judicial decisions by popular vote. The motivation was to cure government of corruption by giving the voters law-making, discharge, and veto powers. It was the recall that Taft found offensive. Taft argued that impeachment laws already empowered states to remove officials, and he held judicial recall to be repugnant. The recall was first instituted in Los Angles and Seattle in 1903 and 1906, respectively, and was adopted by various states, starting with Oregon in 1908. In 1921 North Dakota voters removed the governor by recall. Only the initiative and the referendum, now synonymous terms, have survived.

Insular—Of or pertaining to the U.S. island possessions.

Insurgent—Members of a party or organization that oppose their leadership. In the Senate, the insurgents were generally opposed to the party organization, whereas the concern in the House was over the "Rules Committee." In 1910, the House "rules insurgents" coupled with Democrats and voted to limit Speaker Cannon's powers. In his memoirs, Cannon described those insurgents: "Most of these men were young and ambitious. Some of them had no little ability. All of them had exaggerated opinions of their own importance. Very few of them were amenable to party discipline." "Insurgent" became a catch phrase. There were "insurgents" in the ACA, for example, who voted against Club directors.

Interests—Demagoguery for those who pull the strings, i.e., the monied. Lobbies such as the Grange and the AAA were not considered unto themselves "interests," although they would be termed today "special interests."

Internal Combustion Engine—The internal combustion engine was developed commercially in the United States starting in the 1890s. Fueled by kerosene, gasoline or other petroleum distillates, its primary use was as an alternative to bulky steam engines for stationary engines and water craft. Automobiles required lighter, high-speed engines, and thus created a new type of market. A 1910 estimate held that stationary gasoline engines weighed 320 pounds per horsepower, while the typical automobile engine of 1910 weighed 15 to 18 pounds per horsepower. The exigencies of the automobile revolutionized mechanical power. The dirigible and the airplane were made possible by advances in engine design from the automotive industry.

-isms—Frequently attached to a name, as in Cannonism, La Folletism, Aldrichism, etc. and generally as an insult.

Joy ride—Originally a description for the chauffeur's act of sneaking off with the boss's car off-hours. States enacted laws against the outrage. By 1909 joy riding was a generic term for its literal meaning of the enjoyment of a good, generally fast ride. Taft was the nation's No. 1 joy rider from 1909 to 1913.

Judicial recall—The "recall" when applied to judges and court decisions. See "Initiative, referendum and recall."

Lincoln Memorial Highway—A proposed "living memorial" to Lincoln, a highway from Washington to Gettysburg. For Good Roaders, the Lincoln Highway was the back door to Federal Aid.

Little Governors—Eight western Governors who signed the February 1912 letter to Roosevelt demanding his candidacy. The letter was orchestrated by Roosevelt forces. In fact, Roosevelt prepared his response at the same time the Governors were preparing the letter. Although eight Governors signed it, they came to be known in the press as the "seven little Governors."

Minimum/ Maximum Rates—An important provision of the Payne tariff drawn principally by Senator Root that was demagoged by opponents, especially the mid-western insurgent press. The minimum rate was the normal duty. The maximum rate represented a retaliatory duty to be imposed upon nations that discriminated against the U.S. Opponents disingenuously claimed it was a "joker" that would be used to arbitrarily impose the maximum rates.

Motor—Term for automobile, used as a verb and a noun.

Motor Age—Also, Horseless Age. Also, the title of automobile magazines.

Mud-pikes—Derogatory term for bad roads.

Mugwumps—1884 Republican insurgents who voted for Grover Cleveland over James G. Blaine. The word is Indian for "chief." In politics, it was derogatory. As a young lawyer in Cincinnati, Taft spoke against the Mugwumps, even though he was unsympathetic to Blaine.

National Highways Protective Society—Formed in early 1909, this group was dedicated to fighting the "speed mania." Henry Clews was its first President.

National Monetary Commission—A product of the Panic of 1907, when a market downturn turned hysterical due to a rigid currency system that was unable to provide cover for banks in the form of emergency debt. The Aldrich-Vreeland Act of 1908 authorized a commission to study the monetary and banking system and make a recommendation for a more elastic, responsive currency. Senator Nelson Aldrich headed the National Monetary Commission. It reported its findings to Congress in late 1911 and early 1912. The Commission's plan was the foundation for the Federal Reserve Act of 1913.

National Progressive Republican League — Formed in January 1911 by Robert La Follette, a group dedicated to "popular government." It was La Follette's presidential campaign committee. The League consisted of Senate insurgents, a few House progressives, and private citizens such as Gifford Pinchot and William Allen White.

New Nationalism — From Roosevelt's speech at Osawatomie, Kansas, on August 31, 1910. The speech made inevitable the break with Taft two years later. In it, Roosevelt said that a "New Nationalism," loosely, centralization of power in Washington, was needed to tackle "new problems." In terms of specific proposals, there was little new; what changed was the attitude. Roosevelt compared the challenges of 1910 to those Lincoln faced in 1861. The speech closed with, "We must have progress, and our public men must be genuinely progressive."

Northern Securities Company — A railroad holding company and the object of Roosevelt's first anti-trust case. The trust was a result of a merger of railroads that followed an attempted coup by Edward Harriman in 1901 to gain access for his Union Pacific line to Chicago via a stock raid on the Northern Pacific line. Morgan halted him with the threat of a call on Harriman's preferred stock in the company. Morgan's group, headed by J.J. Hill, settled with Harriman, and the Northern Securities Co. resulted.

Octopus — 1909-speak for a monopoly. Government anti-trust lawyers were called "octopus hunters."

Old Guard — Term for the Republican leadership of 1909. Also, "regular."

Orphan's Day Outing — An event started in New York in 1905 that was mimicked in cities across the nation. As part of the motorists' quest to prove their legitimacy and to fight their bad name, these annual "outings" gave automobile rides to orphans. Today, it'd be like taking poor kids on a luxury yacht. In 1910, the New York "Orphans Automobile Day Association" gave thrilled children the ride of their life. On the way to Coney Island in three hundred autos, from limousines to taxis and trucks, the mostly black and immigrant children cried, "faster! faster!"

Osawatomie — See "New Nationalism."

Oyster Bay — Location of Roosevelt's Long Island home, Sagamore Hill. "Oyster Bay" was a general reference to things Roosevelt.

Patronage — The "spoils system" of giving government jobs to political allies, and one of a president's biggest guns. The "merit system" was its antidote. Taft used patronage and advanced reform of it during his term.

Payne-Aldrich — Officially, the Payne Tariff Bill, the 1909 tariff revision signed by Taft on August 5, 1909, after a special session that started on March 15. Aldrich reported the bill to the Senate and otherwise controlled the Senate version of it, thus the attachment of his name to it. References to it as Payne-Aldrich commenced only after the bill was signed and not generally until 1910. It served critics to associate it with Aldrich.

phone — New word for telephone.

Pierce-Arrow — Originally, the George N. Pierce Co., of Buffalo, New York, an appliance and bicycle manufacturer that became a leading American auto maker by 1909. The 1904 Great Arrow brought the company's fame. Its successor, the Pierce-Arrow, was a tremendous successes, good enough to rename the company for it and to land the car into the White House garage in 1909. Pierces were the mainstay of the White House fleet until FDR's second term. In 1909, the Pierce-Arrow was renowned for its excellent build and smooth six-cylinder engine.

Populists — Variously, a political school, strategy, and organization. The so-called Populist Party came to prominence in the 1892 as the People's Party. It was a western movement that stood for free silver and against the railroads. The party took over one million votes in 1892, but it disappeared as its followers went to the Democrats in 1896 to back William Jennings Bryan. Bryan thereafter represented its original constituents and philosophies. Populism as a way of politics was administered by the Progressives of 1912.

Postal banks—A major Taft-era initiative, Postal banks were retail government banks at Post Offices. The program came of Democratic agitation for Federal guarantees of bank deposits. Instead, Republicans offered government banks. Interest rates were low so as not to compete with commercial banks, and monies deposited were to be reinvested, in part, in local communities. Progressives opposed the bill because they wanted all the money to be reinvested locally, which would have hampered the ability of the banks to pay interest. The largest benefit of the program was to provide a secure place for money outside of the mattress or the back yard for people who would not otherwise use banks. Deposits in the Postal banks, for example, skyrocketed at the beginning of the Great Depression. Postal money orders had long performed the function of a bank, serving as easily transferable and secure holding instruments for cash, even if there was no return on the money.

Primary—1912 was the first instance of "direct primaries" being held for a presidential nomination. In the "direct primary" national convention delegates were named on the ballot. Other primaries named delegates to the state conventions, which named delegates to the national convention. There was a mix of each type, sometimes within a state. In states not having a primary, the delegates were named at the state convention. The method of the primaries were proscribed by state law, which also varied. The political parties controlled their exact form.

Progressive—The word was first used as an adjective during the Roosevelt presidency. It was turned into a noun during the tariff fight of 1909. As a proper noun, it came in the form of La Follette's National Progressive Republican League of 1911 and Roosevelt's 1912 Progressive Party. The progressive impulse was anti-establishment, anti-railroad, anti-courts, anti–Standard Oil, and pro–"the people." The anti-court sentiment came of popular dissatisfaction with local and national court decisions that overturned reform laws based upon their constitutionality, particularly over definitions of what constituted property rights and interstate commerce. Courts held that "manufacture" was not "commerce," which meant that federal laws to regulate the workplace were declared unconstitutional. In the states, courts held that the right of contract was a fundamental property right and based upon this attitude invalidated many reforms such as minimum wage laws. Taft sympathized with this disagreement, but he vehemently opposed the progressive solution to strip the courts of their power. Taft was sympathetic to other progressive reforms but held that they must not violate the Constitution. For example, he signed an 8-hour work day law for government workers, and worker compensation and safety laws for the railroad industry, which fell under the Constitution's "commerce clause" powers of Congress.

Progressive Era—Held to be the period between McKinley's 1901 assassination and the 1921 inauguration of Warren Harding, and frequently said to except the Taft years. More generally, it was a period of transition that came of the late 19th century economic and demographic growth. The general political shift was to the West and the cities.

Railroad Bill—The 1910 Mann-Elkins Act, referred to at the time as the "Railroad bill." The Act enhanced the powers of the Interstate Commerce Commission (ICC, created in 1887, the first federal regulatory agency) over railroad rate making and for its judicial proceedings against railroads. It also created the Commerce Court to handle disputes between shippers and carriers. Taft considered the bill an important part of the Roosevelt legacy set in law. The Progressives hated the bill for not going far enough and for its Commerce Court, which offended their sensitivities for the courts.

Recall—see "Initiative, referendum and recall."

Reciprocity—Taft's free-trade agreement with Canada of late 1910. It was submitted to Congress as a revenue bill in early 1911, and signed into law later that year after a special session of Congress. The political fight for Reciprocity oddly aligned the President with Democrats, and insurgents with regulars. Standpatters and regulars were about evenly split over it. Canadian voters rejected the agreement.

Red Devil—Name of William H. Barnard's Panhard automobile that was one of the fastest cars in American in 1900. "Red Devil" became a derogatory word for scorchers and fast cars.

Regular—vi. Staying the party line. n. Republicans who voted with the leadership. syn. "Old Guard."

Roosevelt Republicans—Not a Roosevelt term, but a self-described distinction of the republicanism of his more extreme supporters in opposition to the Republican leadership. The name was used by individuals and the press.

Rules—House of Representatives deliberations are chaotic and unruly, and require rules to make them less so. The rules are set by the Rules Committee and govern the timing, type, discussion, and amendment of legislation. In 1909, Speaker Cannon held the power to appoint members of the Rules Committee and maintained a seat on the Committee for himself. This power was not new to Cannon, but he exercised it vigorously. It gave him great ability to control legislation and maintain "regularity" in the party.

Rules insurgents—House insurgents who fought against the rules and were otherwise regular. Augustus Gardner was the most prominent of the rules insurgents. The intransigent dissidents, such as George Norris, were called "ultra insurgents."

Schedule—A tariff category.

Schedule K—Tariff category for "Wool, and Manufactures of Wool," which the Payne bill left mostly untouched for the reason that both manufacturers and wool producers held a common interest in that protection. Usually manufacturers and producers were on the opposite side of tariff fights, one looking for cheaper supply and the other looking to protect local production. With wool, everybody was happy with protection except consumers, who footed the bill. Taft recognized the impossibility of touching Schedule K in 1909. Investigation into international wool prices and conditions was the primary focus of his Tariff Board. He presented its findings and demanded a reduction in the wool schedules in late 1911.

Scorch—Scorching, scorcher, etc., also, Speed Mania, Speed Maniacs. To speed. The word came from the bicycle period, but became an imperative in the Motor Age.

Secret Service Affair—One of the worst Roosevelt agitations with Congress near the end of his term. It started in the Spring of 1908 when rumors circulated in Congress that Roosevelt was using the Secret Service to investigate its members. Congress passed a law that specifically limited the Secret Service to protection of the currency and the President. That December, Roosevelt sent a message to Congress stating that the law "has been of benefit only ... to the criminal classes...." Congress took offense and demanded of the President proof of wrongdoing by its members. Roosevelt replied in January without any specific accusations. The House voted to reject the January message, the first censure of its kind since Andrew Jackson.

Selden Patent—In 1895, George B. Selden was issued a patent for an automobile. He had actually built only a one-cylinder motor that differed from the patent entry. He sold the rights in 1899 for $10,000 and a share of royalties to a Wall Street syndicate that had taken over the Pope Mfg. Co., now called the Electric Vehicle Co. The new patent owners set about suing competitors. In 1903, a general settlement was reached and the ALAM was formed. Members were required to pay a 1-1/4% licensing fee over list price. The proceeds went 1/5th to Selden, 2/5ths to the Electric Vehicle Company, and 2/5ths to the ALAM. Henry Ford refused to settle, and a case was proceeded against him. The patent was upheld in 1909. Ford and fellow defendant, Panhard, appealed, and two years later the higher court held that the Selden patent applied only to 2-cycle engines. The industry was liberated from it. The joke was that Selden was henceforth "the Ex-Father" of the automobile.

Self-drive—The act of driving one's own automobile, as opposed to being driven by a chauffeur.

1789—The references to this date in this work concern America, not France. The Constitution was submitted to the thirteen original states on September 17, 1787. It was to be effective upon ratification by the ninth state (two-thirds), which came the following June. The new government was effected in March of 1789, and the first electoral college was held. George Washington won and was inaugurated on April 30, 1789. The first amendments to the Constitution were sent to the states for approval in September of 1789, and ten amendments, known as the "Bill of Rights," were ratified in December of 1791. September 17, 1787, is generally considered the anniversary date of the Constitution. The author celebrates 1789 as the birth of the nation. The United States is the oldest constitutional government in the world.

Sherman Anti-Trust Act—This 1890 law declared, "Every contract, combination in the form of trust, or otherwise, or conspiracy in restraint of trade or commerce among the several States, or with foreign nations, is hereby declared to be illegal." The Act also forbade any "attempt to monopolize" such trade. However, it did not hold up in court, due primarily to a distinction between manufacture and commerce. After a number of state and federal cases were lost in court, enforcement waned. Businesses further avoided the law by incorporating "holding" companies in business-friendly states, which, by 1900, constituted the general form of the "trusts." The ice was broken by the Supreme Court's 1904 ruling that the Northern Securities Company, a railroad trust, violated the Act. The company was dissolved, and Roosevelt's "trust busting" was unleashed. Taft pursued the policy vigorously. In 1911, the government won the Standard Oil case by application of a Court invention, the "rule of reason," which measured whether a restraint of trade was "unreasonable." Conservatives howled at this act of judicial legislation and progressives screamed that it made the Act arbitrary. Taft was satisfied with it, although he felt Congress might further clarify the Act with new laws. This was accomplished under Wilson with passage of the Clayton and Federal Trade Commission Acts of 1914 that better defined "reasonableness" in business practices.

Social Season—January First to Ash Wednesday.

Socialism—As a political party it polled almost 900,000 votes (one in sixteen) in 1912, double its 1908 take. European socialism was "red" back then, as it was tied to various brotherhoods, radical labor and anarchist movements. In America the party sought change through the political process. Socialists took over the city government of Milwaukee in 1910 and put a Representative in Congress. Socialist mayors won at Schenectady, New York, ten Ohio cities and a scattering of other places, including Berkeley, California, and Hartford, Arizona, in 1911 and 1912. Although most of these officials were rejected in the subsequent elections, it seemed at the time that socialism was threatening to become a major political force. Socialists freely called for the abolition of the courts, the Constitution, and private property. The movement's temporary success came of the general discontent of the period, when voters sought change for change's sake and agitation was its own reward. Taft nailed it with the 1912 comment, "The growth of socialism in this country is a noteworthy incident in showing the extreme to which many would go in the solution" of problems. Taft made fun of the socialists by calling them "brother," such as "Brother Gompers...."

Soft Money—In economics, currency that is not backed by gold (see Free Silver). In chauffeur-speak, a bribe. One 1910 story was about the chauffeur "Bateye," who "gets a healthy percentage on the repair bills and tire bills; has a royal time riding the girls and his friends and has the Boss buffaloed with a strangle-lock because of what he found out on him the few trips he actually drove him."

Speedway—A Horse Age description for city roads dedicated to pleasure riding. Into the Motor Age, speedways were converted to motors, but not without a fight, especially in New York.

Standard Oil Co.—Formed in Cleveland, Ohio in 1870 by John D. and William Rockefeller, Henry Flagler, Samuel Andrews, and others. Through aggressive acquisitions and expansion into all aspects of oil refining and sales, such as transportation, pipelines, and storage, it was the epitome of the octopus. The controlling trust moved to New Jersey following an Ohio case of 1890 that ruled that the company illegally held stocks in other companies, which New Jersey allowed. By 1900, Standard Oil controlled upwards of 90% of oil refining in America. Its principal products were heating and lamp oil. The company was the foremost practitioner of railroad "rebates." Leveraging its huge volume, Standard Oil demanded that its rail carriers refund to it a portion of the cost of shipping, including that of competitors. Rebating was the way around price controls set by the Interstate Commerce Commission. Rebating became a huge political issue and was a focus of the Elkins Act of 1903 and the Hepburn Act of 1906. A successful Missouri case ruled by Judge Kenesaw Mountain Landis ordered an almost $30,000,000 fine based upon illegal rebates. It was overturned by a federal court. The federal government commenced a dissolution case against the New Jersey company in 1906. The final ruling came in 1911 with the order to disband the trust into 33 companies.

Standpatter—Generally in reference to the tariff, those who opposed change. Standpattism was embodied in Cannon and Aldrich.

Stanley Steamer—The famous steam car built by the identical twin brothers F.E. and F.O. Stanley. Stanley steamers were the fastest cars on earth. One took that distinction off the earth in 1907 when it went airborbe at some 150 mph at Daytona Beach. The Stanleys' first car was the Locomobile, in which the first presidential motor ride took place in 1899. The Stanleys' soon after sold the company. They returned under their own name in 1902. The company built steamers into the 1920s.

Taft Smile, the—The Taft metaphor coming out of thc 1908 campaign. His laugh, his friend Jack Hammond wrote, "was a form of physical enjoyment. It would start far ahead of the point of an anecdote, when he began to think of something that amused him and was making up his mind to tell it. It began unexpectedly and softly, grew in volume and repetition, and was used to punctuate his sentences. This chuckle startled chuckles in his hearers. One of the most exciting memories of anyone who ever heard him make a speech was his ability to throw huge audiences into spasms of delighted laughter. This was neither a pose nor a trick. Taft was a great lover of laughter—and he liked to share his enjoyment."

Tariff—A tax called "duties" imposed by the federal government on imports or exports based on value or volume. The tariff was the single largest source of revenue for the U.S. Government in 1909. In general, the Republican Party stood for high or "protective" tariffs, and the Democrats wanted low or "revenue only" tariffs, which meant duties only so high as to provide funding for the government. Two important words associated with the tariff are "free listing" and "schedules."

Tariff Board—A board of experts enacted according to the Payne law to investigate the conditions and prices of products and industries overseas in order to determine if American goods were unfairly discriminated against abroad. If so, the Board was to recommend compensatory or punitive rates on U.S. imports in retaliation. Taft used the Board to investigate tariff rates abroad for general advisement on U.S. rates. It started in 1909 and reported its first results in late 1911.

Tennessee Coal & Iron Co.—TC&I. A company purchased in 1907 by U.S. Steel with the tacit approval of President Roosevelt. The necessity of the purchase, Morgan's operatives told the President, was to bail out the stock exchange and certain banks who were collapsing under the falling price of TC&I shares. The purchase and Roosevelt's involvement was the subject of Congressional hearings in early 1909 and 1911. It was also one of the charges in the Taft Administration anti-trust lawsuit against U.S. Steel in 1911. That case was one of the key incidents in the Roosevelt-Taft breakup. The trust was absolved of the anti-trust implications of the purchase in a Supreme Court ruling, which came under Wilson. Whatever the motivation, the purchase was hugely profitable for U.S. Steel, which got the company for less than one tenth its real value.

Tennis Cabinet—Roosevelt's tennis partners who played on a court on the White House grounds. The group contained Incense Swingers, but was not confined to them. Nor was it confined to tennis players, of which there weren't too many, anyway. The court gave way to Taft's West Wing construction. In 1908 *Harper's Weekly* noted, "Mr. Roosevelt is not what you would call a 'crack' at the game."

Turtle—An overturned automobile or to overturn an automobile, as in "to turn turtle." Anti-motorist Senator Bailey described it neatly as when "the top side goes down to the bottom and the bottom side comes up top."

U.S. Steel—A trust formed by the 1901 purchase of Carnegie Steel and other producers. It was the first company capitalized at over one billion dollars. The purchase was organized by Elbert Gary and financed by J.P. Morgan's bank. Its directors were mostly Morgan operatives. Aside from its more adept politics with the Roosevelt administration, the company avoided the offense directed at Rockefeller for its quieter relationship with the railroads. Standard Oil's manipulation of railroad rates offended more than its monopoly.

Uplifters—Term for agents of reform who looked to teach others a better life, especially farmers. In 1909 it was used in reference to Roosevelt's "Country Life Commission" and its adherents. The press and critics ridiculed the term.

Vice President—Just a reminder to readers that the Vice President is an officer of the Senate, where the official title is "President of the Senate." The relevance to this work comes of the Senate budgeting for motor cars for the Vice President in 1909.

West—By 1909 terminology, a reference to the "old" West of the Ohio Valley and today's Midwest. Andrew Jackson, for example, was a "westerner"—he was from Tennessee. Today's West was the "far-West."

White Slavery—Prostitution. A huge issue in Congress during the early Taft administration. Following Taft's recommendation, the Mann Act of 1910 prohibited transport across state lines of women "for immoral purposes." It provided the basis for a Federal police force that later became the FBI.

White steamer—Built by The White Company, Cleveland, Ohio. At first a division of the White Sewing Machine Co., for which the White name was famous, it was set up as a separate entity in 1906. The White family went into automobiles in 1900 and produced the most advanced, highly-engineered steam cars ever. The U.S. Army was an important early client under Secretary of War Taft. In 1909 a White became one of the first two cars in Taft's garage. By 1911, the company dropped steam for gasoline. Into World War I, it dropped automobiles for trucks, of which the company was an important early promoter and commercializer. White was for decades one of the world's largest truck manufacturers. Of its steamers, the Company claimed they would always "get you home." Compared to gasoline, White historian Henry Merkel says that "steam was more forgiving and reliable, but gasoline was more serviceable."

Winona, Minnesota—Hometown of Rep. Jim Tawney and locale of a speech given by Taft that was used against him for calling the Payne tariff "the best tariff bill ever." Actually Taft said it was the best tariff enacted by the Republican Party, and even so it needed much improvement. He was skewered for it. The speech was about Republican regularity more than the tariff.

Glossary of Names

Adams, Henry—Leading American intellect, author, historian, and borderline Incense Swinger. Adams lived at Lafayette Park by the White House, the city's social center until new money moved that epicenter to Dupont Circle. Adams was dismayed that the new President of 1909 was from Ohio. Adams was an enthusiastic motorist.

Aldrich, Nelson W.—Rhode Island Senator, Republican. "High Chauffeur of the Golden Juggernaut," evil force in the Senate and protectorate of industry and the tariff, etc., etc. Historian Carl Hatch called Aldrich "one of the most skilled legislative leaders in American history...." Hatch also called his leadership style, "autocratic." Right on both counts. Aldrich was an easy foil for Taft's opponents. By blaming it all on Aldrich, they could ignore Taft's accomplishments. Senator Dolliver called Taft "an amiable man completely surrounded by men who know exactly what they want." Dolliver couldn't fathom that Taft worked with, not for Aldrich. It was all lubricant for his dissent. Aldrich retired from the Senate in 1911 for health reasons and in order to focus on the National Monetary Commission, whose work led to the Federal Reserve. You may know the name better for Gerald Ford's Vice President, Nelson Aldrich Rockefeller, the Senator's grandson (Aldrich's daughter married John D. Rockefeller's son, John, Jr.).

Aleshire, James—Quartermaster General of the Army. His department managed the Army's automobile fleet.

Anderson, Larz—Taft's ambassador to Japan and major campaign contributor at $25,000 in 1908. Anderson was of the Ohio band. He set up shop in Washington and North Shore, Massachusetts. He was an automobile enthusiast and probably the earliest car collector, having kept most of the cars he bought, starting with an 1899 Winton runabout and another car bought in France in 1902. The fabulous collection is housed at the Larz Anderson Auto Museum at Brookline, Massachusetts.

Archbold, John D.—Director of Standard Oil. Taft was little acquainted with Archbold, although Archbold was a Republican backer.

Bacon, Augustus Octavius—Georgia Senator, Democratic. Fought in the Confederate Army of Northern Virginia. A strict constitutional constructionist and leading Southern states' rights defender. Bacon was respected by all. He owned an automobile as of March 1909.

Bacon, Robert—With the J.P. Morgan company from 1894 to 1903, Assistant Secretary of State, 1905–09, and Secretary of State in early 1909, serving out the final days of the Roosevelt Administration in replacement of Elihu Root, who resigned to join the Senate. He was a Roosevelt Harvard classmate and loyalist, although as Taft's Ambassador to France he stayed clear of the dispute between Taft and Roosevelt in 1912.

Bailey, Joseph W.—Texas Senator, Democratic. Horse breeder and anti-motorist. Bailey condemned automobiles on his way to and from New York horse shows. He was a states' rights Southern conservative, low tariff man, and the leading Democratic proponent of the income tax. He bitterly opposed the recall. He was also a bit of a Democratic insurgent. He was one of two Senate Democrats to vote against Reciprocity, instead demanding free trade with Mexico. Bailey was always in trouble, be it for punching a journalist or for some hazy financial issues back home. After threatening to resign in 1911, he made good on the promise in 1913. The Gridiron joked, "What made Joe Bailey leave the Senate? Someone put a split infinitive in an amendment to the Constitution and it broke his heart!"

Ballinger, Richard A.—Secretary of Interior under Taft and initial object of Incense Swinger outrage at the Taft Administration. Ballinger's problem was that, like Taft, he viewed his authority as expressed, not construed. That is, he did what the law allowed as opposed to following the romantic notions of Pinchot and others that the law was a suggestion and often a hindrance. Ballinger was a Seattle lawyer and Mayor. In between his service to the Roosevelt administration as Land Office Commissioner and becoming Taft's Interior Secretary, he mildly touched the "Cunningham" claims as legal counsel. It was upon this association that the Ballinger-Pinchot affair was based. Ballinger acted prudently throughout, but like Taft, he never was able to overcome the outrage of his opponents or score public relations victories over their high-volume attacks. Taft finally accepted Ballinger's resignation in 1911. Ballinger was not absolved in history until release of Pringle's biography of Taft, which blamed Pinchot and Glavis for the mess and inspired the 1940 *Saturday Evening Post* article, "Not Guilty! Richard A. Ballinger," by Interior Secretary Harold Ickes. Declaring Ballinger innocent after all, Ickes called him the "American Dreyfus."

Bannard, Otto—New York Republican, banker, reformer, and unsuccessful candidate for Mayor of New York City in 1909. Bannard was of the Hughes school of progressive-conservatism. He was a Roosevelt supporter, but remained loyal to the party and Taft during the 1912 campaign. Into 1911, and especially during the 1912 primary, Bannard was one of Taft's most important political advisers.

Barnes, William, Jr.—Albany Republican political boss and Roosevelt antagonist who led the convention floor fight for Taft in 1912. Bannard then called Barnes the "ex-wicked one."

Bell, J. Franklin—Major General, Chief of the General Staff. Automobile enthusiast who took possession of a White limousine in early 1909—on behalf of the Army. In 1910 Bell was in an automobile accident that killed one of his passengers, a Mrs. Slocum. "It was his erratic orders to the chauffeur which caused the accident," wrote Butt, "and yesterday the Coroner's jury relieved the latter of all responsibility and placed the blame on the occupants of the car."

Berger, Victor—Wisconsin Representative, Socialist. Berger won the office in 1910, the year of discontent that also put a Socialist into the Mayor's seat of Milwaukee. Berger's solution to the trust problem was for the government to purchase them. He also proposed to dispense with courts, the Senate, and the Constitution. On a more constructive level, at baseball games between Democrats and Republicans Berger acted as umpire. Berger lost the election of 1912, as did the socialist mayor.

Beveridge, Albert Jeremiah—Indiana Senator, Republican. The middle name says it all. A leading Senate insurgent. He lost the 1910 Senate election and the 1912 Governor's election, in which he ran as a Progressive. He was the opening act at the Bull Moose convention of 1912.

Boardman, Mabel—Taft friend and supreme confidant. She supported Taft always with honest, sometimes brutal advice. Boardman was a leading Washington social figure and in the early days of his Administration, a Roosevelt familiar. She joined Taft on his voyage to the Orient in 1905 along with Alice Roosevelt. Boardman stayed loyal to Taft throughout the split with Roosevelt. Alice called her the "Madame Pompadour" of the Taft Administration. She and Alice were good friends. Boardman rejuvenated the Red Cross, which had languished during the latter years of Clara Barton. She became the first woman Commissioner of the District of Columbia in 1920. Her sister was married to Standpat Senator Murray Crane.

Boardman, William J.—Taft supporter and Ohio friend. Owned a house at the fashionable Dupont Circle area of Washington, D.C., from where President-elect Taft was based when in the city. It was said that Boardman's Columbia touring car was instrumental in the conversion of Secretary of War Taft to the motoring age. In 1909 Boardman owned a Packard limousine.

Borah, William E.—Idaho Senator, Republican and sometime progressive. He was a Roosevelt manager at the 1912 Republican convention. He abandoned the Bull Moose and ran for the Senate as a Republican. Borah was a maverick, not a revolutionary, although with a populist streak. He was against high duties, except for hides, which his state produced. He compromised with Taft, anyway. Borah opposed federal ownership off of Western lands. In late 1911, Borah became a Taft antagonist.

Bourne, Jonathan, Jr.—Oregon Senator, Republican. Early member of Taft's golf cabinet. Bourne and Taft fell out during the Republican implosion. Their split started over the 1910 Postal Banks bill, at the influence of the insurgents. In 1913, Bourne offered Federal Aid legislation, and many of his ideas were adopted in the 1916 Federal Aid Road Act. Perhaps he caught a few ideas while riding in the White steamer. Bourne was President of La Follette's National Republican Progressive League.

Brandeis, Louis D.—Glavis' legal counsel during the Ballinger-Pinchot congressional hearings, paid by *Collier's* magazine. Wilson appointed him to the Supreme Court.

Briscoe, Benjamin—Head of Maxwell-Briscoe Motor Corporation, started in 1904. In 1909 he organized the United States Motor Co., a Wall Street–backed automotive conglomerate that included Maxwell-Briscoe, Stoddard-Dayton and Brush. It went into receivership in 1911. Jonathon Maxwell successfully recommenced under the Maxwell name, which eventually became Chrysler. Briscoe continued with another company under his own name that lasted until 1921. Briscoe was an outspoken proponent of motor cars and protective tariffs for the industry.

Bristow, Joseph—Kansas Senator, Republican. Ultra insurgent, "ranking second only to Senator La Follette," it was said. Bristow was not bitter in his antagonism to Taft. He received the President openly and warmly in Kansas in late 1911.

Bryan, William Jennings—The Peerless Loser, Peerless Promisor, the Commoner, Perennial Contender.... Made his fame with his wild 1896 convention speech, "You shall not crucify mankind upon a cross of gold." He was nominated and was henceforth the leading populist. He lost three national elections, twice against McKinley and once against Taft. Bryan's support for Wilson threw the convention that direction over Champ Clark. Wilson named him Secretary of State.

Burton, Theodore—Ohio Senator, Republican. Member of Aldrich's Monetary commission. Burton stepped into the Senate fight between Charles Taft and Joseph Foraker in late 1908. Charles dropped out in order to defeat Foraker. Burton was a Taft supporter henceforth. He was an important advocate for river and harbor improvements.

Butler, Dr. Nicholas Murray—President of Columbia University and leading Roosevelt advisor until 1908, when Roosevelt became upset at his criticism. Butler took Sherman's place as Taft's vice presidential candidate in the Electoral College elections in late 1912. Butler thereby earned eight electoral votes without placing a foot on the campaign trail.

Butt, Archibald W.—Aide-de-camp for Roosevelt starting in April 1908, and continuing in the same position for Taft. He died on the *Titanic* in April 1912. Butt was beloved by both Roosevelt and Taft, and he was torn by the break between the two men. Taft asked Congress to provide space for a memorial to Butt, which stands today at the foot of the South lawn of the White House. It is dedicated to Butt and his friend, Francis Millet, who was also lost on the *Titanic*. Butt's profuse correspondence offers an important and unique view of the Taft period and daily life.

Butt, Clara—Butt's sister-in-law and the "Dear Clara" of his letters. Following the death of his mother in October of 1908, Butt carried on his copious correspondence with Clara.

Cannon, Joseph Gurney "Uncle Joe"—Illinois Representative, Republican. Speaker of the House and defender of tariffs and the status quo. Standpattism was personified as "Cannonism." Cannon was enormously popular among Republican regulars and in his own, Danville, Illinois, constituents, whom he represented in Congress from 1873 to 1891, 1893 to 1913, and 1915 to 1923 (he lost in 1912 to the party split). Cannon held the Speakership longer than anyone since the Grant presidency and during a time that the post was most powerful. It must be noted that his iron rule covered all of the important reform years of the Roosevelt presidency—a reflection of the political skill of both men. Cannon's personal integrity was never doubted, even by his enemies. He was willing to work with both Roosevelt and Taft, so long as he got something in turn. Roosevelt traded the tariff for railroad legislation. Taft simply sat upon him with the force of the 1908 party platform with payback in the form of Taft's advocacy of regularity, expressed most significantly at Winona. Neither President liked Cannon personally. Cannon was a Good Roads advocate, but felt, like Taft, that the states should pave the way. Butt called him "The Evil One," which means that Taft did, too. Cannon was born in 1836 and died in 1926.

Carnegie, Andrew—1909's richest man, give or take Rockefeller. Carnegie cashed out in 1901 with the formation of U.S. Steel and dedicated himself to philanthropy and peace movements. His share of the sale and bond issues was worth $400,000,000—that's 1909 dollars, folks. In 1909 he told Congress that he could easily have asked for an extra $100,000,000 in the deal. He also said he was by then "blissfully ignorant of the details" of his former company. He gave away some $350,000,000. Carnegie was criticized by some for establishing libraries (over 2,000), for it was thought they would violate copyright and reduce publishing and royalty incomes. Carnegie adored Taft for his peace treaties and his public stand for education for blacks. After being lectured by a socialist on the unjust distribution of wealth, Carnegie instructed his secretary to give him an account of his holdings and the world's population. Carnegie scribbled on a pad, then said to his secretary, "give this gentleman 16 cents. That's his share of my wealth." He took delivery of a "48 horsepower" motor car in March of 1909, probably a Pierce-Arrow.

Clapp, Moses E.—Minnesota Senator, Republican. Insurgent and La Follette ally. He was nominated by the Roosevelt forces for the Temporary Chair at the 1912 Republican convention. The Clapp name became prominent during the Summer of 1912 when he chaired hearings on campaign finances. His committee investigated the 1904 and 1908 elections and aired 1912 expenditures. Roosevelt, Morgan, Charles Taft, and others were hauled before it, making public for the first time the enormous monies raised by the Republicans from U.S. Steel and Standard Oil partners in 1904. Taft stayed clear of it all, as his brother had financed the bulk of his 1908 and 1912 campaigns.

Clark, James Beauchamp "Champ"—Missouri Representative, Democratic. Speaker of the House from 1911 to 1919, one of the longest reigns, along with Cannon and Tip O'Neill. Clark was a good Southern Democrat, that is he was a states' rights conservative who believed in low tariffs. He lost the 1912 nomination to Wilson, even though he won the primaries. He was an anti-motorist, but eventually settled into the cars provided for him by Congress.

Clark, William A.—Montana Senator, Republican, 1901–1907. On June 29, 1902, it was reported that he became an automobilist, one of the earliest politicians to do so.

Clarkson, Coker—Assistant manager of the ALAM and later head of Society of Automotive Engineers (SAE). Clarkson's work at SAE was crucial to the automotive industry for its research, standards, and diffusion of technical information. Clarkson was a tireless promoter of automobiles. His letters and articles made frequent appearances in the New York *Times*.

Cleveland, Grover—The only non-consecutive, two-term President. Cleveland was a conservative reformer and believer in low tariffs. He called tariff protection the "communism of pelf." Cleveland opposed Bryan.

Clifton, Col. Charles—In 1909, Secretary of the Pierce-Arrow Company. The President of the company was George Birge, who was more automobile tourer and socialite than manager. Clifton was the company's guiding personality and force. A 1913 description of Clifton went, "He is the Pierce Arrow and the Pierce Arrow is the Colonel." Clifton was president of the ALAM and its successor organization, the National Automobile Chamber of Commerce. He was President of Pierce-Arrow in 1916.

Cockran, W. Bourke—New York Representative, Democratic. A close Taft friend through his marriage to Anne Ide, the daughter of one of Taft's fellow Philippines Commissioners. Cockran was a great public speaker and leading D.C. gentleman. He had his sights on Alice before she married Nicholas Longworth.

Cocks, William W.—New York Representative, Republican. The automobile-friendly Long Island congressman introduced bills in 1908 and 1910 for federal licensing and registration. He lost the election of 1910.

Corbin, Henry—General. He is to be congratulated for having been caught speeding in England in 1902. He was a close friend of the Tafts.

Cosby, Spencer—Major, Corps of Engineers and Superintendent of Buildings and Grounds in Washington. Cosby was charged with implementation of Taft's keen ideas for the reconstruction of the city of Washington and its monuments. He was also in charge of the White House grounds, including the garage, and the construction of the West Wing and the Oval Office.

Crane, Winthrop Murray—Senator from Massachusetts. The Republican Whip in the Senate. Married to Mabel Boardman's sister. He opposed Taft in the 1908 nomination, but mostly in opposition to Roosevelt. He was otherwise a supporter, family friend, and sometime thorn to Taft, as he was a constant political schemer. He was adept at learning the plans of the insurgents and Democrats.

Dalzell, John—Pennsylvania Representative, Republican. Standpatter and Cannon lieutenant. He lost the 1912 primary.

Depew, Chauncey M.—New York Senator, Republican. Old Guard. He lost the Senate seat to the Democratic takeover of Albany in 1910. His money came from the New York Central Railroad. He was owner of the "Rocket," a Chalmers-Detroit motor car that served as a pathfinder for the "Flag to Flag" tour of 1909 from Denver to Mexico City. Depew was an early automobile supporter and member of the ACA.

Dewey, George—Of Manila Bay fame, for which he was promoted to Admiral, the first since Farragut under whom he served in the Civil War. He was the definitive hero of the Spanish-American war. He was the next door neighbor to the Tafts on K Street during Taft's War Secretary days.

Dickinson, Jacob M.—Taft's first Secretary of War. Taft chose him for his ability as an attorney and because he was a Southern Democrat. Dickinson promoted airplanes, even going up in one while in office. He left the Cabinet in 1911. He managed the government case filed against U.S. Steel that year.

Dolliver, Jonathan P.—Iowa Senator, Republican. A long-time congressman, sometime low tariff man, and insurgent-come-lately as of 1909. He stood for tariff reductions, but not too much. He died in office in 1910.

Durant, William C.—Founder of General Motors. Durant came to automobiles from his family's carriage business. In 1904 Durant took over David Buick's company, which was in financial trouble. Durant went skyward and back several times from there. In late 1908, he formed General Motors with a conglomeration of Buick, Cadillac, and Olds. He lost control in 1910, but was back at it with Chevrolet in 1911, and on top of General Motors again in 1916. Out again in 1920, and back in 1921 with Durant Motors, which eventually included Locomobile, among brands. Durant lost it all again in 1932. In 1909, Durant came out strongly against protection for the industry. He thought high duties protected profits and bad management. He was a tireless business genius whose creations escaped him when he pushed too fast and too hard.

Duryea, Charles and Frank—Automobile pioneers who built their first car in 1891. Younger brother Frank ran the Stevens-Duryea, a top luxury brand of 1909 that introduced one of the first six-cylinder engines in 1905, a huge 9.6-liter affair. While Frank went upscale, Charles kept trying to make the poor man's car with gasoline and electric buggies through the Taft period. A 1913 description of him said the he was the only man who could make cars for 22 years and have "the last one look just like the one he built in 1891."

Dwight, John—New York Representative and Republican House Whip. The Old Guard enforcer, that is.

Edwards, Clarence R.—Major General, close Taft friend, and key member of the Golf Cabinet. They first crossed paths in the Philippines, where Governor Taft was distrusted by the military, and vice versa. Taft won over Edwards. He worked closely for War Secretary Taft as Chief of the Insular Bureau. Edwards oversaw Butt's purchasing of the of the first White House automobiles. Edwards commanded the "Yankee Division" during WWI.

Elkins, Stephen B.—West Virginia Senator, Republican. Taft supporter and Senate sponsor of certain significant Roosevelt and Taft legislation. His daughter was the best Washington catch, and was thought to be a possible Butt paramour. Taft liked her, but Mrs. Taft decidedly did not.

Fisher, Carl G.—Inventor of the Presto-Lite headlamps, which brought him an incredible fortune. Started as a bicycle salesman. Fisher built the Indianapolis Speedway and dreamed of a coast to coast highway. In 1913 he organized the Lincoln Highway Association, which aimed to finance a national road with a one percent royalty on all cars sales by manufacturers. With the Federal Road Aid Act of 1916, the project was abandoned to the states.

Fisher, Walter L.—Taft's second Secretary of the Interior. Fisher arrived following the acrimonious Ballinger episodes. He was a Pinchot friend, reformer, and conservationist. He managed the Department in perfect harmony with Ballinger's policies. He defended Taft with statements such as his call for "real progressives of the middle-of-the-road type, like Mr. Taft..." against "hypocritical, demagogic progressives who opposed every practical progressive policy put forth...." (key word, "practical").

Fitzgerald, John Joseph—New York Representative, Democratic. An iconoclastic, lively force in the House. A key member of the Democratic House leadership following the party's 1910 takeover.

Foraker, Joseph B.—Ohio Senator, Republican. Roosevelt and Taft antagonist. Foraker gave Taft some of his first political support, but the pair never liked each other. Foraker saw himself as Presidential material for 1908, which Taft denied him. He lost the Ohio Senate election after Charles Taft withdrew and threw his support to the third candidate, Burton. Foraker staked his political fortunes on his attacks against Roosevelt over the Brownsville affair. In 1911, Foraker publicly praised Roosevelt, largely of antagonism to Taft.

Ford, Henry—Automobile pioneer starting long before the development of the Model T and the assembly line. For our purposes, Ford led the fight against the ALAM and its Selden Patent, which he won in court in 1911. Ford early on advocated cheap, reliable automobiles. His 1906 Model N runabout was the breakthrough automobile, having far and away the best value and highest power for its price of any automobile anywhere. It immediately became the best selling automobile in the world. However, politics and culture weren't ready for it. When they were, Ford already had the "T," with which he took over the world.

Frick, Henry Clay—Steel industrialist and managerial genius. Made his fortune with "coke" (a coal derivative used as fuel for steel making) furnaces that led to an association with Andrew Carnegie. His fabulous art collection is housed at his Fifth Avenue mansion which he built to be turned into a museum after his and his wife's death. Frick was a Taft supporter and friend. He was not happy about Taft's U.S. Steel anti-trust suit.

Gaines, John Wesley—Tennessee Representative, Democratic. Known for his shrill voice and poor temper. He lost the 1908 election, and spent the rest of his term fighting Cannon and automobiles, among agitations.

Gardner, Augustus P.—Massachusetts Representative, Republican. Son-in-Law of Henry Cabot Lodge. Gardner was an insurgent but not a radical. After the defeat of Cannon he remained regular, and he backed Taft in 1912 with vigorous statements against the radicalism of the progressives, especially the recall.

Garfield, James—Roosevelt's Interior Secretary and leading Incense Swinger and Taft hater. Taft did not offer him a position in his Cabinet "because I knew him," he wrote. Garfield was a political crusader in Ohio, and unsuccessfully ran for the Republican nomination for governor in 1910 on an anti–Taft plank. His entrance to the Roosevelt Administration came as Commissioner of the Bureau of Corporations. His failed negotiations with Standard Oil, with whom he was originally friendly, led to the government suit against the company.

Gary, "Judge" Elbert H.—Organizer and Chairman of U.S. Steel.

Glavis, Louis Russell—General Land Office investigator who with "coal cases on the brain" and charges of "insinuation and innuendo" went after Interior Secretary Ballinger in 1909 for involvement in certain Alaska coal claims. Taft ordered Glavis fired. With Pinchot's help, he took his story to *Collier's* magazine, which caused a furor and hearings in Congress. Later, Glavis got into trouble over, irony of ironies, a conflict of interest between his public office and private deals involving the disposition of public lands (his essential charge against Ballinger) while serving on the California Conservation Commission under Governor Hiram Johnson. The Governor allowed Glavis to resign. Glavis later became an investigator for FDR's Interior Department under Harold Ickes, and he again caused trouble with his overzealousness. He was allowed to resign in 1936.

Goelet, Robert—New York socialite and early motorist, in whose car a shocked Eleanor Roosevelt spotted cousin Alice.

Gore, Thomas P.—Oklahoma Senator, Democratic. Known as the "Blind Statesman."

Grant, F. D.—Major General. Son and exact replica of President U.S. Grant. He was an icon of the U.S. Army. He was a motor enthusiast with an especial liking for White steamers.

Griscom, Lloyd C.—New York political boss. He was Spanish War captain of volunteers and ambassador. In 1910 he became President of a New York County Republican Committee, an important post in state politics. He was friendly with both Roosevelt and Taft. Griscom arranged their disastrous meeting at New Haven in September 1910.

Hadley, Herbert S.—Governor of Missouri, one of the "little governors" of the 1912 primary. Hadley's fame came of his prosecution as Attorney General of Missouri of the Standard Oil Company in a case ruled by Judge Kenesaw Mountain Landis. He declined to resign as Governor to join Taft's Cabinet in 1909. Although a Roosevelt booster in the 1912 primaries and the Convention, Hadley stayed regular after Roosevelt's bolt. Hadley was considered a possible alternative to Taft and Roosevelt at the convention. He was also considered for the Republican Vice President's slot to replace Sherman. He lost the Autumn election to a Democrat and the Republican party split.

Hale, Eugene—Maine Senator, Republican. Old school, long time legislator, standpatter and ardent anti-motorist. He did not stand for reelection in 1910.

Hammond, John Hays "Jack" Mining engineer and inventor. Made his fortune through work with the Guggenheims, then broke off on his own, with mining interests in South Africa, Mexico, and the American West. He regularly advised Roosevelt at the White House and was a close friend to Pinchot. When Taft became Secretary of War, he befriended Taft, who was a classmate of his brother (he was two classes before them). The friendship was worth $100,000 towards Taft's 1908 election. He accompanied Taft on the 1909 Western Tour. His advice, company, and friendship were invaluable to Taft. He served on the Republican National Committee in 1912 on Taft's side of things. Hammond's famous inventor son, John, Jr., built the "Hammond Castle" near Gloucester, Massachusetts, and was a pioneer in radio.

He developed the first radio-controlled motors, one of which he mounted on a boat and scared the folks along the North Shore in 1911.

Harlan, John Marshall—Associate Justice of the Supreme Court. The original "Great Dissenter," he held contrarian views to 316 majority opinions, including *Pollock*, which invalidated the 1894 income tax, *Plessy v. Ferguson*, which legalized segregation with "separate but equal," and the 1911 Standard Oil and American Tobacco cases that defined the Sherman Anti-Trust Act. Harlan wanted Taft to elevate him to Chief Justice when the slot opened up. Harlan died in 1911.

Harriman, E. H.—Railroader, and key player in the formation of the Northern Securities Company. He was a Roosevelt supporter and subsequent chief Roosevelt target. After the relationship became a political liability, Roosevelt called him an "undesirable ... citizen." He was the subject of Roosevelt's infamous "we are practical men" letter, in which he solicited campaign money from Harriman.

Hemphill, Job E.—Charleston newsman and Taft friend. When it was thought that Taft might sail to Panama from Newport News, Hemphill lobbied Taft to have him leave from Charleston. Taft complied, although it meant entering and leaving during high tide, for the harbor could not accommodate the draw of the President's boat. Taft wrote him, "I am coming to your old town, and I am going aboard if I have to float out on a raft." Hemphill was a Democrat. Taft read his newspaper throughout his term.

Heney, Francis—San Francisco lawyer and social crusader. He prosecuted land frauds in Oregon in 1903, and thus earned Roosevelt's endearment as an enforcer of the square deal. Like other reformers during the Taft period, Heney lost his head and found corruption everywhere the name Roosevelt was not invoked. He was a floor leader of the California Roosevelt delegation at the 1912 convention and a Bull Mooser with the bolt. He ended up feuding with his fellow Bull Mooser, Hiram Johnson.

Hengelmüller, Baron von—Austrian Ambassador and senior member of the Washington diplomatic corps, a precedence that was important in those days. He was known as "Hungrymuller," Butt wrote, "on account of his abnormal appetite." When he complained that the President kept him waiting, Taft said, "A man with the name of Hengelmüller should not want me to leave my lunch."

Heyburn, Weldon B.—Idaho Senator, Republican. He was an old school Republican and an anti-automobilist. No tariff was too high for Heyburn. He died in office in 1912.

Hill, James J.—Railroad magnate and dedicated pessimist. Among paranoias, Hill thought automobile lust would drive young men and the country into bankruptcy.

Hilles, Charles D.—Third and most effective of Taft's Secretaries, elevated by Taft to Chairman of the Republican National Committee in 1912. Hilles was a decent man and a good political operative. His job in 1912 was thankless from all but Taft, who was deeply grateful for his Herculean efforts to keep the party intact and solvent.

Hitchcock, Frank H.—Taft's Postmaster General and manager of the 1908 campaign. Hitchcock was the politician in Taft's otherwise mostly lawyer cabinet, which was important as he managed the largest patronage system. During the 1912 campaign, Hitchcock was thought to be sympathetic to Roosevelt. Taft kept him in line.

Hollister, Howard G.—Judge and boyhood friend of Taft

Holmes, Oliver Wendell, Jr.—Harvard and Washington icon, and oldest-ever Associate Justice of the Supreme Court (appointed by Roosevelt, he outlived Taft there). Holmes was another "great dissenter." While in the Court in the 1920s, Taft and Holmes frequently walked together from their homes in Northwest Washington all the way to the Supreme Court on Capitol Hill, a serious hike.

Hoover, Isaac "Ike"—White House usher. Hoover's memoirs are the source of many White House legends, especially certain negative accounts of Taft, some of which the author finds questionable.

Hoyt, Henry M.—Taft Yale friend.

Hughes, Charles Evans—New York Governor,

appointed to the Supreme Court in 1910, Republican candidate for President in 1916, Secretary of State in 1921, appointed Chief Justice of the Supreme Court in 1931, and all-round amazing man. Hughes' fame came of his tenure as Governor when he took on the Equitable Life Assurance Society, which embarrassed Morgan, Harriman, and some key Republicans and their sponsors, including Elihu Root. Roosevelt considered him a rival. Hughes was a Taft associate and friend. As Governor, he was most "progressive" when it came to automotive law.

Johnson, Hiram—California Governor, Republican. He rose to power on the fight against the "Harriman interests" in California. He was the Bull Moose Vice Presidential Candidate in 1912, and remained an independent Republican as Governor and Senator. In 1916 Johnson withheld his influence from the Republican candidate, Hughes, which threw the very tight election to Wilson. Taft called him an "arch-demagogue and fraud."

Johnson, John A.—Governor of Minnesota who was thought a leading Democratic prospect for 1912. He died before he could prove anyone right or wrong. He was a home-State antagonist to Tawney.

Joy, Henry B.—President of Packard Motor Car Company and key industry figure during the Taft period. On behalf of the ALAM, Joy lobbied Congress for the protective tariff in 1909. He walked off with a 45 percent duty and an automotive category unto itself. Joy was a member of the ACA and had Taft's ear. He was also close to Charles Evans Hughes. As a young man, Joy lived up to his name. He lived happily off his father's railroad money and took to automobiles with as much glee and mischievousness as Alice Roosevelt. He was chased by the cops more than she. One night, Joy and a friend hitched a lunch wagon to his car and towed it and the owner around the city of Detroit. Joy was keenly interested and invested in the Wright brothers.

Jusserand, Jean Jules—French ambassador, Washington figure, and important early automobile promoter.

Keifer, Joseph W.—Ohio Representative, Republican, and skilled parliamentarian. Speaker of the House from 1881 to 1883. Lost in the election of 1910.

Knox, Philander C.—Taft's Secretary of State and one of his most reliable advisers. He was a Pittsburgh corporate attorney, McKinley's last Attorney General, carried on by Roosevelt until 1904, when he was appointed to the Senate by the Pennsylvania legislature. He ran the first Roosevelt trust busting case against the Northern Securities Company. As Taft's Secretary of State, Knox negotiated the Canadian Reciprocity deal and Arbitration treaties with France and England. "Dollar diplomacy" was his creation; before it was known as such, the Gridiron called it "Pittsburgh shotgun diplomacy." Knox managed Taft's important overhaul of the Foreign Service. He joined the Senate again in 1917. Knox was an early and enthusiastic motorist.

Kohlsaat, H.H.—Owner of the Chicago *Record-Herald*, a McKinley, Roosevelt, and, lesser so, Taft intimate and 1920s commentator on the McKinley-Harding period. Kohlsaat, who claimed for himself credit for McKinley's "gold" plank in 1896 (others tried to run off with credit, as well), fell out with McKinley over Foraker's Puerto Rican tariff bill of 1900. Kohlsaat was typical of the devoted McKinley Republicans who took to Roosevelt's spell, leaving their old idol behind. Unlike many of those, Kohlsaat kept his head come 1912 and backed Taft, if reluctantly. Kohlsaat was amazed by the megalomania and rationalizations that led Roosevelt into that candidacy. Kohlsaat concluded that Roosevelt was grossly unfair to Taft, both personally and in politics.

La Follette, Robert—Wisconsin Senator, Republican. Leading Senate insurgent. His fame came of his fights against the railroads as Governor of Wisconsin. His philosophy was known as "The Wisconsin Idea." He founded the National Progressive Republican League in 1911, which served as the platform for his unsuccessful 1912 presidential run. Roosevelt took it out from under him. La Follette ran on the third party Progressive-Socialist ticket in 1924 and polled 5 million votes, far less, proportionally, than Roosevelt took in 1912. La Follette was earnest, honest, aggressive, righteous, and maniacally self-absorbed, qualities that are not always endearing in Washington. He could speak for hours. See his autobiography for a good understanding of the hysterical attitudes that came to play during the Taft presidency. La Follette's dissatisfaction with Taft began with the 1908 platform over the railroad plank. La Follette's railroad ideas marked the point at which his progressivism completely departed ways with Taft.

Lodge, Henry Cabot—Massachusetts Senator, Republican. Harvard, Brahmin, Yankee, and all that. He was thought presidential material. He was Roosevelt's political mentor. The student quickly surpassed the master. Lodge was a close friend of Henry Adams. He is most famous for destroying Wilson's entry to the League of Nations. Lodge presided over the 1908 Republican convention. He stayed regular and supported Taft through his Presidency, including during 1912.

Loeb, William—Roosevelt's second Secretary who smoothed the rough edges and kept the office running efficiently. The disposition of Loeb after March 4, 1909, was one of the few favors Roosevelt asked of Taft. Some wanted Loeb in the Cabinet. A solution was found when Loeb was given the chief customs spot in New York City, one of the most powerful positions in the country, both for its management of money and patronage. Republican rivals of Roosevelt in New York were outraged at the appointment. Loeb remained aloof throughout the Taft-Roosevelt controversies, which was detrimental to Taft, as the patronage club was essentially denied him there. Had Loeb turned on Taft, it would have been far worse.

Long, Abel—White House chauffeur, recommended by the Pierce-Arrow Company. He left the White House service in 1913.

Longworth, Alice Roosevelt—First child of Theodore Roosevelt and his first wife, who died at Alice's birth. A teenager when her father became President, she was known as "Princess Alice." Her wedding to Rep. Nicholas Longworth was held at the White House. Despite the domestic collar, she remained a Washington rebel and social fixture. Up until her death in 1980, Presidents visited her and sought her approval. Alice found a sublime rebellion in motor cars.

Longworth, Nicholas—Ohio Representative, Republican. Married Alice. If that's not enough of an accomplishment, he also became Speaker of the House in 1925. Longworth suffered more than any other the Roosevelt antagonisms with Congress in 1908–1909 and the transition between Administrations. While his wife's father screamed at his fellow inmates in Congress, his wife planted a voodoo doll in the White House lawn to curse her father's successor, and his own family fawned over and plotted advantage from their closeness to that successor. In early January of 1909, Butt found Longworth crawling into a bottle at the Metropolitan Club. "I am playing hooky in real earnest today," he said. "They are discussing the resolution to be passed on the President's [Secret Service] message ... I would not have the skin out of the House to prevent voting to censure my own father-in-law." That night Roosevelt slapped Longworth on the back and laughed, "Poor Nick. What is he not suffering for love's sake these days!"

Lorimer, William—Illinois Senator, Republican. His 1909 election was declared invalid by the Senate in 1912 on account of "corrupt methods." Roosevelt's refusal to attend a banquet with Lorimer in 1910 was one of the incidents that prompted his "Return from Elba." During the 1912 election Roosevelt unfairly accused Taft of an association with Lorimer.

MacVeagh, Franklin—Taft's Secretary of the Treasury, where he managed one of Taft's most important reforms, government economizing and budgeting. He supported Aldrich's currency plan. His brother Isaac MacVeagh was a major personality in Washington. During his confirmation hearings, MacVeagh was grilled by the Senate for his low-tariff views, which was one of the reasons Taft chose him.

Mann, James R.—Illinois Representative, Republican. The "Mann" in the 1910 "Mann-Elkins" Act. Mann was an independent but reasonable Republican; that is, he acted on issues and not emotions. He was popular amongst both insurgents and regulars. Taft at first distrusted and was later thankful for him.

Marconi, Guglielmo—Italian physicist who

perfected the transmission of audio signals via "wireless telegraphy," or radio waves. Marconi's system revolutionized communication in the long run; in the immediate, it revolutionized shipping communications. The first practical demonstration of Marconi's radio came in 1899 with news reports of the America's Cup relayed by wireless from offshore. Two years later, he sent signals across the ocean. In early 1909, a sinking ship was rescued after sending radio distress signals. The first federal regulation of radio followed the *Titanic* disaster, when it was learned that nearby ships had not received the ship's wireless SOS messages because radio operators were sleeping.

McKinley, William—U.S. President, 1897–1901, killed by an assassin in 1901 at Buffalo. McKinley's subtle tenacity was often confused for complacence, then and in history. Both supporters and critics ever perceived too late that events, seemingly happening around him, were of McKinley's charge. His uncanny patience and perception of the public mood allowed him to adjust, adopt, and lead, and with a sincerity far deeper than Roosevelt's exultant swings of enthusiasm. McKinley's biographer, Margaret Leech, for example, complained that his industrial stance suffered an "absence of moral vigor." The judgement was premature, and hardly based upon the evidence of McKinley's supreme management of the Spanish American War, colonization, currency issues, labor strife, and the tariff. The trusts were just becoming an issue in 1900, and McKinley was just then applying his quiet eye towards them. Further, he was pronouncing the necessity for tariff revision when he was shot. The author believes that had McKinley served out his second term he would have launched the new Century on surer footing than did Roosevelt, who met it with vigor, certainly, but with excessive agitation.

McKinley, William B.—Illinois representative, Republican, and philanthropist. Taft supporter and key party leader. He lost the 1912 election, but won the following election and later became Senator. He was unrelated to President William McKinley. His fortune came of the world's largest trolley system that he developed around Chicago. He owned an automobile at least as early as March, 1909.

Meyer, George von L.—Taft's Secretary of the Navy, and one of two carryovers from the Roosevelt cabinet.

Miles, Nelson A.—Lieutenant General and Spanish-American War hero. He was an outspoken and brash commander who too frequently strayed into politics and public commentary. He was unfairly though somewhat deservedly attacked by President Roosevelt, and the two hated each other thereafter. Miles was an early and important promoter of automobiles for use by the Army, as early as 1895. He was an honorary member of the ACA.

Morgan, J.P.—Great American financier. Morgan and his associates were closely allied with Roosevelt. Taft met with him on occasion, which was kept secret. Morgan bought Packard and Brewster limousines. ACA member.

Munsey, Frank—Politically active New York banker and merchant who bought and sold magazines and newspapers, owning, among them, the Washington *Times* newspaper. He dropped the La Follette boom for Roosevelt in 1912 and was a major financial backer of the Bull Moose campaign. Munsey was a large investor in U.S. Steel and other Morgan companies.

Murdock, Victor—Kansas Representative, Republican. Ultra-insurgent, called "the noblest Cannon-baiter of them all."

Nagel, Charles—Taft's Secretary of Commerce and Labor. He was a strong Taft supporter in 1908, and the appointment was the reward. He was among the more active of the Cabinet in promotion of Taft in 1912. Nagel was integral to the Taft Administration anti-trust policies, especially as he refused to allow the Bureau of Corporations to act as a substitute to the anti-trust law, which was Roosevelt's ideal.

Nelson, Knute—Minnesota Senator, Republican. Long time Midwest Senator who opposed the Payne and Reciprocity bills. Despite the disagreements, Nelson remained friendly with Taft and otherwise regular to the party. His dissent was constructive not destructive, an example which if followed by the insurgents would have changed things dramatically.

Newlands, Francis G.—Nevada Senator, Democrat. He was a crucial force to the conservation movement, especially as regards protection of coal reserves from fraudulent exploitation. He worked with Taft to reform and legalize the last-minute, extra-legal land withdrawals made by Roosevelt in 1909.

Norris, George W.—Nebraska Representative, Republican. Leading rules insurgent in the House fight against Cannon, and later a relentless insurgent in the Senate. He became an Independent in 1936.

Norton, Charles D.—Taft's second Secretary. Came to the White House through the Treasury Department. Norton was politically ambitious and obtuse about it, and caused Taft no end of trouble. He left in March 1911.

Odell, Benjamin B.—Ex-Governor and Republican boss of New York, and a key figure in Roosevelt's political career.

Oldfield, Barney—Automobile racer. He ran Henry Ford's famous "999" record-setting car.

Owen, Robert L.—Oklahoma Senator, Democratic. Key low tariff advocate.

Page, Dr. Logan W.—Geologist and engineer, Chief of the U.S. Office of Public Roads, Agriculture Department. He arrived to the then-called Office of Public Road Inquires in 1900 from the Massachusetts Highway Commission. Page spearheaded the Office's technological investigations in road building. He was President of the American Association for Highway Improvement. Page was an important advisor to Congress in preparation of the Federal Aid Road Act of 1916. Taft empowered him.

Parsons, Herbert—New York Representative, Republican. Vehemently anti–Cannon and pro–Taft. Parson's argument during the Rules insurgency of 1910 was that Cannon betrayed the party with his Conferees appointments for the Payne bill. He lost the 1910 election.

Payne, Sereno—New York Representative, Republican. Chairman of the House Ways and Means Committee and sponsor of Taft's tariff bill of 1909. Payne was regular and decent about it. He survived both the 1910 and 1912 elections, but died in office in 1914. The author hopes in this work to have restored some honor to his name.

Penrose, Boies—Pennsylvania Senator, Republican. Political boss. Penrose's support was crucial to Taft's nomination victory in 1912. Despite the progressive insurrection, during which he temporarily lost control in his state, Penrose was reelected in 1914. He dominated that state's politics until his death in 1921.

Perkins, George—His resume included work with Northern Securities, New York Life Insurance Co., International Harvester, and U.S. Steel. He was the key financial backer of the Progressive Party of 1912 and its National Executive Committee chairman. Perkins backed Roosevelt's "nationalist" programs to tightly regulate business in, essentially, a partnership with government.

Pinchot, Gifford—The verb in the "Ballinger-Pinchot Affair." Pennsylvania son of privilege, Yale graduate, chief Incense Swinger, and social crusader, frequently under the guise of conservationism. President Roosevelt called him a "useful" socialist. In his autobiography, Roosevelt's friendlier take was that Pinchot "is the man to whom the nation owes most for what has been accomplished as regards the preservation of the natural resources of our country." He served under Roosevelt as Chief Forester. Into 1909, Pinchot traded forestry for politics and turned on Taft for supposedly protecting the "interests" over the "people." Pinchot at first supported La Follette for the 1912 nomination, then dumped the Senator in due haste when Roosevelt declared himself eligible. Pinchot ran for the Senate against Penrose in 1914, but lost miserably. After Penrose died, Pinchot moved back into Pennsylvania politics. He won the governorship in 1922 and 1931, although he lost another Senate bid in 1926. While governor he was a strong advocate of the state's road building program, which Pinchot had by then discovered was a benefit to farmers and the poor.

Platt, Thomas C.—New York Senator, Republican, until 1909. He did not seek reelection and died in 1910. Platt was an Old School political boss and major player in the early political career of Roosevelt.

Pope, Col. Albert A.—Automotive pioneer. He came to the motor through the bicycle, of which his "Columbia" brand was the most famous. He turned that brand into the most important electric automobile, starting in 1896. After some financial troubles, the company was taken over by investors and renamed the Electric Vehicle Company (owner of the Selden patent). The successor brands of Pope and his sons were the Pope-Toledo and Pope-Hartford gasoline cars, and the Pope-Waverley electric. He was an early advocate of the "poor man's" car. His son George became famous for lectures and articles on the history of the automobile.

Pringle, Henry F.—Taft's 1939 biographer. Pringle also wrote a biography of Roosevelt (1931). Pringle's works are incredibly resilient. His view towards the Taft presidency is mixed, citing both failures and successes, which he apologetically labeled, "Forgotten Credits." His treatment of Taft's presidency was otherwise gloomy. The President's brother Horace and son Robert objected to certain of his characterizations of Taft.

Reed, Thomas B.—Maine Representative, Republican. Speaker of the House (1889–1891 and 1895–1899), and the example by which Cannon led the body. When a Democrat complained, "What becomes of the rights of the minority?" Reed replied, "The right of the minority is to draw its salaries, and its function is to make a quorum." Reed opposed the Spanish-American war, over which he lost his hold on the party and the House. McKinley handled him masterfully, an example which Roosevelt failed to match when dealing with Cannon.

Robinson, Francis H.—White House chauffeur, came to the service in 1910 through the White Company in Massachusetts. He served Presidents Taft through Coolidge.

Robinson, George H.—First White House Chauffeur, arrived to the White House from the Quartermaster Corps, where he drove for generals and War Secretary Taft. He managed the White steamer for President Taft until his transfer back to the Quartermasters in 1910.

Rockefeller, John D.—Founder of Standard Oil. Political careers were made and broken over association with or stands against the company. Herbert Hadley of Missouri earned his fame in a state trust-busting case against the company. Foraker of Ohio was accused of an association with the company, as was Lorimer, the removed Senator. Ida Tarbell's *History of the Standard Oil Company* launched a new genre of literature, which Roosevelt labeled the muckrake. Rockefeller died in 1937 at the age of 98. Ironically, he was at first against automobiles. He took to them by 1909. One of his fads was to wear "paper vests" in open-air cars for his health. His son, John, Jr., married Nelson Aldrich's daughter.

Roosevelt, Robert B.—Roosevelt's uncle and a leading New York motorist. Member of the ACA.

Roosevelt, Theodore—The Big Stick, Big Noise, Bwana Tumbo, Teddy, TR, the Hunter, the Colonel and any number of nicknames, complimentary or otherwise. While young government officials, Roosevelt and Taft met in Washington, D.C. Roosevelt and Taft held similar views on reform and government integrity. The key difference between them was amplified (turned up to 11, in fact) when each took the presidency. The following story tells it all: Senator John C. Spooner met with President Roosevelt to discuss some Constitutional issues. Spooner suggested he speak to Taft or Root, who knew more about it. "That's the devil of it," said Roosevelt, "They don't agree with me." Roosevelt employed the phrase, such as "big stick," "hat in the ring," etc., treated everything like a crusade, and publicized his every act. Alice said her father "wanted to be the corpse at every funeral, the bride at every wedding and the baby at every christening."

Root, Elihu—The outstanding character of his day. Secretary of War, 1899–1903; Secretary of State, 1905–1909. New York Senator, 1909–1915. As an attorney, Root worked for Morgan and Carnegie, which kept him from being a viable presidential candidate—which he didn't want, anyway. Root was a crucial Taft ally in the Senate and the force that held the 1912 Republican convention for Taft. *The Concise Dictionary of American Biography* (1964) got it right with, "His success was due to a phenomenal memory, capacity for hard work, mastery of detail, logical conciseness and clarity of argument, and ever-present wit." Root was President of the philanthropic Carnegie Corporation and was recipient of the 1912 Nobel Peace Prize for his work with Latin America, Japan, and international arbitrations.

Shaw, Albert—Owner and editor of the *American Review of Reviews*, an important progressive magazine. The *Review* was pro–Roosevelt and pro–Taft in so far as it viewed Taft as pro–Roosevelt. In late 1910, the *Review* turned against Taft.

Sherman, James Schoolcraft—Not the Sherman of the Sherman Anti-Trust Act. This Sherman was Taft's Vice President. He died in office on October 30, 1912. His spot in the ticket was not filled until December of that year, when Nicholas Murray Butler was placed there as a formality for the Electoral College. Sherman was a leading Republican House member for years (1887–1891, 1893–1909), retiring only to become Vice President. In that role he was adored by the Senate. Taft became the first President to address the Senate in person since John Adams, when, in 1913, he spoke at a memorial service for Sherman. Sherman was not related to John Sherman.

Sherman, John—As Ohio Senator and Secretary of Treasury, he administered much of the turbulent late–19th century monetary policy. Brother of William Tecumseh Sherman, the Civil War general, and no relation to James S. Sherman, Taft's Vice President. John Sherman died in 1900. Sherman's presence carried into 1909 through legislation that carried his name, the Sherman Anti-Trust and Sherman Silver Purchase acts of 1890. Although Sherman believed in a sound currency, based on gold, he caved to Populist politics in the 1890 Silver Act.

Sims, Thetus W.—Tennessee Representative, Democratic. Defender of Tennessee mules and ardent anti-motorist. Sims was a bumbling, beloved member of the House. He was also about Taft's size in body.

Sloan, James, Jr.—Secret Serviceman in charge of the Presidential detail. Butt felt that Sloan was deserving of and headed for higher places. Sloan had a keen political eye and early-on predicted the coming Roosevelt-Taft fight. He was mistaken in the belief that Roosevelt would steal the nomination from Taft. Sloan worked closely with the President's office. He arranged all the details of Taft's trips, and, except for when Taft managed to slip away, he was at the President's side throughout. The other agents on the White House detail were L.C. Wheeler and R.L. Jervis.

Smith, William A.—Michigan Senator, Republican. High tariff man and lukewarm apologist for motor cars in 1909. He defended the industry but not automobiles, especially as regards their effect upon roads, which he deplored. Smith made his fortune in railroads.

Stimson, Henry L.—Taft's second War Secretary (1911), appointed after an unsuccessful run for Governor of New York. Stimson was of the Hughes-Taft school of progressive-conservatism, and was considered the most liberal of Taft's cabinet. Although close to Roosevelt, he remained loyal to Taft in 1912 and was one of the few Cabinet members to actively campaign on behalf of the President. Stimson became former Bull Mooser Herbert Hoover's Secretary of State (1929–1933) and FDR's last War Secretary (1940–1945).

Taft, Alphonso—Taft's father. He was War Secretary and intimate friend to President Grant. He also served as Ambassador to Russia. He was stern and ambitious for his own children, of whom W.H. Taft was the most promising. He died in 1891.

Taft, Charles P.—Taft's half-brother (by his father). Charles married into one of the richest families in Ohio. He was elected to the House of Representatives in 1896, but did not stand for reelection. His most prominent business ventures were the Cincinnati *Times-Star* newspaper and a part interest in the Chicago Cubs baseball team. His wife purchased the "Philadelphia Nationals" baseball park, as well. The Charles Tafts were avid art collectors, their holdings being the foundation of today's Taft Museum of Art in Cincinnati. In 1909 Charles owned a Packard limousine and a Metheson touring car. In 1912–1913 he bought three Pierce-Arrows. Charles funded his brother's political career, giving him stocks, paying for trips, and personally funding his campaigns. He told Congress in 1912 that he funded his brother's 1908 campaign, to some $600,000, to protect his brother's integrity and keep him "free from any embarrassment or obligation.... On that basis I was persuaded to go the limit." He went to the limit again in 1912. He once told Butt, "Huntington thought it came high to get a prince in the family. He ought to have tried getting a President into one."

Taft, Charlie—Taft's youngest son, later Mayor of Cincinnati. At the White House Charlie was playful and loved by all, including the press. He organized baseball games on the South Lawn, ran the White House telephones, held his own press conferences, and learned to drive the Baker Electric. Charlie took over the summer home as he had the White House. Among adventures, he learned the value of a centerboard to sailing — after skimming along the bay sideways he had to be salvaged by Secret Service agents. His name is spelled in his parents' letters and in histories alternatively as "Charley" or "Charlie," the latter being the form used in Mrs. Taft's memoirs.

Taft, Helen—Taft's daughter, referred to at the time as Miss Helen. She was an unusually poised and active First Daughter. She filled in as White House mistress during her mother's illness in 1909–1910, including to carry on her mother's intentions to promote reform of women's labor conditions. She was a Camp Fire girls leader, and an active Washington recreationist, which included horseback riding and the Baker electric. She became Dean of Bryn Mawr College, and afterwards taught history there. From her youth her politics were to the left of her father.

Taft, Helen Herron—Mrs. Taft. Her father, John W. Herron, was law partner and close friend of President Rutherford B. Hayes. When a youth, Mrs. Taft was a frequent visitor to the Hayes White House, which no doubt inspired her ambitions to be First Lady. She attended the 25th Anniversary party of the Hayeses at the White House, which was likewise thought to be the inspiration to the glamorous party she prepared for her own 25th wedding anniversary at the White House in 1911. She remained a grand dame of Washington society until her death in 1943. She called her husband "Will." He called her "Nellie." They were deeply in love.

Taft, Henry "Harry"—Taft's brother. Prominent New York attorney and partner with Wickersham. Taft stayed at the Henry Taft residence when in New York. He owned a Fiat limousine.

Taft, Horace D.—Taft's brother. Founder of the Taft School in Connecticut. He was a leading educator, called the "Headmaster of Headmasters." He was a constant adviser to his brother, the President, although the two did not always agree, especially over the tariff. See his autobiography for an excellent description of his brother President.

Taft, Louise Torrey—Taft's mother. She was greatly interested in her son's career and freely offered her advice. She felt he belonged on the bench. She died in 1907.

Taft, Robert—Taft's oldest son, later prominent Senator from Ohio. While at a party upon his entrance to Harvard Law School, Robert was asked about his background. Where does he live, a woman asked. Ohio, he replied. Does he go there for the holidays? No, the family was now in Washington. What does his father do? He works for the government. Where does your family live? On Pennsylvania Avenue.... Robert learned to drive a White House auto at Beverly. As Senator he was known as "Mr. Republican." The carillon tower dedicated to him behind the original Senate Office Building is the only monument on Capitol Hill.

Taft, William Howard—The biggest of the big guys and a great guy. Born 1857, Cincinnati, Ohio, and died 1930, Washington, D.C.

Tawney, James A.—Minnesota Representative, Republican. "The watchdog of the Treasury." Roosevelt antagonist over Naval appropriations, the "Secret Service" affair, and Roosevelt's commissions. He lost the 1910 primary election to a combination of Democratic crossover votes and the hyperbolic agitations of Pinchot, Heney, and other "Roosevelt Republicans." Roosevelt himself made a caustic, although indirect reference to Tawney in a St. Paul speech just prior to the election. Tawney was a trained machinist and blacksmith before he became a lawyer. In 1910, the progressive *American Review of Reviews* praised him with, "No one in the country, at the present time, is more familiar with the actual practice of Congress in regard to appropriations.... Mr. Tawney's services on the Appropriation Committee have been extremely valuable to the country." Tawney worked closely with Taft to create a budgeting procedure and to advance Taft's budget cutting and government efficiency efforts.

Taylor, Robert—Tennessee Senator, Democratic. Old School Democrat, fiddler, tale-spinner, and great friend of Taft, who loved to listen to his stories late into the night.

Tillman, Benjamin—South Carolina Senator, Democratic. "Pitchfork Ben," an unruly but well-respected Senator. He was the recipient of a Senate censure for hitting another Senator on the floor in 1902. Along with Tawney and Fitzgerald, Tillman was singled out in Roosevelt's "Secret Service" message to Congress. It was just another incident in their longstanding hatred for each other. Tillman was of the founding members of the Ananias Club. With Taft's arrival, Tillman was again welcome to the President's house.

Torrey, Delia—Popularly known as the "Aunt Delia" who sent pies to the White House for her nephew's Thanksgiving celebrations. Taft visited her at Millbury, Massachusetts, at every opportunity. He wrote to her frequently with updates on political situations.

Travis, Walter J.—Golf champion, with whom Taft played at the Chevy Chase links.

Vreeland, Edward B.—New York Representative, Republican. Famous for the Aldrich-Vreeland Act, which created the National Monetary Commission. He did not run for reelection in 1912. Cannon rewarded his "regularity" during the Payne fight with a key committee appointment.

Warren, Francis E.—Wyoming Senator, Republican. Old Guard and strong inside hand at the Senate. Father-in-law of General John J. Pershing.

Washington, Booker T.—Black educator and leader. Founder of the Tuskegee School, supported by Roosevelt, Taft and Carnegie. Taft kept an open door for Washington and appeared with him in public on numerous occasions.

Watterson, Henry—Old School Democratic Kentucky newspaperman and Taft friend. Butt worked for him when he was a correspondent in Washington.

Wheeler, L.C. "Jack"—Secret Serviceman who performed the advance work for Taft's extensive travels. He plotted parade routes, arranged security, investigated local agitators, and secured housing and automobiles for the President. He was a busy man.

White, Edward D.—Confederate soldier, Louisiana Senator, and Associate Justice of the Supreme Court whom Taft elevated to Chief Justice in 1910. The move shocked political circles, as White was a Southerner, a Democrat, a Roman Catholic, and an Associate Justice. Chief Justices were not supposed to come from existing spots on the bench.

White, Rollin H.—The middle of the three White brothers of the family who were engaged in the automobile business and the engineering genius behind their steamer.

White, Thomas—Founder of the White Sewing Machine Company.

White, Walter C.—The youngest of the three White brothers who created and ran the line of steamers. He was a graduate of Cornell and a railroad attorney. He left that career to join the family automobile operation. Walter was in charge of the company's promotions, which included to personally run steamers in tours, trials, races, and, at one point the London mails for a month.

White, Windsor T.—The eldest of the White brothers and manager of the automobile company.

Wickersham, George W.—Taft's Attorney General. Law partner to Taft's brother, Henry. Wickersham enforced the Sherman anti-trust law with vehemence. One of his little-known accomplishments was to explore the legal precedent for the use of White House automobiles across state lines without paying state fees. He prepared a brief after Virginia and Maryland refused to provide gratis licensing for the White House motors.

Taft supporters complained that Wickersham acted without political considerations, which was true. And for exactly that reason Taft liked him.

Wiley, Harvey W.—Chief Chemist at the Department of Agriculture. For his work to enforce the Pure Food & Drugs Act, he became one of the "untouchables" at the Department of Agriculture, along with Secretary Wilson and Forester Pinchot.

Wilson, James—Secretary of Agriculture from 1876 to 1913 (McKinley to Taft), spanning an amazing three administrations. He was one of the "untouchables" in whom the public placed deep confidence. He organized the Department into an effective force for education and agricultural research. Road building technology was among his legacies. Wilson's largest issue during the Taft period was the high cost of farm products. During that time the Department actively promoted road technology and investigated automotive use and its effect upon roads. Wilson was a Republican Representative from Iowa for two terms, 1873–75 and 1883–85. His memorial is a bridge over Independence Avenue between two Department of Agriculture buildings.

Wilson, Woodrow—President of Princeton University. Elected Governor of New Jersey in 1910 and President of the United States in 1912 and 1916. Wilson's historically-as-yet unpaid debts to Taft include tariff, railroad, currency, fiscal, antitrust, foreign policy and other reforms, and the defeat of Roosevelt in 1912 (Wilson and his Secretary of State punted on Taft's Mexico policies, and with ugly result). Oh, and politically-acceptable motoring and a vibrant, world-conquering automobile industry.

Woodruff, Timothy—New York political boss and former Lt. Governor. As the State Chairman, he was the prominent Old Guard player in the 1910 New York Republican convention fight against Roosevelt. Woodruff went Bull Moose in 1912.

Bibliography

The library on the progressive era is huge. Many a Ph.D. has gone towards its understanding, and encyclopedias are full of stock definitions. With this brief look at Taft and his automobiles, your author hopes you will find a new layer to the period. Whatever progress means, it does not always mean charging ahead. Taft found plenty enough progress in the American Constitution, and he saw that drastic changes from it were not progress but retreat. In automobiles, he bursted progress, frequently at some speed himself. At the personal level, Mr. and Mrs. Taft have been skewered in history for many and sometimes any reasons. As you follow this bibliography, the author suggests the salt shaker.

The historical elevation of Roosevelt and Wilson has come at Taft's expense. The most friendly biography of Taft was Duffy's of 1930, which was a eulogy as much as a biography. It is nice to read, as its assumptions are not twisted to bleakness like later works, starting with Pringle, who seems to have written his episode of Taft's presidency in a dark room. Reading Duffy one can almost hear the sneers from the academy; try it, though, and you will have fun. Duffy's work is unstained by the varied emotions of the Butt letters from which historians have readily drawn opposite conclusions, sometimes from the same page. Duffy had access to the Taft papers, but not as extensively as Pringle, a few years later. Pringle was more thorough and exact. His conclusions, however different, were as lofty as Duffy's, and must be understood in the same light. Pringle was particularly poisoned by his enmity towards Republicans of the Harding era, which he unfairly applied backwards to 1910.

The more recent Taft biographies have tended, like Pringle's and this work, to focus on one aspect or another of Taft, rather than to review his life chronologically. As such, the Taft presidency, especially, has been drawn and quartered into the tariff, foreign affairs (which this work leaves to others), the Ballinger-Pinchot lunacy, the 1912 election, and so forth. With apologies to the Big Guy, now we have a chapter on automobiles. This is not a book about automobiles. They are the way we get to Taft. They are a story unto themselves, but no more so than foreign policy or the election of 1912 is important to the Taft presidency. The author's view of Taft differs from others because the author came to Taft differently from the others. The automobile made the introduction. On preparing a chapter on presidential automobiles for a book on the limousine, it occurred to the author that there must be something more to Taft's launching of the presidential garage than a mere change from saddle to gasoline. Further investigation quickly dispelled many of the assumptions of Taft. Suddenly, he was dynamic not fat, fun not dull, proactive not reactionary. It was all very shocking, and the author had to reassess everything he ever learned about the era.

The selections below are the principle sources for this work. Pringle is the most important, but please do enjoy Archie, Alice, and Mrs. Taft. The Butt letters have been mercilessly poked and picked at over the years (including here); nevertheless, a full look at his correspondence will be fresh to even the most learned reader. If you venture to his unpublished papers, the fun truly begins. The reader must beware of two prejudices. First is Butt's loyalty to Roosevelt. Butt resented anything unkind towards the former President, particularly as was heard around Taft during the summer of 1910 when Roosevelt returned to politics. Butt came to understand that Taft's differences with Roosevelt, though mired in emotion, were of politics and philosophy, not personalities. The lesson was fundamental to Butt's final choice of loyalties. Next, there was substantial editing of the published Butt papers. Segments and entire letters were left out not just for space but for political sensitivity. The author's excursion into the unpublished papers, instigated by curiosity about the automobiles, was most revealing.

Your author has spent time with older manuscripts because it is his conclusion that these still influence the Taft history and popular history in general. La Follette's autobiography is full of rancor. The Hoover was simply bitter against Taft. The slant of Roosevelt's autobiography ought be self-evident. Amos Pinchot's "History of the Progressive Party" has been looked upon as a lasting statement on the era; it is incomplete and one-sided, and a fine source of Taft-busting. The author avoided both Pinchot and his literati nemesis, Mark Sullivan, whose work prompted Pinchot's entry into history rewriting. The pair are left here to punch it out on their own. Bull Mooser William Allen White is similarly abandoned here to his Taftian despair. Bowers' work on Beveridge is ridiculously lost in his subject's ego, proof of life-after-death. These works are useful illustrations of the hysterical attitudes of the period. The student must also visit the histories by Champ Clark and Joe Cannon, men who actually wielded power rather than wishing it. Like Roosevelt's, Cannon's is an apologia, and only useful as such. Clark's is fascinating.

The author challenges the history of Taft by Mowry, and beyond the specific instances cited in footnotes, here is why: in the introduction to "The Era of Theodore Roosevelt," his editors call "judicious" his treatment of Taft and conclude, "Taft, for all his good qualities and good intentions, was out of touch with the great movements of his own day and that for the good of his country he had to be repudiated." Come, come, now. Let's start with automobiles, a "great movement" of the day. See how it works?

A must-read is Kolko. With Taft, Kolko almost got it. Almost. Unfortunately he makes the usual mistakes, such as to blame Taft's presidency on his wife, and otherwise to view everything through his thesis on the alliance of government and business. See the first paragraph of Chapter Eight, where he echoes Mowry's editors, as quoted above. The difference is that Kolko almost finds this a good thing, if only because to Kolko it meant that Taft didn't advance the interests of U.S. Steel. Again, the assumption that Taft "blundered tactlessly" causes a severe underestimation of Taft. Kolko ignores Taft's hugely successful philosophic stand against managed competition, what Taft called "State socialism," and the goal of the progressives in regard to the trusts. Nevertheless, the book is always intriguing and must be included for an understanding of the Taft period. Go back to Kolko—with care. Kolko at least understood the ambiguous legacy bequeathed to Taft by his predecessor.

Of the Roosevelt record, the author chose Pringle's as the official account. The choice was deliberate and not meant to ignore subsequent and important other works, such as that by Brands and the ongoing project by Morris. In that Pringle's biography of Roosevelt is historically valid and comprehensive, it serves as an interesting contrast to his work on Taft.

Pringle set the Taft record, and he did little to defend it. The condemnations ring louder than the praise and often exceed the facts. It must be said: it is a great book. Burton's overview of Taft's "public" career is an excellent next start, if only for its compactness and thematic unity. It's like Pringle on Prozac, and a great way to overcome Pringle's depressiveness. Donald Anderson has taken a few hits here, as well, and there is no real reason for choosing him over other modern biographers, such as Coletta, who studied the Taft presidency, other than his book is probably the most accessible of more recent works on Taft. Anderson's assumptions were those of Pringle twisted around a 1970s academic view of a "conservative" which is his thesis and title for Taft. The formulated bias has stuck. The exception is Solvick, who refused the old assumptions of Pringle and, especially, Mowry. Solvick's papers from the 1960s gave a new, direly needed perspective on Taft that subsequent biographers have largely failed to appreciate.

Taft has only himself to blame. As pointed out by Stephen Ponder, Taft was the "nonpublicity" President, and he stayed that way afterwards. Taft's book on the presidency put his own presidency into a cage, which is likely where he preferred it to be. Professor Taft wrote the book not for himself, not for history; he wrote it for good government. Had he published his letters instead, as Pringle points out, he would have provided a far different conception of himself. It's unfair to ask anything else of Taft. As his contemporaries said the thing that made him so great was that he was so good. His critics have gotten away with bashing him because they are louder than he and because he sometimes agreed with them. That's only half the story. Taft was judicial not regal, ponderous not brash, certainly. He was not not aggressive, not not strong. After his death his brother and his friend Jack Hammond tried to explain it, and we would do well to listen better. No more apologies.

To that end, David Burton has recently done more for the Taft history than any biography ever could. His multi-volume "Collected Works of William Howard Taft," arriving as this book is written, will let Taft finally speak for himself. Burton's project is a tremendous service to history. Another work pending completion is a biography of Mrs. Taft by Carl Sferrazza Anthony. The Tafts had a beautiful relationship that has been left untouched by histories that are more concerned with Mrs. Taft's upturned chin than with her heart. Anthony has a remarkable ability to see through personalities and situations, and Mrs. Taft, the first modern First Lady, is to get her monument at last.

Now, what do automobiles have to do with it all? The dominant thesis on the progressive era, Richard Hofstadter's "Age of Reform," mentions automobiles in passing, one among other technologies of the era. It cannot be dismissed. The automobile transcends technology. It was a social and political innovation of definition. The author makes no apologies for the automobile. Yet, just as political history has ignored the automobile, automotive history has ignored politics. The automobile as politics? How could we forget?

Tom McCarthy bravely attempted to accommodate Woodrow Wilson's 1906 remark that "Nothing has spread Socialistic feeling in this country more than the use of automobiles." He found reason in the statement, although he was glad that Wilson had come around to motors by the time he took office, just in time for the Model T. Excusing Wilson, McCarthy swung low, and completely missed Taft's fastball.

The automobile — and politics — now have a new hero. Welcome and go forth!

Books

Adams, Henry, *Henry Adams and His Friends: A Collection of His Unpublished Letters*, compiled by Harold Cater. Boston: Houghton Mifflin Company, 1947.

Adams, Henry, *The Education of Henry Adams*, reprint. Boston: Houghton Mifflin Company, 1974.

Anderson, Judith Icke, *William Howard Taft: An Intimate History*. New York: W.W. Norton & Company, 1981.

Anderson, Donald F., *William Howard Taft: A Conservative's Conception of the Presidency*. Ithica and London: Cornell University Press, 1973.

Anthony, Carl Sferrazza, *First Ladies: The Saga of the Presidents' Wives and Their Power, VOLUME 1, 1789–1990*. New York: William Morrow, 1990.

Bailey, L.S., editor, *The American Car Since 1775: The Most Complete Survey of the American Automobile Ever Published, by the Editors of Automobile Quarterly*. New York: Automobile Quarterly, 1971.

Blackburn, Marc K., *The United States Army and the Motor Truck*. Westport, Connecticut: Greenwood Press, 1996.

Bowers, Claude, *Beveridge and The Progressive Era*. New York: The Literary Guild, 1932.

Boykin, Edward, editor, *The Wit and Wisdom of Congress*. New York: Funk & Wagnalls, 1961.

Brands, H. W., *T.R.: The Last Romantic*. New York: Basic Books, 1997.

Brayman, Harold, *The President Speaks Off-the-Record*. Princeton, New Jersey: Dow Jones Books, 1976.

Brendon, Piers, *Eminent Edwardians*. Boston: Houghton Mifflin, 1980.

Bromley, Michael L. and Mazza, Tom, *Stretching It: The Story of the Limousine*. Warrendale, PA: Society of Automotive Engineers, 2002.

Brough, James, *Princess Alice: A Biography of Alice Roosevelt Longworth*. Boston and Toronto: Little, Brown & Company, 1975.

Burton, David H., *William Howard Taft: In the Public Service*. Malabar, Florida: Robert E. Krieger Publishing Company, 1986.

Busch, Noel F., *T.R.— The Story of Theodore Roosevelt and His Influence on Our Times*. New York: Reynal & Company, 1963.

Butt, Archie, *The Letters of Archie Butt: Personal Aide to President Roosevelt*, Edited by Lawrence F. Abbott. New York: Doubleday, Page & Company, 1924.

Butt, Archie, *Taft and Roosevelt: The Intimate Letters of Archie Butt, Military Aide*. Garden City, New York: Doubleday, Doran & Company, Inc., 1930. (reprint Port Washington, N.Y.: Kennikat Press, 1971.)

Caldwell, Henry, *Hoo's Hoo and Wat's Wat in Gasolene*. New York City: Eaton & Gettinger Press, 1913.

Cannon, Joseph Gurney, *The Memoirs of Joseph "Uncle Joe" Cannon*, transcribed by Helen Leseure Abdill. Danville, IL: Vermilion County Museum Society, 1996.

Clark, Champ, *My Quarter Century of American Politics*. New York: Harper & Brothers, 1920.

Coletta, Paolo E., *The Presidency of William Howard Taft*. Lawrence: University Press of Kansas, 1973.

Collins, Herbert Ridgeway, *Presidents on Wheels*. Washington, D.C.: Acropolis Books, 1971.

Crissey, Forrest, *Theodore E. Burton: American Statesman*. Cleveland and New York: The World Publishing Company, 1956.

Duffy, Herbert S., *William Howard Taft*. New York: Minton, Balch & Company, 1930.

Flink, James J., *America Adopts the Automobile, 1895–1910*. Cambridge, MA: MIT Press, 1970.

Furman, Bess, *White House Profile*. Indianapolis—New York: The Bobbs-Merrill Company, Inc., 1951.

Georgano, G.N., ed., *The Complete Encyclopedia of Motorcars: 1885 to the Present*. New York: E.P. Dutton and Company, 1968.

Hammond, John Hays, *The Autobiography of John Hays Hammond*. New York: Farrar & Rinehart, 1935.

Hatch, Carl E., *The Big Stick and the Congressional Gavel: A Study of Theodore Roosevelt's Relations with his Last Congress, 1907–1909*. New York: Pageant Press, 1967.

Hofstadter, Richard, *The Age of Reform*. New York: Vintage Books, 1955.

Hoover, Irwin Hood, *Forty-Two Years in the White House*. Boston and New York: Houghton Mifflin Company, 1934.

Jaffray, Elizabeth, *Secrets of the White House*. New York: Cosmopolitan Book Corporation, 1926.

Jessup, Philip C., *Elihu Root*. New York: Dodd, Meade & Co., 1938.

Kay, Jane Holtz, *Asphalt Nation*. Berkeley and Los Angeles: University of California Press, 1997.

Kohlsaat, H.H., *From McKinley to Harding*. New York: Charles Scribner's Sons, 1923.

Kolko, Gabriel, *The Triumph of Conservatism: A Reinterpretation of American History, 1900–1916*. New York: The Free Press, 1963.

La Follette, Robert M., *La Follette's Autobiography*. Madison: Robert M. La Follette, 1913.

Leech, Margaret, *In the Days of McKinley*. New York: Harper & Brothers, 1959.

Lindsay, Rae, *The Presidents' First Ladies*, New York: Franklin Watts, 1989.

Link, Arthur S., *Woodrow Wilson and the Progressive Era: 1910–1917*. New York and Evanston: Harper & Row, 1954.

Longworth, Alice Roosevelt, *Crowded Hours*. New York: Charles Scribner's Sons, 1933.

Manners, William, *TR and Will: A Friendship That Split the Republican Party*. New York: Harcourt Brace Javanovich, Inc., 1969.

Mowry, George E., *The Era of Theodore Roosevelt: And the Birth of Modern America, 1900–1912*. New York and Evanston: Harper & Row, 1958.

Nevins, Allan, *Ford: The Times, the Man, the Company*. New York: Charles Scribner's Sons, 1954.

Pringle, Henry F., *The Life and Times of William Howard Taft*. New York: Farrar & Rinehart, 1939. (reprint, Cambden, Connecticut: Archon Books, 1964.)

Pringle, Henry F., *Theodore Roosevelt: A Biography*. New York: Harcourt, Brace and Company, 1931.

Rae, John B., *The American Automobile*. Chicago: The University of Chicago Press, 1965.

Roosevelt, Theodore, *The New Nationalism*, ed. by William E. Leuchtenburg, Peter Smith, Gloucester, Mass., 1971, pp. 36–37 (reprinted from Prentice-Hall, 1961, and The Outlook Company, 1910).

Schlesinger, Arthur M., Jr., editor, *History of American Presidential Elections: 1789–1968*. New York: Chelsea House Publishers, 1985.

Seale, William, *The President's House: A History*. Washington, D.C.: White House Historical Association, 1986.

Strouse, Jean, *Morgan: American Financier*. New York: Random House, 1999.

Sullivan, Mark, *Our Times: 1900–1925*. New York: Charles Scribner's Sons, 1936.

Sward, Keith, *The Legend of Henry Ford*. New York: Rinehart & Company, 1948.

Taft, Horace Dutton, *Memories and Opinions*. New York: The MacMillan Company, 1942.

Taft, Mrs. William Howard, *Recollections of Full Years*. New York: Dodd, Mead & Company, 1914.

Taft, William Howard, *Our Chief Magistrate and His Powers*. New York: Columbia University Press, 1916 (reprint *The President and His Powers*, New York and London: Columbia University Press, 1967.)

Teague, Michael, *Mrs. L: Conversations with Alice Roosevelt Longworth*. Garden City, New York: Doubleday & Company, 1981.

Werner, M.R., *Bryan*. New York: Harcourt, Brace and Company, 1929.

White, William Allen, *The Autobiography of William Allen White*. New York: The MacMillan Company, 1946.

Wik, Reynold M., *Henry Ford and Grass-roots America*. Ann Arbor: The University of Michigan Press, 1982.

Articles

Allison, Hildreth, "Dublin Greets a President," *Historical New Hampshire*, Vol. 35, No. 2, Summer, 1980.

Anderson, Donald F., "The Legacy of William Howard Taft," *Presidential Studies Quarterly*, Vol. XII, No. 1, Winter, 1982.

Anderson, Oscar E., Jr., "The Pure-Food Issue: A Republican Dilemma, 1906–1912," *The American Historical Review*, Vol. LXI, No. 3, April 1956.

Buenker, John D., "The Progressive Era: A Search for a Synthesis," *Mid America*, Vol. 51, No. 3, July 1969.

Carson, Gerald, "Goggles & Side Curtains," *American Heritage*, April, 1967.

Cary, Norman Miller, Jr., "The Use of the Motor Vehicle in the United States Army, 1899–1939," Ph.D. dissertation, University of Georgia, 1980.

Coulter, Merton E., "William Howard Taft's Visit to Athens," *The Georgia Historical Society*, Vol. LII, No. 4, December, 1968.

Fuller, Wayne E., "The Ohio Road Experiment," *Ohio History*, Vol. 74, No. 1, Winter, 1965.

Gatewood, Willard B., editor, "The President and the 'Deacon'," *Ohio History*, Vol. 74.

Gores, Stanley, "Fond du Lac Snubs a President," *Wisconsin Magazine of History*, Vol. 47, No. 2, Winter, 1963–1964.

Gould, Lewis L., "Theodore Roosevelt, William Howard Taft, and the Disputed Delegates in 1912: Texas as a Test Case," *Southwestern Historical Quarterly*, Vol. LXXX, No. 1, July, 1976.

Hendry, Maurice, "Pierce-Arrow: La Premiere Voiture Americaine," *Car Collector*, March, 1980.

Hess, Stephen, "Big Bill Taft," *American Heritage*, October, 1966.

Kimes, Beverly Rae, "Willie K.: The Saga of a Racing Vanderbilt," *Automotive Quarterly*, Vol. 15, No. 3.

McCarthy, Tom, *The Arrogance of Wealth: Woodrow Wilson and Early Mass Automobility in America*, Woodrow Wilson National Symposium, www.woodrow.wilson.org, 2000.

Ostromecki, Walter, Jr., "Helen Herron Taft: Influence and Automobiles," *Manuscripts*, Summer, 1991.

Parker, James R., "Beveridge and the Election of 1912: Progressive Idealist or Political Realist," *Indiana Magazine of History*, Vol. LXIII, No. 2, June, 1967.

Penick, James Lal, Jr., "Louis Russell Glavis," *Pacific Northwest Quarterly*, April, 1964.

Ponder, Stephen,"'Nonpublicity' and the Unmaking of a President," *Journalism History*, Vol. 19, No. 4, Winter, 1994.

Saunders, Steven R., "Charles H. Lee," oral history, Sagamore Hill National Historical Site, National Park Service, Oyster Bay, New York, 1975.

Solvick, Stanley D., "William Howard Taft and Cannonism," *Wisconsin Magazine of History*, Vol. 48, 1964–1965 and "The Conservative as Progressive: William Howard Taft and the Politics of the Square Deal," *Northwest Ohio Quarterly*, Vol. XXXIX, No. 3, Summer, 1967.

Taft, Charles P., "My Father the Chief Justice," *Supreme Court Historical Society*, Yearbook 1977, Washington, D.C., 1976.

Taft, Robert, Jr., "Will and Mabel," *Presidential Studies Quarterly*, Vol. XV, No. 3, Summer, 1985.

Thompson, Jack M., "James R. Garfield: The Making of a Progressive," *Ohio History*, Vol. 74, No. 2, 1965.

Wiebe, Robert H., "The House of Morgan and the Executive, 1905–1913," *American Historical Review*, Vol. LXV, 1960.

Wyman, Roger E., "Insurgency in Minnesota: The Defeat of James A. Tawney in 1910," *Minnesota History*, Vol. 40, No. 7, Fall, 1967.

Periodicals

(Dates indicate periods referenced for this work).

American Motorist, American Automobile Association Publishing Co., Stanford, Conn. & New York, 1909–1916

Auto News Co. oc Washington, 1909.

Automobile, Class Journal Co., New York, 1903–1915. Recommended major articles include: *The Growing Utility of the Automobile*, Sep. 12, 1907; *Experiments of the Office of Public Roads*, May 14, 1908; *What the Wright Brothers are Accomplishing*, Sep. 10, 1908; *Long Island Motor Parkway Has Its Racing Initiation*, Oct. 15, 1908; *What Brains of the Industry Say About Finances*, Jun. 23, 1910; *Selden Patent Not Infringed*, Jan. 12, 1911; *Good Roads, Keynote of Prosperity: Automobile has Forced Issue of Improved Highways* Sep. 28, 1911; *Resume of the Year's Work*, Jan. 26, 1911; *Uniform Automobile Laws in*

All States a Vital Necessity, May 9, 1912, *Wonderful Growth of the Industry*, Jul. 25, 1912

Cincinnati Enquirer

Club Journal, Automobile Club of America, New York, 1909–1913

Evening Star, Washington, W.D. Wallach & Hope, Washington, D.C., 1900–1914

Horseless Age, The Horseless Age Co., New York, 1898–1914

Motor Age, The Horseless Age Co., Chicago, 1909–1910

New York Times, H.J. Raymond & Co., 1899–1914

Pioneer Press Co., St. Paul, Minnesota, 1909–1911.

Vehicle Dealer, Ware Brothers, Philadelphia, 1908–1913

Washington Post Co., Washington, D.C., 1904–1913

Other Sources

Biographical Directory of the United States Congress, U.S. House of Representatives, Office of the Clerk, website, bioguide.congress.gov, 2001.

Butt, Archibald W., Papers, Georgia Department of Archives and History, Atlanta, Georgia.

Congressional Record: The Proceedings and Debates of the Sixty-First Congress, Government Printing Office, Washington, D.C., 1909.

James A. Tawney Papers, Minnesota Historical Society, St. Paul, Minnesota.

Papers of William Howard Taft, Library of Congress, Washington, D.C.

Pierce-Arrow Society website, www.piercearrow.org, 2001.

Sagamore Hill National Historical Site, National Park Service, Oyster Bay, New York.

Taft Summer White House, Beverly Historical Society website, www.members.tripod.com/BevHist/Soc/auto.htm, 2001.

White House Dispersing Officers Accounts, 1894–1924, RG130-50-39-02, National Archives and Records Administration, Washington, DC.

William Howard Taft National Historic Site, National Park Service, Cincinnati, Ohio.

Index

Numbers in **bold** refer to photographs or illustrations.